Granville W. G. L. Gower

A register of all the christninges, burialles & weddinges within the parish of Saint Peeters upon Cornhill:

Beginning at the raigne of our most soueraigne ladie Queen Elizabeth - Vol. 1

Granville W. G. L. Gower

A register of all the christninges, burialles & weddinges within the parish of Saint Peeters upon Cornhill:
Beginning at the raigne of our most soueraigne ladie Queen Elizabeth - Vol. 1

ISBN/EAN: 9783337724412

Printed in Europe, USA, Canada, Australia, Japan

Cover: Foto ©ninafisch / pixelio.de

More available books at **www.hansebooks.com**

THE Publications

OF

The Harleian Society.

ESTABLISHED A.D. MDCCCLXIX.

Registers.—Volume I.

FOR THE YEAR MD.CCC.LXXVII.

LONDON:
MITCHELL AND HUGHES, PRINTERS,
WARDOUR STREET. W.

A Register

OF ALL THE

Christninges Burialles & Weddinges

WITHIN THE

Parish of Saint Peeters vpon Cornhill

BEGINNING AT THE RAIGNE OF OUR MOST SOUERAIGNE
LADIE QUEEN ELIZABETH.

EDITED BY

GRANVILLE W. G. LEVESON GOWER, F.S.A.

LONDON:
1877.

THIS BOOKE CONTAINES THE NAMES OF MORTALL MEN
BUT THEAR'S A BOOKE WITH CHARACTERS OF GOLDE
NOT WRIT WITH INCKE WITH PENSILL OR WITH PEN
WHEARE GODES ELECT FOR EUER ARE INROLDE
THE BOOKE OF LIFE; WHEARE LABOR THOU TO BEE
BEEFORE THIS BOOKE HATH ONCE REGISTRED THEE.

a¹ The initial letter of Burials, 1558 drawn by William Averell, Parish Clerk.
The "Tun" is an allusion to his being a member of the Vintner's Company, the Rose is an emblem of his prosperity in his business and in his family. The verse at the side from Ps 104 should probably be the 15th in our version that text and the following referring to Wine, the last to the Rose. Other initial letters in this Register by the same hand are C for Christenings 1558, an interlaced letter formed of two snakes with a grotesque head in the centre; an initial D. 1558 an interlaced letter on red ground finishing in two snakes with their tongues out barbed, an initial S. 1558, an interlaced letter on red ground with flowers, an initial H. 1558, and an initial W 1558 the outside stems interlaced, the inside twisted with a large Rose in the centre.

THOUGH IN THE GRAVE MENS BODIES SOONE BEE ROTTEN;
YET HEARE THEYR NAMES WILL HARDLIE BEE FORGOTTEN.

This booke was bought at the charge of the parish of St Peeters vpon Cornhill Maister William Ashboold doctor beeing then Parson, and Maister Dauid Powell and Maister Willia' Hartrige beeing then Churchwardens the two and twentith day of September in the yeare of our lord one thousand fiue hundred nynety and eight.

CERTAIN VERSES VPON THIS REGISTER.

Si speculum fluxæ quæris vitæq' caducæ:
  Nobile tumq'; nitens hic liber esse potest.
Hic vitæ vera effigies hic mortis imago:
  Hic iam spirantes mors fera sæpe rapit.
Aluo in materna morientem cernere possis
  Infantem tenerum, cum sibi fata volunt.
Hic iuvenis moritur, sic splendida comptaq'; virgo
  Jam sponsata viro, non sibi nupta dolet.
Hic diues rapitur congestis vndiq'; saccis:
  Fertur ad infernas, Tartareasq'; domos.
Hic qui pauperiem patitur ditatur abunde.
  Nam fruitur cœlis, possidet atq' deum.
Huc grandesq' senes veniunt iam tempore fessi
In folijsq' meis, nomina scripta volunt
Humani generis sors quæ sit sicq' videbis;
  Nomina voluendo quæ tibi forte dabo.

WILLIAM AUERELL, Clarke.

VERSES MADE BY WILLIAM AUERELL CLARKE OF THIS CHURCH, IN WHICH HEE COMPARETH THIS REGISTER TO A GLASSE OR MIRROUR.

Loe heare a christall mirror,
And glas of mannes vaine glorie:
Whose vew may bee a terror,
Gainst pleasures transitorie:
Wheare in each humane creature
May see the course of nature.

See heare the childe now panting,
In wombe of wofull mother:
When life and death is wanting,
How th'on's a grave to th'other:
The wombe that's made to beare it,
Beecomes a tombe t'interre it.

The sucking babe that hangeth,
Vpon the teat so tender:
When fearefull death it pangeth,
Dies like a slip that's slender:
Now born and new baptized,
Now dead and sone disguised.

The youth that's strong and lustie,
Whose face is full of fauor:
May heare see youth vntrustie,
And like a flower in sauor:
Now fresh and sweet new gathred,
Straight stinking, dead, and withred.

The flouring maid beespangled,
With red like damaske roses:
Must leave to bee nowfangled,
And shunne mens flattering glozes.
For heare shee sees her bewtie,
Deathes tribute, debt, and dutie.

The virgin newlie married,
With pompe and wondrous pleasure:
The next day heare is buried
With sorrow passing measure:
Shee meltes and mournes in dying,
Her spouse and frendes with crying.

The riche man that hath scraped,
To fill his bagges with treasure:
Shall see heare none haue scaped,
But death hath had his seazure:
Heare is his name inrouled,
That would not be controuled.

The poore with famine pined,
Once beeing heare recorded
Hath treasures trew assigned,
And heauenlie foode afforded:
In heauen hee's now adorned,
That heare one earth was scorned.

The feeble old man wasted,
With yeares, cares, greef and trouble:
Is glad that death hath hasted,
His death for to redouble:
Though long he liu'd and crooked,
Yet heare hee must be booked.

Thus euery age and calling,
May heare beehold theyr faces:
Theyr rising and theyr falling,
Theyr endes and wretched cases:
Which glasse weare it well vsed,
Life should not bee abused.

PREFACE.

In issuing this, the first I hope of a long series of Parochial Registers that will be printed by the HARLEIAN SOCIETY, a few words are perhaps necessary by way of Preface. The magnitude of such a scheme as the publication of the Parish Registers of England has led many to look with little favour upon the proposal of the Society, and the impossibility of ever completing it is urged as a reason against the attempt. Each Parish Register is, however, a separate work of itself, and even if no more than twenty or thirty were printed a great work would have been achieved, and a vast amount of useful genealogical information secured. I trust, therefore, that the Society will adhere to its resolution, and keep steadily to the object it has in view, viz., that one part of its work shall be the publication of Parish Registers. Our object is to obtain as large a mass of genealogical information as possible in the shortest possible time, and for this reason I trust that any lengthened Annotations, Transcripts of Wills, or of Monumental Inscriptions, will be avoided, and only such notes be given as may be absolutely necessary. A difficult question arises at the outset, and it is one which must be dealt with at once, otherwise I fear that both the interest of our Volumes, and the number that we shall be able to print, will be seriously diminished. It is this—shall we, or shall we not, publish every Register in its entirety? I have no hesitation in saying that to do so will be a very great mistake, and I think that the publication of this Register will go far to support this assertion. We shall encumber our Volumes with a large mass of useless and uninteresting matter, and spend money, both in printing and copying, which might be much better employed; the province of an Editor will be thereby reduced to that of a mere correcting of the letter-press, and much fewer Registers will be published than otherwise might be. To say nothing of the entries of "vagrants," "rogues," persons "ignoti cognominis," and such like, which will fill our pages, I maintain that as a Genealogical Society we are not concerned to find ancestors for families which have risen to the ranks of gentry in later times; our business is only with the record of those who at the time the entry was made were persons of recognized social position. I am aware that to prepare complete and trustworthy abstracts of Parish Registers will require Editors of considerable experience and of local knowledge, and that even then some important entry may occasionally be omitted; but surely this will be a lesser evil than the publication of so many names which have no interest or value whatever. The Registers of large towns will perhaps afford more difficulty, but in most of the country Registers with which I am familiar, there is some distinguishing mark of the gentry, and where such may be wanting the local knowledge of the Editor will enable him to judge what extracts to make. If any class of entries is to be printed in full it should certainly be confined to the marriages, which are less numerous and relatively of more importance.

The Church of St. Peter, Cornhill, is traditionally said to have been the earliest Christian Church in London; its foundation is ascribed to Lucius, the first Christian King of Britain, A.D. 124. The Rev. W. J. Loftie, in a paper on Roman London, in the "Archæological Journal" (vol. xxxiv., p. 177), says: "St. Peter's upon Cornhill is traditionally said to have been the seat of Bishop Restitutus (he was at the Council of Arles, A.D. 314), and the fifteen predecessors and successors assigned to him by the mediæval historians." Whether, as Stow suggests, St. Peter's, at Westminster, is intended or not, this Church is of great

PREFACE. xi

antiquity. The original building was destroyed in the Fire of London, and the present Church was rebuilt on its site by Sir Christopher Wren; it had formerly, as now, a library attached to it.

The Registers consist of eight volumes:—

1. Christenings and Burials - 1536 to 1774.
   Weddings   -   - 1536 to 1754.

Part of this volume is a copy made from an earlier book not now in existence.

2. Christenings and Burials - 1775 to 1812.
3. Weddings   -   -   1754 to 1780.
4. Weddings   -   -   1781 to 1812.
5. Weddings   -   -   1813 to 1837.
6. Weddings   -   -   1837 to present time.
7. Christenings -   -   1813 to present time.
8. Burials   -   -   1813 to 1853; the last year of burial at St. Peter's.

The transcript from the early Register, and the entries up to the year 1605, are made by William Averell, the Parish Clerk. He was probably the son of John Averell, Joyner, and Margaret his wife, the baptisms of several of whose children occur in the Register (p. 2, 3, 4, 5, 7, 8), and whose burials are recorded at page 120 and 126. He was baptized on 12 Feb. 1555 (p. 7), and was married on 2 Nov., 1578, to Gillian, daughter of Robert Goodale, "felix atque faustum conjugium," as he styles it (p. 231). By her he had seventeen or eighteen children,* the baptisms of sixteen of them being recorded in this Register; she was buried on 20 Feb., 1595 (p. 145), and he on 23 Sep., 1605. He was a member of the Merchant Taylors' and Vintners' Company; he was both a Greek and Latin scholar, as appears by the numerous entries in those languages in the margin of the Register. His house was in Corbet's Court, and he had a

* See pp. 45 and 145.

school for pupils, which he probably held in the library attached to the Church. Stow mentions that in his time the place was occupied by a schoolmaster and his usher, for a number of scholars learning their grammar rules. The deaths of some of his scholars are recorded at pages 144, 156, and 158. He was a good draughtsman and penman, as may be seen by the Register, which is a beautiful specimen of writing; the initial letters, one of which is given in the frontispiece, are by his hand, and are of considerable merit. A search in the P.C.C. has not resulted in finding his will.

The present volume brings the Register down to 1666, the year of the great fire; it is proposed to continue it in a second volume down to 1750. The present part contains singularly few entries of persons of rank. One nobleman only, George, Earl of Desmond, whose marriage is recorded (p. 253), one peer's son, William Fairfax, son of Lord Fairfax of Emley *(ibid)*. Two ladies of rank appear as Godmothers (p. 55); the Lady Lucy, Countess of Bedford, and the Lady Elizabeth Darlton, "bewtifull Ladies," as the clerk of the day calls them. Of civic dignitaries we find Sir William Bowyer, Lord Mayor of London 1543, whose burial is recorded on 13 April, 1545, to whom there was formerly a tomb in the south aisle of the choir, the inscription on which is given by Stow ("Survey of London," p. 211). Sir Henry Hubblethorn, Lord Mayor 1546, married in this church to Elizabeth Fuller 26 April, 1552, and buried there 18 Oct. 1556, to whom there was a marble stone under the communion table, mentioned by Stow (p. 212). Mr. William Walthall, Alderman and Sheriff of London 1606, buried 2 Sep. 1608; he left various benefactions to the parish, as recorded by Stow (p. 212). Mr. Thomas Westraw, Alderman and Sheriff 1625, buried in a vault in the chancel 18 December, 1625 (Stow's "Survey," p. 867). Sir Christopher Morris married to Eliza Clifford 18 June, 1543, and buried 3 Feb., 1545; Master Gunner to King Hen. VIII. (Stow, p. 211).

Of Rectors of the parish we have William Ashbold, D.D., Rector in 1560, buried 29 Aug. 1622. Dr. White, Rector in 1622 (see p. 180). William Fairfax, D.D., his successor, buried 20 Nov. 1655. Mr. William

Blackmore, Rector in 1648, whose marriage on 1st May, 1660, is recorded at page 262.

A large number of Dutchmen seemed to have lived in the parish; there are numerous entries of them, and constant mention of the Dutch Church (pp. 17, 19, 21, 23, 31, 43). John Vansalt, an Elder of the Dutch Church, was buried 9 Jan., 1603. James Voulmur, a Dutch Preacher, buried 6 Jan., 1617. This was in Austin Friars, and was part of the old Church of the Friars, and granted to the Dutch in 1550. Some of them were baptized in the French Church (pp. 24, 26, 27); this was part of the old Church of St. Anthony's Hospital, in Threadneedle Street.

Visitations of the Plague are recorded in 1593, 1603, and 1665. The burials of four centenarians, all women, occur, viz., Annes Tibbold, 6 April, 1575; Margery Mane, 14 March, 1596; Annes Lee, 18 Sep., 1597, and Jane Read, 21 Feb., 1632. There are entries of a vast number of foundlings (I have enumerated some forty) who, according to a common custom, were all surnamed Peter, after the Saint to whom the Parish Church was dedicated; one of them bears the name Symon Peter (p. 88).

Of uncommon Christian names we find of Males: Sidrach (p. 12), Gamaliel (p. 19), Bezaleel) (p. 34), Abacucke (p. 36), Hillary (p. 44), Aholiab (p. 47), Nicasius (p. 103), Zephaine (p. 246), Humiliation (p. 253); of Females: Cananell? (p. 9), Ephin (p. 11), Effam (p. 68), Gillian (p. 30), Izan* (pp. 1, 43), Juventa (p. 58), Apoline (p. 59), Appelyna (p. 173), Avice (p. 72), Jacamine (p. 132), Jockaminshaw (p. 169), Nazareth (p. 246), Venus (p. 253).

Among benefactors to the parish we find John Caunt, Fishmonger, buried 22 Oct., 1592; Launcelot Thomson, Draper, buried 14 Jan., 1601; Peter Heelin, buried 21 Feb., 1601; Mr. John Malyn, buried 26 May, 1612.

William Dethick, York Herald, was an inhabitant of the parish; baptisms of his children occur at pages 22, 24, 25, 27, 29.

---

* This name occurs on a monument to Izan Wright, in Allhallows, Lombard Street (Stow's "Survey," p. 220).

The letter "u" being written in the original for "v," has been retained throughout.

The removal of the font from the reading place by the quire is mentioned on 20 Feb. 1604, and on 20 March following John King is entered as "ye first christned in the gilded font."

The description at p. 190 of Mrs. Lucy Edge, as "one of the Widdowes which gives the Lecture at litle Alhallowes," I cannot explain.

The Weigh House is frequently mentioned, with its officers, master porter, porter, carter, etc. (pp. 18, 30, 60, 68, 153, 173, 175). Stow says, that on the north side of Lombard Street "one large house is called the wey-house where Merchandizes brought from beyond the Seas are to be weighed at the Kings beame. Sir Thomas Lovell builded this house which hee gave to the Grocers of London."

It remains to express the thanks of the Society to the Rev. Richard Whittington, M.A., the Rector of St. Peter's, for his kindness in allowing us to transcribe the Register; with him, should our undertaking prove successful, will rest the credit of having been the first to speed us on our way. From others of the clergy we have met with similar encouragement, as the list of our intended publications shews. It is to them in this, as in other antiquarian researches, that we must look for our chief assistance. I am aware that to some of them the prospect of printing Parish Registers appears as if it would seriously diminish the income derived from searchers, and, however willing they may be to forego any advantage to themselves, they feel that they must have regard to their successors. I believe that this is not really a matter of much import to them. In the first place, the searches made in the early years of the Register, say to 1750, with which our Society will be chiefly concerned, are not very numerous, and, in the second place, the fact of these entries being printed will not give them any legal value as evidence; to be of any worth in a Court of law, they will require, as heretofore, a stamp and the certificate of the Rector or other person making the extract. These facts will I trust weigh with the clergy, and induce them to further our undertaking.

The transcript of the Register has been most carefully and accurately made by Mr. J. Eedes. Some errors there must of necessity be, but I trust that they are neither many nor serious.

GRANVILLE LEVESON GOWER.

Titsey Place,
    June 15th, 1878.

Certain Christninges frō the statute of King Henry the eight to the beeginning of her maiestie raigne some thing vnperfectlie kept.

CHRISTNINGES.

Yeare.	Month.	Day.	Names.
1538	Decemb^r	15	Sunday Christning of Hughe Kellsall
		18	Wedensday Christning of Robert Wright
	Januarie	21	Satterday Christning of Richard Pagington
		21	Satterday Christning of Robert Chapman
	February	3	Monday Christning of George Idle
	Marche	11	Tuesday Christning of Robert Rodes
1539	Maye	20	Tuesday Christning of Robert Groue
		20	Tuesday Christned Petronilla ignoti cognominis
	June	19	Thursday Christned William Say, sonne of John Say
		19	Thursday Christned Margaret Munde daughter of John
	Julie	15	Tuesday Christned William Hepworth sonne of Wm Hep.
	August	15	Fryday Christned Etheldra Staper dau. of Rouland Sta.
		15	Friday Christned Ellen James daughter of John James
	Septemb^r	18	Thursday Christned Luce daughter of John Fresingfeeld
		19	ffryday Christned Jane daughter of Jacob Kendall
		20	Satterday Christned Gabella daughter of Robert Jans
	October	30	Thursday Christned Thomas Wanton sonne of Thom
	Nouemb	6	Thursday Christned George Hupton sonne of Thomas
		8	Satterday Christned Emma Horson daughter of Robert
		12	Monday Christned William Weket sonne of Thomas We
		16	ffryday Christned Alice Wintrop daughter of Ade
	Decemb^r	9	Tuesday Christned Edmond Wright sonne of Robert
		29	Christned Thomas Holliwell sonne of William Hol.
	January	4	Sonday Christned William Warren sonne of Ade Wa.'
		17	Christned Thomas Hilles sonne of Thomas Hilles
1539	January	21	Christned Grace Lynsey daughter of John Lynsey
	February	7	Satterday Christned John Chapman sonne of Robert Cha.
	March	12	Thursday Margaret Kirke daughter of John Kirke
1540	Aprill	10	Sonday Christopher Atkinnes sonne of ...*
	Maye	1	Sonday Christned Emma Idle daughter ...
		6	Christning of Katherine Hollis daughter ...
		19	Christning of John Crofton sonne of ...
	June	9	Thursday† of William Munday sonne of ...
		14	Christning of John Brislye sonne of ...
	Julie	3	Sonday Christning of Margaret Tupper

* These marks are put in the original to fill up the line. † Sic.

Years.	Month.	Day.	Names.
1540	August	16	Monday Christning of Mary Heath
		21	Christning of Robert Saunders sonne of ...
		21	Christning of Katherine Myles daughter ...
		29	Christning of Emme Preost daughter ...
	Septemb^r	8	Sonday Christning of Richard Staper ...
	Nouem	5	Fryday Christning of Margaret Vpley
		6	Christning of Robert Hepworth sonne ...
	January	8	Fryday Christening of Annes Hodge daug. of Richard
		16	Christned Annes Kelsie daughter of John Kelsye
		21	Christning of John Wincrappe sonne of ...
	February	21	Sonday Christning of Luce Edwinne
		24	Christning of Katherine Halliwell daug. of W^m
	March	29	Christning of John Wright sonne of ...
		31	Christning of Emme Jance dau. of Robert
1541	Aprill	9	Sonday Christned Robert Chapmanne
		11	Christning of Katherine Hollys daughter ...
		15	Christning of Emme Roodes daughter and ...
	Maye	8	Monday Christning of Ellen Idle daughter ...
	Julie	12	Weddensday Christning of Lettes Groue
		20	Christning of Ellen Gybbinnes daughter ...
		21	Christning of Thomas Kirke sonne of ...
	August	13	Sonday Christning of Mary Bell
		22	Christning of John Atkenson sonne of ...
	August	27	Christning of Elizabeth Lawse daughter ...
		28	Christning of Margaret Segar daughter ...
	Septem	2	Satterday Christning of William Holland
		11	Christning of Emme Pakington daughter of ...
		26	Christning of Annes Heath daughter of ...
		30	Christning of Jone Tipper daughter of ...
	October	21	Satterday Christning of Jane Wicket daugh. ...
		30	Christning of William Crofton sonne of ...
	Nouem	6	Monday Christning of Kathern Gourley
		14	Christning of Emme Borow daughter ...
		17	Christning of John Stauniper sonne ...
		21	Christning of Joane Staper daughter ...
		30	Christning of John Hepworth sonne of ...
	Decemb	13	Wedensday Christning of John Drope sonne ...
		24	Christning of Hercules Huxley sonne of ...
		28	Christning of Elizabeth Averell daughter of John
	January	2	Tuesday Christniug of Christopher Eldrington
		3	Christning of Erasmus Lynsey sonne of John
		7	Christning of Nicholas Hodge sonne of Richard
	March	1	Thursday Christning of Winnefred Kelsam
		7	Christning of Christopher Horwood sonne ...
		16	Christning of Harry Jans sonne of ...
1542	Aprill	24	Wedensday Christning of Elizabeth Horsey
		26	Christning of John Saunders sonne of ...
	Maye	31	Wedensday Christning of Margery Jacksonne
	August	13	ffriday Christning of Katherine Lawes
		21	Christning of Edward Atkinson sonne ...
	October	22	Monday Christning of Constance Haines
	Nouem	13	Monday Christning of Emme Bell
		17	Christning of Izabel Richardson daughter ...
	Decem	8	Satterday Christning of Adam Hepworth
		19	Christning of John Hodge sonne of Richard Hodge
	Ja'uary	7	Monday Christning of Steuen ffelton
		28	Christning of Joan Write daughter of ...

THE REGISTERS OF ST. PETER'S, CORNHILL. 3

Yeare.	Month.	Day.	Names.
1542	Ja'uary	31	Christning of William Holland sonne ...
	Februa	20	Wedeusday Christning of William Street
	March	5	ffriday Christning of Joan Drope daughter ...
		8	Christning of Joane Staper daughter ...
		12	Christning of William ffrisingfeeld sonne ...
1543	Aprill	3	ffriday Christning of Joane Borow daughter of ..
		23	Christning of Denis Goodale sonne of ...
	Maye	3	ffriday Christning of Bridget Wintrope
		21	Christning of Edmund Jance sonne of ...
	June	5	Wednesday Christning of William Gurley
	Julie	14	Sonday Christning of Richard Burton
	Septem	11	Wedensday Christning of Joane Holliwell
1544	Aprill	26	Satterday Christning of John Macrell
	June	1	Sonday Christning of Peeter Packington
		1	Christning of Elizabeth Wrighte daughter
	Julye	30	Wedinsday Christning of William Richardson
	Septem	18	Thursday Christning of Joane Gibbynnes
		19	Christning of William Dicheborn sonne of
1545	Aprill	28	Tuesday Christning of Thomas Saunders
	Maye	1	ffryday Christning of Randoll Saunders
	August	12	Wedeusday Christning of Thomas Drope
		13	Chrestning of Margaret West daughter
		14	Christning of John Jans sonne of ...
	Septem	12	Satterday Christning of William Walker
		13	Christning of Thomas Wright sonne ...
1546	Aprill	26	Monday Christning of Hercules Burton
		28	Christning of Toby Huckslie sonne
	Maye	8	Satterday Christning of Robert Roodes
		10	Christning of Mary ffeeld daughter ...
	Septemb	6	Monday Christning of Mary Borow
		22	Christning of Mary Crafton daughter ...
	October	18	Monday Christning of Elizabeth Gates
	Nouem	6	Monday Christning of John Cater
		13	Christning of Lawraunce Reckener
	Decem	13	Wedensday Christning of Elizabeth Preest
		20	Christning of Margery Jaruis daughter ...
	Februar	5	Sonday Christning of Richard Bell
		22	Christning of Alice Stockemeed daughter
	March	13	Monday Christning of Sara Hodge dau. of Rich.
1547		28	Christning of Joane Hudsonne daughter ...
		28	Christning of Ignatius Price sonne ...
	Maye	12	ffriday Christning of John Lawse sonne
	June	21	Wedensday Christning of Thomas Tipper
	Julie	3	Monday Christning of Annes Madewell
	August	4	Tuesday Christning of the cookes childe
		5	Christning of Thomas Sturman
		8	Christning of John Pullner sonne ...
		15	Christning of Adam Wyntrop sonne of ...
	Septem	5	Tuesday Christning of Tymothy Porter
		5	Christning of Margaret Averell daughter of John
		6	Christning of Katherine Vxley daughter of ...
		16	Christning of Tymothy Barker sonne of ...
		18	Christning of Elizabeth Write daughter of ...
	October	21	Christning of Egbert Dublebeer sonne of ...
		25	Christning of Sara Carter daughter of ...
	Decemb	11	Monday Christning of Jeames Read sonne of ...
		13	Christning of Adam Cater sonne of ...

Yeare.	Month.	Day.	Names.
1547	January	10	Wednesday Christning of Jane Mathew daugh. ...
		11	Christning of Thomas Atkinson sonne of ...
		11	Christninge of Jane Watkinnes daughter of ...
		16	Christning of William Eldertonne sonne ...
		20	Christning of Katherine Preest daughter ...
	March	31	Fryday Christning of Mable Bright daught^r ...
	Maye	12	Monday Christning of Ralphe Edwinne
1548	Maye	30	Christning of John Gates sonne of ...
	June	2	Thursday Christning of Katherine Castle
		15	Christning of Thomas Richardsonne
		25	Christning of John Trotter sonne of ...
	Julie	17	Monday Christning of Thomas Stockmede
		19	Christning of Richard Ball sonne
	August	9	Wednsday Christning of Annes Paintill
		30	Christning of Ralphe Lawse sonne of
	Septem	11	Monday Christning of Elizabeth Walker
	Octob	5	Thursday Christning of Barbara Hatherstoole
	Nouem	14	Monday Christning of Annes Oxley
		15	Christning of Tymothy Pountell sonne of
		28	Christning of Harry Wright sonne of
	Decem	1	Fryday Christning of Nicholas Adames
		5	Christning of William Hutsonne sonne of
		8	Christning of Samson Cater sonne of
		15	Christning of William Tapster alias Aldred
		15	Christning of Katherine Carsey daughter
		15	Christning of Elizabeth Carsey daughter
		21	Christning of Debora Borow daughter
	Januar	16	Monday Christning of Rowand Hodge sonne of Rich.
		26	Christning of William Seller sonne of
	Februa	1	Tuesday Christning of Mary Carter daugh.
		3	Christning of Joane Westraw daughter
		4	Christning of Izabell Preest daughter
		16	Christning of Annes Gyles daughter of
1549*	March	28	Sonday Christning of Mary Thomson daughter of Rich.
		30	Christning of Elizabeth Clerke daughter of
	Aprill	4	Monday Christning of John Lambe sonne
		12	Christning of Thomas Bell sonne and
		30	Christning of Elizabeth Gates daughter
		30	Christning of Rachell Watkinnes daughter
	Maye	5	Wedensday Christned Phebe Atkinson daughter of Edw.
		18	Catherine Wyntrope was Christned daughter of ...
	June	8	Monday Christning of Elizabeth Mathew daugh.
	Julie	2	Tuesday Christning of Edward Castle sonne
	August	16	Thursday Christning of John Dalton sonne
		17	Christning of Edward Idle sonne of
		18	Christning of Joane Averell daughter of John Ave.
		24	Christning of John Atkinson sonne of
	Septem	12	ffriday Christning of Dorothy Evered daughter of
		21	Christning of Anne Phillippes daughter of
	Nouem	16	Sonday Christning of Richard Sturman
		22	Christning of Anne Gunne daughter of
		23	Christning of Grizill Deyne daughter of
		26	Christning of Joane Hallward daughter
	Februa	3	Tuesday Christning of Tymothie Hodge sonne of Ri.
		6	Christning of Joane Wright daughter of

* Year omitted in original.

THE REGISTERS OF ST. PETER'S, CORNHILL. 5

Yeare.	Month.	Day.	Names.
1549	Februa	6	Christning of Joane Cootes daughter of
		12	Christning of Theophilus Adames sonne of
		14	Christning of Joane Lewis daughter of
	March	23	Monday Christning of Prudence Clarke.
		24	Christning of William Brickendale sonne
1550*	Maye	18	Monday Christning of Theophilus Ponder.
		25	Christning of Mary Stockemede daughter
	June	13	Satterday Christning of Sara Mapletonne
	Julie	14	Tuesdaye Christning of Edmund Bagley
		24	Christning of Richard Preest sonne of and
	August	4	Tuesday Christning of Thomas Borrow
		31	Christning of Elizabeth Clarke daughter
	Septem	18	ffryday Christning of Margaret Atkinson
		23	Christning of Phillip Jans sonne of
		28	Christning of Margaret Atkinson daughter
		28	Christning of Joane Westraw daughter
	Octob.	3	Satterday Christning of Jerome Plombaire
		18	Christning of Joane Hayward daughter
	Nouem	4	Wednesday Christning of Mary Dayne
		12	Christning of Sara Gunne daughter
		15	Christning of Emme Lambe daughter
		26	Christning of Sara Keling daughter
	Decem	13	Wedensday Christning of William Mericke
		18	Christning of ffraunces† Molsonne sonne
		28	Christning of Elizabeth Eastfeeld daughter
	Janu.	10	Sonday Christning of Elizabeth Saxfeeld
	Febru	23	Tuesday Christning of Susan Elringtonne
	March	9	Tuesday Christning of Maudlyn Thomsonne
		12	Christning of Joseph Deiane sonne of
		19	Christning of Harry Lewes sonne of
		28	Christning of Richard Clarke sonne of
		30	Christning of Alice Coult daughter of
		30	Christning of Ambrose Clarke sonne of
	May	5	Saterday Christning of James Hodge sonne of Rich.
		12	Christning of Anthonie Jonson sonne of
		23	Christning of Elizabeth Goffe daughter
		23	Christning of Blaze Goodwinne daughter
	June	4	ffriday Christning of Mabell Kyrke daughter
		24	Christning of Joyce Bricket daughter and
	August	9	Monday Christning of Thomas ffletcher
		21	Christning of Margaret Preist daughter
		24	Christning of Garthred Bright sonne of
	Septem	7	Tuesday Christning of Joane Porter
		9	Christning of Nicholas Sturman sonne
	Nouem	20	Satterday Christning of Thomas Swinkfeld
		27	Christning of Sara Mascall daughter
	Decem	7	Tuesday Christning of Judith Stokes
		11	Christning of Susan Wintrope daughter
		11	Christning of Grysell Plommer daughter
	January	1	Satterday Christning of Susan Gunne
		6	Christning of Susan Oxeley daughter
	Februa	5	Satterday Christning of Anne Mathew daughter
1553	Aprill	29	ffriday Christining of Cosse a poulters sonne
	Maye	21	Saturday Christning of Mary Pauefreman
		21	Christning of Salomon Atkinson sonne of Edward

* Years omitted between 1550 and 1553.   † Sic.

Yeare.	Month.	Day.	Names.
1553	June	12	Sonday Christning of Katherine Jonson daugh.
		17	Christning of Joan Knight daughter of John
	August	24	Tuesday Christning of Julie Tratter
		25	Christning of Bartholomew Wright
	Septem	6	Tuesday Christning of Joane Clarke daug. of Tho.
		6	Christning of Nicholas Bricket sonne of
		11	Christning of Richard Clarke sonne of Thomas
	October	9	Sonday Christning of Jane Averell daugh. of John
		11	Christning of Joane Dauisonne daughter of
	October	17	Christning of Thomas Gozhe sonne of
	Nouem	2	Tuesday Christning of William Thomsonne
		17	Christning of Ellen Mapletonne daughter
		27	Christning of Bryde Fannt daughter of
		30	Christning of Alice Clarke daughter of
	Decem	4	Sonday Christning of Judith Hamlet daughter
		19	Christning of Mary Swynkfeeld daughter
		10	Christning of Thomas Gonne sonne of
		21	Christning of Mary Gates daughter
	Janua	3	Tuesday Christning of Alice Porter daughter
		11	Christning of Alice Hampsonne daughter of
	Februa	11	Satterday Christning of John Preest sonne
	March	18	Satterday Christning of Mary Sturmanne
1554	Aprill	4	Christning of Jane Nicholles vpon Tuesday
		4	Christning of Richard Mathew sonne of
		15	Christning of Annes Hill daughter of
		21	Christning of Richard Stokes sonne of
		21	Christning of Katherine Cottes daughter
	Maye	2	Tuesday Christning of Robert Smith sonne
		12	Christning of Elizabeth Williames daughter
	June	16	ffriday Christning of Thomas ffammocke
	Julie	21	Friday Christning of Robert Offley sonne of Tho.
	August	12	Satterday Christning of Elizabeth Goodwynne
		15	Christning of Mary Satchfeeld daughter of Gylbert
	Septem	9	Satterday Christning of Annes Goodale
	Octobe	9	Satterday Christning of Joane Goodale daug.
		22	Christning of John Neuell sonne of
	Decem	30	Satterday Christning of Thomas Lambe sonne of John
	Janua	18	Thursday Christning of Thomas Bagley
	Febru	3	Satterday Christning of Mary Knight daugh.
		9	Christning of John Richemanne sonne of
		9	Christning of William Recknar sonne of
		16	Christning of Elizabeth Daltonne daughter
		16	Christning of John Best sonne of
	March	3	Satterday Christning of John Hole sonne of
		10	Christning Katherine Watkinnes daughter of
		17	Christning of Alice Plommer daughter of
		24	Christning of Nicholas Atkinsonne sonne
1555	Aprill	2	Wednesday Christning of Kathern Goffe daug. of Lawrence
		23	Christning of William ffammocke sonne of
	Maye	3	Thursday Christning of Ellen Preest daughter
		17	Christning of Margaret Barlow daughter
		20	Christning of Phillip Yonge sonne of
	June	3	Sonday Christning of Elizabeth Richmonde
		16	Christning of Cisley Hosseziar daughter
		18	Christning of Susanne Herd daughter of
	Julie	9	Monday Christning of Richard Palfreman
		26	Christning of John Gunne sonne of

THE REGISTERS OF ST. PETER'S, CORNHILL. 7

Yeare.	Month.	Day.	Names.
1555	August	3	Thursday Christning of Mathew Jentyll
		10	Christning of John Sturmanne sonne of
		18	Christning of John Earle sonne of
	Septem	10	Monday Christning of Mary Dowsonne
		12	Christning of John Janes sonne of
		13	Christning of John Hilles sonne of
	Octob.	2	Tuesday Christning of Elizabeth ffletcher
	Nouem	30	ffriday Christning of Isabell Walker
	Decem	31	Monday Christning of Thomas Kyrke
	Decem	31	Christning of Thomas Clarke sonne
	Janua	9	Wedensday Christning of Thomas Awssle
	Februa	12	Tuesday Christning of Richard Bonnell
		12	Christning of William Averell sonne of John
		14	Christning of Jane Baker daughter of
	March	16	Satterday Christning of Dionice Goodwinne
1556	Aprill	17	Wedensday Christning of Ellen Jousonne
	Maye	10	Friday Christning of Richard Porter
		22	Christning of Bryde Stoakes daughter
		23	Christning of John Cottes sonne of
	June	10	Monday Christning of Elizabeth Wrighte
		16	Christning of Izabell Richemonde daughter
	August	12	Monday Christning of Anne Goffe dau. of Lawrence
		24	Christning of Edward Gunne sonne of
	Septem	...	Sonday Christning of Gyles Vxlaye sonne
		10	Christning of Elizabeth Yong daughter
		17	Christning of John Anwicke sonne of
		17	Christning of Elizabeth Trotter daughter
		19	Christning of Aunes Gyles daughter
		20	Christning of John Borrowe sonne of
	Nouem	8	Friday Christning of Thomas Hall sonne of George
		8	Christning of Joane Lynsey daughter
		10	Christning of Gyllian Goodale daughter of Rob.
		15	Christning of Margaret Goodale, twynnes
	Decem	14	Satterday Christning of Annes Wood
		16	Christning of John Saxfeld sonne of Gylbert
		27	Christning of William Jaunce sonne of
		27	Christning of Thomas Preest sonne of
	Janua	20	Monday Christning of Harry Hodge sonne of Rich.
	Februa	14	Friday Christning of Anthony Clarke sonne
	March	14	Friday Christning of Harry Richman sonne
		14	Christning of Mabell Olfley daughter
1557	Aprill	2	Wedensday Christning of Annes Fletcher
		10	Christning of Ellen Dalton daughter and
	Maye	1	Thursday Christning of John Allstone
		21	Christning of Anne Watkinnes daughter
	June	13	Friday Christning of Richard Steeuen
		30	Christning of Anne Coxe daughter of Edward
		30	Christning of Edward Averye sonne
	August	16	Satterday Christning of Vrsula Hill
		26	Christning of Elizabeth Hanscombe daughter
	Septem	29	Monday Christning of Margaret Gunne
	Octobe	1	Wedensday Christning of John Dyxonne
	Nouem	8	Satterday Christning of Margery Lynsey
		21	Christning of John Lister sonne of and
		30	Christning of Richard Whatman sonne and
	Decem	2	Tuesday Christning of William Wroth sonne of Will.
		5	Christning of Phillip Dowson sonne of and

Yeare.	Month.	Day.	Names.
1557	Decem	14	Christning of Paule Lambe sonne of John Lambe
		25	Christning of Peeter Kelly sonne of and
	Februa	14	Satterday Christning of Ellen Mathew daughter
	March	1	Sonday Christning of Annes Goodale daug. of Robert
		10	Christning of Rose Paullmer daughter of and
1558	Aprill	22	Wednesday Christning of Luce Heywood daughter
		23	Cristning of Rachell Yong daughter of
1558	Aprill	28	Christning of Annes Maddesonne daughter
	Maye	6	Wednesday Christning of Annes Baker daugh.
		9	Christning of Marye Judge daughter and
	June	10	Wednesday Christning of Ellen Winckefeeld daughter
	Julie	1	Wednesday Christning of Mary Walker daug. of Edwa.
		6	Christning of John Clarke sonne of
	August	8	Satterday Christning of Katherine Jance daughter
		12	Christning of Richard Flewet sonne of
	August	18	Christning of Richard Parker sonne of and
	Septem	1	Tuesday Christning of Richard Bromefeeld
		9	Christning of Henry Flammocke sonne of and
		25	Christning of Lewce Jacksonne daughter and
	October	1	Thursday Christning of Michaell Nichollson sonne
		1	Christning of Richard Axonne sonne of and
		2	Christning of Elizabeth Harris daughter of
		7	Christning of Izabell Haull daughter of
		12	Christning of Richard Assley sonne of and
		16	Christning of Joane Cuttes daughter of and
		24	Christning of John Gunne sonne of and
		25	Christning of Martha Austonne daughter
	Nouem	2	Monday Christning of Annes Ferychard
		7	Christning of Anne Hylles daughter

HEARE BEEGINNE THE CHRISTNINGES FROM THE REIGN OF OUR GRACIOUS QUEEN ELIZABETH.*

1558	Nouem	18	Christning of Elizabeth Tomsonne daughter of
		22	Christning of Mary Clarke daughter of
	Decem	15	Tuesday Christning of Barbara Cutt daugh.
	Janua	9	Friday Christning of Thomas Porter sonne
		18	Christning of Thomas Masse sonne of and
		20	Christning of Lawraunce Tharpe sonne
	Febru	27	Satterday Christning of Elizabeth Mascoll dau.
	March	5	Friday Christning of Richard Helye sonne of
		9	Christning of Susanne Lambe daughter of John
		14	Christning of Ellen Willsonne daughter of
1559	Aprill	9	Friday Christning of Susanne Goodale d. of Robert
		20	Christning of Martha ignoti cognominis
		26	Christning of Thomas Rosse sonne of and
	Maye	2	Sonday Christning of Margaret Oxgall
		10	Christning of Henry Averell son of John Aver
		20	Christning of Edward Swingfeeld sonne of
		26	Christning of Margaret Richemound daugh.
	June	20	Sonday Christning of Anne Stevens daug.
	Julie	16	Friday Christning of Sara Awnsell dau.
		24	Christning of John Daulton sonne of and

* Each page of the Register until the year 1599 is subscribed Willm Asheboold Robert Warden Mark Scaliet. parson.

THE REGISTERS OF ST. PETER'S, CORNHILL.　　9

Yeare.	Month.	Day.	Names.
1559	August	15	Sonday Christning of Nicholas Burnall
		17	Christning of Susanne Butler daughter and
		20	Christning of Jane Wrath daughter of and
	Septem	10	Friday Christning of Tymothy Chapmanne
	October	20	Wednesday Christning of Elizabeth Affley
	Nouem	5	Friday Christning of Gyles Dudmanne sonne of
		15	Christning of Susanne Wood daughter of and
	Decem	10	Friday Christning of William Coxe son of Edward
	Decem	15	Christning of Richard sonne of and
		24	Christning of Thomas Russell sonne of
	Janua	17	Monday Christning of John Hilles sonne of
		25	Christning of Thomas Thorpe sonne of and
	March	10	Thursday Christning of Mary Heelay daugh.
		30	Christning of Anne Stonehouse daughter of
		30	Christning of William Satchfeld sonne of Gilbert
1560	Aprill	2	Satterday Christning of Margaret Axonne
		13	Christning of Ester Cottes daughter and
		23	Christning of Anthonie Yonge sonne of and
	Maye	3	Tuesday Christning of Susanne Baker
	June	10	Friday Christning of Samuell Gray sonne of Will'.
		25	Christning of John Steuannes sonne of and
	Julie	22	Friday Christning of Cananell Adlingtone.
	Augu	3	Wednesday Christning of Thomas Richardsonne
		24	Christning of Bartholomey Yong sonne of Gregory Yong
	Septem	10	Satterday Christning of Timothy Whittingam son of W^m
		15	Christning of Jane Lambe daughter of and
	Nouem	16	Wedensday Christning of John Ritcheman sonne of
		26	Christning of Elizabeth Paulmer daughter of
		27	Christning of Mary Bricket daughter of Hamlet
		29	Christning of Fraunces Mallisonne sonne of
	De'mbr	10	Satterday Christning of William Cut sonne of Har.
	Janua	16	Thursday Christning of Susanne Wattonne
		12	Sonday Christning of Peeter Wrath sonne of syr Tho., knight
		16	Christning of Susan Auwicke daughter of
		16	Christning of Susan Ferychard the daughter
		19	Christning of John Lister sonne of and
	March	1	Wedensday Christning of Edward Chapman
		1	Christning of Alice Walker daughter of Edward
		8	Christning of William Brownfeeld sonne
1561	Aprill	2	Sonday Christning of Elizabeth Bowmer
		13	Christning of Susan Affley daughter
		23	Christning of Lawraunce Clarke sonne of
		25	Christning of Christopher Leame sonne of
	Maye	18	Thursday Christning of Ellen Westraw daugh.
	June	1	Thursday Christning of John Cursonne sonne
		8	Christning of Lawrence Axtonne sonne
		14	Christning of Susan Pressey daughter
		20	Christning of Margaret Steuannes daughter
		20	Christning of Elizabeth Porter daughter
	Julie	2	Sonday Christning of Richard Burnam sonne of Clem.
		18	Christning of Mary Mascoll daughter and
	August	3	Wedensday Christning of George Stonehouse
		3	Christning of Zachary Heelay sonne of and
		23	Christning of Annes Dowsonne daughter
		24	Christning of Izabell Massey daughter
		25	Christning of George Wrath sonne of and

c

Yeare.	Month.	Day.	Names.
1561	August	25	Christning of Edward Cockes sonne of and
		31	Christning of Mary Shersonne daughter
	Septem	7	Thursday Christning of Martha Gough
		20	Christuing of Thomas King sonne of ...
	Octobe	2	Monday Christning of Edward Cootes
		18	Christning of Edward Wood sonne
	Nouem	15	Wedensday Christning of William Richemond sonne of
		27	Christning of Thomas Cut sonne of Harry Cut Draper
	Decem	7	Thursday Christning of Grislie Malin daughter
		20	Christning of John Yong sonne of Gregory Yong grocer
	Janua	16	Tuesday Christning of Annes Candley daughter
	Februa	10	Satterday Christning of John Swinkfeeld sonne
	March	1	Thursday Christning of William Harris sonne
1562	Maye	28	Monday Christning of William Lambe sonne of Richard
	June	6	Wedensday Christning of Elizabeth Hunter daughter
		14	Christning of Edward Steuannes son of and
		14	Christning of Annes Lightbraiu daughter of and
		24	Christning of Mathew Butler sonne of and
	August	5	Sonday Christning of George Dowson sonne of John
		16	Christning of Robert Leame sonne of and
		20	Christning of John Malen sonne of Thomas Malen
		27	Christning of Thomas Isherwood sonne of and
	Septem	28	Friday Christning of John Jans sonne of and
	Octobe	3	Wedensday Christning of John Steuaunes sonne
		3	Christning of Thomas Wrath sonne of and
		7	Christning of Katherine Clarke daughter of
		11	Christning of Judith Westraw daughter of and
		11	Christning of Annes Inman daughter of John Inman
		11	Christning of Lewes Richardsonne sonne of
		20	Christning of Rachell Axonne daughter of and
		25	Christning of Richard Satchfeeld sonne of Gilbert
	Nouem	6	Tuesday Christning of Samuell Corse sonne of
		26	Christning of Hierome Richmond sonne of and
		26	Christning of Henry Pressy sonne of and
	Janua	8	Thursday Christning of Henry Billingsley sonne
		5	Christning of Nicholas Stonehouse sonne of and
		7	Christning of Daniell Pallmer sonne of William
	Februa	1	Friday Christning of Richard Heywood sonne of
		20	Christning of Henry Heely sonne of
		28	Christning of Annes Yong daughter of Gregory, grocer
	March	15	Friday Christning of Joane Nichollsonne daughter
		20	Christning of Samuel Gough sonne of Thomas Gough, preacher
1563	Aprill	2	Tuesday Christning of George Chapmanne sonne of
	May	9	Thursday Christning of John Burnam sonne of
		30	Christning of Samuell Hayes sonne of and
	June	6	Thursday Christning of Christopher Lambe sonne
		14	Christning of Edward Steuenes sonne of and
		20	Christning of Edward Hill sonne of John Hill, clothworker
	Julie	19	Friday Christning of Susan Adlington daug. of John Adlington
		19	Christning of Katherine Adlington daug. of John, twynnes
		25	Christning of Martha Wattam daughter of and
		25	Christning of John Coote sonne of and
	August	18	Sonday Christning of Ellen Ouerton daughter of John
	Septem	10	Tuesday Christning of Samuell Abowen sonne of John
	October	19	Satterday Christning of Elizabeth Walker daug. of Edward

Yeare.	Month.	Day.	Names.
1563	October	31	Christning of Fulke Hunter sonne of and
	Nouem	20	Wedensday Christning of George Wood sonne of
		22	Christning of Fulke Jorden sonne of Robert Jorden poulter
		23	Christning of Alice Bellanue daughter of and
		27	Christning of Elizabeth Axoune daughter of and
	Decemb	13	Friday Christning of Thomas Malyn sonne of John
		16	Christning of Henry Baker sonne of and
		20	Christning of George Lester sonne of and
	January	20	Monday Christning of Harry Billingsley sonne
	Februa	14	Friday Christning of Elizabeth Westraw daughter
	March	2	Sonday Christning of Elizabeth Offley daug. of Thomas
		12	Christning of Judith Eglesfeeld daughter of and ...
		13	Christning of William Cootes son of and ...
		14	Christning of Ephin King daughter of and ...
		15	Christninges of John Steuennes sonne of and ...
1564	Aprill	9	Wedensday Christning of Thomas Pressey sonne
	Maye	1	Friday Christning of Thomas Yong sonne of Anthonie
		4	Christning of Susanne Richmanne daughter of ...
		10	Christning of Grisell Linsey daughter of and ...
	June	2	Monday Christning of Joane Shearemanne dau.
		30	Christning of Effham Adlington daughter of John
	Julie	10	Thursday Christning of Richard Daulton sonne of Thomas
		13	Christning of Jeames Isherwood sonne of and ...
		27	Christning of Richard Hayes sonne of and
	August	7	Thursday Christning of Mary Coot daughter of ...
	Septem	7	Sunday Christning of Grace Caluar daughter of ...
		20	Christning of Elizabeth Euerton daughter of John
		30	Christning of Margaret Walker daughter of Edward
	October	22	Wedensday Christning of Edward Swingfeeld sonne ...
		29	Christning of William Steuennes sonne of and ...
	Nouem	1	Satterday Christning of Anne Chattertonne daugh.
		3	Christning of Richard Lambe sonne of Adam Lambe
		9	Christning of Rachell Cleent daughter and ...
	Decemb	17	Wedensday Christning of Edward Goffe sonne of Lawrence
	January	7	Wedensday Christning of John Caunt, sonne of Edward
		14	Christning of Walter Stonehouse sonne of Mr Stone
		30	Christning of Jane Clarke daughter of Clarke the cooke
		30	Christning of Susanne Dowson daughter of John Dowson
	February	5	Thursday Christning of George Gough sonne of Thomas pcher
		5	Christning of Edward Jordain sonne of Robert Jorden, poulter
		6	Christning of Elizabeth Morris daughter of and ...
	March	7	Satterday Christning of Elizabeth Baxter daughter
		17	Christning of Robert Coorfe sonne of John Coorfe
		24	Christning of Willfred Brown sonne of and ...
1565	Aprill	3	Friday Christning of Elizabeth Richardsonne daughter
		5	Christning of Nicholas Wallay sonne of and ...
	Maye	12	Tuesday Christning of Mary Lambe daughter and
		12	Christning of Sara Bowing daughter of and ...
		12	Christning of Elizabeth Turner daughter and ...
		27	Christning of Robert Pressey sonne of and
	Julie	1	Wedensday Christning of John Mascoll sonne of
		8	Christning of Katherine Yong daughter of and ...
		8	Christning of Elizabeth Ilbraine daughter of and ...
		20	Christning of Haniball Adlington sonne of John and ...
		26	Wedensday Christning of Rebecca Paulmer daughter

Yeare.	Month.	Day.	Names.
1565	August	28	Christning of Thomas Westraw sonne of Thomas
		28	Christning of Peeter Smith sonne of and ..
		28	Christning of John Dehouay sonne of and ..
		28	Christning of Sidrach Dehouay sonne of and ...
	Septem	12	Satterday Christning of John Yong sonne of Gregory Yong
		23	Christning of Hester Harris a dutch child daughter
	October	17	Satterday Christning of Luke Hayes sonne of
	Nouem	14	Satterday Christning of a weake child of Mr Steuens
	Decem	3	Thursday Christning of Dionice Satchfeeld sonne of Gilbert
	Janua	10	Sonday Christning of Sara Chattertonne daughter
		12	Christning of John Inmanne sonne of Inman hosier
		25	Christning of Judith Barnard daughter of Libias
		25	Christning of John Straunge son of and ...
		30	Christning of Richard Clarke sonne of Clarke ye cooke
	Februa	12	Friday Christning of Thomas Cockes sonne of Edward
		18	Christning of Harry Jordan sonne of Robert Jordan
	March	19	Christning of Grace Hilles the daughter of ...
1566		25	Christning of Anne Thomson daughter of Richard ; cooke
		30	Christning of Robert Burnam sonne of Clement Bur.
	April	14	Wednesday Christning of Harry Lodge sonne of Sy^r Thomas L.
	Maye	6	Thursday Christning of Robert Wood sonne of ...
		12	Christning of John Turner sonne of and ...
		16	Christning of Elizabeth Yong daughter of and ...
	June	29	Tuesday Christning of Peeter Bennet
	Julie	7	Wednesday Christning of Thomas Walley sonne
		13	Christning of William Mascoll sonne of
		21	Christning of Robert Knight sonne of and ...
		21	Christning of John Malen sonne of and ...
	August	10	Tuesday Christning of William Lambe sonne of
		21	Christning of William Paulmer sonne of Willia'
	Septem	5	Sonday Christning of Sara Axonne daughter
		6	Christning of Katherine Woodcocke daughter and
		12	Christning of Annes Jorden daughter of and ...
		22	Christning of John Bowen sonne of John Bowen
		23	Christning of Richard Hannam sonne of and ...
		29	Christning of Thomas Sckott sonne of and ...
	October	6	Wednesday Christning of Mathew Cut sonne of Hary
		8	Christning of Phillip Steuens sonne of Richard, Armoro^r
	Nouem	1	Monday Christning of Richard Baynes sonne of
		6	Christning of William Anger sonne of and ...
		23	Christning of Ruth Gough daughter of Mr Gough prech^r
		24	Christning of Anne Brown daughter of and ...
	Decem	1	Monday Christning of Thomas Satchfeld sonne of Gil.
		9	Christning of Thomas Adlington son of John Adling.
		12	Christning of William Mese son of Mr Mese grocer
		12	Christning of William Yong sonne of Anthonie Yong
		30	Christning of Jeames Stonehouse sonne of Mr Stone
	Februa	2	Wednesday Christning of Mary Hayes daughter
		17	Christning of Mary Yong daughter of Gregory Yong
	March	16	Wednesday Christning of John Jordain sonne of Robert
1567	Aprill	6	Wednesday Christning of Ellen Walker daughter of Edw.
		17	Christning of Charitie Burchenshaw daug. of Randoll
	Maye	1	Sonday Christning of Doritie Richemond daughter
	June	8	Wednesday Christning of Elizabeth ffecie daughter
	Julie	20	Wednesday Christning of Elizabeth Goffe daughter of and ...

Yeare.	Month.	Day.	Names.
1567	Julie	24	Christning of Maudelin Clarke daughter of and ...
	August	3	Tuesday Christning of Alice Lambe daughter of ...
		10	Christning of Thomas Axtonne sonne of and ...
	Septem	16	Thursday Christning of Sara Cut daughter of Harry
		18	Christning of a weake child of Richard Steuenes
	Nouem	2	Christning of George Milles vpon a tuesday
	Decem	21	Tuesday Christning of a child of Mr Wakefeeld
	January	8	Satterday Christning of Elizabeth Byllam daug.
		10	Thursday Christning of Richard Richardsonne
1568	March	28	Monday Christning of William Clint sonne
		28	Christning of Mary Cockes, daughter of Edward
		28	Christning of Alice Hill daughter and ...
	Aprill	10	Sonday Christning of Daniell Abowen sonne of John
		10	Christning of Mary Jordain daughter of Robert Jord.
		25	Christning of Alice Yong daughter of Anthonie Yong
	Maye	2	Monday Christning of Daniell Barnard sonne of
		9	Christning of Annes Wilkinsonne daughter of and ...
		9	Christning of Anthonie Hern sonne of and ...
		16	Christning of John Gough sonne of Thomas, pcho^r
		16	Christning of William Sekot sonne of and ...
	June	6	Monday Christning of Harry Cullymer sonne
		27	Christning of Mary Auling daughter of and ...
	Julie	9	Satterday Christning of John Courson son of Rich., Arnore^r
		9	Christning of Elizabeth Wood daughter of and ...
		14	Christning of John Fewterell sonne of and ...
		29	Christning of Christopher Turner sonne of
	August	20	Satterday Christning of Jane Goffe dau. of Lawrence
		29	Christning of Gregory Axonne sonne of
	Septem	19	Monday Christning of William Clarke sonne of Siluester
	October	3	Monday Christning of Joane Malin daughter of John
		3	Christning of Katherine Porter daughter of
		24	Christning of Phebe Cut daughter of Harry Cut
		24	Christning of Jane Knight daughter of and ...
	Nouem	21	Monday Christning of Sara Jordain dau. of Robert
		30	Christning of Richard Hayse sonne of and ...
	Decem	16	Friday Christning of a child of Mrs Wakefeeldes
		19	Christning of Richard Westrawe sonne of ...
		21	Christning of Frauncos Steuennes sonne of Richard
		25	Christning of William Mascoll sonne of Mr Mascoll smith
	Janua	17	Tuesday Christning of Thomas Thomson sonne of Richard
	Februa	2	Thursday Christning of Mary Banes daughter of ...
	March	5	Sonday Christning of Rosamund Mylles daughter
1569		27	Christning of Joane Wheeler daughter of and ...
	Aprill	10	Monday Christning of a childe of Ellen Smithes which died
	Maye	27	Satterday Christning of Katherin Satchfeeld daugh. of Gilbert
	June	19	Monday Christning of Winnefred Harrisone daug.
	August	7	Monday Christning of Mabell Wroth daughter of ...
		9	Christning of Robert Yong sonne of Anthonie Yong
		14	Christning of Richard Ager sonne of and ...
		14	Christning of John Adlington sonne of John Adlington
		27	Christning of Edward Browne sonne of and ...
		31	Christning of Richard ffinar sonne of and ...
	Septem	4	Monday Christning of Richard Richardson sonne of
		4	Christning of Susanne Taylor daughter of and ...
		18	Christning of Margaret fflower daughter of Richard

Years.	Month.	Day.	Names.
1569	Septem	18	Christning of Elizabeth fflower daughter of Richard
		28	Christning of Thomas Brown sonne of Thomas
		30	Christning of Anne Jordane daughter of Robert
	October	9	Monday Christning of George Sckot sonne of and ...
	Nouem	27	Monday Christning of Luce Axsonne daughter of
		27	Christning of Elizabeth Cut daughter of Harry Cut
		30	Christning of Daniell Woodcocke sonne of and ...
	Decem	4	Monday Christning of Luce Rogers daughter of
	Janua	1	Monday Christning of Josua Bowen sonne of John
		15	Christning of Katherine Steuens daughter of Richard
	Februa	5	Monday Christning of Katherine Goffe dau. of Laurence
		18	Christning of Jesper Warren sonne of and ...
	March	19	Monday Christning of Edward Burnam sonne of
1570	Aprill	13	Friday Christning of Vrsula Jud daughter of John Jud
		23	Christning of Martha Audly daughter of William
		29	Christning of Thomas Bricket sonne of Hamlet
	June	7	Thursday Christning of Margaret Malin daug: of John
		18	Christning of Benjamin Stokes sonne of and ...
	Julie	9	Monday Christning of Edward Bleache sonne of W^m
		14	Christning of Judith Smith daugh. of John Smith, hosier
		23	Christning of Suzanne Linsey daughter of John
		24	Christning of John Mascoll sonne of Mr Mascoll smith
	August	8	Wedensday Christning of Grace Phillips dau. of Thom.
		20	Christning of Susan Hill daughter of John Hill
		21	Christning of James More sonne of James More
		24	Christning of Susanne Yong daughter of Gregory Yong
	Septem	3	Christning of John and Marye Turner children of John
		24	Christning of Dorothy Billam daughter of Richard
	October	1	Monday Christning of Richard Curson sonne of Richard
		1	Christning of Elizabeth Fewterer daughter of Fraunces
	Nouem	25	Monday Christning of Edward Cut sonne of Harry Cut
	Decem	17	Monday Christning of Grace Jordain daugh. of Robert
	Januar	7	Monday Christning of Jeames Steuens sonne of Richard
		14	Christning of Elizabeth Borow daughter of Thomas Bor.
		15	Christning of John Porter sonne of John Porter
		21	Christning of John Warren sonne of John Warren Armorer
		28	Christning of Phillip Tibbald sonne of William Tibbald
	Februa	19	Tuesday Christning of John Yong sonue of John Yong
	March	11	Monday Christning of Thomas Gardner sonne of Thomas
		24	Christning of Harry Adlington sonne of John Adlington
1571	Aprill	1	Sonday Christning of William Morgraue sonne of John Morgraue
	August	4	Satterday Christning of Samuell Goffe sonne of Laurence
		19	Christning of Isbell Hayes daughter of John Haies and
	Septem	21	Friday Christning of Elizabeth Baynes daughter of John
	October	14	Sonday Christning of Mary Bowen daughter of John
		21	Sonday Christning of William Bilborough sonne of Robert
		28	Sonday Christning of Rowland Standly sonne of John
	Nouem	11	Sonday Christning of Anne Scot daughter of Willm
		30	Friday Christning of Richard Billam sonne of Richard
	Decem	26	Wedensday Christning of Elizabeth Milles dau. of Robert
		30	Sonday Christning of Steuen sonne of Gregory Yong grocer
	Janua	27	Sonday Christning of John Cuttes sonne of Harry
	Februa	6	Wedensday Christning of Joane Judge daugh of Wm Judge
		13	Wedensday Christning of Richard Woodcocke sonne of W^m
	March	16	Satterday Christning of Joane Hayse daugh. of Steuen
1572	Maye	18	Satterday Christning of Jane Adlin daugh. of John Adlin

Yeare.	Month.	Day.	Names.
1572	June	22	Sonday Christning of Joane Knight daugh. of John Kni.
		29	Sonday Christning of Margaret Adlington dau. of John
	Julie	1	Tuesday Christning of John Malin sonne of John Malin
		27	Sonday Christning of Elizabeth Durdant dau. of Thomas
	Septem	2	Tuesday Christning of Susan Barrow daugh. of Tho'
		8	Monday Christning of Annes Burnam daugh. of Clement
		21	Sonday Christning of William Turner sonne of John Tur.
	October	10	Friday Christning of Alice Thomlinson daugh. to Mathew
		12	Sonday Christning of Margery Parton daugh. to ffraunces
		20	Monday Christning of William Yong sonne of Anthonie
	Nouem	2	Sonday Christning of John Stanly sonne of Thomas
		3	Monday Christning of Anne More daugh. of Jeames More
		23	Sonday Christning of John Phillippes sonne of Thomas
		23	Christning of Annes Hayes daughter of Annes Haies a single woma'.
	Decem	7	Sonday Christning of John Scot sonne of William Scot
		21	Sonday Christning of Agatha Smith daugh. of John Smith
	Janua	14	Wedensday Christning of Margaret Goffe daug. of Lawraunce
		15	Thursday Christning of William Tibbold sonne of William
		22	Thursday Christning of Robert Bilborough sonne of Robert
	Februa	8	Sonday Christning of Alexander Norris sonne of John
	March	5	Sonday Christning of William Warren sonne of John Warren
1573	June	27	Satterday Christning of Mary and Susan Beston at Mr Luntloes
		28	Sonday Christning of John Gunby sonne of George
	Julie	18	Friday Christning of John May sonne of Robert May
		25	Satterday Christning of Mary Walker daughter of John
	August	9	Sonday Christning of Anne Hassall daughter of John
		16	Sonday Christning of Mary Knight daughter of John
	Septem	6	Satterday Christning of Martha Porter daug. of William
		28	Sonday Christning of Godfry Rombat a duch childe
	October	2	Thursday Christning of Thomas Durdant sonne of William
	Nouem	1	Sonday Christning of Nicholas Adlington sonne of John
		6	Friday Christning of Jane Stokes daughter of William
		8	Sonday Chri: Thomas Hassall sonne of Perciuall: born the 5 day
		15	Sonday Christning of Thomas More sonne of Jeames More
		22	Sonday Christning of Martha Cuttes daughter of Harry
		30	Monday Christning of Margery Axon daughter of Lawrence
	Decem	22	Monday Christning of Annes Hailes daughter of Jeames
	Janua	11	Monday Christning of William Stayner sonne of Harry
		14	Thursday Christning of Kathern Yong daughter of Gregory
	Februa	7	Sonday Christning of Jane Borrow daughter of Thomas
		8	Monday Christning of Elias Edwardes sonne of Edward
		14	Sonday Christning of John Parton sonne of ffraunces
		14	Sonday Christning of Katherine Miles daughter of Robert
		24	Wedensday Christning of Mathias Phillippes sonne of Thomas
	March	21	Sonday Christning of Jeames Kelley sonne of John Kelley
1574	Aprill	4	Sonday Christning of Christopher Gardner son of Mr Thomas
	May	17	Monday Christning of Thomas Adlyn sonne of Mr Adlyn
	Julie	7	Wedensday Christning of Maudelin Barbar daughter of Paule
		11	Sonday Christning of Tobias Abowen sonne of John Abowen

Yeare.	Month.	Day.	Names.
1574	August	23	Monday Christning of Edmond Nicholles sonne of Edmond Ny:
		23	Monday Christning of Blaunch Locke daughter of John Locke
	October	12	Tuesday Christning of Margery Gunby daughter of George
		31	Sonday Christning of Joane Porter daughter of Gregory
	Nouem	7	Sonday Christning of Martha Hassald daugh. of John Ha.
		15	Monday Christning of John Hewgen sonne of John Hewgen
		28	Sonday Christning of Fraunces Goffe daughter of Lawrence
		30	Tuesday Christning of Edward Yong sonne of Anthony Yong borne ye 27
	Decem	11	Satterday Christning of Robert Durdant sonne of Thom. borne ye 9 Decem
		18	Satterday Christning of Paul Vanhocke at the duch church : sonne of Bartholomew : but borne heare. Witnesses Mr Ashbold parson, Mr Yong, Mr Heath
	Janua	2	Sonday Christning of Richard Hayles sonne of Steuen born ye first day
		6	Thursday Christning of Anne Hamlyn daug. of John born the 2 day
		9	Sonday Christning of Robert Adlington son of John born the 8 day
		25	Tuesday Christning of Jesper Tibbold sonne of William born the 20 day
	Februa	13	Sonday Christning of Christopher Blower, son of Robert, born ye 3 day
	March	13	Sonday Christning of Elizabeth Salsbury daug. of Robert born ye 7 day
		20	Sonday Christning of Anne Parton dau. of Fraunces born the 18 day
1575		27	Sonday Christning of Fraunces* Dylton son of Richard, born ye 25 day
		27	Sonday Christning of Susan Axon, daug : of Lawrence born ye 24 day
	Aprill	3	Sonday Christning of Jeremy Gardner sonne of Mr. Thomas Gardner, Grocer the child born the 30 of March
	Maye	1	Sonday Christning of Joane Cut daughter of Harry Cut Draper, the childe borne the 24th daye of Aprill
	June	10	Friday Christning of Rachell Phillippes daughter of Thomas Phillippes grocer, the child born the ninth of this month of June
	Julie	3	Sonday Christning of John Joden sonne of William Joden, Inholder, the childe was born the second day of this month of Julie
	August	19	Friday Christning of Foulke Bromely sonne of William Bromly, Poulter, the childe was born the 14th daye of August
		21	Sonday Christning of Julian Bording daughter of Nicholas Bording, the childe was born the 17th day of August
	Septem	8	Thursday Christning of Elizabeth Hassald daughter of Perciuall Hassald sckinner born the 7th day wedensday
		18	Sonday Christning of Edward Smith sonne of John Smith Draper, the childe was born the same day it was Christned

* Sic.

Yeare.	Month.	Day.	Names.
1575	Septem	25	Sonday Christning of Thomas Stanly, sonne of John Stanly Draper, the childe was born the 22th day of September
	October	12	Wedensday Christning of George Lynsey sonne of George Lynsey, Haberdasher, the childe was born the 9th of October
	Nouem	27	Sonday Christning of Alice Willy daughter of Richard Willy Grocer, the childe was born the 21th daye of Nouember
	Decem	9	Friday Christning of Ellen Durdant daughter of Thomas Durdant Skynner, the childe was born the 5th day of December
		11	Sonday Christning of Mathew Brugge sonne of Mr. Anthonie Brug Esquire of London Draper, the childe was borne the 8th day of December
		15	Thursday Christning of Ambrose and Richard Porter sonnes of Gregory Porter, the children weare born the same day of the month being the 15
	Februa	2	Thursday Christning of Susan Warren daughter of John Warren Armoror the childe was born the first day of the month of February
		17	Friday Christning of Elizabeth Lister daughter of John Lister Barbor, the childe was born the 13th daye of this month of Februarye
	March	11	Sonday Christning of Elizabeth Holsworth daughter of Harry Holsworth of London Mercer the childe was born the 8th daye of Marche
1576	Aprill	19	Thursday Christning of Daniell Vanhocke at the duche church sonne of Bartholomew : the childe was born in this parish of St. Peeters
	Maye	27	Sonday Christning of Harry Cut sonne of Harry Cut, Draper the childe was born the 17th day of this month of Maye
		27	Sonday Christning of Edward Porter sonne of William Porter the childe was born the 24th daye of this present month of May
		27	Sonday Christning of Elizabeth Adlington daughter of John Adlington Poulter the childe was born the 25th daye of this mouth.
	Julie	1	Sonday Christning of Anne Blower daughter of Robert Blower the childe was born the six and twentith day of June.
		1	Sonday Christning of Anne Cornelis daughter of Hierome Cornelis of London, Joyner the childe was born the 29th day of June
1576	August	5	Sonday Christning of John Walker sonne of Edward Walker of London Carpenter the childe was born the 29th day of Julie
		13*	Sonday Christning of Hamlet Bricket sonne of William Bricket of London Sc'vener the child was born the 9th daye of August
		13	Monday Christning of Rebecca Kellet daughter of John Kellet Haberdasher, the childe was born the 12th day of this present August
		26*	Monday Christning of Bartholomew Cooke sonne of Richard Cooke seruingman the childe was born the 23th daye of August

* Sic.

Yeare.	Month.	Day.	Names.
1576	Septem	2	Sonday Christning of John Astmore sonne of John Astmore Baker the childe was born the 27th of August
		9	Sonday Christning of Elizabeth Curson daughter of Richard Curson Armorer the childe born the 7th daye
		16	Sonday Christning of Thomas Phillip sonne of Thomas Phillip Grocer, the childe was born the 10th of September
		29	Satterday Christning of Richard Smith sonne of John Smith Merchaunt Tayler the child born the 24th Septem.
	October	25	Thursday Christning of Sara Margraue daughter of Nicholas Morgraue Merchaunt Tailor, the child born ye 24 Octob^r
	Nouem	4	Sonday Christning of Thomas Chaderton sonne of Robert Chaderton, Fishmonger the child born the 30th day of October
	Decemb	10	Monday Christning of Ellen Atkinson daughter [of] Peeter Atkinson Draper the childe was born the first day of December
		16	Sonday Christning of Robert Lecroft sonne of Robert Lecroft Armorer the child was born the thirteenth day of December
		27	Thursday Christning of Susan Jordane daughter of Jeames Jordane Porter in the waygh house; born the 25th of December
		30	Sonday Christning of Margery Lockson daughter of Richard Lockson, Armorer the childe born the 29th day of December
	Janua	20	Sonday Christning of Elizabeth Hippe, daughter of John Hippe wooll winder the child born the 16th day of January
	Februa	24	Sonday Christning of Margery Woodcocke daughter of John Wookcocke Skynner the child born the 22th day of February
	March	10	Sonday Christning of Perciuall Hassald sonne of Perciuall Hassald Skynner the childe was born the second of Marche
		17	Sonday Christning of Robert Gardner sonne of Thomas Gardener Grocer the childe was born the 12th day of Marche
		24	Sonday Christning of Lawrence Gofe sonne of Lawrence Gofe Draper, the childe was born the twentith of Marche
1577	Aprill	21	Sonday Christning of Mary Fidens daughter of John Fidens minister of this church the childe born the 14th of Aprill
	Maye	1	Wedensday Christning of Alice Holsworth daughter of Henry Holsworth Mercer the childe born the 29th of Aprill
		24	Friday Christning of Elizabeth Axon daughter of Lawrence Axon the childe was born the 19th of Maye
		26	Sonday Christning of Elizabeth Dilling daughter of Richard Dilling Poulter the childe borne the 23th day of May
	June	12	Wedensday Christning of Katherine Graunger daughter of Symon Graunger Grocer the childe born the 10th of June
		23	Sonday Christning of Fraunces Baines daughter of Richard Baines, merchaunt of ye Staple, born the 19th daye of June

THE REGISTERS OF ST. PETER'S, CORNHILL.

Yeare.	Month.	Day.	Names.
1577	August	28	Wedensday Christning of Alice Mager daughter of William Mager Merchant Tailor the childe born the 24th of August
	Septem	15	Sonday Christning of Annes Willy daughter of Richard Willy Grocer, the childe was born the 11th daye of September
		20	Friday Christning of Sara Wiffen daughter of John Wifen Husband-man, the childe was born the 18th of September
		22	Sonday Christning of Judith Cut daughter of Harry Cut, Draper the childe born the 20th day of Septemb.
	Nouem	18	Monday Christning of Edward Noble sonne of Thomas Noble of Nottingham, the childe born the 16th daye of Nouembr
		24	Sonday Christning of Alice Bromely daughter of William Bromely Poulter, the childe born the 18th day of Nouember
		24	Sonday* of Annes Wenwright daughter of Thomas Wenwright, the childe born the 19th day of this Month Nouembr
	Decem	8	Sonday Christning of Agatha Gold daughter of Hugh Gold Grocer, the childe born the fourth day of December
	Janua	15	Wedensday Christning of Thomas Wodford sonne of Gamaliell Woodford, Grocer, the childe born the 13th of January
	Februa	2	Sonday Christning of Richard Powell sonne of David Powell Merchant Tailor the childe born the 30th of January
		9	Sonday Christning of Adam Watson sonne of Barnaby Watson Merchaunt Tailor the childe born the 8th of february
	March	9	Sonday Christning of Joane Finche daughter of John Finche Carpenter the child was born the seventh day of March
		16	Sonday Christning of Zachary Hassald sonne of Perciuall Hassald Skinner the childe born the 11th daye
1578		30	Sonday Christning of Paule Scaliot sonne of Marko Scaliot Blackesmith the childe was born the 15th day of March
	Aprill	20	Sonday Christning of Peeter Lyster sonne of John Lister of London, Barbor, the childe born the 19th of this p'sent March*
	June	1	Sonday Christning of John Corser sonne of John Corser, Clothworker, the childe was born the 29th daye of Maye
		1	Sonday Christning of Bright daughter of Sallomon Bright, Haberdasher, the childe was born the 28th of Maye
		1	Sonday Christning of Dauid Pope sonne of Waldron Pope Duchman, the child born heare ye 30th of May, but Christened at the Duche Church the day and date afore mentioned
		15	Sonday Christning of Fulke Phillip sonne of Thomas Phillip, Grocer, the Childe was born the 13th of this present June
		22	Sonday Christning of Margery Stanly daughter of John Stanly Draper the childe was born the 17th day of June

* Sic.

Yeare.	Month.	Day.	Names.
1578	Julie	16	Wedensday Christning of Mary Holdsworth daughter of Henry Holdsworth Mercer the childe born the 14th of July
		27	Sonday Christning of John Hunt sonne of Robert Hunt, Waterman the childe was born the 23rd of Julye
	August	17	Sonday Christning of Joane Graunger daughter of Symond Graunger, the childe was born the 15th of this month
		22	Friday Christning of Steuen Hales, sonne of Steuen Hales Pewterer, the childe was born the 19th of August
		27	Wedensday Christning of Jeames Gunby sonne of George Gunby the childe was born the 24th day beeing Bartholmew day
	Septem	28	Sonday Christning of William Hippey sonne of John Hippey wooll-winder the childe was born the 24th day of Septem
	Nouem	23	Sunday Christning of John Walker sonne of John Walker, Armorer the childe was born the 21th daye of Nouember
	Decem	4	Wedensday Christning of Anne Cockes daughter of Harry Cockes Clothworker the childe was born the 23th of Nouembr
		12	Friday Christning of Robert Hubbersted sonne of George Hubbersted Taylor the childe born the 7th day of Decembr
		21	Sonday Christning of Thomas Jones sonne of Thomas Jones Grocer, the childe born the 18th day of December
	Januar	4	Sonday Christning of Anne Powell daughter of David Powell Merchant Taylor, the child born ye 3 of Janu
		10	Satterday Christning of Robert Cotton sonne of George Cotton of London Grocer the childe born the same day
		28	Wedensday Christning of Richard and John Gold sonnes of Hugh Gold Grocer, ye children born the 24th of January
	Februa	1	Sonday Christning of Cibell Mewter daughter of John Mewter of London Taylor the childe born the 26th of January
		2	Monday Christning of Annes Averell daughter of William Averell Merchaunt Taylor the childe born the 26th of January
		13	Friday Christning of Judith King daughter of Richard King Grocer the childe was born the 7th day of February
1579	Aprill	12	Sonday Christning of Alice Bennet daughter of Melchisedech Bennet Poulter, born the 9th of Aprill
		19	Sonday Ester day Christning of William Porter sonne of William Porter Clothworker born the 15th of Aprill
		20	Monday Christning of Richard Cut sonne of Harry Cut the childe born the 16th of Aprill; ye father a draper
	Maye	24	Sonday Christning of Anne Woodford daughter of Gamaliell Woodford Grocer the childe born the 17th of this present May
		24	Sonday Christning of Fraunces Cornelis daughter of Jerome Cornelis Joyner the childe was born the 17th of this present May
	June	7	Sonday Christning of Perciuall Hassald sonne of Perciuall Hassall Skynner the childe was born the 31th of May, being sonday

Yeare.	Month.	Day.	Names.
1579	June	11	Thursday Christning of Thomas Haukes sonne of John Haukes, Draper, the childe born the 6th of this month beeing Satterday
		11	Thursday Christning of Richard Gunby sonne of George Gunby Scriuenor, the childe was born the same day
	Julie	10	Friday Christning of Anne Randoll daughter of John Randoll Draper, the childe was born the 6th of this month of Julye
	August	16	Sonday Christning of Thomas Yong sonne of Gregory Yong, Grocer, the childe was born the 10th day beeing Monday
		30	Sonday Christning of Daniell Pope sonne of Waldron Pope, Duchman at ye duch church, born heare the 23th of August being sonday
	Septem	18	Friday Christning of Nicholas Hailes sonne of Steuen Hailes, Pewterer, the childe was born the 14th of Septembr beeing Monday
		27	Sonday Christning of Rebecca Hippey, daughter of John Hippy Wooll winder, the childe was born the 24th day beeing Thursday
	October	4	Sonday Christning of Elizabeth Finche daughter of John Finch, Carpenter, the childe was born the first of October Thursday
		18	Sonday Christning of Marget Holsworth daughter of Harry Holsworth Mercer, the childe born the 13th day beeing Tuesday
		25	Sonday Christning of Richard Willy sonne of Richard Willy, Grocer the childe born the 18th day of October beeing sonday
	Nouem	22	Sonday Christning of Jeames Stanley sonne of John Stanley Draper, the childe born the 19th of Nouember being Thursday
		29	Sonday Christning of Rebecca Ball daughter of Humphry Ball white baker, the childe born the 26th day being Thursday
		29	Sonday Christning of William Robinson sonne of Richard Robinson, Skynner the childe born the 23th day being Monday
	Decemb	6	Sonday Christning of Katherine Vandort daughter of Cornelis Vandort ducheman and goldsmith born the 5th of December, satterday
		22	Tuesday Christning of William Lister sonne of John Lister barbor the childe was born the 21th of December being Moneday
		27	Sonday Christning of Susan Averell daughter of William Averell Merchaunt Taylor, born the 24th of December Thursday
	January	24	Sonday Christning of Richard Warren sonne of John Warren Armorer, the childe born the 15th of January beeing Friday
	Februa	2	Tuesday Christning of William Watson sonne of Barnaby Watson Merchaunt Taylor born the 29th of January being Fryday
		11	Thursday Christning of Phebe Gold daughter of Hugh Gold, Grocer the childe born the 6th of February being Satterday
1580	Aprill	5	Tuesday Christning of Robert Bennet sonne of Melchisedech Bennet Poulter the childe born the 3d of Aprill being Ester day

Yeare.	Month.	Day.	Names.
1580	Aprill	10	Sonday Christning of Alice Hubbersted daughter of George Hubbersted Merchaunt Tailor born the 4th daye beeing Monday
	Maye	1	Sonday Christning of Elizabeth Gunby daughter of George Gunby Scriuenor the childe born the 27th of Aprill being Wedensday
		5	Thursday Christning of Phillip Brisket sonne of Ledewicke Brisket gentleman the childe born the 28th of Aprill being Friday
		20	Friday Christning of Robert Brian sonne of John Brian Tailor the childe born the 16th of Maye beeing Monday
		30	Monday Christning of Margery Willsonne daughter of Daniell Willson butterman, born the same day in Mr. Tibaldes house
	June	5	Sonday Christning of Thomas Kynaston sonne of Thomas Kynaston Merchaunt Tailor, born the 3 of June being friday
		12	Sonday Christning of John Wenewright sonne of Thomas Wenewright Carter, the childe born the 6th day being Monday
	Julie	10	Sonday Christning of Katherine Corzer daughter of John Corzer Clothworker, the childe born the 5th of Julie being tuesday
		30	Satterday Christning of John Sutton sonne of John Sutton Carpenter the childe born the 28th of Julie beeing Thursday
		31	Sonday Christning of Judith King daughter of Richard King, Grocer the childe born the 28th day of July being Thursday
		31	Sonday Christning of Gregory Jones sonne of Thomas Jones Grocer, the childe born the 27th of July being wedensday
	Septem	21	Wedensday Christning of Anne Miller daughter of Richard Miller Clothworker the childe born the 18th day beeing Sonday
		29	Thursday Christning of Elizabeth Cornelis daughter of Jerom Cornelis Joyner the child born the 24th day this month : satterday
	October	9	Sonday Christning of John Randoll sonne of John Randoll, Draper the childe was born the 6th of October beeing Thursday
		23	Sonday Christning of Joane Cooper daughter of Thomas Cooper Armorer the childe was born the 19th of Octobr being Wedensday
	Nouem	1	Tuesday Christning of William Sturman sonne of Richard Sturman fishemonger, born the 28th of October being friday
		6	Sonday Christning of Vrsola Baynes daughter of Richard Banes Merchant Stapler; born the first of Nouember being tuesday
		13	Sonday Christning of Gilbert Dethicke sonne of Mr. William Dethick alias Yorke Harold of Armes; born the 6th of Nouember being sonday
	Decem	4	Sonday Christning of Thomas Robinson sonne of Richard Robinson Skynner, the childe was born the same day in the fore-noone
		15	Thursday Christning of Vincent Atkinson sonne of Edward Atkinson Merchaunt Tailor ye queenes man : born the 11th day beeing sonday

Yeare.	Month.	Day.	Names.
1580	Decem	18	Sonday Christning of Susan Pope daughter of Waldron Pope duche man at the duche church, born heare the 17th day being satterday
		21	Wedensday Christning of Anthonie Bright sonne of Salomon Bright Haberdasher, born the 18th of December: sunday
		21	Wedensday Christning of Elizabeth Averell daughter of William Averell Merchaunt Taylor, born friday the 16th day
		25	Sonday Christning of Diana Holsworth daughter of Harry Holsworth : Mercer the childe born the 22th day beeing Thursday
		25	Sonday Christning of Vrsula Stanly daughter of John Stanly Draper, the childe was born the 20th day beeing Tuesday
		25	Sonday Christning of Elizabeth Hubbersted daughter of Robert Hubbersted Merchaunt Tailor, born the 19th of December
	Januar	2	Monday Christning of Susanna Scaliot daughter of Marke Scaliot blacke smith the childe born Wedensday the 28th day
		15	Sonday Christning of William Woodford sonne of Gamaliell Woodford Grocer, the childe was born the 8th day being sonday
		15	Sonday Christning of Audrian Bromely daughter of William Bromely Poulter the child born thursday ye 12th day
	Februar	19	Sonday Christning of Maudlyn Powell daughter of Dauy Powell Merchaunt Tailor, the child born the 12th day : sonday
		24	Friday Christning of Margaret Lister daughter of John Lister Barbor, the childe was born the 19th day of february : sonday
	March	12	Sonday Christning of Joane Bennet daughter of Melchisedech Bennet Poulter, the child born the 9th day beeing Thursday

SUMME OF THE YEARE—33.

1581		25	Satterday Christned Susan Androwes daughter of Robert Androwes Goldsmith, the childe born the 21th day being Tuesday
	Maye	14	Whitsonday Christning of Robert Gunby sonne of George Gunby Scriuenor, the childe born the 9th day being Tuesday
1581	June	3	Satterday Christning of Susan Stanly daughter of John Stanly Draper the childe was born the first of June being Thursday
		22	Thursday Christning of Margaret Gould daughter of Hughe Gold Grocer, the childe born the 19th day of June being Monday
	Julie	7	Friday Christning of Owen Kynnaston sonne of Thomas Kynnaston Merchant Taylor, ye childe born Monday the third daye
		30	Sonday Christning of Mary Thornell daughter of Thomas Thornell Draper the childe was born the 27th day in St Mychells p'ish
	August	6	Sonday Christning of Elizabeth Ball daughter of Humphry Ball White baker, the child born the 3d day of August, at ye bull

Yeare.	Month.	Day.	Names.
1581	Septem	21	Thursday Christning of William Pingle sonne of Richard Pingle Mercer the childe born the 13th day being Wedensday
	October	22	Sonday Christning of John and Josua sonnes of Perciuall Hassald sckynner: the children weare born the 14th of October boeing satterday
		22	Sonday Christning of Thomas Sturman sonne of Richard Sturman fishmonger, the childe borne the 15th day being sonday
	Nouem	21	Tuesday Christning of John Watson sonne of Baruabe Watson Merchant Taylor the childe born the 19th day of Nouem: sonday
		26	Sonday Christning of John Averell sonne of William Averell Merchaunt Tayler, the childe born the 21th day being Tuesday
	Decem	17	Sonday Cristning of Em Bowyer daughter of Harry Bowyer Grocer the childe born the 10th day being Sonday
		24	Sonday Christning of Abraham Pope sonne of Waldron Pope Ducheman born the 22 day in this p'ish: Christned at the french church
	January	7	Sonday Christning of Edward Hubbersted sonne of George Hubbersted Taylor the childe born the first day, new yeares day
		21	Sonday Christning of William Dethicke sonne of William Dethicke alias Yorke Harrold at Armes born ye 17th day, Wedensday
	Februa	2	Friday Christning of John Joanes sonne of Thomas Joanes Grocer the childe born the 29th of January being Monday
		23	Friday Christning of Susan Holdsworth daughter of Henry Holsworth Mercer the childe born the 19th day being Monday
	March	25	Sonday Christning of Fraunces Gunstone the daughter of Robert Gunstone Inholder the childe born the 21th day: Wedens

SUMME OF THE YEARE—20

1582	Aprill	1	Sonday Christning of Melchisadeck Bennet sonne of Melchizadeck Bennet poulter, ye child born ye 25th day march being sonday
		1	Sonday Christning of Thomas Haukes sonne of John Haukes Draper, the childe born the 31th of March being satterday
		8	Sonday Christning of Elizabeth Bromely daughter of Wm Bromely poulter, the childe born the 5th day being Thursday
	June	3	Sonday Christning of Elizabeth Willy daughter of Richard Willy Grocer the childe born the 31th of May being Thursday
	Julie	21	Satterday Christning of Elizabeth Sutton daughter of John Sutton, Carpenter the childe born the 18th day being Wedensday
	August	26	Sonday Christning of Abraham Jordan sonne of Jeames Jordane porter of ye Waygh house: born ye 25 day being sattterday
	Septem	8	Satterday Christning of Margery Rayment daughter of John Rayment poulter, yonger, born the same day afore the tyme

Yeare.	Month.	Day.	Names.
1582	Nouem	11	Sonday Christning of Harry Hassald sonne of Perciuall Hassald Skynner the child born the 8th day being Thursday
	Decemb	16	Sonday Christning of Jane Pingle daughter of Richard Pingle Mercer, the childe born the 12th day being Wedensday
	Janua	1	Tuesday Christning of Thomas Powell sonne of Dany Powell Merchant Tailor born the 29th of December being satterday
		20	Sonday Christning of George Gunby sonne of George Gunby, scriuener, the child born the 15th of January. Tuesday
		27	Sonday Christning of Jeames Sturman sonne of Richard Sturman Fishmonger the child born the 26th day beeing satterday
	Februa	24	Sonday Christning of Mathias Averell sonne of William Averell Merchant Tailor, born the 18th day being monday
	March	17	Sonday Christening of Katherine Bennet daughter of Mellchisedeck Bennet poulter, born the 14th being Thursday
		24	Sonday Christning of William And Richard Houlsworth twynnes of Henry Holdsworth Mercer, both born the 19th day being Tuesday
		24	Sonday Christning of Anne Bryan daughter of John Bryan Taylor the childe was born the self same day beeing weake

SUMME OF THE YEARE—16

1583		31	Sonday Christning of Elizabeth Warren daughter of John Warren Armorer, the childe born the 23 day being satterday
	Aprill	2	Tuesday Christning of Thomas Jones sonne of Thomas Jones barbor, the child born the 26th of March being Tuesday
		7	Sonday Christning of Lucres Lister daughter of John Lister Barbor the child born the second of Aprill beeing Tuesday
		14	Sonday Christning of Paule Scaliot sonne of Marke Scaliot Blacksmith, born the 8th day of Aprill beeing monday
	Maye	1	Wedensday Christning of Thomas Wood sonne of William Wood Jentleman the child born 30th of Aprill being Tuesday
		5	Sonday Christning of John Cornelis sonne of Hierome Cornelis Joyner the child was born the 28th of Aprill being sonday
		16	Thursday Christning of William Dethike 6th sonne of William Dethicke Esquire herrold yorke, ye child born this day being weake
	June	23	Sonday Christning of Elizabeth Androes daughter of Robert Androes Goldsmith the child born the 15th day being satterday
		24	Monday Christning of Peeter Prestly sonne of John Prestly Carpenter the child born the 28th of June being sonday
	Julie	14	Sonday Christning of Thomas Walthall sonne of William Wallthall Mercer, the chile born the 10th of July beeing Wedensday

Yeare.	Month.	Day.	Names.
1583	August	4	Sonday Christned at the french Church Salamon Pope sonne of Waldron Pope duchman the child born with vs y⁰ 28ᵗʰ of July sonday
		25	Sonday Christning of Thomas Pigot sonne of Thomas Pigot Grocer the child born the 19ᵗʰ of this moneth beeing Monday
	Septem	8	Sonday Christning of John Hartridge sonne of William Hartridge Draper, the childe was born the 4ᵗʰ day of this month beeing Wedens
		22	Sonday Christning of Edward Atkinson sonne of Edward Atkinson purueior of the Queenes wines: born the 18ᵗʰ of septem: wedensday
	October	13	Sonday Christning of Rose Cooper daughter of Robert Cooper Armorer, the childe was born the second day of October being wodens
		20	Sonday Christning of Elizabeth Corzer daughter of John Corzer Clothworker the child born the 18ᵗʰ day of October being friday
	Nouem	8	Sonday Christning of Thomas Jones sonne of Thomas Jones, Grocer, the child was born the second of Nouember being satterday
		10	Sonday Christning of William Gunstone sonne of Robert Gunstone Inholder the child born the 5ᵗʰ of this month: Tuesday
		24	Sonday Christning of William Kynnaston, sonne of Thomas Kynnaston Merchant Taylor, born the 20ᵗʰ day being Wedensday
		24	Sonday Christning of Cibill Atkinson daughter of Nicholas Atkinson seruingman, the child born the 11ᵗʰ day of Nouem: Monday
	Decemb	15	Sonday Christning of Mary Gunby daughter of George Gunby seriuener, the child born the 9ᵗʰ of December being Monday
	Februar	2	Sonday Christning of John Sollomon sonne of Thomas Sollomon Sadler, the child was born the first of February: satterday
		9	Sonday Christning of Anne Wroth daughter of Mʳ Robert Wroth Justice of the peace, the child born the 3 day of February being Monday
		16	Sonday Christning of John Hubbersted sonne of George Hubbersted Tailor, the child born the 12ᵗʰ day of February being Wedensday
	March	8	Sonday Christning of Richard Parchement, sonne of Peter Parchment weuer, the child born the 4ᵗʰ day being Wedensday

SUMME OF THE YEARE—25

1584	Aprill	5	Sonday Christning of John Watson sonne of Barnaby Watson Merchaunt Tailor, the childe born the 30ᵗʰ of March Monday
		5	Sonday Christning of Luce Hassald daughter of Perciuall Hassald Skinner the child born the 12ᵗʰ day beeing Sonday
		20	Monday Christning of Fraunces Gardner sonne of Mr. Richard Gardiner Esquire of Surry born the 14ᵗʰ of Aprill, Tuesday

Yeare.	Month.	Day.	Names.
1584	Maye	3	Sonday Christning of Thomas and and John Crant sonnes of John Crant Haberdasher, the children born the first of May friday
		21	Thursday Christning of John Haukes sonne of John Haukes Draper the childe was born the 18th of May beeing Monday
		24	Sonday Christning of Lyonell Pingle sonne of Richard Pingle Mercer, the childe was born the 21th day of May beeing Thursday
		31	Sonday Christning of Katherin Houldsworth daughter of Harry Holdsworth Mercer, the child born the 28th day beeing Thursday
	June	28	Sonday Christning of Lawrence Genninges sonne of Mihell Genninges Grocer, the childe born the 19th of June being friday
		29	Monday Christning of Robert Hunter sonne of Edward Hunte^r, Poulter the child was born the 27th day of June being satterday
	Julie	12	Sonday Christning of Harry Dethike sonne of Wm Dethike alias Yorke Esquire Herrold of Armes, the child born the 4th day being satterday
	August	2	Sonday Christning of Elizabeth Pigot daughter of Thomas Pigot, Grocer, the child born the 25th day of July beeing satterday
		16	Sonday Christning of Susan Sutton daughter of John Sutton, Carpenter, the child was born the same daye in the Morning
		23	Sonday Christning of John Willy sonne of Richard Willy Grocer the childe was born the 22th daye of August beeing Satterday
		23	Sonday Christning of Katherin Allin daughter of Thomas Allen Carpenter the child was born the 19th day of this month being Wedensday
		25	Tuesday Christning of Mary Pope daughter of Waldron Pope duchman the child born the 23th day in this p'ish : Christned at ye french church
	Septem	25	Thursday Christning of Thomas Rayment sonne of John Rayment Poulter the yonger the childe was born the 20th day of Septemb: sonday
	Nouem	22	Sonday Christning of George Gunstone sonne of Robert Gunstone Inholder the childe was born the 19th day of Nouemb^r : Thursday
	Decem	13	Sonday Christning of Alice Brian daughter of John Brian Tailor, the childe was born the 10th day of December being Thursday
		20	Sonday Christning of John Grean sonne of John Grean Cooke the childe was born the 18th day of this month being friday
		25	Friday Christniug of Mary Preast daughter of Robert Preest doctor of phisike, the child born the 24th day being Thursday
		27	Sonday Christining of Fulke Bromely sonne of William Bromly Poulter the child was born the 22th day being Tuesday
	Janua	15	Friday Christining of Elizabeth Wallthall daughter of Mr. William Wallthall Mercer the child born the 7th day being Thursday

Yeare.	Month.	Day.	Names.
1584	Janua	17	Sonday Christining of Anne Kynnaston daughter of Thomas Kynnaston Merchaunt Taylor the child born the 11th day Monday
		24	Sonday Christining of John Smith sonne of William Smith, Poulter, the child was born the 19th day of January being Tuesday
		24	Sonday Christining of Katherine Rande daughter of Mr. Wm Rand gentleman, the child was born the 18th day being Monday
	Februa	21	Sonday Christining of Susan Randoll daughter of John Randoll Draper, the child born the 11th of February Thursday
	March	2	Tuesday Christining of William Averell sonne of William Averell Merchaunt Tailor the child born ye 25th of Febru: Thursday

SUMME OF THE YEARE—28

1585	Aprill	4	Sonday Christining of Peeter Cater sonne of John Cater Skynner: the child was born the 29th of March being Monday
		4	Sonday Christining of John Orton sonne of Randoll Orton Merchaunt Tailor, the child born the 30th of Marche, Tuesday
	Maye	9	Sonday Christining of Frauncos Hickmot sonne of Edward Hickmot Sadler, the child born the 7th of May beeing Friday
		9	Sonday Christining of Joane Powell daughter of Dauid Powell Merchaunt Tailor, ye childe born the 4th day Tuesday
		12	Wedensday Christining of Ciprian Pingle sonne of Richard Pingle Mercer the childe born the 6th day being Thursday
		16	Sonday Christining of Grace Sturman daughter of Richard Sturman fishmonger the childe born the 9th day: sonday
	June	6	Sonday Christining of Perciuall Gunby sonne of George Gunby Scriuener the childe born the 3 of June beeing Thursday
		13	Sonday Christining of Perciuall Hassald sonne of Perciuall Hassald, Sckinner the childe born the 8th day Tuesday
		13	Sonday Christining of John Rogers sonne of John Rogers Grocer, the childe born the 5th day being Satterday
	Julie	11	Sonday Christining of Susan Houldsworth daughter of Henry Houldsworth Mercer the childe born the 4th day being sonday
		25	Sonday Christining of Christopher Gardner sonne of Mr. Richard Gardner Esquire the childe born the 17th day being satterday
	August	8	Sonday Christining of William Seyr sonne of Ralph Seyr Tallow chaundler the child born the 30th of Julie being fryday
		15	Sonday Christining of Nicholas Joanes sonne of Thomas Jones Grocer, the childe born the 8th of this month being Sonday
		15	Sonday Christining of Dina Lister daughter of John Lister, Barbor the childe was born the 9th of this month: Monday

THE REGISTERS OF ST. PETER'S, CORNHILL.

Yeare.	Month.	Day.	Names.
1585	Septem	5	Sonday Christining of Robert Allin sonne of Thomas Allin, Carpenter the childe born the 31th of August being Tuesday
		26	Sonday Christining of Robert Dethicke sonne of Mr. Wm Dethicke alias Yorke herrold the childe born the 22th being Wedensday
	October	3	Sonday Christining of Elizabeth Atkinson daughter of Edward Atkinson, Merchaunt Taylo^r born ye 28th september : tuesday
		10	Sonday Christining of Susan Hunter daughter of Edward Hunter the child born the 6th day of October being Wedensday
		20	Wedensday Christining of Peeter Leden Hall ignoti patris matrisque hee was found left alone in Leden haule
	Decem	12	Sonday Christining of Katherine Raiment daughter of John Rayment the yonger, born the seuenth day being Tuesday
	Janua	30	Sonday Christining of Ann Record daughter of John Record Merchaunt Taylor, born 22th day Janua : being satterday
	Februa	13	Sonday Christining of Jeames Randoll sonne of John Randoll, Draper the childe was born the 4th of February, being friday
	March	6	Sonday Christining of Libeus Orton sonne of Randoll Orton Merchaunt Tailor born the 26th of February being satterday .
		15	Tuesday Christining of Anne Smith daughter of William Smith, Poulter, the childe born the 12th day being friday
1586	Aprill	4	Monday Christining of Fraunces Kynnaston sonne of Thomas Kynnaston Merchaunt Tailor, born the first of Aprill : friday
		17	Sonday Christining of Parnell Averell daughter of William Averell Merchaunt Tailor, born the 9th day being Satterday
	Maye	1	Sonday Christining of William Hartridge sonne of Willia' Hartridge Draper, the childe born the 25th day being Monday
		21	Satterday Christining of Peeter Grace sonne of Katherine Dauis an harlot. Witnesses John Jeames, John Stanly Annes Richardson
	June	12	Sonday Christining of Thomas Sollomon sonne of Thomas Sollomon Sadler the childe born the 6th day being Monday
	Julie	15	Fryday Christining of Martingue Billowes daughter of Peeter Van Billowes strange^r born the 11th day : Monday
		17	Sonday Christining of Mary Joanes daughter of Thomas Joanes Barbor, the childe born the 12th day being Tuesday
	August	7	Sonday Christining of Elizabeth Cater daughter of John Cater Sckinner the childe was born the 5th day being friday
		14	Sonday Christining of Margaret Sturman daughter of Richard Sturman ffishmonger the childe born the 9th day being Tuesday
	Septem	4	Sonday Christining of Elizabeth Watson daughter of Barnaby Watson Merchaunt Tailor, born the 28th of August Sonday

Yeare.	Month.	Day.	Names.
1586	Septem	11	Sonday Christining of Alice Lewes daughter of Thomas Lewes Armoror, the childe was born the 3 day being satterday
		25	Sonday Christining of John Holdsworth sonne of Henry Holdsworth Mercer, the childe was born the 20th day being Tuesday
	October	2	Sonday Christining of Martha Hassald daughter of Perciuall Hassald Sckinner, the childe born the 17th of Septem: satterday
		9	Sonday Christining of Annes Wigges daughter of William Wigs Glouer the childe born the 5th day of October being Wedensday
		17	Tuesday Christining of Richard Hunter sonne of Edward Hunter, Poulter, the childe born the 15th daye beeing Sonday
		30	Sonday Christining of Margaret Walthall daughter of Mr. William Walthall Mercer the child born the 24th day being sonday
	Nouem	6	Sonday Christining of Margery Lecroft daughter of William Lecroft Armorer, the child born the 4th of Nouember Friday
		20	Sonday Christining of Thomas Gold son of Hugh Gold Grocer, the childe was born the 13th of Nouember being sonday
		20	Sonday Christining of John Pigot sonne of Thomas Pigot, Grocer, the childe was born the 15th day being Tuesday
	Decem	11	Sonday Christining of Frances Hodgesonne sonne of William Hodgesonne Skynner born the 7th day of Decem: being Wedensday
	Februa	5	Sonday Christining of Gillian Jones daughter of Thomas Jones Grocer, the childe was born the 3d day of Februa: being Friday
		19	Sonday Christining of Anne Parchment daughter of Peeter Parchment Weuer the child born the 9th day being Thursday
		21	Tuesday Christining of Elizabeth Busby daughter of John Busby Merchaunt Tailor, born the same day 'twas Christned
	March	5	Sonday Christining of Mary Willy daughter of Richard Willye Grocer, the childe was born the 27th day of February: Moneday
1587		26	Sonday Christining of Elizabeth Powell daughter of Dany Powell Merchaunt Tailor born the 18th day being satterday
	Aprill	9	Sonday Christining of Edward Green sonne of John Green Carter in the Weigh house, born the 6th daye of Aprill being Thursday
		11	Tuesday Christining of Fraunces Reddish daughter of Fraunces Reddish seruing man, the childe born the 8th day being Satterday
	Maye	14	Sonday Christining of Martha and Ellen Cage daughters of Anthonie Cage Draper, the children born the 10th day Wedensday
		14	Sonday Christining of Fraunces Smith daughter of William Smith Poulter, the childe born the 9th day being Tuesday

Yeare.	Month.	Day.	Names.
1587	Maye	21	Sonday Christining of Jerome Pope sonne of Waldron Pope straunger the childe born heare ye 18th day Christned at ye duch church
	June	4	Sonday Christining of William Haukes sonne of John Haukes, Draper, the childe born the 30th of Maye being Tuesday
		18	Sonday Christining of Jeames Atkinson sonne of Edward Atkinson Merchaunt Tailor, the childe born the 8th day Thursday
	Julie	11	Tuesday Christining of John Wessell sonne of John Wessell Duche man born heare ye 8th of Julie Christned at ye duch Church
		23	Sonday Christining of Margery Hyne daughter of William Hyne Labourer, the childe was born the same day Sonday
	August	16	Wedensday Christining of John Rayment sonne of John Rayment Poulter the younger, born the 13th day of August, Sonday
		27	Sonday Christining of Dorithie Kynnaston daughter of Thomas Kynnaston Merchaunt Tailor born ye 22th day Tuesday
	Septem	24	Sonday Christining of Mathew Averell sonne of William Averell Merchaunt Tailor, the childe born ye 5th day Friday
	October	1	Sonday Christining of John Thorogood sonne of Jeames Thorogood, the child born the 28th day being satterday
		1	Sonday Christining of Ellen Cater daughter of John Cater, Skynner the childe born the 23th day of September: Satterday
		15	Sonday Christining of Sara Hare daughter of John Hare, Salter, the childe was born the 13th daye beeing Friday
	Nouem	5	Sonday Christining of Anne Houldsworth daughter of Henry Houldsworth Mercer, the childe born the 31th day of Octobe^r
		26	Sonday Christining of William Lecroft sonne of William Lecroft Armorer, the childe was born the 19th day being Sondaye
	Decemb	10	Sonday Christining of Hugh Gold sonne of Mr. Hugh Gold Grocer the childe was born the 30th Nouember being Thursday
		10	Sonday Christining of Edward Hunter sonne of Edward Hunter Poulter, the childe was born the 3 of this month. Sonday
		17	Sonday Christining of William Wallthall sonne of Mr. William Wallthall Mercer the childe born the 11th daye being Monday
	Januar	21	Sonday Christining of Mary Sturman daughter of Richard Sturman Skynner the childe born the 19th daye being Monday
	Februa	4	Sonday Christining of Mary Sheppy daughter of Robert Sheppy, Poulter, the childe born the 28th day being Sonday
		18	Sonday Christining of Jane Robinson daughter of Richard Robinson Skynner, the childe born the 11th day being Sonday
		25	Sonday Christining of John Price sonne of William Price Shoemaker, the childe born the 22th day being Thursday

Yeare.	Month.	Day.	Names.
1587	Februa	25	Sonday Christining of Katherine Caunt daughter of Edward Caunt Fishmonger, born the 22th day being Thursday
	March	3	Sonday Christining of Jeames Hodge sonne of Jeames Hodge White Baker, the childe was born ye 28th day Wedens.
		3	Sonday Christining of Martha Ratsdale daughter of William Ratsdale ale Brewer, born the 26th day Monday
		17	Sonday Christining of Elizabeth Busby daughter of John Busby the childe was born the 11th day beeing Monday
1588	Aprill	14	Sonday Christining of Ellenor Hassald daughter of Perciuall Hassald Skynner born the 6th day Satterday
		28	Sonday Christining of Walter Smith sonne of Mr. Humphry Smith Esquire iudge of ye sheriues court born ye 20th day satterday
	June	9	Sonday Christining of Harry Waight sonne of Richard Waight, Poulter, the childe was born the 6th day of June being Thursday
		9	Sonday Christining of Elizabeth Hodgesonne daughter of Peeter Hodgesonne vpholster, ye childe born ye 4th day Tuesday
		23	Sonday Christining of Mary Marrall daughter of George Marrall Carpenter, the childe born the 16th day Sonday
	Julie	7	Sonday Christining of Thomas Randoll sonne of John Randoll Draper the childe born the 3 day being Wedensday
		7	Sonday Christining of Jane Randoll daughter of John Randoll Draper, the childe born the 3 day being Wedensday
		14	Sonday Christining of Katherine Smith daughter of William Smith Poulter, born the 9th of July being Tuesday
		24	Wedensday Christining of John Thorogood sonne of Mr. John Thorogood gentleman, the childe was born ye 12th day being friday
	August	4	Sonday Christining of Alexander Toomes sonne of John Toomes Haberdasher, born the 31th of July being Wedensday
		4	Sonday Christining of Elizabeth Hartridge daughter of William Hartridge Draper, born the 29th day being Monday
	October	27	Sonday Christining of Bridget Ashbold daughter of Mr. William Ashbold our parson, born the 18th day of this month
	Nouem	1	Friday Christining of Katherine Kynnaston daughter of Thomas Kynnaston Merchaunt Tailor, born ye 28th october Monday
		3	Sonday Christining of Elizabeth Satchfeld daughter of John Satchfeld white Baker born the 30th day October being Wedensday
		10	Sonday Christining of Edward Thrower son of Robert Thrower Vintner born the 4th of this month beeing Monday
	Januar	5	Sonday Christining of William Sheppy sonne of Robert Sheppy, Poulter, the childe born the 31th day being Tuesday
		5	Sonday Christining of Mary Gold daughter of Mr. Hugh Gold Grocer, the childe born the 29th of December being sonday

Yeare.	Month.	Day.	Names.
1588	Januar	19	Sonday Christining of Jonas Holdsworth sonne of Henry Holdsworth Mercer the childe born the 17th day being friday
	Februar	2	Sonday Christining of Judith Lister daughter of William Lister, Barbor, the childe born the 25th day being satterday
		9	Sonday Christining of John Thorowgood sonne of Jeames Thorogood Poulter the childe born the 31th of January being Friday
		16	Sonday Christining of Susan Parchment daughter of Peeter parchment Weuer the childe born 10th day being monday
		23	Sonday Christining of Anne Sallomon daughter of Thomas Sallomon Sadler the childe born the 18th day being Tuesday
		23	Sonday Christining of Mary Lewis daughter of Thomas Lewis Armorer the childe born the 16th day being Sonday
	March	9	Sonday Christining of Barnabe Watson sonne of Barnabe Watson Merchaunt Tailor, born the 7th day being Friday
1589		30	Sonday Christining of Foulke Woodford sonne of Mr Gamaliell Woodford Grocer the childe born the 23th day being Sonday
	Aprill	6	Sonday Christining of Peeter Cater sonne of John Cater, Skinner the childe born the 31th day of March being Monday
		11	Friday Christining of Robert Martin son of Robert Martin a bachelor, begotten of a maide an harlot, born ye 31th of March Monday
		13	Sonday Christining of Peeter Coling sonne of Fraunces Coling, Fishmonger, the childe born the 7th day of Aprill being Monday
	Maye	4	Sonday Christining of Marten Cooper sonne of Richard Cooper Haberdasher, the childe born the 29th of Aprill being Tuesday
		4	Sonday Christining of Anne Thorton daughter of Robert Thornton Barber Surgion, born the 28th of Aprill being Monday
	June	1	Sonday Christining of Thomas Wallthall sonne of William Walthall Mercer, the childe born the 30th of May being Fryday
		14	Satterday Christining of William Turner sonne of Hillary Turner Draper the childe was born the 13th day being Friday
	Julie	27	Sonday Christining of Anne Hartridge daughter of William Hartridge Draper, the childe born the 21th day Christ: at St Michells
	August	3	Sonday Christining of William Hunter sonne of Edward Hunter, poulter, the childe born the 29th of July beeing Tuesday
		3	Sonday Christining of Elizabeth Hallwood daughter of Edward Hallwood Barbor Chirurgian, born the 29th of July being Tuesday
		17	Sonday Christining of Susan Powell daughter of Dauid Powell Merchaunt Tailor, the childe born the 14th day being Thursday

F

Yeare.	Month.	Day.	Names.
1589	Septem	7	Sonday Christining of William Averell sonne of William Averell Merchaunt Tailor, the childe born the 30th day of August Satterday
		21	Sonday Christining of Thomas Waight sonne of Richard Waite poulter the childe born the 16th day of September Tuesday
		28	Sonday Christining of Perciuall Hassald sonne of Perciuall Hassald Skynner, the child born the 19th day being Fryday
		28	Sonday Christining of Mary Lecroft daughter of William Lecroft Armorer, the childe born the 26th day being friday
	October	5	Sonday Christining of Margaret Morow daughter of George Morow Carpenter the childe born the 30th of September Tuesday
		12	Sonday Christining of Jerome Wroth sonne of Mr Richard Wroth gentleman, the childe born the 3 day being ffriday
		26	Sonday Christining of John Hodgeson sonne of peeter Hodgsonne Vphoulster the childe born the 24th day being Friday
	Nouem	2	Sonday Christining of Bezaleell Nicholson sonne of Michaell Nichollson Cordwayner born the 26 of October sonday
		9	Sonday Christining of John Morris sonne of John Morris Clothworker, the childe was born the first day beeing Satterday
		9	Sonday Christining of Anne Sturman daughter of Richard Sturman Fishmonger, the childe born the 5th day Wednesday
	Decemb	7	Sonday Christining of Robert Thrower sonne of Robert Thrower Vintner, the childe was born the 29th of Nouember, satterday
		14	Sonday Christining of William Sutton sonne of John Sutton Carpenter the child was born the 9th day being Tuesday
		28	Sonday Christining of Elizabeth Green daughter of John Green carter of the Weigh house, born the 25th day beeing Thurs.
	Janua	11	Sonday Christining of Joyce Steward daughter of Robert Steward Barbor Chirurgian born the 2 day being Friday
		25	Sonday Christining of John Bray sonne of William Bray White Baker, the childe born the 15th day being Thursday
		25	Sonday Christining of Harry Purleuant sonne of Thomas Purleuaunt Grocer, the child born the 17th day being Satterday
	Februa	15	Sonday Christining of William Ashbold sonne of Mr William Ashbold of this Church parson, the childe borne the 8th daye Sonday
		22	Sonday Christining of Katherine Randoll daughter of John Randoll Draper, the childe born the 14th day being Satterday
	March	8	Sonday Christining of Dennis Partridge daughter of Steuen partridge Goldsmith, born the first of March being Sonday
1590		29	Sonday Christining of Vrsula Jones daughter of Thomas Jones, Grocer, the childe born the 20th day of March being Friday

Yeare.	Month.	Day.	Names.
1590	Aprill	26	Sonday Christining of John Gold sonne of Mr Hugh Gold Grocer, the childe was born the 21th of Aprill being Tuesday
	Maye	17	Sonday Christining of Dorithy Ratsdale daughter of William Ratsdale, Brewer, the childe born the 9th daye being Satterday
		31	Sonday Christining of John Toomes sonne of John Toomes Haberdasher, the childe was born the 29th day being ffriday
	June	7	Sonday Christining of Margaret Holdsworth daughter of Henry Holdsworth Mercer, born the 31th of May being Sonday
		14	Sonday Christining of Edward Caunt sonne of Mr Edward Caunt Fishmonger, the childe born the 4th day being Thursday
		14	Sonday Christining of Christian Cater daughter of John Cater Skynner, the childe born the 3 day being Wedensday
		14	Sonday Christining of Alice Rayment daughter of John Rayment the yonger Poulter, the childe borne the 8th day being Monday
		21	Sonday Christining of Harry Haukes sonne of John Haukes Draper, the childe was born the 12th day being ffriday
		21	Sonday Christining of John Satchfeeld sonne of John Satchfeeld White Baker, the childe born the 14th day being Sonday
	Julie	26	Sonday Christining of William Hodgesonne sonne of Wm Hodgeson Skynner, the childe born ye 18th day being satterday
	August	16	Sonday Christining of Mary Hartridge daughter of Wm Hartridge cittizen and draper Lon: born the 6th day Thursday
		23	Sonday Christining of Bartholmew Averell sonne of Wm Averell Merchaunt Tailor, the childe born the 17th day Monday
		23	Sonday Christining of Elizabeth Vertu daughter of Christopher Vertu vintner, the child born the 21th day Friday
		30	Sonday Christining of Thomas Hazelfoote sonne of Wm Hazelfoote Grocer the childe born the 28th day being friday
		30	Sonday Christining of Cibell Ouerton daughter of Lawraunce Ouerton, Bowyer born the 25th day being Tuesday
	Septem	13	Sonday Christining of Anne Thorogood daughter of Jeames Thorogood Poulter, the childe born the 9th day being Wedensday
	October	4	Sonday Christining of Robert Jones sonne of Thomas Jones Carpenter the childe born the 2 day of October being friday
		4	Sonday Christining of Edward Jones sonne of William Jones Merchaunt Tailor the childe born the 27th of Septembe^r sonday
		11	Sonday Christining of Jane Morris daughter of John Morris Clothworker, the childe born the 4th day being sonday

36   THE REGISTERS OF ST. PETER'S, CORNHILL.

Yeare.	Month.	Day.	Names.
1590	October	25	Sonday Christining of Lucas Walthall sonne of Mr. William Wallthall Mercer, the childe born the 17th day being satterday
	Nouem	1	Sonday Christining of Robert Lecroft sonne of William Lecroft Armorer, the childe born the 26th day Octob^r Monday
		8	Sonday Christining of Maudelin Challener daughter of Mr. Fraunces Challener gentleman, born the 31th October, satterday
		22	Sonday Christining of Foulke Waight sonne of Richard Waight Poulter, the childe born the 17th day being Tuesday
	Decem	6	Sonday Christining of Ellen Gunby daughter of George Gunby Scriuenor, the childe born the first day Tuesday
		13	Sonday Christining of Mary Coling daughter of Fraunces Coling Fishmonger, the childe born ye 2 day Wednesday
		20	Sonday Christining of Abacucke Tailor sonne of John Tailor, Merchaunt Tailor born the 14th day being Monday
		27	Sonday Christining of Thomas Bray sonne of William Bray White Baker, the childe born the 21th day being Monday
	Janua	3	Sonday Christining of Moyses Steward sonne of Robert Stuard Barbor Surgion, the child born ye 31th December Thursday
		3	Sonday Christining of Margaret Sheppy daughter of Robert Sheppy Poulter, born the 27th day December, sonday
	Februa	7	Sonday Christining of Jane Morrow daughter of George Morrow Carpenter, born the 3 day of February Wedensday
		7	Sonday Christining of Anne Hodgesonne daughter of Peter Hodgesonne Vpholster, the child born ye 6th day being satterday
		7	Sonday Christining of Susan Turner daughter of Hilarie Turner Draper, the childe born the 30 Janua: satterday
		14	Sonday Christining of Samuell Willy sonne of Richard Willy Grocer the childe born the 8th day of February being Monday
		17	Wedensday Christining of Ellen Gooche daughter of Robert Gooche Merchant of Yarmoth, born the 10th day beeing Wedensday
		21	Sonday Christining of Joseph Munke sonne of Richard Munke Clothworker, the childe born the 19th day in St. Michaelles p'ish
	March	7	Sonday Christining of Elizabeth Hunter daughter of Edward Hunter Poulter, the childe born the first day being Monday
		14	Sonday Christining of Elizabeth Rider daughter of Adam Rider Vintner, the childe born the 9th daye being Tuesday
		16	Tuesday Christining of Richard Lucy sonne of Mr. Thomas Lucy Esquire rider of her Maties horse, born the 4th daye being Tuesday
		21	Sonday Christining of Richard Sallomon sonne of Thomas Sallomon Sadler, the childe born the 12th daye beeing Friday

Yeare.	Month.	Day.	Names.
1591	March	28	Sonday Christining of Blanch Record, daughter of John Record Merchaunt Tailor, the child born the 20th daye being Satterday
	Aprill	4	Sonday Christining of Randoll Lewis sonne of Thomas Lewis Armorer, the childe born the 29th of March beeing Monday
	Maye	9	Sonday Christining of John Cooke sonne of Walter Cooke Merchaunt Tailor, the child born the 4th daye being Tuesdaye
	June	20	Sonday Christining of William Ratsdale sonne of William Ratsdale Brewer, the childe born the 16th daye being wedensday
		24	Thursday Christining of Robert Gold sonne of Mr. Hugh Gold Grocer, the childe born the 16th daye being Wedensday
	Julie	4	Sonday Christining of Katherine Wallthall daughter of Mr. Thomas Walthall Mercer, born the 29th daye June being Tuesday
	August	22	Sonday Christining of William Hartridge sonne of William Hartridge Draper, the childe born the 16th day being Monday
	Septem	5	Sonday Christining of Katherine Powell daughter of Dauid Powell Merchaunt Tailor, born the second day being Thursday
		5	Sonday Christining of Martha Averell daughter of William Averell Merchaunt Tailor, born the 31th of August being Tuesdaie
		29	Wedensday Christining of Katherine Hudson daughter of William Hudsonne Fishmonger, born the 22th day being Wedensday
	Octobe	3	Sonday Christining of Martha Norden daughter of Mr. John Norden gentleman, born the first of October being ffridaye
		24	Sonday Christining of Jeames Vertu sonne of Christopher Vertu Vintner, the childe born the 17th daye being Sondaye
	Nouem	1	Monday Christining of William Steuens sonne of John Steuens Embroderer, the childe born the 28th of October. Thursday
		14	Sonday Christning of Mary Lecroft daughter of William Lecroft Armorer, the childe born the 7th day being Sonday
		21	Sonday Christning of Susan Eueling daughter of Robert Eueling Armorer the childe born the 9th daye being Tuesdaye
	Janua	9	Sonday Christning of Elizabeth White daughter of Thomas White Letherseller, born the 7th of January being fridaye
		12	Wedensday Christning of Beniamin Holland sonne of one Holland a professed gentleman base born in Mrs Jordanes house by Ledenhaull
		23	Sonday Christning of Henry Drables sonne of Robert Drables Fishmonger, the childe born the 17th day of January beeing Monday
	February	6	Sonday Christning of Susan Hudson daughter of George Hudson Vpholster, the childe born the 2 of February being Wedensday

Yeare.	Month.	Day.	Names.
1591	February	13	Sonday Christning of Henry Thrawer sonne of Robert Thrawer Vintner, the childe was born the 5th of February beeing Satterday
	March	5	Sonday Christining of Daniell Thorogood sonne of Jeames Thorogood Poulter, the childe born the 29th of February being Tuesday
		5	Sonday Christining of Elizabeth Turner daughter of Hillarye Turner Draper the childe born the 24th of February being Thursday
		5	Sonday Christining of Vrsula Smith daughter of Robert Smith, Draper the childe born the second of March beeing Thursdaye
		19	Sonday Christining of Margaret Kyunaston daughter of Thomas Kynnaston Merchaunt Tailor born the 10th of March being fridaye
1592	Aprill	2	Sonday Christning of Robert Smith sonne of William Smith Poulter, the childe was born the 28th of March being Tuesday
		2	Sonday Christining of John Randoll sonne of John Randoll Draper sexton of this Church, the childe born the 28th of March being Tuesday
		25	Tuesday Christining of Alice Cooke daughter of Walter Cooke Merchaunt Tailor, the childe born the 21th of Aprill being friday
	Maye	7	Sonday Christining of Symon Waight sonne of Richard Waight Poulter, the childe was born the 29th of August* being Satterday
	June	18	Sonday Christning of Richard Hubberd sonne of John Hubberd, Tailor, the childe was born the 14th of June beeing Wedensday
		25	Sonday Christning of Elizabeth Haukes daughter of John Haukes draper the childe born the 20th of June beeing Tuesday
		25	Sunday Christining of John Wallthall sonne of Mr Thomas Wallthall Mercer, the childe born the 20th of June being Tuesdaye
		29	Sonday Christining of Harry Ashbold sonne of Mr William Ashbold parson of this Church, born the 23th of June, friday Midsomer eue
	Julie	23	Sonday Christining of Elizabeth Record daughter of John Record Merchaunt Tailor, the childe born the 15th of Julie being Satterday
		30	Sonday Christining of Willfred Spalding sonne of Willfred Spalding Cutter, the childe was born the 22th of Julie being Satterday
	August	2	Wedensday Christning of Roger Peeter so named of our Church, the mother a rogue, the childe was born the 22th of July at Mr Lecrofts dore
		6	Sonday Christining of Christopher Gold sonne of Mr Hugh Gold Grocer, the childe was born the 25th of Julie being Wedensdaye
		20	Sonday Christining of Henry Satchfeeld sonne of John Satchfeeld White Baker, born the 13th of August being Sondaye
	Septem	3	Sonday Christining of Gabriell Coling sonne of Fraunces Coling Fishmonger, the childe was born the 25th of August being friday

* Sic, ? for April.

Yeare.	Month.	Day.	Names.
1592	Septem	3	Sonday Christning of Jane Hudson daughter of William Hudson Fishmonger, the childe was born the 26th of August Satterday
		3	Sonday Christining of Mary Cater daughter of John Cater Skinner, the childe born the 29th day of August being Tuesday
		10	Sonday Christning of Henry Daldron sonne of John Daldron a Broker, born in a part of Mr Thomas Malens house ye bell
		17	Sonday Christining of Mary Caunt daughter of John Caunte Fishmonger, the childe born the 8th of September being Friday
	October	22	Sonday Christining of Fraunces Ratsdale son of William Ratsdale ale Brewar, the childe born the 5th* of October being Sonday
		29	Sonday Christining of Maudelin Parchment daughter of Peter Parchment Weuer, the childe born the 21th day being Satterday
	Nouem	26	Sonday Christning of Thomas Holdsworth sonne of Henry Holdsworth, the childe born the 21th of Nouember Tuesday
	Decem	17	Sonday Christining of Christian Towerson daughter of William Towerson Skynner, the childe born the 10th of December Sonday
		31	Sonday Christining of Thomas Bray sonne of William Bray White Baker, the childe born the 21th of December being Thursday
		31	Sonday Christining of William Acton sonne of Fraunces Actonne Chirurgian, the childe born the 22th of December being Fridaye
	Januar	7	Sonday Christned Thomas Averell sonne of William Averell Merchaunt Tailor the childe born the 3 day of January being Wedensday
		28	Sonday Christining of Elizabeth Hunter daughter of Edward Hunter Poulter the childe born the 20th of January being Satterday
		28	Sonday Christining of Katherine Sheppy daughter of Robert Sheppy Poulter the childe born the 22th of January being Mondaye
	Februa	4	Sonday Christining of Katherine Marrow daughter of George Morrow Carpenter, the childe born the 29th of January being Mondaye
		11	Sonday Christining of George Eueling sonne of Robert Eueling Armorer, the childe was born the 31th of January being Wednesday
1593	Maye	6	Sonday Christning of Abell Tailor sonne of John Tailor Merchaunt Tailor, the childe born the 2 of Maye beeing Wedensday
		10	Thursday Christining of Thomas Lillie sonne of Thomas Lillie Draper, the childe born the 5th of May in St. Michaelles p'ish Christned hea^r
		24	Thursday Christning of Katherin Smith daughter of Mr Robert Smith gentleman, born the 17th of Maye beeing Thursdaye
		30	Wedensday Christning of John Steward sonne of Robert Stuard Chirurgian, the childe was born the 28th of May being Mondaye

* Sic.

THE REGISTERS OF ST. PETER'S, CORNHILL.

Yeare.	Month.	Day.	Names.
1593	June	3	Whitsonday Christining of Robert Bland sonne of Peeter Bland Skynner, the childe born the 25th day of Maye beeing Fryday
		5	Tuesday Christning of Thomas Hartridge sonne of William Hartridge Draper, the childe born the 30th of May being Wedensday
	Julie	8	Sonday Christning of Cisly Willy daughter of Richard Willy, Grocer, the childe was born the 5th of Julie being Wedensday
		29	Sonday Christning of Anne Walthall daughter of Mr Thomas Wallthall Mercer, born the 24th of Julie beeing Tuesday
		29	Sonday Christning of Margery Waight daughter of Richard Waight Poulter, born the 26th daye of Julie, being Thursday
	August	24	Friday Christining of Sara Cokaines daughter of Mr Thomas Cokaines Skynner, born the 16th of August being Thursday
	Septem	16	Sonday Christining of Erasmus Record sonne of John Record, Merchaunt Tailor, the childe born the 8th day being Satterday
		30	Sunday Christning of Robert Hudsonne sonne of William Hudson Fishmonger, the child was born the 24th day Monday
		30	Sonday Christning of Susan Gunby daughter of George Gunby, Scriuener born the 25th of September Tuesdaye
	Novem	11	Sonday Christning of Mary Sallomon daughter of Thomas Sallomon Sadler, born the first day Thursday All saints
		25	Sonday Christining of Anne Gold daughter of Mr Hugh Gold, Grocer the child born the 18th day being Sonday
	Decem	2	Sonday Christning of Hugh Mole sonne of Richard Mole, Merchaunt Tailor and sexton heare born ye 23th November friday
		23	Sonday Christning of Richard Averell sonne of William Averell Merchant Tailor, born the 14th of December Friday
	Janua	13	Sonday Christining of Apeline Moris daughter of John Moris Clothworker, the childe born the 6th January Sonday
		20	Sonday Christning of Hillary Turner sonne of Hillary Turner, Draper, the childe born the 13th day being Sonday
		20	Sonday Christining of Alice Harris daughter of John Harris Scriuener, the childe born the 14th day being Monday
		20	Sonday Christining of Richard Lecroft sonne of William Lecroft Armorer, the childe born the day afore dyed morow after
		27	Sonday Christining of Thomas Symons sonne of Nicholas Symons Whitebaker, born the 24th of January being Thurs :
	Februa	3	Sonday Christining of Annes Hunter daughter of Edward Hunter Poulter, born the ffrst of february friday
		10	Sonday Christning of John Cooke sonne of Walter Cooke, Merchaunt Tailor, born the 8th of February being friday

Yeare.	Month.	Day.	Names.
1593	Februa	17	Sonday Christining of Effam Thorogood daughter of Jeames Thorogood, Poulter born the 8th of February friday
	March	3	Sonday Christned Richard Satchfeeld sonne of John Satchfeeld white baker, born the 24th of February Sonday
1594	Maye	5	Sonday Christning of Ellen Pedder daughter of John Pedder Merchaunt Tailor, born the 29th of Aprill Monday
	June	2	Sonday Christining of Richard Powell sonne of Dauid Powell Merchaunt Tailor born the 27th of May Monday
		2	Sonday Christining of Anne Bray daughter of William Bray Whitebaker, born the 21th of May Tuesday in Whitson week
		16	Sonday Christining of Hellenor Sheppy daughter of Robert Sheppy Poulter, born the 12th of June Wednesday
	Julie	14	Sonday Christning of Anne Drables daughter of Robert Drables Fishmonger, born the 7th of Julie being Sunday
	August	18	Sonday Christning of Arthur Leake sonne of Arthur Leake Merchaunt Tailor, born in Mr Hassaldes house in controuersie ye 11th day
	Septem.	1	Sonday Christning of Roger Shaw sonne of Ralph Shaw vintner at the sunne in Cornhill born the 26th of August Monday
		8	Sonday Christining of Frannces Coling sonne of Frannces Coling Fishmonger, born the 31th of August Satterday
		8	Sonday Christning of Harry Waight sonne of Richard Waight, Poulter the child was born the 2 of September
		15	Sonday Christining of Parnell Griphin daughter of John Griphin Felt maker, the childe born the 13th day being friday
		22	Sonday Christining of Leonard Pallmer sonne of Sebastian Pallmer Merchaunt Tailor, born the 13th day being friday
		22	Sonday Christining of Mary Hudsonne daughter of George Hudsonne Vpholster, born the 16th of September Monday
		22	Sonday Christining of Joane Roberts daughter of Steuen Roberts, Cooke, the childe born the 13 of September friday
		25	Wedensday Christning of William ignoti cognominis base born of one widow Smith in mother Manes house the lute: shee stole away
		29	Sonday Christining of Mary Askew daughter of William Askew Cooke, the childe born the 22th of Septem: sonday
	October	13	Sonday Christning of John Ratsdale sonne of William Ratsdale Ale Brewar, born the 6th of October being Monday
		13	Christned Sara Skeell daugh: of Wm Skeell, Draper, born ye 8th day
	Decem	15	Sonday Christned Sara Pywell dau: of John Pywell, born ye 8th Decem: sond
		29	Sonday Christining of Rebecca Averell daughter of William Averell Merchaunt Tailor his 16th child, born the 22th Decemb: Sonday
	Janua	26	Sonday Christining of Elizabeth Gold daughter of Mr Hugh Gold Grocer, the childe was born the 17th of January Friday

G

Yeare.	Month.	Day.	Names.
1594	Februa	16	Sonday Christining of Richard Willis sonne of Richard Willis, Grocer the child was born the 10th day of February Monday
		16	Sonday Christned Mary Stuard daugh. of Robert Stuard, born ye day afore
	March	12	Son: Christned Marget Caunt dau: of John Caunt born ye same day weake
		16	Sonday Christining of Thomas Satchfeeld sonne of John Satchfeld white Baker, born the 10th of March being Tuesday
		23	Sonday Christining of George Marrow sonne of George Marrow Carpenter, the childe was born the 14th of March friday
1595	Aprill	6	Sonday Christining of Dorite Cokain daughter of Mr Thomas Cokain Skynner, born the 26 of March being Wedensday
	May	18	Sonday Christning of Sara Nicholson daughter of Michaell Nichollson Cobler, the childe born the 10th of May satterday
	June	1	Sonday Christning of Elizabeth Pigot daughter of Mr Thomas Pigot Grocer born the 26th of May Monday
		15	Sonday Christining of Henry Needam sonne of Henry Needam Barbor Chirurgian, born the 8th of June sonday
		15	Sonday Christning of Elizabeth Hales daughter of Thomas Hales gentleman, born the 12th of June Thursday
	Julie	7	Wedensday Christuing of Richard Bray sonne of William Bray White Baker, born the 6th of July being Tuesday
		20	Sonday Christining of Mary Turner daughter of Hilla Turner Draper, the childe born the 13th of July Sonday
		30	Wedensday Christning of Elizabeth Crofte daughter of perciuall Crofte Merchaunt Tailor born ye 27th of July sonday
	August	3	Sonday Christning of John Naddle sonne of Rowland Naddle Brewar born the 31th July being Thursday
		3	Sonday Christning of John Leake sonne of Arthur Leake Merchant Tailor, born in ye north tenement of Mr Hassald ye 29th July
		3	Sonday Christining of John Web sonne of Elis Web Haberdasher the child born the 30th of July Wedensday at ye Bell
		31	Sonday Christning of Ralph Skeell sonne of William Skeell Draper, born the 24th day of August being Sonday
	October	5	Sonday Christning of Prudence Chapman daughter of Wm Chapman Haberdasher born the 27th of September being satterday
		26	Sonday Christning of Anne Thorogood daughter of Jeames Thorogood Poulter born the 22th day of October Wedensday
	Nouem	9	Sonday Christning of Jane Shepy daughter of Robert Shepy poulter, the childe born the 3 of Nouember beeing Monday
		23	Sonday Christning of Elizabeth Parchment daughter of Peeter Parchment Weuer the child born ye 18th day Tuesday
	Decem	7	Sonday Christining of John Edmondes sonne of Euannes Edmondes Clothworker, born the 30th Nouember Satterday

THE REGISTERS OF ST. PETER'S, CORNHILL. 43

Yeare.	Month.	Day.	Names.
1595	Janua	18	Sonday Christining of Elizabeth Ashbold daughter of Mr William Ashbold Doctor in diuinitie & parson of this Church, born ye 10th day satterday
		18	Sonday Christining of Elizabeth Palmer daughter of Sebastian Palmer Merchaunt Tailor, born 8th of January being Thursday
		23	Friday Christining of Ellen Caunt daughter of John Caunt Fishmonger the childe was born two dayes afore weake, dyed shortly after
		25	Sonday Christining of John Harris sonne of John Harris Scriuenor, the childe was born the * of January being
		25	Sonday Christning of Margery Averell daughter of William Averell Merchaunt Tailor my 17th childe, born the 14th day, being Wedens.
	Februa	29	Sonday Christning of Izan Dorington daughter of Mr John Dorington, the childe was born the 22th of February being sonday
1596	Aprill	11	Sonday Christining of Anne Coling daughter of Fraunces Coling Fishmonger, the child born the 5th of Aprill being Monday
	May	9	Sonday Christning of Mary Hudson daughter of William Hudsonne Fishmonger, the childe born the first day being satterday
		20	Thursday Christning of William Munday sonne of Richard Monday Sawyer, the childe born the 19th of Maye being Wedensdaye
		23	Sonday Christning of John Vertu sonne of Christopher Vertu Vinter, the childe was born the 18th of Maye being Tuesday
	June	20	Sonday Christning [of] Christian Tailor daug: of John Talo^r, born ye 10th day thursday
		20	Christned at the duch church Isacke Vansalt sonne of John: born heare ye 11th June
		27	Christned at the duch Church Peeter Vanvphouen sonne of Gylbert Vanvphouen of Deuontree, born in this parish the 18th day of June
	Julie	4	Sonday Christning of Mary Mole daughter of Richard Mole Merchaunt Tailor, born the 10 day of June beeing Thursday
		25	Sonday Christning of Margaret Ratsdale daughter of William Ratsdale ale Brewer, born the 23th day dyed ye day after Christning
	August	8	Sonday Christining of Elizabeth Waight daughter of Richard Waight Poulter, born the first of August being Sonday
		22	Sonday Christning of Susan Parker daughter of John Parker Poticary, the childe was born the 17th of August beeing Tuesday
		29	Sonday Christining of William Stuard sonne of Robert Stuard Barbor Surgion, the childe born the 27th day friday
	Septem	5	Sonday Christning of Abraham Griphin sonne of John Griphin Feltmaker, born the first of September Wedensday
		5	Sonday Christning of Anne Skeell daughter of William Skeell Hosier, the childe born Satterday beeing the 28th of August

* Sic.

Yeare.	Month.	Day.	Names.
1596	Septem	13	Sonday* Christining of Lettice Goodwin daughter of Richard Goodwin Carter of the waygh house born the 9th day Wedensday
		13	Sonday* Christining of Edward Spalding sonne of Willfred Spalding Cutler, the childe born the 4th day of September Fridaye
		17	Friday Christining of Jane Naddle daughter of Rowland Naddle a Browers seruant, dwelling in the Church ally gainst ye wall
		19	Sonday Christning of Henry Sallomon sonne of Thomas Salomon a Sadler, the childe born the 15th day of Septembe^r wedensday
		26	Sonday Christning of Jane Willis daughter of Richard Willis Grocer, the childe was born the 22th day of September Wedensday
	October	3	Sonday Christining of John Hill sonne of John Hill Merchaunt Tailor, the childe was born vpon the 30th day of Septem: Wedensday
		17	Sonday Christning of William Turner sonne of Hillary Turner Draper, the childe was born the 3 of October beeing Sondaye
		24	Sonday Christning of Elizabeth Web daughter of Ellis Web Vintner, the childe was born the 23th of October beeing Satterday
		24	Sonday Christning of Annes Wright daughter of John Wright Poulter, the childe was borne the 15th of October friday at ye spred egle
	Nouem	7	Sonday Christning of Anne Needam daughter of Henry Needam Barbor Chirurgian, born the 30th of October being Satterday
		21	Sonday Christning of Elizabeth Oldam daughter of Robert Oldam Seruing man, the childe born the 15th of Nouember being Monday
		28	Sonday Christning of Andrew Satchfeeld sonne of John Satchfeld White Baker, the childe born the 18th of Nouember being Thursday
		28	Sonday Christining of Alice Thorogood daughter of Jeames Thorogood Poulter, the childe born the 20th of Nouember being satterday
	Decem	26	Sonday St Johns day Christning of Joseph Cokain sonne of Mr Thomas Cokain Skynner, born the 13th of December beeing Tuesdaye
	Janua	6	Tuesday Christning of Thomas Wallthall sonne of Mr Thomas Wallthall Mercer and Marchaunt, the childe born the first January
		16	Sonday Christining of two twynnes of Fraunces Persey Labourer viz. John Persey and Thomas Persey born the 10th daye Mondaye
		30	Sonday Christning of Michaell Nicholson sonne of Michaell Nicholsonne Cordwainer, born the 28th of January being then Monday
	Februa	2	Wedensday Candlemas day Christning of Peeter Chapman sonne [of] William Haberdashe^r born the 26th of January Wedensdaye
	March	4	Friday Christning of Dauid Tailor sonne of one John Tailor

* Sic.

Yeare.	Month.	Day.	Names.
			as the mother said, born at Meg Jordanes dore by leaden haule corner one St Dauids day
1596	March	6	Sonday Christning of Thomas Powell sonne of David Powell Merchaunt Tailor, born the 27th of February beeing Sondaye
1597	Aprill	3	Sonday Christning of Barbara Dorrington daughter of Mr John Dorrington Merchaunt, born the 27th of March Sonday
		17	Sonday Christning of Elizabeth Cumbars daughter of Thomas Cumbars Cooke, born the 12th of Aprill beeing then Tuesdaye
		24	Sonday Christning of Elizabeth Burchewood daughter of Thomas Burchewood Cordewainer, born ye 16th of Aprill satterday
	Maye	8	Sonday Christning of Jane Bray daughter of William Bray White Baker the childe born the second of May beeing Monday
		24*	Sonday Christning of Sara Jacobsonne daughter of Peeter Jacobson Duche man, born in the house next Mr Thomson Grocer
	Julye	24	Sonday Christning of Mary Brewin daughter of Roger Bruin, Skinner, the child born the 14th of Julie beeing then Thursday
	Julie	24	Sonday Christning of Susan Witter daughter of George Witter Vintner, the childe was born the 14th of Julie allso being Thursday
	Septem	18	Sonday Christning of Robert Friar sonne of Symon Friar, Skynner, the childe was born vpon the 9th day of September being friday
	October	2	Sonday Christning of William Webbe sonne of Ellis Webbe Vintner the childe was born vpon the 29th of September Thursday, Michellmas day
		8	*Sonday Christning of William Heton son of Thomas Heton Merchaunt, born the 29th of September being Thursday in Mr Goffes house
		30	Sonday Christning of Anne Spalding daughter of Willfrid Spalding Cutter, born in Randolles house sexton, the 3 of October Monday
	Nouem	6	Sonday Christning of William Ratsdale sonne of William Ratsdale ale Bruer, the childe was born the 3 of Nouember Wedensday
		16	Wedensday Christning of Marget Skynner daughter of John Skynner as the mother said in Bridewell, base begotten in the Minorites by hym
	Decemb	2	Friday Christining of Alice Waight daughter of Richard Waight Poulter, the child was born the 26th of Nouember being satterday
	Decemb	4	Sonday Christning of Elizabeth Averell daughter of William Averell his 18th childe, Merchant Tailor & Clarke heare, born ye 28th Nouem : Mon.
		25	Sonday Christmas day Christning of John Caunt sonne of John Caunt Fishmonger, the childe was born the 13th of December being Tuesday
	Januar	1	New yeares day Sonday Christning of Cisly Ashbold daughter of Mr William Ashbold Doctor of Diuinitie & parson of this church born ye 22th Thurs :

* Sic.

Yeare.	Month.	Day.	Names.
1597	Januar	22	Sonday Christning of Ellen Marrow daughter of George Marrow Carpenter, the childe was born the 13th of January beeing friday
	Februa	19	Sunday Christning of Daniell and Nathaniell Willys twynnes of Richard Willyes Grocer, born the 12th of February being Sonday
		19	Sonday Christining of John Maxfeeld sonne of John Maxfeeld Armorer, the child was born the 12th of February beeing Sondaye
		23	Thursday Christning of John Pedder sonne of John Pedder Merchaunt Tailor, the childe was born the 22th day Wedensday
	March	12	Sonday Christning of Barbara Coling daughter of Frances, Fishmonger, the childe was born the 2 of March beeing Thursday
1598	June	4	Sonday Christining of Edward Parker sonne of John Parker Potticary, the childe born the 27th of Marche beeing satterday
		11	Sonday Christining of Thomas Burchwood sonne Thomas Burchwood Cordwainer born the 4th of June beeing Sonday
		18	Sonday Christning of Thomas Cumbars sonne of Thomas Cumbers Cooke, the childe born the 9th of June beeing friday
	Julie	2	Sonday Christning of Ellen Lecroft daughter of Samson Lecroft Armorer, the childe born the 26th of June beeing Monday
		2	Sonday Christining of Elizabeth Brittain daughter of Walter Brittain Merchaunt Tailor, born the last of June beeing friday
		9	Sonday Christining of Samuell Cokaines sonne of Mr Thomas Cokaines Skynner, the childe born the 27th of June Tuesday
		27	Thursday Christning of Mary Satchfeld daughter of John Satchfeeld white Baker, born the same daye beeing very weake
	Julie	30	Sonday Christning of Susan Hardwin daughter of Jeames Hardwin Blacksmith the childe born the 20th of Julie beeing Sonday
	August	6	Sonday Christining of Thomas Dorington sonne of Mr John Dorington Merchaunt born the 2 day of August beeing Wedensday
		18	Friday Christning of John Westly sonne of Robert Westly vpholster the childe born vpon the 17th day of August, Thursday
	Septem	3	Sonday Christning of Marget Shepy daughter of Robert Shepy Poulter the childe born the 25th of August Fridaye
		10	Sunday Christning of Margery Harris daughter of John Harris Scriuener born the first of September being Thursday
		24	Sonday Christning of Mary Tailor daughter of John Tailor Merchaunt Tailor born the 16th of September being Satterday
		29	Friday Christning of Jeames Grace sonne of Richard Grace deceased an Attorny, born the 20th of September being Wedensday

THE REGISTERS OF ST. PETER'S, CORNHILL. 47

Yeare.	Month.	Day.	Names.
1598	Octobe'	22	Sonday Christning of John Griphin sonne of John Griphin Felt maker born the 15th of October beeing then Satterday
		29	Sonday Christning of Humphry Turner sonne of Hillarye Turner Draper, born the 22th of October beeing Sonday
	Nouem	19	Sonday Christning of Christopher Witter sonne of George Witter Vintner, born the 12th of Nouember being Monday
		26	Sonday Christining of John Friar sonne of Symon Friar Skynner, the childe was born the 16th of Nouember being Thursday
		26	Sonday Christining of Harry Warman sonne of William Warman Cooke, the childe born the 12th of Nouember Sonday
		29	Wedensday Christning of Edward Rigely sonne of Edward Rigely one of the Sherifes officers, born the 24th day Nouember friday
	Decem	10	Sonday Christning of Alice Bromly daughter of William Bromly the yonger, Poulter, born the 4th day beeing Monday
		17	Sonday Christning of Thomas Faringdon sonne of Edward Farringdon Mercer, the childe born the 10th of December sonday
	Janua	1	Monday Christning of Marget Goddard daughter of Edward Goddard Armorer, the child born the 21th day being S^t. Thomas day
	Februa	2	Friday Christning of Anthony Waight sonne of Richard Waight Poulter, born the 24th day of January beeing Wedens
1599	Maye	6	Sunday Christning of Edward Marrow sonne of George Marow Carpenter born vpon May Day beeing Tuesday
	Julie	1	Sunday Christning of Julius Brooke sonne of William Brooke Pewterer, born the 26th of June being Tuesdaye
		11	Wedensday Christning of Walter Maude sonne of William Maude of Ratclif sailor borne the 4th of July Wedensday
		25	Wedensday St Jeames day, Christ: Jeames Gold sonne of Mr Hugh Gold Grocer, the child born the ...day of Julie bing
		29	Sunday Christning of Robert Brewin sonne of Roger Brewin, Skynner born the 18th of July beeing Thursday
	August	12	Sunday Christning of Anne Burchewood daughter of Thomas Burchwood Cordwainer born ye 4th of August satterday
		19	Sunday Christning of Margaret Ratsdale daughter of Wm Ratsdale ale Brewer the child born the 15th daye Wedensday
	Septem	2	Sunday Christning of Bartholomew Maxfeld sonne of John Maxfeld Armorer born the 23 of August. Thursdaye
		2	Sunday Christning of John Williames sonne of Roger Williames Cooke the child born the 28th of August. Tuesday
		23	Sunday Christning of Aholiab Nicholson sonne of Michaell Nicholson Cordwainer, born the 19th of September, Wedensday
	October	2	Tuesday Christning of Walter Persy sonne of Fraunces

Yeare.	Month.	Day.	Names.
			Persy Skynner, the child born the 28th day of Septem : Friday
1599	October	14	Sunday Christning of Martha Cokaine daugh: of Mr Thomas Cockaine, Skynner, the child born the 5th of October beeing friday
		21	Sunday Christning of Peeter Goodwyn sonne of Richard Goodwin Seruant in ye waigh house born ye 13th of October, satterday
		21	The same day Christned Ellen Tillner daughter of Nicholas Tyllner, Ironmonger, born the 16th day of October. Tuesday
		21	The same day Christned Joane Shepy daughter of Robert Shepy Poulter, born the 12th day being friday
		28	Sunday Christning of Frannces Parker daughter of John Parker Potticary born the 24th day of October, Wedensday
	Nouem	11	Sunday Christning of Jane Colyng daughter of Fraunces Colyng Fishmonger, born one the second of Nouember : Friday
		25	Sunday Christning Richard Lecroft sonne of Samson Lecroft Armorer, the childe born the 19th of Nouember being Monday
	Decemb	16	Sunday Christning of Mary Friar daughter of Symon Friar Skinner, the childe born the 9th of December being Sonday
	January	6	Sonday Christning of Richard Bromly sonne of William Bromly Poulter: the childe born the 30th of December Sonday
	Februar	3	Sunday Christning of Martha Satchfeld daughter of Richard Satchfeld Grocer the child born the 28th of January being Monday
		10	Sunday Christning of Parnell Reynoldes daughter of Rouland Reynoldes Skinner the childe born the 3 of February Sonday
		17	Sunday Christning [of] Elizabeth Caunt daughter of John Cant Fishmonger, the childe born the 9th of February, one Satterday night
		24	Sunday Christning of Edward Pigot sonne of Thomas Pigot, Grocer, the childe born the 16th of February being Satterday
1600	March	25	Tuesday our Lady day Christning Joane Warman daughter of William Warman Cooke the child born ye 18th of March. Tuesday.
		30	Sunday Christning of Thomas Hardwin sonne of Jeames Hardwin Blacke-smith the child born the 20th of March. Thursday
		30	Sunday Christning of Susan Brittain daughter of Walter Brittain Merchant Tailor, born the 27th of March. Thursday
	Aprill	6	Sunday Christning John Record sonne of John Record Merchant Tailor the child was born the 28 of March beeing Fryday
		9	Wedensday Christining of Robert and Sara Kelly twinnes of a vagrant woman named Elsabeth, born in Leden Hall the day afore
		20	Sunday Christning of Robert Webbe sonne of Elis Webbe vintner the childe born the 17th day of Aprill beeing the Wedensday afore

THE REGISTERS OF ST. PETER'S, CORNHILL. 49

Yeare.	Month.	Day.	Names.
1600	Maye	13*	Monday Christned Henry Roberts sonne of Samuell Roberts vpholder, born in St Michaells in Cornhill, but for weaknes Christned heare
	Julie	13	Sunday Christned Elizabeth Downes daughter of Thomas Dounes Fishmonger, the Childe was born 3 daies afore, & dyed the morow after
		20	Sunday Christned Thomas Burchwood, sonne of Thomas Burchwood Cordwainer: born vpon the day afore beeing Monday
	August	30	Sunday Christned Jone Haruey daughter of Symon Haruy Groce^r the childe was born vpon friday being the 21 of August
	Septem	7	Sunday Christned Thomas Morris sonne of Thomas Morris Clothworker, the childe born † the † of August
		21	Sunday Christned Elizabeth Mercer daughter of John Mercer Habberdasher, the childe was born the 15th of September Monday
	October	5	Sunday Christned Thomas Turner sonne of Hillary Turner, Draper, the childe was born one Sunday the 29th of September
		12	Sunday Christned Wm Chapman son of William Chapman Habberdasher, born vpon Sunday the 5th of October
		12	Sunday Christned William Meares sonne of Walter Meares Skynner, the childe born Thursday the second of October
		12	Sunday Christned Christian Harris daughter of John Haris Scriuener, the childe was born one tuesday September the 30
		26	Sunday Christned Jeames Persy sonne of Fraunces Persy Skynner, the Childe was born one friday the 24th of October
		28	Tuesday Symon and Judes day Christned Symon Pedder sonn of John Pedder Merchaunt Tailor born friday the 24th of October
	Nouem	7	Friday Christned Samuell Turke sonne of † Turke the childe born vpon the 3 of Nouember. Monday
	January	1	Thursday Christned Jeames Symmones sonne of Thomas Symmones Vintner, born vpon the satterday before
		4	Sunday Christned Elizabeth Shepheard daughter of Thomas Shepheard Merchaunt Tailor born the 25th of December
		6	Tuesday Christned Anne Bowen daughter of Edward Bowen Vpholder, the childe was born vpon friday the 2 January
	Februa	1	Sunday Christned Edward Tilman sonne of Nicholas Tilman Ireonmonger, the childe was born tuesday the 27th January
		1	Sunday Christned Cisly Thorogood daughter of Jeames Thorogood, Poulter the childe born monday afore Candlemas
		22	Sunday Christned John Heeling sonne of Peeter Heel: of London Grocer the childe was born the † of february
		22	Sunday Christned John Maxfeld sonne of John Maxfeld Armorer the childe was born wedensday the † of february

* The Register from October 28, 1599, to September 6, 1601, is subscribed Will'm Asheboold and Mark Scaliet.
† Sic.

Yeare.	Month.	Day.	Names.
1600	March	8	Christned Mary Brown daughter of William Browne fishmonger the child born at the Angell now, once the sunne in question in Cornhill
1601		25	Monday Christned Rebecca Satchfeld daughter of Richard Satchfeld Grocer, the childe born the 17th of March Tuesday
		29	Sunday Christned Robert Record sonne of John Record, Merchaunt Tailor, the childe was born the * of Marche
	Aprill	7	Sunday Christned Richard Swifte sonne of Richard Swift Merchaunt Tailor the child was born vpon the 1 of Aprill
		13	Monday Christned Mary ignoti nominis daughter of a vagrant woman brought to bed at the church dore in Cornhill
	Maie	3	Sunday Christned Fraunces Dorington sonne of John Dorington Grocer the childe was born tuesday the 21th of Aprill
		10	Sunday Christned Daniell Tailer sonne of John Tailer Marchaunt Tailor, born vpon the 3 of May being sonday
		17	Sunday Christned William Marrow sonne of Georg Marow Carpenter; the childe was born the 8th of May beeing friday
		17	Christning of Susanne Warman daughter of William Warman Cooke, the childe born the 11th of May beeing Monday
		24	Sunday Christned Thomas Daniell sonne of Walter Daniell Tailor, the childe born the 15 of May beeing friday
	Julie	26	Sunday Christned Sara Lecroft daughter of Samson Lecroft Armorer the child born the 17th of Julie beeing friday
	August	30	Sunday Christned Ralph Varnam sonne of Ralph Varnam Merchauntailor born at the lute the 25 of August beeing tuesday
	Septem	6	Sunday Christned Gerson Peeter a boy 2 yeares old found one Jeames Thorogoodes stall about 3 weekes old, not Christned till now, Mr Doctor named hym
		6	Sunday Christned Allice ffenton daughter of Roger ffenton Founder, the child was born one Satterday the 29th of August
	Nouem	8†	Sunday Christned John Parker sonne of John Parker Grocer the Child was born one sunday the first of Nouember
		8	Sunday Christned Marget Congrey daughter of Richard Congrey, Glasier, the child was born satterday the 31th October
		29	Sunday Christned Thomas Hudson sonne of George Huddson vpholder, the child born tuesday the 24th Nouember
		29	Sunday Christned Fraunces Goddard daughter of Edward Goddard Armorer the child born Monday the 23 of Nouember

* Sic.

† The Register from November 8, 1601, to July 4, 1602, is subscribed Will'm Ashboold, parson, John Caunt, churchwarden, John Marrys.

Yeare.	Month.	Day.	Names.
1601	Decem	6	Sunday Christned William Forringdon sonne of Edward Forringdon Mercer, the child born * the * of Nouember
		13	Sunday Christned Alice Wright daughter of John Wright Poulter, the child was born one satterday the 5th of December
		27	Sunday Christned Saraa Burchwood daughter of Thomas Burchwood Cordwainer: born satterday the 19th December
	Janua	12	Wedensday Christned Richard Billingslie sonne of Harry Billingsly Merchant, born in Mr Stockes house wedens: ye 29th December
		17	Sunday Christned John Dickenson the sonne of Widow Dyckenson of Nedingworth Huntingshire born in Edward Hunters house ye 9th Jan:
	Februa	2	Tuesday Christning Mary Bourn daughter of Thomas Bourn Salter, the child born Thursday last the 28th of January in Mrs Powells house
		14	Sunday Christned ffraunces Haruey daughter of Symon Haruey ye Queenes Grocer, born wedensday the 3 of February
		28	Sunday Christned John Turner sonne of Hillary Turner Draper: the child was born Sunday the 21th of February
1602	March	28	Sunday Christned Jeames Pickborn sonne of Jeames Pickborn Merchaunt Tailor born in widow Bromlies, ye 18th March Thursday
		28	Sunday Christned Giles Hardwin sonne of Jeames Hardwin Blacke smith the child born Tuesday the 23th of March
		28	Sunday Christned Robert Brittain sonne of Walter Brittain Merchaunt Tailor: the child born satterdaie the 20th March
	Aprill	4	Easter day Christned Jane Ashboold daughter of Mr William Ashboold Doctor of diuinitie & parson heare: born ye 17th March Monday
		18	Sunday Elizabeth Page daughter of Thomas Page Armorer the child born one Easter tuesday in Mr Loxons house
	Maie	2	Sunday Christned Bartholomew Thorogood sonne of James Thorogood Poulter: the childe born friday beeing the 23th of Aprill
	Julie	4	Sunday Christned Rachell Satchfeld daughter of Richard Satchfeld Grocer, the child born Wedensdaie the 30th of June
		4	Christned Bennet Warman daughter of William Warman Cooke: the child was born friday beeing the 21th of June
		11†	Sunday Christned Alice Symmon daughter of Thomas Symmon Vintner The childe born one Wedensday ye 7th of Julie
	Septem	19	Sunday Christned William Tillman sonne of Nicholas Tyllman Ironmonger the childe was born Satterday the 4th September

* Sic.
† The Register from July 11, 1602, to March 13 following. is subscribed Will'm Ashcboold, parson, Thomas Galouwy.

Yeare.	Month.	Day.	Names.
1602	Septem	26	Sunday Christned Dorothy Rainoldes daughter of Rowland Reynoldes Skynner, the child was born *
	October	24	Sunday Christned Jane Swift daughter of Richard Swift Merchaunt Tailor: born vpon Tuesday the 19th day of October
	Decem	19	Sunday Christned William Elmhurst sonne of William Elmhurst of the Custom House born sunday the 12th of December
	Janua	6	Thursdaie twelf daie Christned Georg Dauis sonne of Thomas Dauis Tailor: the childe born one new Yeares day night last
Shee was punished in Bride well		29	Satterday Christned Annes Odium alias Cartwright born in Mr Morris his house of his servant Cisley Hartfordshire beegotten by John Odium in St Gyles parish in ye feld
		30	Sunday Christned Edward Parker sonne of John Parker, Grocer and Poticary the childe was born one Monday the 24th of January
	Februa	2	Wedensday Candlemas day Christned Nicholas Record sonne of John Record Merchaunt Tailor born vpon Satterday the 22th of January
		13	Sunday Christned William Lecroft sonne of Samson Lecroft Armorer. The childe was born the * of February beeing
	March	13†	Sunday Christned Walter Wright sonne of John Wright poulter the child was born one Sunday the syxt day of Marche

Heare end theyre birthes by her sweet death:
Vnder whose raigne they tooke theyr breath,
A peereles prince a Virgin Queen:
Whose like one earth was neuer seen.
England put one sad sable black:
With brynish teares lament her lack
And mourn for her that now hath been
Fourtie fiue yeares thy nurse and Queen.
Whose golden vertues to recite
No tongue can tell, no penne can write.
Elizabeth thy glorious name:
Shall liue while earth doth keep her frame.
And when the earth shall melt and wast:
In heauen thy fame shall liue and last.
Queen Elsabeth is gone and dead,
King James now raigneth in her stead.
Her vertues sounded weare by fame,
The world ringes of his princelie name.
A Queen and King so to succeed,
I neuer heard nor none did reed.

Quoth William Averell.

Spes mea Christus erit sine quo spes nulla salutis.
W. A.

* Sic.

Iam noua progenies, ô rex sequitur tua proles,
Nam sub te dicant ortus habere suos.

CHRISTNINGS 1603.

So now beeginnes a new ofspring
At entrance of a vertuos king.
King James the first preseru'd by fate
For Englandes crowne and regall state.
Long maie hee swaie the diadem,
Of princes all the princelie gemme.
For men, nay angelles crie and sing.
God saue thee James thrise famous king.

Yeare.	Month.	Day.	Names.
1603	Maie	8*	Sundaie Christned Elizabeth Liddington daughter of Thomas Liddington Armorer, born thursdaie the 28th of Aprill
		15	Sunday Christned James Hardwin sonne of James Hardwin blacksmith, born one Monday the ninth of Maye
	June	19	Sundaie Christned Thomas Turner sonne of Hillarie Turner Draper, the child was born one Sundaie beeing the 12th of June
	Julie	31	Sundaie Christned Steuen Warman sonne of William Warman Cooke, the child was born one the Fridaie seuenth night afore
	August	16	Wedensdaie Christned Peeter Bourn sonne of Thomas Bourn who wedded Mrs Powells daughter: born one satterday last past
		31	Wedensdaie Christned Marie Goddard daughter of Edward Goddard Armorer, born one Sundaie last the 28th of August
	October	3	Mondaie Christned Sara Stauelie daughter of James Stauelie Pewterer, the child was born to bee Christned beefore the father when hee was carried to bee buried, and died soone after
	Nouem	6	Sundaie Christned Anne Hudson daughter of George Hudsonne Vpholder. the child was born one satterdaie the 29 October
		9	Wedensdaie then Christned Edward Powell sonne of Humfry Powell Tailor, the child was born thursdaie last the 3 of Nouember
	January	6	Fridaie twelf daie Christned Elizabeth King daughter of † King Mercer, the child born wedensdaie the 28th of December
		15	Sunday Alice Pickborn daughter of James Pickborn Merchant Tailor, the childe born the † of Januarie beeing then ...
		29	Sunday Ellis Norton sonne of Henry Norton by a vagrant named Elizabeth Dauis the childe born at ye pewterers dore, by ye plattes
	February	21	Tuesdaie Marie Cason daughter of John Cason Grocer, the childe born but late beefore, and dyed that daie it was Christned

---

* The Register from May 8, 1603, to November 16, 1606, is subscribed Will'm Asheboold, parson, Chrystopher Verteu, and ffraunces Colynge.

† Sic.

Yeare.	Month.	Day.	Names.
1603	February	25	Satterday Susan Pane daughter of William Pane Skynner the childe was born vpon Tuesday beeing the 21th of February
		26	Sunday Katherin Lecroft daughter of Samson Lecroft Armorer, the childe born the 14th day of Februarie beeing tuesday
	March	11	Sunday Thomas Burchwood sonne of Thomas Burchwood Cordwainer, the childe born the 5th of March beeing Monday
		18	Sunday Ruth Leigh daughter of Thomas Leigh Pewterer the childe born the 6th of March beeing then Tuesday
1604		25	Sunday beeing our Lady day William Satchfeeld sonne of Richard Satchfeld Grocer the child born vpon tuesdaie the 20th day
		25	Sunday: Daniell Maxfeeld sonne of John Maxfeld Armorer The childe was born vpon the sunday afore beeing the 18th day
	Aprill	8	Easter day: Elizabeth Coling daughter of Frauncos Coling, Fishmonger, born one Maunday Thursday beeing the 5th of March
	Maie	28	Tuesdaie in Whitsunweeke: Thomas Wellen sonne of Nathaniell Wellen Lynen Drap': born the sunday seuennight beefore beeing ye 19th
	June	3	Sunday: William Robinson, sonne of Arthur Robinson Marchant Stapler: the childe born one Satterday the 26th of Maye
		3	Sunday George Seaman sonne of Thomas Symon or Seaman Vintner at the bell and hauke born the 31th of Maye beeing Thursday
		3	Sunday Anne Williames daughter of Roger Williames Cooke the childe was born one monday last beeing the 28th of May
		9	Satterday: Katherin Barley daughter of William Barley Draper, the childe born one satterday fourteenth night afore. The godfather Syr Edward Stanhop Knight, godmother ye Lady Granger
		17	Sunday: Katheryn Herby daughter of Edward Herby Grocer the child born in St Mychaelles parish next, the 9th of June beeing satter:
	Jvlie	29	Sunday James Synnocke sonne of James Synnocke Clothworker the child born in St Michaells parish the church repayring the 27 of July
	August	19	Sunday Anne Marsh daughter of Thomas Marsh a porter the childe born in St Michaells parish the church in repairing
		29	Wedensday: Henry Ashbold sonne of Mr William Ashboold Doctor of Diuinitie and parson of this parish: The childe born one friday fourteunight afore: The godfathers Syr Henry Billingsly and Syr John Deane Knights, ye Lady Hayes Godmother
	Septem	1	Satterday, Jone Okely daughter of Thomas Okely, Waxchandler, the childe born the daye afore beeing friday
		2	Sunday. Thomas Hardwyn sonne of James Hardwyn Blackesmith, the childe born one the sunday afore
	Decemb	9	Sundaie: Joseph Cowes sonne of William Cowes Pewterer the child was born vpon satterday was seuen night the first day

Yeare.	Month.	Day	Names.
1604	Decemb	21	Friday St Thomas Day. Christ: Elizabeth Wenman daughter of Syr Ferdinando Wenman Knight, the childe born in th'ally by the Platterer in Gratious street the 10th of this month being Monday the Godfather the Lord William Knowelles, one of his Maties priuie counsell; Godmothers, the Lady Lucie Countes of Bedford, and the Lady Elizabeth Darlton, bewtifull Ladies
	Februa	6	Thursday: Ellen Palmer daughter of Ellen Pallmer an vnmaried Woman syster to John Palmer body maker, it was gotten by one Edmund Welsh a seruingman, they weare presented to Doctor Creeke
		20	Wedensday: Elizabeth Webbe daughter of Richard Webbe Grocer, the Childe was born wedensday the 13 of February; the first child Christned in the font remoued from the reading place by the quire
	March	20	Wedensday: John King sonne of John King Mercer, born the 12th of March being tuesday: ye first Christned in the gilded font
1605	Aprill	1	Monday: Kathern Woodall daughter of John Woodall Chirurgian the child born vpon Sunday the 24th of March last past
			Monday: Anne Hickman daughter of Joseph Hickman Carpenter, the child born 20th of March past beeing Wedensday
	May	5	Elizabeth Maxfeild daughter of John Maxfeild Armorer dwelling in Cornhill
	July	21	William Barley the sonne of William Barley drap' yett a booke Seller dwelling in gratious streete
		28	John Parker the sonne of John Parker Apoticary dwellinge in Gratious streete
	August	11	Rowland Reynoldes the sonne of Rowland Reynoldes Skynner and Vpholder dwellinge in Cornhill
		29	Effam Okely the daughter of Thomas Okelye Waxchandler dwellinge in gratious streete
	Septemb^r	22	Ann Barrowe the daughter of Richard Barrowe who lodged att Mr Kettels in Cornhill and came from Graues eude
		27	Edward Ridgley the sonne of Edward Ridgley seargyant dwellinge in Corbets Courte in gratious streete
	October	18	Hughe Barnard the sonne of Richard Barnard haberdasher, dwellinge Cornhill*
		20	Thomas Leigh the sonne of Thomas Leigh Pewterer dwellinge in Leaden Hall streete
		27	Elizabeth Warman the daughter of William Warman Cooke, dwellinge in Leaden Hall streete
	Nouemb	3	Palmer Turner the sonne of William Turner Grocer, dwellinge in Cornhill
		10	Henrye Palmer the sonne of William Palmer Marchant dwellinge in Leaden Hall streete
		24	ffrauncies Holdsworth the daughter of Thomas Holdsworth, Inholder dwellinge in gratious streete
	Decemb	15	Sarah Jennings the daughter of Robert Jennings Vpholster dwellinge in Cornhill
	Januarie	5	Ann Weston the daughter of Roberte Weston Vpholster dwellinge in St Peters Alye

* Sic.

THE REGISTERS OF ST. PETER'S, CORNHILL.

Yeare.	Month.	Day.	Names.
1605	Januarie	15	William Boulton the sonne of Robert Boulton
		26	Elizabeth Younge the daughter of George Younge Musitian dwellinge in Read Cross Alye
		30	Roger Walthall the sonne of Thomas Walthall Marchaunte and Mercer in gratious streete
	Februar	9	Thomas Mathew the sonne of Thomas Mathewes
		9	Hellen Stone the daughter of Thomas Stone Poulter in gratious streete
		28	Elizabeth Hunter the daughter of Edward Hunter, Poulter in gratious streete
	March	16	Elizabeth Weightman the daughter of Peter Weightman Vintner in gratious streete
		16	Isabell Seirle the daughter of John Seirle Lawier
1606	Aprill	13	Ann Mortimor the daughter of John Mortimor from Mrs Kinnstons Poulter in gratious streete
		28	William Robinsonne the sonne of Arthur Robinsonne Marchaunt in Bishopsgate streete
	May	11	Elizabeth Luddingtonne the daughter of Vallintonne Luddingtone Smith in Leaden Hall Streete
		18	Margret Bourne the daughter of Thomas Bourne from Mr Richardsones the Clothworke in Leaden Hall str:
		22	Hable Brittane the daughter of Walter Brittane Tapstreworker in Leaden Hall streete
	Julie	20	Ann Porter the daughter of Lewis Porter whoe loged att Mr Turners in Cornhill
	Septemb	7	Hanna Cowsley the daughter of William Cowsley Pewterrer in Leaden Hall streete
	October	11	Walter Ridgley the sonne of Edward Ridgley sea^{r}g: dwellinge in Corbets Courte in gratious streete
		13	William Webb the sonne of Richard Webb grocer in Bishopsgate streete
		15	Peter Keyes a Child Laid in this p'ishe in Leaden Hall streete and pute to nurse to Goodman Woodine att vatford
		19	Margret Vdall als Woodall daughter to John Vdall Barber Chirurgion in Cornhill
		26	Richard Sachfeild the sonne of Richard Sachfeild Baker in Bishopsgate streete
	Nouemb	16	Ann Kinge the daughter of John Kinge dwellinge in Leaden Hall streete
		30*	Peter Ward the sonne of Thomas Ward Vpholster Whoe loged att the blacke bull in Leaden Hall streete
	December	21	Elizabeth Greenhall the daughter of ffrauncis Greenhall Linnen Drap: dwellinge in Cornhill
	Februarie	8	Richard Goodwine the sonne of Richard Goodwine dwellinge in Cornhill in the Kinges ware house yarde
	March	8	Thomas Holdsworth the sonne of Thomas Holdsworth Late Inholder dwellinge in gratious streete
		8	Marie Androws the daughter of William Androws Late Grocer dwellinge in Leaden Hall streete
1607	Aprill	5	Richard Barnard the sonne of Richard Barnard habe^r. of small wayers dwellinge in Cornhill
		9	Marie Barley the daughter of William Barley Drap^r yett a booke seller dwellinge in gratious streete

* The Register from November 30, 1606, to July 31, 1608, is subscribed Will'm Asheboold, parson. ffraunces Colynge, John Parker.

THE REGISTERS OF ST. PETER'S, CORNHILL.

Yeare.	Month.	Day.	Names.
1607	Aprill	12	Ann Turner the daughter of Hillarie Turnere Grocer dwellinge in Cornhill
	May	24	Marie Askew the daughter of Tobias Askew haberdasher dwellinge in gratious streete
	June	24	John Casonne the sonne of John Casonne Grocer dwelling in Cornhill
	Julie	26	Margret Hardcastle the daughter of Richard Hardcastle dwellinge in Cornhill
	August	31	Robert Prime the sonne of Thomas Prime scriuener dwellinge in Leaden Hall streete
	September	6	John Whitman the sonne of Peter Whitmann Vintener dwellinge in gratious streete
		13	Marie Jennings the daughter of Robert Jennings Vpholdst^r. dwellinge in Cornhill
		29	John Stone the sonne of Thomas Stone Poulter dwellinge iu gratious streete
	October	18	Barbara Mathews the daughter of Thomas Mathewes ffishmonger whoe loged att Mr Hardcastle in Cornhill
	Nouember	15	Ann Maxfeild the daughter John Maxfeild Braszer dwellinge in Cornhill
	Januarie	3	Ellen Hickman the daughter of Joseph Hickman Carpenter dwellinge in gratious streete
		3	Richard Leycraft the sonne of Sampson Leycrafte Braszer dwellinge in gratious streete
		24	Edward Sachfeild the sonne of Richard Sachfeild Baker dwellinge in Bishopsgate streete
	Februarie	2	Susanna Luddington the daughter of Valentine Luddington Smith dwellinge in Leaden Hall streete
		28	Arthur Robinson the sonne of Arthur Robinsonne Marchant dwellinge in Bishopsgate streete
	March	19	John Ridgsley the sonne of Edward Ridgsley seargyant dwelling in Corbettes Courte in gratious streete
1608		26	Hester Harley the daughter of Jeames Harley Cooke keepinge Poulter dwellinge in gratious street
	Aprill	10	Thomas Reynoldes the sonne of Rowland Reynoldes Vphodste^r dweinge* in Cornhill
	May	15	Ann Okeley the daughter of Thomas Okeley waxchandl^r but vsing Poulter dwelling in gratious streete
	June	3	Jeames Goodwine and Walter Goodwine the sonne of Richard Goodwine porter dwellinge in Cornhill in the kinges warehouse yard
		5	John J'ansonne the sonne of William J'ansonne Vintener dwellinge in Cornhill
		24	Thomas Kinge the sonne of John Kinge Marchante dwellinge in Leaden Hall streete
		26	Amie Turner daughter of Hillarie Turner grocer dwellinge in Cornhill
	Julie	24	Ann Garritt the daughter of Thomas Garritt Inholder dwellinge in gratious streete
		24	Grisogo Launglee the daughter of John Launglee Linen Drap: dwellinge in Cornhill
		31	Jeane Weightman the daughter of Peter Weightman Vintener dwellinge in gratious streete
	August	7†	Tobias Weston the sonne of Robert Weston Vpholdst^r: dwellinge in St Peters Alie in gratious streete

* Sic.
† The Register from August 7, 1608, to June 10, 1610, is subscribed Will'm Asheboold, parson, John Parker, Stephen Roberts.

I

Yeare.	Month.	Day.	Names.
1608	Septemb^r	11	Elizabeth Westcoott the daughter of Thomas Westcoott Baker dwellinge w^tin Mr Osbornes in Cornhill
		25	Jeane Parker the daughter of John Parker Apothicarie dwellinge in gratious streete
	October	2	John Jenoure the sonne of Henrye Jenoure Marchant whose wif being a guest att Mr Launglees in Cornhill was d'd of Child
		22	Margret Parker the daughter of Joh: Parker a Soiorne^r [at] m^r Hardwins the Smith
	Nouember	16	Marie Hunter the daughter of Edward Hunter Poulter dwellinge in gratious streete
		18	Hughe Peregrine a Child laid in St Peters Church Alie beinge in gratious streete
	Januarie	29	Arthur Wakefeild the sonne of Arthur Wakefeild haberdasher dwellinge in Cornhill
		29	ffrauncies Lea the sonne of ffrauncies Lea haberdasher dwellinge in Cornhill
	Februarie	24	Allice Stone the daughter of Thomas Stone Poulter dwellinge in gratious streete
		24	Elizabeth Blofeild the daughter of Richard Blofeild Brazer dwellinge in gratious streete
1609	May	13	Elizabeth Robinsonne the daughter of Arthur Robinso': Marchant in Bishopsgate streete
	June	21	John Chatwine the sonne of Thomas Chatwine Yeoma' dwelling in Corbets coorte in gratious streete
	Julie	11	Isackey Cason the sonne of John Cason, grocer dwellinge in Cornhill
		16	John Garrit the sonne of Thomas Garrit, dwellinge att the spread egle in gratione* streete
		23	Marie Hudsonne the daughter of George Hudson Vpholster, dwellinge in Cornhill
	August	2	Valintine Luddingtonne the sonne of Valentine Luddingtonne Smith dwellinge in Leadenhall streete
		2	Edward Middletone the sonne of Robert Middletonne Inholder dwellinge in Leaden hall streete
		2	Margrett Ridgley the daughter of Edward Ridgley Sergeant, dwellinge * Corbets Coorte in gratious streete
		6	Jeane Greenhalf the daghter of ffrauncies Greenhalf Linnen drap: dwellinge in Cornhill
	October	8	Robert Younge the sonne of George Younge Musition, dwellinge in read crose Alie in Cornhill
	Nouember	12	Richard Askew the sonne of Tobias Askew haberdasher dwellinge in gratious streete
		21	George Warman the sonne of William Warman Coocke, dwellinge in Leaden hall streete
	December	3	George Harlowe the sonne of Jeames Harlowe poulterer, dwellinge in gratious streete
		17	Elizabeth Dorton the daughter of William Dorton gent. dwelling in Leaden hall streete
	Januarie	27	Juventa Peter a Child Layed in o^r p'ishe in Leaden hall streete
	Februarie	25	Elizabeth Whitlocke the daughter of Robert Whitlocke, pourter dwellinge in Cornhill
	March	4	Grace Hunter the daughter of Edward Hunter, Poulterre, dwellinge in gratiouse streete

* Sic.

THE REGISTERS OF ST. PETER'S, CORNHILL. 59

Yeare.	Month.	Day.	Names.
1609	March	11	Apoline Burton the daughter ef William Burton Marchant dwellinge in gratious streete
1610	Aprill	1	William Prime the sonne of Thomas Prime Scruiner, dwellinge in gratious streete
		9	Thomas Charter the sonne of Richard Charter Taylor, dwellinge in Cornhill
	June	10	Thomas Reynolds the sonne of Rowland Reynolds Vpholder dwellinge in Cornhill. the Child a Twinne
		10	Elizabeth Reynolds the daughter of the aforesaid Rowland Reynolds dwelling in Cornhill : Twin
	July	10*	Sammuell Carltonne the sonne of Bigley Carlton, Marchant dwellinge in Corbets Coorte
	August	5	Prudent Weightman the daughter of Peter Weightman, Vintener dwellinge in gratious streete
	August	9	Marie Arnwaye the daughter of Richard Arnwaye, Vintener, dwellinge in Leaden hall streete
	Septemb^r	6	Luke Robinsonne the sonne of Aurthur Robinsonne, Marchant, dwelling in Bishopsgate Streete
	Septemb^r	12	Edward Ridgley the sonne of Edward Ridgley s'gant. dwelling in Corbets Coorte
	October	21	Elizabeth Satchfeild the daughter of Richard Satchfeild, Baker in Bishopsgat streete
	Nouemb^r	4	Robert Garrit the sonne of Thomas Garrit Inhold^r in gratious streete
	Nonemb^r	11	Briant Dod the sonne of Will'm Dod Poulter at her mothers howse in gratious streete
	Nouemb^r	11	Katherin J:anson the daughter of William J:anson, Vintener in Cornhill
	Nouemb^r	25	Ann Laungley the Daughter of John Langley Linnen Drap' in Cornehill
	Decemb^r	16	Thomas Leycrafte the sonne of Thomas Leycrafte, from his ffathers, M^r. Jones barber in Bishopsgat streete
	December	16	Doritie More, the daughter of Thomas More, Haberdasher in Cornehill
	Decemb^r	30	Ralph Wetwood the sonne of Robert Wetwood Pewtere^r in Bishopsgate Streete
	January	27	Elizabeth Hvggins the daughter of Ann Huggins dwelling in Gratious streete wth Mr Evans Cutler And one George Clerkson and Widdow Pristie & Hager Smith were witnesses
	March	7	Abraham Helmes the sonne of Edward Helmes Groc^r in Cornehill streete
	March	10	Judith Blofeild, the Daughter of Richard Blofeild Brasier in Gratious streete
	March Twins	17	Richard Westone the sonne of Robert Westone Vpholder in the Church Allie Nicholas Westone, the sonne of Robert Westone. Vpholder in the church Allie
1611	March	31	Thomas Hudson the sonne of George Hudson Vphold^r in Cornhill
	Aprill	7	Thomas Mercer the sonne of Steephen Mercer in Cornhill
		9	Dionis Peeter A maiden Child laid in the weighouse yeard in this p'ish the 31th of March last

* The Register from July 10, 1610, to July 11, 1618, is subscribed Will'm Asheboold, parson, John Cason, churchwarden.

Yeare.	Month.	Day.	Names.
1611	May	26	William Hill the sonne of Nicholas Hill Linnen Drap' in Cornehill
	June	12	Charles Stone the sonne of Thomas Stone, Poulter in Gratious streete
	June	18	George ffoster the sonne of John ffoster of St Gyles p'ish in the feildes, the child borne at Mrs Kennestons howse widd' whoe, wth her sonne entred into bond to secure the p'ish of the chardg therof
	August	7	Ann Chapman the Daughter of Henry Chapman sonne to William Chapman in the weighouse
	August	7	Hanna Dolton the Daughter of Wm Dolton in Leadenhall streete
		18	Will'm Reynoldes the sonne of Rowland Reynoldes vpholder & free of the skiners in Cornhill
		25	Beniamine Lamebt the sonne of John Lamebt
	Septemb^r	1	Marie Robinson, the Daughter of Miles Robinson Brasier in Gratious streete
		1	Margrett Westcott, Daughter of Thomas Westcott Baker in Cornhill
		5	Sarah Prime the Daughter of Thomas Prime Scrivner in Leaden hall streete
		8	Henrie Robinson the sonne of Arthur Robinson Marchant in Bishopsgate streete
	October	6	Richard Arnwaie the sonne of Richard Arnwaie Vintner in Leadenhall streete
	Nouemb^r	1	Jean Peter a child laid in this p'ish the 26th of October last
		10	Hester Satchfeild the Daughter of Richard Satchfeild Baker in Bishopsgate streete
		24	George Burkett the sonne of George Burkett Brasier in Cornehill
		24	Elizabeth Garret the Daughter of Thomas Garret Inholder in Gratious streete
	January	5	Margret Whitlock the Daughter of Robert Whitlock one of * carmen of the kinges weighouse
		26	John Bennet the sonne of Michell Bennet M^{r}chanttalo^r
		27	ffrancis lee the daught^r of ffrancis lee haberdasher Cornhill
		28	Elizabeth Leycroft Daughter to Thomas Leycroft deceased sometime cittizen and free of the Turners of London, but by trade a Linnen Drap: in Leaden hall streete but dwelt with Mr Jones his wiues father in Bishopsgate streete barb^r
	ffebruary	16	Prudence Moore the daughter of Thomas Moore hosier in Cornhill
1612	March	31	Elizabeth Lancaster the daughter of a poor woman that was Deliuered in the streete neere Leaden hall borne the 29 day of the month, before
	Aprill	15	Peeter Weightman the sonne of Peeter Weightman Vintn^r in Gratious Streete
		19	John Mercer the sonne of Stephen Mercer in Cornhill belonginge to the kinges weighouse
	May	3	Christened Jefferie Slater the sonne of John Slate^r in Gratious streete
	June	30	Edward Helmes the sonne of Edward Helmes Grocer in Cornhill

* Sic.

THE REGISTERS OF ST. PETER'S, CORNHILL. 61

Yeare.	Month.	Day.	Names.
1612	August	9	Sarah Dolton the daughter of William Dolton Seafarer, dwelling in Leadenhall streete
		30	John Hill the sonne of Nicholas Hill Linnen Drap. in Cornhill
	Septemb^r	6	William Chapman the sonne of Henery Chapman dwelling in the Weighouse
		28	Margret Robinson the daughter of Arthur Robinson Marchant in Bishopsgate streete
		29	Robert Preene the sonne of Thomas Preene Scrivner in Leaden hall streete
	October	4	William Hinde the sonne of Thomas Hinde Inholder in Leaden hall streete
		27	Elizabeth Androws Daughter of Richard Androwes M^rchaunt in Leadenhall streete
	Decemb^r	6	Marie Norman the daughter of Robert Norman Painter in bishopsegate streete
	January	6	Susan Graues the daughter of Joseph Graues Vintener at the nagges head ye corner house betweene cornhill & bishopsgat' born 24 decem^r

Att this time & one this daye was James Jenntts made clarke of ye p'ish. A° 1612.

	January	9	Ellice Geyst the sonne of Elice Geyst supposed: She was brought a bedd in her fathers howse whose name is Robert Steward surgion, dwellinge at the Bull ouer against leaden hall
		16	Nicholas Sutton the sonne of Isacke Sutton M^rchant dwelling in Leaden hall streete Borne the third of January 1612
	February	7	Jeane Sheppard the daughter of Will'm Sheppard Inkeeper at the bull ouer against leaden hall: borne the 30 of January
		14	Sarah Reynoldes the daughter of Rowland Reynoldes vpholder in Cornhill borne the 8th of ffebruary 1612
		28	Mary Walthall Daughter of Luke Walthall M^rchant in gratious streete; borne one ffriday being the 19th of ffebruary 1612
	March	7	Sond: Jone Prentize the daughter of Arnold Prentize Vintner in Leaden hall streete borne the 25th of ffebruary 1612
1613		28	Sond: John Laugly the sonne of John Laugly Linnen drap' in Cornhill & borne the 17th of March anno 1612
	Aprill	11	Sond: Ann Payste daughter of Audrian Payste M'chant stranger dwelling in the Church ally: borne the 3 of Aprill Satterd:
		21	Wensd: Richard Slater the sonne of John Slater Brasyer in Gratioustreete borne the 12th of Aprill Monday
		25	Sond: Marie Blowfeild daughter of Richard Blowfeild, Braysier in Gratious streete born the 18 of Aprill Sond:
	May	23	Sond: Clement Bakon the sonne of Clement Bakon Taylor in Bishopsgate streete, & borne ye 15th of said mouth of May
	June	6	Sond: Mary More the daughter of Thomas Moore Ma'chan^t in Cornhill and borne 28th of Maye 1613 ffryday
		24	Thursd: Margret Hellmes the daughter of Edward Hellmes Grocer in Cornhill and borne ye 19 of June 1613

Yeare.	Month.	Day.	Names.
1613	July	11	Sond: Anne Luddington the daughter of Valentine Luddington Victler in Leaden hall strete, and borne the 8th of July 1613 Thurs:
	August	18*	Wensday. Anne Gewen the daughter of Xpofer Gewen crewell seller in Gratioustreete, and borne the 11th of August being Thurs:
	August	22	Sonday Elizabeth Lusher the daughter of Thomas Lusher Lynnen drap' in Cornhill: and borne the 15th of August being Sonday
		—	Sonday Mary Westkoot the daughter of Thomas Westkott Baker in Cornhill and borne the 19th of August being Thursday
	Septemb	12	Sonday Susan Morton the daughter of George Morton Lynnen drap' in Cornhill: and borne the 5th of September being Sonday
		19	Sonday Elizabeth Weightman daughter of Peter Weightman Vintn^r in Gratioustreete. borne one Monday night being the 13th of Septm^r
		—	Sonday Symon Willimott the sonne of Symon Willimott Vintn^r in Leadenhall streete, borne ye 12 of Septem^r being Sonday
		26	Sonday Stephen Mercer the sonne of Stephen Mercer one belongin' to the Kinges Weighouse dwelling in Redcrose ally borne ye 16th of Sept
	October	10	Sonday Margerie Whitlocke the daughter of Robt. Whitlocke one of the porters of the kinges weighouse borne one Wen': the 6th of Octob^r
		31	Sonday Thomas Hinde the sonne of Tho. Hinde Inholder at the Bull in Leadenhall streete born the 24th of October being Sonday
	Nouemb^r	7	Sonday Sarah Robinson the daughter of Myles Robinson Braysier in Gratioustreete, borne the 31th of October being Sonday
	Decemb^r	12	Sonday Ellyn Graues daughter of Joseph Graues Vintner in Cornhill, borne the 5 of December being Friday
		19	Sonday John Sutton the sonne of John Sutton Vpholdster dwelling wthin his ffathers howse in corbittes co'rte borne 12 of D
		26	Sonday Sarah Burkett the daughter of George Burkett Braysier in Cornhill, and borne the 19th of December
	January	16	Sonday Elizabeth Sutton daughter of Isacke Sutton M^{r}chant and f^{r}ee vintener in Leadenhall streete borne ye 4 of January Tu.
		23	Sonday Rebecca Carleton daughter of Biglie Carlton M^{r}chan^t in Corbites Coorte borne the 11th of January being wensday
		30	Sonday Luke Pease the sonne of William Pease, Sadler in gratioustreete, and dwelling wth Mr Auerill in Corbites courte
	March	1	Tuesday, William Walthall sonne of Luke Walthall M^{r}chant in gratioustrete, and borne the 21th of ffebruary being Monday
		27	Sonday Sara Prentize the daughter of Arnold Prentize Vintner in Leadenhall streete borne the 13th of March

* The Register from August 18, 1613, to April 25, 1614, is subscribed Will'm Asheboold, parson, Robert Bell, John Pywall.

THE REGISTERS OF ST. PETER'S, CORNHILL.

Yeare.	Month.	Day.	Names.
1614	Aprill	25	Monday Caudewell Slauter the sonne of John Slauter Braysier in Gratiousteete borne the * of Aprill
		—	Monday Anna Peter a foundeling, beinge laide at Mr Reynoldes dore 5 daies before it whas Christned
	July	10†	Sonday Thomas Ranking the sonne of Thomas Ranking shomak^r in Corbittes Courte: borne one thursday beinge the first of July
	Septem^r	11	Sonday Thomas Preenn the sonne of Thomas Preenn Scryno^r dwelling in Leadenhallstreete: born the * of August
		—	Sonday Thomas Wharton the sonne of Thomas Wharton Grocer in Bishopsgatestreete: borne the * of August
		11	Sonday Mary Jones the daughter of William Jones Taylo^r. in Bishopsgatestreete: borne the * of *
		18	Sonday Moudie Lusher the sonne of Thomas Lusher Lynnen drap' in Cornhill: borne one friday the 9th of Septem^r
		25	Sonday William Moore the sonne of Thomas Moore M^rchante dwelling in Bishopsgatestreete
		—	Sonday Richard Taylor the sonne of John Taylor free Mercer dwelling in Corbittes Courte in Gratioustret
	October	23	Sonday Henery Barnett the sonne of Henery Barnett Inholder at the Spred Eagle in Gratioustrette
		28	Thursday William Symondes the sonne of Mr Thomas Symondes M^rchaunt dwellinge in Bishopsgatestreete
	Nouemb^r	20	Sonday Nicholas Hill the sonne of Nicholas Hill Lynnen drap' dwelling in Cornehill
	Decemb^r	18	Sonday Katherin Helmes the daughter of Edward Helmes Grocer, borne the 4th of December being Sunday
	January	1	Sonday Mary Sutton daughter of Isack Sutton M^rchaunte in Leadenhallstreete borne the 17th of dece' being So:
		8	Sonday Thomas and John the sonnes of Clement Bakon Taylo^r
		22	Sond. Mary the daught^r of George Morton Lynnen drap' in Cornhill
	Februaj	9	Thursday Thomas Andrew the sonne of Richard Andrew Marchant in Leadenhall streete. borne the 28 of January Satterd.
		26	Sonday John Mercer the sonne of Stephen Mercer one belonginge to the kinges weighouse, borne ye 28th of ffebruary Satterd.
1615	Aprill	30	Sonday Margrett Graues daughter of Joseph Graues Vintner in Cornhill at the nagges heade
	May	29	Monday Elizabeth Langlie daughter of John Langlie Lynnendrap' in Cornehill
		—	The same day was Christned John Peeter this child was found one Mr Okelyes stall one wensday night before
	Jvne	8	Thursday Robert Jennettes the sonne of James Jennettes Clarke of this p'ishe dwellinge in Corbitt Courte in Gratioustreete
		11	Sonday Katherine Botlie the daughter of Anthony Botlie Lynnen drap' in Leadendall streete

* Sic.
† The Register from July 10, 1614, to May 27, 1616, is subscribed Will'm Asheboold, parson, p' me Ric. Sachfilde.

Yeare.	Month.	Day.	Names.
1615	July	9	Sonday Mary Whitelocke daughter of Robarte Whitelocke one of the porters of the Waighouse
	August	16	Wendensday Anna Hardwine the daughter of Matthias Hardwine Taylor dwellinge in Leadenhallstreete
	Septemr	3	Sonday John Westcott the sonne of Thomas Westcott Whight baker in Cornhill
		17	Sonday John Willimott the sonne of Symon Willimott Vintner in Leadenhall streete
		24	Sonday John Euans the sonne of John Euans Cutler dwellinge in Gratioustreete
	Octobr	8	Sonday John and Samuell the sonnes of Robert Norman Paynterstayner in Bishopsgatestreete
		12	Thursday Elizabeth Whorton the daughter of Thomas Whorton Grocer and ffree of the Bowyeres in Bishop:
		29	Sonday Ellixsander the sonne of Ellixsander Symondes Cooke in Leadenhall streete
	Nouembr	5	Sonday Hughe Taylor the sonne of John Taylor ffree of the Mercers Dwellinge in Corbittes Courte in Gratious:
	Decembr	3	Sonday Ann Lee the daughter of ffrauncis Lee ffree of the Sadlers Dwellinge in Redd Crosse ally in Cornhill
		17	Sonday Mary Johnson the daughter of Will'm Johnson lodger wthin James Butler, Potter in Bishopsgatestreete
		18*	Sonday Isacke Sutton the sonne of Isacke Sutton Mrchaunt ffree of the Vintners Dwellinge in Leadenhall streete
		23	Satterday Stephen Huchinson the sonne of Jaruice Huchinson one of the porters of the kinges weighouse
		28	Thursday Elizabeth Gewen the daughter of Xpofer Gewen one who sold Cruell Dwellinge in Gratioustreete
	January	7	Sonday Mary Sutton the daughter of John Sutton vpholdr and ffree of the Drap' Dwellinge in Corbittes Courte in Gratious:
	February	18	Sonday Martha the daughter of Miles Robinson Brasyer Dwellinge in Gracechurch streete
	February	25	Sonday Sybbell Lusher the daughter of Thomas Lusher Lynnen draper Dwellinge in Cornhill
	March	6	Wendesday Luke Warren the sonne of Richard Warren Cutler in Gracechurch streete
		10	Sonday Jerremy Bakon the sonne of Clement Bakonn Taylor in Bishopsgate streete
1616	May	1	Wendensday John the sonne of a poore weoman who was Deliuered of her child in Mr Parradines doore in Bishopsgate
		26	Sonday Richard Hatton sonne [of] Roger Hattonn Glasyer Dwelling in Bishopsgate streete borne the 22th of May
		27	Monday Elizabeth Andrew the daughter of Richard Andrew Dwelling in Leadenhall streete Merchaunte
	June	16*	Sonday John Morton the sonne of George Morton Lynnendraper Dwellinge † Cornhill
		16	Sonday Mary the daughter of Biglie Carlton free of the Grocers Dwellinge in Gracechurch streete
		16	Sonday Hanna Moore the daughter of Thomas Moore free of the Haberdashers dwellinge in Bishopsgatestreete

* The Register from June 16, 1616, to March 6, 1617, is subscribed the mark of ⟨W⟩ Michell Webb, churchwarden, John Langley, churchwarden.
† Sic.

THE REGISTERS OF ST. PETER'S, CORNHILL.

Yeare.	Month.	Day.	Names.
1616	June	27	Thursday Sarah the supposed daughter of George Billing Ostler at the Bull in Leadenhallstreet and borne of the body of Alice Hubbersteid daughter of George Hubbersteid Deceased
	Julie	16	Tuesday Mary Church daughter of William Church Haberdasher dwellinge in harro allie in Gracechurch street
	August	14	Wendsday Lawrence Dawson the sonne of Edward Dawson Wollen draper Dwellinge in Cornhill
	Septem^r	8	Sonday John Goffe the sonne of Allen Goffe lyinge at Mr Hills howse Lynendrap in Cornhill
		11	Wendsday Thomas Smiththicke the sonne of Thomas Smiththicke M^{r}chaunte Dwellinge in Corbites Courte
		15	Sonday Joseph Graues the sonne of Joseph Graues Vintner dwellinge in Cornhill & free Haberdashe^{r}s
	Nouem^r	3	Sonday John Burket the sonne of George Burket Brasyer dwellinge in Grace Churchstreete
		10	Sonday Robert Hill the sonne of Nicholas Hill Lynnen draper in Cornhill and free of the Vintners
		12	Twesday Martha Jennettes daughter of James Jennettes parish Clarke and free of the Goldesmithes in Corbitt C.
		20	Wensday William a bastard child borne of the boddie of Mary Cuttes servant to Robart Whitelocke porter
	January	1	Wensday Joyce the Daughter of Xpofer Grymes ffishmong^r and Merchaunt dwellinge in Bishopsgate streete
		26	Sonday Martha the daughter of Thomas Whorton Grocer in Bishopsgate streete
	February	5	Wensday William Mullet the sonne of Thomas Mullet Poulter in Grace Church streete
		9	Sonday John Taylor the sonne of John Taylor free of the Mercers dwelling in Corbites Court in Gratioustreet
		12	Wensday Edward Peeter a foundelinge layed in ye sexto' stall
	March	19	Wensday Mary Slauter the Daughter of John Slauter Brasyer in Cornhill at the Helmett
		23	Sonday Thomas Helmes the sonne of Edward Helmes Grocer at the Corner howse of Leadenhall streete
		23	Sonday William Whitelocke the sonne of Robarte Whitelocke porter belonginge to the kinges weighowse
1617	Aprill	27	Sonday Judie Langlie the daughter of John Langlie free of the ffishmongers dwelling in Cornhill
		27	Sonday Ann Southwell daughter of Raph Southwell free of the Mercers dwelling in Cornhill
	May	25	Sonday Margret Rochdale daughter of Thomas Rochdale free of the Brewers dwelling in Cornhill
		30	Friday John Peeter a child gest to be one yeare and $\frac{1}{2}$ found at Thomas Ashlies dore in Cornhill a the shipp
	June	8	Sonday Xpofer Willimott the sonne of Symon Willimot free of the Haberdashers dwelling at y^e kings head leadenhall
		15	Sonday Honno^r Tyther the daughter of Edward Tyther free of the Grocers dwelling in Cornhill in y^e weigh house yeard
		29	Sonday Samuell Symones the sonne of Allexander Symones free Cooke dwelling in grace church streete
	July	6	Sonday Elizabeth Evans the daughter of John Evans free of the Gyrdlers dwilling in grace church streete

K

Yeare.	Month.	Day.	Names.
1617	Septem^r	7	Sonday William Andrew the sonne of Richard Andrew free [of] the Merchantaylors dwelling in Leadenhall streete and a M^{r}chant
		23	Tuesday ffrauncis Butler daughter of James Butler free of the ffishmongers dwelling in Bishopsgate streete
	October	15	Wensday Abbigale Webb the daughter of John Webb Inmate wth goodwife Boomers howse in the Church Allie shomak^r
		18	Satterday Luke Huchins the sonne of Thomas Huchins and Ann his wife the said Ann was brought a bead in the cadge at L.*
		24	Friday Katherin Dawson the daughter of Edward Dawson free of the Drapers dwelling in Cornhill warde
	Nouem^r	9	Sonday Judeth Bridges the daughter of Nicholas Bridges free of the Mercers dwelling in Gracechurch streete
		16	Sonday Edmond Bingham the sonne of Thomas Bingham free of the Cookes dwelling in Leadenhall streete
		23	Sonday George Morton the sonne of George Mortoun free of the ffishmongers dwellinge in Cornhill
	Decem^r	14	Sonday Thomas the sonne of Tho: Lusher fishmong^r in Cornhill
	January	6	Tuesday John the sonne of Roger Hatton Glasyer in Bishopsgate st.
		15	Thursday Mary the daughter of Mr Anthony Partridge gent brother in law to Edward Helmes Grocer in leadenhall st
		25	Sonday Ezekyell Culuerwell the sonne of Mr Richard Culuerwell minister dwelling in barrow allie in graceeh
	ffebrua^r	15	Sonday Martha Reynoldes daughter of Rowland Reynoldes free of the Skynners dwelling in Cornhill
		19	Thursday John ffearen the sonne of Godphery ffearen free of the Haberdashers dwelling in Cornhill
		26	Thursday Elizabeth Mullet the daughter of Thomas Mullet free of the Poulters Dwell' in Gracechurch st.
	March	6	Friday Mary Stodder the daughter of Richard Stodder Inmate in Harry Richardes his howse in Bishopsgate st.
		15†	Sonday Katherin Gybbins the daughter of Daniell Gybbins M^{r}chaunt dwelling in Leadenhall streete
		16	Monday Mary Grimes the daughter of Xpofer Grimes free of the ffishmongers dwelling in Bishopsgate street
1618	April	9	Thursday Nicholas Bakon the sonne of Clement Bakon free of the Drapers dwelling in Bishopsgate streete
		11	Satterday Hester Harding the daughter of Mathias Harding Taylor dwellinge in Leadenhall streete
	May	31	Sonday Alice Sutton the daughter of John Sutton Vpholder dwelling in Corbittes Courte in Gratioust^{r}eet
	June	7	Sonday Ann Mercer the daughter of Stephen Mercer one belonging to the kinges weighhowse in Cornhill
	Julie	19	Sonday Thomas Robinson the sonn of Miles Robinson Brasyer dwelling in Gracechurch streete
	August	22	Satterday Emanuell Whitelocke the sonn of Robert Whitelocke one of the porters of the kinges weighhouse
		23	Sonday Hanna Carleton the daughter of Biglie Carleton Grocer dwelling in Gracechurch streete

* Leadenhall.

† The Register from March 15, 1617, to January 5, 1618, is subscribed John Langley, churchwarden.

THE REGISTERS OF ST. PETER'S, CORNHILL.

Yeare.	Month.	Day.	Names.
1618	August	30	Sonday William Gewen the sonne of Xpofer Gewen one that selleth Crewill dwelling in Cornhill
	Septem^r	6	Sonday Thomas Gattwood the soun of Thomas Gatwood free of the Mercers dwelling in Gracechurch streete
		20	Sonday Joseph Moore the sonn of Thomas Moore free of the Haberdashers dwelling in Bishopsgate streete
		20	Sonday Edward Martin sonn of J^o Martin of Broxborne in the Com. of Hertford mealeman ther was suerties put in
		28	Monday William Jones the sonu of Wm Jones Taylor dwelling in Bishopsgate streete ye childe baptized at home
	October	18	Sonday Mary Taylor the daughter of John Taylor free of ye Mercers dwelling in Corbittes coart in gratio'
	Nouemb^r	8	Sonday James Willmot the sonn of Symon Willmott Vintner dwelling in Leadenhall streete at ye kinges head
		8	Sonday Thomas Bingham sonn of Thomas Bingham free of ye Cookes dwelling in Leadenhall streete
		15	Sonday Sarah Burkehead daughter of George Burkehead Brasierr dwelling in Gracechurch streete
		22	Sonday Jacob Mempris sonn of Thomas Mempris Lynnen Drap dwelling in gracechurch streete free Haberdash^{rs}
	Decemb^r	6	Sonday Ann Church daughter of Thomas Church free of the Clothworkers dwellinge in Harrow Ally in gracechurch
		8	Tuesday Mary the daughter of Thomas Whorton Grocer dwelling in Bishopsgate baptized at howse
	Janua^{r}y	5	Tuesday ffrauncis Tyther sonn of Edward Tyther Grocer dwelling in the weigh house yeard in Cornhill
		10*	Sonday Elizabeth Barnes daughter of Thomas Barnes dwelling in Leadenhall streete
		17	Sonday Katherin Boyce daughter of Sr Edward Boyce knight dwelling in Leadenhall streete
		17	Sonday Joseph Hatton sonn of Roger Hatton free of the Glasyers dwelling in Bishopsgatstreete
		17	Sonday John the sonn of Richard Denman Taylor lying wthin J^o Charkes howse in Cornhill Lynnendrap'
		24	Sonday James Evans sonn of John Evans Cutler dwellinge in Gracechurch streete
	ffebrua^{r}y	11	Thursday Ann Andrew daughter of Richard Andrew Merchaunt dwelling in Leadenhall streete free M^{r}chantaylo^r
		11	Thursday John the sonne of Edward Helme Grocer dwellinge in Leadenhall streete in the corner howse
		14	Sonday Susan Symons daughter of Alixander Symons Cooke Dwelling in Gracechurch streete
		21	Sonday Margret Buckocke daughter of Daniell Buckocke Lynnen Drap' dwelling in Cornhill
		26	Fryday Susan Dauis daughter of Richard Dauis free of the Vintners dwellinge in Leadenhall streete
	March	13	Sonday Robert Williams sonn of Elizabeth Williams late the wife of Anthony Williams pewterer deceassed in leadenhall
		21	Sonday Margret Southwell daughter of Ralph Southwell Lynnendrap' and free of the Mercers dwelling in Cornhill
1619	Aprill	4	Sonday Robert Sanforde sonn of Robert Sanford Lynnendrap' and free of the Skynners dwelling in Cornhill

* The Register from January 10, 1618, to March 4, 1620, is subscribed francis White.

68   THE REGISTERS OF ST. PETER'S, CORNHILL.

Yeare.	Month.	Day.	Names.
1619	Aprill	9	Fryday James Harlow sonn of James Harlow Cooke Dwelling in Gracechurch streete borne ye same daye
	May	5	Wensday Mary Webb daughter of John Webb Shomak^r Dwelling wthin Goodwife Boomer in St Peeters allye
		9	Sonday Sarah Cartewright daughter of Edward Cartewright Poulter dwelling in Gracechurch street
		18	Tuesday Margret Hodgeson the daughter of Wm Hodgeson free of the Skynners dwellinge in Cornehill
		18	Tuesday Katherin Mullett daughter of Thomas Mullett Poulter Dwelling in Gracechurch streete
		30	Sonday Edward Morton the sonn of George Moreton free of the ffishmongers Dwelling in Cornehill
	August	1	Sonday Peeter Jennettes sonne of James Jennettes Goldesmith dwelling in Corbitts coarte the childe borne 25th of Julie
	Octob^r	10	Sonday Margret Pease the daughter of William Pease Sadler in Grace Church streete he dwelte
		10	Sonday Jeane Billinge daughter of George Billinge the mother of the child was daughter to Widd. Hubbersteed
		30	Sonday Bridget Burr daughter of Nicholas Burr free of the Poulters dwelling in Bishopsgatestreete
		30	Sonday Dorritie Tayloy daughter of John Tayloy free of the Mercers Dwelling in Corbittes courte in grace Ch'
	Nouem^r	14	Sonday William Austine sonn of Thomas Austine Sheiregrinder Dwelling in Leadenhall streete
		21	Sonday Richard Langlie sonn of John Langlie ffree of the ffishm'gers dwelling in Cornehill
		21	Sonday George Bingham sonn of Thomas Bingham free of the Cookes dwelling in Leadenhall streete
	Decem^r	19	Sonday Susanna Tyther the daughter of Edward Tythe^r free of the Grocers dwelling in Cornhill in ye Weigh howse yeard
		19	Sonday Jeane Mercer daughter of Stephen Mercer M^r of the Kinges weighowse dwelling in Cornhill
		19	Sonday Anna the daughte^r of Clement Bakon free of the Drapers Dwelling in Bishopsgatestreete
	Janua^{r}y	14	Fryday James the supposed sonne of Conradus Chills Stanger* borne in the streete the mothers name Eliza
		16	Sonday William the sonne of Wm Jones Taylor and Maudlin his wife dwelling in Bishopsgatestreete
	ffebruary	11	Fryday Ann the daughter of John Slanter Armorer and Mary his wife dwelling in Cornhill
		17	Thursday Thomas the sonne of Thomas Gatward Mercer & Elizabeth his wife dwelling in Gracechurch streete
		25	Fryday Tabbitha the daughter of Thomas Tyggins Skynner & Elizabeth his wife dwelling in Harrow ally
	March	5	Sonday John the sonne of George Burkehead Armorer and Jeane his wife dwelling in Gracechurch streete
		5	Sonday James the sonne of Richard Holmes Carpenter & Mary his wife dwelling in Corbites courte in gatious'
1620		30	Thursday ffrauncis the sonne of Allexander Brounescome & Effym his wife brought a head at Mr Vowelles howse
	Aprill	15	Satterday Walter the sonne of William Meires and Sarah his wife dwelling wth his Mother in gratioustreete

* Stranger.

Yeare.	Month.	Day.	Names.
1620	Aprill	16	Sonday Debborah the daughter of Thomas Whaly vintn^r & Debborah his wife Dwelling in Cornhill at ye Mermayd
	May	14	Sonday Ralphe the sonne of Ralph Southwell M^rcer and Ann his wife dwelling in Cornhill
		25	Thursday Hanna the daughter of Matthias Harding and Elizabeth his wife dwelling in Leadenhall streete
	June	22	Thursday Jane the daughter of Robert Sanford free of the Skynners and Phillis his wife dwelling in Cor'
	Julie	27	Thursday ffranncis ye sonne of William Hodgeson free of the Skynners and Elizabeth his wife dwelling in Corn'
		30	Sonday Ann the daughter of Edward Helme Grocer and Margerie his wife dwelling in Leadenhall streete
	August	10	Thursday Anna ye daughter of Thomas Lusher free of ye ffishmongers and Sybbell his wife dwelling in Corn'
		13	Sonday Elizabeth ye daughter of John de Clarke a Stranger and Elizabeth his wife dwelling in Harrow ally
	Septemb^r	3	Sonday John the sonn of John Heather M^rchaunt & Jeane his wife from Mrs Blowfeilds howse in Bishop'
		14	Thursday John the sonne of Edward Dawson Drap' in Cornhill and Marge^{rt} his wife
		17	Sonday Richard the sonne of Richard Harris M^rchaunt dwelling in Leadenhall streete
		21	Thursday John the sonne of William Chenery Ironmonger and Jone his wife in leadenhallstret
		27	Wedensday Martha the daughter of John Webb and Abbigall his wife dwelling wth goodwife Boom^r
	October	8	Sonday William the sonne of Allixander Symons Cooke and Susan his wife dwelling in Gracechurch str'
		15	Sonday George the sonne of Roger Hatton Glasyer and Rebecca his wife dwelling in Bishopsgate streete
		29	Sonday Thomas the sonne of Thomas Mullet poulter and Elizabeth his wife in Gracechurch str'
	Nouem^r	5	Sonday Thomas the sonne of Thomas Churche Clothworker & ffrauncis his wife in Gracechurch str'
		5	Sonday Edward the sonne of Edward Cartewright poulter & Susan his wife in Gracechurch streete
		23	Thursday Andrew the sonne of John Burton free of the Tallowchandlers in Gracechurch stree'
	Decemb^r	3	Sonday Richard the sonne of John Taylor and Jone his wife free of the Mercers in Corbites coarte
		30	Satterday Ann the daughter of James Harlow and Elizabeth his wife free of the Cookes in Gracechurch stree'
	January	12	Fryday Elizabeth a Child found in redd crosse ally in a Bakers baskett ye 2 day of January about 9 of ye clocke at night
		18	Thursday John the sonne of Biglie Carleton Grocer and Rebecca his wife dwelling in Gracechurch streete
	ffebrua^ry	25	Sonday William the sonne of Thomas Gatward and Elizabeth his wife free of the Mercers in gracechurch stree'
	March	4	Sonday Katheren the daughter of Splenden Warner and Ellyn his wife M^rchaunt in Bishopsgate streete
		7*	Wedensday Elizabeth the daughter of Daniell Chapman and Isbell Marshall she was brought a bead in ye cadge
		11	Sonday Abbigall the daughter of Miles Robinson Armorer and of Sara his wife dwelling in Gracechurch streete

* The Register from March 7, 1620, to December 10, 1621, is subscribed Ro. Dumvile, curat.

Yeare.	Month.	Day.	Names.
1620	March	18	Sonday Debborah the daughter of Thomas Mempris Haberdasher and of Elizabeth his wife dwelling in Gracechurch streete
		22	Thursday ffrauncis the sonne of Daniell Buckocke Lynnen Drap' and of Debborah his wife dwelling in Cornhill
1621	Aprill	15	Sonday Ellyn the daughter of Thomas Smiththicke free Skynner and of Margret his wife dwelling in Corbites courte
	May	6	Sonday John the sonn of William Pease Sadler and of Marie his wife dwelling in Gra^echurchstreete
	June	5	Tuesday Ann the daughter of John Euans Cutler and of Elizabeth his wife dwelling in Gracechurch streete
		5	Tuesday Ann the daughter of John Harman keep' of ye greene yearde in Leadeu hall and of Elizabeth his wife
		10	Sonday John the sonne of Mathias Harding Taylor and of Elizabeth his wife dwelling in Leadenhall streete
	Julie	1	Sonday Thomas the sonne of Ralph Southwell Mercer and of Ann his wife dwellinge in Cornehill
		29	Sonday ffrauncis the sonne of ffrauncis Hall Taylor and of Elizabeth his wife dwelling in Leadenhall streete
	August	5	Sonday William the sonne of William Hodgeson skynn^r and of Elizabeth his wife dwelling in Cornhill
		19	Sonday Ann the daughter of Thomas Braddocke M^rchan^t and of Elizabeth his wife dwellinge in Bishopsgate stree'
	Septem^r	2	Sonday William the sonne of Edward Helme grocer and of Margery his wife dwellinge in Leadenhall street
		2	Sonday Ann the daughter of Thomas Barnes and of Elizabeth his wife dwellinge in Leadenhall street
		23	Sonday Thomas the sonne of Thomas Whaly Vintner and of Debbora his wife dwellinge in Cornhill
	Nouem^r	4	Sonday Thomas the sonne of John Masters and Ann his wife she was brought a bead at Mr Midletons dore ..... wgetyne (?)
		18	Sonday John the sonne of Allixander Symondes Cooke & of Susan his wife dwelling in Gracechurch streete
		18	Sonday Elizabeth the daughter of John Sutton and of Elizabeth his wife dwelling in Corbittes courte
	Decem^r	9	Sonday Ann the daughter of Joseph Graues free Haberda^r and of Ann his wife dwelling in Leadenhall streete
		10	Monday Margret the daughter of Robert Sanforde free of ye Skynners & of Phillis his wife dwelling in Cornhill
	Decemb^r	23*	Sonday Sarah the daughter of Thomas Byngham Cooke and of Judeth his wife; dwelling in Leadenhall stret
		25	Tuesday Jeane the daughter of John Taylor Mercer and of Jone his wife Dwelling in Corbittes Courte
		30	Sonday Ellyn the daughter of James Butler free of ye ffishmongers and of ffaith his wife dwelling in Bishopsgat'
	Februay	3	Sonday John the sonne of Thomas Austine Sheyregrynd^r and of Elizabeth his wife dwelling in Leadenhall streete
		7	Thursday Jeane the daughter of Richard Midletou M^rcha'nte and of Jeane his wife dwelling in Leadenhall streete
		24	Sonday Martha the daughter of John Langley free of the ffishmongers and of Martha his wife dwellinge in Cornhill

* The Register from December 23, 1621, to January 1, 1623, is subscribed francis White.

THE REGISTERS OF ST. PETER'S, CORNHILL. 71

Yeare.	Month.	Day.	Names.
1622	Aprill	14	Sonday Hester the daughter of Richard Harris M^{r}chante and of Hester his wife dwellinge in Leadenhall streete
		21	Sonday Samuell the sonne of Bryan ffell Pewterer and of Elizabeth his wife dwellinge in Leadenhall streete
	Maye	1	Weddensday Allixander the sonne of William Meires Skynner & of Sara his wife dwelling in Gracech'rch stree'
		12	Sonday Ann Mullet daughter of Thomas Mullet Poult^r and of Elizabeth his wife dwelling in Gracechurch street
		19	Sonday Elias the sonne of John Sappes ffactor and of Mary his wife dwelling in Harrow ally in Gracechu^{r}ch st'
	June	2	Sonday Elizabeth daughter of John Wenlocke Haberdashe^r and of Elizabeth his wife dwelling in Harror ally in Gracechu^{r}ch st'
		23	Sonday Thomas the sonne of John Middelton Inholder and of Margaret his wife dwelling in Leadenhall streete
	Julie	1	Monday William the sonne of Henery Watson Barber and of Ann his wife dwellinge in Bishopsgate streete
		28	Sonday John the sonne of Thomas Gatward Mercer & of Elizabeth his wife dwelling in Gracechurchstreete
	August	4	Sonday ffrauncis the sonne of George Billinge Shipcarpent^r and of Alice his wife dwelling in Leadenhall streete
		11	Sonday Roberte the sonne of Roberte Hodgeson Skynne^r and of Elizabeth his wife dwelling in Cornhill
		11	Sonday Elizabeth the daughter of ffrauncis Burte Poult^r and of Elizabeth his wife dwelling in Gracechurch streete
		16	Friday Nehemia the sonne of John Webb Shoomaker and of Abbigall his wife dwelling in St Peeter allie
	Septem^r	22	Sonday Thomas the sonne of Clement Bakon Talo^r and of Martha his wife dwelling in Bishopsgate streete
		22	Sonday Roger the sonne of Roger Hatton Glasyer and of Rebecca his wife dwelling in Bishopsgate streete
	October	7	Sonday John the sonne of John Sharpe Armorer & of Elizabeth his wife dwelling in Bishopsgate warde in gra'
		14	Sonday Susana the daughter of Ralph Southwell free of ye Merceres & of Ann his wife dwelling in Cornhill
		28	Sonday Richard the sonne of Thomas Lusher ffishmong^r & of Sybbell his wife dwelling in Cornhill
	Nouemb^r	10	Sonday Henrie the sonne of John Mole Gentelman & of ffra'nces his wife dwelling wth his father in Leadenhall str'
		10	Sonday Allixander the sonne of Thomas Smith Hnberdash^r & of Joyce his wife dwelling in Harrow ally in Gracechurch st'
		10	Sonday ffra'nces the daughter of Thomas Church Clothworker & of ffrances his wife dwelling in Cornhill
		29	Friday Thomazine ye daughter of Edward Dawson Drap' and of Margaret his wife dwelling in Cornhill
	Decemb	5	Thursday Margerie ye daughter of Edward Helme Grocer & of Margerie his wife dwelling in Cornhill
		8	Sonday William ye sonne of John Harman laborer to ye Cittie & of Elizabeth his wife dwelling in ye greene yeard
		29	Sonday William the sonne of John Burton Tallowchandler & of Mary his wife dwelling in Gracechurch street

Yeare.	Month.	Day.	Names.
1622	Janua'y	19	Sonday Thomas the sonne of Henery Tompson Haberdasher and of Tomazine his wife dwelling in Bishopsgate st^r
		22	Friday James the sonne of Will'm Jones Taylor and of Maudlin his wife dwelling [in] Corbittes Coarte in Gracioust'
		26	Sonday Amie the daughter of Joseph Graues Haberdasher and of Ann his wife dwelling in Leadenhall streete
		26	Sonday Anna the daughter of Thomas Whalie Vintner and of Debborah his wife dwelling in Cornhill
	March	23	Sonday Susan the daughter of Thomas Haggar Drap' and of Ann his wife dwellinge in Gracechurch streete
1623	Aprill	9	Weddensday Jane the daughter of Richard Holmes Carpent^r and of Marie his wife dwellinge in Corbites Coarte
		16	Friday Sara a childe founde at Mr Casons doore in Cornhill
	May	11	Sonday Elizabeth the daughter of Edward Cartewright poulter and of Susan his wife dwelling in Gracechurchst'
		25	Sonday Hugh the sonne of Thomas Mullet poulter and of Elizabeth his wife dwelling in Gracechurchst'
	June	8	Sonday Richard the sonne of Richard Harris M^{r}chaunt and of Hester his wife dwelling in Leadenhall streete
		23	Monday Elizabeth the daughter of George Morton ffree of the ffishmongers and of Elizabeth his wife dwellinge in Cornhill
	Julie	13	Sonday James the sonne of Matthias Harding Taylo^r and of Elizabeth his wife dwelling in Leadenhall street
		27	Sonday Jacob the sonne of Thomas Mempris Haberdasher & of Elizabeth his wife dwelling in Gracechurchst'
	August	5	Tuesday Thomas the sonne of James Jennetts p'ishe clarke and of Avice his wife dwelling in Corbittes Coarte
		13	Wedensday Elizabeth the daughter of (a) poore woman whose name was Elizabeth Coleman, she was brought a bead in Leaden hall
		19	Tuesday Thomas the sonne of Henerie Chapman free of the Haberdashers & of Elnor his wife dwelling in Cornhill
		22	Fryday Rebecca daughter of Thomas Bingham Cooke and of Judeth his wife dwelling in Leadenhall streete
	Septemb^r	3	Wedensday Thomas the sonne of Robert Edwardes M^{r}chantaylo^r and of Susan his wife dwelling in Gracechurch street
		12	Fryday John the sonne of Robert Hodgeson free of the Skynners & of Elizabeth his wife dwelling in Cornhill
		19	Fryday Prissylla daughter of Margrett ffryerson s^{r}vant to Peeter Rogers who was suposed to be father of ye said child
		28	Sonday Thomas the sonne of Bryan ffell Pewterer and of Elizabeth his wife dwelling in Leadenhall streete
		28	Sonday Jeane the daughter of ffraunces Hall Taylor and of Elizabeth his wife dwelling in Bishopsgate streete
	October	7	Fryday Mary the daughter of Stephen Mercer free of ye Grocers and of Mary his wife dwelling in Cornhill
		19	Sonday Ann the daughter of John Midelton free of the Inholders & of Margret his wife dwelling in Leadenhall streete

THE REGISTERS OF ST. PETER'S, CORNHILL. 73

Yeare.	Month.	Day.	Names.
1623	Nouem^r	1	Satterday Elizabeth ye daughter of Josua Wenlocke free of ye Haberdashers & of Elizabeth his wife dwelling in Gracech'
		16	Sonday Miles the sonne of Miles Robinson Armorer dwellinge in Gracechurchstreete and of Sarah his wife
	Decemb^r	5	Fryday Mary the daughter of Ralph Southwell Merc^r dwelling in Cornhill and of Ann his wife
		21	Sonday Alice the daughter of Thomas Barnes Haberdasher dwelling in Leadenhall streete & of Elizabeth his wife
	January	1	Thursday Edward the sonne of John Sharpe Armorer dwelling in Gracechurchstreete & of Elizabeth his wife
		11*	Sonday Edward the sonne of Edward Bawcombe Tallow chandler dwelling in Leadenhall streete & of Sara his wife
		18	Sonday Richard the sonne of Thomas Austine Sheiregrind^r and of Elizabeth his wife dwelling in Leadenhall streete
		25	Sonday Howard the sonne of Mr John Mole Gentelman and of ffrauncis his wife dwelling wth his ffath^r in Leadenhallst'
		30	Friday Thomas the sonne of Thomas Sergant Vpholder and of Bridget his wife dwelling in Cornhill
		30	Friday James the sonne of James March Carpenter and of Ellyn his wife dwelling in Corbitts Court in Gratioustree'
	ffebrua^r	29	Sonday James the sonne of John Evans Cutler and of Elizabeth his wife dwelling in Gracechurchstreete
	March	14	Sonday Thomas the sonne of Thomas Hagger free of the Drap' and of Ann his wife dwelling in Gracechurchstreete
		21	Sonday Sara the daughter of Joseph Graues Haberdasher and of Ann his wife dwelling in Leadenhall streete
1624		25	Thursday Henery the sonne of Thomas Gatward Mercer and of Elizabeth his wife dwelling in Gracechurch streete
		25	Thursday Mary the daughter of Alixander Symondes Cooke and of Susan his wife dwelling in Gracechurchstreete
		25	Thursday Sara the daughter of John Sutton Draper and of Elizabeth his wife dwelling in Corbittes Courte in Grace Ch'
	May	2	Sonday Jeane the daughter of Phillip Meade ffishmong^r and of Dorritie his wife dwelling in Cornhill
	June	20	Sonday Thomas the sonne of William Pease Sadler Dwelling in Gracechurchstreete and of Mary his wife
		20	Sonday Thomas the sonne of Thomas Smith Haberdasher and of Joyce his wife dwelling in Gracechurchstreete
		27	Sonday Abraham the sonne of Roger Hatton Glasyer and of Rebecca his wife dwelling in Bishopsgatestreete
	Julie	2	Fryday Martha a Child found on Mr Dawsons staule
		25	Sonday James the sonne of Richard Harris M^{r}chaunt & free of the Grocers and of Hester his wife dwelling in leaden hall st'

* The Register from January 11, 1623, to May 26, 1631. is subscribed William Hudson, churchwarden.

L

Yeare.	Month.	Day.	Names.
1624	August	1	Sonday Andrew the sonne of John Langlie ffishmonger and of Martha his wife dwelling in Cornhill
	September	3	Friday Lyonell the sonne of Ralph Maddison Me'rchant and of Elizabeth his wife dwelling in Bishopsgate streete
		12	Sonday Paule the sonne of Thomas Bingham Cooke and of Judeth his wife dwelling in Leadenhall streete
		19	Sonday William the sonne of William Tompson Haberdasher and of Thomazine his wife dwelling in Bishopsgatestr'
		21	Tuesday Elizabeth the daughter of William Hodgeson Skynner and of Elizabeth his wife dwelling in Cornhill
	October	3	Sonday Marie the daughter of Brian ff'ell Pewterer and of Elizabeth his wife dwelling in Leadenhallstr'
		7	Thursday William the sonne of William Meires Skynne'r and of Sarah his wife dwelling in Gracechurch str'
		10	Sonday James the sonne of Henery Chapman Habe'rdasher and of Elnor his wife dwelling in Cornhill
	Nouemb'r	24	Weddensday Isabell y'e daughter of William Gratrix and of Jone his wife servantes to M'r Cason dwelling in Cornhill
		26	Friday Mary the daughter of Ralphe Pettie Barbershu'rgion and of Effam his wife dwelling in Gracechurchstr'
	Decemb'r	5	Sonday Martha the daughter of Clement Bakon free of y'e Drap' & of Martha his wife dwelling in Bishopsgate-str'
		12	Sonday Mary the daughter of Will'm Whittingham free of y'e Salters & of Elizabeth his wife dwelling in Bishopsgate str'
		27	Monday Katherine y'e daughter of Andrew Harvie a Marryn'r & of Ann his wife daughter to George Hudson deceased
	January	2	Sonday Elizabeth the daughter of Josua Wenlock Haberdash'r and of Elizabeth his wife dwelling in Gracechurchstrecte
		7	Fryday John the sonne of Ralphe Southwell Mercer and of Anne his wife Dwelling in Cornhill
		16	Sonday Thomas the sonne of Edward Bawcombe Tallowchandler and of Sarah his wife dwelling in Leadenhall-street
		21	Fryday Martha the daughter of John Webb Shoomaker dwelling in S't Peeters ally and of Abbigall his wife
		23	Sonday Elizabeth the daughter of Vmphery Woodward free of y'e Woodmongers & of Elizabeth his wife dwelling in Bish:
		28	Fryday Martha the daughter of William Dynn Scriuon'r and of Margrett his wife dwelling in Gracechurch streete
	ffebruary	6	Sonday Anne the daughter of ffrauncis Burte Powlter and of Elizabeth his wife dwelling in Gracechurch streete
		13	Sonday Anne the daughter of M'r John Mole Gentelman & of ffra'nces his wife dwelling w'th his ffather in Leadenhall street
	March	8	Tuesday Humphrey y'e sonne of Daniell Batten m'chantaylo'r and of Katherine his wife dwelleing in Leadenhall streete
		13	Sonday Thomas the sonne of Will'm Aude free of the Inholders and Suzanna his wife dwelleing in Leadenhall str'

THE REGISTERS OF ST. PETER'S, CORNHILL. 75

Yeare.	Month.	Day.	Names.
1625	March	25	Friday George ye sonne of George Alsop free of the Stac'oners & of * his wife dwelling in Leadenhall str.
		27	Monday Elizabeth the daughter of Robt. Madison gent. and Deborah his wife dwelling with his brothe^r in Buishopsgate str'
	Aprill	24	Sonday Mary the daughter of John Harman keeper of Leadenhall greene yard and Elizabeth his wife
		27	Weddensday Dyna ye daughter of Rob'te Edwardes m'chant Taylo^r & Suzanna his wife dwelling in Pewter platter Alley in Grace Church streete
		26	Tuesday Christned at home in the howse of Thomas Hulce in Buishopsgate streete Patience the daugher of Will'm ffrancklin gent & of Edie his wife dwelling in Glocestersheir
		31*	Tuesday Richard the sonne of ffraunces Coling ffree of the ffishmongers dwelleing in Cornehill
	June	7	Tuesday Mary the daughter of Joseph Graue Habb'd' & Anne his wife dwelling in Leadenhall str.
		29	Weddensday Thom' ye sonne of Tho: Hagger free of ye Drap's and Anne his wife dwelling in Gracech: str'
	July	15	Friday Raphe sonne of Rob'te Cramphorne Taylo^r and Elizabeth his wife dwelling in Bishopsgate str'
	August	26	Paule the sonne of Allexander Bronscom & * daughter to Mrs Powell Poulter dwelling in graceeh: str'
		28	Sonday Henry ye sonne of Henry Watson Barber and * his wife dwelling in Bishopsgat str'
	Septemb	25	Sonday Christopher ye sonne of George Morton ffishmong' & Elizabeth his wife dwelling in Cornhill
	Nouemb'	12	Sonday Elizabeth ye daughter of Bryan ffell Pewterer dwelling in Leadenhall str': & Eliz: his wife
		20	Sonday Margarett ye daughter of ye sonne of Tho: Tiggins dwelleing in Harrow Alley
	Decemb'	16	ffryday Will'm ye sonne of Thomas Smith free of the Habb'ds dwelling in Gratious streete
	January	20	Sonday John the sonne of Thomas Tixtofer Poulter dwelling in Gratious streete
			Charles the sonne of a poore woman brought a bed in the Cage
			Sonday Antbony an Indian aboute the age of sixteene yeres
	March	5	Sonday Anna ye daughter of Mr Bigley Carlton and * his wife dwell: in Gratious str'
		17	ffryday John sonne of Edward Bawcombe and Sarah his wife dwelleing in Leadenhall str'
		18	Satterday Will'm, and John, twins sonnes of Raph Southwell Drap' dwell: in Cornehill
		19	Sonday Raph sonne of Henry Chapman & Ellen his wife dwelleing in Cornehill
1626		26	Sonday ffraunces the sonne of John Buttris free of the Turners & Anne his wife dwelling in Leadenhall streete
	Aprill	7	ffryday John the sonne of X'popher Vertue and Bridgett his wife dwelling in Cornehill
	May	8	ffryday ffraunces the sonne of ffr. Coleing dwelleing in Cornehill

* Sic.

Yeare.	Month.	Day.	Names.
1626	July	30	Sonday Anne ye daughter of Thomas Lusher Lynnen drap' dwelleing in Cornehill
	August	11	ffryday John the sonne of Will'm Pease free of the Sadlers and Mary his wife dwelleing in Grace Churchstreete
		13	Sonday, Sarah the daughter of Mathyas Harding Marchantayler and Elizabeth his wife dwelleing in Gracech: strete
		18	ffryday Will'm ye sonne of Humphrey Woodward dwelleing in Bishopsgate streete
	Septemb'	7	Thursday twoe Twins, Will'm and Sarah Children of John Conway and Elizabeth his wife dwelleing in Bishopsgate str'
		8	ffryday John the sonne of Edward Cason and Dorcas his wife dwelling in Cornhill
		20	ffryday Elizabeth daughter of Thomas Gatward free of the m'cers dwelling in Gratious str' & Eliz: his wife
			George sonne of John Mole gent dwelling in Leadenhall str' and ffraunces his wife
	October	1º	Sonday Elizabeth daughter of John Sapp & Mary his wife dwelling in Leadenhall streete
		4	Weddensday James the sonne of Henry Harris Cutler dwelling in Grace church str' & * his wife
		14	Sonday Henry the sonne of Thomas Hagger dwelling in Gracechurch streete
			William sonne of James Butler dwelling in Bishopsgate streete
		18	Weddensday Myles the sonne of Myles Robinson and Mary his wife dwelling in Grace Church streete The Childe was borne ye xith of October, wensday
		22	Sonday Paule the sonne of Joseph Graue free of the Habb'dashers & Anne his wife dwelling in Leadenhall str'
	Nouemb	5º	Sunday Elizabeth daughter of Thomas Plomer free of the Habb'dashers dwelling in Leadenhall streete
		12	Sonday Barbara daughter of John Clarke Stationer dwelling in St Peters Alley
			Margaritt daughter of Bryan ffell Pewterer and Eliz: his wife dwelling in Leadenhall str'
		19	Sonday John the sonne of ffrauncis Walcott & Elizabeth his wife dwelling in Harrow Alley in Grace church str'
	Decemb'	10	Sonday Jane daughter of Raph Maddison dwelling in Bishopsgate streete
	ffebruary	4	Sonday James sonne of Henry Chambers Cooke dwelling in Grace church streete
			Dorithy daughter of Will'm Morris Taylo^r dwelling in Buishopsgate streete
		11	Sonday Mary the daughter of Thomas ffenn dwelling in Corbettes Courte
		11	Elizabeth daughter of Thomas Tixtover Pulter dwelling in Grace church streete
	March	4	Sonday John sonne of George Alsopp Stac'oner and Jane his wife dwelling in Leadenhall streete
		9	ffryday Nicholas sonne of Thomas Gaynesford and Mary his wife, free of the Inholders dwelling in Buishopsgate streete

* Sic.

Yeare.	Month.	Day.	Names.
1626	March	18	Sonday Dorithy the daughter of Phillip Meade and Dorithie his wife dwelling in Cornehill
1627		27	Twesday Elizabeth ye daughter of ffrauncis Colinge and Elizabeth his wife dwelling in Cornehill
	May	4°	ffryday Mary the daughter of Will'm Meares Skynner dwelling in Harrow Alley in Gratious str'
		15	Twesday John the sonne of Thomas Bingham free of the Cookes dwelling in Leadenhall str'
		17	Christned Mary the daughter of Theophilus Boulten Lynnen Draper dwelling in Lea: Hall
	July	1°	Sonday George sonne of Roberte Edwards Milliner dwelling in Harrow Ally
		8	Sonday William sonne of James Chamb' dwelling in Leaden Hall streete
			Thomas sonne of Thomas Walstall Vintne^r dwelling in Cornehill
		25	Wensday Mary daughter of Thomas Alkin dwelling in Bishopsgate streete
		27	ffriday Jane the daughter of John Midleton Inholder dwelling in Leadenhall str'
	August	10	ffriday Thomas sonne of John Tayler dwelling in Corbetts Court
		15	Wensday Elizabeth daughter of Alexander Brumstone dwelling in Gracecious streete
		25	Sonday William sonne of Clement Bacon free of the Draper^s and Clarke of the said parish the 17th on ffriday
		31	ffriday Rebecca daughter of Richard Browne Glover dwelling in Harrow Ally
	Septem^r	2°	Sonday Bartholomew sonne of Humphrey Woodart dwelling in Bishopsgate streete
		2°	Ann daughter of John Padmoore dwelling in Leaden Hall streete
		9	Sonday Suzanna daughter of William Hall Brasier dwelling in Gracious streete
		14	ffriday Mary daughter of John Rutter Tayler dwelling in Bishopsgate stre'
		16	Sonday Samuell sonne of Henry Chapm' Haberdasher dwelling in Cornehill
		19	Wensday Elizabeth daughter of Raph Southwell Draper dwelling in Cornehill
	October	3	Wensday Nathaniell sonne of Samuell Norris sadler dwelling in Harrow Ally
		7	Sonday Walter sonne of Thomas Smith Leatherseller dwelling in Gracious streete
		14	Sonday Robert sonne of Edmond Tulie Inholder dwelling in Gracecious streete
		21	Sonday Elizabeth daughter of Robert ffisher Cutler dwelling in Bishopsgate streete
		28	Sonday Elizabeth daughter of John Buttris Cooke dwelling in Leadenhall str'
	Novemb^r	4	Sonday Jane daughter of Peter Warren skinner dwelling in Gracious str'
		22	Thursday Phillip sonne of John Langley Draper dwelling in Cornehill
	Decemb^r	9	Sonday ffrancis sonne of Joseph Graves dwelling in Leaden Hall

Yeare.	Month.	Day.	Names.
1627	Decembr	13	Thursday Susanna daughter of Willi': Mothall skinner
		14	ffriday Elizabeth daughter of a poore woman being brought to bed in the streete her fathers name being John Hudson
		30	Sonday William sonne of William Tiestover dwelling in Gracious str'
	January	13	Sonday Margarett daughter of Bryan ffell Pewterer dwelling in Leadenhall str'
		27	Sonday Henry sonne of Thomas ffen Cheesemonger dwelling in Corbetts Court
		27	Martha daughter of Thomas Plomer Haberdasher dwelling in Leaden Hall str'
	March	16	Sonday Mary daughter of John Jeames dwelling in Gracious streete A Child of a poore womans brought to bed in the Cage the name is Christian
		23	Sonday John sonne of John Johnson Haberdasher dwelling in Gracious str'
			Mary daughter of Henry Chambers dwelling in Gracious str'
		27	Thursday Elizabeth daughter of Edward Linsey dwelling in Bishopsgate:
1628		28	ffriday Mary daughter of William ffairfax Parson of the p'ish dwelling in Parsonage house
		30	sonday Jane a Child which was laid vnto George Buckinghams sonne in law in Allhallowes p'ish in Gratious streete being brought a bed in the streete and appointed by an order at Gwild Hall before the Lord Maior, that they should beare all Charges and keepe the Child
			Mary daughter of Thomas Lusher Lynnen Draper dwelling in Cornehill
	Aprill	4	ffriday Benjamen sonne of Willia' Dun Scrivenor dwelling in Gracious str'
		6	sonday John the sonne of Thomas Carter free of ye Sadlers dwelling in Cornehill
	May	4	sonday Robert sonne of John Clarke free of the Stationers dwelling in Peters Ally
		16	sonday Ann daughter of John Moorehowse Wollen Draper dwelling in Cornehill
	July	9	Wednesday Elizabeth a child laid at Mr Lushers doore Churchwarden
		16	Mary daughter of Robert Tompson dwelling in Bishopsgate streete
		20	sonday James sonne of Walter Gollifer Clothworker dwelling in Cornhill
		27	sonday Elizabeth daughter of Simon ffreeman Cloth worker dwelling in harrow ally
	August	03	Thursday Nathaniell sonne of William Winch Grocer dwelling in Cornehill
		10	sonday George sonne of George Mole Gent dwelling in Leaden hall streete
			Mary daughter of William Pease sadler dwelling in Gracious streete
		21	Elizabeth daughter of Stephen Banister dwelling in Harrow Ally
	Septembr	28	sonday Robert sonne of John Mason dwelling at the platter in Gracious streete
	October	07	Tuesday Edward sonne of Thomas Gatwood Mercer dwelling in Gracious streete

THE REGISTERS OF ST. PETER'S, CORNHILL. 79

Yeare.	Month.	Day.	Names.
1628	Nouembr	23	sonday John sonne of ffrancis Burt Poulter dwelling in Gracious streete
		30	sonday Debora daughter of Thomas Wastall Vintner dwelling in Cornehill
	Decembr	06	satterday Dorothie daughter of Phillip Meade ffishmongell* dwelling in Cornehill
		07	sonday Ann daughter of William Ticstopher Poulter dwelling in Gracious streete
		14	sonday Suzan daughter of Thomas Serieant Skinner dwelling in Cornehill
	January	06	Richard sonne of Raph Southwell Linn' Draper dwelling in Cornehill
		18	Thursday Lidia daughter of Richard Harris Marchant dwelling in Leaden hall streete
	february	01	Sonday Sara daughter of Thomas Chetta' Inholder dwelling in Cornehill
		04	Wednesday Mary daughter of Thomas ffenn dwelling in Corbetts Court
	March	03	Tuesday Elizabeth daughter of Robert Shaw Vintner dwelling in Leadenhall streete
			Ann the daughter of William Hudson Skinner dwelling in Cornehill
		04	Wednesday John the sonne of Edward ffoaldington Sexton of this parish
		08	sonday ffrancis sonne of John Padmore Cheesemonger dwelling in Leaden hall streete
		22	sonday Thomas sonne of Thomas Astine Shoere grinder dwelling in Leaden hall streete
1629	Aprill	02	ffriday James the sonne of Theophilus Boulton Marchantaylor dwelling at Leaden hall Corner
		05	Monday Simon sonne of Thomas Smith Haberdasher dwelling in Gracious streete
		06	Tuesday John soune of John Silke Pewterer dwelling in Leaden hall streete
		15	Tuesday Suzanna daughter of George Hamor dwelling in the Nacks head yard
	May	03	sonday Humphrey sonne of Thomas Phillips Taylor dwelling in Harrow Ally
		07	Thursday Thomas sonne of Edmond Tooley Inholder dwelling in gratious streete
		26	Monday Elizabeth daughter of Joseph Graues Haberdasher dwelling in Leadenhall streete
		31	sonday John sonne of Mathias Harding dwelling in Gracious streete
			Ann daughter of Thomas Bingham Cooke dwelling in Leaden hall streete
	June	24	Wednesday Robert sonne of Thomas Carter sadler dwelling in Bishopsgate streete
	July	04	sonday Jerimy sonne of Myles Robinson Armourer the child borne the 27th of June
	August	04	Wednesday John sonne of John Younge Grocer dwelling in Gracious streete
		07	sonday Margery daughter of Robert Chamberlaine
		30	sonday Robert sonne of Steven Grove Poulterer dwelling in Gracious streete

* Sic.

Yeare.	Month.	Day.	Names.
1629	September	02	Wednesday Suzanna daughter of Nicholas Seares Stationer dwelling in Bishopsgate streete
		27	Sonday Thomas sonne of Thomas Johnson ffishmonger dwelling in Gracious streete
		29	Tuesday Sara daughter of Thomas Lusher ffishmonger dwelling in Cornehill
	October	22	Thursday Bigley sonne of Mr Bigley Carlton Grocer dwelling in Gracious streete
	November	05	Thursday George sonne of Robert Tompson Armourer dwelling in Bishopsgate streete
		08	Sonday Anna daughter of William Hall Armourer dwelling in Gracious-streete
		15	sonday John sonne of John Midleton Inholder dwelling in Leadenhall streete
		22	sonday Jonathan sonne of William Browne dwelling in Gracious streete
		29	sonday Sara daughter of Humphry Woodard Woodmonger dwelling in Bishopsgate streete
	December	12	sonday James sonne of Henry Chambers Cooke dwelling in Gracious streete
		14	Tuesday Raph sonne of Simon ffreeman Clothworker dwelling in Gratious streete
		19	sonday Henry sonne of William Ticstopher Poulter dwelling in Gracious streete
	January	03	sonday Rebecca daughter of Peter Warren Skinner dwelling in Gracious streete
		10	sonday Anne daughter of Walter Goollifer dwelling in Red crosse Ally in Cornehill
	March	03	Wednesday William sonne of William Duin free of ye Poultereres dwelling in Gracious streete
		07	sonday Henry sonne of Henry Perkinson Cordwayner dwelling in Bishopsgate streete
		10	Wednesday Symon the sonne of a poore woman which was brought to bed the 8th of March in St Peters Ally
		11	Thursday Elizabeth daughter of Raph Southwell Linnen Draper dwelling in Cornehill
		18	Thursday Suzan daughter of Symon Thorowgood Draper dwelling in Cornehill
		25	Elizabeth daughter of Mr George Henly Leatherseller
1630	Aprill	04	sonday Samuell sonne of John Moorehowse Marchantaylor dwelling at Leaden Hall Corner
		11	sonday John sonne John Warner Marchantaylor dwelling in Leadenhall streete
		12	Monday John sonne of Elizabeth Smith a poore woman brought to bed at the Cage on Thursday the 8th day which as shee saith dwells at Grauesend
		18	sonday Elizabeth daughter of John James Armourer dwelling in Gracious streete
	May	16	sonday Thomas sonne of Thomas Smith Draper dwelling in Leadenhall streete
		28	ffriday Edward sonne Ann Skidmore dwelling in St Georges parish in Southarke shee was brought to bed at Leaden hall gate the 20th day
	June	15	Susan daughter of Robert Edwards in Harrow Alley
		19	Saturday Josias sonne of Thomas Bingham, Cooke, dwelling at Leaden hall

THE REGISTERS OF ST. PETER'S, CORNHILL.

Yeare.	Month.	Day.	Names.
1630	June	20	Sonday Jonathan sonne of Joⁿ Butteriss Cooke dwelling in Leadenhall streete
		27	Sonday Elizabeth daughter of Joⁿ Clarke Stac'oner in St Peters alley
	July	11	Sondaie Judith daughter of Joⁿ Cheswick Cooke in Gratious streete
			The same day Rose daughter of Edmond Tooley Victualler in Gratious streete
		23	ffridaie Peter sonne of Joⁿ Taylo^r in Corbittes Courte
		28	Wensdaie Nathaniell sonne of Richard Harris March^t in leadenhall streete
	August	17	Tuesdaie Esther daughter of Thomas Wastell Vintner in Cornhill
		30	Sondaie Lawrence sonne of Nicolas Sporlynge wch lay at Joⁿ Rutters in Bishopsgate streete. Mr Holliday in Gratious street passed his word to ye Churchwarden to free ye p'rish of the child
	October	8	ffridaie Michaell sonne of Lawrence Ticknor dwelling in Harrow alley
			The same day Joⁿ sonne of Marie Fisher a poore woman brought to bedd in the Cage at Leadenhall street ye 3° of Octob^r
		24	Daniell sonne of Wm Hudson Vpholder dwelling on Cornhill
	Nouember	7	Sondaie James sonne of Joⁿ Padmore Cheesmong^r Dwelling in leadenhall streete
		19	ffridaie George Grace a poore child being taken vpp on Sunday night the 14th of ye said month at Mrs Satchfeildes stall
		26	ffridaie Phillis daughter of Jane Crowder whoe as shee saith dwelleth at Dover being brought to bedd at the Cage on Saturday night being ye 20th of this month
		28	Sondaie Marie daughter of Roger Hooke lying at Mr Battens in Leadenhall streete
		30	Tuesday George sonne of M^r W^m ffairfax p'son of this p'ish Parrish* the child was borne on wensday morning the 17th of this month
	December	25	Saturday Marie daughter of Wm Peas Sadler in Gratious streete
		27	Mundaie Elizabeth daughter of Thomas Carter Hosier in Bishopsgate streete
		30	Thursdaie John sonne of Joseph Graves Vintner in Leaden hall streete
	January	16	Sondaie Sarah daughter of Thomas Smithe Leatherseller in Gratious streete
			The same day George the sonne of John Silk Pewter in leadenhall streete
	February	6	Sondaie Isaac sonne of Wm Bramich Brasier in Gratious streete
		11	ffridaie Marie daughter of Henrie Custings Vphoulder in Cornhill
		13	Sondaie Susanna daughter of Thomas ffenn in Corbettes Courte
		20	Sondaie Thomas sonne of Thomas Lusher & Sibell his wife lynnen Drap' in Cornhill

* Sic.

Yeare.	Month.	Day.	Names.
1630	February	27	Sondaie Isabell daughter of Symon Freeman Clothworker in Harrow Alley
1631	Aprill	24	Sondaie Elizabeth daughter of Jo^n Middleton Inholder dwelling in Leaden Hall streete
	May	1	Sondaie John sonne of George Henley Marchaunt dwelling in Gratious streete
		8°	Sonday Thomas sonne of Robert Thompson Armo'rer dwelling in Bishopsgate streete
		18	Wensdaie Marie daughter of Humfrie Woodward Woodmonger in Bishopsgate streete
		19	Thursdaie Thomas sonne of Symon Thorowgood lynnen draper dwelling in Cornhill
		26	Wensday Walter sonne of William Meares Skynne^r dwelling in Harrow alley
	June	15*	Wensdaie William sonne of John Mynn dwelling in Leadenhall streete
	July	10	Sondaie Peter sonne of Thomas Smithe Draper dwelling in Leaden Hall streete
		20	Sonday Phillipp sonne of Phillipp Mead dwelling in Cornhill Lynnen Draper
			The same day George sonne of Theophilus Bolton Lynnen draper dwelling at Leaden hall corner
			The same daie Anne daughter of Robert Shawe Vintner at the Kings head in Leadenhall streete
	Septemb^r	9	Frydaie Elizabeth daughter of John Buttrisse Cooke Dwelling at Leaden Hall
		25	Sondaie Elizabeth the daughter of ffrauncis Burt Poulterer dwelling in Gratious streete
	October	9	Sondaie Thomas sonne of William Tixtover Poulterer dwelling in Gratious streete
		9	The same daie Anne daughter of Jo^n Chiswicke Cooke dwelling in Gratious streete
		26	Sondaie Margarett daughter of Giles Harding whitebaker dwellinge in Cornhill
	Novemb^r	8	Tewsdaie Sarah daughter of Sarah Digby whoe was brought to bedd at Mr Moseleis house, dwelling in Cornhill
		20	Sondaie John sonne of Henrie ffeake Gouldsmith Lodging at Mr Wollastons house in Cornhill
		30	Wensdaie Raph sonne of Raph ffyrth Draper dwelling in Bishopsgate streete
	Decemb.	17	Sondaie William sonne of William Hall Armorer dwelling in Gratious streete
	January	8	Sondaie Jane daughter of Henrie Perkinson Cordwayner dwelling in Bishopsgatestreete
		15	Sondaie Suzan daughter of Arthur Rhodes Sadler in Gratious streete
		29	Sondaie William sonne of Thomas Bingham Cooke in Leadon hall streete the said William being a Twynn the other being still borne
	February	19	Sondaie Elizabeth daughter of John Warner Marchaunttaillo^r dwelling in Leaden hall streete
		24	firiday Jane daughter of Thomas Tococke Dwelling in Corbettes Court

* The Register from June 15, 1631, to March 11 following, is subscribed Phillipp Meade, churchwarden.

THE REGISTERS OF ST. PETER'S, CORNHILL. 83

Yeare.	Month.	Day.	Names.
1631	February	29	Saturday Mathias son of Mathias Harding Marchaunt-tailloʳ dwelling in Gratious streete
	March	11	Sonday Joseph sonne of Raphe Southwell Lynnen draper in Cornhill
1632		29*	Thursdaie William sonne of Joseph Graves vintuer dwelling at the naggs head in leadenhall streete
	Aprill	19	Thursdaie Marie daughter of the wor^{ll} William ffairfax doctor of Divinity and Parson of the parish church of St Peter on Cornhill She was borne on Sonday morning the 11th day of ye said month
		22	Sondaie John sonne of John James Armorer dwelling in Gratious streete
			The same day Robt. sonne of John Middleton Inholder in Leaden hall streete
		24	Tewsdaie Suzan daughter of Roberte Edwards Marchaunt-taillo^r dwelling in Harrow alley
		29	Sundaie Anne daughter of William Sykes Cloathworker dwellinge in Peters Alley
	Maie	8	Tuesdaie William sonne of William Dwight Tallowchandler at Leadenhall Corner
		13	Sundaie Anne daughter of William Gulleuer Cloathworker in Red crosse alley
		20	Sundaie Thomas sonne of Thomas Hansonn Grocer dwellinge in Leadenhall streete
	June	6	Wednesdaie John sonne of Simon ffreeman Clothworker dwelling in Harrowe alley
		15	Fridaie Elizabeth daughter of Henrie Custinges, vphoulster dwellinge in Cornehill
	Julie	8	Sundaie Marie the daughter of Thomas Carter sadler dwellinge in Bishoppesgate streete
	August	5	Sundaie Dorothie the daughter of George Henlie merchant dwellinge in Gracious streete
			The same daie Margaret daughter of Philipp Mead, Linnendraper dwelling in Cornehill
			The same daie Elizabeth daughter of Richard Stretch Grocer dwellinge in Bishopesgate streete
		12	Sundaie Marie daughter of Richard Harris merchant dwellinge in Leadenhall streete
	Septemb	7	Fridaie Henric and Katherine beinge twinns and children of William Meares Skinner dwellinge in Harrowe Alley
		16	Sundaie Isacke sonne ef Peeter Warren skinner dwellinge in Graciousstreete
		23	Sundaie Marie daughter of Thomas Wills Cordwainer dwellinge in Corbettes Courte
	October	26†	Fridaie Peeter sonne of Theophilus ffellowes servant of John Chiswick Cooke, in Graciousstreet borne out of wedlocke
		28	Sundaie Sara daughter of Robert ffisher Cutler dwellinge in Bishopesgate streete
	Novemb	18	Sundaie Sarah daughter of John Morehowse Draper dwellinge at Leadenhall Corner
	December	26	Wednesdaie John sonne of a vagrant borne in the streete last sundaie morninge

* The Register from March 29, 1632, to September 23 following, is subscribed George Henlie, churchwarden.

† The Register from October 26, 1632, to October 27, 1633, is subscribed Thomas Birkehead, churchwarden.

84   THE REGISTERS OF ST. PETER'S, CORNHILL.

Yeare.	Month.	Day.	Names.
1632	December	30	Sundaie William sonne of William Tixover poulter dwellinge in Gracious streete
		31	Mundaie Ellinor Peeter of vnknowne parents found in the streetes
	January	10	Wednesdaie Dorothie daughter of John Clarke Stationer dwellinge in St Peeters Alley
	February	17	Sundaie George sonne of Thomas Smith Haberdasher dwellinge in Gracioustreete
			The same daie Hanna daughter of Thomas ffenn porter dwellinge in Corbettes Courte
		24	Sundaie Charles the sonne of Henrie Chambers Cooke dwellinge in Gracioustreete
			The same daie William sonne of Giles Harding Baker dwellinge in Cornehill
1633	Aprill	17	Wednesdaie Elizabeth daughter of a vagrant brought to bedd in ye Cage
		18	Thursdaie Thomas sonne of Theophilus Boulton linnendraper dwellinge at Leadenhall Corner
		28	Sundaie James sonne of John Chiswick Cooke dwellinge in Gratioustreete
	Maie	15	Wednesdaie vinsint sonne of John Silke a pewterer dwellinge at Leadenhall
		23	Wednesdaie Anne daughter of Thomas Gatward mercer dwellinge in Gracioustreete
	June	5	Wednesdaie Anne daughter of John Spencer Millener dwellinge in Cornehill
		12	Tuesdaie Sara daughter of Thomas Smith vphoulster dwellinge in Leadenhall streete
		30	Sundaie Thomas sonne of Thomas Birkhead Armorer dwellinge in Cornehill
			The same daie Elizabeth daughter of Henry ffeake gent. lyinge at Mr Wollastonns in Cornehill
	Julie	3	Wednesdaie Peter sonne of William Dweyght Tallowchandler dwellinge at Leadenhall
		19	Fridaie Christopher sonne of John Warren Haberdasher in Leadenhall street
		25	Wednesdaie Elizabeth daughter of Christopher Broome in Bishoppesgate streete borne ye 12th
		28	Saturdaie ffraunces sonne of ffraunces Cooling ffishmonger in Cornehill
			The same daie John ye sonne of Humfry Woodward Grocer in Bishopesgate streete
	August	1	Thursdaie William sonne of William ffearfax Doctor of Divinitie and Parson of this parish
		4	Sundaie Isack sonne of Isack Jones Gouldsmith in Leadenhall streete
		11	Sundaie Mary daughter of Ralph Blacklie Dier brought to bedd at Mr Griffins ye Glasier
		25	Sundaie Marie daughter of John Padmore Cloathworker in Leadenhall street
	Septemb	5	Thursdaie ffraunces sonne of ffraunces Burt Poulterer in Gratioustreete
		22	Sundaie Walter sonne of Walter Guillefer Cloathworker in Redcrosse alley
			The same daie Henrie ye sonne of Henric Perkinson shoemaker dwellinge in Bishopesgatestreete
		29	Sundaie Anne daughter of William Hornebuckle Tailor lyinge at Goodman Whiteheads Cobler

THE REGISTERS OF ST. PETER'S, CORNHILL. 85

Yeare.	Month.	Day.	Names.
1633	October	6	Sundaie Hanna daughter of Joseph Graves free of ye haberdashers dwellinge in Leadenhall streete
		13	Sundaie Margarett ye daughter of John Royce victualer dwellinge in Cornehill
		20	Sundaie Marie daughter of William Pease sadler dwellinge in Gratioustreete
		27	Sundaie John sonne of Thomas Reynoldes Skinner dwellinge in Cornehill
			The same daie Robert sonne of Wm Meares Skinner dwellinge in Gratioustreete
	Novemb	20*	Wednesdaie Sibill daughter of Timothie younge ffishmonger dwellinge in Cornehill
		24	Sundaie Robert sonne of Martin Higgins Scrivener in Gratioustreete
	Decemb	5	... Isabell daughter of Simon ffreeman Clothworker dwellinge in Platter alley
	January	12	Sundaie William the sonne of William Hall Armorer dwellinge in Gratioustreete
		15	Wednesdaie Dorothie daughter of William Browne glover and Sextoun of this parish
	ffebruary	11	William Peter a ffoundlin laid on Mr. Wm Hudsonns stall the second of ye same moneth
		13	Wednesdaie Thomas sonne of Thomas Spilsburie Smith dwellinge in Bishopesgate street
		18	Bridgit Peeter a ffoundling left at Mr Deputie Bells doare and was judged about two yeeres old
1634	Aprill	19	Raph sonne of Martha Daie beinge a poore woman and brought to bed in ye Cage
	Maie	1	Jane daughter of Josias Sparrow Iremonger in Platter alley
		18	Fridaie Elizabeth daughter of Simon Thorowgood ffishmonger dwellinge in Cornehill
			The same daie Thomas a poore child laid at Mr Wastells doare the 6th day of Aprill
	June	7	Fridaie Rebecca daughter of Thomas Smith haberdasher in Gratioustreet
	Julie	6	Sundaie Alice daughter of Thomas Handsonn Grocer in Leadenhall streete
		27	Sundaie Benjamin ye sonne of George Henlie Letherseller dwellinge in Gratioustreete
	August	1	ffridaie Robert sonne of William Sikes Cloathworker dwellinge in St Peters alley
		10	Sundaie George sonne of M^r † Hardestee clothwork^r
		13	Wednesdaie Samuell sonne of Henrie Chambers Cooke
		20	Wednesdaie Marie daughter of a poore woman brought to bedd in ye Cage
			The same daie Marie daughter of John Spenser merc^t tailo^r
		24	Sundaie George sonne of Thomas Birkett Armorer and Bridgitt his wife
	September	6‡	Sundaie Elizabeth daughter of John Clarke minister

---

* The Register from November 20, 1633, to August 24, 1634, is subscribed Theophilus Boulton, churchwarden.

† Sic.

‡ The Register from September 6, 1634, to August 30, 1635, is subscribed John Mead, churchwarden.

Yeare.	Month.	Day.	Names.
1634	September	11	Fridaie Margarett daughter of Richard Harris Grocer
		13	Sundaie Anna daughter of Wm Hammond Ironmong^r
		30	Tuesdaie Joyce a poore child takeu up at Mr Simonds his doare ye 28th present
	October	2	Thursdaie Elizabeth daughter of William Dwoit Tallow-chandler
		10	Fridaie Sara daughter of John Warner haberdasher
			The same daie Susan daughter of Thomas Reynoldes skynner
	November	1	Saturdaie Alice daughter of Raphe ffrith Scrivener
		19	Wednesdaie Margarett daughter of Edward Rayne merch^t
		28	Fridaie Margarett daughter of Isack Jones Goldsmith
	Decemb	26	Fridaie Thomas sonne of John James Armorer and Alice his wife
	Januar	21	Wednesdaie Beniamin sonne of Wm Hudson Skinner and Elizabeth his wife
	ffebruar	2	Mundaie Henrie Hanna Peter foundlinges: ye boy esteemed a yeere old and ye girle a moneth old
		8	Sundaie Barberie daughter of Jno Chesworth Cooke
		25	Wednesdaie Marie daughter of Arthur Roades Sadler
	March	1	Sundaie Marie daughter of John Silke Pewterer
		8	Sundaie Elizabeth daughter of Timothy young ffishmong^r
		22	Sundaie Katherine daught^r of John Royse victualer
1635	April	9	Thursdaie George and Anne Meares Twynns being children of Wm Meares Skinner
		12	Sundaie Jacob sonne of Wm Croone Clothworker
			The same daie Rebecca daugh^r of Wm Pease Sadler
		22	Wednesdaie Hanna daught^r of Robt. ffisher Cutle^r
	May	10	Elizabeth daught^r of Jo^n Morehouse Marchanuttailo^r
		24	Sundaie Elizabeth daughter of Walter Golefer Clothworker
	June	19	Fridaie Dennis daught^r of Mr John Mynn gent
		28	Sondaie Giles sonne of Giles Harding Whitebaker
	July	24	Fridaie Elizabeth daught^r of Tho: Higgenbotham Sadle^r
		29	Isaack sonne of Peeter Warren Skynner
	August	2	Sondaie Jo^n sonne of Henrie Hurt Marchanuttailo^r
		16	Sondaie Marye daught^r of Wm Dweyght Tallow Chandler
		30	Elizabeth daughter of Wm Hall Armorer
	October	11*	John the sonne of Richard Wollastone lynnendrap'
		18	Sara daughter of Henry Chambers Cooke
		25	John sonne of Jo^n Burton Vintner
	November	8	Ann daughter of William Browne, Sexton
		16	Ann daughter of John Spencer Milliner
		29	Sondaie John sonne of Thomas Birkhead Armori
	Januarie	13	Johanna daughter of Wm Watson Apothecary
		16	Deborah daughter of Hen: Perkinson Cordweyno^r
		27	Wensdaie Erasmus sonne of Erasmus Mucey March^t
		29	Brian sonne of Josias Plumpton of Eastham
		31	Martin sonne of Martin Higgins Scriuene^r
	February	2	Sara daught^r of Mathias Harding Taylor
		9	Hanna daughter of Wm Bramw^{ch} Armore^r
		19	Raph sonne of Richard Poole Labourer, aud marye his wyfe
	March	6	Josias sonne of Josias Sparrey Ironmonge^r
		20	Ann daughter of Jo^n Silk pewtere^r
1636	Aprill	27	Esther daughter to Timothie young & Elizabeth his wife

* The Register from October 11, 1635, to February 18, 1637, is subscribed Francis Burt, churchwarden.

THE REGISTERS OF ST. PETER'S, CORNHILL. 87

Yeare.	Month.	Day.	Names.
1636	Maie	6	Mary a foundling taken vp in Corbettes Court
		15	John sonne of Thomas Jakes Brickleyo^r
		26	Thomas sonne of Tho: Willes Cordweyno^r
	June	16	Marie daughter of Robt. Ingram Iremong. & Ann his wife
	August	27	ffra: Peter a foundling at Mr Higg^{ins} his doore
	Septem	18	Jo^n sonne of John Roys Victualler
	Novem	11	Andrew sonne of John James Armorer
	January	12	John sonne of John Harrman & Dorathie his wife
1637	May	21	Ann daughter of Thomas Jakes Brickleyor
	June	8	Richard sonne of Richard Kingsman Grocer
		17	John sonne of Erasmus Mucey Habberdash^r
		30	Christopher sonn of Timothie Young & Eliz. his wife
	August	20	Thomas sonne of Thomas Osborne Brickley^r & Ann his wife
	Septem^r	3°	Thomas sonne of Thomas Hatrill Cordweyner
		24	Ann daughter of Robert Ingram Iremong & Ann his wife
	Octob^r	4	Rebecca daughter of Thomas Smith Habberdasher
		29	Samuel sonne of William Hall Armorer
	Novem^r	29	John sonne of John Hiron Cooke
	Decem^r	3	Elizabeth daughter of William Watson Apothecary
		18	Judith daughter of Giles Harding Whitebaker
		17	Nathaniel sonne of Raph Frith Draper
			William sonne of Wm Abbot Lynnen drape^r
	January	9	Ann daughter of Margaret Patty a poore woman in ye Cage
		21	Elizabeth daughter of Martin Higgins Poulter
	Febru:	2	John sonne of Lewis Biker Grocer
		4	Edward sonne of Thomas Moseley Turner
		18	Thomas sonne of Thomas Reynolds Skynner
1638	Aprill	29*	Christned Henrie sonn of Walter Golefer clothworker
	May	3	Christned a female Infant laid at Mr Mums his doore
		13	Christned Ann daughte^r of Jo^n Silk pewterer
			Ann daught^r of Thomas fenn Sexton
		24	Christned W^m sonne of Wm Croone Clothworke^r
		27	Christned flora daughter of Thomas Hill Taylo^r
	July	29	Christned Mary daught^r of Samuel Ward Stac'oner
	Septemb	14	Lidia daughter of Robert ffisher Cutle^r
	January	1	W^m sonne of Wm Hamond Ironmonge^r
		3	Ann daught^r of Lewis Biker Grocer
		6	Elizabeth daughter of Rich. Johnson
		16	Edmond sonne of Jo^n Harriman Haberdashe^r
	february	10th	Jo^n sonne of Robert Whitney Barbor
		17	Susanna daughter of John Wells Inhold^r
		24	Alice daughte^r of Wm Bibbey Inholder
	March	3	Thomas sonne of Thomas Lee Marchantailo^r
		10	Sarah daughte^r of Ben Pauck Haberdasher
1639		28	Christopher sonn of Christo: Desborough Merce^r
		29	Samuell sonne of Thomas Penn Grocer
	Aprill	21	Henry sonne of John Robinson
	May	5	John sonne of Thomas Conn Scriuene^r
		23	Mary daught^r of Wm Watson Apothecary
		29	Peter the supposed sonn of John & Ann lee brought to bed in leadenhall
		30	Samuell sonne of George Henley leatherselle^r
	June	24	W^m sonne of Raph frith Scriuener

* The Register from April 29, 1638, to June 24, 1640, is subscribed Henry Watson, churchwarden.

Yeare.	Month.	Day.	Names.
1639	July	14	Thomas sonne of Thomas Bedum Apothecary
	August	5	Peter sonne of Peter Newton Armorer
	Septem	8	Joseph sonne of Xpofer Chatterisse Cooke
		18	Elizabeth daughter of Beniamyn Claridg Potter
	Octob{r}	15	Gabriell sonne of Thomas Osborne Brickleyo{r}
		30	Susanna daughter of Richard Sea
	Nouem{r}	10	Peter sonne of John James Armore{r}
	Decem{r}	15	John sonne of Henry Perkinson Cordweyno{r}
	January	1	John sonne of Walter Golefer clothworker
		12	George sonne of Rich Turfrey Marchantailo{r}
		19	Sarah daughter of Geo: Long M'chantaillor
			Robert sonn of W{m} Hall Armorer
		28	Elizabeth daughter of Thomas Hanson Grocer
	february	1	Alexand sonn of Alexand Butler Inholder
	March	15	W{m} sonn of Jo{n} Warner Marchantailo{r}
		18	Martha daughter of W{m} Peas Sadler
1640		26	Sara daughter of Rich. Kingsman Grocer
	Aprill	19	W{m} sonn of Will' Saby Blacksmith
	May	1	Henry son of Henry Cowper Cordwcyn{r}
		26	Richard sonn of Thomas Hill Marchantailo{r}
	June	24	Mary daughter of Lewis Byker Grocer
	August	18*	Thomas sonne of Timothy young fishmonger
	Septem{r}	13	William sonne of Nathaniell Hawkeridge Vintner
		20	Peter sonne of Peter Newton Armorer
		29	Raph sonne of Thomas Reynolds Skynner
	Novem{r}	2	Mary daughter of Christopher Desborough Mercer
		11	John sonne of Martin Higgins Poulter
			Joseph sonne of George Henlye leatherseller
	Nouember	29	Symon Peeter A foundlin ....
	Decemb{r}	13	John sonne of John Witherall Iremonger
		20	John sonne of John Silke Pewterer
		27	Thomas sonne of Robert Whitney Barborchirurgion
			Will'm sonne of Thomas Lee Marchantaillo{r}
	January	3	Anne daughter of John Cotterell Glasier
		24	Mary daughter of William Bibbey Inholder
	February	2	Samuel sonne of William Watson Apothecary
		14	francis daughter of Alexander Butler Inholder
		25	James sonne of Thomas Penn Chandler
	March	5	Samuell sonne of William Hamond Ironmonger
1641		28	Emme daughter of William Hall Armorer
	Aprill	11	Sarah daugher of John Rolfe Goldsmith
	May	26	Symon sonne of Richard Thorowgood fishmonger
	June	14	Elizabeth daughter of Henrie Humpden leatherseller
		27	Rebecca daughter of Walter Golefer clothworker
	July	3	Richard sonne of John Langley fishmonger
		11	Henry sonne of Henry Gilpin Armorer
	August	29	Richard sonne of Richard Kingsman Grocer
	Septemb	15	William sonne of Mephibosheth Robins
		30	Nathaniell sonne of Nathaniell Hawkeridge Vintner
	October	13	Hannah daughter of Beniamyn Claridge Potter
	Nouemb	21	Mary daughter of Thomas Osborne Brickleyo{r}
		30	Priscilla daughter of Peter Newton Armorer
	Decemb	2	Thomas sonne of Henry Haughton gentleman
		9	† sonne of Moodey Lusher fishmonger

* The Register from Augnst 18, 1640, to May 1, 1642, is subscribed George Longe, church-warden.

† Sic

THE REGISTERS OF ST. PETER'S, CORNHILL. 89

Yeare.	Month.	Day.	Names.
1641	Decemb	10	Mary daughter of John Warner Marchauntaillo^r
		12	Margaret daughter of Thomas Ward Grocer
		28	John sonno of James Blott Draper
	January	5	Elizabeth daughter of Thomas Reynolds Skynner
		25	James sonne of William Saby Blacksmith
		29	Elizabeth daughter of Alexander Butler Inhold^r
	february	2	Mary daughter of Henry Cowper Cordweyner
		11	Anna daughter of John James Armorer
		15	Martin sonne of Jo^n Hudnoll Vintner
		24	Jane daughter of Thomas Handsonne Grocer
	March	12	John sonne of Mr Katch Leatherseller
1642	Aprill	14	Mary daughter of Thomas Norman Haberdasher
	May the ffirst		Margaret a foundlin left at Mr Hudsons doore
			Henry a foundlin left at Mr Masons doore
	May the ffirst		Rebecca daughter of William Watson Apothecarie
	May	19*	John sonne of John Langley fishmonger
		22	Richard sonne of Richard Thorowgood fishmonger
	June	16	William sonne of William Tapping Vintner
	August	2	Jane daughter of Thomas fenn Tallowchandler
	Septemb	18	Mary daughter of John Cottrell glasier
	October	30	Robert sonne of Robert Whitney barber
	November	8	Jonathan sonne of Beniamine Clarridg potter
	December	9	Edward sonne of Mephibosheth Robbins
		12	Ann daughter of Robert Margerets fishmo'ger
		8	Sarah daughter of John Am'y draper
		27	Mary daughter of John Gorum butcher
		29	John sonne of William ffisher in platter alley
	February	5	Ann daughter of John Booker Vintener
		9	Judeth daughter of Christopher Desborrough
		9	Thomas sonne of Thomas Hanson grocer
		14	Ann Daughter of William Chamberlaine dier
		23	Thomas sonne of Walter Golefer Clothworker
	March	4	Susan daughter of John Silke pewterer
		5	Margeret daughter of William Holmes winecoop'
1643	May	4	Jno son of Lewes Biker grocer
		9	Grace daughter of Thomas Osborne bricklayer
		10	Dorethy daughter of William Bibbey Inholder
		14	William sonne of Richard Kingsman grocer
	June	1	Jeames sonne of William East grocer
			Elisabeth daughter of Jeames Blott Drap'
	Julie	2	Elisabeth daughter of Edward Clarke Vintener
		17	Magdelayne daughter of William Sabey smith
	October	3	Mary daughter of John Warner m'chantaylor
		10	Henry sonne of John Robinson haberdasher
	August	28	John Peter a foundling
	November	2	William sonn to William Watson Apothecary
		27	Margaret daughter of Randolph Isaackson haber'sher
	December	30	Mary Peter found at Mr Renolds his doore
	Novemb	10	Thomas sonn of Thomas Penn grocer
	Decemb	10	Hanna daughter of John Rolph scrivener
		20	Ann daughter of John Briscow grocer
			Same day Mary Peeter foundlin
			Judith daughter of Willia' Hamon Iremonger
	January	28	John sonne of William Tappin Vintener

* The Register from May 19, 1642, to April 2, 1644, is subscribed Walter Golifer, churchwarden.

Yeare.	Month.	Day.	Names.
1643	February	17	Phillip sonne of John Wetherall
		18	Phebey daughter of Peter Newton armorer
		24	Mathew sonne of John Jeames armorer
1644	Aprill	2	Samuell sonne of William Pease saddler
		26*	Thomas son of Wm Perry Drap'
	May	12	Thomas son of Thomas Norman habb'
		14	William son of Wm Hinton Iremonger
	June	11	Daniell son of George Henly leatherseller
		13	Edward son of Wm Chamberline Dyer
	July	05	Elisabeth Peter a foundling
	August	27	Thomas son'e of Henry Coop' Cordwinder
	September	28	Lettis daughter of Lewis Biker grocer
	October	31	Beniamin son of Thomas Hanson grocer
	November	5	Sarah daughter of Rapho Trunket Cooke
	December	5	Ann daughter of Howgh Best vintener
	February	11	Samuell son of Thomas Renolds skinner
		25	Nicholas son of Christofer Desborrow mercer
	March	2	Samuell son of W^m ffisher barber surgeon
		3	Martha daughter of John Langley ffishmonger
		16	W^m son of Wm Bibbey Inholder
1645	May	15	W^m son of Wm Sabey blacksmith
		27	W^m son of Wm Chamberlayne dyer
	June	6	Ann daughter of Thomas Osborne, bricklayer
		24	Thomas son of Thomas Boothe leatherseller
		25	Mary daughter of Wm Tappin vintener
	July	6	Elizabeth daughter of Wm East m'chantalor
		29	Thomas son of Robert Whitney Barber
	August	10	Joseph son of Walter Golifer clothworker
		14	W^m and John sons of Jeames Blott drap' being Twines
		24	John son of John Cotterell glasier
		31	Christian daughter of Robert Whitbourn Cooke
	Septemb	14	Katherine daughter of John Galhampton Vintener
			Mary daughter of Wm Chamberlayne poulter
	Novemb	16	Hanna daughter of † Stallord
	Decemb	3	Sarah daughter of Lewis Biker grocer
		7	Josua ye son of Mathias Harding m'chantailor
		25‡	Christian daughter of John Silke pewterer
	January	18	Samuell son of John Jeames armorer
		23	Thomas son of Thomas ffiges haberdasher
	February	5	Martha & Mary two twines of Richard Kinsman free of the Grocers
		6	Henry son of Henry Robinson Mercer
		8	Edward son of Andrew Pearse haberdasher
		13	John son of John Amis Draper
		24	W^m son of Robt Hudson Skinner
	March	1	John son of Wm Hinton Iremonger
1646	Aprill	20	Thomas son of Walter Tappin Vintener
	May	6	Edward son of John Wetherall
	June	11	Joanna daughter of Henry Clarke barbar
	July	2	Samuell son of Thomas Haudson grocer
		4	John son of John Parrey m'chantaylor
		8	Rose daughter of Georg Kempe Inholder

* The Register from April 26, 1644, to December 7, 1645, is subscribed Mr. John Langley, churchwarden.

† Sic.

‡ The Register from December 25, 1645, to March 29, 1647, is subscribed Thomas Hanson, churchwarden.

THE REGISTERS OF ST. PETER'S, CORNHILL.

Years.	Month.	Day.	Names.
1646	July	9	Richard son of Richard Thorowgood fishmonger
		21	Joseph son of Allexander Grey scholmaster
		20	Richard son of Richard Archer tallow chandler
	August	14	Beniam'e son of Wm Chamber Dyer
	Septemb	6	Jeames son of Wm Tappin Vintener
	Octob	25	Thomas son of Thomas Lake m'chantayler
	Novemb	15	Jeane, daughter of Hew Best vintener
		22	Mary daughter of Ralph Trunket Cooke
	Decemb	27	John, son of Jeames Blott Draper
	January	11	Dorithy daughter to Mr Henry Robinson gent
	february	7	Elisabeth daughter * Wm Chamberlaine Poulterer
		28	Benet * of Wm Hamond Iremonger
	March	10	W^m son of Wm Mabbet pewterer
		14	Simon son of John Cotterell glasier
		19	Rebecka daughter of Phillip Brocke dyer
1647		28	Mathew son of Tho. Norman haberdasher the child borne ye last of february
		29	Joseph soonn of Thomas Yong Tallowchandler
	Aprill	2†	Elizabeth Peeter left att Mr Bikers Dore
		12	Stephen Sonn of Walther Vigor Comfetmake^r
		20	Allexander Son of Andrew Peirce Vintner
	May	16	Henry Sonn of Henry Robinson Habberdasher
		25	William Sonn of Charles Burgis Clothworker
		27	Robert Sonn of Robert Hudson Skynner
	June	24	Susanna Daughter of John Budd Poulterer
	July	11	Sara Daughter of Henry Cooper Cordwinder
		16	Jane dauto^r of Robert Parrey Clothworker
		18	Samuell Sonn of Lewis Biker Grocer
	Augu^t	8	Mary Daughter of George Barker Cooper
			Mary Daughter of Richa'd & Marrian Dodsall
		12	William Sonn of William East Marchantayler
	Octob	2	Richard Sonn of Richard Kinsman Grocer
		10	Mary Daughter of William Lawson Marriner
		13	John & Gabrill two twinns sonns of Baptist Croft M'chantayl^r
		14	Richard Sonne of Robert Whitney Marchantayler
		28	John Sonn of Henry Clarke Chirurgion
	Decemb^r	2	Margarett Daughter of Henry Robinson gentill'
		28	Beniamine Sonn of Thomas Leacocke Merchantayler
			Susanna Daughter of James Abrathatt Merchant
	Janua'	6	John son of Robert Houghton Drap' & Dorothy vxor
			John Sonn of John Chevall Drap' & Susan ei vxo'
		18	Sara Daughter of John & Mary Amie his wife
		22	John Sonn of Thomas Lake Mercha'tayler & Abigale vxo'
	Februar'	3	Leonard Sonn of Peeter Towers Drap' & Katherine ei vxo'
	March	5	Mary daughter of ffrancis Walker Irem'nger
		19	John Sonn of William Tapping Vintner
		21	Beniamine Sonn of Richard Thorowgood ffishmonger
1648	Aprill	2	Beniamine Sonn of William Hinton Iremonger
		6	James Sonn of John Wetherall Laborer
		16	James Sonn of James Gallantly Habberdasher
	May	5	Elizabeth Daughter of John James Armorer
		24th	Mary Daughter of Robert Hudson Skynner
		30th	Elizabeth Daughter of William Chamberline Dyer

* Sic.

† The Register from April 2, 1647, to July 30, 1648, is subscribed Mr John Silke, churchwarden.

Yeare.	Month.	Day.	Names.
1648	June	8th	A ffoundling Mary Peeter aged halfe a yeare
		19	John Peeter ffoundling aged two yeares
	July	16	Thomas son of John Budd Poulterer
		30th	Abell Sonn of Ralph Trumkitt Cooke
	...	30*	Andrew sonn of William West Merchantayler
	October	1	Sara daughter of Mr William Blackmore Rector
		8	Jaine daughter of William Chamberline Polterer
	Novem	5	Hanna daughter of Hunt Grace Cooke
		7	Rebecca daughter of Andrew Peirce Vintener
	Decembr	2	Grace Daughter of John Hall Clothworker
		31	John Sonn of John Smith Clothworker
	January	25	Thomas Sonn of Thomas Griffine Pewterer
	ffebru	14	John Sonn of Henry Robinson Gentleman
		20	Ann Daughter of Thomas Hilliard Mercer
		22	Ann Daughter of Thomas Hanson Grocer & Ann vxor
		26	Daniell Sonn of William Saby Blacksmith
	March	2	Leonard Sonn of Peeter Towers Draper
		16	Thomas Sonn of Thomas & Isabella Lushar ffishmonger
		22	A ffoundling Susan Peeter aged f... weekes
1649	Aprill	1	Elizabeth Daughter of Willia' & Elizabeth Harmer Painter Stainr
		2	Elizabeth Daughter of James & Elizabeth Blott Draper
		3	Henry Sonn of James Gallatley Perfumer
		8	Sara Daughter of Thomas & Mary Norman Habbrdasher
	June	14	Thomas Sonn of Thomas & Appulonia Tickner Grocer
		22	Hanna Daughter of Lewes Biker Grocer
	July	2	John Sonn of John Sturt Letherseller
		3d	Symon Sonn of Richard Blackborne Draper
	August	9th	Sara Daughter of William Tapping Vintner
	Septemr	2	John Sonn of Phillip Brocke Dyer
		15	John Sonn of John Gore Merchant
		25	Rebecca daughter of Ralph Trumkett Cooke
	Octobr	20	Sara Daughter of William Hamon Ironmonger
	Novemr	7	Elizabeth & Ann Daughters of ffra'ces Walker Iror
	October	26	Robert Sonn of Robert Hudson Skynner
	Novemr	20	Elizabeth daughter of John Wright Mercha'tayler
These two are entered in the margin.			Jane daughter of Edmund Williamson ffletcher & Katherine his wife borne the 8th and Christned the 11th of december 1649
			Robert sonn of Robt Nulm the 24th M'ch 1649 borne the 16th
	ffebruar'	19	Ellinor daughter of John Sawell Talloweha'dler
		28	Elizabeth daughter of Robert Halton draper
	March	17	Susanna daughter of Henry Cooper Cord'nder
1650	Aprill	3d	James sonn of John Cotterill Glasier
		9	Elizabeth daughter of Thomas Leacocke Mercha'tayler
		10	Ann Daughter of John Romney Armorer
		11	Thomas sonn of Thomas Hanson and Ann ei vxo' Grocr
		14	ffrancis sonn of Nicholas and Elizabeth Bendey Salter
			Margey Daughter of William Lawson Marriner
	May	6	Mary Daughter of James Blott drap'
	June	6	Susanna Daughter of Huntgrace, Cooke
		†8th	Dorcas daughter of John Hix Cordwinder

* The Register from July 30, 1648, to June 6, 1650, is subscribed Mr. Richard Thorowgood, churchwarden.

† The Register from June 8, 1650, to August 10, 1651, is subscribed Mr. Lewis Byker, churchwarden.

THE REGISTERS OF ST PETER'S, CORNHILL.

Years.	Month.	Day	Names.
1650	June	9	Rebecca daughter of Richard Woodnorth Stationer
		23	Jonas Sonn of Thomas Griffine Pewterer
	July	14	Elizabeth Daughter of William Hinton Ironmonger
	August	8	Martha Daughter of Mr William Blackmore or Minister
		19	Esdras sonn of Esdras Mills Plasterer
	Septemr	3	William soun of John Aymis Draper
		8	Elizabeth Daughter of Willia' Chamberline powlter
	Octobr	1	Elizabeth daughter of John and Susanna Choval drap'
		3	Thomas sonne of William East Marchant taylor
		13	John sonne of John Sturt Leather seller
		31	William sonne of Richard Thoroughgood fishmongr
	Nouembr	12	mary daughter of James Abrathat goldsmith
		18	mary daughter of Ralph Trunkett Cooke
	Decembr	8	deborah daughter of George Barker Cooper
		18	sarah daughter of John James Armourer
	Januar'	19	Hester daughter of James Gallatle haberdashr
	Januar 30th 1650		Elisabeth daughter to Thomas Godfrey Goldsmith
	februa'	1	susan Peter a foundling at mr Hansons stall
		23	John sonne of Robert Hudson skinner
		28	Robert sonne of Thomas Tickner Grocer
	March	2	mary daughter of John wright mercht taylr
		12	Elizabeth daughter of John & sarah fowler vintnr
		20	martha daughter of John and Grace Hall mercht taylr
1651	Aprill	3	John sonne of Thomas and Ann Hanson groc'
		17	Sibilla daughter of John and sibilla Turner free of the fishmongers
		25	Two Twinnes martha & Elizabeth daughters to William Tapping vintner
		29	Elizabeth daughter to Edward Buttler draper
	May the ffirst		John son of John Rumleye Armorer
		3	mary daughter of Walter and Elizabeth Garford mercer
		17	Beniamin sonne of Thomas Lecock mcht taylr
	July	16	Henry sonne of Radolfe Pateman Iremongr
		17	Anne daughter of Robert selwin vintnr
		19	William sonne of William Perry draper
			sarah Peter a foundling in ye greene yard aged three yeares
		22	Elizabeth daughter of James Blott drap'
		31	margarett daughter to Robert whituey m'chtay; James sonne of Richard Emmes Cooper
	August	3	Richard sonne of Richard Blackborne drap'
		5	Mary daughter of John Simons Cooke
		10	John sonne of John Ratcliffe vintur
	Septemr	3*	William sonne of William Phillips vintnr
		14	Phineas sonne of John Athey Haberdashr
	Octobr	5	mary daughter of William East mercht taylor
		12	Joseph sonne of William Lawson marriner
	nouemr	12	Joseph & Elizabeth Children of Richard Thorogood fishmonger
		28	Rebecca daughter of Richard husbands fishmongr
	Decemr	7	mary daughter of Joseph dix Poulterer
	Febr	12	sarah daughter of John fowler vintner
	March	1	Penelope daughter of William and Amy Hillarsdin Clothworker

* The Register from September 3, 1651, to December 30, 1652, is subscribed Mr. John James, churchwarden.

Yeare.	Month.	Day.	Names.
1651	March	9	vrsilah daughter of Thomas and Anne Handson Grocer
		21	Elizabeth daughter of Robt hudson skinner
1652	Aprill	15	Marie Daughter of John Witherall Laborer
		20	Richard Sonne of Richard Hill Gent.
		26	Elizabeth Daughter of John Turner fishm'
	May	11	Elizabeth Dawghter of Nicholas Bendy
		14	Elizabeth Dawghter of John Catterell glasier
		17	Grace Dawghter of William Halle Draper
	June	2	Marie Dawghter of Thomas Griffen Pewterer
		8	Jane Dawghter of Richard Kinsman Groc^r
		17	Abraham Sonne of Ralph Truket Cooke
		19	Richard Sonne of John Cheuell drap^r
		29	John Sonne of Walter Garford Merser
	Augus	9	Elizabeth daughter of Henry Jordan Chirurgion
		29	James sonne of Robert Hyatt merch^t taylor
	Septe^r	12	William sonne of William Chamberlane poulterer
		19	Richard sonne of Ralph stocking merch^t taylor
	October	11	Mary Peter a foundling laid by m^r . . . ells his shopp on a stall aged 3 weekes
		17	Katherine dawghter to william Lenford Cordwiner
	Nouemb'	20	John Peeter Aged 6 weekes, a fondlinge
		25	Mary Dawghter of Richard Thorogood ffishmong^r
		28	Elizabeth dawghter of William Tapping
		30	Beniamin sonne of William East m'chant
	Decemb^r	2	Ester dawghter of Richard Eames wineCooper
		8	William sonne of Wiliam Hammond Ironmg^r
		9	William sonne of Will' Parker Clotworker
		16	James sonne of Anthony Start haberdash^r
		30	Rebeckah dawghter of John Gray Haberdasher
	January	11*	Katherne dawghter of Edmo'd williamson fletcher
		18	Elizabeth dawghter of Nathanell Sedgwick
		25	Mary dawghter of Randolph Pateman
	ffebruary	10	Phillip sonne of Thomas Jefferisse Apoth'y
		16	Robert sonne of Robert Selman Vintener
		23	Mary dawghter of Thomas Auddy : Clot^r
		25	Lydia Peter a foundling month age
		27	Samuell sonne of William Hynton Irem^r
	March	6	Elizabeth daughter of William Inglott free of the Wine Coopers
		10	Edward sonne of Thomas & Ann Hauson free of the Groc^{rs}
1653		27	Richard sonne of Richard Woodnorth haberd'sh'
		30	Ann dawghter of John Smith Clothworker
	Aprill	18	Hannah dawghter of Gilbert Maddokes Baker
	May	19	Martha dawghter to Mr William Blakmore
		30	George Sonne of John Rumle Armor^r
	June	19	James Sonne of John Ratliffe vintener
	July	6	Mary Dawghter to Heury Jorden Cerre'gion
		10	Christopher Sonne of John Simons Cooke
		17	Thomas sonne of Thomas Jeninges habberdasher
		19	Sammuell sonne of James Blott Drap'
		21	Elizabeth daughter of ffrancis Marwood Merser
		27	Marie daughter of John & Sibbell Turner ffish'
	August	12	Robert sonn of Robt and Rebecca Warrin : Sadler
		12	Sarah Daughter of John and ffrancis Russell : Cooke

* The Register from January 11, 1652, to January 19, 1653, is subscribed Mr. William Hamon, churchwarden.

THE REGISTERS OF ST. PETER'S, CORNHILL.

Yeare.	Month.	Day.	Names.
1653	Septemb	30	Mary Daughter of Robert and Elizabeth Hyet: Merchant Taylor. borne ye 27th day
	Novemb'	17	Thomas sonne of Thomas Griffin Peuterer
		28	Rebecca Daughter of Ralph and Ann Trunckett Cooke borne the 20th
	Decemb'	20	ffrancis Daughter of William and Amey Hillersden Clothworker borne the 12°
		22	John sonne of Thomas Tickner Grocer
		26	Sarah daughter of John Saywell tallow Chandler
		27	Abraham: sonne of Henry and Agnis Chittie, vint:
	*Jan:	8°	John sonne of Dudley and Bridgett Harrood M'chant, borne ye 2°
	Jannu:	12	John sonne of John ffouler Vintner borne ye 6
		21	Eliz: Buzbie alias Coghin a Basterd child brought to bed at the wayhouse gate. the child 3 q'ters ould
		19	Joane Daughter of Samuell Shenton Sadler
		26†	Hanna Daughter of Nicholas Bendie Salter
	March	2	Sarah Daughter of Robt. Hudson: Skinner, born 16th ffeb
		16	Danniell son'e of John Athie habberd: borne ye 8th day
1654	Aprill	06	Sammuell son of Tho: Lecocke borne the 22° March 1653
		11	Anna Daughter of James Okes Drap' borne ye 8 day
		21	Deborah: Daughter of Simon and Eliz: Read Puterer borne the 13th day
	May	11	James sonne of John Langely ffishmonger borne ye 29th day
		18	Mary Daughter of Thomas Powell Armorer borne ye 3^d day
	June	11	Anthony sonn of John Stert Leatherseller
		20	Lawrence sonn of John Chevill: Draper borne ye 12th Day
	July	2	Thomas sonne of Thomas Hanson: Groser born ye 27° June
		4	Elizabeth daughter of Edmund Williamson: free of ye flletchers
		6	William sonn of Richard Thorowgood Drap born y^c 20th of June
		13th	Robert sonn of Robert Whitney borne the 3 day
		17	Sarah daughter of John Gray habberdasher borne ye 2th day
		18	William sonn of Gilbert Madox Habberdasher
	August	3	Joseph sonn of Thomas Jeninges Habberdasher
		8	Elizabeth daughter of John Hall Merchant taylor borne the 24th of July
		11	Rebecca daughter of Robert Warenn sadler
		25	Ann: Daughter of Nicholas and Martha Dun Cooke
	Septemb:	9	ffrances daughter of ffrancis and Mary Leonard ffishmonger
		21	John sonne of William Bookey Merchant Tayler
	Octob.	8	Robert sonne of William Chamberlin: poulterer borne the last of September
		9	ffrances sonn of Richard Blackborne Drap' borne the therd day
		9	Katherine daughter of James Bissill Butcher borne ye 5th
	Novemb:	5	Elizabeth Daughter of Henry Cooper Sexton
		5	Thomas sonne of Sammuell Purchis: Vphoulster borne the 21th of Octob^r

* Entered in margin.
† The Register from January 26, 1653, to May 7, 1655, is subscribed Mr. Thomas Wells, churchwarden.

Yeare.	Month.	Day.	Names.
1654	Novemb:	16	Mary Daughter of William Parker Clothworker borne ye 10th day
	Decemb^r	4	Elizabeth: Daughter of Thomas and Sarah ffrith ye sa: day
	February	5	Mary: Daughter of William East Merchant tayler born ye 22° Jan:
		11	Sammuell sonn of Sammuell Shenton Sadler
	March	20	James sonne of Anthony Stert habberdasher
1655	Aprill	3	Elizabeth daughter of James Okes Draper, born 26 March
		5	Elizabeth daughter of Walter Garford Merser
		8	Mary Daughter of Robert Hudson: Skinner borne 28th March
		23	Mary Daughter of John Simonds Cooke
		24	Judith Peeter a foundling of a yeare ould at Mr Lecocks stall
	May	7	Ann Daughter William ffearne Cordwinder
	June	3*	John sonne of Richard and Mary Porter Poulterer borne ye 25th of May
		5	Elizabeth Daughter of Thomas Griffin: Pewterer borne the 3: day
		10	Thomas sonne of Thomas Hickockes borne the same Day
		14	Thomas sonne of Thomas Leacocke Skinner borne the 9th Daye
		19	Thomas sonne of Thomas Adye Clothworker borne the 17th Day
	July	1	Elizabeth Daughter of Henry and Allis Jorden Chururgion, borne the 23° of June last
	August	19	Hugh sonne of Nicolas Dunn borne 12
		24	Sarah Daught^r of John Wright Marchant Taylor borne ye s^d day
		26	Jemes sonne of Robert Hyatt borne 24
	Septemb:	6	Josuah sonne of John Fowler vintn^r borne 24th August
		17	Samuell sonne of Tho: Jennings hab^{r}dasher borne ye same day
		20	Jeane daught^r of John Rumney Armorer borne 11 day
	August	2	Mathew daught^r† of John & Sarah Trasler borne & crisned 2th August
		28	Elizabeth daught^r of Simon Reade Pewterer: borne 18th
	Octob^r	9	Hannah daught^r of John & Grace Hall Marchantaylo^r: borne 25th sept^{br}
		10	Darcas daught^r of Jaruice Smith Marchantayl^r: borne 21th septemb^r
		18‡	Mary daught^r of William and Izabell Blagrow Pewterer borne 23th of Septemb^r
		14	Mathew Sonne of William Lawson Marrin^r borne 5th day
		29	Jesper sonne of Richard Kinsman Gros^r: b: 24th
	Nouemb^r	18	George sonne of Thomas Tickner Gros^r: borne 29th of Octob^r
		21	William sonne of Jemes Blott Drap^r: bo^{rne} 11
		18	Elizabeth daught^r of William Parker Clothwork^r: borne 12th

* The Register from June 3, 1655, to October 10 following, is subscribed Capt. William Easte, churchwarden.

† Sic.

‡ The Register from October 18, 1655, to April 29, 1657, is subscribed Mr. William Williams, churchwarden.

THE REGISTERS OF ST. PETER'S, CORNHILL. 97

Years.	Month.	Day.	Names.
1655	Decemb[r]	8	Susannah daught[r] of Samuell Purchass vpholst[r]
		10	Elizabeth daught[r] of George Only Vintn[r]
		23	Isack and Jacob: two sonnes of John Athy vint[r] being Twinns borne 15th
		19	Elizabeth daught[r] of Jonathan and Mary Botham Marchantayl[r]: borne 19th Decemb[r] and Christued 4th January
		28	Thomas sonne of John Gray Haberdash[r]: borne 28 Decemb[r] and Christned 4[th] January
	January	20	Martha daught[r] of Ralph Trunckett Cooke borne 9[th]
		20	Samuell sonn of John Sturt Lethersell[r] bo[rn] 2
	February	10	Mary daught[r] of Francis Leonard fishmong[r] borne January 30[th]
		12	Ann daught[r]: of Tho: Eells Hab[r]dasher borne 25[th] of Jan
		28	Thomas sonn of Tho: Frith Pewterer borne 11[th]
	March	16	Agnis daught[r] of Hen: Chitty viutn[r]: borne 2[th]
		23	Robert sonn of Robert Waring sadl[r]: borne 18
1656	Aprill	18	William sonn of John Chevell drap[r]
	May	6	John, sonn of John Smith borne 28[th] of Aprill
		25	Mary daught[r] of Richard Porter poulterer
	June	5	Elizabeth daughter of William Bookey Marchant tayler
			Dorothy daughter of Thomas Lecock Marchant tayler
		6	Elizabeth Daughter of Thomas and Susanna Powell
		21	John sonne of John Symondes Cooke
	July	29	Colinge sonn of Nicholas Bendie salter born y[e] 17th July
	August	27	Jacob sonn of Edward Ash Cutler borne y[e] 19[o]
		31	William sonne of William Chamberlin
		31	ffrances Daughter of John Saywell: borne y[e] 27[o]
	Septemb[r]	1	Mary Daughter of John Peck Leatherseller
		14	Elizabeth Daughter of Henry and Allis Jorden Chururgion: borne the first day
		15	Elizabeth Daughter of Richard Blackburne Drap' borne the 11th Day
		21	Phillip Daughter of Sammuell Hynton: Ironmonger
	October	12	Margaret Daughter of William Ingoll Coop'
		23	Elizabeth Daughter of Robt: Hyet: Merchant tayler
	November	3	Edward sonn of Edward ffranckton Habberdasher
		3	Mary Daughter of John ffowler vintner
		9	Sarah daughter of Thomas Pistoll ioyner
		5	Thomas son of James Oakes Draper
		14	Sammuell son of William Parker Cheese monger
		22	Mary Daughter of John Alder Draper
	Decemb[r]	11	Susanna Daughter of W[m] and Sarah Shepheard
		16	Alice daughter of Richard Armstone Osler
	January	4	Mary Daughter of Thomas Godfry born 28 Dec:
		19	William son of Barnabe Dench born y[e] 11th day
		25	Jeane Daughter of John Athie born y[e] 14th day
	February	1	Richard sonn of William Lauson Marriner
		3	Mary Daughter of John Hall Drap' born 19th Janu:
		13	John sonn of Thomas Griffin borne y[e] ffirst
		14	A foundlinge laied in Red Cross yard Aged 6 months named Barbery Peeter
	februarj 1656	25	{ Margret Peeter Laid at M[r] Rosses dore aged ten months
	March y[e]	29	Mary daughter of Robert and Robecka Waring sadler
			Mary daughter of Thomas Woodward Cooke

o

THE REGISTERS OF ST. PETER'S, CORNHILL.

Yeare.	Month.	Day.	Names.
1657	Aprill y^e	5	Thomas son of Thomas Elles Haberdasher
		19	Charles son of Thomas Jennings march^t Tayler
		29	Jane dawghter of Ralph Stoken march^t Tayler
	May	*13th	Willyan† soun of Wm Rugby
		20	Edward sonne of Thomas Hickhack porter
		25	Ann Daughter of Richard Porter Poulterer
		23	George sonne of John Rumney : Armorer
	June	1	Mary Daughter of Thomas Lecocke, Merchant tayler
		4	Eliner Daughter of Robert Baker founder
	June	11	John sonn of Richard and Sarah Kinesman : Grocer
	August	16	Richard sonn of William Hynton : Ironmonger. borne the 3^d Day
		23	John sonn of Tho: Blackborne M^rchant taylor borne ye 12th of August
		29	Edward sonn of John Symonds Cook : bapt : Sept : 1°
	Sept	19	Hannah Daughter of Thomas and Susanna Powell Armorer borne ye 5th Day.
	October	18	John sonn of Walter Yonge Sexton of ye p'ish
	Decemb^r	13	Henry sonn of Henry Jorden borne ye 29th of November
			Joseph sonn of John Chevill Drap^r borne ye same day
		22	Judith Daughter of Abraham Sayon and Judith his wife M^rchant
		28	Thomas sonn of Wm Chamberlyn Poulterer
	Jannuary	1	Elizabeth daughter of Sammuell Purchis vphoulster
		19	Elizabeth ye 2^d daughter of Anthony Bayler Clothworker
			John sonn of John Gray Habberdasher. born ye 10th day
	February	2	Andrew sonn of Henry Quelch born January ye 19th day
		2	James sonn of James Okes borne ye 28th of January
		23	Judith Peeter taken vp at Mr Woodnoths doore
	March	5	Ann Daughter of Richard Burd born ye 22° ffeb' :
		7	Sammuell sonn of John Sturt borne ye 23° ffeb'
1658	April	5	Amie Daughter of Joseph and Katherin Evins
		20	Katherin Daughter of John and Mary Peck Leatherseller
		21	Sarah Daughter of Thomas and Sarah ffrith pewterer
	May	2	Susanna Daughter of Ralph Truncket Cooke
	June	2	James sonn of Sammuell Kinge borne ye same day
	Julye	4	Edward sonn of Edward ffrankton & Susannah his wyfe Habberda :
		25	Richard son of Richard Portor poulterer borne the 10th
		26	Elizabeth daughter of Edward Aish cutler borne the 20th
		27	John son of John Hall Draper borne the 14th day
	August	5	Nicholas son of Nicholas Bendye borne the 21th of July
		19	William son of John Symonds borne the same day
	Septemer	21	John son of John wright Milliner borne ye same day
		12	Nathaniell Sonn of Thomas Woodward Cooke borne the 5th day
	October	12	Ann daughter of Willyam Parker borne the sam fifte month
	december	10	Paule late Sonn of Richard Blackburne draper borne sam day
			Walther peeter A ffoundling taken vp at m^r Leacocks dore

* The Register from May 13, 1657, to April 2, 1659, is subscribed Mr. Richard Richman, Churchwarden.
† Sic.

THE REGISTERS OF ST. PETER'S, CORNHILL. 99

Yeare.	Month.	Day.	Names.
1658	ffebevary	4	willyam sonu of willyam Sherrington fishemonger ffree
	Marche	15	John sonn of Thomas Eles ffree Habberdasher
1659	Aprill	20	William sonn of John Saywell Clotheworker
		2	Willyam Soun of willyam Ingall wyne Cooper
		10*	John son of Samuell Purches vphoulder borne the 08 of March
		20	Daniell Sonn of m^r John Chevell draper borne the same daye
	Maye	6	Thomas Sonn of John Rumey Armorer
		10	ffrances Sonn of m^r Leanord flishemonger
		12	Richard son of Richard may girdler borne 23 of Aprill
	June	15	Sarah daughter of Robert Hict marchantaylor And Elizabeth his wyfe borne the 23th of June
		24	Richard sonn of John And Ann Smithe Clothwor:
		29	Mary daughter of Anthonye baylye Clothworker born the 28 of the same monthe
		28	Barnaby sonn of Barnaby denche Clothwork'
	September	2	John sonn of Thomas Tredway ffree of the Grosers borne the twenty too of August 1659
		4	Elizabeth daughter of Richard Porter Poulterer
		10	John Waring sonn of Robert Waring ffree Sadler
		18	Elizabeth daughter of W^m & Elizabeth wright borne 13 day
		20	Samuell Bendy the sonn of Nicholas Bendy borne 5th day
	Nouembe^r	5	Susan daughter of m^r John Symonds ffree Cooke
		6	Ann daughter of Thomas & Mary Woodward Cooke
	8†	17	Beniamen sonn of m^r Richard Ordway bornth 14th
			willyam sonn of John Hall borne the 29th of october
	december	2	willyam Peeter A ffoundling at m^r Hamond dore month ould
		31	Edward Sonn of Thomas Everall borne the 30th
	January	15	Susannah daughter of Edward ffrankton born the 6
		22	martha daughter of Alce and waltor yong born 11 day
	ffeberary	5	Grace wilkes daughter of willyam wikkes† born 26 of Janu^{ary}
		12	beniamin Lawson sonn of willyam Lawson borne
		11	willyam Sonn of willyam Hopkins borne the same day
1660	Septemb^r	30	Humphry Sonn of Thomas Eles Habberdasher
	October	7	Thomas sonn of Thomas & Susan Blackborn borne the 26th of September
		31	Judith daughter of Thomas Griffin borne the 28th
	Nouembe^r	6	Elizabeth Stokin daughter of Raph Stokin
		15	willyam Bendy sonn of Nicholas Bendy borne the 2 of the same month
		29	John ffuller sonn of Willyam ffuller borne the 19th
	december	16	Thomas sonn of thomas Whichcoke ffree Cooke
		19	Matthow Bayly sonn of Anthony Bayly borne the 14th
		30	willyam sonn of Henry Quelch born the same day
	January	8	Charles sonn of Richard Blackborne born the same
		13	Elyzabeth daughter of John Smith Clothworker
		15	John sonn of willyam Chamberline & Elizabeth
		13‡	Elybath† the daughter of John Smith

* The Register from April 10, 1659, to January 15, 1660, is subscribed Mr. Willyam Hynton, churchwarden.
† Sic.
‡ The Register from January 13, 1660, to June 6, 1662, is subscribed Mr. John Chevall and Mr. James Blott, churchwardens.

Yeare.	Month.	Day.	Names.
1660	January	27	Edward son of John Alder ffree of the drapers
		31	Allice daughter of Henry & Allice Jorden
	ffeberary	1	Hannah daughter of Thomas Leacocke Marchantaylor
		10	Susanna daughter of m^r John & Susanna Chevall draper borne the 29 of Jannuery
		24	Sarah daughter of Henry Smith born the 15
		23	Robert peeter young ffondling Infant layd att m^r Smithes In S^{tt} peeters Allye
	March	6	Marcye the daughter of John ordwaye
			Marye daughter of Willyam Hinton born the 8 of ffeberry
		13	Robert waring the sonn of Robert waring borne the 3
		20th	Katherin Pecke the daughter of Pecke borne the 13 marche
1661	Aprill the	2	Issabell the daughter of willyam Blagraue
		28	Nathon sonn of willyam Ingall Cooper and wyfe
	May	1	Charles the sonn of John Symonds ffree Cooke borne the 22 of Aprill 1661
		20	Ann daughter of Richard & mary porter
	June	17	Judith peter A ffoundling Infant that was layed A m^r Leacockes stall
		23	mary daughter of Edward & Susannah ffranklin
		24	mary daughter of Jarvis & dorcas Smith marchant
	Julye	16	Joseph and beniamin too sonns of willyam varnham being twinns were baptised
		28	Thomas sonn of John Smith porter borne 21th
	September	12	Elizabeth daughter * willyam & Elizabeth Sherrinton
		18	Sarah daughter of willyam And Sarah Hopkins Chyrurgion
	Septemb^r	8	Ann daughter of Edward Biston borne 8 day
	October	13	ffrancis sonn of Samuell & Ann Shute dyer ffree
	novemb:	18	mary daughter of walter and Alce young Cordwaynor
		26	Thomas the sonne of John Sturt Leatherseller
	Decemb:	25	Nicholas Peeter a foundling laid at widd: Smiths dore adged about 2 yeares
	January	12	Margret the daughter of w^m Lawson Mariner
	ffeberary	9	Willyam sonn of John brathwyth vinterer
		23	George ye sonne of John Rumney Armorer
	March	13	Elizabeth the daughter of John Peck letherseler
		19	Evans Peeter a foundling laid vpon m^r Clarks stall
1662	Aprill	11	William ye sonne of Symon Coules Cooke
	May	6	William ye sonne of John Smith Clothwo^{rk}:
	June	5	Sara the daughter of Richard & Sara Ordway vintner
		6	Joseph ye son of Henry Quelch drap^r
		8†	Susan ye daughter of Thomas & Susan Blackburne Marchant tayl^r and borne the 24th of May 1662
		28	William ye sonne of William Evans
	July	18	Elizabeth ye daughter of John Price skiner and Elizabeth his wife
	August	3	Ann ye daughter of Thomas Eeeles haberdasher
		3	Tho: the sonne of Anthony Bayly
		17	Sarah ye daughter of william fforster
		27	Elizabeth the daughter of John Symons borne Monday the 18th of August
		25	Grace peter a foundling left on Mr Chamberlins stall

* Sic.

† The Register from June 8, 1662, to June 4, 1663, is subscribed Mr. James Blott, churchwarden.

THE REGISTERS OF ST. PETER'S, CORNHILL.

Years.	Month.	Day.	Names.
1662	October	7	Judeth ye daughter of John Scott clothwork^r
	Novemb:	2	Richard ye sonne of Wm Ingoll Mariner
		27	Henery ye Sonne of Henery Jordaine
	Decemb	14	Anna ye daughter of Edward ffrancton
		21	Edmund ye sonne of Robt Porter
		28	Rebecka ye daughter of william Chamberlin Poulterer
		24	Joseph ye sone of Tho: Wodward
		28 ·	Sara ye daughter of Tho: Wodward
	Jan:	2	Chewning ye sonne of Mr William Blackmore Clerke and Mary his wife borne the 1th of January
		11	Elizabeth ye daughter of Henery Smith Clothworker and Sarah his wife
			Margret ye daughter of Thomas Barbor Scrivener and Margret his Wiffe
		20	Richard Sonn of Thomas Hickocke in* margrett his wyfe
		22	Margerett Nicholas daughter of Thomas & Elizabeth Nicholas his wyfe was borne the 11th of January
	ffeberary	15	Richard sonn of willyam & Sarah Hopkins Chyrurgion
		26	Joshua son of Jacob Hadley borne same day
			debberah daughter of Robert Rowland Armorer
	Marche	11	Susan daughter of John Alder vphoulder And ffree draper
		17	Charles sonn of John Hall Lyning draper
1663	May	29	Allexander ye sonne of Allexander and Elizabeth Venner Marchantayler
	June	4	John ye sonne of John Cottram grocer & Sarah his wiffe borne 25th may
		4	Mary ye daughter of Mr William Sherington fishmonger and Elizabeth his wiffe
		20†	A ffemale Infant lefte at m^r purchases dore named Doruthy wedster Aged six weekes
		28	Ann daughter of Willyam & Ann Evans Inhoulder dwelling att Mr Burkes
	Julye	18	Henry soun of Edward Biston & his wyfe
		1	Willyam sonn of Russell grocer borne the ffirst
	August	6	Temperance the daughter of Walter and Bridgitt young Sexton & Cordweaned*
		9	Elyzabeth daughter of John Ireland kallinder
		10	Ann daughter of James fferland Weaver
		30	Claree daughte^r of William Wise Vintner & ffrances his wife
		30	Elizabeth daughte^r of John Harbert Feltmaker and Elizabeth his Wife
	Septem:	1	Hannah daughte^r of William Knight Haberdashe^r and Sarah his Wife
	Octob^r	11	Thomas sonn of Christopher Tillard and Ann his wife vintner
		13	Walter sonn of John Smith and Ann his wife, Clothworker
	No: ber	15th	Robart Cheuall Sonne of Mr John Cheuall Draper
	Septemb^r	13	Dorothy Daughter of Robert Welch Marchant and Elizabeth his wife
	Novemb:	19	Simon sonn of Simon Coles Cooke
	Decemb:	20	Timothy sonn of Thomas Blackborne Marchantaylor and Susan his wife borne the 7th day

* Sic.
† The Register from June 20, 1663, to March 27, 1664, is subscribed Mr. Nicholas Bendy, churchwarden.

Years.	Month.	Day.	Names.
1663	Decemb:	20	George sonn of John Ordway vintner
	ffebr:	9	John Sonn of Thomas Eeles Haberdasher and Anne his wife borne the 27 January
		10	John Sonn of John Vtting Marchant and Amy his wife borne the 22 January last
		21	Dorothy Daughter of Thomas Lacock vpholster
	March	2	Constant the daughter of Christopher Kember Merchantaylor and Constant his wife
		24	Thomas the Sonne of Thomas Barber and Margarett his wife borne the 18th
1664	March	27	Ralph the Sonne of Ralph Stockinge and Barbarah his wife
	Aprill	11*	Thomas the Sonne of Robert Rowland and Elizabeth his wife borne the same day
		13	Joseph Sonne of John Sturt and ffrances his wife
	July	3	Edward sonne of Edward ffrankton Haberdasher borne 19th June
		5	Martha daughter of Henry Jorden Barber chirurgeon and Alice his wife borne the 21th June
		8	William sonne of Thomas Nicholas Ironmonger and Elizabeth his wife borne the 23th June
		17	William sonne of William Chamberlen Poulterer and Elizabeth his wife
		28	Elizabeth daughter of William and Isabella Blackgrave borne the 14º
	August	7	John sonne of John Mason ffruterer and Anne his wife
		11	Edward sonne of Nicholas Bendy Salter and Elizabeth his wife by Deane Hodges, borne the 29th of July
		11	Mary daughter of Abraham Saijon Marchant and Judith his wife by Deane Hodges
		11	Samuell sonne of William Hopkins Barberchirurgeon dec'd and Sarah his wife by Deane Hodges borne the 9th
		16	Steven Peter a ffoundling left att mr Staples doore in Gracechurchstreete
		18	John sonne of Tobias Garbrand ffishmonger and Margarrett his wife
	October	4	Thomas sonne of John Smith Clothworker
		16	ffrances daughter of Jacob Clarke and ffrances his wife
		23	Anne daughter of John Holland Chirurgeon and Anne his wife
		23	Joseph and Mary Price Twins the Children of John Price Skinner and Elizabeth his wife, borne the same day
	December	11†	Elizabeth daughter of Richard Babington Ironmonger and Margarett his wife
	January	1	Joseph sonne of Thomas Eeles Haberdasher and Anne his wife
		12	Alice daughter of Richard Ordway Vintner and Sarah his wife
		15	Mary daughter of Walter Younge Joyner and Briggitt his wife
		22	Mary daughter of William Merrill Inholder and Anne his wife
	March	12	Richard sonne of Alexander Venner Marchantaylor and Elizabeth his wife borne the 25º ffebruary

* The Register from April 11, 1664, to October 23 following, is subscribed Mr. Ralph Trunckett, churchwarden.

† The Register from December 11, 1664, to March 11, 1666, is subscribed Mr. Richard Blackburne, churchwarden.

Yeare.	Month.	Day.	Names.
1665	Aprill	2	William sonne of William Warthan Haberdasher and Deborah his wife
		2	Anne daughter of Richard Armstronge
		16	Christopher sonne of Christopher Tillard Vintner and Anne his wife
			Anna daughter of Samuel Shute dier borne the 12° and baptized the 21th May 1663*
		30	Elizabeth daughter of Thomas Hickocke Cooke and Margarett his wife
	May	14	Robert sonne of Robert Rowland Armorer and Elizabeth his wife
		21	Thomas sonne of Cornelius Cage Vintner and Margaret his wife borne the 11th
		28	John sonne of John Herbert ffeltmaker and Elizabeth his wife borne the 14th
	June	1	Elizabeth daughter of William Sherrington Marchant borne the 15° May
			Samuell sonne of John Cockeram and Sarah his wife borne the 9° and baptized the 14° June 1665
		18	Nicholas sonne of Richard Porter Poulterer and Mary his wife borne the 8th
	July	13	Mary daughter of John Ireland Clothworker and Mary his wife
	October	16	Richard sonne of Nicasius Russell Clockemaker and Anne his wife
		19	ffrancis Blackburne sonn of Richard Blackburne Draper & Elizabeth his Wife Octob' 19th 1665
	August		Elizabeth daughter of Edward ffranckton Haberdasher
	Novemb:	12	Anne daughter of Richard Holden Cordwyner
	Decemb:	17	Richard sonne of John Mason and Anne his wife
	March	8	Anne daughter of Anthony Bayley and Joice his wife borne the 26° ffebr
		21	Joseph sonne of Thomas Eeles Haberdasher and Anne his wife
1666	Aprill	7	Jane daughter of Thomas Barber and Margarett his wife. borne the same day
	May	6	John sonne of John Clarke Grocer and Bridgett his wife borne the 21° Aprill
			John and Elizabeth Alder Twins children of John Alder Draper and Mary his wife borne the same day
			Sarah daughter of Henry Jordan borne and baptized the 17° May 1666
		31	Henry sonne of Richard Ordway Vintner and Sarah his wife
	June	5	Elizabeth daughter of Robert Rowland Armorer and Elizabeth his wife
	July	20	John sonne of John Harris ffishmonger and Anne his wife borne the 14°
		20	Sarah daughter of John Price Skinner, and Elizabeth his wife borne the same day
		30	Letitia Daughter of John Cockeram Grocer and Sarah his wife
	Augt	4	Richard Sonn of Edward ffrancklin Haberdasher and * his wife
		11	Ann Daughter of Robert Clarke Victualler and Ann his wife

* Sic.

Yeare.	Month.	Day.	Names.
1666	Nov:	6	Richard Kemble Sonn of Thomas Kemble Draper and Ann his wife
	Jan:	13	Susan the Daughter of George Grigman Victualler and Susanna his wife
		23	Mary the Daughter of Tobias Garbrand ffishmong^r and Margarett his wife
		26	Susanna the daughter of Thomas Wickersham ffishmonger and Elizabeth his wife
	Feb	26	Elizabeth Daughter of John Roberts * and Mary his wife
	March	11	Mary the daughter of William Packer, Salter & Mary his wife

CHRISTNED THIS YEARE 17.

Mr. Richard Blackburne, churchwarden.

* Sic.

1538.

Diuers burialls in the raignes of King Henry, King Edward, and Que'ne Mary.

BURIALLES.

Yeare.	Month.	Day.	Names.
1539	Janua	7	Burying of John Jonsonne the 17th of January Anno 39
		7	Burying of Thomas Preest the 7th of Januarie 39
		11	Burying of Symond English the 11th of January
		29	Burying of John Lambe the 29th of January 39
	Februa	12	Buryed the wif of William Friar the 12th of Februa.
	March	14	Burying of Richard Burnam the 14th of March
1540	Maye	15	Burying of Robert Saunders the 15th of Maye 40
		28	Burying of Thomas Hepworth sonne of Wm Hepworth
		31	Burying of John Federston the 31th of Maye 1540
	August	18	Burying of William Saye sonne of John Saye the 18
	Septem	2	Burying of Fraunces Preste, sonne of Thomas Preste
	Februa	4	Burying of John Jonson, the 4th of February 1540
		9	Burying of Randulphus Reed the 9th of Februarye
1541	May	8	Burying of Margaret Kyrke the 8th of Maye
		18	Burying of Elizabeth a gentlemans wif the 18th
		23	Burying of John Louell the 23th of May Anno 41
	Julie	2	Burying of Emme Idle, the 2th of July Anno 1541
		31	Burying of Annes Thornton the 31th July Anno 41
	August	8	Burying of John Nichollson, the 8th day of August
		25	Burying of Edward Innocent the 25th
		26	Burying of Thomas Marten, a preist 26th day
	Septem	1	Burying of Robert Saunders September the first
		7	Burying of Elizabeth Tipper, September the 7th
		8	Burying of John Bently September the 8th
		13	Burying of Katherine Lindsey September ye 13th
		23	Burying of Thomas Linsey September the 23th
		27	Burying of John Scriuen September the 27th
		29	Burying of Thomas Vbanke September the 29
		30	Burying of Alice Welles September the 30th
	Octobe	8	Burying of Symond Byrd October the 8th
		9	Burying of Robert Spert, October the 9th
		9	Burying of Syr Richard Fetherstone, the 9th day
		9	Burying of John Shippe, October the 9th day
		9	Burying of Katherine Miles. October the 9th daye
		13	Burying of Thomas Thorpe. October the 13
		22	Burying of Elizabeth Browne. October the 22

Years.	Month.	Day.	Names.
1541	Octobe	29	Burying of Joane. her syr name not known
	Decem	1	Burying of Margaret Kamymam. December 1
		21	Burying of Lawrence his syr name not set downe
	Janua	9	Burying of Harry Crostaud January the 9th
		11	Burying of Andrew Warde: January the 11th
		29	Burying of John Horton, January the 29th
	Februa	7	Burying of Alice Twistleden. February the 7th
		17	Burying of Katherine Downes. February the 17
	March	26	Burying of Ellen Speed, March the 26th
1542	Aprill	8	Burying of Fraunces Downes. Aprill the 8th
	Maye	4	Burying of Alice Wanton: Maye the 4th
		13	Burying of Elizabeth Fundling. May the 13th
		16	Burying of Jane Thornton. May the 16th
		19	Burying of Robert Westerbe May the 19th
	July	4	Burying of Roger Halle: July the 4th
		15	Burying of Lettice Groue. July the 15
		22	Burying of Maye Lamymam. July the 22
		26	Burying of Dorothy Hart. July the 26th
		29	Burying of Jeames Kendall. July the 29th
	August	2	Burying of Edward Warrington. August the 2
		10	Burying of William Atkinson August the 10
		24	Burying of my Lady Margery Morris the 24th
	Septem	6	Burying of William Munday September the 6th
	Octobe	9	Burying of Charles Thomson: October the 9th
		17	Burying of John Afort: October the 17th 1542
		20	Burying of Margery Idle October the 20th
	Nouem	7	Burying of Joane Barton: Nouember the 7th
	Decem	13	Burying of John Drope: December the 13th
		26	Burying of William Laister December the 26th
	Janua	18	Burying of Elizabeth Midleton. January the 18th
	Februa	15	Burying of Annes Norman: February the 15th
		24	Burying of Roger Lylly: February the 24th
		27	Burying of John Bankes called Kerner. Februa 27
	March	17	Burying of Harry Speed. March the 17th
1543	Aprill	4	Burying of Annes Mosse: Aprill the 14th 1543
	Julie	15	Burying of Margery Eliot: July the 15th 1543
		19	Burying of Rowland Seger: July the 19th 1543
		22	Burying of Emme Horsey: Julye the 22th 1543
	August	10	Burying of Robert Frere: August the 10th 1543
		16	Burying of Ellen Tuchborn: August the 16th
		20	Burying of William Hepworth: August the 20th
		25	Burying of John Atkynson: August the 25th
	Septem	2	Burying of Peeter Gaith: September the 2
		17	Burying of Joane Sourall: September the 17th
	Octobe	8	Burying of John Willson. October the 8th 1543
		20	Burying of John Taylor. October the 20th
	Nouem	3	Burying of Jane Walker. Nouember the 3
		28	Burying of John Averell: Nouember the 28th
	Janua	1	Burying of Margaret Daulton January the first
		18	Burying of Bose Felton: January the 18th 1543
	Februa	9	Burying of Annes Hoult February the 9th
	March	17	Burying of Robert Carnaden the 17th of March
		18	Burying of Radegund Maruell March the 18th
1544	Aprill	6	Burying of Thomas Portington. Aprill the 6th
		16	Burying of Robert Paynter: Aprill the 16th
		20	Burying of Roger Person: Aprill the 20th
		25	Burying of George Hynton: Aprill the 25th

Yeare.	Month.	Day.	Names.
1544	Maye	4	Burying of Erasing Busay: May the 4th
	June	20	Burying of John Pattinson: June the 20th
		29	Burying of Thomas Casebolt: June the 29th
		30	Burying of Anne Warde: June the 30th
	Julie	10	Burying of Mary Feeld: July the 10th 1544
		14	Burying of Wynfred Gylstone the 14th June*
		19	Burying of Griphet Hyntonne the 19th
		22	Burying of Anne Heylyn. July the 22th
		28	Burying of Griflet Tailor. July the 28th Anno 1544
		28	Burying of Thomas Owen. the 28th of July Anno 44
	August	8	Burying of Katherine Hayward. the 8th of August
		9	Burying of Anne Giger. the 9th day of August
		10	Burying of Katherine Harwood the 10th day of Augu.
		13	Burying of Jeames Blackemore the 13th of August
		20	Burying of Richard Avery. the 20th day of August
		27	Burying of Annes Bertonne the 27th of August
		27	Burying of Ellen Parsonne, the 27th of August
	Septem	7	Burying of William Gerard, the 7th of September
		9	Burying of Jone Edwin the 9th day of September
		11	Burying of Mary Cocher the 11th daye of September
		15	Burying of Joane Reynoldes, the 15th of September
		23	Burying of Katherine Horsley the 23th day Septem.
		24	Burying of Mary Stamford, the 24th day of Septem.
		24	Burying of Joane the seruant of Mr Atkynnes the 24th
		30	Burying of Robert Jonsonue the 30th of September
	Octobe	6	Burying of Alice Fryre the 6th day of October
		6	Burying of Thurstone Langdone the 6th daye
		9	Burying of William Barker, the 9th day October
		10	Burying of Jone Groue the 10 daye of October
		13	Burying of Izaboll Norris the 13th day of October
		14	Burying of Margaret Ball, the 14th day of October
		17	Burying of Leonard Walker, the 17th day October
		20	Burying of Emme Edwin the 20th of October 1544
		20	Burying of John Saunders, the 20th day of October
1545	Aprill	1	Burying of Robert Greane the first of Aprill
		4	Burying of Julyan Sakary the 4th daye of Aprill
		13	Burying of Syr William Bowyer late lord Maior of London
		24	Burying of John Wallis. the 24th day of Aprill
	Maye	6	Burying of John Reason the 6th of May Anno 1545
		8	Burying of Joane Lalache the 8th day of Maye
		9	Burying of William Sommer the 9th daye of May
		11	Burying of Lewes Vaghan the 11th of Maye 1545
		29	Burying of John Mackerell the 29th day of Maye 45
		31	Burying of John Adames the 31th daye of Maye
	Julie	2	Burying of Thomas Briseley the 3 daye of Julye
		3	Burying of William Sliuge the 3 day of July 1545
		20	Burying of Richard Briseley the 20th day of Julie
	August	7	Burying of John Jance, the 7th daye of August
		14	Burying of Joane Sommers the 14th day of August
		22	Burying of Steuen Sommers the 22th day of August
		31	Burying of Edwarde Groue the 31th day of August
	Septem	17	Burying of Richard Houster, the 17th day of Septem.
		19	Burying of Annes Packyngton the 19th day of Septem.
		21	Burying of Jane Lambe the 21th of September
	Octob	9	Burying of John Genninges, the 9th daye of October

* Sic.

Yeare.	Month.	Day.	Names.
1545	Nouem	17	Burying of Richard Blage. the 17th day of Nouember
	Februa	3	Burying of Syr Christopher Morris Knight, Februa 3
1546	Maye	3	Burying of Thomas Whighte a Preest, May the 3
		3	Burying of one Semer a Spanniard, May the 3 day
		6	Burying of George Stamper, the 6th day of Maye
		7	Burying of Elizabeth Roodes the 7th daye of Maye
	Julie	27	Burying of Phillip Baylye the 27th day of July
		29	Burying of Edward Edwin the 29th daye of Julye
		31	Burying of Thomas Cockes the 31th day of Julye
	August	6	Burying of Annes Judde, the 6th daye of August
		15	Burying of John Ball, the 15th daye of August
		25	Burying of Alice a stranger the 25th day of August
		29	Burying of Haunce Doublebeare the 29th of August
	Septem	1	Burying of Leonard Edwyn. the first day of September
		10	Burying of William Edwyn, the 10th daye of September
		10	Burying of Alice Payne, the 10th daye of September
		11	Burying of Ellen Bell the 11th daye of September
		12	Burying of Agense Rudcarke the 12th of September
		20	Burying of Maude Weller the 20th day of September
		21	Burying of John Decheborn the 21th day of September
		22	Burying of Elizabeth Roddocke the 22th day of September
		26	Burying of John Tepkyn the 26th day of September
		28	Burying of John Vales the 28th daye of September
	Octobe	1	Burying of Margaret Lasselles, the first of October
1547	June	2	Burying of John Bower; the second of June. Anno 47
		7	Burying of Goodman Haselbury the 7th of June 47
		27	Burying of Anne Rowse the 27th day of June
		27	Burying of Oliuer Porter of the Weygh House
	Septem	13	Burying of Mary Borow the 13th of September
	Octobe	15	Burying of Anne Sparrat the 15th of October
	Nouem	7	Burying of John Cartar the 7th of Nouember
		18	Burying of Larenco Rekener the 18th of Nouember
		27	Burying of Anne Fowler the 27th of Nouember
	March	1	Burying of John Linsay the first of Marche
		24	Burying of William ffoster the 24th of Marche
		24	Burying of Ralphe Saunders the 24th of Marche
1548		31	Burying of John Cockes the 31th of March
	Aprill	5	Burying of Barbara Weller the 5th of Aprill
		8	Burying of Anne Eatonne the 8th of Aprill
		10	Burying of Robert Thornton the 10th of Aprill
		29	Burying of William Segar the 29th day of Aprill
	Maye	1	Burying of one of Mr Brightes men, the first Maye
		9	Burying of Harry Penifather, the 9th of Maye
		29	Burying of Goodman Haselberry, the 29th Maye
	June	30	Burying of Thomas Tipper the 30th of June
		30	Burying of Jales yong childe the 30th of June
	Julio	6	Burying of Reynold Downes: July the 6th 1548
		12	Burying of Elizabeth Speed: July the 12th Anno 48
	August	15	Burying of Alexander Stoke: August the 15th
		15	Burying of Richard Atkinson. August the 15
		16	Burying of Harry Gonne: August the 16th
		17	Burying of Rose Myller: August the 17th 1548
		17	Burying of Rowland Atkinson the 17th day August
		19	Burying of Margaret Borrow, August the 19th
		19	Burying of Master Borrowes man. August the 19
		20	Burying of Audrian Walker: August the 20th
		22	Burying of Maister Parkers mayde the 22th day

THE REGISTERS OF ST. PETER'S, CORNHILL. 109

Yeare.	Month.	Day.	Names.
1548	August	22	Burying of Elizabeth Connyers : August the 22th
		22	Burying of Margaret Mathew. August the 22th
		25	Burying of John Mathew: August the 25th
		25	Burying of Mr Stokes mayde August the 25
		26	Burying of John Stokes : August the 26th
		31	Burying of John Connyers. August the 31th
		31	Burying of Marmaduke Connyers the 31th daye
	Septem	4	Burying of John Irish. September the 4th daye
		5	Burying of Richard Seely September the 5th
		7	Burying of Thomas Croughton. September the 7
		8	Burying of John Burton, the 8th day of September
		8	Burying of John Croughton September the 8th
		9	Burying of John Dychebourn. the 9th daye
		9	Burying of Margaret Parker the 9th of Septem.
		10	Burying of John Carpenter. the 10th of Septem.
		17	Burying of Harry Drope the 17th day September
		25	Burying of William Hynton the 25th of Septem.
		29	Burying of Gabriell Croughton the 29th Septem.
		30	Burying of Elizabeth Thrower the 30th day
	Octobe	7	Burying of Elizabeth Caryon the 7th of October
		8	Burying of John Horton, October the 8th daye
		11	Burying of Griffet Hynton October the 11th
		18	Burying of Father Bell. the 18th of October
		20	Burying of Richard Blackborn : the 20th day
		24	Burying of Fraunces Trougton the 24th daye
		30	Burying of Sara Cartar the 30th of October
	Nouem	11	Burying of John Richardson. Nouember the 11th
		12	Burying of Rafe Whighthed. Nouember the 12th
		18	Burying of John Stabbye. Nouember the 18th
		20	Burying of John Stott the 20th daye of Nouember
	Decem	7	Burying of Thomas Askew. December the 7th
		14	Burying of Adam Cater the 14th of Decembr
	Janua	13	Burying of Thomas Atkynson. January the 13th
		29	Burying of Robert Idle. January the 29th
	Februa	16	Burying of Thomas Fryar the 16th of January
	March	2	Burying of George Judde the second of Marche
1549	Aprill	11	Burying of Annes Idle, the 11th of April 49
	Maye	28	Burying of Robert Horsley the 28th of Maye
	June	30	Burying of George Rower the 30th of June
	Julie	12	Burying of Thomas Goodale July the 12th
		17	Burying of the Joyners seruant the 17th of July
		19	Burying of Rychard Ball the 19th of Julye
		22	Burying of William Comptonne the 22th of Julye
		23	Burying of Robert Grobbe the 23th of Julye
	August	3	Burying of Anthony Addis the 3 of August
		12	Burying of John Burton the 12th day of August
		13	Burying of John Poyntell the 13th day of August
		26	Burying of Richard Bell the 26th day of August
		27	Burying of John Thompson the 27th of August
	Septem	1	Burying of Ellen Happy : the first of September
		9	Burying of Julyan Atkinson the 9th of September
		12	Burying of John Bell the 12th of September
		24	Burying of Elizabeth Bell the 24th of September
		27	Burying of Thomas Bell the 27th of September
	Nouem	7	Burying of Elizabeth Lawdry the 7th of Nouember
		16	Burying of John Gybbens, the 16th of Nouember
	Decem	14	Burying of Annes Marten the 14th of December

Yeare.	Month.	Day.	Names.
1549	Decem	22	Burying of Katherine Coorse the 22th of December
	Janua	3	Burying of Mr Gybbons maide the 3 of January
		10	Burying of William Segar, the 10th of January
		30	Burying of Mrs Gaune the 30th of January
		31	Burying of Thomas Turnpeny the 31th Januarie
	Februa	3	Burying of Joane Westra: the 3 of February
		19	Burying of Annes Gyles the 19th of February
	March	9	Burying of Maude Petelyn the 9th of Marche
1550	May	7	Burying of Mr Harrison merchant of Hull. May 7
		12	Burying of Roger Hoyton the 12th of Maye
		19	Burying of Walter More the 19th of Maye
	June	2	Burying of Peeter Smith the second of June
		6	Burying of Mary Mabletonne the 6th of June
	Octobe	3	Burying of Dorithe Dured the 3 of October
		7	Burying of Joane Lawse, the 7th of October
	Nouem	18	Burying of Thomas Hayse the 18th of Nouember
	Decem	7	Burying of John Hawward the 7th of December
		11	Burying of Annes Coolefox the 11th of December
	Janua	30	Burying of Joane Hayleward the 30th of January
	Februa	5	Burying of Joane Hodge, the 5th of February
		6	Burying of William Mushrempe the 6th of February
		7	Burying of Joane Lotis the 7th of Februarye
		8	Burying of Joane Harlow the 8th of February
		14	Burying of Lettonish Cayne, the 14th of February
1551	March	24	Burying of Harry Swingfeeld the 24th of March
	May	9	Burying of Robert Stokes the 9th day of Maye
		14	Burying of My Lady Hubblethorn the 14th day
		14	Burying of Richard Sucklyne the 14th day of May
		22	Burying of my Lady Morris the 22th day of May
	June	14	Burying of Thomas Scherly, 14th of June
		18	Burying of Gouldstoues wif the 18th day of June
	Julie	4	Burying of Joane seruannt to Mr Roger Ponder
		5	Burying of Edward Sheyfeld the 5th of Julye
		9	Burying of Valentine Brockell the 9th of Julye
		10	Burying of Chareles Vandeweruen the 10th daye
		11	Burying of Thomas Lewis, the 11th of Julye 1551
		11	Burying of John Keling the 11th daye of July 1551
		11	Burying of Joane Thomas the 11th daye of July
		11	Burying of Charles Gunne the 11th daye of July
		11	Burying of Joane Dyxon the 11th daye of Julye
		11	Burying of Joane Mascoll the 11th daye of Julye
		11	Burying of Thomas Marshall the smithes seruannt
		12	Burying of William Tailer the 12th daye of July
		12	Burying of Symond Cassell the 12th daye of Julie
		12	Burying of Joane Mr Foulers maide the 12th daye
		12	Burying of Annes Mr Foulers maide the 12th daye
		13	Burying of Edward Clarke Mr Herdes man the 13th
		13	Burying of Steuen Brond, the 13th daye of Julye
		13	Burying of Richard Lawrence, the 13th day of Julye
		13	Burying of Mr Moore, brother to Mrs Adames
	Septem	18	Burying of Margaret Atkinson : September the 18th
	Octobe	7	Burying of a still born childe of Robert Wrightes the 7th
		8	Burying of Joane Webbe the 8th daye of October
	Nouem	28	Burying of Harry Baall, Nouember the 28th
	Februa	2	Burying of Annes Willey the second of Februarye
		22	Burying of Margaret Gunne, the 22th of February
1552	Aprill	8	Burying of William Crafton the 8th daye of Aprill

Yeare.	Month.	Day.	Names.
1552	Aprill	27	Burying of Joane Thornton the 27th day of Aprill
	May	12	Burying of Joseph de Jane, the 12th daye of Maye
		22	Burying of Anthony Jonson the 22th daye of Maye
	July	29	Burying of William Clarke Skynner the 29th Julye
	Septem	7	Burying of Joane Porter September the 7th daye
	Nouem	27	Burying of Thomas Swingefeeld the 27th day Nouem.
		29	Burying of Thomas Nicholson Clothworker
	Decem	7	Burying of Thomas from the Flower de luce the 7th
		12	Burying of William Latheman the 12th of Decem.
	Februa	13	Burying of Anne Mathew, daughter of Richard Mathew
1553	May	17	Burying of William Bulson the 17th daye of Maye
	August	26	Burying of Barthollmew Wright the 26th August
	Septem	2	Burying of John Battes September the 2 of the same
	Octobe	20	Burying of John Averell sonne of John Averell Joyner
	Nouem	9	Burying of Grace Clearton wif to Mr Eldertonne
		13	Burying of Robert Gibbon Poulter the 13th Nouem.
	Decem	8	Burying of Steuen Riche, Mr Eldertones seruannt
	Janua	1	Burying of John Fletcher the first of January
		1	Burying of Margaret Manuering the first January
		3	Burying of Robert Forest the 3 of January
		5	Burying of Emme ffletcher wif of Anthony Fletcher
		12	Burying of Margaret Tompson the 12th January
	Febru	16	Burying of Mary Sturman February the 16th
1554	May	15	Burying of Tymothy Westraw the 15th of May
	June	20	Burying of Edward Barnsdale the 20th of June
	Julie	29	Burying of Katheryne Jance July the 29th
	Octob	18	Burying of William Lawse October the 18th
	Nouem	12	Burying of Thomas Flye of Bostone Draper
		19	Burying of William Pye a water man the 19th
	Februa	29*	Burying of Thomas Heelys a porter February 29
1555	Aprill	10	Burying of Joane Westraw wif of Robert Westraw
	Julie	11	Burying of John Partridge the 11th of July
	August	18	Burying of Jane Tauernor the 18th of August
		28	Burying of John Earle the 28th daye of August
	Septem	24	Burying of Mary Pearse the 24th day of Septem.
	Octobe	3	Burying of John Wood the 3 of October Anno 55
		22	Burying of Joyce Roddes October the 22th daye
	Janua	30	Burying of John Hatte, the 30th day of Januarye
1556	Aprill	5	Burying of Alice Daldron the 5th of Aprill
		20	Burying of John Hyde, the 20th day of Aprill
	May	22	Burying of Alleyn Goldstone the 22th of Maye
	June	8	Burying of Richard Lister the 8th of June 1556
		30	Burying of Annes Chidley the 30th of June
	Julie	5	Burying of Misteris Annes Hubblethorn July ye 5
		10	Burying of Anne Gunby the 10th of Julye
	Septem	1	Burying of Thomas Goffe the first of September
	Octobe	15	Burying of John Quiby the 15th of October
		18	Burying of Syr Henry Hubblethorn Knight of London
		20	Burying of Dorothy Needam the 20th of October
	Decem	28	Burying of Jeronomy Mondye December the 28th
	Janua	20	Burying of Emme Lambe Wif of the elder Lambe
		23	Burying of Isabell Hodge: January the 23th
	Februa	3	Burying of Dorethy Satraw the 3 of February
		6	Burying of William Dolfin the elder February 6th
		6	Burying of Morgan Turberfeld, February the 6th

* Sic. The year 1554 was not a Leap Year.

Yeare.	Month.	Day.	Names.
1556	Februa	18	Burying of Roger Avery the 18th of February
	March	7	Burying of Maister Jeames Apot, March the 7th
		15	Burying of Margery Parkar, March the 15th
1557		30	Burying of John Rookesech the 30th day of March
	Aprill	4	Burying of John Medelyn, the 4th of Aprill
	May	6	Burying of Joane Allstone the 6th of Maye
	June	13	Burying of Joane Palmer the 13th of June
		28	Burying of Richard Jonson the 28th day of June
	Julie	5	Burying of Phillip Yong, the 5th daye of Julye
		12	Burying of Edward Avery the 12th day of Julye
		14	Burying of Anne Westgate the wif of John Westgate
		16	Burying of Alice Avery the 16th day of Julye
	Septem	1	Burying of John Westgate the elder, September 1
		1	Burying of Annes Cottering the first of September
		8	Burying of Annes Pearson the 8th of September
		12	Burying of John Brislye the elder the 12th daye
	Octobe	20	Burying of Thomas Lilliard October the 20th
		21	Burying of Edward Knight the 21th of October
		23	Burying of Annes Trisse the 23th of October
	Nouem	5	Burying of Lady Anne Bower Nouember 5
		21	Burying of Margery Thwaites the 21th of Nouember
		28	Burying of Frannces Nicholson the 28th of Nouember
	Janua	3	Burying of Isabell Pearsye, the 3 of Januarye
	Februa	13	Burying of Robert Hadlyn the 13th of Februarye
		16	Burying of William Euerite the 16th of Februarye
		18	Burying of Margaret Allen the 18th of February
		25	Burying of Leonard Richeman, the 25th of Februa.
		26	Burying of Harry Eyre the 26th of Februarye
		26	Burying of Richard Mathew the 26th of Februarye
1558	Maye	4	Burying of Elizabeth Gardner the 4th of Maye
	June	10	Buring* of William Jackson the 10th of June 1558
		13	Burying of William Tailor the 13th of June
		23	Burying of Margaret Leueman the 23th of June
		26	Burying of Susanne Gonne the 26th of June
	Julie	12	Burying of Isabell Willsonne the 12th daye of Julie
		15	Burying of John Aunsell the 15th of Julye
		17	Burying of A scottish man seruant to Mr Hodge
	August	15	Burying of Robert Dixon: August the 15th
		19	Burying of Annes Maddestone the 19th of August
		29	Burying of John Auskame, the 29th day of August
		31	Burying of John Gorley seriant of the Queenes house
	Septem	1	Burying of William Parker Iremonger September 1
		5	Burying of William Cut the first of September
		14	Burying of Thomas Porter the 14th of September
		15	Burying of Thomas Weller the 15th of September
		16	Burying of Luce Weller the 16th day of September
		22	Burying of Richard Leycrofte the 22th of Septembr
		23	Burying of Mary Groobbe the 23th of Septembr
		25	Burying of Richard Humphrey the 25th of Septembr
	Nouem	10	Burying of Richard Walker the 10th of Nouember
		15	Burying of Harry Hodge the 15th of Nouember

Breue tempus et irreparabile.

* Sic.

1558.

Burialles beeginning at ye raigne of our most gracious Queen Elizabeth.

Yeare.	Month.	Day.	Names.
1558	Nouem	17*	. . . .
		23	Burying of George Cutt vpon the 23th of Nouember
		24	Burying of Margaret Symmes the 24th day of Nouember
		27	Burying of Annes Burnell the 27th day of Nouember
	Decem	3	Burying of Thomas Gonne the third day of December
		16	Burying of Thomas Personne the 16th day of December
		18	Burying of Elizabeth Dowues the 18th day of December
		20	Burying of John Sturman th'elder the 20th day of December
		22	Burying of Barbara Cut the 22th of the month December
		29	Burying of Joane Cut the 29th daye of the month December
	Janua	2	Burying of Margaret Adlyn the 2 day of Januarye
		21	Burying of Edward Dytchborn the 21th of January
		23	Burying of Annes Austen the three and twentith of Janua.
	Februa	3	Burying of William Chapman Poulter the 3 of February
		3	Burying of Elizabeth Bland the 3 day of February
		10	Burying of John Hollifeeld the tenth day of February
		20	Burying of Edward Eluerington the 20th day of February
		27	Burying of Mr John Judde, the 27th day of february
	March	17	Burying of one John no parishioner his name not set doune
		19	Burying of Jeames Treaton the 19th daye of March
			SUMME—20.
1559		26	Burying of Elizabeth Vxly the 26th daye of Marche
		29	Burying of John Daulton the sonne of John Daultonne
		31	Burying of Susan Hodge daughter of Mr Hodge baker
	Aprill	4	Burying of Edward Hodge the 4th day of Aprill
		8	Burying of Katherine Sodaine the 8th of Aprill
		24	Burying of Steuen Recknoll the 24th of Aprill Anno 2°
	Maye	10	Burying of Edward Gonne the 10th of May Anno 2° Eliz.
		30	Burying of Robert Michaell the 30th of May Anno 2° Eliz.
	June	18	Burying of Rowland Hodge the 18th of June Anno 2° Regni
		30	Burying of Elizabeth Yong the 30th of June Anno 2° Regni
	Julie	6	Burying of Anne Bacon the 6th of July Anno 2° Regni
		22	Burying of William Megges the 22th of July Anno 2° Regni
		28	Burying of John Clarke the 28th of July Anno 2° Regni
		30	Burying of Mr John Richmond the 30th of Julie Anno 2° Regni
	Septem	6	Burying of Elizabeth Symondes widow the 6th of Septem.
		9	Burying of Richard Curling the 9th of September Anno

* The Register from November 17, 1558, to April 16, 1600, is subscribed Wm Asheboold parson, Robert Warden, Marke Scaliot.

Yeare.	Month.	Day.	Names.
1559	Septem	18	Burying of Margery Johnson the 18th of September Anno 2
		19	Burying of Phillip Dowson the 19th of September Anno
		21	Burying of Margery Wright the 21th of September Anno
		24	Burying of Elizabeth Wyng widow ye 24th of September Anno
	October	2	Burying of Robert Goodale the 2 of October Anno Regni Eliz.
		5	Burying of John Watkynnes the 5th of October Anno Eliz.
		5	Burying of Augustine Dumber the 5th of October Anno Eliz.
		9	Burying of Elizabeth Olliuer the 9th of October Anno Eliz. 2
	Decem	1	Burying of Edmond Elmer the first of December Anno Eliz. 2
		24	Burying of Mary Boulstone the 24th of December Anno 2°
	Februa	4	Burying of Margery Sturgion th 4th of February Anno 2°
	March	6	Burying of Richard Lamerson the 6th of March Anno 2°

SUMME OF THE YEARE—29.

1560		30	Burying of Ralph Lawse the 30th of March Anno Eliza.
	Aprill	29	Burying of Harry Lawse the 29th of Aprill Anno Eliza.
	Maye	24	Burying of Ellen Tippe the wif of Harry Tippe, the 24th day
		26	Burying of Anne Stonehouse the 26th of May Anno Eliza.
	June	26	Burying of valentine seruannt to Nicholas the Cobler
	Julie	4	Burying of Ellen Willsonne the 4th of Julie Anno Eliza.
		18	Burying of Thomas Waite the 18th of Julie Anno Eliza.
	Septem	1	Burying of Richard Allen the first of September Anno Eliz.
		6	Burying of Thomas Mase the 6th of September Anno Eliz.
	Octobe	13	Burying of Katherine Midletonne the 18th of October
			Burying of Jone Dytchborn the 14th daye of October
	Decem	4	Burying of Edward Cockes the 4th day of December
		18	Burying of Jane Haiborn the 18th of December
	Janua	3	Burying of Luce Hayward the third day of Januarye
		17	Burying of Harry Flammocke the 17th of Januarye
	Februa	23	Burying of Annes Goffe the 23th day of Februarye
	March	7	Burying of Jonas Richeman the 7th of March Anno Eliz.
		19	Burying of John Browne the 19th day of Marche

SUMME OF THE YEARE—19.

1561	Aprill	12	Burying of William Carre the 12th of Aprill Anno
		22	Burying of John Walker the 22th of Aprill Anno
	May	3	Burying of Annes Leame the 3 of Maye Anno
		17	Burying of John Cursonne the 17th of May Anno
	Julie	16	Burying of John Tomson the 16th of July Anno
		16	Burying of Margaret Recknoll the 16th of July Anno
	August	16	Burying of George Stonehouse the 16th of August
	Septem	5	Burying of Susan Butler the 6th of September
	Nouem	18	Burying of Richard Axam the 11th of Nouember
		18	Burying of Joane Coates the 18th of Nouember
		20	Burying of a still born childe of Mr Binlyes the 20th
		23	Burying of Gylbert Mader the 23th of Nouember
	Decem	31	Burying of Elizabeth Gourley, the 31th of December
		10	Burying of George Heiborn the 10th day of December
		16	Burying of Joane Jackson the 16th day of December

SUMME OF THE WHOLE YEARE—15.

THE REGISTERS OF ST. PETER'S, CORNHILL. 115

Yeare.	Month.	Day.	Names.
1562	Maye	1	Burying of William Hodge the first of May Anno
		28	Burying of Thomas Leame the 28th of May Anno
	June	1	Burying of William Lambe the first of June Anno
		6	Burying of John Dauldorn the 6th of June Anno
		25	Burying of Elizabeth Willow the 25th of June Anno
	Augu	16	Burying of Margaret Richmond the 16th of August
		8	Burying of Thomas Isharwood the 8th of August
	Septem	12	Burying of Joane Jordane the 12th of September
	Octob	3	Burying of George Hill the sonne of John Hill the 3 day
		21	Burying of Harry Tipper the 21th of October Anno
	Decem	5	Burying of Anne Hinton the 5th day of December
		7	Burying of Susan Pressie the 7th day of December
		9	Burying of Joane Pallmer the 9th of December Anno
	Janua	6	Burying of Elizabeth Hunter the 6th day of January
		7	Burying of Harry Billingslie the 7th of January
		14	Burying of Mary Mascall the 14th day of January
	March	16	Burying of Annes Heywood the 16th day of Marche
		20	Burying of John Lambe the 20th day of Marche
		21	Burying of Lawraunce Axton the 21th of Marche

SUMME OF THE WHOLE YEARE—19.

1563		24	Burying of Richard Heiwood the 24th of Marche
	May	21	Burying of William Adames the 21th of Maye
	June	1	Burying of Ellen Maunsfeeld the first of June Anno
	Julie	15	Burying of Jane Coursonne the 15th of Julye Anno
		21	Burying of Mathew Gough daughter of Mr Gough parson
		24	Burying of Susan Adlington the 24th of July Anno
		25	Burying of Mary Goodale the 25th day of Julie
	August	2	Burying of Elizabeth Plasterer the second of August
		3	Burying of Margaret Bostocke the third of August
		12	Burying of Thomas Curteys the 12th of August
		12	Burying of Ellen Johnson the 12th day of August
		18	Burying of Joane Williamson the 18th of August
		19	Burying of Ellen Personne the 19th of August
		21	Burying of Anne Steuens the 21th of August
		23	Burying of Robert Byche the 23th of August
		28	Burying of John Steuens the 28th of August 1563
		28	Burying of John Bricking the 28th of August
		30	Burying of Elizabeth Matram the 30th of August
	Septem	1	Burying of Harry Auerell the sonne of John Averell
		1	Burying of John Syngerly the first of September
		1	Burying of Augustine Cursonne the first of Septem.
		1	Burying of John Cursonne the first day of Septemb.
		2	Burying of Mary Thwaite the second of Septem.
		2	Burying of Joane Lynsay the second day of Septem.
		2	Burying of Elizabeth Edwardes the second day of Septem.
		2	Burying of Richard seruannt to Mr Hodge the 2 day
		5	Burying of Bryde Stokes the 5th daye of September
		6	Burying of Judith Stokes the 6th daye of September
		6	Burying of Richard Waylye the 6th day of September
		7	Burying of Alice Thwaite the 7th day of Septem.
		7	Burying of Elizabeth Butler the 7th day of Septem.
	Septem	9	Burying of George Bateman the 9th of Septemb.
		9	Burying of Prudence Clarke the 9th of Septembr
		10	Burying of Thomas Affenne the 10th day of Septembr
		10	Burying of Margaret Yong the wif of Mr Gregory Yong
		10	Burying of Elizabeth Dauldron the 10th of September

Yeare.	Month.	Day.	Names.
1563	Septem	12	Burying of Susan Yong daughter of M[r] Gregory Yong
		12	Burying of Hugh Lynne seruannt to M[r] Hodge
		13	Burying of Anne Jacob daughter of M[r] Jacob
		13	Burying of Thomas Ames the 13th of September
	Septem	13	Burying of Joane Chapman the 13th of September
		14	Burying of Steuen Thomsonne the 14th of Septem.
		14	Burying of Marian Daldronne the 14th of Septem.
		14	Burying of William Elkin the 14th day of September.
		14	Burying of Christopher Lambe the 14th of Septem.
		14	Burying of Jeames Sound the 14th of September
		15	Burying of Margaret Lecroft the 15th of Septem.
		15	Burying of Richard Porter the 15th of Septem.
		15	Burying of William Pepper the 15th of Septem.
		16	Burying of Elizabeth Mascoll the 16th of Septem.
		17	Burying of Thomas Borrow the 17th of September
		17	Burying of John Doodman the 17th of September
		19	Burying of Robert Wright the 19th of September
		19	Burying of William Green the 19th of September
	Septem	19	Burying of Annes Vpperhend the 19th of September
		20	Burying of Wynnefred seruaunt to M[r] Drope the 20th
		21	Burying of Martha Keely the 21th of September 63
		21	Burying of Rose Pallmer the 21th of September 63
		21	Burying of Margaret seruaunt to M[r] Pepper the 21
	Septem	23	Burying of George Hepworth the 23th of September
		23	Burying of Thomas Clarke the 23th of September
		23	Burying of Ellen Welch the 23th day of September
		23	Burying of John Clarke the 23th day of September
		26	Burying of Hugh Ashe the 26th day of September
		26	Burying of Lawrence Heyes the 26th day of September
		27	Burying of John Gough sonne of M[r] Gough Parson
		27	Burying of Elizabeth Clarke the 27th of September
	Septem	27	Burying of Ambrose Clarke the 27th day of September
		27	Burying of Elizabeth seruaunt to M[r] Beane the 27th
		27	Burying of Haunce Weuer the 27th day of September
		27	Burying of Anthonie Clarke the 27th day of September
		28	Burying of John Borrow the 28th day of September
		29	Burying of Joane Porter the 29th day of September
		29	Burying of Elizabeth Porter the 29th day of September
		29	Burying of Joane Aunswell the 29th day of September
		29	Burying of George Chapman the 29th day of September
		30	Burying of Margaret Inman the 30th day of September
		30	Burying of Susan Jackson the 30th daye of September
		30	Burying of Ralphe Sheding the 30th day of September
1563	Octobe	1	Burying of Mathew Wattam the first day of October
		1	Burying of Thomas Porter the first day of October
		1	Burying of William Page the first of October. 1563
		2	Burying of Thomas Richardsone the second of October 63
		2	Burying of Steuen Matram the second of October Anno 63
		2	Burying of John seruaunt to M[r] Lynsay the second of October
		3	Burying of Annes Hercocke the third of October Anno 63
		3	Burying of John Lister the third of October Anno Reg. 7
	Octobe	5	Burying of Edmond Bagley the 5th of October Anno
		5	Burying of John Inman the fift of October Anno 63
		7	Burying of Susan Wattam the 7th of October Anno 63
		7	Burying of John Robottam the 7th of October Anno 63
		9	Burying of John Heywood the 9th of October Anno 63

THE REGISTERS OF ST. PETER'S, CORNHILL. 117

Yeare.	Month.	Day.	Names.
1563	Octobe	9	Burying of Edward Staple the 9th of October Anno 63
		12	Burying of Katherine Ilbraine the 12th of October Anno
		12	Burying of Sara Keely the 12th of October Anno 63
		13	Burying of John Richardson the 13th of October Anno 63
		13	Burying of Robert Hunter the 13th of October Anno 63
		13	Burying of William Rigge the 13th of October Anno
		14	Burying of Vincent Badcooke the 14th of October 63
		15	Burying of John Chapman the 15th day of October 63
		15	Burying of John Chapman of the waigh house yard the *
		16	Burying of John Chapman the father the 16th of October
		16	Burying of Robert Christmas the 16th of October Anno 63
	Octobe	18	Burying of Anthonie Eastfeeld the 18th of October 63
		18	Burying of John Lister the 18th of October Anno 63
		18	Burying of Johan Heyes the 18th of October Anno 63
		19	Burying of John Cutt the 19th daye of October Anno
		19	Burying of Margery Offley the 19th of October Anno
		19	Burying of Jeames Verney the 19th of October Anno
		20	Burying of Elizabeth Eastfeeld the 20th of October Anno
		21	Burying of William Sturman the 21th of October Anno
		21	Burying of Judith Lawrence the 21th day of October Anno
		23	Burying of Lewes Richardson the 23th day of October Anno
		23	Burying of Thomas Wattam the 23th day of October Anno
		23	Burying of George Dauid the 23th day of October Anno
		24	Burying of Elizabeth Averell the 24th day of October 63
		24	Burying of Anne Dobes the 24th day of October Anno 63
		24	Burying of Elizabeth Harris the 24th of October Anno
		25	Burying of Annes Swingfeeld the 25th of October Anno
	October	25	Burying of Maudelyn Thomson the 25th of October Anno
		25	Burying of Roger Newman the 25th of October Anno 63
		26	Burying of John Burkin the 26th day of October Anno 63
		26	Burying of Robert Kendall the 26th day of October Anno 63
		27	Burying of Hugh Craft the 27th day of October Anno 63
		27	Burying of Ellen Townsend the 27th day of October Anno
		29	Burying of Symond Barbar the 29th day of October
		29	Burying of Margaret Mewes the 29th day of October
		30	Burying of Edward Gonne the 30th daye of October
		30	Burying of Mary Pallfryman the 30th day of October
		30	Burying of Annes Ilbrain the 30th daye of October
	Nouem	2	Burying of John Longshaft the second day of Nouember
		9	Burying of Margaret Wistow the 9th day of Nouember
		9	Burying of William Craft the 9th daye of Nouember
		10	Burying of Elizabeth Atkinson the 10th day of Nouember
		12	Burying of Anne Swyngfeeld the 12th day of Nouember
		13	Burying of Christopher Pepper the 13th day of Nouember
		15	Burying of Ellen Mathew the 15th daye of Nouember 63
		16	Burying of Vincent Heywood the 16th of Nouember 63
		16	Burying of Richard Walker the 16th of Nouember 63
		17	Burying of Elizabeth Thompson the 17th of Nouember
		18	Burying of Joane Sawfor the 18th day of Nouember
		18	Burying of John Cotes the 18th daye of Nouember 63
		19	Burying of Mary Walker the 19th daye of Nouember 63
		20	Burying of Elizabeth Needam the 20th of Nouember 63
		23	Burying of Richard Mathew the 23th day of Nouember
		26	Burying of Elizabeth Offly the 26th of Nouember
		28	Burying of Fraunces Mallison the 28th day of Nouember

* Sic.

Yeare.	Month.	Day.	Names.
1563	Nouem	28	Burying of Elizabeth Walker the 28th day of Nouember
	Decem	1	Burying of John seruaunt to Mr Beanes the first day
		2	Burying of William Lawse the second day of December
		3	Burying of Allice Pepper the third day of December
		5	Burying of William Laysee the 5th day of December
		8	Burying of John Eastweeke the 8th day of December
		8	Burying of Nicholas Warren the 8th day of December
		9	Burying of Gillian Wilkinson the 9th daye of December
		12	Burying of William Bellinger the 12th of December
		16	Burying of John Lambe Habberdasher the 16th day
		16	Burying of Samuell Haise the 16th day of December
		20	Burying of Hester Cootes the 20th day of December
		28	Burying of William Cootes the 28th day of December
	Janua	5	Burying of Mary Tomson the 5th day of January
		17	Burying of Harry Hutton the 17th day of January
		20	Burying of Thomas: from out Mr Daultons house
		22	Burying of Elizabeth Mascoll the 22th of January
	Februa	4	Burying of John Hancocke the 4th day of Februarye
		16	Burying of John Cootes the 16th daye of February
	March	3	Burying of Oliuer Midleton the 3 day of March 63
		6	Burying of John Hunte the sixt day of March
		7	Burying of Joan Tomson wif to Richard Tomson

SUMME OF THE WHOLE YEARE—169.

1564	Aprill	3	Burying of Rouland Johnson the third daye of Aprill 64
		6	Burying of John Hinde the syxt daye of Aprill 64
		7	Burying of Harry Bowyar the seuenth of Aprill
		27	Burying of Jeames Isharwood the 27th of Aprill
	Maye	10	Burying of Tymothy Chapman the 10th of Maye
		15	Burying of John Lambe the sonne of John Lambe the 15
	June	10	Burying of Thomas Jackson Baker the 20th June
	Julie	27	Burying of Daniell Pallmer the 27th day of Julye
	Augus:	16	Burying of Richard Hayse the 16th of August 64
		28	Burying of Gyllian Warren the 28th of August
		29	Burying of Grace Haise the 29th daye of August
	Octobe	22	Burying of a still born childe of Thomas Clarkes
		24	Burying of Allice Hodge the 24th of October
	Janua	30	Burying of a childe out of the Waigh house the 30th
	March	3	Burying of Grace Caluar the third of March 64
		19	Burying of Margaret Bucher the 19th of March
		21	Burying of William Ratting the 21th of March 64
		22	Burying of Thomas Dale the 22th of March

SUMME OF THE YEARE IS—18.

1565	Maye	12	Burying of William Richeman the 12th of Maye 65
	Juune*	16	Burying of Annes Dowsonne the 16th of June 1565
		25	Burying of John Nihell the 25th of day of June 65
	Julie	12	Burying of John Mascoll the 12th daye of Julie 65
		20	Burying of Edward Swinkfeeld the 20th day of July
	Decem	2	Burying of Zachary Caunt the second of December
		23	Burying of Joane Pagington the 23th of December
	Janua	10	Burying of Widow Heywood the 13th of January Anno 65
		17	Burying of Mr Edward Fowler the 17th daye of January
		21	Burying of Annes Borrow the 21th day of January
		24	Burying of Samuell Gough the 24th day of January

* Sic.

Yeare.	Month.	Day.	Names.
1565	Janua	25	Burying of Annes Sympsonne the 25th day of January
	March	6	Burying of Elizabeth Turner the 6th day of March
		9	Burying of Anne Chattertonne the 9th of Marche

SUMME OF THE YEARE IS—14.

1566	Aprill	8	Burying of Edward Wood the 8th daye of Aprill Anno 66
		20	Burying of Steuen Pownter the 20th of Aprill Anno 66
	Maye	28	Burying of John Dodman the 28th daye of May Anno 66
	June	22	Burying of George Merricke the 22th of June Anno 66
		23	Burying of Robert Valler the 23th of June Anno 66
	Julie	17	Burying of Thomas Wally the 17th of July Anno 66
	August	31	Burying of William Paullmer the 31th of August 66
	Septem	4	Burying of Sara Axton the daughter of Mr Axton Tailor, buryed the fourth daye of September Anno 66
	Nouem	18	Burying of Gyles Swinkfeeld the 18th day of Nouember

SUMME OF THE YEARE IS—9.

1567	March	29	Burying of John Malyn sonne to John Malyn the 29th
		30	Burying of Richard Apprice the 30th daye of Marche
	Maye	19	Burying of John Kynsman the 19th daye of Maye 67
	Julie	13	Burying of William Merricke the 13th daye of Julie
		26	Burying of Thomas Yong sonne to Anthonie Yong
	August	19	Burying of Misteris Pott Widdow the 19th of August
	Septem	28	Burying of Joane Wheeler the 28th of September
	October	30	Burying of John Inman sonne of John Inman the 30th
	Nouem	16	Burying of William Mascoll the 16th day of Nouember
	Decemb	10	Burying of John Euertonne the 10th day of December
		19	Burying of William Mease the 19th day of December
		25	Burying of Misteris Clarke widdow the 25th of Decemb.
	Januar	8	Burying of Clement Byllam wif of Mr Byllam
	Februar	14	Burying of Ambrose Harris Merchaunt the 14th
		25	Burying of a yong childe name Sara Caluar
	Marche	1	Burying of a still born childe of William Woodcocke
		16	Burying of John Gill woodpacker the 16th of Marche
		17	Burying of Joane Mericke Widdow the 17th of March

SUMME OF THE YEARE IS—10.

1568	Aprill	29	Burying of Margaret Caruet the 29th day of Aprill 68
	Maye	11	Burying of the Wif of John Brickhed the 11th of May
		21	Burying of Elizabeth Axon the 21th of Maye Anno 68
	June	13	Burying of Josua Abowen sonne to John Abowen ye 13th June
		24	Burying of Mathew Cootes the 24th daye of June 68
	Julie	29	Burying of Katherine Brislye the 29th of Julye
		31	Burying of Richard Richardson the 31th of Julye 68
	August	23	Burying of Margaret Bleache the 23th of August
	Nouem	24	Burying of Christopher a Waterman the 24th Nouem'
	Decemb	16	Burying of Elizabeth Richardsonne Wif to George Rich'
		20	Burying of Widdow Euerid the 20th of December
		30	Burying of Grizell Lynsay the 30th of December
	Januar	3	Burying of Robert Grassham the third daye of Januarye
		15	Burying of Mother Michaell widdow the 15th of Januarye
	March	13	Burying of Siluester Clarke: And of Fraunces Talmach ye 23 May

SU'ME 16.

120   THE REGISTERS OF ST. PETER'S, CORNHILL.

Yeare.	Month.	Day.	Names.
1569	June	10	Burying of Anne Tillowe the 10th daye of June 69
	Julie	9	Burying of Annes Ladbrooke y[e] 9th day of Julie Anno 69
		18	Burying of John Averell of London Joyner the 18th of Julie 69
		26	Burying of Elizabeth Treser the 26th of Julie Anno 1569
		27	Burying of Joane Knight the 27th of Julie Anno domini
		27	Burying of Misteris Flammocke widdow the 27th of Julie
		28	Burying of Joane Jance daughter of John Jance the 28th day
	August	7	Burying of Annes seruaunt to goodman Hease the 7th day
		10	Burying of John Turner the 10th daye of August the 10th*
	Septem	6	Burying of Annes Staines wif of William Staines the 6th
		10	Burying of Doritie Wroth the tenth daye of September
		12	Burying of Elizabeth Wroth the 12th daye of September
		13	Burying of Edward Cockes the 13th daye of September
		19	Burying of Thomas Butler the 19th daye of September
		19	Burying of John Richman sonne of Lenard Richeman y[e] 19th
		21	Burying of Alice Oton the 21th daye of September Anno 69
		22	Burying of Harry Snowe the 22th daye of September 69
		22	Burying of Alice Lambe daughter of Adam Lambe
		24	Burying of Harry Richman the 24th daye of September
	Octobe	1	Burying of John ffewtrell the first of October Anno 69
		2	Burying of a still born childe of Edward Walkers the 2 day
		3	Burying of Jane Haire the third day from M[r] Wrothes
		6	Burying of Susan Barnard the 6th daye of October
		14	Burying of John Daldron the elder the 14th daye of October
		21	Burying of John Thwaites the 21th day of October Anno 69
	Nouem	9	Burying of Alice Haruy the 9th daye of November 69
		11	Burying of Joane Nichollson the 11th daye of Nouember
		13	Burying of Anne Jacksonne the 13th daye of Nouember
		13	Burying of Thomas Ager the 13th daye of Nouember
	Decem	7	Burying of Elizabeth fflower the 7th daye of December
		13	Burying of Hamlet Cooke the 13th daye of December
		16	Burying of Richard Hixe tbe 16th daye of December
	Febru	25	Burying of a poore man which dyed in the streete the 25 of feb.
	March	19	Burying of Jeames Milles tbe 19th daye of Marche Anno 69
		20	Burying of Anne Jacksonne the 20th daye of Marche 1569
		20	Burying of Annes Colle the 20th day of Marche Anno
			SUMME OF THIS YEARE IS—36.
1570		29	Burying of Jeames seruannt to M[r] Jance the 29th daye
	Aprill	5	Burying of Abraham Taylor the 5th day of Aprill 1570
		9	Burying of Rosamund Milles the 9th day of Aprill 79
		29	Burying of Annes ffyner the 26th daye of Aprill Anno 70
		28	Burying of Richard ffyner the 28th daye of Aprill Anno 70
	Maye	26	Burying of a still born childe of Steuen Hailes y[e] 26th
		29	Burying of John Jouson the 29th daye of May Anno 70
	June	17	Burying of Lawrence Cosby the 17th daye of June Anno 70
	Julie	13	Burying of Katherin Watkyn the 13th day of Julye
		13	Burying of Emme Euannes tbe 13th daye of Julye
		21	Burying of John Lynsey the 21th daye of Julie
		22	Burying of Mary Pallmer the 22th of Julye
		25	Burying of John Glouer the 25th daye of Julye
		28	Burying of Thomas Rosse the 28th daye of Julye

* Sic.

THE REGISTERS OF ST. PETER'S, CORNHILL.

Yeare.	Month.	Day.	Names.
1570	August	4	Burying of Beniamin Stookes the 4th of August
		7	Burying of Thomas Thorpe the 7th day of August
		11	Burying of Joane Phillippes the 11th day of August
		11	Burying of John Hopkynnes the 11th day of August
		25	Burying of Catheryne Porter the 25th of August
		29	Burying of Thomas Morrell the 29th day of August
		31	Burying of Harry Cradle the 31th daye of August
	Septem	7	Burying of Ralph Oxley the 7th daye of September
		16	Burying of Harry Hensonne the 16th of September
	Octob	18	Burying of Anne Hill the 18th daye of October Anno
		19	Burying of George Harris the 19th day of October
	Nouem	10	Burying of George Barker the 10th day of Nouember
		22	Burying of Richard Pagington the 22th of Nouember
	Decem	22	Burying of Edward Burnam the 22th of December
		24	Burying of Mr Thomas Luntley the 24th of December
	Februa	12	Burying of Thomas Westraw Clothworker the 12th febru.
		26	Burying of John Cotts the 26th day of ffebruarye
	March	12	Burying of Edward Bleach the sonne of William
			SUMME OF THIS YEARE—32.
1571	Aprill	10	Burying of Anne Tompson the 10th of Aprill Anno 71
		26	Burying of John Adling the 26th daye of Aprill 71
		29	Burying of Robert Selman the sonne of Robert Selman
	May	4	Burying of Jeames Jennynges the 4th daye of Maye
		21	Burying of Sibell Goffe the 21th daye of Maye 71
		26	Burying of Joane Preist the 26th daye of Maye 71
		26	Burying of Alexander Sheres the 26th daye of Maye 71
	June	7	Burying of Emme Stookes the 7th day of June Anno 71
		10	Burying of John Hill Clothworker the 10th day of June
		11	Burying of Jeames Steuens sonne of Richard Steuens
	August	7	Burying of William Yong sonne of John Yong the 7th day
		19	Burying of John Mascoll Armorer the 19th of August
	Septem	10	Burying of Joseph Abowen sonne of John Abowen the 10th
		17	Burying of Harry Jefferson Girdler the 17th of Septem.
	Octobe	28	Burying of John Turner the sonne of John Turner
	Nouem	13	Burying of Mr Gardner Seriant of the Queens sellar
	Decem	26	Burying of Joane Tailer wif of Thomas Tayler
	Janua	20	Burying of John Vandenhamble a Douche man
		29	Burying of Jeames the Deuill Ducheman the 29th day
			SUMME OF THIS YEARE—19.
1572	Aprill	26	Burying of John Parker the 26th of Aprill Anno 1572
	June	19	Burying of Mr Thomas Cullimer the 19th of Aprill* Anno
		28	Burying of Alice Neale the 28th daye of Aprill* Anno
	July	18	Burying of John Malyn sonne of John Malyn the 18th
	August	17	Burying of Alice Blunt the 17th daye of August
		17	Burying of Garret Catche the 17th daye of August
		18	Burying of Robert Blunt the 18th daye of August
		18	Burying of Joan Wrenche the Wif of John Wrenche
		22	Burying of John Dowson Clothworker the 22th of August
		29	Burying of Richard Richardson the 29th day of August
		29	Burying of Andrew Hall the 29th day of August
	Septem	6	Burying of Joane Wistow the 6th daye of September
		13	Burying of Thomas Richardson the 13th daye of Septem.
		14	Burying of Ellen Dauldron the 14th daye of September

* Sic.

Yeare.	Month.	Day.	Names.
1572	Octobe	13	Burying of Elizabeth Phillippes the 13th of October
		25	Burying of Mary Vpton the 25th day of October
	Nouem	1	Burying of Annes Burnam the first of Nouember

SUMME OF THIS YEARE IS—17.

1573	Aprill	25	Burying of Rowland Hurst the 25th daye of Aprill
		26	Burying of a french Woman from Mr Cullimers
	June	1	Burying of George Fryar the first daye of June
	Julie	20	Burying of George Stonehouse at St Andrewes
		30	Burying of Adam Lambe the 30th day of Julye Anno
	Augus	1	Burying of John Maye the first of August Anno 73
		7	Burying of Annes mother Burches maide the 7th day
		11	Burying of John Clynt the 11th daye of August 1573
		24	Burying of Mary Knight the 24th daye of August
	Septem	7	Burying of Elizabeth Burche the 7th daye of Septem.
		24	Burying of William Mense the 24th of September
	Octobe	10	Burying of Thomas Sueton the 10th day of October
	Nouem	26	Burying of Allice Wendrit the 26th daye of Nouember
	Decem	23	Burying of John Wendrit the 23th daye of December
	Janua	25	Burying of Dorothy Jordan, Monday the 25th January
	Februa	16	Burying of Thomas Mayne a stranger Tuesday ye 16
		16	Burying of Edmond Nicholson the 16th of February
		18	Burying of Marrian Axon the 18th day of February
		19	Burying of John Parton the 19th day of February
	March	4	Burying of Thomas Joanes Thursday the 4th of March

SUMME OF THIS YEARE IS—20.

1574	Aprill	15	Thursday Burying of Robert Fishman the 15th of Aprill 74
		20	Burying of Alice Stone the 20th daye of Aprill Anno 74
	May	3	Burying of Annes Goulsonne the 3 of Maye being Monday
		8	Burying of William Steuens the 8th daye of Maye
		10	Burying of John Abowen the 10th daye of Maye Anno 74
	May	18	Burying of Thomas Addames the 18th daye of Maye
		30	Burying of Richard White the 30th daye of Maye Anno 74
	June	29	Burying of Mr Richard Steuens Armorer one Tuesday
	Julie	21	Burying of Jeames Nicholson Cobler one Wedensday
	August	21	Burying of Margaret Corzer wif of John Corzer Clothwor
		21	Burying of Susan Fremond daughter of John Fremond. Satterday
		30	Burying of John Cursonne sonne of Richard Curson Armorer. Mond.
	Septem	9	Burying of Mr Richard Porder parson of this Church: one Thursday
		17	Burying of Alexander Sawllmond seruant to Rowland Railton Armo:
		21	Burying of Clement Railton nephew of Rowland Railton Armorer Tues.
		26	Burying of John Carter seruaunt to Mr Fuller the 26th day
		27	Burying of Elizabeth Futrell daughter of Fraunces Futrell. Mon.
	October	5	Burying of Richard Judsonne sonne to John Judson; on Tuesday
		8	Burying of Cisly weanewright ye carters wif of ye weygh house
		9	Burying of Mrs Margaret Malyn wif of John Maliu Armo: satter:

THE REGISTERS OF ST. PETER'S, CORNHILL. 123

Yeare.	Month.	Day.	Names.
1574	October	13	Burying of Annes Kelly daughter of John Kelly. Wedensday
		14	Burying of Colly Chamberlain daughter of John Chamberlain
	Nouem	8	Burying of Joane Porter daughter to George Porter. Monday
		9	Burying of Briget Judson daughter of John Judson, one Tuesday
		13	Burying of Blanch Lockey daughter of John Lockey Satterday
		13	Burying of Robert Kelly sonne to John Kelly, the 13th daye
		14	Burying of Mr John Brizely vintner the 14th daye Sonday
		23	Burying of Robert Stokes Clarke of St Clements Eastchep. Tuesd.
	Decem	10	Burying of John Porter sonne to William Porter : fridaye
		17	Burying of a still born childe of John Smith Merchant tailor
		23	Burying of Constant Morris daugh : of Richard Morris Thursday
	Janua	23	Burying of Mary Houghton a french woman, one Sondaye
	Februa	13	Burying of Thomas Borow Clothworker the 13th day Sonday
	March	6	Burying of William Coorse sonne of John Coorse Sondaye

SUMME OF THIS YEARE IS—34

1575	Aprill	6	Burying of Annes Tibbold widow a 100 yeares old : Wedensday
	Maye	10	Burying of John Warren sonne of John Warren Armorer. Tuesday
		17	Burying of Joice Turner seruant to John Warren Armorer Tuesday
		31	Burying of a still born childe of Fraunces Dynne : Tuesdaye
	Julie	3	Burying of Anne Yong daugh. of Antony Yong Skynner. Sonday
		9	Burying of Robert Jance Poulter the 9th day being Friday*
	August	29	Burying of Walter Vpton waterman the 29th day August Monday
	Septem	7	Burying of Anne Hassall daughter of John Hassall wedensday
		7	Burying of Thomas Locksonne sonne of John Lockson Armorer
		10	Burying of Amy Clawyer seruant to Hamlet Bricket : Satterd.
		19	Burying of Mr John Hassall Mercer and Merchaunt Venturer : Monday
		19	Burying of Edward Smith sonne of John Smith Merchant tailor
		26	Burying of Joane Rutter daughter of John Rutter one Mondaye
		28	Burying of Georg Lynzey Habberdasher one Wedensdaye
	Octobe	1	Satterday Buryed Margery Lockson daughter of Richard Loxon
		3	Moonday Buryed Joyce Bricket daughter of Hamlet Bricket
		6	Thursday Buryed Joan seruant vnto John Adlington poulter

* Sic.

Yeare.	Month.	Day.	Names.
1575	Octobe	10	Sonday Buryed Hamlet Bricket Skynner the 10th day
		22	Satterday Buryed Elizabeth Hyckmote Widow the 22th
		25	Thursday Buryed Jone Chadwicke daugh: of Charles Chad:
	Nouem	7	Monday Buryed John Adlington sonne of John Adlington
		13	Sonday Buryed Mary Cut daughter of Harry Cutt
		15	Tuesday Buryed Mary Bricket daugh: of Hamlet Briket
	Decem	19	Monday Buryed Elizabeth Steward daugh: of Edward Stuard
		25	Sonday Buryed Mathew Brudges sonne of Anthony Brudges Drap^r
		26	Monday Buryed Margaret Durdant wif of Thomas Durdant
	Janua	2	Monday Buryed Richard Porter sonne of Gregory Porter
		6	Friday Buryed George Richardson sexton of this Church Clothwo^r
	Februa	5	Sonday Buryed William Coxon sonne of William Coxon
	March	5	Monday Buryed Mary Hill daughter of John Hill ye 5th
		21	Weddensday Buryed Annes Perryn Widow from Mr Maiors
		24	Satterday Buryed Joane Abowen widow the 24th of March
			SUMME OF THIS YEARE IS—32.
1576	Aprill	13	Fryday Buryed George Masonne Skynner the 13th Aprill
		30	Monday Buryed Alice Dany daugh: of Edmond Dauy
	June	23	Satterday Buryed Mr Robert Lecroft Armorer ye 23th
		25	Monday Buryed Sara Margraue daugh: of Nicholas Mar:
		27	Wedensday Buryed Owen vp Dauy ap Gryffen Tailor
	Julie	11	Wedensday Buryed a still born childe of John Beckinsalles
	August	19	Monday Buryed a still borne childe of George Gunby
		23	Thursday Buryed Elizabeth Gunby wif of George Gunby
	Septem	7	Fryday Buryed* of Awdry Seward the Widow of *
		16	Sonday Buryed Anne Blage wif of William Blago Imbrodro^r
		16	Sonday Buryed William Blage sonne of William Blage
	Nouem	18	Sonday Buryed Mathew Coxon sonne of Mathew Coxon
	Decem	16	Sonday Buryed Margery Atkinson wif of Peeter Atkinson Drape^r
		23	Sonday Buryed Anne Cleffe daughter of William Cleffe
	Februa	23	Satterday Buryed Thomas Stanly sonne of John Stanly
			SUMME OF THIS YEARE IS—15.
1577	Aprill	5	Goodfriday Buryed a still born childe of Steeuen Hailes
		8	Monday Buryed Mrs Elizabeth Luntly wif of Mr Thomas Luntly
	May	23	Thursday Buryed Susan Kelly daughter of John Kelly
		28	Tuesday Buryed Susan Axon daughter of Lawrance Axon
	June	19	Burying of a still born childe of John Smith one Wedensday
	Julie	2	Tuesday Buryed Mr Edward Cockes grocer & Merchaut ventrer
		22	Monday Buryed Judith Thwait daughter of Steuen Thwait, vintne^r
		27	Satterday Buryed Edward Cut sonne of Harry Cut ye 27th
		28	Sonday Buryed Edward Porter sonne of William Porter
		29	Monday Buryed Lawrence Axsonne Merchaunt Tailor
	August	4	Sonday Buryed Luce Axsonne daughter of Lawrence Axon
		5	Monday Buryed Dauy Joanes sonne of John ap Edwardes
		6	Tuesday Buryed Mr Oliuer Couper Clothworker
		7	Wedensday Buryed Jone Cutt daughter of Harry Cutt
		9	Friday Buryed Pheby Cutt daughter of Harry Cut

* Sic.

THE REGISTERS OF ST. PETER'S, CORNHILL. 125

Yeare.	Month.	Day.	Names.
1577	August	10	Satterday Buryed John Cutt sonne of Harry Cutt
		11	Sonday Buryed Thomas Axsonne sonne of Lawrence Axon
		15	Thursday Buryed Rachell Axsonne daughter of Lawrence Axon
		17	Satterday Buryed Robert Tibbold sonne of William Tibbold
		18	Sonday Buryed William Dilling sonne of Richard Dilling
		19	Monday Buryed Samuell Abowen sonne of John Abowen
		24	Satterday Buryed Briget Beckinsall Wif of John Bekinsall
		27	Tuesday Buryed Susan Mihell daughter of Symon Mihell
	Septem	2	Monday Buryed Mary Abowen daughter of John Abowen
		7	Satterday Buryed Daniell Abowen sonne of John Abowen
		8	Sonday Buryed Tobith Abowen sonne of John Abowen
		8	Sonday Buryed Susan Jordane daughter of Jeames Jordan
		12	Thursday Buryed Thomas More sonne of Jeames More
		14	Satterday Buryed Thomas Thompson sonne of Richard Tomson
		19	Thursday Buryed John Cooke, sonne of Robert Cooke
		20	Fryday Buryed Nem Carye daughter of Harry Carye
		21	Satterday Buryed Robert Lockson sonne of Richard Lockson
		23	Monday Buryed Margery Lockson daugh: of Richard Loxon
		30	Monday Buryed Mathy More wif of Jeames More
	Octobe	2	Wedensday Buryed Jeames More Skynner the second Octo.
		2	Wedensday Buryed Hugh Green : sonne of Richard Green
		9	Wedensday Buryed Alice Lockson daughter of Richard Loxon
		10	Thursday Buryed William Cooke sonne of Thomas Cooke
		11	Friday Buryed Nicholas Docket sonne of John Docket
		12	Satterday Buryed Thomas Lockson sonne of Richard Loxon
		14	Monday Buryed Christopher Willson sonne of John Willson
		30	Wedensday Buryed Margery Porter daug: of Frances Porter
	Nouem	26	Tuesday Buryed Harry West: sonne of John West the 26th
	Decem	16	Monday Buryed Mr William Barbor Baker Aldermans Deputy
		22	Sonday John Plummer Tailor the 22th daye
	Janua	3	Friday Buryed of* Mr Gilbert Satchfeld Baker
		6	Monday Buryed Griphin Ap Thomas, the 16th of Janua.
	Februa	1	Satterday Buryed Jesper Vandeleare born in Anwarp
		16	Sonday Buryed Dauy Gittens of London Draper
		24	Moneday Buryed Valentine Tompson sonne of Christopher Tom.
		25	Tuesday Buryed John Haddon a Porter the 25th day
	March	1	Satterday Buryed Nicholas Sturman sonne of John Sturman
		2	Sonday Buryed Margery Rayman Widdow the second day
		14	Friday Buryed Doggon Jones sonne of Euan Jones

SUMME OF THIS YEARE IS—54.

1578	March	.28	Buryed a still born childe of John Smithe, Merchant Tailor
		31	Monday Buryed Ellen Smith wif of th'afore said John Smith
		31	Monday Buryed Maudelyn Frezingfeld widow the 31th day
	Aprill	10	Thursday Buried Mr Edward Ellerington her Maties pentioner
		13	Sonday Buryed Alice Mager daughter of William Mager
		14	Monday Buryed Jeames Benet Clothworker the 14th
	Maye	2	Friday Buryed Katherine Billing daughter of John Billing
		8	Thursday Buryed Ellen Corzer daughter of John Corzer

* Sic.

Yeare.	Month.	Day.	Names.
1578	Maye	24	Satterday Buryed John Wilkinson Sy^r Rowland Clarkes se^{r}uant
	Julie	2	Wedinsday Buryed Steuen Yong sonne of Mr Gregory Yong
		6	Sonday Buryed Margaret Averell Widow of John Averell Joyne^r
		12	Satterday Buryed Nicholas Sporling Mr Gregory Yonges seruant
	August	1	Fryday Buryed Mrs Mary Walthall wif of Mr William Walthall Merce^r
		8	Friday Buryed Ellen Cranaway daughter of Thomas Cranaway
		14	Thursday Buryed George Boghhan sonne of Robert Boghhan
		20	Wednesday Buried John Foden sonne of William Foden
		22	Friday Burying of Mathias Marsball the 22th day Friday
		23	Satterday Buryed John Wickham the 23th day of August
		26	Tuesday Buryed Joane Granger daughter of Symon Grange^r
		27	Wedinsday Buryed Richard Richardes sonne of Dauye Richardes
		28	Thursday Buryed Margery Sanly* daughter of John Stanley
	Septem	4	Thursday Buryed Richard Faith sonne of Thomas Faith
		8	Monday Buryed Joan Steuens daugh: of John Steuens
		10	Wednesday Buryed John Hunt sonne of Robert Hunt
		27	Satterday Buryed Thomas Atkins sonne of John Atkins
	October	5	Sonday Buryed Thomas Fables a stafford shire man
		8	Wedinsday Buryed John Smith Merchaunt Taylor
		9	Thursday Buryed Elizabeth Wright daugh: of Edward Wright
		11	Satterday Buryed Margery Spence daugh: of Fraunces Spence
		20	Monday Buryed Mary Yong daugh: of Gregory Yong Grocer
		20	Monday Buryed Cisly Currant seruant of Widow Cosby
		22	Wedinsday Buryed Mrs Anne Palphreman wif to Mr Thomas Pal: of ye Chapell
	Nouem	4	Tuesday Buryed William Tibbold sonne of William Tibbold
		4	Tuesday Buryed Joane seruant vnto William Tibbold
		9	Sonday Buryed Richard Franklyn seruant to Thomas Daldron
		11	Tuesday Buryed Mrs Agatha Cockes once wif of Mr Edward Cockes Grocer
		12	Wedinsday Buryed Mrs Joan Lambert wif of Mr Lambert
	Decem	22	Monday Buryed Anne Cockes daugh: of Harry Cockes Clothwo^r
	Janua	11	Sonday Buryed a still born childe of Jeames Jordane Porter
		12	Monday Buryed Robert Cotton sonne of George Cotten Groser
		29	Thursday Buryed Edward Goffe sonne of Lawrence Goffe Drape^r
		30	Friday Buryed John Berryman sonne of Wm Beryman seruant to Mr Goffe
	Februa	5	Thursday Buryed Mr Edward Atkinson Purueyor of ye Queens Wines
		6	Friday Buried Elizabeth Worrall daughter of Mr John Worrall

* Sic.

Yeare.	Month.	Day.	Names.
1578	Februa	8	Sonday Buryed Margaret Allam ye widow of Fraunces Allam
		16	Monday Buryed a still born childe of Thomas Thorp Grocer

SUMME OF THIS YEARE IS—46.

1579	March	29	Sonday Buryed Mr Richard Adams Mercer, hee dyd ye 27th day 75 yeares old
	Aprill	1	Wedensday Buryed Wm Dowlphin sonne of Wm Dolphin 90 yeares old
		10	Friday Buryed Susan Stanly daughter of John Stanly Draper
	Maye	16	Satterdaye Buryed a still borne childe of George Bartleye
	June	12	Friday Buryed Thomas Haukes sonne of John Haukes; in ye south chapell
		15	Monday Buryed Robert Gardner sonne of Mr Thomas Gardne^r, 3 yeares old
	Julie	22	Wednesday Bu: William Porter sonne of Wm Porter Clothworke^r 14 wekes old
	Augus	27	Thursday Buryed Mrs Margery Avenon wif of Mr Alisander: 26 yeares old
	Decem	22	Tuesdaye Mrs Anne Adames widow, late wif of Mr Richard Adames Merce^r: 66 yeares
		22	Tuesday, a still borne Childe of George Cotton Grocer, ye 22th day
		23	Wedensday, Jeames Stanly sonne of John Stanly draper, 5 weekes old
	Janua	7	Thursday Buryed a still born childe of Edward Atkinson, Merchant tailo^r
		29	Friday Elizabeth a poore creature dying in ye streetes lousye 40 yeares old
	Februa	1	Monday Dauy vp Beuan sonne of Beuan vp Dauy Mr Smithes man. 30 yeares
		11	Thursday Edward Walker Carpenter of th'age of 51 yeares
	March	9	Wedensday Elizabeth Kynnaston daugh: of John Kynnaston. 14 yeares

SUMME OF THIS YEARE IS—17.

1580	Maye	5	Elizabeth Gunby daugh: of George Gunby scriuene^r 8 dayes old
		30	Monday Margery Wilson daughte^r of Daniell Wilson; a day old
	Julie	2	Satterday John Abowen white baker, dying of the stone 63 yeares old
		9	Satterday Ellen Cooke wif of Richard Cooke seruing man 53 yeares old
		10	Sonday William Preston sonne of Richard Preston of 34 yeares age
		11	Monday John Hollywell Skynner, he dyed being 85 yeares old
		12	Tuesday Mrs Grace Phillip wif of Mr Thomas Phillip, Grocer 44 yeares old
		13	Wedinsday Phillip Wattam sexton of this church, he dyed 55 yeares old
		20	Wednesday Mr Richard Bright of Loth in Lincolnshire, from ye spred Egle. 36 yeares
		22	Friday Judith King daugh: of Richard King Grocer. 18 months 8 dayes old

Yeare.	Month.	Day.	Names.
1580	August	14	Sonday Buryed a still borne childe of Richard Westwood Merchant taylo^r
	Septem	8	Thursday Buryed a still born childe of John Dixon Armorer. a sonne
		23	Friday a still borne childe of Jeames Jordane Porter of ye waigh house
	Octobe	1	Satterday Jeames Commyn sonne of Robert Commyn Tanne^r 7 yeares old
		8	Thursday Thomas Jones sonne of Thomas Jones Grocer. 18 monthes old

SUMME OF THE YEARE IS—15.

1581	Aprill	23	Sonday Susan Androwes daugh: of Robert Androes Goldsmith. a month old
	June	5	Monday Jone Corzer daugh: of John Corzer Clothworker. 10 yeares old
		9	Friday. Buryed a still borne childe of John Bryant Merchant tailo^r
		14	Wednesday. Mrs Jone Rayment wif of John Rayment, th'elder, purueyo^r. 56 yeares
		21	Wednesday. Richard Willy sonne of Richard Willy Grocer 20 monthes old
		27	Tuesday Mrs Dionise Wroth wif of Mr William Wroth Mercer. Yeares 54
		28	Wednesday Buryed a still born childe of Georg Cotton Grocer
	Julie	25	Tuesday Buryed Johu Green from Richard Bondes vintne^r yea^res 18
	August	1	Tuesday Mr Jeames Haruy Iremonger, & merchant from John Malins. 50
		11	Friday Margaret Warner daughter of Robert Warner, from Chattertons 25
		15	Tuesday William Hippy sonne of John Hippy Wooll winder. yeares 3
		15	Tuesday Elizabeth Stanton daugh: of John Stanton Gyrdler. yeares 16
		15	Tuesday Susan Dowson daugh: of John Dowson Clothworker. yeares 17
		26	Satterday Elizabeth Blage daugh: of Wm Blage cuntryman: yeares 24
		31	Thursday Barnaby Stanley sonne of John Stanly Draper of yeares 3
	Septem	4	Monday Anne Holland daugh: of John Holland of Lodlow, of yeares 24
		4	Monday John Gyrling sonne of Robert Gyrling, from John Stanly years 24
		5	Tuesday, John Day from Mr Dauldrons, hee dyed being of yeares 23
		10	Sonday Agatha Gold daughter of Mr Hugh Gold Grocer, her years 4
		10	Sonday Elizabeth Mager, daugh: of William Mager Merchant Tailo^r 14
		10	Sonnay Mrs Anne Parker, Widow of Mr John Parker Grocer, bur: in ye south chapell
		15	Friday Jane Trase daugh: of William Trase Cooke, from Fodens of yeares 18

THE REGISTERS OF ST. PETER'S, CORNHILL.

Yeare.	Month	Day.	Names.
1581	Septem	15	Friday Alice More daugh: of William More of Oxford, of the age of 17
		16	Satterday Alice Hill daughter of John Hill Clothworker being of years 11
		19	Tuesday Friz Stanly daughter of John Stanly Draper of yeares 7
		19	Tuesday Phillip Steuens sonne of Richard Steuens Armorer of years 15
		20	Wedensday Fraunces Cornelis daugh: of Jerom Cornelis Joyner years 3
		22	Friday Katherine Yong, daugh: of Robert Yong of Bristow of yeares 13
		24	Sonday Joane Pennelton daugh of Wm Pennelton of Shropshire, years 21
		25	Monday William Dethicke sonne of Wm Dethicke alias Yorke Herrold ye^{r}s 3
		27	Wedensday Annes Green daughter of William Green of Suffolk years 19
		29	Friday Grace Hill daughter of John Hill Clothworker, her years 13
	October	1	Sonday Robert Walton sonne of Richard Walton of Yorke his years 24
		20	Friday Robert Malison laborer to ye Chamber, he dyed of a fall from a lader. 74
	January	31	Wedensday Mr Robert Chatterton Fishmonger: purueyor of ye Queens Wines

SUMME OF THE YEARE IS—35.

1582	Maye	6	Sonday Mrs Elizabeth Thomas wif of Mr Thomas, Mercer, in ye south ile. 30
		15	Tuesday a still born child of William Hartridge Draper: in ye east yard
		19	Satterday George Cotton Grocer, of a consumption, lying in ye new cros ile 33
	June	12	Tuesday Richard Meredith sonne of Dauy Meredith, from Wistoe's west yard. 23
	August	25	Satterday Ellen Harwood daughter of Patrike Harwood of ye plague. yers 10
		25	Satterday Nicholas Adlington sonne of John Adlington poulter, of ye plague. 7
		28	Tuesday Melchisedecke Bennet poulter, of a surfet: bu: in ye south ile. yers 31
	Septem	2	Sonday William Lyne sonne of John Lyne; hee dyed of ye plague. yers 29
		8	Satterday William Fisher sonne of William Fisher, he dyed of ye plague, 10
		9	Sonday Margery Rayment daughter of John Rayment the yong^r a day old
		12	Wedensday Ellen Kynnaston daughter of William Kennaston her yeares 15
		13	Thursday Katherine Androw wife of Godfry Androw, of an agew yers 46
		15	Satterday Susan Goodale daug: of Robert Goodale Brownbaker, in ye south ile. 23
		15	Satterday Jane Painter daugh. of Nicholas Painter, bu: in ye west yard 16

s

Yeare.	Month.	Day.	Names.

1582, Septem, 16 — Sonday Debora Payne daugh: of William Payne, bu: in ye west yard. 7

17 Monday Paule Scaliot sonne of Marke Scaliot Blacke Smith, in ye new ile, old 5 yeares

25 Tuesday Richard Wright dwelling with Mr Mager, he dyed of ye plague at Coxons. 18

29 Satterday Elizabeth Averell daughter of William Averell Merchant tailo^r 2

30 Sonday Thomas Preest Bricke Layer, hee lyeth in ye west yard, years 82

Octobe 1 Monday John Swan sonne of Libeus Swan husbandman, in ye west yard 20

1 Monday Elizabeth Watson daugh: of John Watson in Bedford shire weue^r 19

8 Monday Marke Scaliot sonne of Marke Scaliot Blacke Smith, in ye new ile 6

9 Tuesday Alice Bayly widow from Mr Edward Cauntes; In ye Library 60

15 Monday William Lister sonne of John Lister, Barbor, of 2 Yeares 3 q^rt^rs

17 Wedensday Isacke Rodemaker sonne of John Rodemaker ducheman, of yeares 5

19 Friday Anne Rodemaker daugh: of John Rodemaker duchman, of yeares 10

22 Monday Abraham Rodemaker, sonne of John Rodemaker ducheman, his Yeares 8

26 Friday Sarah Morgraue daugh: of Nicholas Morgraue Merchant Tailor. Yeares 6

29 Monday Jone Worthington daugh of John Worthington cuntryman. Yeares 17

31 Wedensday Harry Portas sonne of Wm Portas a captain, being of Yeares 19

Nouem 9 Friday Cadwallader Robertes Baker, from John Malens Armorer. Yeares 30

11 Sonday John Clarke sonne of John Clarke, hee dyed of the plague. Yeres 22

17 Satterday, a still born child of John Rodemaker duchman; from Lynzeys

24 Satterday John Rodemaker duchman, from Lynzeys, of the plague

28 Wedensday Robert Bennet sonne of Melchisedecke Benet poulter: Yeares 2 & half

Decem 3 Monday John Walker sonne of Edward Walker Carpenter, of Yeares 6

5 Wedensday Georg Hartridge sonne of Mr John Hartridge of Crambrooke. Yeares 24

7 Friday Anne Randoll wif of John Randoll Draper sexton, being of yers 36

14 Friday John Hill sonne of Jeames Hill cuntryman, hee was of Yeares 46

Januar 28 Monday Thomas Vyner sonne of Harry Vyner Mercer, being of Yeares 20

28 Monday Hugh Mosse sonne of Richard Mosse, hee dyed of ye plague. Years 20

Februa 12 Tuesday Peeter Lister sonne of John Lister Barbor, of Yeares 5

THE REGISTERS OF ST. PETER'S, CORNHILL.

Yeare.	Month.	Day.	Names.
1582	March	9	Satterday Margaret Androes daughter of Robert Androes goldsmith 4
		10	Sonday Robert Bryan sonne of John Bryan Taylor, of Yeares 3

SUMME OF THE YEARE IS—44.

1583		27	Wedensday Catherine Bale daugh: of William Bayle, of Yeares 14
	Aprill	3	Wedensday Elizabeth Warren daughter of John Warren Armore^r, old dayes 10
		16	Tuesday Drew Hewat sonne of Nicholas Hewat, from John Malens. Yeares 30
		30	Tuesday Alice Nicholson widow of Jeames Nicholson: being of Yeares 63
	Maye	5	Sonday John Gylder, hee dyed at Coxons of the collicke and stone. Yeares 60
		9	Thursday Alice Hudson wif of William Hudson Brewer, of Yeares 60
		14	Tuesday Mr Fraunces Lambert Grocer, M^r of the weigh house, of Yeares 70
		17	Friday Catherine Parchment daugh: of Peeter Parchment Weuer 7
		19	Sonday John Inman of London Draper and hosier, being of yeares 63
		21	Tuesday Harry White, sonne of Harry White, from Watsons, Yeares 14
		27	Monday Jerome Cornelis Joyner, hee dyed of the plague. Yeares 38
	June	11	Tuesday John Cornelis sonne of Jerome Cornelis Joyner, being old weekes 6
	Julie	23	Tuesday William Ball of London Gyrdler, hee dyed being of yeares 82
		24	Wedensday Mrs Joane Wodford wif of Mr Gamaliell Wodford Grocer, & m^{r}chant 28
	Septem	22	Sonday Gregory Jones soone of Thomas Jones Grocer, being of years 3
		23	Monday Thomas Walthall sonne of Mr William Walthall Mercer, being old wekes 10
		25	Wedensday Grace Mager daughter of John Mager, beeing of yeares 11
	October	4	Friday Mr Foulke Heath Skynner, he lyeth buryed vnde^r ye co'munion table 54
		11	Friday Anne Burch daughter of John Burch, being of ye age of 18
		30	Wedensday Celitie Lipson a duch maide daugh: of Peeter Lipson 19
	Nouem	13	Wedensday Thomas Ireland Bacheler, out of Mr Heathes, of years 24
	March	8	Sonday Foulke Phillip sonne of Thomas Phillip Grocer five yers 3 q'ters
		9	Monday John Hassall sonne of Perciuall Hassall sckynner, 2 yeares a q'ter
		13	Friday Cibell Burnam widow of Clement Burnam, of yeares 40
	March	18	Wedensday a still born childe of William Averell Merchaunt Tailor

SUMME OF THIS YEARE IS—25.

Yeare.	Month.	Day.	Names.
1584	Aprill	9	Thursday Amery Marten, widow, of Wilsdon; from Edward Hunters. yers 80
		22	Wedensday John Gold sonne of Mr Hugh Gold Grocer, 5 Yeares & a quarte^r
	Maye	5	Tuesday Richard Gold sonne of Mr Hugh Gold Grocer. 5 yeare a qua^{r}ter
		5	Tuesday John Crant sonne of John Crant Haberdasher, 4 daies old
		11	Monday William Sturman sonne of Richard Sturman Fishmonger 3 yeares d'
		12	Tuesday Phebe Gold daughter of Hugh Gold grocer, 4 yeares 4 monthes
		13	Wedensday John Reuses sonne of Edward Reuses yeoman, seruant to Willis 14
		18	Monday Adrian Bromly daugh: of Wm Bromly poulter; 3 yeres 4 mouth
		19	Tuesday Margaret Gold daugh: of Mr Hugh Gold, 2 Yeares 11 monthes
	Julie	7	Tuesday William Watson sonne of Barnaby Watson Tailor 4 years d'
		28	Tuesday William Foden Inholder, at ye platter, pit in ye south ile years 48
	August	9	Sonday Katherin Jones daugh: of Thomas Jones Barbo^r, of Yeares 5
	Septem	17	Thursday William Lewkner sonne of Mr Edward Lukner Esquire, north ile 26
	Octobe	1	Thursday Edward Gold sonne of Mr Hugh Gold grocer, one Yeare & half
		4	Sonday Robert Noble sonne of Thomas Noble of Lyncolnshire, of yers 22
		10	Satterday John Titlow, a M^r porter of ye weygh house, pit in north ile 52
		14	Wedensday Thomas Mansfeld sonne of Thomas Mansfeld, wheell write 14
		30	Friday Phillip Stodderd, Tailor, from ye platter, pit in the west yard yers 49
	Nouem	1	Sonday Thomas Dowle a seriant, of an impostume, pit in ye east yard 42
		2	Monday Mrs Margaret Hodge Widow of Mr Ric. Hodge baker. in mid ile 62
		13	Friday Walter Hancocke sonne of John Han: from Loxons ally, of ye plague 20
		14	Sat: a still born childe of Jacamine Sadler a harlot, got by one Purret lite^{r}man
	Decem	14	Monday Anne Malison Widow of Robert Malison labore^r, pit in west yard 68
	Janua	10	Sonday Elizabeth Sutton daug: of John Sutton Carpente^r. a year & d'
	March	26	Friday an Infant of Jone Percifall a harlot, seruant to Wm Hartridge. west yard

SUMME OF THE YEARE IS—25.

1585	Maye	2	Sonday Jone Segers widow of one Segers of Pittam, from Popes; yers 61
	June	9	Wedensday Elizabeth Gunby wif of George Gunby: in child bed; north ile 29

THE REGISTERS OF ST. PETER'S, CORNHILL. 133

Yeare.	Month.	Day.	Names.
1585	Julie	1	Thursday a still born childe of William Hartridge Draper, East yard
		17	Satterday Alice Masson daugh: of John Masson, from Fryers: west yard 16
		30	Friday Wynefred Hayes late Wif of Edward Hayes Joyner, pit in mid ile 43
	August	3	Tuesday Blanch Robinson daugh: of Rich: Robinson, from Fryers skynne^r 3
		5	Thursday William Robinson sonne of Richard Robinson Skynner: of yeares 6
		9	Monday John Rayment sonne of John Rayment ye yonger a poulte^r. yers 6 & half
		19	Thursday John Bently one of ye Queens players, pit in ye north ile. yers 32
		24	Tuesday Fraunces Heath sonne of Thomas Heath of a pluresie—from Fryars 19
	Septem	12	Sonday John Warren Armorer, of the plague, his pit in ye west yard. 50
		21	Tuesday Katheryn Williames daugh: of Harry Williames, west yard. 19
		27	Monday, John Grey Merchant, from Wm Dales, bur: at ye new church yard: yers 52
	October	3	Sonday Randoll Orton Tailor of ye plague from Warrens house: East yard 32
		23	Satterday Maudlyn Powell daug: of Dauy Powell merchant tailor iij quarters old
		30	Satterday Elizabeth Orton daug: of Randoll Orton, pit in ye west yard yers 2
	Nouem	2	Tuesday Edward Skolding sonne of John Skolding yeman, from Galles yers 20
		5	Friday Robert Burnam sonne of Clement Burnam baker, from John Moris 19
		12	Friday Thomas Gall, Draper, sonne of Robert Gall: pit in the south chapple 30
		20	Satterday a still born childe of Harry Tompson Grocer, pit in ye east yard
	Decem	2	Thursday, Rowland Railton Armorer, pit in the myd ile, vper end. Yeares 38.
		30	Thursday Christian Crow daugh: of John Crow Inholder in Norfolke, west yard. 22
	Janua	1	Satterday Mary Jordan daugh: of Robert Jordan Poulter, pit in ye west yard 17
		11	Tuesday Mrs Elizabeth Barbor widow of Mr Wm Barbor Baker, pit in ye quire 71
	Februa	12	Satterday Katherin Allin daugh: of Thomas Allin carpenter, a yeare & a half
		13	Sonday Fraunces Gunston daugh: of Robert Gunston Inholder, beeing of yers 4
		28	Monday Grace Bryan daugh: of John Bryan Armorer, three dayes old
	March	15	Tuesday Mr Richard Hodge white Baker, hee dyed ye 11th day, pit in ye mid ile. Yers 85

SUMME OF THE YEARE IS—28.

| 1586 | Aprill | 8 | Friday Mr Richard Pingle Mercer, his pit in the mid ile ye vpper end, yeares 46 |

Yeares.	Month.	Day.	Names.
1586	Maye	24	Tuesday Jone Chaunce daugh: of Adam Chaunce cuntry man, of Yeares 24
		29	Sonday John Dauis from St Katherine Colmans his pit in the north chapell 66
	June	27	Monday Mrs Anne Satchfeeld widow of Mr Gilbert Satchfeld Baker. Yeares 59
	Julie	16	Satterday Martingue Billowis daug: of Peeter Billowis duchman: 6 dayes old
		20	Wedensday Mrs Fraunces Barnard wif of Libeus Barnard Mercer in ye west yard 64
	August	23	Tuesday Walter Stodderd sonne of Phillip Stodderd Tailor, in ye west yard yers 2 di
		23	Tuesday Barnard Lambe Draper, pit in the library: his yeares were 59
	Septem	1	Thursday William Satchfeld bachelor soonne of Gilbert: whitebaker: in north ile 27
		11	Sonday Annes Newman daug: of Mr Thomas Newman, a maiden of yers 38
		23	Friday a still born childe of John Sutton Carpenter, pit in ye west yard
	Octobe	30	Sonday Libeus Barnard Mercer of a burning agew, pit in ye west yard yers 66
	Nouem	6	Sonday Gyllam de vleskchawer of Gaunt; from ye weigh house, pit in ye library 46
		7	Monday Elizabeth Clifton daug: of Wm Clifton cuntryman, from Mr Palphremans 19
		9	Wedensday Elizabeth Richmond widow of Wm Richmond Armore^r: in ye east yard. 51
	Januа	7	Satterday a still born childe of William Ratsdale of London Brewer
	Februa	3	Friday Mrs Margaret Caunt, late wif of Mr Edward Cant Fishmon: south chapell 66
		22	Wedensday Elizabeth Busbey daugh: of John Busby merchant Tailor, one day old

SUMME OF THE YEARE IS—18.

1587	Aprill	4	Thursday Robert Coueny Fishmonger, from Mr Wrothes, pit in ye west yard yers 60
		15	Satterday Anne Turke late wif of Harry Turke, shomaker; from Birchenshas 30
		26	Wedensday Thomas Jones sonne of Thomas Jones Grocer, west yard. yeares 3
		30	Sonday Richard Byrd sonne of Wm Byrd cuntryman, from Wardens. yeares 3.
	Maye	7	Sonday John Slake a rogue: hee dyed in Grasse street at Leden hall: west yard 16
		11	Tuesday* Alice West late wif of Thomas West, husband man, from Mr Moris 32
		23	Tuesday Martha & Ellen Cage twynnes of Anthony Cage Draper, from Euans. 13 daies.
	June	8	Thursday Robert Nicholson sonne of Edward Nicholson cuntryman: pit libra yers 26
		10	Satterday Annes Scot widow, shee dyed beeing of the age of seuenty yers

* Sic.

Yeare.	Month.	Day.	Names.
1587	June	11	Sonday Gesper Graffam sonne of John Graffam Grocer; pit west yard 30
		12	Monday Robert Jordan Poulter, his pit in the north ile beeing of yeares 72
		15	Thursday Daniell Bellowis sonne of Peeter Bellowis duchman, 14 dayes old
		16	Friday a still born childe of John Satchfeld white Baker, pit in ye east yard
		21	Wedensday Richard Bond vintner sonne of John Bond, pit in ye mid ile 36
		24	Satterday John Adlington Poulter, his pit in the myd ile, his yeares 50
	Julie	9	Sonday Nicholas Ouerton sonne of Wm Ouerton of Yarmoth, pit west yard 35
		9	Sonday William Hill Stationer son of Wm Hill from Oliuer Coopers years 24
		10	Monday William Maier Merchant Tailor, his pit in the mid ile aboue 68
		11	Tuesday Thomas Gold sonne of Mr Hugh Gold grocer ye pit in ye mid ile. yers 8
		15	Satterday a still born childe of Thomas Tailor Tallow Chandler
		22	Satterday Richard Hubberd sonne of John Hubberd born in Harby in Lecester 22
		27	Thursday Katherin Wiges late wif of Wm Wiges, her pit in the west yard 24
		31	Monday a still born Childe of Thomas Allins Carpenter, pit in ye east yrd
	August	5	Satterday Alice Allen wif of Thomas Allen Carpenter, pit in ye south ile 30
		20	Sonday William Porter Clothworker, his pit in the East yard, his yeres 74
	Septem	4	Monday Tymothy Heard sonne of John Heard Bucher, his pit in ye west yard 19
		10	Sonday Jone Tibbold wif of Wm Tibbold Dyer, her pit in the east yard, yers 21
		14	Thursday John Busbey Merchant Tailor sonne of John Busby of Oxford 39
		15	Friday Mrs Margaret Hodgson late wif of Wm Hodgson Skynner, in ye mid ile 29
		15	Friday Alice Bricket daugh : of George Bricket cuntryman; in ye west yard 22
		20	Wedensday Jeames Randoll sonne of John Randoll Draper, in ye belfry. one year d'
		25	Monday Rooke Hayward sonne of Hugh Heyward, from Bromlyes: west yard 20
		26	Tuesday Katherin Presson a maiden daughter of John Presson from Mascoll 88
		27	Wedensday Jone Burchenshaw daug: of Rouland Burchenshaw Draper 28
	Nouem	2	Thursday Richard Paulmer sonne of John Paulmer wooll winder: from Mascols 20
		9	Thursday Ralfe Bird sonne of Harry Bird white baker, pit in ye west yard yers 24
	Decem	21	Thursday Margery Hyne daugh : of William Hine laborer, pit in ye west yard
	Februa	8	Thursday William Crow of a consumption, from Mr Goffes, pit in ye west yard yers 91

Yeare.	Month.	Day.	Names.
1587	March	12	Tuesday Mrs Anne Madocke late wif of Mr John Maddocke Salter, pit in ye east yard 60

SUMME OF THIS YEARE IS—39.

1588	Aprill	20	Satterday Samuell Appelby sonne of Wm Appelby cuntryman, pit in ye east yard 4
	Maye	4	Satterday Jone Inman daugh: of Jeames Inman cuntryman, a mayd. in west yard 46
		13	Monday Thomas penny batcheler sonne of John Penny cuntryman, in west yard 21
	June	20	Thursday Elizabeth Holliwell widow of John Hollywell Skynner, pit in ye east yard 94
		29	Satterday Eue Delasse daugh: of Nicholas Delas duchman, pit in ye west yard 22
	August	19	Monday William Milles sonne of Tobith Milles cuntryman, beeing of Yeares 4
		22	Thursday Giles Esfeld botcher duchman of ye yellow iau'dice, pit in ye west yard 82
	Septem	27	Friday a still borne childe of John Rayman yonger, poulter, pit in ye west yard
	October	10	Thursday Catherin But daugh: of John But Costermonger, from Corbetes court 30
		17	Thursday Joyce Taylor wif of Nicholas Taylor Tallow Chandler: west yard 47
		28	Monday Richard Androes sonne of Mathew Androes cuntryman: west yard 17
	Nouem	11	Monday Annes Robinson daugh: of Marke Fryar Skynner, pit in ye south ile yeres 28
		21	Thursday Anne Smith daugh: of Wm Smith Poulter, pit in ye west yard. yeares 3
		30	Satterday Anne Hunter daugh: of Thomas Hunter, Fishmonger. west yard 19
	Decem	3	Tuesday Mr Richard Baynes Merchant of the Staple, pit in ye south Chapell yers 56
		5	Thursday Anne Frizingfeld a mayden daug: of John Friz: haberdasher: west yard 68
	Janua	8	Wedensday Symon Busby sonne of John Busby cuntryman; from Mr Wodfords 22
		26	Sonday a still born childe of Richard Willy of London Grocer
	March	4	Tuesday William Sauage a father of great Yeares from ye spread Egle 93
		25	Tuesday Richard Sturman Fishmonger, his pit is in the Library. yers 39

SUMME OF THE YEARE IS—20

1589	Aprill	1	Tuesday Jeames Williames, an old soldier, from Corbetes court: west yard 70
		2	Wedensday Ellis Walmesly a packer, from Corbetes court, pit in west yard 73
		3	Thursday Alice Turner widow of Richard Turner a smith of ye cuntry 88
		5	Satterday Jeames Hodge white Baker, his pit in the midle ile, his yeres 37
	May	3	Satterday Mrs Mary Atkinson widow of Mr Edward Atkinson, Merchant tailor 77
	Julie	31	Thursday Margery Watlam widow of Phillip Watlam late sexton heare 72

THE REGISTERS OF ST. PETER'S, CORNHILL. 137

Yeare.	Month.	Day.	Names.
1589	Septem	16	Tuesday Nicholas Tailor Tallow Chaundler, his pit in the East yard. yeares 30
	Octobe	1	Wedensday Mr Humphrey Smith Esquire. Justice of peace, his pit and coat armo^r in ye quire 58
		14	Tuesday Mrs Luce Hassall wif of Mr Perciuall Hassall Skynner, in north ile : years 39
		20	Monday Peeter van Aske duchman, from ye weighhouse : pit in the east yard 45
	Decem	11	Thursday Mr Thomas Palphreman Esquire synger in ye Queenes Chappell : mid ile 77
		13	Satterday John Lister Barber : of an impostume, his pit in the east yard yeres 50
		20	Satterday Thomas Munke sonne of George Munke of Burntwood, in ye library 22
	Februa	2	Monday Jeames Hodge sonne of Jeames Hodge Tallow Chandler, pit, mid ile, a yea^r 3 q'
	March	16	Monday Mrs Anne Hammersly late Wif of Mr Wm Ham'ersly, Fishmonger : south ile 67

SUMME OF THE YEARE IS—15.

1590	May	13	Wedensday Mrs Susan Thrower wif of Robert Thrower vintner, in ye mid ile 23
		17	Sonday Margaret varne, wif of John varne Grocer ; her pit in the east yard 54
		24	Sonday Thomas Cooper Armorer, hee dyed of a consumption, pit in ye east yard 58
	June	1	Monday Roger Finard Goldsmith a sumner of Canterbury court : being of yers 76
		4	Thursday Marke Wardman sonne of William Wardman cuntryman, from Throers 24
		4	Thursday John Toomes sonne of John Toomes Haberdasher, in ye west yard : old daies 6
	Julye	2	Thursday John Lynsey Armorer, of the Strangury, hee dyed being of yeares 68
		16	Thursday a still born childe of Thomas Kynnaston Merchant Tailor
		21	Tuesday Margaret Marrow daughter of George Marow Carpenter one yeare old.
		24	Friday Mrs Sara Seger late wife of Mr John Seger gentleman, of yeares 39
	August	8	Satterday Vrsley Jones daugh : of Thomas Jones Grocer in ye west yard : old weekes 20
	Septem	27	Sonday Susan Ratsdale daugh : of Wm Ratsdale Bruer, of a burning agew. yers 10
	Octobe	13	Tuesday Barnabe Watson Merchant Tailor, of a consumption, in west yard 38
		17	Sonday Maudelyn Lambe widow of Barnard Lambe Draper : in west yard 42
	Nouem	3	Tuesday Mr. Thomas Gardner Grocer, his pit and coat Armor, in ye quire yers 59
		13	Friday Mrs Marion Walthall widow of Mr Roger Walthall : pit in ye mid ile. yers 94
	Decem	22	Tuesday Annes Wigges, daugh : of Wm Wiges Goldsmith, pit in the east yard. yeares 4
		27	Sonday Leonard Thickpenny Minister of Enfeld brought from the Kinges bench in a coffen with a flap to open,

T

Yeare.	Month.	Day.	Names.
			with a writing one it in verse, laid at Ledenhall gate by night
1590	Janua	6	Wedensday: two children still born of Robert Drables Fishmonger of London
		18	Monday Peeter Hodgeson vpholster of a consumption. pit in ye south ile. yeares 35
	Februa	12	Friday Katherin Linsey widow of Thomas Linsey of Lancashire, from Ratsdales. 63.
		26	Friday an infant of Jone Nicholson, contracted to william Wooden
	March	15	Monday Fraunces Sacheuerell a maid, daugh: of John Sacheuerell: west yard 50

SUMME OF THE YEARE IS—24.

1591		27	Satterday Hellen Dauis widow of Humphry Dauis from Randolles. of yers 33
	April	2	Goodfriday Mr John Malin Armorer, his pit in ye south Chappell. his yeares 65
		3	Satterday Maudlyn Euans a rogue dying in Gracious street, years 18
		11	Sunday Elias Wethers sonne of Mr. Harry Wethers Doc: of Diuinitie: yers 16
		12	Monday Ellen Gouch daugh: of Robert Gouch of Yarmoth from ye spred Egle.
	Maye	22	Satterday George Carter sonne of Wm Carter cuntryman, from Coopers 19
	June	5	Satterday, a still born childe of John Rayment ye yonger, Poulter, west yard
	Augu	21	Satterdaay Mrs Dina Walthall wif of Mr Wm Walthall, Mercer, a vertuous yong woman, religious, and good to ye poore, pit in ye south Cha: 30
		24	Tuesday Mr Anthonie Yong Skynner, his pit in the south ile, yeares 68
		27	Friday Alice Parchment wif of Peeter Parchment Weuer, north ile 35
	Septem	6	Monday Fraunces Steuens sonne of Richard Steuens Armorer from Lecrofts 22
		23	Thursday John Hancocke sonne of John Hancocke cuntryman. yeares 19
	Octobe	10	Sonday a still born childe of Nicholas Symones White Baker
		12	Tuesday Mrs Elizabeth Mascoll, wife of Robert Mascoll Carpenter, mid ile 48
		18	Monday Mr Edward Caunt Fishmonger, his pit in the Library: his yeares 62
		22	Friday Katherine Pedder daug: of John Pedder Merchaunt Tailo^r a yeare 3 qr.
		28	Thursday Alice Gunstone wif of Robert Gunston Inholder, pit in north ile 48
	Nouem	1	Monday Wm Steuens sonne of John Steuens Embroderer from ye spred egle 4 daies
		24	Wedensday Mr Wm Pateshall gentleman of Hartfordshire from Mr Atkinson: north ile 50
	Decem	2	Thursday Elizabeth Perry daugh: of John Perry of Cumberland. yeares 23
		15	Wedensday Richard Fells sonne of Edward Fell cuntryman, from ye spred Egle 48
	Janua	11	Tuesday Elizabeth Juggle daugh: of John Juggle bucher: dying in childbed 30

Yeare.	Month.	Day.	Names.
1591	Janua	24	Monday John Cater sonne of John Cater Bucher of ye cuntry 38
		26	Wedensday Edward Pauet sonne of John Pauet cuntryman, pit, west yard 21
	Februa	22	Tuesday Mrs Blanch Fryar wif of Marke Friar Skinner, pit south ile 64
		27	Sonday Susan Parchment daugh: of Peeter Parchment weuer; east yrd. 3
	March	13	Monday William Parchment sonne of Peeter Parchment Weue^r, east yrd 9
		21	Tuesday Alice Lucy daugh: of Mr Thomas Lucy gentleman, pit in ye Chancel old 10 days

SUMME OF THE YEARE IS—28.

1592	Aprill	11	Tuesday John Smith Cooper, a Bruars Clarke, his pit in ye east yard 30
	May	17	Wedensday Annes Hisfeld widow of Gyles Hisfeld Botcher, west yard 66
	May	18	Thursday Maudlyn Ball widow of William Ball, Girdler, pit east yard 82
	June	30	Friday Katharine Walthall daugh: of Mr Thomas Walthall Mercer, south ile 1 yer
	July	10	Monday Katherine: Mr Mascolls maid born in the North, her pit in ye east yard
		12	Wedensday Elizabeth Sutton widow, from her sonnes John Sutton, in ye west yard 80
		30	Sonday Elizabeth Hunter daugh: of Edward Hunter poulter, in ye east yard 1 d.
	August	10	Thursday Alice Wilson Mr Goffes maid daug: of Jeames Wilson of Baldocke; west 25
	Septem	12	Tuesday Katherine Randoll dau: of John Randoll Draper & sexton: in ye belfry
		25	Monday Katherine Hafford from Mr Gardners, buryed in ye new church yard 13
		26	Tuesday a still born childe of John Pedder Merchant Tailor
		26	Tuesday Mathew Averell sonne of Wm Averell Merchant Tailor: and Clarke of this Church; his pit in the West yard toward the church wall. yers 5
Mathew Auerell*			
			Hunc puerulum quem ego charissimum habui, olim in cœlesti gaudio me inuenturum esse confido: post quam ab antro sepulchri, rediuiua eius caro tanqua' nouus Phœnix, frumentiq': granum reuinescens, non tanta facilitate, quam fœlicitate resurget. Inquit G: Auer. pater φιλόσοργος.†
	Septem	26	Tuesday Mary Caunt daug: of John Caunt Fishmonger; pit in Library
	October	4	Wedensday Annes Stokely from Friars, her pit in the east yard yers 7
		8	Sonday Jone Woodard Mr Thorowgoodes maid. her pit in the west yard 25
		12	Thursday Dorite Lister widow of John Lister Barbor, pit in ye east yard 40
		18	Wedensday John Chamberlin upholster, his pit in the mid ile, his yeares 60

* Entered in margin.
† This is an obsolete word, but is given by Aldus in his Greek Dictionary, and is explained as 'indulgens,' 'amans.' The last letter in the original is a contraction which stands for *os*.

Yeare.	Month.	Day.	Names.
1592	October	22	Sonday John Caunt the yonger; Fishmonger; this yong man by his fruites showed his faith, which older yeld not: Hee gaue bountifully to both Vniuersities, to the Hospitall: to the poore of this parish xij^{li}, with many other legacies, his pit in the south Chappell by Sy^r Wm Bowyers tombe. yers 24
	*Lucerna, lucens facem alijs. John Caunt		
	Nouem	2	Thursday Mrs Elizabeth Hewet widow of Mr Huet Clothworker: South Chap
		22	Wedensday Daniell Cloise sonne of Mr John Cloise duchman: pit: east yard i yer
	Decem	28	Thursday Mrs Isabell Welles wif of Mr John Wells a messenger, shee came from Bishopes gate street next the bull, her pit by her father Mr Mase in ye quire
	Janua	5	Friday Mr William Hammersly Fishmonger, his pit in ye south ile. yeares 60
		15	Monday John Daldron Brokar, his pit in the west yard, his yeares 50
		22	Monday Mrs Margaret Goffe wif of Mr Lawrance Goffe Drape^r: north ile 60
		30	Tuesday Robert Thrower vintner, his pit in the mid ile; his Yeares 36
	March	11	Sunday Margery Bird, from the sunne in Cornhill, her pit in ye west yard 24
		12	Monday Henry Daldron sonne of John Daldron Brokar, west yard, old 7 monthes

SUMME OF THE YEARE IS—27.

1593		25	Sonday Lawraunce Shingleton Mercer, & of ye custome house, pit in west yard 72
		31	Satterday Robert Mascoll Carpenter, his pit in the midle Ile, his yeares 59
	Aprill	2	Monday Thomas Wall seruant to John Ashly vpholster: pit in the west yard 22
		25	Wedensday Edward Burchly sonne in law of Mr Thomas Pigot: in ye south ile 14
		26	Thursday Fulke Waight sonne of Richard Waight Poulter, pit in ye east yard 3
	Maye	1	Tuesday Jeames Burchly sonne of Mr Thomas Pigot Grocer; in ye south ile 10
		8	Tuesday John Ashly Skynner, of the plague, pit in the crosse ile by ye belfry 48
		10	Thursday Henry Satchfeld an infant of John Satchfeld Baker, in ye north ile
		17	Thursday Dauid Harris tapster at the Bull, his pit in the east yard yeares 24
		30	Wedensday Rose Jacob from John Raymentes Poulter, her pit in the east yard. 12
	June	17	Sunday Jeames Nicholson Lynnen Draper, his pit in ye north ile vnder ye buckete 32
		19	Tuesday, Margaret Shepy daugh: of Robert Shepy Poulter, in ye east yard 2
	Julye	1	Sonday Barbara Shepy Wif of Robert Shepy Poulter, pit in ye east yard 30
		1	William Shepy sonne of Robert Shepy Poulter, his pit in ye grave wth her

} pla.

* Entered in margin.

Yeare.	Month.	Day.	Names.
1593	Julye	5	Thursday Katherine Fishman widow in ye Church ally: her pit in ye east yard 80
		5	John Scremsby sonne of Mr Scremsby of the cuntry from Wm Towersons, east yrd 20
		7	Satterday Josias Robertes seruant to George Hubbersteed Tailor, pit east yard 20
		7	Thomas Feeld sonne of Mr Feeld Lynin Draper in Grasse street, pit by ye vestry dore 16
		9	Monday Katherine Shepy daugh: of Robert Shepy Poulter, in th'east yard 7 mon
		11	Wednesday Susan Salsbury daugh: of Robert Salsbury vpholster; in th'east yard 16
	Julye	19	Thursday Thomas Hassall seruant to Mr Symons Baker, in th'east yard 18
		20	Friday Robert Salsbury vpholster an vpright & iust man, of ye plague; by ye vestry 50
		20	Daniell Salsbury his sonne, buryed in the same graue, hee dyed of ye plague 10
		20	Ellen Rowell Mr Swannes maid, her grave in the east yard, her yeares 18
		23	Monday Peeter Ratsdale sonne of Wm Ratsdale Brewar, pit in th'east yard
		28	Satterday William Skeell Draper, hee dyed suddainly, his pit in ye crosse ile 64
		29	Sunday Fraunces Smith daughter of Wm Smith Poulter; pit in ye east yard 6
		30	Monday Robert Gold sonne of Mr Hugh Gold Grocer, his pit in the midle ile 4
		31	Tuesday Richard Hubbersted brother of George Hubbersted Tailor: west yard 24
	August	1	Wedensday Martha Ratsdale daugh: of William Ratsdale Brewar, pit in th'east yard 6
		4	Satterday Phillip Price born in Bristow Mr Powells man; in th'east yard 22
		6	Monday Wm Blalocke sonne of John Blalocke carter of ye weigh house; east yrd 2
		13	Monday Elizabeth Hare a vertuous maiden, dau: of John Hare Salte^r, in ye crosse ile 16

*Non tam bella quam bona κ' σοφὴ κ' καλή.

1593	August	14	Tuesday John Scath Ostler at the spread Egle, pit in the east yard, yeares 26
		14	Dorothy Ratsdale daughter of William Ratsdale Brewar; in th'east yard 4
		16	Thursday Katherin Owen Mr Bromlyes maid, her pit in ye east yard. yeares 18
		17	Friday Margery ignoti cognominis, Mr Lecraftes mayd, of ye plague, in ye east yrd 26
		18	Satterday William Smith Poulter, his pit in the east yard; yeares 40
		19	Sunday John Blalocke Carter in ye weigh house, of ye plague. east yard 30
		19	Sonday Bu: Hugh Gyttins George Hubbersteedes man, pit in th'east yard 18
		25	Satterday Thomas Wisewald Ostlier, from Ratsdales, pit in

* In margin.

Yeare.	Month.	Day.	Names.

ye north Chappell   56.   hee paid duble charges because hee was no parishioner; he gaue ye poore 30^s

1593   August   27   Monday: John Gryphin seruant to Mr Satchfeld Baker, pit in th'east yard   17

28   Tuesday: John Rayment sonne of John Rayment Poulter, pit in th'east yard   6

29   Wednesday, Ellen Hewet seruant to Mr Carles of ye weygh house; in th'east yrd   10

Septem   1   Satterday Sara Hare daugh: of Mr John Hare Salter; pit in the crosse ile   6

4   Tuesday Alice Robertes wif of Steuen Robertes Cooke, pit in the east yard   26

4   Robert Fox seruant with Mr Dancaster, his pit is in the east yard   yers 28

4   Jone Pike seruant with Mr Rayment Poulter, her pit in th'east yard   26

5   Wednesday: Josua Hassall sonne of Perciuall Hassall Skynner, in th'est yrd   12

6   Thursday: George Drables sonne of Robert Drables Fishmonger; in th'est yard   6

6   Balthasar Pope sonne of Waldron Pope Duchman; pit in the east yard   19

7   Friday Adam Baker Tailor, from his mother Hisfeldes house; in west yard   40

8   Satterday: Harry Hassall sonne of Perciuall Hassall, Skynne^r, pit in north ile   11

8   Harry Drables sonne of Robert Drables Fishmonger, his pit in ye east yrd   2

10   Monday Ellen Cater daugh: of John Cater Skynner, deceased; in th'est yard   6

11   Tuesday Ellen Taylor seruant to Mrs Malyn: her pit in the east yard   23

13   Thursday: Mary Pope daugh: of Waldron Pope Ducheman; pit in th'est yard   9

16   Sonday John Careles a M^r porter of the weigh house; pit at ye south dore in ye church   80

16   John Randoll sonne of John Randoll sexton heare; his pit in the bellfry   14

21   Friday Elizabeth Whitehead Mr Hunters maid; her pit in the east yard   18

24   Monday: Morris Griphin Mr Powells man, his pit in the east yard   24

27   Wednesday: Agnes Pope daugh: of Waldron Pope Duchman; in th'east yard   17

30   Sonday: Alice Willson Mr Gunbys mayd: her pit in the east yard, yers 28

Octobe   1   Monday: Jeremy Pope sonne of Waldron Pope Duche man; pit in th'east yard   6

2   Tuesday Christian Cater dau: of John Cater deceased: pit in th'east yard   3

2   Mary Gunby daughter of George Gunby Scriuener: pit in th'east yard   10

5   Friday: Alice Wallmesly widow, from Corbetes court, pit in the east yard   80

12   Friday an infant dying at Mr Thomas Wallthall his dore; - in east yrd

17   Wedensday Thomas Powell sonne of Dauid Powell Merchant tailor; in west yrd   16

Yeare.	Month.	Day.	Names.
1593	Octobe	19	Thursday, Gregory Stancer, Mr Powells man, his pit in the west yard 24
	Nouem	5	Monday Susan Pope daugh : of Waldron Pope Ducheman, in the west yard 13
		9	Friday : Marget Parchment wif of Peeter Parchment weuer; pit in ye library 36
		16	Friday : Richard Powell sonne of Dauid Powell Merchant Tailor ; in ye west yard 16
	Decem	13	Thursday : Mary Parchment daughte^r of Peeter Parchment weuer, in the west yrd 13
		26	Wedensday : a Chrisome Childe of John Randolles sexton heare ; pit in ye west yrd
	Janua	1	Tuesday : Annes Parchment daugh : of Peeter Parchment Weuer, in ye new churchyrd 8
		21	Monday Mathew Lecroft wif of Wm Lecroft Armorer, pit in ye south Chapell ; her years 30
		25	John Randoll Draper and sexton of this Church : his pit in the belfrye years 45
	Februa	7	Thursday : Jeames Lyngar Mr Thomas Gardners man, pit in the belfrye 40
		21	Thursday : William Wickam gentleman of Willshire, buryed in the new church yard 80
		21	Richard Averell an infant of William Averell Merchant Tailo^r, in west yard
		27	Wedensday : William Parchment sonne of Peeter Parchment ; in ye east yard 22
	March	3	Sonday Nicholas Meriall of North Hampton from M^r friars, pit in th'east yard 50

SUMME OF THIS YEARE IS—88.

*δόξά σοι κύριε Δόξά σοι, πάσης
φιλανθρωπίας ἀβυδος† παρά
σοι. πασης ἀνεξικακίας‡ πλοῦτος.§

Thear dyed in London in all,   25886
Of them of the plague in all,   15003
Within the walles & liberties,   8598
Without, in & out of liberties,   17288

*Innumeros quamuis consumpsit morbida pestis
Seruauit dominus meq' domumq' meam.

In a thousand fiue hundred ninety and three,
The lord preserued my house and mee.
When of the pestilence theare died,
Full manie a thousand els beeside.

1594	June	6	Thursday Susan Hudson daugh : of George Hudson vpholster ; in th'east yard 2
	Julye	17	Wedensday William Averell sonne of William Merchant Tailor Clarke of this Church, his pit in the west yard : hee was of yeares 4
		17	Joane Lawraunce daughter of Jeames Lawrance Merchant, pit in west yard 3
		21	Sonday Thomas Brown Packer ; his pit in the west yard, his yers 30
		25	Thursday Sara Hartridge wif of Mr Wm Hartridge Draper, in ye church at ye south dore

* Entered in margin.   † Explained by Aldus to mean depth.
‡ Clemency, patience.
§ The same contraction occurs at the end of this word as was noted at page 139.

Yeare.	Month.	Day.	Names.

1594 Octobe 23 Wedensday: William Ashboold sonne of Mr William Ashboold Parson of this Church, a toward yong child, and my scholler, he lieth buried in the Chauncell vnder a small blewish stone, hard by the south dore: whose death wroong from mee these suddain verses, viz.

> My sweet and little boy, my lif, my ioyfull sight,
> Thou wast thy fathers earthly ioy, and mothers chief delight
> Though heauy destinyes haue ta'ne thee soone away,
> Yet enuious death shall giue thee ioyes that neuer shall decay
> Thou wast my scholler deare, but henceforth thou shalt bee,
> A scholler of thy maister Christ through all eternitie.

> Dulce caput mi parue puer mea lux, mea vita ; *
> Patris deliciæ tum genetricis amor.
> Et si te subito iam tristia fata tulerunt,
> Inuida nunc tibi mors gaudia multa dabit.
> Tu mihi discipulus charus fueras, tamen at nunc
> Christi discipulus postea semper eris.

In mortem Gulielmi Ashboold.

1594	Decem	..	Sunday Ellen Martine, from Ferns house, her pit in the west yard, her yeares 6
	Janua	21	Tuesday Nicholas Symons Baker, his pit in the north ile by his pew: yers 42
		25	Satterday John Stewart sonne of Robert Stuart Surgion: in th'east yard yers ..
	March	10	Monday, a Chrisome male childe of Richard Robinson Armorer; in th'east yard
		14	Friday John Woodleaf soone of Mr Woodleaf Haberdashe^r; of wormes: in east yrd 5

SUMME OF THIS YEARE IS—11.

1595	March	28	Friday, Marget Caunt an infant of Mr John Caunt Fishmonge^r, in ye south Chapell
	Aprill	2	Wedensday, Anne Record daug: of John Record Merchant Tailor: in ye entry of ye mid ile 5
		7	Monday, Elizabeth Wratting Widow; her pit in the west yard: her yeares 70
	Maye	18	Sonday Susan Randoll daug: of John Randoll sexton heare, pit in ye west yrd 10
		21	Wedensday, Katherine Inman widow, her pit north by ye little pewes by ye belfry 68
		24	Satterday, John Sallomon sonne of Thomas Sallomon Sadler, pit in th'east yrd 12
	June	12	Thursday, Annes Warden wif of Robert Warden Poulter, pit in the north ile. years 60
		22	Sonday, Randoll Burchenshaw Draper, his pit in the west yard, his yeares 80
		22	Mrs Marget Hartridge, wif of Mr William Hartridge Draper: pit in ye mid ile
	Julye	26	Satterday: John Holdsworth sonne of Henry Holsworth Mercer: in ye west yard 9
		29	Tuesday: Annes Bray Wif of Wm Bray Baker, her pit in the south ile. yeares 30

* Entered in margin.

THE REGISTERS OF ST. PETER'S, CORNHILL. 145

Yeare.	Month.	Day.	Names.
1595	August	15	Friday: John Naddle sonne of Rouland Naddle Brewer: ye infantes pit in ye east yrd
	Octobe	2	Wednesday: Margery Shingleton widow, her pit in the west yard, her yeares 80
		25	Satterday, B: a Chrisome child of Mr Askew Cooke, pit in the west yard
		31	Friday: Buryed Ellen Pedder daughter of John Pedder Merchant Tailor, the infant dyed of a consumption: her pit in the west yard
	Nouem	2	Sonday Bu: Katherine Marow daug: of George Marow, Carpenter: in west yard 3
		20	Thursday: a still born childe of Robert Oldam seruingman, pit in ye west yard
	Decem	22	Monday: a chrisome male childe of Steuen Robertes Cooke, pit in th'east yard
	Janua	5	Monday: Jone Tod an old mayd, from St. Lawrance ye Jury, pit in th'east yard 60
	Februa	20	Friday, Gillian Averell wif of William Averell Merchant Tailor and Clarke of this Church: Huius mulieris virtutem fidem, pudicitiam, castitatem, probitatem, ceterasq. animi dotes, quibus perpulchre erat ornata, mihi si centum essent ora, totidemq. linguæ, exprimere nullo modo possem: Domi frequens erat non multiuaga: vicinis amabilis non morosa: viro obsequens atq. fida; deo obediens, et religiosa bene vixit et bene mortua est; iamq. omnibus malis liberata, ac leuata, eam vitam assecuta est, qua nihil est beatius: shee died of her 17th child; pit in ye west yard by her children, at the right hand toward the church wall, where ye bay tree stood.

In vxorem suam Tetrastichon.
Vxor casta, pudica viro subiecta fidelis
Præmia virtutis, iam tibi larga manent.
Meus tua stelliferum retinet castissima cœlu,'
Heu mihi quod tecum, non licet ire viam.

1595	Februa	24	Tuesday: William Dale Letherseller, his pit in the mid ile, his yeares wea^r 80
		24	Vrsly Persy wif of Fraunces Persy Porter, her pit in the west yard. 40
	March	1	Monday: Ellen Caunt daug: of Mr John Caunt Fishmonger, pit in south Chappell

SUMME OF THIS YEARE IS—22.

1596	April	5	Monday: Mary Hudson wif of George Hudson vpholster, pit in mid ile 30
		9	Goodfriday: Cibell Ouerton daugh: of Lawrance Over: Merchant: in north ile 5
		22	Thursday: Barbara Record wif of John Record Merchant Tailor: in mid ile 39
	May	8	Satterday. Marget Parkins wif of Frances Parkens Skynner: in th'east yard 80
		10	Monday: Briget Brawdy of Essex, widow; her pit in the east yard. yeares 82
		22	Satterday: William Munday an infant sonne of Richard Mun: sawyer: in east yrd
		29	Satterday: Mr Thomas Boston of Lynne, from ye spread Egle; pit in ye chancel 48
	June	25	Friday, William Barnfeld Porter; of a cough; his pit in the west yard 58
		29	Tuesday: Richard Collect, Mr Raymentes man: his graue in ye west yard 24

U

Yeare.	Month.	Day.	Names.
1596	Julie	3	Satterday: Elizabeth Hales, daugh: of Thomas Hales gent: in ye west yard 1
		21	Wedensday: Elizabeth Parton dau: of Frances Parton, in th'east yard 11
		26	Monday: William Strachie of Safron Walden soldier, pit in th'east yard 30
		26	Marget Ratsdale daughter of William Ratsdale Brewer: an infant
	Septe	9	Thursday: Anne Skeel an infant of William Skeell hosier; in th'east yard
		14	Tuesday: Abraham Griphin an infant of John Griphyn; in th'east yard
		21	Monday: Sarah Skeell wif of William Skeell hosier: shee died in childbed 30
	Octobe	4	Monday: Annes Hunter daug: of Edward Hunter Poulter, in ye east yard 3
		27	Wedensday: Elizabeth Web, an infant of Elis Web vintner, in the east yard
	Novem	12	Friday: William Hudson Skynner, an vpholster, his pit in the crosse ile. years 45
		15	Monday: John Barret Grocer, from Mrs Banes house, in ye crosse ile. years 36
		16	Tuesday: Susan Scaliot wife of Marke Scaliot Blacksmith: in ye mid ile. yers 46
		16	Elizabeth Neuby Mr Cockaines maid: her pit in the east yard, her yeares 18
	Decem	28	Tuesday: Thomas Alise Mr Deputy Wodfordes man; his pit in ye library. yeares 26
		31	Friday: a still born childe of John Pedders Merchant Tailor: in th'east yrd
	Janua	1	Satterday: Katherine Dekisar wif of Peeter Dekisar duchman in cros ile 40
		11	Tuesday. William Sedall Mr Goldes man; his pit is in the west yard. yers 20
		16	Sonday: Nicholas Sallomon sonne of Thomas Sallomon; sadler, in ye east yrd 16
		19	Wedensday: Mrs Katherine Foulke gentlewoman; her pit in ye north Chappell 28
		20	Thursday: Elizabeth Dowson widow: her pit toward the belfry: years 70
		22	Satterday: John Persy an infant of Fraunces Persy porter, pit in th'east yrd
	Februa	6	Sunday: Buryed a begger wench which dyed at Leden Hall bench
		11	Friday Richard Sallomon sonne of Thomas Sallomon sadler, in ye east yrd 6
		13	Sonday: John Westgate a porter of Leden Hall; his pit in the west yard 80
		14	Monday: Michaell Vale Mr Vertues man, his pit is in the east yard 20
		22	Tuesday: Cisly Satchfeld wif of John Satchfeld Baker: in ye north ile 35
	March	11	Friday: Bu: poore Michaell lying in ye Library: but hee dyed in Lewes house 50
		14	Monday: Margery Mane widow, old, yet deuout in often hearing ye word: iu ye cros ile 100

SUMME OF THIS YEARE IS—37.

THE REGISTERS OF ST. PETER'S, CORNHILL.   147

Yeare.	Month.	Day.	Names.
1597	March	30	Friday: Thomas Powell sonne of Dauid Powell Merchant tailor: west yard
	June	2	Thursday: Abraham Jacobson sonne of Peeter Jacobson, pit in ye east yard 6
		7	Tuesday: Robert Cokain sonne of Mr Thomas Cockain skynner: in south chapell 5
		12	Sonday: valentyne Weston: from Mother Manes house: pit in the east yard 18
	Julie	7	Wednesday: a still born childe of Steuen Robertes Cooke, pit in the east yard
		19	Tuesday: Jone Robertes wif of Steuen Robertes Cooke, pit in ye mid crosse ile 26
		28	Thursday. William Skeel Draper, hee sold hose: his pit in the myd ile 34
		30	Satterday: Sara Jacobson dau: of Peeter Jacob: duchman: in th'east yard 0
	August	15	Monday Elizabeth Stonar Mr Witters maid: pit in the east yard 21
		25	Thursday: Mrs Grace Banes widow, her pit in the south Chappell 50
		26	Frday John Cutterell Mr Hassalles man: his pit in the east yard 26
	Septem	6	Tuesday Morgan Jones Mr Powells man: his pit in the east yard: yeares 22
		18	Sonday: Annes Lee an old woman from Mr Raymentes, pit in th'east yard 100
		20	Tuesday: Buryed a still born childe of John Hilles Lynnyn Draper 0
	Octobe	1	Satterday: Sara Atkinson, from Mr Stocke Lynnyn Draper: east yard 10
		1	Satterday: Thomas Dixon father of John Dixon Armorer in ye south ile 80
		21	Friday: Katherine Rigely an infant of Edward Rigely yeoman: pit in east yrd 2
	Nouem	27	Monday: John Dixon sonne of Thomas Dixon aforesaid: in ye south ile: years 53
	Decem	4	Sonday: Alice Waight an infant of Richard waight Poulter: pit in th'east yrd
	Februa	7	Tuesday: Rebecca Bannester from Lawrance Euannes: pit in the east yard 9
		16	Thursday: Thomas Cumbars Cooke at the Lambe; pit in the church by ye west dore 35
		24	Friday; John Pedder an infant of John Pedder Merchant Tailor

SUMME OF THE YEARE IS—22

1598	Aprill	6	Thursday: Adam Dixon Armorer at ye Helmet, pit in the south ile: his yeares 28
		18	Tuesday: John Griphin Feltmaker, his pit in the East yard: his yeares 30
	May	4	Thursday: William Price Cobler: his pit in the East yard: his yeares 60
		24	Wedensday: Annes Malen wif of Thomas Malen Brown baker: in ye north ile 88
		25	Thursday: Daniell Pope sonne of Waldron Pope Duchman: pit in the east yard 19

Yeare.	Month.	Day.	Names.
1598	May	25	William Heton sonne of Mr Thomas Heton Merchant: his pit in ye north ile 0
	June	8	Thursday: Jerard Yopus Duchman from John Maxfeldes; pit in the east yard 30
	Julye	5	Wednesday: Richard Grace an Atturny of the kinges bench, pit in the crosse ile 42
		26	Wednesday: Thomas Brown sonne of Thomas Brown Packer, in ye west yrd 5
	August	6	Sonday: Mary Satchfeld an infant of John Satchfeld Baker: in ye east yard 0
		17	Friday: a still born childe of Robert Westlyes vpholster, in the west yard 0
		23	Wedensday: a still born child of Ellis Webb, vintner: pit in the east yard 0
		25	Friday; John London Robert Westlies seruant: his pit in the east yard 16
		27	Sonday: John Westly an infant of Robert Westly vpholster: in the west yard 0
	Septem	2	Sonday: Elizabeth Cumbers daug: of Thomas Cumbars Cooke; in th'east yrd i d'
	Nouem	7	Tuesday: Oliuer Groome Clothworker; his pit in the north ile, his years 67
		18	Satterday: Susan Hardwin an infant of Jeames Hardwin: Blacke smith
	Decem	2	Satterday: a Chrisome childe of Jeames Thorowgood Poulter: in ye east yrd 0
		9	Satterday: a Chrisome childe of John Morris Clothworker; in th'east yard 0
		12	Tuesday: Margaret Fordom Mr Wardens maid: her pit in the east yard yeres 14
		31	Sonday: Elizabeth Vpton Widow: her pit in the West yard: her years 93
	Janua	18	Friday: Margaret Shepy daugh: of Robert Shepy Poulter; in th'east yard 3
		24	Wedensday: Thomas Persy sonne of Fraunces Persy Porter, in th'east yard 2
	Februa	14	Wednesday. Thomas Yong keeper of the green yard, his pit in the east yard 80
		17	Satterday: Anne Thorogood daugh: of Jeames Thorogood Poulter: in east yrd 3
		18	Sonday: William Lecroft Armorer: his pit in the Library at ye east yrd dore 50
		19	Monday: William Lecroft sonne of Wm Lecroft Armorer; pit in th'east yard 10
		20	Shroue Tuesday: John Satchfeld white Baker: his pit in the north ile yers 42

SUMME OF THE YEARE—28.

1599	April	5	Thursday: A still born childe of John Rikecord sonne of Malliard Rikecord strainger, in Mr Hassalds house in controuersy, one the north side of his capitall tenement, claymed by St Mar: Outwich
	Maye	13	Tuesday: Buryed Elizabeth Averell daughter of William Averell Clarke of this church, her pit in the West yard by the spoute. 1 & a half
	June	11	Monday. Buried Barbara Dorington an infant of Mr John Dorington, Merchant, her pit in the mid ile by his pew

THE REGISTERS OF ST. PETER'S, CORNHILL.   149

Yeare.	Month.	Day.	Names.
1599	June	12	Tuesday Buryed William Holdsworth sonne of Henry Holsworth Mercer, of 16 yeares of age; pit in the west yard
		21	Thursday Buried Henry Thomson Grocer of 62 yeares, his pit in North Chappell vnder the foure square stones
	Julie	19	Thursday Buried William Bromly the elder Poulter of 60 yeares of age, his pit in the Library by the east yard dore
		26	Thursday Buryed Richard Carlill Tallow Chandler of 46 yeares; his pit was made in the East Church Yard against ye dore
	Augus	1	Wedensday Buryed Robert Brewin an infaut of Roger Brewin Vpholder by his trade 14 daies old. Pit in the east yard
		6	Satterday Buried Christopher Warrenan* 3 Yeares old sonne of William Warren † Cooke, his Pit in the East Church Yard
		7	Sunday Buried Marget Treuis daughter of Andrew Trevis, Plummer deceased, of 4 Yeares, her Pit in the East yard
		14	Tuesday‡ Buried Thomas Holdsworth sonne of Henry Holdsworth Mercer, of 7 Yeares of age, his Pit in the West Yard
		25	Satterday Buryed John Norton Jornyman with John Maxfeld Armorer, of 25 Yeares, burnt wth pouder; his Pit in the East Yard
	Septem	6	Thursday, Buryed Elizabeth Oliuer, Wif of Isacke Oliuer Stranger, of 28 yeares of age, her Pit beehind ye south dore in ye church
		7	Friday Buryed George Ange seruant to Mr Woodford of the age of 19 Yeares of an Ageu: his Pit in the Library by the East dore
		9	Sunday Edward Forringdon an infant of Edward Forringdon a Mercer beeing 3 quarters old, his Pit in the East Church Yard
	October	3	Wedensday: Buryed Walter Persy sonne of Fraunces Persie, of 7 dayes old, the infantes pit in the East Church Yard
		12	Friday. Buryed Joane Westly wif of Robert Westly Vpholder of 41 Yeares of age, her Pit in the West yard against his dore
	Nouem	1	Thursday Buryed Rebecca Nicholson daughter of Michaell Nicholson Cordwainer of 13 Yeares of age; Pit in the west Yard
	Decem	8	Satterday: Buried Mrs Katherine Chambers widow of 80 yeares; her pit in the south Chappell under the middle pew
		30	Sunday: Harry Waight sonne of Richard Waight Poulter the childe 5 yeares old his pit in the east Church Yard
1600	April	10	Thursday: Buryed Robert Kelly a twyn christned the day afore. the mother a uagrant, deliuered in Leden haule
		13	Sunday. Buryed Elizabeth the mother of th'afore saide Robert Kelly, shee dyed in the cage in Leden haule market

* Sic. Should be Warman. See under 1605 and 1607.
† Sic.   ‡ Sic.

Yeare.	Month.	Day.	Names.
1600	Aprill	16	Wedensday: Buryed John Maxfeld sonne of John Maxfeld Armorer 3 yeares old, his pit in the north ile by the pewe number
	Maie the 26*		Buryed Harry Warman a yeare old sonne of William Warman Cooke: his pit is the east church yard, hee dyed of an agew
	Julie	1	Beryed a still born woman childe of Robert Brewin vpholder, & free of the Skinners, her pit is in the east church yard
		15	Tuesday: Buryed Downes daughter of Thomas Downes, Fishmonger being an infant, his* pit in west yard in a boxe
		21	Monday: Buryed Thomas Burchwood an infant of Thomas Burchwood Cordwayner, his pit in the West Church yard
	August	26	Tuesday Buryed Fraunces Starling daughter of Jeames Starling in ye County of Cambridge 16 years old, pit in the east yard
		29	Friday Buryed Mary Forringdon daughter of Edward Forringdon Mercer, 3 yeares old of a pyning sicknes; pit in the east yard
	Septem	10	Wedensday: Buryed John Caudell from Mr Loxones 25 yeares of age, hee dyed of a flux, his pit is in the east Church yard
		10	Buryed the same day John Brewin seruant and brother to Roger Brewin Skynner, 17 yeares old of a flux, pit in the east yard
	Octobe	24	Friday Buryed Alice Askew wif of Edmund Askew, Habberdasher: 67 yeares old, her pit is in the west Church yard
	Nouem	10	Monday: Buried Edward Childe Salter of the age of 40 Yeares, hee dyed of a Pthisis, his pit is in the East Church yard
	Decemb	4	Thursday Buryed Richard Satchfeld sonne of John Satchfeld Baker, 6 yeares old his pit in the east yard to Mr Lecroftes
	Februa	2	Monday Buryed Thomas Hardwin sonne of Jeames Hardwin Blackesmith the childe dyed of teeth, pit in ye east yard
1601	Aprill	3	Friday Buried John Green one of the M^{rs} of the weighhouse 50 yeares of age his pit in the crosse ile to the vestry dore
		6	Monday Buried Anne Byrchwood daughter of Thomas Byrchewood Cordwainer, pit in the West yard, 2 yeares old
		14	Tuesday: Buryed Margery Harris daughter of John Harris Poulter 3 Yeares of age, her pit in the West church yard
	Maye	7	Thursday Buryed John Caunt sonne of John Caunt fishmonger 3 yeares and a half old, his pit in the south Chappell
		13	Wednesdaie Buryed a still born childe of Edward Ridgely Cyttizen and Draper of London, pit in the East yard

* The Register from May 26, 1600, to July 22, 1601, is subscribed William Asheboold, Mark Scalict.

† Sic.

THE REGISTERS OF ST. PETER'S, CORNHILL.   151

Yeare.	Month.	Day.	Names.
1601	June	15	Friday Buried Annes Clifford widow of the age of 84 yeares Her pit is in the East yard toward the Church wall. Coff.
		10	Wedensday Buried Margery Avison alias Parten daughter of Goodwife Parton in Skynners ally 17 yeares old, pit in the west yard
		10	Wedensday Buried Walter Danniell an infant of a month old: sonne of Walter Daniell Merchant Tailor in ye west yard
	Julie	22	Tuesdaie Buryed John Rikeworth stranger out of Mr Hassaldes house long in strif of law wth martens outwitch, in the crosse ile his pit. Out of the north tenement of Mr Perciuall Hassald
		30*	Thursday: Buryed Saran Lecroft daughter of Samson Lecraft Armorer. The child was buryed in the East yard
	August	30	Sunday Buryed Margaret Westgate of the age of 80 Yeares Widow. Her pit is in the West church Yard
	Septem	18	Friday Buried Alice Pain Mrs Lockes syster soiourning in Mr Lockes house, 20 Yeares old; pit in the east yard
		18	Friday Buryed Margaret Cooke wif of Walter Cooke Merchaunt Tailor 30 years old, her pit in the south ile
		21	Tuesday Buried Nicholas Sayer 18 Yeares old seruant to Mr Symmones at the bell and faucon, pit in the East yard
ἀνὴρ ἀγαθός καὶ καλὸς		22	Wedensday Buryed Dauid Powell Clothworker but free of ye Merchant Tailors: 54 Years old, his pit in the mid ile

This† Powell was a plaine man and led an honest life,
Hee loued peace and amitie, and shun'd debate and strife.

1601	Septem	25	Fryday Bur: Thomas Kynnaston Merchant tailor 50 yeares old, in ye mid ile
		26	Satterday Bu: Elizabeth Poulter Mr Lecroftes maid: 30 yeares old. East yard
	October	16	Buried this day beeing friday Annes Willis wif of Richard Willis Grocer, an honest painfull woman, of 46 yeares, in the south ile
		16	The same day Buryed Jeames Rowley, seruant to Samson Lecroft Armorer: 28 yeares old, his pit in the East yard Coff
		20	Tuesday: Buried Sara Sauill Mr Waightes Maid of the age of 20 yeares, Her pit is in the East Church Yard
		27	Tuesday Buried Elizabeth Shepie wif of Robert Shepie Poulter of 40 Yeares, her pit in the East Church yard
	Nouem	1	Sunday Buried a Wench found dead in the Cage at Ledon Haull not known how she came thether, in the East Yard
		20	Friday Buryed Mr Nicholas Myn gentleman of Walsingam in Norfolke 38 Yeares old, from Mr Hassaldes, pit in the Chancell
		21	Satterday Buryed Marget Porter Widow of 50 Yeares of age from Skynners alley. Her pit is in the East Church yard

* The Register from July 30 to February 21, 1601, is subscribed William Asheboold, parson, John Caunt, churchwarden, John Marrys.
† Entered in the margin, underneath the Greek sentence.

Yeare.	Month.	Day.	Names.
1601	Nouem	24	Tuesday Buried Edward Bowen vpholder of the age of 30 yeares. His pit is in the North ile by his pew by the pewes 7. 8
	Decem	6	Sunday Buryed Walter Cooke Merchant Tailor of the age of 44 Yeares. His pit is in the South Chappell vnder ye second pew
	Janua	1	Friday Buryed William Green seruant to Mr Askew Cooke of the age of 20 years. His pit is in the East Church yard
		14	Thursday Buried Launcelot Thomson Draper of 36 years of age A good benefactor to our poore: his pit in the High Chancell wth Mr Ade. Hee gaue 5^{li} yearlie to our poore in bread and coales
		25	Monday Buryed a still born Childe of Mr John Cauutes fishmonger born the morning afore, her pit in the South Chappell
	Februa	10	Wedensday Buryed Perciuall Hassald Skynner of 60 yeares of age, hee was brought from Grace church, his pit in the North ile
		16	Tuesday Buryed Mrs Cisly Walthall of the age of 50 Yeares the Wif of Mr William Walthall Deputie, a woman godly and charitable. Her pit is in the vault wheare Sy^r William Bowyer is
		21	Monday Buried Peeter Heelin Grocer of 46 yeares of age, a good benefactor to our poore. His pit is in the Highe Chauncell. He gaue fagottes to our poore yearelie
		24*	Thursday Buryed Christoper Redman a souldier of the age of 30 Yeares fro' Widow Jordanes, his pit in the East yard
	March	11	Thursday Buryed Jane Buttler Wif of Jeames Buttler Chaundler: her pit in the Church by her first husband John Randoll
		15	Monday Buryed Mary Fryar daughter of Symon Fryar Skynner: 3 yeares old. Her pit in the West Church yard
1602		26	Friday Buryed Ellen Elmhurst daughter of William Elm-Hurst Haberdasher, a yeare old, her pit by Jane Buttlers in ye Church
	Aprill	5	Monday Buried Mrs Ellen Caunt wife of Mr John Caunt Fishmonger, 30 Yeares old, her pit in the south chappell by her children
	May	22	Satterdaie, Fraunces Goddard daughter of Edward Goddard Armore^r: 6 monthes
		23	Sundaie, James Gold sonne of Mr Hugh Gold Grocer, pit mid ile, 3 yeares old
	June	10	Thursdaie, Symon Cooper seruant to William Campe Cutler 20 yeares
		19	Satterdaie. Margaret Clarke wife of Thomas Clarke a poore pencione^r: 87 yeares
		23	Wedensdaie. A Chrisome male chile of Nathaniell Wellen linnin draper
		25	Fridaie. Thomas Clarke Girdler, pit by his wif in the west yard 86 yeares

* The Register from February 24, 1601, to August 21, 1603, is subscribed Will'm Asheboold parson, Henry Holdsworth, Thomas Salomon.

THE REGISTERS OF ST. PETER'S, CORNHILL. 153

Yeare.	Month.	Day.	Names.
1602	June	25	Eadem die: Sophia Poole, alias vander la poole wif of Daniell vanderlapoole Duchman; her pit in the north Chappell; vnder the tiles 27 yeares
		29	Tuesdaie: Richard Swift sonne of Richard Swift, Tailor, a yeare & a quarter
		30	Weddensdaie, Elizabeth Page an infant daughter of Thomas Page
	Septem	9	Weddensdaie, Edward Ridgley sonne of Edward Ridgley Draper 3 yeares
		21	Tuesdaie, a still born male childe of Fraunces Coling, Fishmonger
		30	Thursday, Katherin Hughson widow, pit in the chancell by her other husband Mr Fulke Heath Skinner, vnder Mr Porders stone: 77 yeares
	October	6	Weddensdaie. Margerie Waight, daughter of Richard Waite poulter 7 yeares
		25	Monday. Ellen Malen widow of John Malen Armorer, pit in the Chancell vnder the stone of Mr Steuens her first husband 70 yeares
		30	Satterdaie Jane Turner wif of Jeffry Turner Tailer 30 yeares
	Nouem	20	Sunday: Alice Jordan wife of James Jordan M^r porter of the waigh house in Cornhill, pit in the west yard by her daughter 60 yeares
		27	Wedensdaie: a still born child of William Ratsdale Brewer: east yard
	Decem	10	Fridaie James Seaman sonne of Thomas Seaman Vintner 2 yeares
		17	Friday Elizabeth Hunter daughter to Edward Hunter poulter 12 yeares
		23	Thursdaie, Edward Tillman an infant of Nicholas Tillman Ironmonger
	Februa	4	Fridaie Mrs Mary Forest wife of William Forest gentleman 50 yeares
		9	Wedensdaie, Phebe Wellen from white Chappell, her pit in ye north ile 19 yeares
	March	3	Thursdaie. Joane Androwes wife of Robert Androwes Goldsmith 63 yeares
		7	Shroue tuesdaie, William Askeu Cooke, in the north Chappell 56 yeares
		12	Satterdaie. Mrs Elizabeth Holsworth wif of Mr Henry Holdsworth Mercer, her pit by Mrs Yonges pew by the south Chappell dore yeares 52
		15	Tuesdaie, James Swithens Mr Parkars man, pit in the west yard 20 yeares
		20	Sunday, Marke Scaliet Blackesmith, pit in the mid ile by his wif 64 yeares
		22	Tuesdaie. Elizabeth Hudson: daughter of Wm Hudson skynner 18 yeares
1603	Aprill	17	Buried Palme Sonday: John Tailor sonne of John Tailor Marchant tailor, pit in the west yard 16
The first buried in this parish in the king his tyme.		30	Satterdaie. William Elmhurst an infant of William Elmhurst 20 Weekes old
	Maie	3	Tuesdaie, John Tailor th'elder Marchant Tailor, pit by his sonne, beeing yeares 48
		4	Wedensday: Marie Tailor daughter of John Tailor, pit by her father 5

x

Yeares.	Month.	Day.	Names.
1603	Maie	13	Fridaie, John Griffith sonne of John Griffeth Feltmaker deceased yeares 5
		23	Monday: Fraunces Dorington sonne of Mr John Dorington Grocer yeares 3
		23	Eadem die. Parnell Griffith daughter of John Griffith about th'age of 9 y^{rs}
	June	6	Monday Elizabeth Braddington, daughter in law to Fraunces Persy 12
		14	Tuesday. William Probe Skynner, his pit in the east yard, beeing 50
	Julie	7	Thursday. Mary Stewart daughter of Robert Stewart Chirurgian 9
		8	Friday: Moses Stewart sonne of Robert Stewart Barbor Surgeon 13
		10	Sunday: Robert Stewart sonne of the same Robert Stuart, beeing*
		19	Tuesday Edward Goddard Armoror, his pit in the east yard, being 43
		20	Weddensday Nicholas Holden seruant to John Sutton Carpenter 22
		21	Thursday, William Stewart sonne of Robert Stewart Barbor Sur: 7
		24	Sunday William Knight seruant to Edward Goddard Armorer 20
		27	Wedensday Jozen Weebrooke daug: of Fraunces Weebrooke duchman 8
		29	Friday Ellen Brown daughter of Thomas Brown porter deceased 14
		2	Tuesdaie. Elizabeth Pigot daug: of Mr Thomas Pigot grocer, pit in ye north chap: 7
	August	4	Thursdaie Susan Sutton daug: of John Sutton Carpenter in ye east yard 18
		5	Fridaie. Edward Goodwin sonne of Edward Goodwin in Mrs Yonges house 55
		5	Fridaie Ellen Tillman wif of Nicholas Tyllman Ironmonger of years 30
		6	Satterdaie Thomas Banes seruant to James Hardwin Blackesmith 16
		7	Sundaie Margaret Averell daugh: of Wm Averell Clarke of this church, her pit in the West yard by her mother shee was 16 yeares old: Laudetur dominus deus.
		8	Mondaie Sara Chart out of one Hilles house in Mr Loxons alley age 14
		8	Fraunces Weebrooke the same day, a duchman 40 yeares old: from Popes:
		8	Katherin Weebrooke the same day his wif buried both in one pit in th'east yard 40
		8	Kathern Weebrooke the same day her daughter in the same pit, beeing old 12
		9	Tuesday Jane de Hay born in Gaunt all these out of Popes house of age 65
		9	William Sutton sonne of John Sutton Carpenter buried in her* pit east yrd 12
		9	James Hardwin sonne of James Hardwin Smith in her* pit allso: months 3
		10	Wedensday Peeter Jacobson sonne of Peeter Jacobson stranger beeing years 14

* Sic.

Yeare.	Month.	Day.	Names.
1603	August	14	Sunday Ellen Marrow daughter of Georg Marrow Carpenter beeing yers 6
		15	Monday Thomas Page sonne in law to Thomas Liddington Armorer Yers 5
		15	Thomas Whorewood seruant to Mr Pigot Grocer, pit in th'east yard : yeares 24
		17	Wedensdaie Robert Tailor seruant to John Sprenter Clothworker Yeares 18
		17	John Gunby sonne of George Gunby Scriuener: pit in the east yard 30
		17	Wedensdaie Anne Hunter wife of Edward Hunter poulter, yeares 48
		17	Ellen Willson kinne to Mr Pigot Grocer, her pit in north Chappell years 13
		18	Thursdaie Elizabeth Web wif of Richard Web Grocer, pit in the Church 40
		18	Susan Goodwin daughter of Edward Goodwin Merchant, pit with Mrs Web 20
		19	Friday. Mrs Katherin Swan wif of Libeus Swan Fishmonger, 48 Yeares of age, her pit in the mid ile by her hushandes pew. shee dyed of a consumption
		19	Peeter Stansall kin to Mr Sprentar Clothworker in Mr Hassaldes house 18
		20	Satterdaie Richard Symson seruant to Mr Sprenter Clothworker : Yeares 20
		20	Jane Lester seruant to Mr Goodwin Marchant, her pit in th'east yard 20
		20	Lea Barkar wif of William Barkar and daughter of Edward Goodwin Merchaunt. shee sickned the same daie shee was married beeing monday afore 21
		20	Susan Binkes seruant to John Bomer Garberler. in ye west yard 16
		21	Sundaie Richard Cowlie officer in Leaden haule, pit in the east yard 63
		21*	Sunday: Thomas Wilson, kyn to Mr Pigot Grocer, being of Years 10
		22	Monday: buried one Mathew a cutter-out of a shop by Mr Hassaldes house 20
		24	Wedensdaie Marie More Mr Waightes maid seruant beeing of years 17
		25	Thursdaie. Roger Bradshaw 30 Yeares old Carpenter from Skinners ally
		25	William Marrow sonne of George Marrow Carpenter beeing about 3 yers
		26	Friday James Pickborn poulter, his pit in the North ile, his Yeares 36
		26	Edward Marrow sonne of George Marrow Carpenter, in the west yrd 3
		27	Satterdaie Perciuall Gunby sonne of George Gunby Scriuener 3 ye^s
		27	Samuell Smith seruaunt to M^r vertew Vintner, pit in th'east yard 19
		28	Sunday. Daniell Jonson out of Mr Jacobson his house, pit in ye north Chap. 30

---

* The Register from August 21 to September 15, 1603, is subscribed Will'm Asheboold, parson, Thomas T I Jones marke, ffrauncos Colynge.

Yeare.	Month.	Day.	Names.
1603	August	29	Sara Walker seruant to Mr Record Marchant Tailor, pit in theast yard 25
		30	Tuesday. William Kinson seruant to George Marrow Carpenter. Yeares 30
		30	Elizabeth Willet seruant to Widow Walker; her pit wth Wm Kinson. Years 18
		30	Elizabeth Hawes, Mrs Jordan Widow kept her in her house, her Yeares 40
	Septem	1	Thursday Abraham Stepney from Mr Richardson his house. Yeares 14
		2	Friday. John Janes born in this parish, dyed at Mr Wardens dore, there born 46
		2	George Marrow of London Carpenter, his pit in the North Chappell 50
		2	Edward Goodwin Merchaunt from Widow Yonges house, pit by his daugh: 55
		2	Elizabeth Watson daughter of Barnabe Watson deceased her Years 17
		3	Satterdaie Edward Pigot sonne of Mr Thomas Pigot Grocer, yers 3
		3	Jane Warren Mr Recordes wiues sister, from his house, pit in the south chapell 17
		3	Elizabeth Liddington an infant of Thomas Liddington Armorer defunct
		3	Roger Twist, from Mr Wooldridges house poulter being 3 yeares old
		4	Sundaie. George Gunby publique Notarie his pit in the east yard yeares 60
		4	Susan Gunby daughter of George Gunby aforesaid; pit wth her father ye^{rs} 9
		5	Monday. Marie Mole daughter of Richard Mole our sexton, pit in ye west yard 7
		5	Richard Lecroft sonne of Samson Lecroft Armorer, pit in ye library. yeares 4
		5	Peeter Vertu sonne of Christopher vertu Vintner: pit with Rich: Lecroft yers 18
		6	Tuesdaie. John Wright Poulter, his pit in the West yard vnder the spout: 36
		6	Fraunces Westlie daughter of Westlie vpholder in the Church allye yers 8
		6	Alice Cooke daughter of Walter Cooke Merchant Tailor: pit south Chapell 12
		8	Thursdaie Katherin Adames Mr Lecroftes maid, pit in the east yard: 14
		8	Richard Willis Grocer, his pit in the south ile by the library dore years 56
		9	Fridaie Henrie Ashboold my scholler sonne of Mr Doctor Ashboold parson of this church, a youth composed and framed out of the mould of vertu; for learning and modestie in so yong Yeares admirable, hee lieth buried in the high Chauncell vnder a small blewish stone wth his brother 10

Henrie Ashboold

O happie Henry thou hast runne thy race,
The graue thie corpes, the heauens thy soule embrace.

ὃν γὰρ φιλεῖ Θεὸς, ἀποθνήσκει νέος.

THE REGISTERS OF ST. PETER'S, CORNHILL. 157

Yeare.	Month.	Day.	Names.
1603	Septem	12	Mondaie John Lewes Peeter Richardson his man, pit in th'east yard yers 19
		12	John Record Marchaunt Tailor, his pit in the south Chappell; yeares 48
		12	Ellis Minors from John Record his house, his pit in the east yard years 5
		14	Wedensdaie Henry Bromlie Mr Warmans seruant Cooke, in th'east yrd 18
		15	Thursday Nicholas Record sonne of John Record Marchant Tailor: yer & a half
		15	Hugh Mole sonne of Richard Mole sexton of this church: pit west yard: 9 y^{ers}
		15	Ananias Warren sonne of George Warren in Recordes house, pit east yrd 17 yers
		15*	Weston Cabbage seruant to Mr Cooper sheere grinder, pit east yrd 19
		16	Fridaie Robert Record sonne of John Record Merchant Tailor, east: 3 yers
		16	Thomas Tailor sonne of John Tailor Merchant Tailor, west yard 18
		16	Richard Powell sonne of Dauid Powell Marchaunt Tailor, west yrd 9
		17	Satterdaie Elizabeth Rainscroft from Mrs Linseyes, pit in the west yrd 26
		18	Sunday Harry Wilkinson George Marrow his man: in the west yard 20
		19	Monday Katherin Powell daughter of Dauid Powell, merchant tailo^r 10
		21	Wedensdaie Thomas Fox seruant to Web Blacksmith, pit in ye east 18
		22	Thursdaie Jone Robertes wif of Steuen Robertes Cooke, pit in the south chap 30
		22	Robert Hunter sonne of Edward Hunter Poulter, pit in the West yrd 21
		23	Fridaie John Randoll sonne of John Randoll draper, pit in the east yard 10
		23	Michaell Nicholson sonne of Michaell Nicholson Cobler, in ye west yrd 7
		26	Monday William Ben Mr Thomas Wallthalles man, in ye south chapell 20
		28	Wedensdaie Symon Pedder sonne of John Pedder Marchant tailor 3 yers
		28	A still born childe of Thomas Plummer Grocer, pit by Pedders child west
		29	Thursdaie Edmond Cooper Armorer, pit in the west yard by ye vine 46
		29	John his man ignoti cognominis, his syr name not known, in theast yrd 19
		30	Friday Cutbert Hutchenson John Maxfeldes man, pit in the east yard 24
		30	Kathern Plummer wif of Thomas Plummer Grocer, in the south chap: 24
	October	1	Satterday Thomas Plummer Grocer, his pit with his wif in ye south chap: 30

* The Register from September 15, 1603, to February 7, 1604, is subscribed Will'm Asheboold, parson, T I   L E.

Yeare.	Month.	Day.	Names.
1603	October	1	Marget Goddard daughter of Edward Goddard Armorer, in ye east y^rd 4
		1	John Walton seruant to John Pedder Tailor, his pit in the east yard 18
		2	Sunday, Alice Thorogood daughter of James Thorogood Poulter years 7
		2	Sara Hickman daughter of Joseph Hickman Carpenter, an infant
		3	Monday James Stauelie Pewterer, his pit in the east yard his yers 30
		5	Wedensday Abell Tailor sonne of John Tailor Marchant tailor: yers 10
		6	Thursday Robert Bladwell Clothworker, his pit in the Library, yeres 76
		8	Satterday Anne Lecroft daugh: of Samson Lecroft Armorer in library 7
		8	Ralph Alcocke Edward Newelles man, Tailor, pit in the east yard: 19
		8	Peeter Bourn sonne of Thomas Bourn an infant beeing 8 weekes old
		9	Sunday James Thorogood Poulter, his pit in the east Yard, yeres 42
		19	Wedensday, Cisly Thorogood daugh: of James Thorogood Poulter: 3 yers
		19	Sara Stauelie an infant of James Stauelie Petwerer, pit wth her father
		21	Fridaie Rachell Powell daughter of Humfry Powell Tailer, of Yeares 3
		22	Satterday Marget Rochedale daughter of Wm Rochdale Brewer. yeares 6
		23	Abigaill Staulie daughter of James Staulie pewterer, an infant yers 2
		27	Thursday William Ratsdale* sonne of William Rochedale Brewer. Yeres 13
		28	Fridaie. Anne Kempton Mrs Plummers wench: pit in the west yard. 13
		28	Elizabeth Write daughter of John Wright Poulter, pit in ye west yard. 4
		29	Satterdaie. Richard Swifte Merchant Tailor, pit in ye church by ye poores box. 30
		22	Robert Michem seruant to Peter Haule Grocer, beeing about of yers 20
	Nouem	3	Thursdaie. William Rochedale sonne of William Rochedale, his yeares are: 6
		6	Sondaie Samuell Jackson seruant to Mrs Tailor widow, his yeares 23
Jonas and Richard Holdsworth my schollers.		5	Satterdaie. Jonas Holdsworth sonne of Henry Holdsworth Mercer, a boy very toward in learning, his pit in the west yard, hee was about 15 yrs
		9	Wedensday: Richard Holdsworth a youth vertuouslie giuen sonne of Henry Holdsworth Mercer, his pit by his brother, his yeares about 21

These vertuous youthes with guifts of nature blest,
Haue left this life and now doe liue at rest.

| | Novem | 11 | Friday: Williame Rodes seruant to William Warren, Cutler: his Yeares 16 |

* Sic.

Yeare.	Month.	Day.	Names.
1603	Novem	11	Aholiab Nicholson sonne of Michaell Nicholson Cobler, beeing of yeares 4
		13	Sunday, Robert Seaman brother to Thomas Seaman Vintner, yers. 20
		15	Tuesday: Jane Swifte, widow of Richard Swifte Tailor, pit by her husband. 26
		15	A Chrisome childe of hers new born, and buryed with her in the coffen
		18	Friday: Jane Swift daughter of Richard Swift, Tailer, a yeare & quarter old
		22	Tuesday: Christopher Askew Swiftes man in lif, beeing about yers 18
		26	Satterday: Sara Nicholson daughter of Mychaell Nicolson cobler: yers 9
	Decem	7	Wedensdaie, Isacke Vausalt sonne of Mr John Vansalt stranger his pit in the church in the North ile in the middle, hee was of yeares: 9
		22	Thursday: Mary Newell wif of Edward Newell Tailer; and the daughter of Mr Holdsworth. Mercer: a prety and modest woman her pit in the Library at th'entry in to the church dore, her Yeares: 26

From the 23 of December 1602 to the 22 of December 1603 buried in this parish in all; num :   158

Of them of the plague   87

Buried in all this yeare both without and w'in the liberties; and in the 8 out parishes from the 14th of Julie   38244

Of them of the plague: 30578

1603	Decem	28	Wedensdaie Elizabeth Farmer Mrs Askewes maid, in the east yard: 16
	Janua	2	Mondaie William Towers Mrs Askewes seruant, pit by her: yeares 18
		3	Tuesdaie Hamlet Rigsby Mrs Askewes man, pit by hym. Yeares 26
		9	Mondaie Mr John Vansalt Duchman, his pit in the Chancell vnder the stone of Mr Breton, hee was a good man & an elder of the duche church 52
		24	Tuesdaie Elizabeth Wigganhance a duch maid. his seruant, her pit in the Chancell by hym vnder Mr Bewchampes stone. Yeares 21
	Februa	6	Mondaie: Rachell Ridgeley wif of Edward Ridgeley Draper, her pit in the Librarie next the stones by the Church dore. her yeares 40
		13	Monday. Thomas Birchwood Cordwainer, pit in ye mid ile, his yers 42
		22	Wedensday. Mary Cason daughter of John Cason Grocer, an infant Christned but the daie beefore, her pit in the North ile by his pew.

Yeare.	Month.	Day.	Names.
1603	March	17	Satterday: A beggar boy ignoti nominis, which dyed in Leaden haule, brought out of St Andrewes parish next, by Braughton Constable
1604	June	3	Monday: Anne Williames an infant of Roger Williames Cooke
	July	15	Sunday: Susan Parker daughter of John Parkar Appoticary 7 yeares old, pit in the librarie by the West yard dore 7
	Septem	30	Sunday: Martha Satchfeld daughter of Richard Satchfeld Grocer: 4 yeares old, pit at the vpper end of the North ile 4
	October	12	Friday: Mr Thomas Malen, Browne baker, 80 Yeares old; 80 a man very discreet and wellbeloued; his graue in the North ile vpon his Wif vnder the stone against the Writing O sancta trinitas
	Decem	18	Tuesday Edward Steuens Jorniman to John Maxfeld 26 yeares old, his pit in the West yard hard by the Wall neare the gutter
	Februa	7	Thursday John Gray sonne of Mr William Gray Balif of Yarmouth out of Mr Sacheuerelles house the goat, his pit in the south Chappell vnder a long stone in the middest, age 22
	February	17*	Sunday: an infant named Ellen Palmer, beegotten of Ellen Palmer an vnmarried woman, by one Edmu'd Welsh a seruing man
		18	Monday: a Chrisome Childe of Richard Satchfeldes Grocer the pit in the North ile at the vpper end by Mr Pigots pew
	March	7	Thursday: Mr Richard Loxon Armorer 76 Yeares old one of the Maisters of Bridewell his pit in the Chauncell vnder the stone Wheare Mrs Ellen Lukener Wife of Mr Roger Lukener Esquire lyeth
		16	Satterday: Ellen Lecroft daughter of Samson Lecroft Armorer 7 Yeares old the childes pit in the Library, one this syde th'east yard dore
1605		27	Wedensday: Margaret Vertu mother of Christopher Vertu vintne^r 100 yeares old, her pit in the Crosse ile by the poores box
		28	Maundy Thursday: Thomas Leigh Pewterer 80 Yeares old, hee dyed of a feuer rather of greef: his pit in south Chapell vpon Mr Gray
	Maye	16	Thomas Hudsonne the sonne of George Hudsonne Vpholster dwellinge in Cornhill
	June	27	Peter Colinge the sonne of ffrauncies Colinge Linendrap' dwellinge in Cornhill
		28	A Crisome Child the daughter of Edward Newelles Marchant dwellinge in Gratious streete
	Julie	11	Jone Warman the daughter of William Warman Cooke dwellinge in Leaden hall streete
		15	Jeames Persey the sonne of ffraunces Persey porter dwellinge in Gratioustreete
		16	Thomas Wellen the sonne of Nathnioll Wellen Linendrap: dwellinge in Cornhill
	Auguste	11	Jone Reynoldes the Wif of Rowland Reynoldes Skinner dwellinge in Cornhill

* The Register from February 17, 1604, to February 7, 1605, is subscribed Will'm Asheboold, parson, L E, Chrystopher Vertew.

THE REGISTERS OF ST. PETER'S, CORNHILL. 161

Yeare.	Month.	Day.	Names.
1605	August	11	ffrauncies Humstone a guest from Thomas Holdsworth Inholder dwellinge in gratious streete
		22	A stillborne Child of one Alice Jones as shee sayth the wife of one Rowland Jones dwellinge in Huntington shire
		24	Eve Draper a Dutch Wench from ffishers the Cobler dwellinge in Bishiopsgat streete
	September	6	Jone Weller auncient p'ishioner an almes woman dwellinge in Corbets Coorte
William Auerell parish clarke		23	William Averell Clarke of this p'ishe dwellinge in Corbetes Courte in Gratious streete
	Nouember	28	Sarah Strafford the daughter of Jeames Strafford of Abbington in Oxfordshoere and sy'vant to Libbeus Swane
	December	6	Katherin Vdall Alias Woodall the daughter of John Vdall Alias Woodall barber sargant dwellinge in Cornhill
		27	Luce Anderson Widd': shee died in Childbed and her Child stilborne shee was seruant to Mrs Walker in Corbetes Courte gra' street
	Januarie	20	William Ap Robertes servant to Peirce Richardsonne Clothworker dwellinge in Leaden hall streete
		21	John Boomer the Husband of Jone Boomer dwellinge in St Peters Alie in gratious streete. ali' in the Church allie
		31	William Stone
	February	7	Elizabeth Ashboold the daughter of Mr William Ashboold dwellinge in St Peters Alie in Gratious streete
		23*	John Milner the sonne of Robert Milner
	March	7	John Williames the sonne of Roger Williames Cooke dwellinge in Gratious streete
		17	. . . † Adlingtonne Widdow dwelling in gratious streete
		16	Hellen Stone the daughter of Thomas Stone Poulterer dwellinge in Gratious streete
1606	April	7	Joseph Cowes the sonne of William Cowes, Pewterer dwellinge in Leaden hall street
		15	Allice . . . † of Deptforde an Ancient Maid that fell suddenlie downe dead att the spread Eagle in gratious streete
	Maye	6	Richard Barron seruant to Joseph Granes Vintner dwellinge in Bishiopsgat streete
		9	An Kerbee who Lodged att Goodman ffishers the Cobler dwellinge in Bishopsgat streete
		23	Hable Brittan the daughter of Walter Brittane Tapstreworke^{r} dwellinge in Leadenhall stteete
	June	12	Elizabeth Parton the Wif of Edward Parton dwellinge in gratious streete
		18	Henric Palmur the sonne of William Palmur Marchant dwellinge in Leaden hall streete
	August	8	Margret † sy'vant to Edward Hunter poulter dwellinge in Gratious streete
		10	Thomas Laurence whoe Lodged att Edward Hunters dwellinge in Gratious streete
		13	William Chadocke in the Librarie the sy'vant to Rowland Reynoldes Vpholster, dwelling in Cornhill
		14	Alice Pickborne on hir ffather Jeames Pickborne dwellinge in Bishopsgate streete

* The Register from February 23, 1605, to November 13, 1606, is subscribed Will'm Ashcoold, parson, Chrystopher Vertew, ffraunces Colynge.
† Sic.

Yeare.	Month.	Day.	Names.
1606	August	20	William Charlton sy'vant of William Jaunsonne Vintner dwellinge in Cornhill
		27	An Weston the daughter of Robert Weston Vpholster dwellinge in St Peters Alie in gratious streete
	Septem	16	Peter Turner Grocer, dwellinge in Cornhill
	October	29	Allice Jurdaine Widd': dwellinge in gratious streete
		30	William Androwes Grocer dwellinge in Leadenhall streete
		31	A poore ffraukticke Womanne found in Leaden hall streete
	Nouemb	5	Anne Poulter the seruant to William Wellinge Linen draper dwellinge in Cornhill
		13	Thomas Holdsworth Inholder att the spread Eagle in Gratious street
	Decemb^r	29*	An Obortiue the sonne of William Jansonne Vintner dwellinge in Cornhill
		31	Edmund Sesmer Mearcer whoe Lodged att Robert Weston dwellinge in St Peters Alie in gratious streete
	Februar	3	Boniface Tatam Vintner whoe dwelte in marke laine
		13	Elizabeth Colinge the daughter of ffraunces Colinge Linen drap': dwellinge in Cornhill
	March	3	Ann Cloinge† the wiffe of ffrauncies Cloinge† Linen Draper dwellinge in Cornhill
		5	Edward Planckney sy'vant to the L. Buckurst T^r whoe lodged att Walter Brittans dwelling in Leadenhall street
		21	A stil borne Child the sonne of John Caunt Linen drap' dwellinge in Leaden hall streete
		21	Thomas Sutle a poore man that Lay att the spred Egle in Gratious streete
		21	Jone Barley Widd': Mother to William Barley Stationer, dwelling in Gratious streete
1607	Aprill	9	Richard Goodwine the sonne of Richard Goodwine Porter dwellinge in Kinges ware house Yard
		14	Anthonet ffarninean duchman dwellinge in burchin laine
		19	William Normavell, Lodger att the spred egle in gr: streete
		26	Walter Wright the sonne of John Wright Poult^r dwellinge in gratious streete
	Julie	10	ffraunces Askew the daughter of William Askew Cooke dwellinge in Leaden hall streete
		12	Richard Barnard haberdasher dwellinge in Cornhill
		12	Marie Askew the daughter of William Askew Cooke dwellinge in Leaden hall streete
		21	ffrauncies Pywell the daughter of William Pywell in the Countie‡ Clothworker
	Auguste	1	Marie Sacker the daughter of Richard Sacker of Cambridge and sy'vant to Peter Weightman in grat: str.
		3	Edward Rowles from M^{ris} Askew dwellinge in Leaden hall streete
		24	Elizabeth Luddingtonne the daughter of Valintine Luddingtonne smith dwelling in Ledon hall streete
		27	Hughe Barnard the sonne of Richard Barn' haberdasher dwellinge in Cornhill

* The Register from December 29, 1606, to July 1, 1608, is subscribed Will'm Ashebooold, p'son, ffraunces Colynge, John Parker.
† Sic.   ‡ Sic.

THE REGISTERS OF ST. PETER'S, CORNHILL. 163

Yeare.	Month.	Day.	Names.
1607	September	1	A poore souldier that died in the Cage in Leaden hall street
		2	Robert Prime the sonne of Thomas Prime Scrivener dwellinge in Leaden hall streete
		8	Lucressa Clarke the wiffe of Robert Clarke with hir Child stil borne Marchand dwellinge in Cornhill
	September	15	John Whitman the sonne of Peter Whitman Vintner dwellinge in gratious streete
	October	19	* sy'vant to Jeames Hardwine smith dwellinge Bishopsagat streete
	November	5	Bennet Warman the daughter of William Warman Cooke dwelling in Leadenhall street
		25	Cisley Harte an Auncient Maide lyinge att m^r Butlers the Potter dwelling in Bishopsgat streete
	Januarie	16	Robert Piggott the sonne of Richard Piggott from m^r Piggott grocer dwellinge in Cornhill
		27	Richard ffussett Tapster at the spead* Eagle in Gratious streete
	March	11	Maudeline Williams Widd': the Mother of Roger Williams Cooke dwellinge in gratious streete
		13	Richard Allen the ffather of Mr Woldrigs Wiffe Poulter dwellinge in gratious streete
1608		29	Roger Walthall the sonne of Thomas Walthall Marchant dwellinge in gratious streete
	Aprill	11	Androwe Lannglee the sonne of John Lannglee Linen Draper dwellinge in Cornhill
		12	Basshaw Travesse sy'vant to Mr Bell marchant dwellinge in Leaden hall streete
		30	Anne Kinge the daughter of John Kinge Marchant dwellinge in Leaden hall streete
	Maye	4	Nicholas Casonne grocer dwellinge in the King's ware house Yard in Cornhill
		10	John Snape the sonne of † Snape how loged att Mr Stockes in gratious streete
		12	Thomas Vowell the ffather of John Vowell Poulter dwellinge in gratious streete
		30	Jone Okeley the daughter of Thomas Okeley Poulter dwellinge in gratious streete
	June	4	Walter Ridgley the sonne of Edward Ridgley sy'gante dwellinge in Corbetes Courte in gratious streete
		4	Jeames Goodwine the sonne of Richard Goodwine Poter dwellinge in the Kinges ware house yard in Cornhill
		7	Walter Goodwine the sonne of Richard Goodwine Potter dwellinge in the Kinges ware house yard in Cornhill
		18	John Maxfeild Brasier dwellinge in Cornhill
		24	Sampson Leycrofte Brasier dwellinge in gratious str:
	Julie	1	An abortiue the sonne of ffrances Scotte the sonne in law to Edward Kittle dwelling in Cornhill
		10‡	An abortiue the sonne of George Younge musitiane dwellinge in read crose Alie in Cornhill
		16	Robert Androwes dwellinge in Leaden hall streete
		16	Thomas Piggott Grocer dwellinge in Cornhill
		24	Susanne Brittane the daughter of Walter Brittane Tapstre worker dwellinge in Leaden hall streete

* Sic.   † Sic.
‡ The Register from July 10, 1608, to October 9, 1609, is subscribed Will'm Ashebolde, parson, John Parker, Stephen Roberts.

Yeare.	Month.	Day.	Names.
1608	Auguste	9	Elizabeth Brittane the Wiffe of Walter Brittane Tapstre worker dwellinge in Leaden hall streete
		22	Beasee Nickolles the sonne of * Nickolles dwellinge in Bishopsgate streete
		23	Susan Kinnistone the Wiffe of * Kinnistone Poulter dwellinge in Gratious streete
		27	Thomas Holdsworth the sonne of Thomas Holdsworth Inholder dwellinge in gratious streete
	September	2	Marie Wellen the wiffe of Nathaniell Wellen Linen Draper dwellinge in Cornhill
		2	Mr William Wallthall Alderman, and free of the Mearcers dwellinge in Gratious streete
		6	Owen ffisher Cobler dwellinge in Bishopsgat streete
		17	John ffisher the sonne of Owen ffisher Cobler dwellinge in Bishopsgat streete
		21	Margerie Jurdan the wif of Jeames Jurdan Potter dwellinge in the Kinges ware house yard in Cornhill
	December	22	Prudence Weightman the daughter of Peter Weight: Vintner dwellinge in gratious streete
	Januarie	20	A Child of Sir Anthonies Agers whoe lodge in Leadenhall
		25	Jeames Jurdan Mr Potter in the Kinges Ware house Yard in Cornhill
	Februarie	3	Margrett Dickson Widd': dwellinge in Cornhill
	March	12	Anne Purlevant the Wif of Thomas Purlevant dwellinge in Kinges Ware house yard in Cornhill
		15	ffrauncies Sheffeild seruant to Mr Vertue Vintner dwellinge in Leaden hall streete
		19	Grace Arnwaye the wif of Richard Arnwaye Vintner dwellinge in Leadenhall streete
1609		29	Ralph Leese seruant to peirce Richardson Cloworker* dwellinge in Leadenhall streete
			A stilborne Child the sonne of Thomas Prime Scrivener dwellinge in Leaden hall streete
			Marie Purlevant the daughter of Thomas Purlevant dwellinge in the Kinges Ware house yard in Cornhill
	Aprill	12	William Evanes seruant to Peirce Richardson Cloworker* dwellinge in Leaden hall streete
		16	Robert Jones seruant to Peirce Richardson Cloworker* dwellinge in Leaden hall streete
	May	11	Angnis Toolie Widdowe that came from Greenwiche and died att m^r Jones the Barber in Bishoppsgate streete
		13	Arthur Robinsonne the sonne of Arthur Robinsonne Marchant dwellinge in Bishoppsgat streete
		23	William Weston, ffree of the Grocer, dwellinge in Bishoppsgat streete
	June	1	Robert Hearon, of Meldonne in the Countie of Northumberland gent: Lodged att the spread Eagle in gratious streete
		4	Annes Richardson, Widdow. dwellinge in gratious streete
		8	Isabel Loxon, Widdow. dwellinge in Leaden hall streete
		9	Nicholas Melway seruant to m^r Tucker, Marchantalor dwellinge in gratious streete
		25	John Caunte, ffree of the ffishmonger. Linen Drap': dwellinge att the Corne* of gratious streete
		28	Richard Lucnst, servant to Widdow ffisher Cobler, dwellinge in gratious streete

* sic.

Yeare.	Month.	Day.	Names.
1609	July	4	Adam Shipp in the New Church Yard the sonne of John Shipp dwellinge in gratious streete
		11	Christian Harries the daughter of John Harries Scriuener, dwellinge in Bishopsgat streete
		19	William Webb the sonne of Richard Webb grocer dwellinge in Bishopsgate streete
	Auguste	4	Richard Webb, ffree of the grocers and dwellinge in Bishopsgate streete
		16	Margrett Ridgley the daughter of Edward Ridgley Seargent, dwellinge in Corbetts coorte in gratious streete
		24	Marie Barley the daughter of William Barley stationer, dwellinge in gratious streete
	September	22	Sarath Jacobsonne the daughter of Peter Jacobsonne straunger dwellinge in Bishopsgate streete
		26	Richard Paine seruant to Arthur Wakefeild haberdasher, dwellinge in Cornhill
	October	9	Susan Charter the daughter of Richard Charter Taylor, dwellinge in Cornhill
		11*	A stilborne Child of Mr Kinges, Marchand dwellinge in Leaden hall streete
	Nouember	4	Mathew Wakefeild the wif of Arthur Wakefeild haberdasher dwellinge in Cornhill
		6	Arthur Wakefeild, haberdasher dwellinge in Cornhill
		11	Jone Casonne, from mr Weight, in gratious streete
		24	Annes Goldinge the wif of Henry Goldinge stockingepresser, dwellinge in Bishopsgate
		28	Robert Warden, poulterer, dwellinge in Bishopsgat str
	December	7	A stilborne Child the sonne of Thomas Leycraft from mr Jones Barber, dwellinge in Bishopsgat str
		16	ffraunces Pearce, porter dwellinge gratious str'
	Januarie	17	Robert Rates, seruant to William Burton Marchant, dwellinge in gratious streete
	Februarie	24	Richard Lendall, seruant to Heurye Goldinge stockinge presser dwellinge in Bishopsgate streete
	March	9	Robert Sanders, seruant to Jeames Hardwine Smith, dwellinge in Bishopsgat streete
1610		29	Isackey Cason the sonne of John Cason Grocer dwellinge in Cornhill
	Aprill	25	Richard Weight, ffree of the Poulterer dwellinge in gratious streete
	Maie	2	Thomas Luddington, ffrom Valintine Luddington Smith, dwellinge in Leaden hall streete
	June	11	Gregorie Younge Grocer dwellinge att the corner house of the north side of Leaden hall streete
		18	A stilborne Child the daughter of Thomas Chatwine Sergant dwellinge in Corbets Coorte
	July	11	Katherine ffeildinge, seruant to William Chapmanne, dwellinge in Cornhill
		24	Elizabeth Blofeild, the daughter of Richard Blofeild, Brasier, dwellinge in gratious str
		24	Thomas Phillips, A poore Laberinge man dwellinge in Corbets Coorte in gratious streete
		31	Tobias Weston the sonne of Robert Weston, Vpholdster, dwellinge in the Church alie

* The Register from October 11, 1609, to July 31, 1610, is subscribed Will'm Asheboold, parson. Stephen Roberts.

Yeare.	Month.	Day.	Names.
1610	August	1*	Susan Scuinnge, shee dwellt at Mr Webbs Smith, dwellinge in Bishopsgat streete
		31	John Ridgley, the sonne of Edward Ridgley Sergant, dwellinge in Corbets Coorte
	Septemb^r	6	Richard Charter, Taylor dwellinge in Cornhill
		11	Prudent Weightman, the daughter to Peter weightman, Vintener, dwellinge in gratious st^r
		11	Edward Ridgley, Seyrgant, dwellinge in gratious† in Corbets Coorte
		12	Edward Ridgley, And Edward† Ridgley the Sonnes of Edward Ridgley as aforesaid
		16	Alice Higgines, the Sister of Mrs Ridgley dwellinge in Corbets Coorte
		17	Margrett Ridgley, the Wif of Edward Ridgley dwellinge in Corbets Coorte
		21	Elizabeth Morries the daughter of Hugh Morries shee dwelt att Mr Chamb^rlines the Brickler in Platter alie in Gratious streete: pit ye East yeard Coff
		29	Richard Ardinge s^rvant to John Pedder Taylor in corbites Coort in gratious streete: his pitt in ye East yeard
	October	1	Mathew Jones Mrs Charters man the Taylor in Cornhill hee died of the plague, his pitt at the new church yeard
		20	Edward Chapman, ffree of the bricklayers dwelling in Bishopsgate streete he died of a greefe. his pitt at the going in at the belferrie neere the founte
		21	Jone Pywell the wife of John Pywell her pitt in the North capple
	Decemb^r	24	A poore man from Mr Midletons house at the black bull in leadenhall streete being brought thether by the constable of ffarthing ward
	February	2	Edward Eachell s^rvant to Mr Pywell in Leadenhall streete
		19	John Leake keeper of Leaden Hall
	March	8	Thomas Leycroft the sonne of Thomas Leycroft a Lynnen drap'
		20	A poore boy that died of a fall from a horse by the Cage in Leaden hall streete
1611	Aprill	12	John Lemott the sonne of John Lemott Ma^rchaunt strang^r
	June	5	Thomas Charter the sonne of Richard Charter sometime M^rchantaylor in Cornehill Deceased
		11	Isbell Grauenor the wife of Thomas Grauener Lynnen Drap' in Gratious streete
	July	10	Margaret Haunis the wife of Richard Hannis silkweauer in the Harrow alie in Gratious streete
		16	John J'anson the sonne of William J'anson Vintner in Cornehill
	August	18‡	Thomas Brewin the sonne of Roger Brewin Vpholder in Leadenhall streete
		19	Peeter Goodwine the sonne of Richard Goodwine one of the porters of the kinges weighouse
		23	Christopher Vertue Vintener in Leaden hall streete
		31	Roger Brewin Vpholder and free of the Skynners in Leadenhall streete

* The Register from August 1, 1610, to July 16, 1611, is subscribed Will'm Asheboold, parson.
† Sic.
‡ The Register from August 18, 1611, to October 14, 1613, is subscribed Will'm Asheboold, parson, John Cason, churchwarden.

THE REGISTERS OF ST. PETER'S, CORNHILL.

Yeare.	Month.	Day.	Names.
1611	Septem	2	Anthony Pigine s`vant to M`r` Brewin Vpholder in Leadenhall streete
		5	Susan Sauidge wife to * Sauidge Haberdasher in Leade*hall streete, whoe desperatelie hanged herselfe the Daye before
		6	Thomas Leycroft free of Turners and Linnen drap' in ledenhall streete
	Septemb`r`	7	Hellen Williamson wife to James Williamson lodger at M`r` Helmes the Brasier in Cornehill
		20	Mary Brewine daughter to Roger Brewine deceased
	October	6	Susan Lddington* the daughter of Valentine Luddington Armorer in Leaden hall streete
	October	12	Richard Westonn sonne of Roberte Westonn Vpholder in Church allie
		13	A poore boy that died in the Cadge in Leaden hall streete
	Nouemb`er`	4	John Chare servant to M`r` Jones Barber in Bishopsgate stret
		4	Jane Peeter a poore child laide in this p'ishe
		9	Marie Askew the daughter of * Askew haberdasher in harrow Allie in Gratious streete
	Decemb`r`	6	Thomas Jones the sonne of Thomas Jones Barber in bishopsgate stree'
	January	2	John Kinge the sonne of John Kinge M`r`chante in leadenhall stree'
		5	Mary Lemott the daughter of John Lemott M`r`chante in bishopsgat stree'
	February	8	Nicholas Weston sonne of Robert Weston Vphold`r` in y`e` church ally
		18	Elizabeth Leycroft Daught`r` of Thomas Leycroft sometime drap' of london
	March	3	Jone Prisley widdow & searche`r` dwelling at y`e` Bull in leaden hall street
		8	Arther Tucker sonne of Thomas Tucker M`r`chantalo`r` in harrow ally gratious*
		21	Annis Hadley s`r`vant to M`r` Barley Stacioner in gratious streete
1612	Aprill	4	Abraham Helmes the sonne of Edward Helmes Grocer
		10	* Hall y`e` wife of M`r` Hall grocer in leadenhall Streete
		24	Ma`r`y Price widdow whoe died of a Consumption
	May	10	Joseph Hickman Carpenter dwellinge in Corbittes coorte in gratious street
	June	26	Rob`t`. Weston Vpholder in the Churchallie his ¦pitt in the west yeard
		28	Symon Cleanlie M`r`chantalor from his brother Westons howse aforesaid
		30	Jefferie Salte`r` the sonne of John Salte`r` Brasye`r` in gratious street
	July	18	Edward Hunter Poulter in Gratious streete
	August	11	Elizabeth Snape daughter of Edward Snape sometyme lying at M`r` Stockes howse
		13	A Child newborne the daughter of John Morten linnen drap' in Cornhill
		28	John Hutton s`r`vant to Thomas Grauener Linnen draper at Leaden hall Corner
	October	1	Edward Thorowgood s`r`vannt to Thomas Lusher Lynnen drap'

* Sic.

Yeare.	Month.	Day.	Names.
1612	October	2	Elizabeth Robinson the wife of Arthur Robinson Marchant in bishopsga'
		23	Lettice Euans the wife of Lawrence Euans Cutl{r} in gratious street
	Nou{e}mber	22	Margret Whitlocke Daughter of Robert Whitlocke of y{e} kinges weigho'
	December	10	James White s{r}vaunt to M{r} Helmes Brasyer in Cornhill
		13	M{rs}* Hopkins the wife M{r} Will'm Hopkins ffishmonger in New fish street
	December	21	Robert Haxsbee Clarke of this p'ish and free of the ffishmongers Dwelt in Corbittes Courte in gratioustreete
	January	26	Will'm Edwardes s{r}vant to Tho: Salloman Sadler in Gratioustreete his pitt in the East yeard: died of a Consumpc'on
	ffebru{a}ry	2	Ellice the supposed sonne of Ellice Gest: the mother of the saide childe dwelleth w{th} her ffather Rob{t} Steward w{th}in the bull y'
	Aprill	14	M{rs} Vertue sometime dweller in this p'ish was buried in the Chancell vnder the bradeston ouer against y{e} dore in the midle ile
		28	Walter Dayrell ffrom M{r} Colinges his pitt in the lyberary. aboue the dore going into the west yeard howers knell 4{th} bell
	May	1	Honery Bunny s{r}vant to John Holmes Shomaker in Bish: died of a surphit pitt in the West yeard hou{rs} knell w{th} y{e} 3 bell
		fri 14	M{r} Thomas Walthall Mercer in Gratioustreete, age 75 yeares. his pitt in the chancell coffined greate bell afternoone po{r}e mo{r}nrs
		17	Monday M{rs} Woodford the wife of M{r} Gamalioll Wodford somtime p'ishon{r} buried in the valte in y{e} North chappell by night
		18	Tuesday Elizabeth Huggins from M{r} Euans Cutler in grat't† pitt in the west yearde coff next the co{r}ner of the church East
		25	Tuesday M{r} John Malyn Practicon{r} in Phissicke dweling in Byshopsgate Streete pitt in the North Ile greate bell 6 ho{rs} coffen. He gaue 12{d} euery weeke in bread to y{e} poore of this parrish
		28	Friday M{rs} Anne Payne mother to M{rs} Socke Lynnen drap' of the age of 74 yeares died of a consumption her pitt in South Chappell
	August	16	Monday Richard Bromly a Shropshire man, brought w{th} a passe from Algate ward and died in Cornhill streete buried in y{e} new church yeard
	Septem{r}	4	Satterday M{r} John Morrice free of the Clothworkers dwelling in Cornhill of the age of 64 yeares died of a consumption pitt in the Chancell
		17	Friday M{rs} Barbarah Cason the wife of M{r} Jo: Cason Grocer dwell' in Cornhill died of a Consumption being of the* 44 yeares pit Chancell
		25	Satter: Elizabeth Weightman daughter of Peter Weight: Vintne{r} in Gratioustreet being a Crysum pit in the West yeard
		28	Tuesday: Sarah Dolton the daughter of William Dolton

* Sic.   † For "Gratious street."

THE REGISTERS OF ST. PETER'S, CORNHILL.

Yeare.	Month.	Day.	Names.
			Seafarer dwelling Leadenhall streete being of a yeare old pit in the W : y :
1613	October	4	Monday ffrauncis Brett from Mrs Weightes of the age of 24 yeares her pitt in the liberary betweene the church yeard do^r & ye stret S
		—	The same daye buried a stilborne child of Mr Gatwoodes in Gracious streete at the pew do're marked wth the figure 8 in the midle Ile coffe : N
		14	Thursday Jeane Demaie mother to Mrs Payne dwelling in Gracioustreete in the valte vnder the Communion table of the age of 64 yeares great bell 6 howres
	Nouemb^r	20*	Buried a man childe still borne of Mr Jesper ffowler M^{r}chant dwelling in Bishopsgate streete Mid Ile
		23	Buried Mrs Coop' sister to Mrs Ashboold in the valte vnder the Communion table by night who died of Consum'
		26	Buried a man childe still borne of Robarte Jeninges vphold^r in Cornhill pitt in the mid Ile vnde^r the pew wth the fig : 7
		—	Buried the wife of Mr Jesper ffowler M^{r}chant she died in childebedd her pit in the Chancell against the mid Ile doore one the left hande goinge in, greate bell 6 how^{rs} Duch wo'
	Decemb	9	Buried Dorrity Parrott s^{r}vant to Mr Chapman in the weighowse yeard her pitt in the mid Crosse Ile vnder ye 3 stone N
		13	Buried Martin Bradford s'vant to Mr Luke Walthall his pitt in the West yeard and died of a burning feau^r
		17	Buried Susan Kenniston of ye age of 9 yeares coffened her pitt in the South Ile one right hand at the vp' end
	Janua^{r}y	5	Buried Steuen Robartes free of the cookes dwelling at the plat^r in gratioustreete his pitt in the south chapple. died of ye palse
		7	Buried Mrs Clarke out of Mynsinge layne her pit in the Chancell one south side of the Communion table of age
		10	Buried Alce Weightman the wife of Peeter Weightma' vintner in Gratioustreete her pit in the south Ile of ye kinges†
		13	Buried Joane the daughter of Arnold Prentize vintner in Leadenhall streete, of the age of 9 month' pit in the east yeard
	Februa	13	Buried William Strayne s^{r}vant to Mr Holmes Shomaker in Bishopsgate streete pit in ye east yeard died of a bur'ng feau'
		18	Buried Richard Congrie free Glaysier dwelling in bishopsg' streete, his pit in the midle Ile one North side, of the goute
		19	Satterday Michell Brunskyll s^{r}vaunt to Mr Lynthwaight vpholdster in Cornhill pit in the east yeard coff : age of 21 yea'
	March	13	Buried William Yeates s^{r}vaunt to Mr Richardson Cloth worker in leadenhall streete, pitt in the East yea'
1614	Aprill	16	Buried Jockaminshaw Butler the wife of James Butler Potter in Bishopsgate streete, pit in the South chappell great bell

* The Register from November 20, 1613, to June 24, 1614, is subscribed Will'm Asheboold, Robert Bell, John Pywall.
† Sic.

z

Yeare.	Month.	Day.	Names.
1614	May	14	Buried Sara the daughter of George Burket braysier in Cornhill: pitt in the Midd: Ile being of the age of ¼
	June	8	Buried Dorritie Moore the daughter of Thomas Moore M^rchaunt in Bishopsgatst': pitt in the Midd Ile right hand
		24	Buried William Hynde sonne of Thomas Hinde Inholder at the Bull in Leadenhall streete pitt in Midd Ile one the North side of the said Ile 3 bell 1 ho^r
	July	29*	Buried Rich: Blowfeild free of the Armoro^{rs} in Gratioustreete his pitt in the Cross Ile one hether side the poore boxe greate bell 6 ho^{rs}
	August	11	Buried Richard Goodwine servante Mr Webb, smith in Bishopsgate st^reete, his pitt in the West yearde, coff, 22 years old
		—	Buried a still borne child of John Evans Cutler in gratioust^rete pitt in the East yeard at the doore coming in small bell on ho^r
		24	Buried Elizabeth Hannis daughter of Rich: Hannis silkeweauer in Harrow Allie of the age of x yeres pitt in the Cloyst^r
	October	31	Buried Margarett Slauter s^rvant to Mr Lee haberdasher dwellinge in Cornhill, age 25 yeres, pitt in the east yeard
	January	31	Buried Elizabeth Clyfton s^rvant to Raphe Southwell Lynnendrap' in Cornhill, age 30 yeres pitt in the east yeard
	February	14	Buried a poore weoman that was founde dead in Mr Wrothes entrie she was buried in the new church yearde
		12	Buried Elizabeth Andrew the daughter of Richard Andrew M^rchaunte in leadenhall streete pitt in the church North Ile
1615	April	25	Buried Margaret Graues widdo' of the age of 88 yeares her pitt in the Church in ye North Ile one the left hand greate bell 6 ho^{rs} Coff'
	May	6	Buried Edward Walker ffree Clothworker dwelling Bish: his pitt in the Cloyster great bell 1 ho^r Coffened
		15	Buried Gyles Bostocke ffree Scriueno^r of the age of 24 yeares who dwelte in Mr Hills in Cornhill Lyndp'
		18	Buried Peeter Hall Grocer but free Drap' his pitt in the Chancell his age 76 yeares greate bell 6 howe^{rs}
		22	Buried Sarah Reynoldes the daughter of Rowland Reynoldes her pitt in the Midd Ile in the body of the church
	June	12	Buried Clement Bakon the sonne of Clement Bakon Taylor of the age of 2 yeares dweling in Bishop.
		15	Buried Widd: Younge a poore pencioner who dwelte in the greene yeard at leaden hall her pitt in the S: yeard
		17	Buried Katherine the daughter of Anthony Botly Lynnen drap' in the liberary her pitt was next† the church doo^r
		20	Buried Anne Crouch servant to Tho: Gottwod in Gratioustreete her pitt in the Crosse Ile by ye poore boxe
		22	Buried Petter Sommers ffree of the Iremongers from Martine Bondes in leadenhall streete age 25 ye^{rs}

* The Register from July 29, 1614, to June 3, 1616, is subscribed Will'm Asheboold, parson, p' me Ric. Sachfilde.
† Sic.

Yeare	Month.	Day.	Names.
1615	Julie	1	Buried Ellyn Hickman daughter of Joseph Hickman deceased who dwelt in Corbites Courte she was of 8 yeares
		3	Buried George Hubberstead of the age of 58 year^{rs} his pitt in West yeard vnder the vine 4 bell 1 hore coff'
		5	Buried Robarte Jennettes sonne of James Jennettes p'ish Clarke of the age of 6 weekes 2 dayes in the West yeard
		7	Buried Thomas Hinde the sonne of Thomas Hinde Inholder in the midle Ile Coff" of the age of 2 yeres
	August	14	Buried Edmund Parton ffree of the Skynners dwellinge in Harrow ally of the age of 106 yeares Coff"
	Septem^r	14	Buried a Childe still borne of Thomas Gatwood free of the Mercers in the midle Ile Coff" 3 bell 1 ho^r
	October	24	Buried Ellen Graues the daughter of Joseph Graues Vintner her pitt in the North Ile Coff' 3 bell 1 ho^r
	Noumb^r	16	Buried Margrett Warden widd' she dwelte in Bishopsgate streete her pitt in the Chancell vnder her husbands ston
	Decemb^r	15	Buried Susan Yong widd' she dwelte in the Corner house of leadenhall streete her pitt in the Chancell by her husband
		23	Buried a Crysome childe of Debborah Trulace she was brought a bedd of it in the Cage in Leadenhall streete
		24	Buried Stephen Huchinson ye sonne of Jaruis Huchinson one of the porters of the kinges Waighouse
	Janua^{r}y	9	Buried Thomas Ogar brother to William Ogar Grocer in Leadenhall streete: pitt in the East yeard Coff" 3 bell 1 ho^r
		13	Buried Robarte Steward free of the Barbersurgeons dwelling in Leadenhall streete his pitt in the East yeard Coff" 3 bell 1 ho^r
		22	Buried Robarte Standish free of the Haberdashers dwelling in Bishopsgate streete his pitt in the Crose Ile by the alminacke
	Februa^{r}y	11	Buried Anne Charles seruant to Nicholas Hill Lynnendrap' in Cornhill her pitt in the East yeard Coff' smale bell 1 ho^r
		22	Buried Ellen Walker of the age of 44 yeares she died of a dropsey her pitt in the east yeard Coff" 3 bell 1 ho^r
	March	15	Buried Richard Taylor the sonne of John Taylor free Mercer dwellinge in Corbittes Corte in Gracechurch streete pitt in ye east yea^{r}d
1616		25	Buried a Crysome childe of John Slauters ¡Braysier in Cornhill a* the Helmet his pitt in the West yeard vnder the vine
		30	Buried John Graye borne in the p'ish of Charford in Essex hee died in the streete. his pitt in the East yeard
	Aprill	17	Buried Ann Ambrose widd' she died at Mr Stockes howse her pitt in the East yearde Coff' she died of a Consumption
		25	Buried Anthony Bullardine free of the A^{r}morers delling* in Gracechurch streete his pitt in the Cloyster age 37 yeres
		29	Buried Ann the wife of John ffearen free of the Skynnes* dwelling in Harrow ally in Gracechurch streete

* Sic.

Yeare.	Month.	Day.	Names.
1616	May	16	Buried Mary the daughter of Robarte Whitelocke one of the porters of the kinges weighouse pitt in ye west y'
		17	Buried Mary Steward widd' and pen'coner of this p'ish she dwelt in Leadenhall streete her pitt in the east yeard
	June	3	Buried Wilmore Knowleman s^{r}vant to Mr Norman Paynter in Bishopsgate streete her pit in the east yeard
	Julie	18*	Buried Marie Jones the daughter of Richard Jones Taylo^r in Bishopsgate streete pitt in the west yearde
		25	Buried Richard Maddox seruant to Robart Chamberlyn Bricklayer in Gracechurchstreete pitt in the East yeard
	August	24	Buried fflowrance Slauter the sonne of John Slauter Brasier in Cornhill pitt in the West yearde
		31	Buried Marg^{r}et Rochdale the wife of Will'm Rochdale Bruer her pitt in the north Ile by the Collecto^{rs} pew
	Septemb^r	16	Buried Richard Sachfeild free of the Grocers his pit in the North Ile ouer against the pew nomber 4 by night
		24	Buried Thomas Bingham the sonne of Thomas Bingham Cooke dwellinge in Leadenhalle streete pitt in the East yeard
	October	10	Buried Ellinor Graues the Wife of Joseph Graues vintne^r her pitt in the Midle ile vnder ye pewes number 4 & 5 right side
		31	Buried Martha Norton widd' she died at Allixande^r Symondes Cooke in leadenhall streete her pitt in the East yearde Coff'
	Nouem^r	8	Buried Hanna Hardinge daughter of Matthias Hardinge Taylo^r in leadenhall streete her pitt in the East yearde Coff'
		19	Buried Robarte Hill the sonne of Nicholas Hill Lynnen Drap' in Cornhill pitt in the East yearde coff'
		26	Buried Margret Wellen the wife of Nathaniell Wellen sometime dwelling in this p'ishe pitt in the North Chappell
	Decemb^r	24	Buried John Burket the sonne of John Burkett Armorer in Gracechurch streete pitt in the Midle ile nom^r 9
	January	1	Buried John Kinge servante to M^r J:anson vintener in Cornhill. his pitt in the West yearde Coff' 3 bell 1 how^r
		10	Buried Elizabeth Lynzey widd' pitt in the lib^r next to ye church doo^r
	Marche	19	Buried Edward Orde servante to Mr Hinde pitt in ye east yeard
1617	Aprill	3	Buried Alixander Symondes the sonne of Alixander Symondes Cooke in Gracechurch streete. pitt in the Midle ile vnder his stone
		12	Buried Will'm Myntton carrier from Mr Hills Lynnen drap' in Cornhill pitt in the West yearde 3 bell 1 hou^r
		14	Buried Elizabeth Cade widd' pitt in the lib^r in the midle to ye east
		24	Buried James Symondes servante to M^r J:anson the saide s^{rv}' stabbed himselfe wth a knyfe pit in the east yeard wthout seruice
	May	19	Buried John Wibo a duchman, pitt in the chancell vnder Mr Stephens stone greate bell 6 ho^{rs} single duties
	June	9	Buried John ffearen free of the skynners pitt west yearde

* The Register from July 18, 1616, to June 29, 1617, is subscribed Will'm Asheboold, parson.

THE REGISTERS OF ST. PETER'S, CORNHILL. 173

Yeare.	Month.	Day.	Names.
1617	June	12	Buried Jeane Peacoke daughter in law of Rob[t] Jeninges drap' her pitt in the midle Isle vnder y[e] pew nomb[r] 7 one the right hand
		29	Buried Appelyna the wife of Thomas Church her pitt in the Chancell vnder M[r] Stephens ston great bell 6 ho[rs]
		29	Buried William Whitlocke y[e] sonne of Rob[t] Whitlocke one of the porters of the kinges Weighowse pit in y[e] west yeard
	Aug'st	16*	Buried a still borne child of Robt. Normans in the west yea'
	Septemb[r]	14	Buried John Rogers s[r]vant to M[r] Williams cooke in the west yea'
	October	4	Buried John Sutton Carpent[r] dwellinge in Corbites corte in Gracechurch streete pit in the lib' 4 bell 1 ho[r] Coff'
		31	Buried a still borne child of Will'm Jones talo[r] in the west y'
	Nouemb[r]	1	Buried Will'm Rochdale free of the Bruers he dwelt in Cornhill pit vnder y[e] 3 stone coming in one y[e] North sid 6 ho[r] g†
		6	Buried Will'm Corker Inholder dwellinge in Gracechurch streete his pitt in the Chancell vnder bewchamps stone
		14	Buried Robarte Kyndall s[r]vant to M[r] Dams in Leadenhall streete pitt in the south Ile vnde[r] the pew nomb[e] one left
		16	Buried John Bridges the sonne of Nicholas Bridges M[r]cer in Gracechurch streete pitt in the midell Ile vnder y[e] pew n[o] 3
	Decem	1	Buried Thomas Hannis servan[t] to M[r] Hannis pitt in the east yea'
		6	Buried John Peeter who was kepte of the p'ish pit in the east yea'
	Janua[r]y	6	Buried James Voulmu[r] a duch preacher who died at M[r] Bakons howse in Bishopsgate streete pit in the Chancell great 6 ho[r] doble
	February	11	Buried a stillborne childe of Edward Cartewright in y[e] east yeard
		16	Buried John the sonne of Roger Hatton glasyer in y[e] west yeard
		17	Buried a stillborne childe of Raphe Southwell free Mercers pitt in the North Ile vnder the little pew behinde the piller
	March	2	Buried Thomas Engeham gent father to Peeter Rogers his wife pitt vnder M[r] Hodges stone buried by night
		6	Buried Mary the wife of Thomas Ingham free clothwork[r] her pit in the lib' by the east doore 3 bell 1 ho[r] Coff'
		17	Buried Mary the daught[r] of Rich' Goddard in the west yeard
1618	Aprill	9	Buried Roger Williames Cooke dwellinge in Gracechurch streete hee died being churchwarden before his comptes was made, his pitt in the Cloyster or lib' neere to the church do[r] great bell 6 ho[rs]
		11	Buried Godfery ffearen free Haberdasher dwellinge in Cornhill pitt vnder M[e] Hodges stone midle Ile greate 6 ho[rs] coff'

* The Register from August 16, 1617, to June 6, 1618, is subscribed the marke of ⟨ω⟩ Michell Webb, churchwarden, John Langley, churchwarden.
† For great bell.

Yeare.	Month.	Day.	Names.
1618	May	5	Buried Alice Yonge widd' her pitt in the South Ile vnder the pew nomber 2 greate bell 6 ho^{rs} died of age
		17	Buried Jerromy the sonn of Clement Bakon in ye east yeard
		20	Buried Martha the daughter of James Jennettes clarke her pitt in the West yearde vnder the vine coff' age ¼
		21	Buried Mathew Meirs lawyer in the west year* coff'
		29	Buried Clare Bedford servant to Mr Smiththicke, her pit in the west yeard Coff' she died of a feauer
	June	6	Buried William Lawrence s^{r}vant to Mr Smiththicke his pit in the south Ile next to M^{rs} yonge Coff"
		9†	Buried .... ‡ Bridges the wife of Nicholas Bridges free of the Mercers her pitt in the Chancell
	Julie	5	Buried Duncan Dundas scotchman in the west yeard
		12	Buried a stillborne child of Joseph Cockes in ye west yeard
		14	Buried Robart Nortly s^{r}vaunt to M^r vowell in ye east yeard
	August	20	Buried Ann Potter wife of Symon Potter her pitt in the South Ile vnder the pew nomb^r 1 one ye south side
		20	Buried Richard the sonn of Symon Potter in ye west yeard
		22	Buried Elizabeth the wife of Robert Whitlocke in ye west yeard
		23	Buried Anthony Williams Pewterrer dwelling in Leadenhall streete pitt in the south Ile one the south side vnder ye pew 1
		30	Buried Dyna the wife of James Sturdy in ye west yeard
	Septem^r	19	Buried Ann the daughter of Thomas Tyggins in ye west yeard
		30	Buried William sonn of Will'm Jones Talor in the west yeard
	Octob^r	5	Buried John the sonn of Thomas Weskott in the libary
	Nouem^r	4	Buried John the sonn of John Piggot his pit in the South chapple in the midle of the chapple at the vpp' end
		17	Buried Walter Meires Skynner in the South Chapple under Burnells stone neere the stepps entring ye vault
		19	Buried Blanch Bryan widd' and penco' her pit in ye east yeard
	Decemb^r	3	Buried Thomas Ingerham Clothworker in ye liberary
		9	Buried Mary the daughter of Thomas Whorton in ye W: yeard
		11	Buried Thomas sonn of Thomas Bingham in ye east yeard
		25	Buried Susan White s^{r}vant to Mrs Meires in ye west yeard
	January	6	Buried ffrauncis sonn of Edward Tyther grocer pit in the midle Ile vnder the pew nomber eight one the north
		6	Buried Umphery Yeates s^{r}vant to M^r J:anson, west yeard
		8	Buried Thomas sonn of Thomas Gatwood in ye midle Ile
		10	Buried Joseph sonn of Thomas Moore pit in ye midle Ile
		19	Buried John ye sonn of Richard Denman Taylor lodging wthin John Clarkes howses pit in the east yeard duble duties
		28	Buried Elizabeth Bufyll s^{rv} to M^r J:anson in ye west yeard
		29	Buried Jelyan the wife of Thomas Salloman sadler dwelling in gracechurch stree' her pitt in the south Chaple
	ffebrua^{r}y	12	Buried Elizabeth Batcheler widd' in the west yeard
		14	Buried John Vdoueall Paynter pitt in the west yeard doble duties

* For 'yard.'
† The Register from June 9, 1618, to September 23, 1621, is subscribed Ro: Dumvile, cur.
‡ Sic.

THE REGISTERS OF ST. PETER'S, CORNHILL. 175

Years.	Month.	Day.	Names.
1618	ffebruary	17	Buried Thomas Edhowse Merchantaylo^r dwelling in gracechurch streete pitt in the Midle Ile vnd^r ye second stone coming done
		21	Buried a wooman child of John Slauters in ye west yeard
	March	5	Buried Emmory Piggot widd' dwelling in Cornhill her pitt in the south Chappell at ye vpp^r ende in ye midle
		17	Buried Edward Caunt ffishmonger dwelling at the corn^r howse next to leaden hall pit in the liberary ye 2 stone to ye dore
1619	Aprill	10	Buried Elizabeth the wife of James Harlow free of the Cookes her pitt in the libary vnder the stone next the Church
		10	Buried in the same pitt wth his mother James the sonn of the aforesaid James Harlow Cooke dwelling in grace'
		11	Buried Thomas the sonne of Thomas Bingham Cooke his pitt in the west yearde Coff'
		23	Buried Margrett the wife of Richard Goodwine one of Mr Porters of the kinges weighouse in ye west yeard
	May	5	Buried Robert Dweight father of Wm Dweight free of the Tallowchandle^{rs} pitt in ye midle Ile double dutes
		14	Buried Mr John West free of the Grocers sonn in law to Mr Docto^r Ashboold pitt in ye Chauncell double dutes
	June	5	Buried Alice the wife of James Lynthweight M^{r}chantalo^r dwelling in Cornhill pitt in ye midle Ile pewes 6 and 7
		16	Buried Elizabeth ye daughter of John Piggott Grocer dwelling in Phynch layne in ye South Chapple
	Julie	3	Buried Isacke Hinde free of the Leathersello^{rs} dwelling in Bishopsgate streete. pitt in the New church yeard
		20	Buried Thomas Tucker free of the Merchantaylors dwellinge in Gracechurch streete. pit in the Liberary
	August	8	Buried Thomas Basse servant to Thomas Berrie Cheesemong^r in Leadenhall streete. pitt in ye west yeard
		23	Buried Cyslie the wife of Peeter Weightman Vintn^r in Gracechurch streete. pit in ye South Ile
	Septem^r	21	Buried Thomas Wotton free of the Mercer brother to Mrs Alice Linthweight deceased pitt in the midle Ile
		27	Buried William Warren free of the Armorers pit in the West yeard hee dwelte in Bishopsgate streete
	October	5	Buried John the sonne of Edward Helme Grocer pitt in the North Ile close vnder the vppermost pillo^r
	Nouem^r	19	Buried John Pedder sexton free of the Merchantaylo^{rs} pitt in the belfrie vnder a smale stone wth his name
		22	Buried John Styrman free of the Skynners his pit in the chauncell vnder Porders stone funerall by night
	Decemb^r	12	Buried John Rowland servant to William Jones taylo^r his pitt in the West yeard he died of a Consumption
		12	Buried Elizabeth Bedhouse of the age of 14 yeares she died in Leaden hall, pitt in the east yeard, of Could
	January	6	Buried Mr Thomas Coleman gentelman pitt in the Chauncill vnder p'son Porders stone, fath^r to Mrs Southwell
		25	Buried John the sonne of Richard Dauis free of ye vintners, pit one the North side of ye Communion table in the Chauncell
	March	1	Buried George Smith Whitebaker, pitt in the North Ile one the vpper end one the right hand of the age of 63 yeares

Yeare.	Month.	Day.	Names.
1619	March	3	Buried James Boofeild free of the ffishmongers his pitt in the West yearde. he died of a dropsy: smale bell Coff'
		23	Buried Ann the wife of George Morton free of the ffishmongers her pitt in the North Ile. she died of a Consump^{tion}
1620	Aprill	3	Buried Marie the daughter of William Pease Sadler dwelling in Gracechurch streete: pitt in the West yeard Coff'
		23	Buried Henery Thompson free of the Drap' dwelling wthin Mr Bakons howse in Bishopsgatestreete: pitt in the west yea^{r}d
		28	Buried Joane Walker widdow from William Shippes howse in Corbitts coorte her pitt in the east yeard Coff'
		30	Buried John Wilson s^{r}vant to one Mr Wodderoffe Mercer in Cheapeside. hee died in the streete; pitt in ye East yearde Coff'
	May	15	Buried William Wolridge Poulter dwelling in Gracechurch streete; pitt in the South Ile greate bell 6 hou^{rs} Coff'
	June	9	Buried George Burkehead Armorer dwelling in Gracechurch streete, pitt in the Midle Ile; greate bell 6 hou^{rs} Coff'
	Julie	16	Buried Sarah Wolgate kynswoman to Mrs Berrie dwelling in Leadenhall streete, pitt in the West yeard Coff' small bell
		17	Buried James the sonne of John Evans Cutler in Gracechurche streete, pitt in the south Ile vnder the broken stone
		20	Buried Susan the daughter of Alixand^r Symons Cooke in the Midle Ile vnder a litle stone wch hee formerly had laide
		29	Buried ffrauncis the sonne of William Hodgeson free of the Skynners, pitt in the Libarry 3 bell 1 ho^r Coff'
	August	6	Buried Robert Williams late sonn of Anthony Williams Pewterrer deceased, hee died of the teeth pitt in ye South Ile
	Septem^r	16	Buried Elizabeth Warren late wife of William Warren deceased she died of a consumption pitt in the West yeard Coff'
		18	Buried Robert the sonn of Robert Sanford free of the Skynne^{r}s, pitt in the midle Ile one ye left hand pew nom^r 6
		18	Buried Hester the daughter of Matthias Harding Taylo^r dwelling in Leadenhall streete pitt in the East yeard Coff'
	October	6	Buried a man child of John Piggottes Grocer dwelling in ffinch layne pitt in the South Chappell in ye midle p^{t}te
	Nouemb^r	3	Buried ffrauncis Corbit s^{r}vant to Mr Cole dwelling in Harrow ally in Gracechurch streete pitt in the West yeard
		18	Buried Paule Jarmice s^{r}vant to Mr John Wroth M^{r}chant dwelling in Leadenhall, pitt in the library wth a Coff
		22	Buried Elizabeth Phillipes widdow whilst she liued she was a pentioner of this p'ishe pitt in the West yea^{r}d Coff'

THE REGISTERS OF ST. PETER'S, CORNHILL. 177

Yeare.	Month.	Day.	Names.
1620	Nouembr	22	Buried a woman Child still borne of James Butlers free of the ffishmongers pitt in the West yeard Coff'
		22	Buried Alice Kenniston Widdow dwelling in Gracechurch streete her pitt in the South Ile. she died of age Coff'
		30	Buried John the sonne of George Morton free of the ffishmongers dwellinge in Cornhill, pitt in ye North Ile
	January	1	Buried James Abbott srvant to William Tomson Haberdasher in Bishopsgate streete pitt in ye west yd
		16	Buried Audrian the sonne of Audrian Henricke Merchaunt stranger pitt in the Chauncell. Coff'
		16	Buried X'pofer the soun of Symon Willamot free of the Haberdashers pitt in the Midle Ile
		22	Buried Elizabeth a child found in Redcrosse ally in a bakers baskett pitt in the West yeard
	February	15	Buried Sarah Hannis the daughter of Robert Hannis ye child was nurssed at Tho: Tyggins east yead
		21	Buried Margrett the daughter of Mr Robert Dumuile minister of this p'ishe pitt in ye Midle Ile
	March	3	Buried Margery Barnett widdow a poore weoman
		7	Buried Jeane the daughter of Robert Sanford free of the Skynners pitt in the Midle Ile one ye left hand
		12	Buried Martha the daughter of John Webb Shomakr
1621		25	Buried Splenden Warner Merchant: dwelling in Bishopsgate streete pitt in the South Ile in the midle thereof
		30	Buried Peeter Edward srvant to Mr Cason pitt in ye W: yeard
	Aprill	9	Buried John Spann srvant to Mr Tompson pitt in ye W: yeard
		20	Buried Ann the daughter of Edward Helme Grocer in Leadenhall streete pitt in the North Ile vnder a broad sto'
		22	Buried Mary the daughter of John Taylor in ye East yeard
		24	Buried Margery Brumlie Widdo': pitt in ye Liberary
	May	1	Buried Micheall Webb free of the Blacksmithes dwelling in Bishopsgate streete pitt in the South chaple
		17	Buried ffrauncis the sonne of Daniell Buckocke Lynnen Drap' in Cornehill pitt in the midle Ile one the left hand
	June	5	Buried Margret the daughter of Wm Pease in ye W: yeard
		16	Buried a man child of Edward Tythers being a Crysome pitt in the midle Ile vnder the pew nomber 9 Coff'
	Julie	28	Buried John the sonne of Steeuen Mercer, Grocer and Clarke of the kinges weighouse pitt in ye North Ile
	August	27	Buried Thomas the sonne of Thomas Church Clothworker dwelling in Cornehill pitt in the North Ile
		28	Buried Thomas the sonne of Edward Dawson Drap' dwelling in Cornehill pitt in the midle Ile vndr ye pew 7
		28	Buried Richard the sonne of Richard Harris Merchant dwelling in Leadenhall streete, pitt in ye Midle Ile
	Septemr	13	Buried Ann the daughter of Thomas Church Clothworker dwelling in Cornehill pitt in ye North Ile no: 7
		23	Buried a Crysom being a man Childe of John Piggottes in finch lane Grocer pitt in the South Chapple
	October	10*	Buried Anne the wife† Richard Warner Ironmonger daughter to Mr Leechland pitt in the midle Ile Coff'

* The Register from October 10, 1621, to November 29, 1623, is subscribed francis White.
† Sic.

2 A

Yeare.	Month.	Day.	Names.
1621	October	19	Buried John Baker s^{r}vant to Allixand^r Symons Cooke E yeard
		24	Buried Tomazine Webb widd': late wife to Michealle Webb deceased her pitt in the South Chappell wth her husband
		26	Buried John Kinge s^{r}vant to Thomas Hinde, East yeard
	Nouemb^r	6	Buried Mrs Jeane Gardner wife of Mr Robert Gardner free of the Mercers, & daught^r of Mr Docto^r Ashboold in ye Cha'ncell
		6	Buried a man child still borne of Thomas Churches free of the Clothworkers, pitt in the North Ile Coff'
		23	Buried George the sonne of Thomas Bingham, East yeard
	Decemb^r	21	Buried William Leechland M^{r}chaunt dwelling in Leadenhall streete pitt in the Midle Ile wth his daughter Warner
		24	Buried Anne Masters a poore woman out of ye Cadge, East yeard
		25	Buried Jeane the daughter of John Taylo^r Mercer, East yeard
	January	3	Buried Mrs Bridget Thayres wife of Mr Anthony Thayres free of the Leathersello^{rs} & da. of M^r Do: Ashboold p'son, Chancell
		16	Buried John Lambe free of the Haberdashers dwelling in Cornhill, pitt in the South Chappell buried by night Coff'
		22	Buried John the sonne of Alixander Symones Cooke dwellinge in Gracechurch streete, pitt in the Midle Ile
		23	Buried John Newball servante to John Slauter Armorer pitt in the East yeard Coff' smale bell 1 ho^r
	Februa^{r}y	16	Buried Thomas Holland servant to Peeter Weightman vintner pitt in the west yeard Coff': smale bell 1 ho^r
	March	6	Buried Elizabeth Dauie the daughter of Jeane Dauie widd' lying wthin Thomas Braddocks pitt west yeard
		22	Buried a man child of a daye old of one Dorrite Lawrence a poore woman y^t was brought to bead in Mr Wrothes ent^{r}y
1622	Aprill	26	Buried Ann Mercer wife of Stephen Mercer one of the Masters of the kinges weighouse; pitt in the Midle Ile
		27	Buried William ye sonne of Thomas Gattward free of ye Mercers dwelling in Gracechurch streete; pitt in ye midle Ile
	May	4	Buried Walter the sonne of William Meires Skynner dwelling in Gracechurch streete, pitt in the West yeard
		7	Buried Thomas Sallomon Sadler dwelling in Gracechurch streete of age 76 yeares, pitt in the south chapple
		7	Buried John Harris free of ye Inholders dwelling in Bishopsgate streete, age 60 yeares, pitt in ye South chapple
		14	Buried Peeter the sonne of William Jones Taylo^r lying in Goodwife Partons howse in Harrow allie pit in ye west yeard
		15	Buried Margret a poore mayde she died in Leaden Hall
	June	10	Buried Symon the sonne of Symon Willimott free of ye Haberdashers dwelling in Leadenhall streete, pitt in ye midle Ile
	June	12	Buried Elizabeth the daughter of John Wenlocke Habe^r-

Yeare.	Month.	Day.	Names.
			dasher dwelling in Gracechurch streete pitt in the west y:
1622	June	19	Buried Joseph the sonne of Roger Hatton Glasyer in Bishopsgate streete pitt in the west yeard died of ye teeth
		20	Buried Thomas the sonne of Thomas Lusher ffishmong^r dwelling in Cornhill, pitt in ye Middle Ile nomb^r 4 right hand
	Julie	26	Buried Sarah Berriman a poore weoman she died in the Cadge wheare she was borne or from whence she came we *
	August	8	Buried Ellen the wife of Henery Burkehead free of ye Girdle^{rs} & late wife of Roger Williams deceased pitt in ye liberary
		24	Buried Jacob the sonne of Thomas Mempris Haberdash^r dwelling in Gracechurch street, pitt in ye west yeard
		29	Buried Wm Ashboold dot^r & parson of this church, vnd^r ye com' table
		30	Buried a child still borne of Mathew Moyce a poore woman out of ye Cadge, pitt in the East yearde
	Septem^r	25	Buried Peeter Weightman Vintner dwelling in Grace-Church streete, pitt in the West yearde Coff'
	October	2	Buried Sarah the daughter of Thomas Bingham Cooke dwelling in Leadenhall streete, pitt in ye East yearde
	Nouemb^r	12	Buried John Lapley s^rvant to Biglie Carleton Grocer dwelling in Gracechurch streete, pitt in ye Midle Ile neere ye belfry
		22	Buried a man child stilborne of Thomas Barnes free of the Haberdashers dwelling in Leadenhall streete east yeard
		24	Buried a man child of Joshua Wenlockes an abortiue
		24	Buried Edward Williames s^rvant to Philip Meade ffree of ye ffishmongers pitt in the lib'ary Coff'
		25	Buried Elizabeth ye wife of John Warren Skynner dwelling in Harrow allie in Gracechurch streete, in ye same grau'
	Decemb^r	13	Buried Peeter the sonne of James Jennetts p'ishe clarke dwelling in Corbitts Coarte pit in the west yearde Coff'
		20	Buried Elizabeth ffry s^rvant to Thomas Whalie vintner dwelling in Cornhill pitt in the East yeard Coff'
	January	16	Buried Ann the daughter of John Slauter free Armore^r dwelling in Cornhill pitt in the West yeard Coff'
		24	Buried a woman child of Wm Jones taylo^r being an Infant
		25	Buried James ye sonne of Wm Jones taylo^r pitt in ye west yeard
	ffebruary	1	Buried Jone Hannis daughter of Elbright Hannis Silke-weaver dwelling in Harrow ally pitt in the lib'ary Coff'
		6	Buried John Wallen a poore child found at Leadenhall & kepte wth goodie Webb being of 4 yeares of age, pit east yea'.
		8	Buried ffraunces ye daughter of Thomas Church Cloth-worke^r dwelling in redd C^rosse ally in Cornhill pitt in ye North Ile right hand

* Sic.

Year.	Month.	Day.	Names.
1622	ffebruary	15	Buried George the sonne of Roger Hatton Glasyer dwelling in Bishopsgate streete, pitt in the west yeard vnd^r ye vestrie windo'
	March	1	Buried Cisly Ashboold daughter to the late reverend father m^r Wm Ashboold Doctor of diuinitie & parson of this church her pitt vnd^r ye com'uni: table
		15	Buried Bartholmeu Maxfeild gent sonne of Mr John Maxfeild cittizen and Armorer, pitt in ye North Ile at y^o foote of ye stepes Coff'
		16	Buried ffrauncis the sonne of ffrauncis Hall Taylor dwelling in Bishopsgate streete, pitt in the West yeard coff' smale bell 1 ho^r
		18	Buried Margret Sutton widdow, pencioner of this parish dwelling in Corbittes Courte in Gracechurch streete; pitt in the west yeard Coff'
1623		30	Buried Wy'niffrett the daughter of Alice Rose of Acton in the Countie of Midd'. a poore woman; pitt in the East yeard
		31	Buried a Crysome child of Thomas Gattward Mercer dwelling in Gracechurch streete pitt in the Midle Ile, left hand
	Aprill	14	Buried Marie the daughter of Miles Robinson Armorer dwelling in Gracechurch streete pitt in the Midle Ile, vnder ye pew no: 7
		23	Buried John Vowell free of the Poulters dwelling in Gracechurch streete, pitt in the East yearde coff' buried by night
	May	29	Buried John the sonne of Thomas Austine Sheiregrinder dwelling in Leadenhall streete, pitt in the East yeard coff'
	June	12	Buried Ellyn Collyns s^rvant vnto docto^r White parson of this church her pitt in the midle Crosse Ile with a Coff' age 44
		19	Buried Thomas Preagle s^rvant to Symon Willimott in Leadenhall streete Haberdasher, pitt in the East yeard Coff'
		20	Buried a woman Child still borne of George Mortons ffishmonger dwelling in Cornehill pitt in the North Ile Coff'
	August	2	Buried Margret the wife of Henery Barnard Inholder dwelling in Gracechurch streete pitt in the Midle Ile Coff'
		4	Buried Jeane Leechland widdow of Wm Leechland M^rchant deceased whoe dwelte in Leadenhall streete; pitt in ye Midle Ile
	Septem^r	4	Buried Ann the wife of Henery Watson Barber dwelling in Bishopsgate streete, pitt in the South Ile Coff'. of a feave^r
		19	Buried Zacary Healinge free of the Haberdashers and dwelt in Bartholmewlane, pitt in the Chauncell one the south side
	October	5	Buried Prissylla the daughter of Margrett ffryerson servant to Peeter Rogers Clothworker and supposed to be ye said Peeters child
		8	Buried Thomas Purlivent free of the Grocers hee was owne of o^r Pention^{rs} of this parrish pitt in the West yeard coff' of a feauo^r

THE REGISTERS OF ST. PETER'S, CORNHILL. 181

Years.	Month.	Day.	Names.
1623	October	13	Buried Joyce * servant to Henery Watson Barber
	Nouemb^r	5	Buried Thomas Okely Waxchandler dwelling in Gracechurchstreete his pitt in the South chapell vnder Mr Gochyns stone
		14	Buried Thomas the sonne of Clement Bakon Draper pitt in ye east yea^{r}d
		17	Buried Elizabeth the daughter of John Wenlock Haberdasher
		29	Buried John Slauter Armorer his pitt in the South chapell vnder M^r Jo. Richmonds stone hee dwelt in Cornhill, died of a feav^r
		29†	Buried Richard Taylor servant to Elbright Hannis Silkeweauer dwellinge in Gracechurchstreete pit East yea^{r}d
	Decemb^r	25	Buried Thomas Waygood free of the Cookes dwelling in Leadenhall streete, pitt in the South Ile buried by night
		27	Buried Sarah Hamlet s^{r}vant to Thomas Burkehead dwelling in Cornhill, pitt in the West yeard Coff'
	January	2	Buried Thomas Goldwell s^{r}vant to Thomas Bingham Cooke dwellinge in leadehallstreete pit east yearde
		5	Buried Samuell the sonne of Brian ffell Pewterrer dwelling in Leadenhallstreete, pit in the South Ile
		8	Buried Sarah Jeninges servant to Thomas Mullet Poulter dwelling in Gracechurchstreete pit west yeard
		14	Buried Ann the daughter of John Evans free of the Gyrdelo^{rs} dwelling in Gracechurchstreete pit in ye south Ile
		15	Buried ffrauncis Mumford a child of Mr Powells daughters wch she kepte pit in East yearde Coff'
		22	Buried Thomas Lambe s^{r}vant to George Alsop free of the Sta'cioners dwelling in leadenhall streete
	February	5	Buried Edward Sherman free of the Poulters dwelling in Gracechurchstreete pitt in the West yearde Coff'
		26	Buried Mr John Cason free of the Grocers dwelling in Cornhill, pitt in the Chauncell against ye Commun' table
	March	4	Buried two yonge children of Will'm Jones Taylor
1624	Aprill	4	Buried Jeane the daught^r of Will'm Whittinghams
		15	Buried Richard Goodwine one of the Mr Porters of ye kinges Weighowse pitt in the lib' one the right hand
	June	4	Buried Mr Thomas Allyblaster gent. from Edward Tythers howse his was in Chauncell vnder Poynes stone
		19	Buried George Barber a poore vagrant in ye East yeard
		25	Buried Allixander Symonds Cooke dwelling in Gracechurchstreete his pitt in the Midle Ile vnd^r ye 2 & 3 pewes No^{r}th
	Julie	24	Buried William Horne a Scotch M^{r}chant dwelling in Gracechurchstreete; pitt in the South Ile vnd^r ye 6 & 7 pewes
	August	2	Buried an Abortiue child of John Mideltons free of the Inholders dwelling in Leadenhall streete in ye lib'
		7	Buried Henery sonne of Thomas Gatward Mercer dwelling in Gracechurchstreete pitt in the Middle Ile
		13	Buried James sonne of Richard Har^{r}is M^{r}chaunt dwelling

* Sic.
† The Register from November 29, 1623, to April 24, 1632, is subscribed Phillipp Mead, churchwarden.

Yeare.	Month.	Day.	Names.
			in Leadenhallstreete pit in the Midle Ile one ye right hand
1624	August	27	Buried William Gylman kynsman to John Holmes Cordewayno^r dwelling in Bishopsgatestreete pitt in ye W: yeard
		28	Buried John: sonne of Robert Gardner M^{r}chaunt dwelling in Bassingshaw and grandchild to Mr Ashboold the child was buried in the vault vnder ye Communion table
	Septemb^r	11	Buried M^r ffrauncis Coling free of the ffishmongers dwelling in Cornhill pit in the Midle Ile one lefte hand vnde^r ye pews no: 2 & 3
		12	Buried Ann Willimot sister to Symon Willimot free of the Haberdashers dwelling in Leadenhall streete pit in ye M: Ile
		14	Buried Katherin the wife of Anthony Botly M^{r}chantaylo^r some* dwelling in this parrish her pitt in the lib' one her brothe^r E: Gant
		30	Buried William Seuerne servant to Thomas Spilsberie Blacksmith dwelling in Bishopsgatestreete pit in ye East yeard
	October	4	Buried Anne the wife of Edward ffouldington Sexton free of the Merchantaylo^{rs} her pit in the Crosse Ile next ye belfrie
		9	Buried Margerie Bristow servant to Mrs Johnson widd' dwelling in Gracechurchstreete. pit in the East yeard
		17	Buried ffrauncis sonne of George Billing dwelling in Leadenhall streete shipwright pit in the West yeard
		24	Buried ffrauncis sonne of William Dynn Scriueno^r dwelling in Gracechurchstreete pit in the liberary
	Nouembe^r	2	Buried Ann Drawater sister to John Piggots wife Grocer dwelling in ffynch lane pit in the south Chaple
		16	Buried George Hudson free of ye Vpholders dwelling in Cornhill pitt in the Midle Ile vnder ye side of ye last pew
		16	Buried Richard Warren free of the Cutlers dwelling in Gracechurchstreete pit in the Liberary Coff'
		23	Buried ffraunces daughter of James Butler free of ye ffishmongers dwelling in Bishopsgatestreete pit in ye W: yeard
	Decemb	7	Buried Austine Synagree a poore Souldier out of Leadenhall he dyed of a feaver Pitt in the Easte yard
		10	Buried Hellen the daughter of James Butler free of the ffishmongers dwelling in Bishopsgate str' pit in ye west yarde
		11	Buried Katherine the wife of George Hudson Vphold^r deceased her pitt in the middle Ile, she dyed of a feaver
		14	Buried William Pratt a poore Souldier out of Leadenhall he dyed of a feaver Pitt in the East yarde
		24	Buried Alice the wife of Will'm Shippe Carpenter dwelleing in Corbettes Courte hir pitt in the South Ile
		28	Buried Sampson ye sonne of Raphe Edmondes free of the Drap's dwellinge in Bishopgate streete pit in the South Ile

* Sic.

Yeare.	Month.	Day.	Names.
1624	January	16	Buried a woman Child still borne of Symon Willymotts in the Middle Ile of the Church
	ffebruar'	5	Buried Elizabeth the daughter of George Morton free of the ffishmonge^{rs} dwelling in Cornhill pitt in ye North Ile
		11	Buried Will'm Bell one of the vnder Porters of the waigh howse his pitt in the Weste Yard
		18	Buried Anna ye daughter of Thomas Lusher free of ye ffishmongers pitt in the middle Ile
	ffebuary	20	Buried Johan the wife of John Taylo^r free of the Mercers, dwelling in Corbetts Court pit in ye East yard
1624	March	4	Buried Thomas the sonne of Rob'te Edwards Marchant Taylo^r dwelleing in Harow alley pit ye Library
		20	Buried Thomas Rankin Shomaker dwelleing in St Peters alley Pitt in the West yard
1625		26	Buried Mary the daughter of Suzan Symons widow dwelleing in Gracechurch streete pitt ye midle Ile
	Aprill	9	Buried John the sonne of Will'm Pease Sadler dwelleing in Grace-church streete pitt in ye Library
		26	Buried Will'm Nicolls s^{r}vant to Will'm Dwight Chandler his pitt in the East yarde
		27	Buried Raph Edmondes free of the Drap's dwelleing in Bishopsgate streete pytt in the South Ile
	May	2	Buried Jane Edmondes daughter of the said Raphe Edmondes Draper pitt in the South Ile
		13	Buried Richard the sonne of Richard Harris Marchunt dwelleing in Leadenhall streete pit in ye midle Ile
		20	Buried Elizabeth the daughter of Edward Cartwright poulter dwelleing in Gratious streete pitt in ye west yard
	June	4	Buried Mary daughter of ffrannces Walcott Habbd' in Harrow Alley pitt in ye Crosse Ile
		10	Buried Tho: Jelley a lodger at m^r Binghams howse in Leadenhall streete pitt in the Easte yard
		25	Buried Thomas Church free of ye Clothworkers dwelleing in Redcrosse Alley pit in ye Chancell North Ile
		26	Buried Tabatha Tiggins daughter of Thomas Tiggins free of ye Skynn's, in Harrow alley pit in ye East yard
	July	7	Buried M^{ris} Pigott ye wife of John Pigott Grocer dwelleing in ffinch lane pitt in ye South Chappell
			Buried Thomas the sonne of Roger Hatton Glasier Pitt in the Weste Yarde
		12	Buried Suzan Procter daughter to Mrs Midleton dwelleing in Leadenhall streete pitt in the Chancell
		13	Buried George Hinde s^{r}vant to Mathew Gillam Tayler in the New Church yard Buishopsgate
		14	Buried Abigall the daughter of Myles Robinson Armorer dwelleing in Gratious streete pit in ye midle Ile
		15	Buried Sarah the daughter of ffraunces Walcott Habbd' pitt in the Crosse Ile
			Buried Thomas Eaton s^{r}vant to Joseph Denman Grocer at Leadenhall pitt in the East yard
		17	Buried Johan the wife of Rob'te Chamberlyn Bricklayer dwelleing in Harrow Alley in new ch: Yard
		19	Buried John Moore s^{r}vant to m^r Hannis dwelling in Harrow Alley pitt in the new Church yarde

Yeare.	Month.	Day.	Names.
1625	July	19	Buried Thomas Bateman free of the Armorers and dwelle* in Grace Church strett pit in the new church Yard
		20	Buried John Dover s^rvant to Myles Buckstone Hostler dwelling in Corbetts Court pitt in ye new ch: yard
		25	Buried Anne daughter of Clement Bacon Taylor dwelleing in Buishopsgate streete pit in ye East yard
		26	Buried Christopher Watson Silkeweaver dwelling in Corbetts Court pitt in the Library
		27	Buried Katherine ye wife of John Conway Cooke dwelleing in Gratious streete pitt in ye Library
			Buried an Abortiue Child of Henry Harris Cutler dwelleing in Grace Church streete
		31	Buried Margarett wife of Will'm Shorte Cheesemonger dwelleing in Leadenhall, pit East yard
			Buried Elizabeth * s^rvant to Thomas Hulce free of the Silkeweavers, pit in new church yard
	August	1	Buried Elizabeth the wife of Thomas Mullett Poulter dwelleing in Grace Church str', pit in ye west yard
			Buried Dorithie * s^rvant to Humfrey Woodward Grocer dwelleing in Bishopsgate streete, pit in new Ch: Yard
		2	Buried George Billin sonne in law to Widd' Hubb^rsted dwelleing in Leadenhall streete, pitt in ye Easte yard
		3	Buried Robert Whitlocke Porter of the Waighe howse pitt in the Easte Yard
			Buried Elbright Hannis free of the Weavers dwelling in Harrow Alley pitt in the Library
			Buried Will'm & Dorithy Holmes the Children of Richard Holmes dwelling in Corbets court, pit East yard
		5	Buried James the sonne of Richard Holmes dwelleing in * Courte pit in the East yard
		7	Buried Anne the wife of Henry Harris Cutler dwelleing in Grace Church streete pit in ye Library
		7	Buried Jane the daughter of Richard Holmes Carpenter dwelleing in Corbets Court pit East yard
		8	Buried Raphe Pettite dwelleing wth m^{ris} Tucker in Harrow Alley Pitt in the Easte Yarde
			Buried Sarah Billing late daughter of George Billing deceased Pitt in the East yarde
		9	Buried Randall Smith s^rvant to Humphrey woodward grocer in Bishopsgatstr' pit in ye East yard
		10	Buried Richard Holmes Carpenter dwelling in Corbetts Courte pitt in the East yard
		12	Buried Elizabeth daughter of Humfrey woodward dwelleing in Bishopsgate streete pitt in the Easte Yarde
			Buried Samuell sonne of Thomas Bradocke dwelling in Bishopsgate str' pit in the East yard
		13	Buried Thomas Hulce free of ye weavers dwelleing in Buishopsgate str' pit in ye Library
			Buried Roberte Hilton one of the vnder Porters in the wey howse pit in ye Est yard
			Buried Nicholas Burr free of the Poulters dwelleing in Buishopsgatstr' pit in ye Library

* Sic.

| Yeare. | Month. | Day. | Names. |

1625 August 13 Buried Johan the daughter of Will'm Aude Inholde^r dwelleing in Leadenhall street pit West yard
Buried Tho: Kendall s^{r}vant to wid' Symons dwelleing in Grace Church str' pit in ye East yard
15 Buried Alice the wife of John Whiteshead Cordwayn' dwelleing in Leadenhall str' pit in ye East yard
Buried Anne the daughter of Tho. Bradocke dwelleing in Bishopsgate str' pit in ye East yard
Buried Jane the daughter of Widd' Billing dwelling in Leadenhall streete pit in the East yard
17 Buried Thomas Wescott whitebaker dwelleing in Cornehill pit at the Cloyster doore
Buried Mary the daughter of Widow Petite dwelling in Harrow Alley pit in ye East yard
17 Buried Samuell * the s^{r}vant of Tho: Bosworth Brasier dwelling in Gracechurch str' pit in ye East yard
Buried James Taven' s^{r}vant to Will'm Dwight Chandler dwelling in Leadenhall str' pit in ye East y:
18 Buried Hester daughter of Mr Easton dwelling in Harrow Alley pitt in the East yard
19 Buried Elizabeth the wife of Tho: Braddocke dwelling in Bishopsgate str' pit in ye East yard
Buried Margery the daughter of Robt Whitlocke Porter pitt in the Easte Yard
Buried Mary the s^{r}vant of Tho: Bosworth Brasier dwelling in Gracechurch str' pit in ye East yard
20 Buried Harman Haynes s^{r}vant to m^{ris} Church in Redcrosse Alley pitt in the East yard
Buried Vrsula Holmes daughter of Wid' Holmes dwelling in Corbetts Court pit in ye East yard
21 Buried John Sutton Drap' dwelleing in Corbetts Courte pit in the Library
Buried Elizabeth Heyley widow dwelling in Corbetts Court pit in the East yard
Buried Nehemiah sonne of John Webbe shomaker dwelling in Corbetts Court pit East y:
23 Buried Rob't Wharton s^{r}vant to m^r Burton vint: dwelleing in Gracechurch str' pit in ye Crosse Ile
24 Buried Peter Rogers free of ye Clothworkers dwelling in St Peters Alley pit in ye Midle Ile
Buried Elizabeth the wife of the said Peter Rogers her pit wth her husband
Buried Richard Sachfeild sonne of Widd' Sachfeild dwelling in Buishopsgate streete Pit in the North Ile
Buried Allexander Baker brother to widow Symons dwelling in Gracechurchstr' pit in ye East yard
Buried Edward wyner s^{r}vant to ffrances Walcott dwelleing in Harrow Alley pit in ye East y:
Buried Martha webb daughter of John webb Shomaker dwelling in Corbets Court pit East y:
25 Buried Thomas Braddocke dwelleing in Buishopsgate streete pit in ye New church yard
26 Buried Will'm Aude free of the Inholders dwelling in Leadenhall streete pit in ye west yard

* Sic.

Yeare.	Month.	Day.	Names.
1625	August	26	Buried Martha Lile widow, mother to m^{ris} Aude dwelleing in ye howse wth them pit in ye East y:
		28	Buried Anne Spence widow lyeing at m^{ris} Warrens in Gracechurchstr' pit in ye East yard
		29	Buried Katherine Reader s^{r}vant to m^r Hinde Inholder dwelleing in Leaden hall str' pit in ye midle cr.* Ile
			Buried Johan Mare s^{r}vant to Thomas Whaley vintn' dwelling in Cornhill pit in ye East yard
			Buried Thomas the sonne of Will'm Tompso habb' dwelleing in Buishopsgate str' pit in ye East yard
		30	Buried Will'm Tompson Habb' dwelling in Buishopsgate streete pit in ye East yarde
		31	Buried George the sonne of George Alsopp free of the Stacioners dwelleing in Leadenhall streete pit in the Easte Yarde
			Buried Thomas ye son of Tho: Bradock dwell' in Bishopsgate streete pit in ye East yard
	September	1	Buried Rebecca daughter of Jo: Watson son in law to m^r Mould dwell' in Cornhill pit in ye west y:
		3	Buried Thomas the sonne of Widdow Aude dwelleing in Leadenhall streete pit in ye west y'
			Buried Mary the daughter of John Webbe Shomaker dwelleing in Corbetts Court pit East y'
			Buried Debora ye daughter of Tho: Whaley vintn' dwelleing in Cornehill pit in ye midle Ile
		5	Buried Thomas the son of James Jennetts p'ish Clarke dwelleing in Corbets Court pit in ye west y'
		6	Buried Mathew Dod m'chantaylo^r dwelleing in Corbetts Court pit in the East yarde
			Buried Samuell ye son' of Nicholas Burden Taylo^r dwelling in Gracechurch streete pit in ye East ya:
			Buried Paule ye son' of Allexande^r Brumston dwell' in Grace Church streete pit in the East yard
			Buried John Smith free of the m'cers dwelling wth m^{ris} Sachfeild in Bishopsgatstr' pit in ye North Ile
		10	Buried Thomas ye son' of Tho: Whaley Vintn' dwelling in Cornhill pit in the Midle Ile
		11	Buried Thomas Whaley Vintn' dwelleing in Cornhill pit in the middle Ile by his Children
		12	Buried Suzanna Symons widow dwelleing in Grace Church streete pit in the South Ile
			Buried John Weste free of ye Grocers s^{r}vant to m^r Bigly Carlton dwelleing in Grace Church streete, pit in the South Ile
			Buried Cokely s^{r}vant to m^{ris} Whaley dwelling in Cornehill pit in the East yard
		13	Buried William Horne Scotchman lyeing at Mr Burtes howse pitt in the East yard
			Buried Nicholas Amys s^{r}vant to Miles Robinson Armorer dwelling in Gracechurchstr' pit East y'
		14	Buried Rob'te the son' of Thomas Memprisse Habbd' dwelling in Gracechurch str' pit in ye west y'
		15	Buried John Granger s^{r}vant to Tho: Memprisse Habbd' dwelling in Gracechurch str' pit in ye west y'

* Cross.

Yeare.	Month.	Day.	Names.
1625	September	15	Buried Richard Hinde s^rvant to Tho: Hind Inholder dwelleing in the Leadenhall str' pitt in ye west y'
		16	Buried * s^rvant to Edw: Bawcomb Chandler dwelleing in Leadenhall str' pit in ye East y'
			Buried Suzanna Vandebrooke wife of Mr Vandebrooke dwelleing in Dukes place Pitt in the Crosse Ile
			Buried Elizabeth Rickworth sister to the said Suzanna Vandebrooke dwelleing in Dukes place pit in the same graue
		21	Buried Nicholas Burden m'chantaylo^r dwelling in Gracechurch str' pitt in the East yard
			Buried James Jennetts sonne of James Jennetts p'ish Clarke dwelling in Corbets Court pitt vnder the Vine in the west yarde
			Buried John Yeomans lodgeing in John Conway the Cooke his howse in Gracechurch streete pitt in the East yarde
		22	Buried John the sonne of Raph Southwell free of ye m'cers dwelleing in Cornhill pit in ye midle Ile
			Buried Thomas Mason s^rvant to Mr Joseph Graue Habbd' dwelleing in Leadenhall str' pit in ye east y'
		24	Buried John ye son' of James Jennetts p'ish Clarke dwelleing in Corbets Court pit in ye west y'
			Buried John ffenricke s^rvant to m^r Madison m'chant dwelling in Bishopsgat str' pit ye cros Ile
			Buried Myles ye son' of Myles Robinson Armorer dwelleing in Gracechurch str' pit ye midle Ile
			Buried Will'm Goner s^rvant to Tho: Bingham Cooke dwelling in Leadenhall str' pit in ye East y'
		25	Buried * daughter of Henry Chapman Habbd' dwelling in ye wey howse yarde in Cornhill pit in the East yard
			Buried * a maid s^tvant of Myles Robinson dwelling in Gracechurchstr' pit in ye East y'
	October	1	Buried * the daughter of Tho: Mempris Habb' dwelleing in Gracechurchstr' pit in ye west y'
		2	Buried Roger Hatton ye son' of Roger Hatton Glasier dwelleing in Bishopsgat str' pit in ye west y:
			Buried John Reynolds free of ye ffishmongers brother to Rowland Reynolds dwelleing in Cornhill pit in ye Crosse Ile
		5	Buried Roger Hatton Glasier dwelleing in Bishopsgate str' pit in the west yard
			Buried * the daughter of John Harman Laborer to ye Citty dwelleing in Leadenhall in the Greene yard pitt in the West yard
		7	Buried Elizabeth s^rvant to Mr Graue dwelleing in Leadenhall streete pit in the East yard
	October	9	Buried John the sonne of John Harman Laborer to the Citty pit in the weste yarde
		10	Buried Prosper Pye s^rvant to m^r Joseph Graue Habb', pit in the East yard
		21	Buried Margarett Meires s^rvant to Wid' Meires in Grace Church streete pit in the West yard
		23	Buried Henry Parkinson s^rvant to m^r Graue dwelling in Leadenhall str', pit in the East yard

* Sic.

Yeare.	Month.	Day.	Names.
1625	November	2	Buried James Jennetts p'ish Clarke free of ye Goldsmithes dwelleing in Corbetts Court pit at ye vestry doore
		12	Buried m^{ris} Richardson dwelling at London stone her pit in the middle Ile
			Buried Will'm Shorte free of the Girdlers dwelling in Leadenhall streete pit in the East yard
	December	13	Buried a Crisom Child of John Middletons dwelling in Leadenhall str' pit in the Library
			Buried Suzanna the Wife of Edward Cartwright Poulter dwelling in Grace Church streete pit in the East yard
		14	Buried a Kinswoman of widow Hannises dwelleing in Harrow alley in gracechurch str' pit in ye East y'
			Buried Alice ye wife of Tho: Jones Barber dwelling in Buishopsgate streete pit in the South Ile
	Tuesday	18	Buried m^r Thomas Westraw Alderman and Sheriffe of the City of London sonne of Tymothy Westraw sometyme a p'ishon' in this p'ish and free of ye Grocers pit in the Chancell
	January	29	Buried Rebecca late wife of Raphe Edmond deceased free of ye Drap's dwelling in Bish'-str' pit in ye south Ile
	ffebruary	7	Buried Elizabeth Allaby wife of Edward Allaby Marryn' kinswoman to m^r Holmes pit in ye midle Ile
	March	4	Buried ffraunces Coling son' of ffraunces Coling free of the ffishmongers dwelling in Cornhill, pit in ye Libra:
1626		27	Buried Johan wife of John Boomer deceased she was one of the Pentioners pit in the west y'
	April	8	Buried William sonne of Raphe Southwell free of the Mercers dwelling in Cornhill pitt in ye midle Ile
	May	15	Buried John Webb Shomaker dwelling in Corbetts Courte Pitt in the East yarde
		19	Buried Mary the daughter of Mr Alderman Westraw deceased her pitt in Chancell wth her ffather
	July	3	Buried Margarett ye wife of Will'm Dynne free of the Pulters dwelling in Gracechurch str' pit in ye south Ile
		13	Buried Grace wife of X'pofer Vertue free of ye Vintners dwelling in Cornhill pit in North Ile
	August	3	Buryed Johan s^rvante to X'pofer Vertue Lynnen Draper pitt in the west yard
		5	Buryed Elizabeth daughter of Bryan ffell Pewterer pit in the South Ile
		26	Buried Martha ye daughter of m^r Rowland Reynolds dwelling in Cornehill, pit in ye body of ye Church
	Septemb:	4	Buryed William ye sonne of Humphrey Woodward grocer dwelling in Bushopsgate streete pit in the Easte yarde
		8	Buryed Elizabeth the wyfe of John Mountford free of the Pewterers, pit in ye Chan: south Ile
		16	Buried James the sonne of Henry Chapman dwelleing in Cornhill pit in ye south Ile
	October	5	Buryed Mary ye wife of Edward ffoldington Sexton her pit by the Belfr^ey
		27	Buryed an Abbortiue Child of widow Webs dwelleing in Corbetts Court pit in ye Este y':
		29	Buryed John Addison free of ye Glasiers dwelleing in Gratious str' pit in ye new ch': y':
	Nouemb'	2	Buried Anne daughter of Stephen Ham'ond dwelling in Bishopsgat str' pit in ye East yard

THE REGISTERS OF ST. PETER'S, CORNHILL. 189

Yeare.	Month.	Day.	Names.
1626	Nouemb'	30	Buried Rowland Reynolds free of the Skynn's dwelling in Cornehill pitt in the Chancell
	January	9	Buried m^{ris} Anne Collman widow dwellinge in Cornchill pitt in the Chancell
		27	Buried Elizabeth the daughter of Thomas Gatward free of ye M'cers dwelling in Gratious str' pitt in body Ch:
	ffebruary	1°	Buried ffraunces Pennicke s'vaunt to Thomas ffenn dwelling in Corbetts Court pitt in the Easte yard
		8	Buried James sonne of Henry Chambers dwelling in Gracechurch str' Pitt in the East yard
	March	16	Buried Henry Chapman Habbd' dwelling in Cornehill pitt in the South Chappell
1627	Aprill	4	Buried Edward ye sonne of Thomas Carter free of the Sadlers dwelling in Cornehill pitt in ye Library
		10	Buried Mary the daughter of Thomas Wescott White baker dwelling in Cornhill pitt at ye south dore
		20	Buried a Child of m^r Plomers Chandler dwelling in Leadenhall str' pitt in the Easte yard
	July	1°	Buried Widdow Moorehen one of the Penc'oners pitt in the East yard
		9	Buried William sonne of James Chambers Cutler dwelling in Leadenhall str' pit in ye east yard
		31	Buried Jane daughter of Thomas Midleton dwelling in Leadenhall str': pitt in the Library
	Septemb^r	22	Buried a stilborne Child of Henry Watson Barber dwelling in Bishopsgate str' pit in ye west y^d
		26	Buried Elizabeth daughter of Raph Southwell drap^r pit in the body of ye Church by her Pewe
	November	28	Buried Joane Rankin Widdow on of ye Pencone^{rs} pitt in the West yard
	December	9	Buried Thomas Tiggin free of the skinners pit in the West yard
	January	18	Buried John sonne of John Connoway one of the Twins pit in the East yard
		19	Buried Elizabeth wife of John Burton Chandler pit in the South Chappell
			Buried Rebecca daughter of Lawrence Anthonie Haberdasher pitt in Newchurchyard
		24	Buried John sonne of Christopher Vertue Linnen Draper. pitt in the North Ile
	ffebruary	8	Buried Elizabeth daughter of Elizabeth Winch Grocer pitt in the Library
	March	11	Buried William sonne of William Meares Skinner pitt in the West yard
1628	Aprill	16	Buried Samuell Key servant to Mr Hurt Drap' pit in the West yard
		19	Buried Suzan Goodwin Widdow dwelling in Broad streate pit in the South Ile
		27	Buried John Kenricke servant to Mr Holmes shoemaker pitt in the West yard
	May	31	Buried ffrancis daughter of George Mole gentl. pit in the body of the Church
	June	22	Buried Jone daughter of Raph Hampton shee was servant to Mr Mole. pit in the East yard
		23	Buried Richard sonne of Thomas Lusher Draper pit in the body of the Church

Yeare.	Month.	Day.	Names.
1628	June	30	Buried Ann daughter of ffrancis Burt Poulter pit in the South Ile
	July	16	Buried a still borne Child of Robert Tompson pit in the East yard
	August	05	Buried Walter sonne of Thomas Smith Haberdasher pit in the East yard
		19	Buried Sr Jasper ffouler Mercer dwelling in Westminster pit in the Chancell
		30	Buried Christian Harris widdow pit in the South Chappell
	September	11	Buried Mary daughter of James Chambers Cooke pit in the East yard
		17	Buried Nathaniell sonne of Samuell Norris sadler pit in the East yard
	October	10	Buried James sonne of James Marsh Carpenter pit in the West yard
	December	06	Buried Dorothie wife of Phillip Meade Drap' pit in the Chancell
	February	18	Buried Arthur Isby stranger pit in ye west yard
		25	Buried Mrs Luce Edge one of the Widdowes which giues the Lecture at little Alhallowes
	March	03	Buried Joseph sonne of Robert ffisher Joyner pit in the East yard
		06	Buried William sonne of Clement Bacon Clarke pit in the East yard
		09	Buried Mary daughter of John Buttres Cooke pit in the East yard
1629		26	Buried John Warren Skynner pit in the Library
	Aprill	20	Buried Mrs Boulton wife of Theophilus Boulton ffishmonger pit in the North Ile
	May	09	Buried a still borne Child of Mr Griffins Glasier pit in the West yard
	July	0i	Buried Edmound Shipdon servant to m^r Edwards pitt in the Library
	August	07	Buried John sonne of John Younge Grocer pit in ye Church South Ile
		13	Buried M^{ris} Johnson widdow in Hackny Church by her husband
	Novemb^r	05	Buried M^{ris} Anne Mole Widdow pitt in the East Chappell by her pew
		23	Buried Jonathan sonne of William Browne pit in the East yard
	January	11	Buried Mary wife of John Younge Grocer pit in the Church south Ile. shee deceased in the parish of Whitechappell
1630	Aprill	0i	Buried Thomas sonne* Edward Spradbury pit in East y^d
		20	Buried Jarvis Hutchinson Porter to the East India Companie pit in the East yard
	Maie	07	Buried a poore man a Lincolneshire drover who died suddenly in the streete pitt in the West yard
	June	11	Buried James Butler ffishmonnger pitt in the Library
		18	Buried Suzan daughter of Robert Edwards pitt in ye Library
	July	7th	Buried Dorathie Oulden servant to Mrs Morris widdow pitt in the North Ile by her Mistres her pue
		15	Buried ffrancis Allison servant to Mrs Westcott widd' dwelling in Cornhill pitt in the East yard

* Sic.

THE REGISTERS OF ST. PETER'S, CORNHILL. 191

Yeare.	Month.	Day.	Names.
1630	July	20	Buried Thomas sonne of Thomas Smith draper in leaden hall street pitt in the Librarie
		24	Buried Robert sonne of Steven Grove Poulter in Gratious streete pitt in the East yard
	August	20	Buried Christopher Gewin Marchauntaillo^r dwelling vpon Cornhill Pitt in the North Chappell by ye furthest pue
		29	Buried a poore boy that died in the street pit in ye East yarde
	October	10	Buried a stillborne Child of M^r ffeakes in ye north Ile
		22	Buried William sonne of ffrancis Coling Lynnen Draper dwelling in Cornhill pitt in the librarie
	Novemb^r	23	Buried Edmonde sonne of Edmond Dawney wch lay at Mr Bramich his house in Gratious street pitt in ye East yarde
		23	Buried Elizabeth wife of Thomas Birkheade Armor^r dwelling in Cornhill pitt in the bodie of the Church by her pue
	December	25	Buried Marie daughter of Roger Hooke lying at Mr Pattens in Leadenhall street pitt in ye east church yard
		29	Buried Mary daughter of William Peas Sadler in Gratious street pitt in the East church yard
			Buried the wife of Mr Jacob Gardner lecturer the 20th of Decemb^r 1630 pitt in the North chappell
	Januarie	7	Buried Elizabeth daughter of Edmonde Tooley Inholder in Gratious street pitt in ye librarie
		10	Buried Marie the wife of Wm Peas Sadler in Gratious streete pitt in the South chappell by her father
		14	Buried Wm Dynn Scriven^r dwelling in Gratious street pitt in the South chappell
		26	Buried Joane Watson kinswoman to Mrs Tooley pitt in the Librarie by her Childs
	February	6	Buried Margarett daughter of Wm Hudson Churchwarden pitt in the bodie of the church
		11	Buried Mrs Meares widdow in Harrow alley pitt in the South chappell by her husbands
		22°	Buried Isaac sonne of Wm Bramich Brasier in Gratious street pitt in the South Ile
		24	Buried Elizabeth daughter of ffrancis Burt Poulter in Gratious street pitt in the South Ile
	March	1	Buried Ann daughter of Mr Jo^n Langley Draper vpon Cornhill pitt in the Chauncell
		5	Buried John Macree servant to Jo^n Morehouse Wollen Drap': pitt by the churchwardens pew
		7	Buried Davy Price Draper at leadenhall Corner pitt by the Churchwardens pue
		23	Buried Isabell daughter of Symon ffreeman in Harrow alley. Pitt in ye East yard
1631	Aprill	1°	Buried Marie ffoster seruant to M^r ffeake. pitt in ye East yard
		9	Buried Richard sonne of George Wood Tallowchandler pitt in the East yard
		11	Buried a child wch was taken vp at Mrs Vowells stall aged one half yere pitt in the East yard
		28	Buried Ann daughter to Mr John Maxfeild Armore^r pitt in ye North Ile by her father
	May	4	Buried Katharine wife of Gawen Helme Armore^r pitt in the middle Ile in ye Church

Yeare.	Month.	Day.	Names.
1631	May	5	Buried Samuell Hurt wch lay at Mrs Westcotts Baker dwelling in Cornhill pitt in ye middle Ile
	June	2°	Buried Mary wife of William Bramich Armore^r dwelling in Gratious street pitt in ye South Ile
		21	Buried William Shipp Carpenter. pitt in the South Isle
	July	8	Buried Elizabeth daughter of William Hopkins Armorer pitt in the east yard
		25	Buried Ellen Gray seruant to Phillipp Mead Lynnen draper pitt in the east yard
	Septemb^r	8	Buried Thomas sonne of Thomas Carter Sadler pitt in the Library nere ye Church dore
		9	Buried Ann daughter of Walter Golefer Clothworker. pitt in the north Ile by his wifes pewe
		27	Buried Ann wife of William Moseley pitt in the north chappell at the end of the pewes
	Novemb^r	5	Buried Giles Eglestone Groce^r dwelling in Corbites court pitt in the South Isle by his pew doore
		8	Buried Thomas Hitchcock sonne of Thomas Hitchcocke pitt in the east yard neere the cloister
		23	Buried Sarah Symcock widdow lodging at Mr Rutters pitt in the West yard
	Decemb^r	3	Buried Alice Waterhowse widdow mother in law to Mr J^{no} Piggott pitt in ye south chappell by his wife
		10	Buried a still borne child of Henry Chamb^s Cooke pitt in the east yard
	January	3	Buried Tobiah Austen daughter of Thomas Austen dwelling in Leadenhall streete
		9 14*	Buried twoe Children of Mrs Rastells lodging at Mr Bells in Leadenhall street at Garlickhith
			The same day buried William sonne of the said Thomas Austen pitt in the east yard
		17	Buried William sonne of Thomas Jones Marchanttaillo^r pitt in the West yard
		29	Buried a still borne child of Thomas Bingham pitt in the east yard
			Buried the same day Ann daughter of John Chiswick Cooke in Gratious street pit in ye west yard
	February	20	Buried Elizabeth daughter of John Warner in Leaden Hall street pitt in the west yard
	March	12	Buried Mathias sonne of Mathias Hardinge Taylo^r in Gratious street pitt in ye east yard by his windowe
1632		26	Buried Jane daughter of Thomas Tocock pitt in the east yard
	Aprill	21	Buried John sonne of J^{no} Warner Haberdashe^r in leaden hall streete pitt in the west yard
		24	Buried Elizabeth daughter of Robt. Shawe vintner in leadenhall streete. pitt in the middle Ile by her pew doore
	Maie	1†	Buried Susan the daughter of Robert Edwards Haberdasher, pitt in ye Librarie
		3	Buried Marie the daughter of William Pease sadler, pitt in the south Chapple
		9	Buried a still borne child of Mr Wastells vintner pitt in the bodie of the church

* Sic.
† The Register from May 1, 1632, to July 14, 1633, is subscribed Thomas Birkhead, churchwarden.

THE REGISTERS OF ST. PETER'S, CORNHILL.

Yeare.	Month.	Day.	Names.
1632	Maie	10	Buried John the sonne of Roger ffisher Cutler pitt in the East yard
		16	Buried William the sonne of Sr Mathew Brand Knight, pitt in the South Chappell
		19	Buried Marie the daughter of Thomas Gatwood mercer pitt in the bodie of ye Church
	Julie	29	Buried Elizabeth the wife of Allen Baker poulter, pitt in ye west yard
	August	18	Buried Marie ye daughter of Thomas Lusher linnendraper, pitt in the middle Ile
	Septemb'	14	Buried Joane Warde servant to Mr Hord Tailor, pitt in the west yard
		24	Buried Henrie sonne of William Meares Skinner one of the twinns pitt in the west yard
	October	11	Buried William sonne of William Dwight tallow chandler pitt in the middle Ile
		28	Buried Phillipp sonne of Phillip Mead linnen draper pitt in the North Ile
	Novemb'	17	Buried Thomas Hawkes merchant in Hackney church by his father
	January	16	Buried a still borne child of John Middletonns Inholder pitt in the East yard
		19	Buried Elie Wyborne at Enfeild in ye Churchyard
		20	Buried John Graunt porter in ye South Ile by ye doare
	February	14	Buried Grace Whitlocke widowe pitt in ye East yard
		21	Buried Jane Read widowe of the age of one hundred yeeres and vpwards a vagrant, came from Chapsott in Leicestersheere, died in ye Cage, pitt in ye East yard
1633	Aprill	2	Buried Marie Barker widowe pitt in the East yard
	Maie	3	Buried Margarett wife of Phillip Mead Linnen draper pitt in ye North Ile
		12	Buried Elizabeth daughter of John James Armorer pitt in the South Ile by her mothers pew
	June	10	Buried James Toolie servant to o^r soveraigne Lord the Kinge, pitt in ye Librarie
		12	Buried Clement Egleston pitt in ye South Isle
	Julie	6	Buried Henrie sonne of Henrie Perkinson pit in the west yard
		8	Buried Peter sonne of Wm Dwoight pitt in ye bodie of ye church
		9	Buried Sr Wm Bishop of Dublin in Ireland pitt in ye chancell
		14	Buried John Harman pitt in ye East yard
		19*	Buried Charles sonne of Henrie Chambers Cooke pitt in ye East yarde
		27	Buried Christopher sonne of John Warner merchantailor pitt in ye west yard
	August	2	Buried Barbarie Bates a child at M^r vncles pitt in ye west yard
	Septemb.	1	Buried Hanna daughter of Thomas ffenn Porter pitt in ye west yard
		8	Buried W^m sonne of William Hall Armorer pitt of† ye bodie of ye church
		9	Buried Wm Hopkins Armorer pitt in ye East yard

* The Register from July 19, 1633, to September 11, 1634, is subscribed Theophilus Boulton, churchwarden.
† Sic.

Years.	Month.	Day.	Names.
1633	Septemb.	28	Buried James sonne of John Cheswick Cooke pitt in ye west yard
	October	9	Buried a Chrisome child of Mr Roads pitt in ye west yard
		21	Buried Marie ye daughter of Wm Pease sadler pitt in the south chappell
		30	Buried Isack sonne of Peter Warren Skinner pitt in ye bodie of ye church
	Novemb'	8	Buried a child taken out of ye vault at leadenhall New borne pitt in ye East yard
		20	Buried a male child still borne of Mr James's Armorer pit in ye South Isle
		29	Buried M^{ris} James wife of John James Armorer pitt in the south Isle
	January	13	Buried Miles Smith servant to Mr Homes pit in ye west yard
	February	4	Buried Elizabeth Dye servant to Mr Wroth, west y^d
		19	Buried Mr James Dawson schoolem^r, in ye Chauncell
		21	Buried Marie ye daughter of Wm Sikes in ye bodie of ye church
1634	Aprill	8	Buried Thomas sonne of Thomas Spilsburie pit in ye west y^d
		9	Buried Roger Robuck y^t died at Mr Moorehowses, pit in ye south Isle
	Maie	11	Buried Alexander Stephens servant to Mr Hall pitt in ye Librarie
	June	14	Buried a Stilborne child of Wm Brommidge pitt east y^d
	Augest	7	Thursdaie James Swinehoe servant to Robert Edwards pit in the librarie
		16	Buried Samuell sonne of Henrie Chambers Cooke pitt in ye East y^d
		21	Buried a poore child in ye East yard
	Septemb	2	Buried Wm Sonne of Nicholas Seres stacion' pitt middle Isle
		5	Buried Christopher Burt Skinner pitt in ye North Isle
		11	Buried John sonne of Jno Sutton Draper pitt librarie
		11	Buried Walter sonne of Wm Meares Skynner pitt east y^d
	October	1†	Buried * sonne of Mr Hardestee clothworker pitt in west yard
		8	Buried Jonathan Gowers servant to Mr Wills Cordwainer pitt east yard
			Buried Susann wife of Tho. Reynolds skinner pit chancell
		14	Buried George Boulton servant to Mr Shawe vintn^r pitt crosse
			Buried Thomasin Thompsonn widowe pitt East y^d
		16	Buried a stilborne child of Mr Hazards bodie of ye Church
		18	Buried Katherine daughter of Wm Meares Skinn^r pitt west y^d
		21	Buried Henrie Carendine serv^t to Mr Guillefer clothwor^r pitt in ye east y^d
		28	Buried Richard Stretch Grocer pitt in ye North chapple
		30	Buried W^m sonne of Wm Hall Armorer Pitt in ye middle Isle
	Novemb'	3	Buried Margarett daughter of Jo: Royce victuall^r pit east y^d

* Sic.
† The Register from October 1, 1634, to August 19, 1635, is subscribed John Mead, church-warden.

THE REGISTERS OF ST. PETER'S, CORNHILL. 195

Yeare.	Month.	Day.	Names.
1634	Nouemb'	13	Buried M^{ris} Hazard in ye Bodie of ye Church
		18	Buried Abigall daughter of Henrie Robinsonn merc^t pitt in ye north Isle
		28	Buried Tho. White sonne of Walter White merch^t of Exon
	Decemb'	1	Buried Susann Horne kineswoman to Mrs Brommidg pitt East y^d
		5	Buried Robert Hudsonn Skinner pitt in ye South chapple
		11	Buried W^m sonne of M^r W^m ffarefax doctor and parsonn of ye parishe. . . . . . Chauncell
		12	Buried Nicholas Seres stationer pit in ye middle Isle
		19	Buried Mr Hemmings fishmonger pit East y^d
	January	20	Buried Jane Peeter widowe pitt vnder ye great Bell
	March	5	Buried a still borne child of Sr Peter Bettesford pit East y^d
		9	Buried George sonne of Theophilus Boulton linnendrap' pitt in ye middle Isle. 4 y^r age
		10	Buried ffrances sonne of ffrances Burt Poulter pit south Isle
		12	Buried Jonathan sonne of Wm Browne sexton pit west y^d
		18	Buried Thomas sonne of Thomas Hanson Grocer pit south Isle
		19	Buried Dorothie daughter of Wm Browne sexton pit west y^e
		24	Buried Sr Peter Bettesworth knight pit in ye chancell at ye end of ye pewes, hee died at Mr Wille his howse
1635		28	Buried M^{ris} Agnes Done widowe dwellinge in ffanchurch street whitebaker pitt in ye library by her husband
	Aprill	9	Buried Marie wife of Robert Norman painter pitt middle Isle
		13	Buried Robert sonne of Martin Higgins scriven^r pitt library
	Maie	7	Buried Mathew Gillam M^{r}chauuttailo^r pit in ye north chappell
		25	Buried Nicholas Challeno^r serv^t to m^r young pit in ye middle Ile
	July	3	Buried Marie daught^r of Arth^r Rodes Sadler pit in ye west yard
		6	Buried Sara daught^r of Jo^n Warner m'chanttailo^r pit in ye west y^d
		24	Buried Rebecca daught^r of Tho. Smith Haberdash^r pit in ye east y^d
	August	8	Buried Simon Thorowgood drap' pit in ye South chappell
		14	Buried William sonne of Joseph Graues Vintu^r pit in ye South chappell
		19	Buried Mary daughter^r of Richard Harris M^{r}chaut pit in middle Ile
	November	3*	Buried Ann Langley a poore maid pit in ye west yard
		5	Buried Henrie Chambers Cooke pit in ye South Isle
	Decemb'	1°	Buried Tho: Hind Inhold^r pit in ye South chappell
	January	14	Buried Mrs Ashpoole widdow pit in the Chauncell
		28	Buried Mrs Biker wif of lewis Biker Groce^r pit in the South Ile
			Buried Epham Vowell widdow pitt in ye middle Ile
	February	9	Buried Sarah daughter^r of Hen: Chamber^s cooke pit in ye east y^d
		17	Buried Andrew Ward serv^t to Giles Harding pit in ye west y^d
		29	Buried Rebecca daughter^r of Hen: Robinson pit in ye west y^d

* The Register from November 3, 1635, to March 22, 1638, is subscribed Francis Burt, churchwarden.

Yeare.	Month.	Day.	Names.
1636	March	29	Buried Stephen Grove Poult^r pitt in ye East yard
	April	10	Buried Joⁿ Smith s^rv^t to Mr Watson pit in ye west y^d
		24	Buried James ffarewell s^rvant to Mr Barnard pit in the east yard
		28	Buried Ann daughte^r of John Silk Putere pit in ye west yard
	May	5	Buried Thomas Gilman s^rv^t to Mr Barnard pit in ye east yard. Plague
	June	4⁰	Buried Joⁿ Selby s^rv^t to Mr Satchfeild pit in ye west yard
	July	3⁰	Buried a still borne child of Tho: Hill pitt in ye west yard
	August	11	Buried George Goodwyn Habberd' pit in ye South chappell
		24	Buried Katharine daught^r of Joⁿ Roys pit in ye East yard
	Septem^r	13	Buried James Armit s^rv^t to Mr Hurt pit in ye East yard. Plague
		14	Buried Ann Mackaris s^rv^t to Mr Hiron pit in ye west yard
		19	Buried Margarit wife of Joⁿ Roys pit in ye East yard Plague
		22	Buried John Roys pitt in the said east yard Plague
	October	1	Buried John sonn of Joⁿ Roys pitt in the East yard Plague
		6	Buried Amy wife of Mr Hen :Barnard pitt in ye middle Isle
		9	Buried Ann mother of Joⁿ Roys pit in the east yard
		23	Buried Rich: White. pitt in ye North chappell Plague
	Nouem^r	2	Buried Jasp' brother to Mr Robt. Shaw pitt by ye church doore
		8	Buried Samuell srv^t to Mr Silk pewterer pit in ye west yard. Plague
		21	Buried Nicho: Browne sv^t to Mr Bramw^{ch} pit in ye west yard
		24	Buried Joⁿ Hackett Shoomaker pit in ye west yard
	Decemb'	1	Buried Marie Bofeild widdow pit in ye west yard
		29	Buried a chrisome child of Walter Golefer pit in ye North Ile
	January	26	Buried Mrs Hacket pit in the west yard plague
	February	18	Buried Sara Clark widdowe pitt in the west yard
	March	21	Buried Wm Cockings sv^t to Mr Hurt pit in ye east yard. plague
1637		28	Buried Joⁿ Burton Tallowchandl^r pit in ye west yard
	Aprill	15	Buried Joⁿ Wheele^r sv^t to Mr Bingham pit in ye east yard plague
		18	Buried William Dwight Tallowchandl^r pit in ye middle Ile
	May	2	Buried Josias & Ann children of Mr Bingham pit in ye east yard
		7	Buried Mrs Mary Seaman widdow pit in the South chappell
		21	Buried Rebecca daughter of Tho: Bingham pit in ye east yard plague
	June	8	Buried Isabell Ward mother of Mrs Burt pit in ye South Ile
		11	Buried Thomas Bingham Cooke pit in ye South chappell plague
		18	Buried Mrs Miers. pit in the west yard plague
		25	Buried William Living s^rv^t to Mr Peas pit in ye east yard plague
		28	Buried Joⁿ Leave pitt in the West yard
	July	7	Buried the wife of Joⁿ Thorpe in Christchurch plague
		17	Buried Mary daughter of Humfrie Woodward pitt in ye east yard. plague
		20	Buried a female child of Jone Ashby murthered pit in the east yard

THE REGISTERS OF ST. PETER'S, CORNHILL.

Yeare.	Month.	Day.	Names.
1637	July	29	Buried Jo^n sonn of Hum: Woodward. pit in the east yard
	August	2	Hanna daughter of Robert fisher Cutler pit west yard
		9	William Stanton serv^t to Mr Graves pit by the poores box in ye church
		13	Sara daught^r of Hum: Woodward pit in ye East yard
		15	Martha Dynn, pitt in the East yard of ye plague pl'
		16	Mary daughter of Raph Frith pit in ye East yard pl'
		30	Thomas Spilsbery Smith pitt in the South Ile pl'
			Alice daughter of Raph Frith pit in the East yard
	Septemb'	4	W^m sonne of James Butler pit in the Library
		8	Elizabeth Woodcocke a poore woman diing* in ye street pit east yard
		31	Jo^n sonne of John Warner Habberd' pit in ye West yard
	Novemb'	10	Buried fraunces Coston widdowe at Aldersgate Church
	Decemb'	5	John soune of John Hieron pit in ye east yard
	January	12	Elizabeth Mote pitt in the East yard
		26	Margaret King widdowe buried at Creechurch
	February	24	Christopher Sener s^{rt} to m^r Langley pit in ye west yard
	March	15	Elizabeth Perkins widd', Pit in the West yard aged 92
1638	Aprill	1°	Thomas sonne of Thomas Lushe^r pit in y^c Middle Ile
		9	Thomas sonne of Jo^n Glynn pitt in the east yard
		18	Thomas sonn of Jo^n White pit in ye North Chappell
		20	Sarah daughte^r of John White pit in ye North Chappell
		25	Katharin Hubbersted widd' pit in ye West yard
	May	9	Bridget wife of Thomas Birkhead Armor pit in ye middle Ile
		16	Elizabeth daughte^r of Walt^r Golefer clothworker pitt in the north Ile
		28	Thomas Jones Penc'one^r Pitt in ye West yard
	June	14	Mr Jo^n Wroth. aged 74. pitt in the South Ile
		16	Edward Roberts serv^t to m^r Biker pit in ye Library
		20	Daniell Witham serv^t to Mr Kingsman pit in ye Library
			Ann daughte^r of Tho: fenn Sexton pit in ye west yard
		22	Thomas sonne of Alice Hennag pit in ye east yard
	July	15	Elizabeth daught^r of Wm Watson pit in ye east yard
		25	A male chrisom child of Jo^n Harding pit in ye North Ile
		28	Sarah wife of Jo^n Witherall pit in ye North chappell
		29	A male still borne child of Wm Abotes pit in the east yard
	August	12	Jo^n Browne Inholder pit in the South chappell
	Octob^r	5	Jo^n Portler serv^t to Mr Desbrough pit in ye Library
		16	Fra: sonn of fraunces Walcot pit in the North Ile
		22	Will'm Norton a foot poost dying in the street pit in ye east yard
	Nouemb'	9	An abortiue male child of Jo^n Brownes pit in ye east yard
		4	Perciuall How serv^t to Mr Birkhead pit in ye West yard
		11	Jo^n sonn of fraunces Walcot pit in the South Ile
	Decemb'	24	Osman Vuckles Cooke pit in ye North chappell
	January	23	Dorathie wife of John Hariman pit in ye North Ile
	February	2	John Whitesbead Cobler pit in ye East yard
		14	Mary Chaplin widdow pit in the Middle Isle
	March	22	Ellen Hill widd' pit in the South Chappell
1639	Aprill	14†	Nathaniel sonn of William Cole m^{r}cer pit in ye west yard
		25	Jo^n sonne of Jo^n Silk petwerer* pit in the west yard aged 10 yeres

* Sic.
† The Register from Aprill 14, 1639, to March 24, 1642, is subscribed Thomas Sergeant, churchwarden.

Yeare.	Month.	Day.	Names.
1639	May	3	The wife of Henry Robinson pit in the west yard
		15	Agnes daughter of Jo^n Booth Letherselle^r pit in ye South chappell
		20	A still borne child of Thomas Royse pit in the east yard
	June	25	Joane ye wife of fra: Walcott Habb' pit in the south Ile
	July	11	John Langley esq^r Pit in ye Chauncell by his daughte^r
	August	1	Samuell Ward Stac'on^r pit in the Librarye
		8	Peter a chrisom child of Peter Newton pit in ye east yard
	Septem^r	26	Thomas Izard s^{r}vant to Hen. Perkinson pit in ye West yard
	Octob'	18	Wm Meares Skynner pitt in the west yard
	Nouem'	18	Thomas sonn of Tho: Bedum pit in ye North Isle
	Decemb'	4	George Roise Skynn^r pit in the East yard
		19	Wm Hill Grocer pit in the South Ile p' the vestry dore
		29	A male child still borne of Mr Wards pit in the East yard
	January	31	Jane Morris widd' pitt in the middle Isle aged 75 yeres
	February	2	Alexand^r sonn of Alex Butle^r pit in ye North Isle
		14	Henry Loton sv^t to Wm Bibbey pit in ye East yard
		23	Ann daught^r of fra: Wilkins pit in ye East yard
	March	10	James son of Jo^n Padmore Clothworker pit in ye midd' Ile
		20	Eliz. wife of Tho: Austen pit in the East yard
1640	Aprill	18	Jo^n sonn of Lewis Biker pit in the South Isle
		25	Judith Keech widdow pit in the North chappell
	June	16	Jo^n sonn of Tho. Osborne Brickleyo^r pit in ye west yard
	July	17	A still borne child of Jo^n Poole Minister pitt in ye middle Isle
		18	Elizabeth wife of Timothy Young pitt in the middle Isle
		22	Richard Denham Inholder pitt in the west yard
	Septemb'	1	Robert Meares pitt in the West yard
	October	15	William sonne of Samuell Ward pitt in the Librarie
	Nouemb'	9	Thomas sonne of Theophilus Bolton pitt in ye North Isle
	Decemb'	3	Hugh Tresse Turner pitt in the South chappell
		4	Mary wife of George Henley buried in Algate church
		20	Christian Hannys widdow pitt in the Library
		16	William Stubbs Ironmonger pitt in ye south Isle
		29	Henry sonne of Walter Golefer pitt in ye North Isle
	January	24	Margaret wife of Jo^n Bowker pitt in ye South chappell
	February	5	Jeromy Gardner Esquier pit in the chauncell
		17	John sonne of Thomas Birkett Armorer pitt in ye middle Isle
	March	5	Raph sonne of Tho: Reynolds Skynne^r pitt in ye middle Isle
1641		31	Ann daughter of Richard Cleaton pitt in the East yard
	June	8	Richard sonne of Rich: Croone Clothworker pitt in the North Isle
		14	Paull sonne of Thomas Bingham Cooke pitt in the East yard
		17	Joannah daughter of Wm Watson pitt in the East yard
	July	1	Martha Langley widdow pitt in the Chauncell
		14	Constance Katch, pitt in the north Isle
		28	Elizabeth Acklande widdowe. pitt in the East yard
		31	Lawrence sonne of Lawrence Goffe pitt in ye South chappell
	August	7	Thomas Smith Haberdasher pitt in ye East yard
		16	Jo^n Harman serv^t to Mr Holmes pitt in the east yard
	Septemb'	1	Henry sonne of Henry Gilpin Armorer
	Octobe^r	16	Thomas Mullat Inhold^r. pitt in the west yard
	Nouemb'	6	Sarah Greenick pitt in ye East yard

THE REGISTERS OF ST. PETER'S, CORNHILL.

Yeare.	Month.	Day.	Names.
1641	Nouemb'	10	Ann daughter of Joⁿ Cottrell pitt in the East yard
	Decemb'	10	John sonne of Martin Higgins pitt in yᵉ Library
		19	Margaret daughter of Thomas Ward pitt in yᵉ middle Ile
		23	Elnor wife of James Marsh pitt in the West yard
		20	John Gore: Lecturer pitt in the Chauncell
			Thomas sonne of Robert Whitney pitt in the east yard
	January	17	William sonne of Tho: Smith pitt in yᵉ east yard
	February	11	George Harding Vintener pitt in yᵉ North Isle
		15	Mary daughter of Henry Cowp' pitt in the east yard
		21	Samuell sonne of Wᵐ Hamond Ironmongʳ pit in yᵉ west yard
		24	Elizabeth Satchfeild widdow pitt in yᵉ North Ile
	March	2	Thomas Pywell Salter pitt in the North Ile
1642	Aprill	15	Elizabeth Gatward Widdow pitt in yᵉ middle Ile
		21	John Burton Skynner pit in the West yard
	May	20	George Burton gent. pit in yᵉ West yard
		21	Elizabeth daughter of Tho: Reynolds pitt in yᵉ middle Ile
	June	1	Edward Peter sʳvᵗ to Mʳ Sibley pit in yᵉ east yard
		27	Robert Bourne sʳvᵗ to Mʳ Watson pit in yᵉ east yard
	July	5	John sonne of James Blott pitt in yᵉ South Ile
		8	frances sonne of frances Coling pitt in ye middle Ile
		15	Joⁿ Hudnoll Vintnʳ pitt in yᵉ South chappell
		26	Wᵐ sonne of William Saby Blacksmith pitt in yᵉ east yard
	August	4	Mathew Sibley Cooke pitt in yᵉ South chappell
		7	Jane daughter of Tho: ffenn pitt in the West yard
		8	Joⁿ sonne of Wᵐ East grocer pitt in yᵉ east yard
		10	Alice daughter of Tho: Hanson grocer pitt in yᵉ South Ile
	Septemb'	19	Dorathie daughter of Joⁿ Clark stac'onʳ pitt in yᵉ West yard
		24	Richard Turfrey linnen drap' pitt in yᵉ south Ile
		25	Mary daughter of William Bibbey in yᵉ East yard
	October	2	Barbary ⎫ daughters of John Clarke stacioner pitt west
			Elisabeth ⎭ yard
		14	Elisabeth Burt widd'. pitt in the North Ile
		15	Mary daughter of John Padmore In new Church yard
		18	John Cowp' servᵗ to mʳ Clark pitt in yᵉ west yard
		19	Elisabeth wife of John Evans girdler pitt In yᵉ south Ile
		27	Arthur Awbery servant, pitt in yᵉ south Ile
	November	22	Christian Tomelay Widd' pitt in yᵉ south chappell
	December	17	Grace Chandeler pitt in yᵉ west yard
		21	John Gleene larrimore* pitt in the East yeard
		23	Joane wife of Zachary Speck pitt in yᵉ East yeard
	February	10	Elisabeth Hill widd'. pitt in the Chansell
		14	Henry Mason pitt in the south Ile
		28	Elisabeth Whiteshead widd' pitt in yᵉ East yeard
	March	8	Sarah wife of Laurence Goffe pitt in yᵉ south chappˡˡ
		24	Wᵐ sonne of Hewghe Best pitt in yᵉ East yeard
1643	June	23†	Henry sonne of Henry Cowp'. pitt in the East yeard
	July	11	Richard sonne of Richard Kingsman grocer pitt in yᵉ west yard
	August	14	ffrancis Derham labourer pitt in ye west yeard
		15	Johnathan sonne of Beniamine Clarridg potter pitt in the west yeard

* Of the Lorimers' Company.
† The Register from June 23, 1643, to June 21, 1644, is subscribed Walter Golliver, churchwarden.

Yeare.	Month.	Day.	Names.
1643	August	17	Nicholas sonne of Clement Bacon pitt in ye East yard
		19	William Watson potticary pitt in ye south Ile
		22	Jeames Gutter serv^t to m^r Kingsman pitt in ye West yard
		23	A souldier at the Bull pitt in ye west yeard
		27	Jeane daughter to m^r Hanson grocer pitt in ye south Ile
	September	10	A mayd servant of m^r Shaws pitt in ye west yard
		14	Rebecka Wife of Beniamin Clarridg potter pitt in ye west yeard
		19	John Kitche linnen drap' pitt in ye North Chappell
	October	4	Mary daughter to Lewis Byker grocer pitt in ye north Ile
		14	John sonne of Lewis Biker grocer pitt in ye north Ile
		17	Mary Thikneys pitt in ye south Chappell
		24	Ann daughter of Wm Hall armorer pitt in ye East yeard
		26	Mary daughter of John Warner m'chautailor pitt in ye west yard
		30	A poore woman pitt in ye East yeard
		31	Thomas sonne of Willia' Pease saddler pitt in ye south chapp^{ll}
	November	5	Samuell son of Wm Hall armorer pitt in ye East yard
		8	Ann Gilbert pitt in ye West yeard
		14	Emm daughter to Wm Hall Armorer pitt in ye East yard
		21	ffrancis Doyley pitt by the com'union table
	December	8	Hanna daughter of Thomas Speed drap' in ye west yeard
	January	4	Anne daughter of Robert Shaw Vintener pitt in ye middle Ile
		9	Christopher Hanbury servant to Captayne Woleston pitt in the middle Ile
		12	Humphry Stirt letherseller pitt in ye north Ile
	March	2	M^{ris} Chapman pitt in ye Library
1644	Aprill	27	Elisabeth daughter of Jeames Blott pitt in ye south Ile
	June	11	Sarah daughter of Robt ffisher pitt in west yard
		16	Jeames Gold serv^t to m^r Rolf dyed here but was buried in St Andrews Vndershafts church yard
		18	Sarah Stirt Widd': pitt in ye north Chappell
			John serv^t to m^r Desborrow pitt in ye Library
		19	Bridget Norton Widd'. pitt in ye south chappell
		20	Elisabeth Wife of John Hyrou pitt in ye south chapp^{ll}
		21	George Henly leatherseller pitt in ye Chancell
		22*	Jeane Hynde Widd' pitt in ye south Chapp^{ll}
		22	John Croone packer pitt in ye south Ile
		22	Mis Lusher wife to m^r Tho. Lusher fishmonger pitt in ye middle Ile
		23	Judith Sibblis Widd' pitt in ye north Chapp^{ll} by her husband.
		23	Robert † servant to m^r Cooling pitt by ye churchwardens pew
		24	Sarah Seller widd' pitt in ye West yard
		24	Mary Ward widd' pitt in the library
		24	Elisabeth Satchfeild pitt in ye north Ile
		25	Elisabeth wife of ffrancis Burt pitt south Ile
		25	Mary daughter of John Silke aged 9 yeares pitt in ye west yard
		25	Ann Dyeath serv^t to m^r Pease pitt in the West yard

* The Register from June 22, 1644, to April 14, 1645, is subscribed John Langley, churchwarden.

† Sic.

THE REGISTERS OF ST. PETER'S, CORNHILL.

Yeare.	Month.	Day.	Names.
1644	June	26	Henry Hurt m'chantailor, pitt in ye middle Ile
		27	Ann Wife of Willia' Sikes clothworker pitt in the middle Ile
		28	Jeames * servant to Wm East grocer pitt in the East yard
		29	Christopher Desborrow mercer in ye south Chappell
	July	2	Sarah Wife of John Harrima' in ye north ysle
		25	Sarah Wife of Beniamin Clarridg in ye west yard
	August	8	Samuell Procter m'chant in ye Chancell
	September	22	John Mountford pewterer in ye Crosse Ile
	October	11	Susan Wife of Thomas Cole Drap' in ye Chancell
		25	Elisabeth Wife of Mathias Harding in new church yard
	November	16	Luce wife of Tho: Holland in ye west yard
	December	10	Elisaboth Tomson Widd' in ye west yard
	January	7	Beniamin son of Tho: Hanson grocer in ye south yle
		23	William Bibbey inholder in ye east yeard
	March	7	Martha daughter of John Langley in ye Chancell
		14	Barbara Lock Widd' in the middle Ile
		21	Steven Helme armorer In ye middle Ile
1645		28	Ann daughter of John Silk pewterer in ye west yard
	Aprill	4	William Sikes Clothworker pitt in y^o middle yle
		14	A femal Crissome of Mary Smith brought on bedd in ye streete pitt in ye East yard
		23†	Thomas son of Thomas Hanson groc' south Ile
	May	5	Mary daughter of John Cotterell glasier East yard
		22	Mary ye wife of Nicholas Chowney minister West yard
		29	* son of Thomas Ward grocer middle Ile
	July	7	ffaith Buttler pitt by her husband In ye library
		9	Mary daughter of Mr Gorom pit in ye East yard
		19	Edward son of Mephibosheth Robons, factor East yard
	August	30	Thomas Natt Marriner pit in ye East yeard
	October	18	John Taylor free of ye Mercers pitt East yeard
	Novemb	18	John Harriman haberdasher pitt North yle hy his wife in his pew near a grocer
		20	Robert Pennington pitt middle yle by his pew near a grocer
	D'ember	5	Alse daughter of Wm Bibby Inholder pitt in ye East yard
		25	Thomas Boothe letherseller pitt South chapp^{ll} by his mother
	January	2	John Busbey souldier of mowsam by chensoford‡ pitt east yard
		12	John son of John Cotterell glasier pitt East yard
		18	Mary Wescott widd' pitt at Cloyster dore
	February	10	W^m & Jeames sons of Jeames Blott drap' pitt south yle
		15	Willia' son of Mephibosheth Robins pitt East yeard
		18	Abraha' Clay Cooke pitt east yard
	March	3	Willia' Hudson skinner pitt in ye south chapp^{ll}
		16	Tho: son of Thomas Bothe letherse^r pitt South Chap^{ll}
		18	Mrs Jeane Thorowgood pitt in south yle
		25	Susa' daughter of Nicholas Seros pitt middle yle
1646	March	30	Our Reverent pastor m^r Tho: Colema' pitt in ye vpper end of ye Chancell
		31	Thomas son of Thomas Coop' Cordwayner pitt in ye East yard
	Aprill	22	Thomas, son of Thomas Walter Tappin Vintener East yard

* Sic.
† The Register from April 23, 1645, to February 4, 1646-7, is subscribed Thomas Handson, churchwarden.
‡ Moulsham by Chelmsford. Moulsham is one of the divisions of the town of Chelmsford.

Yeare.	Month.	Day.	Names.
1646	Aprill	22	Ann, daughter of Wm Chamberlayne dyer, pitt East yeard
		30	m^{rs} Margaret Cooling Widd', pitt in ye middle Ile, aged 90
	May	10	Ann wife of Thomas ffenn sexton pitt in ye Liberary
	June	20	Richard Cowp' servant to m^r Thomas Lusher free of ye fishmongers, pitt in ye middle Ile
	June	29	Thomas Whaylsley servant to John Hiron cooke pitt East yard
		30	Robert Griffin servant to Thomas Sergeant vpholdster pit East yeard
	July	4	William Holmes labourer pitt East yeard
		10	Hanna wife of Gilbert Maddox baker pitt in ye south Ile
		11	Rose daughter to Edmond Tooley Inholder pitt in ye library
		15	Margery wife of m^r Edw: Helm grocer pitt in the North Ile
		19	A female still borne child of William Parreys clothworker pitt East yeard
		23	Anne daughter of Allexander Meers chirurgian pitt in ye west yard
	Septemb	4	Margaret daughter of m^r Pasmore pitt lyber'*
	October	2	A female childe of Robt. Whitburnes pit in East yeard
		21	John Holmes cordwayne' pitt in ye south chapp^{ll}
	Novemb	14	John son of Wm Sabey, blacksmith pitt East yeard
		30	Martha, daughter to m^r w^m Blackmore our Minister pitt in the Library
	Decemb	1	Thomas son of Thomas Wills cordwayner pitt in ye Library (of ye plague)
		9	Elisabeth wife of Thomas ffiges pitt in ye middle yle
		9	A male Infant of m^r Jeames Abrathaps marchant pitt in ye middle yle
		22	Elisabeth daughter of Robert Holton draper pitt in the north yle
		25	Thomas son of Robt. Whitney barber pitt in . . . yard
		28	Henry son of Henry Robinson Mercer pitt in the south yle
	February	4	John Evens Cutler aged 80 pitt in ye south yle
	March	2†	John sonn of William Tapping Vintner pitt in the North Ile by his Mothers pew
		19	Joane the Wife of Richard Moule Merchantay' pitt in the West yard in the Middle
1647	Aprill	6	Mathias Harding Merchantayler pitt in the Nuchurch yard by his Wife
		8	John Agnies a Contremau pitt in the south Ile by Mr Blotts Children
		26	Elizabeth Daughter to Mr Thomas Booth Letherseller pitt in the south Chappell by her ffather
	June	8	Izabell the Wife of James Marsh Carpinter pitt in the West yard
		11	Joanna Daughter of Henry Clarke Chiru^{r}gion pitt in the South Ile by her Mothers pew
		21	Henry sonn of Henry Robinson Habberdasher the yonger pitt in the south Ile aged A month
		27	Susanna daughter of John Budd powlt' pitt in the East yard
	July	13	John sonn of John Silke Pewterer pitt in the West yard

* Library.

† The Register from March 2. 1646-7, to March 2. 1547-8, is subscribed Mr John Burdsall, churchwarden.

THE REGISTERS OF ST. PETER'S, CORNHILL.   203

Yeare.	Month.	Day.	Names.
1647	July	22	Richard sonn of Edward Archer Tallow cha'dler pitt in the West yard
	Septem	25	John Smith s^{r}vant to Mrs Gatha'pton pytt in the North Ile by her piew
		26	Alice Hill se^{r}vant to Mr Whittington pitt in the East yard
		30	Symon sonn of John Cotterill Glasie^r pitt in the East yard by the Windoe
	October	13	John and Gabrill two twynns the sonns of Baptist Croft M'cha'tayler p^{tt} West y^d
	Novemb^r	17	Mrs Jaine Wife of Mr Thomas Hanson Groce^r pitt in the South Ile by her Children
		26	Edward Sonn of Edward Archer Tallowcha^r pitt in the West yard
	Decemb^r	14	Tusday Mrs Jaine the Wife of M^r Rc'd Midleto^n Grocer pitt in the Chancell Vault by Alderman Westraw
		16	Robert Marsh Vintene^r pitt in the West yard
		17	Robert Sonn of Edmund Tooley Inholder pitt in the Library
			Mrs Poole the Wife of Mr Poole Minister by Epping pitt in the North Chappell
		23	Henry Perkinson Cordwinder pitt in ye West yrd
	ffebruar'	15	Leonard sonn of Peeter Towers Drap' pitt in the East yard
	March	2	Mrs Elizabeth Cooling the Wife of Mr ffrancis Cooling pitt in the Middle Ile
1648	March	28*	Sarah Daughter of Thomas Stollard pitt in the West yard
		30th	Edward Sonn of William Chamberline Dyer pitt in the Middle Ile
	Aprill	9	Leonard Sonn of Marsh Vintener pitt in the West yard
		11	Jonne Winne schott in the head by acsidente pitt in the East yard
		28	Mr Henry Tanner Minister pitt in ye No^{r}th Iyle
	May	9th	Mary Daughter of George Barker Cooper pitt in the East yard
		16th	Thomas Austine Sheeregrinder pitt East yrd
	June	3^d	Susan Daughter of James Abrathapp pitt in the middle Ile
	June	6th	Mrs Jaine Williams Daughter to Mr Richard Midleton Merchant pitt in the Chansell vaute
		23	Katherine Daughter of Galhampton Vintener pitt in the South Iyle by her Mothers pew
	August	9	Mr Allexander Butler Inholder pitt in the south Chappell
		27	Ann Bray Widdow Pitt in East yard
	Septem	2	Mary daughter of Jerremy Daniell West yrd
		4	Elizabeth daughter of Jerremy Daniell West yrd
		5	Dorothy s'vant to Mr Croone pitt in East yrd
		15	Rebecka Daughter of Phillip Brocke dyer pitt in the Cross Ile
		20	Robert sonn of Robert Whitney pitt in East yrd
	November	14	Sara Daughter of Mr William Blackmore Rector pitt in the Library
	October	5	Mr Peeter Hassard ffishmonger pitt Middle Ile
		22	Mrs Elizabeth ffrith pitt in the South Ile. Mr Hansons Wifes Mother

* The Register from March 28 to November 24, 1648, is subscribed Mr John Silke, churchwarden.

Yeare.	Month.	Day.	Names.
1648	October	23	Jaine Wife of Edmund Tooley Inholder pitt in the Library by the Church yrd dore
	Novemr	6	William Sonn of William Mabbutt pitt East yrd
		21	Mrs Ann Mote Vidua' pitt in the Middle Ile
			Mary Daughter to Mr Abrathatt in the same grave
		24	Mrs Ann Westbrucke spinster Gent' pitt South chappll
	Januar	2*	Mr Richard Wolleston flishmonger pitt in the South Chappell
	ffebruar'	1	Barnabee Watson pitt in the West yard
		27	John Sonn of John Smith Clothworker pitt in the Midd' Ile
	March	5	Thomas Mvn s'vant to Mr Ostler pitt in the East yard
1649	Aprill	1	Beniamine Sonn of Thomas Leacocke Merchantaylor Pitt in the South Chappell vnder the Deske
		22	Tabitha Daughter of James Bucke Vicker of Stradbrooke in Suffolke pitt in ye North Ile by the wall
	June	18	Mary Daughter of John Webb pitt in the East yard
		26	Mr ffrancis Burt Polterer pitt in the south Ile
	July	3d	Symon Sonn of Richard Blackborne Draper pitt in the East yard
			A Male Child of Mr Barkers Coop' pitt in the East yrd
		8	William Sonn of William Saby Blacksmth pitt in the East yard
		12	Elizabeth daughter of Mr Chamberline Dyer pitt in the Middle Ile
		24	Mr Thomas Walthall Mercer pitt in the Chancell
		25	Thomas Sonn of Thomas Griffine Pewterer pitt in the East yard
		27	Mary Wife of Gilbert Maddox Bak'r pitt in the Library
	Augu'	7	A Male Crisome Child of Mr Husba'ds pitt in the Midd Ile
		24	Mary Daughter of ffra'ces Walkur Ironmonger pitt in the South Chappell by her Aunt
	Septemr	17	John Gore Merchant pitt in the North Chappell
	October	7	Debora Butler se'vant to Mr Best pitt in the East yrd
		10	A ffemale Child of Mr Claridges pitt in the West yard
		11	Ann Brocke pitt in the Middle Ile
		14	Katherine Pembrooke s'vant to Mr Dodson pitt in the West yard
	the second of Novr		Charles Burgis Cheesmonger pitt in the Midd' Ile
		9	Elizabeth Nurse Widd: pitt in the North Ile
			Joane Stranguidge s'va't to Mr Pearce pitt East y'd
		22	Mary Daughter of Ralph Trunckitt Cooke pt East y'd
	Decem'	3	Lettis Daughter of Luis Biker Grocer pitt in ye south Ile
		3	Thomas Sonn of Allexa'der Smith Scoolma' pit East y'd
		24	Elizabeth Daughter of Mr Blott Drap' pitt in the south Ile
		25	A Male Child of John Smithes Clothwor: pitt Midd Ile
	Januar	13	A ffemale Child of Mr Haules pitt in the East y'd
	March	7	Mr James Abrathatt Gouldsmith pitt in the Midd Ile
1650		29†	Jaine Daughter of Hugh Best Vintener pitt in the Library
	Aprill	16	Judith the Wife of Willia' Perry Grocer pitt in the South Chappell in the Vaught

* The Register from January 2, 1648, to March 7, 1649, is subscribed Mr John Clarke, churchwarden.

† The Register from March 29, 1650, to June 4, 1651, is subscribed Mr Lewis Biker, churchwarden.

Yeare.	Month.	Day.	Names.
1650	Aprill	24	Martha Daughter of John Glynn Larramore* pitt in the East Yard
	May	19	Joyce Smith Vidua' pitt in the East yard
		31	Mary Chamberline pitt in the West yard
	June	1	Twoe ffemale Twinnes of M*r* Clarridges p*t* West yard
		24	Mary Acton daughter to M*r* Jerremy Gardner Gent'. pitt in the Chansell
		25	James sonne of James Ellison. pitt in the East y*rd*
	July	25	M*r* ffrancis Cooling ffishmonger p*tt* in the Midd. Ile
	Augu*t*	5	Elizabeth Daughter of Willia' Harmar p*tt* East ya*rd*
		15	Jn*o* Middleton Inholder pitt in the West yard
		28	Martha Daughter of M*r* Willia' Blackmore our Minister in the Library by the East yard dore
	Septem*r*	2	Mary Daughter of William Russell Painter Stayner pitt in the West Yard neere the Wall
		24	Robert Chamberlaine aged 88 pit west yard
	Octob*r*	1	M*rs* Joane flaxmoore by her brother m*r* John Casun in the south Chappell
	Nouemb*r*	22	ffrancis Pickering in the west yard
	Decemb*r*	20	sarah daughter of John James in south chapel
		23	Hannah daughter of Thomas Norman west yard
			A femal Chrisom Child of John smith midle Ile
		28	Christopher sibthorpe of Chelmsford west yard
	Janua*y*	10	John sonne of John Coppocke west yard
		18	Dorcas daughter of John Hickes East yard
	febru*y*	5	Jane daughter of M*r* John Langly fishmong*r* pit in the Chancell by his fathers stone
	March	7	Richard Biker mercer pit in the Library
		19	John sonne of Robert Holton draper pit in the North Ile aged three yeare & half
1651	April	10	John Dow seruant to Ralph Trunkett Cooke pitt in the East yard
		30	m*rs* Alice sparrow pitt in south Chappell
	May	5	mary daughter of Walter and Elizabeth Garford Mercer pitt in the midle Ile
		13	Anne one of the twins of m*r* Walkers Iremonger pitt in the south Chappell
		23	Anne daughter of James Gallatle haberd*r* in lib*y*
	June	2	Elizabeth daughter of m*r* Husbands midle Ile
		4	Henery sonne of James Gallatle haberd*r* library
		11†	Barberry daughter of Edward Archer pitt in the West yard
		18	Dorothy Crowder seruant to m*r* Butler pitt in the East yard
		20	Richard Mould marchant taylor pitt in the west yard, by his wife aged 95 yeares
	July	15	m*r* William Pease was buried at the bath aged 68 yeares
	August	12	Thomas sonne of Thomas Piggott Grocer pitt in the south chappell aged 60
	Septem*r*	12	Ignatius Gibbs s*r*uant to m*r* Birdsol pitt midle Ile
		14	James sonne of John Witherall pitt midle Ile
			William sonne of william Phillips pitt west yard
		25	Robert Whiteborse Clothworker pitt west yard
	Octob*r*	2	John Wright kinsman to Edward Archer pitt west yard
			Thomas seriant skinner pitt in the south chapel

* Of the Lorimers' Company.
† The Register from June 11, 1651, to March 17, 1652-3, is subscribed M*r* John James, churchwarden.

Yeare.	Month.	Day.	Names.
1651	Octob^r	19	A male Child of Robert Holtons in ye north Ile
	Nouem^r	12	Elizabeth daughter of Esdras Mils East yard
		13	Robert Eaton Vpholder pitt north Ile
		14	Elizabeth Woodgate pitt East yard
		19	A male Child of John smith pitt midle Ile
	Decem^r	4	Elizabeth daughter to ffrancis Walker Iremonger pitt in ye south Chappel
			Tomasin daughter of Sr Anthony Luther pitt in ye north Chappel
	Janua^y	9	Grace daughter of William hall midl. Ile
		11	Susan wife of John Brickland west yard
		21	Elenor daughter of John saywel west yard
	March	13	Moody Lusher pitt in the midle Ile
		21	William Nutt s^{r}uant to m^r miller pitt in the north Chappell 18 year
		23	Thomas Merrick s^{r}uant to m^r figes west y^{r}d
1652	Aprill	3	Margret the wife of James Marsh: Est yeard
		19	Lawrence Goffe Marchant in ye south vaught
		22	Edward Sonne of Edward Tither Chancell
		30	Sarah Carter S^{r}vant to m^r Norman in ye west yeard
	May	23	Ann daughter of Tho: Hanson Groc^r south Ile
		24	William Hall Armorer in the est yeard
		29	Joane Whorde in the south Ile
	June	14	Edward sonne of Edward Archer west yerd
	Julij	25	Grace dawghter to william Hall middle Ile
		31	Elizabeth wife of william Hudson Chirurgion south chapel
	Augus	2	John Pennill of Norwich in the County of Norfolke hossier pitt in the midle Ile
		9	Mary Higgins seruant to m^r Holton pitt west yard
		10	Robert sonne of Thomas Tickener grocer pitt south Ile
		19	Mary daughter to William East pitt East yard
		20	Thomas Grigge s^{r}uant to m^r Nuttall sadler pitt Middle Ile
		21	Jane daughter to Richard Kinsman pit west yard
		22	Elizabeth daughter to Henry Jordan West yard
		29	Elizabeth hunt s^{r}uant to m^r Lecock pitt west yard
			Henry Oner s^{r}uant to m^r Tarleton west yard
	Septe^r	1	John dodson girdler pitt in the middle Ile
		9	m^r Richard Midleton free of the Grocers his pitt in the Chancell vault by his wife
		16	Mary daughter of Joseph Cooke Scriu'ner pitt in the North Ile by her grandmoth^r
		19	Marssy daughter of Richard Russell in Library
		20	Robert ffisher Cutler pitt west yard
		23	ffemale Chrisom infant of m^r Claridges pitt in the west yard
	Octob^r	1	James sonne of Robert Hyatt m^{r}ch^{nt}tayler pitt in the south Ile by his wiues brother
		20	Mary daughter of Henry Jordan Cherergion pitt in the west yeard
		29	John sonne of Walter Garford mercer pit in the Middle Ile
	Nou:b^r	4	Thomas Birkhead Armorer pitt in the Middle Ile by his Pew
		17	Hanna Peter pit east yeard
	Janua^{r}y	1	Anna daughter of John Russell Cook pitt in the west yeard
		13	Beniamin sonne of Ralph Stokin m^{r}chant Tayler pit in the west yeard
		15	Abigall wife of Allen Baker Poulterer pitt in the East yeard
		21	Iddyr Payne widdow pit North Ile

Yeare.	Month.	Day.	Names.
1652	January	28	Sarah Craftes Granchild to m^r John Clarke pit in the west yeard
	ffeb:^{r}y	12	Prissilla Wife of Peter Newton Armorer pit in the North Ile
		13	Jane Groue widdow pit in the South Ile
		25	Thomas osborne Briklaier Collidg hill
	March	5	Thomas sonne of francis Walcote Haberdasher pit in the south Ile
		14	Elizabeth daughter of Nathaniell Sidgwicke Grocer pit west yeard
		17	Mrs Dorothy ffairfax wife of Docter william ffairfax pitt in the Chancell by her Ch'lden
1653	March	29*	Susanna Dawghter of Richard Emms wine Coop^r pit in the middle Ile
	Aprill	19	Mary Dawghter of Thomas Adey clothworker pit in the east yeard
		24	Elizabeth Dawghter of Edward Archer pit in west yeard
	May	5	John Blagroue in the south Chapell
		16	George Tarlton inholder west yeard
		18	Thomas ffenn Sexston in the west yeard
		19	Anne Armestrong serv^t to m^r Hucheson west
		28	ffrancis Sonne of Nicholas Bendy linnen draper, pitt in the middle Ile by the Granffather Colinge
		30	George Sonne of John Rumley Armorer South Chap'le
		31	Martha dawghter of Mr William Blackmore pit in the Library by the East dore
	June	8	Jone Stowell widdow pit in ye east yeard
		15	James Sonne of Anthony Start in ye North Ile
	July	6	Mr John ffowler pit in the south Chapel valt
	August	12	Thomas sonne of Tho: Dixon poulterer in ye South Ile
		17	Robert sonne of Robt. Warrin Sadler in ye West yard
	Septemb^r	1	Katherin Daughter of Edmund Williamson: Sepulchers
		2	Connoway: Saull: of Brittain in ye Countie of Summersetsheir Pitt in ye west yard
		7	Mephibosheth: Robbins: Pitt in ye South Chappell
		16	Bridggett: Daughter of Thomas Birkehead Armorer Pitt in the middle Isle by her father
		23	Robert: Whittaker servant to Mr Hutchinson pitt in the west yard p^r ye maide
		29	M^{ris} Husbands the wife of Richard Husbandes pitt in the south Chappill: p^r Bro: Wolliston
	October	5	Richard Warrin Skiner pitt in ye East yard
	Octob:	11	Judith Daughter of Tho: Rott Blacksmyth East yard
		15	John: Elme: Leatherseller Pit in ye sowth Chappill
	Decemb'	5	Stephen sonne of Wm Dorman Cordwinder. Librarie
		14	Abraham sonne of Henry Chittey In Cros Ile vintener
		24	Thomas Nutt souldier in ye new church yard
	January	10	William sonne of William Chamberlyn poulterer Pitt in the south Isle. Aged on yeare & halfe
		13	Thomas sonne of Tho: Smyth Marriner West yard
		26†	Mary: Smyth widdow Pitt in Cross Ile
		28	Ann: Newman: servant to Mr Emmes west yard
		28	Mr Edward Thurman Shoolem^r in the Chansell by thebench

* The Register from March 29. 1653. to January 13, 1653-4, is subscribed Mr William Hammon, churchwarden.

† The Register from January 26, 1653, to November 13, 1654, is subscribed Mr Thomas Wells, churchwarden.

Years.	Month.	Day.	Names.
1653	ffebruary	3	Christian Williams, daughter of Mr Williams Draper in the Chancell vault p^r mother
		7	Sarah Daughter of Thomas: Smyth habberdasher in the East yard p^r mother
	March	6	Eliz: Stert widdow pit in ye North Ile p^r her sonn
1654	April	29°	ffrancis Daughter of Wm Hillersden Clothworker pit in the North Isle
	May	5	Richard sonne of Richard Woodnoth in ye south Ile
		6	Abraham sonne of Henry Chittey Cross Ile
	June	6	Adrian wife of Henry Clarke pitt in ye south Ile
		18	Anthony son of John Stert pit in ye North Ile
	July	22	Walter Gullifer Clothworker pitt in the North Chappill by the steps
	August	3	Allin: Baker poulterer pit in ye East yard
		4	Hanna Daughter of Nicholas Bendie Drap pitt in the middle Ile by Grandfather
		6	Joane Crouch, servant to Mr Botham pit in the East yard
		18	Mary Daughter of Robert Hudson skinner pit in the south Chappill by her Grandfather
		18	Margaret Thompson widdow pit East yard
	Sept.	18	William sonn of ffrancis Marwood pitt in the North Ile
		20	Vrsley daughter of John: ffipps pit Est yard
		21	Elizabeth: Daughter of Wm Williamson
		24	Dorothy: Capell servant to Mr Marwood pitt west yard
	Octob.	2	James Yates servant to Mr Hillersden pitt in the North Ile
		20	William son of Thomas: Pistoll ioyner East yard
		27	George son of Thomas: Smyth: Habberdasher East yard
		31	Mr John: Walltholl: Esqr pit in the Chansell
	Novemb^r	6	Robert son of Robert: Davis pit in the West yard
		9	John son of Henry Stetfeild Dyer pit in the library
		13	Elizabeth: Daughter of Henry: Coop' pit in ye East yard
	Decemb.	25*	Elizabeth Daughter of Thomas: ffrith. pit in ye library
	January	13	Elizabeth Wellham: sert. to Mr Wright pitt west yard
		25	Sarah: Daughter of Henry: Coop' Sexton pitt East yard
	February	5	Ann: Daughter of William Mabbott pitt East yard
		15	James sonne of John: Ratliff: pitt west yard
		25	Michaell Vauhon: Cordwinder pit west yard
	March	1	James sonn of George: Ownly pit west yard
		2	Lawrence Tickner Grocer pitt west yard
		19	John: sonne of Thomas: Jenings pit Est yard
		20	Elizabeth: Daughter of John Smyth pit midd' Isle
		23	Susanna Daughter of Henry Cooper Sexton pit Est yard
		23	Thomasin procter Widdow pitt in ye North Isle
1655	April	7	Elizabeth wife of William East M^rchant tayler midd' Isle
		11	Rebecca and Bethia Daughters of Benjamen Clarridge west yard
		13	Elizabeth Daughter of Walter Garford pitt midd' Isle
		27	Maudlin wife of William Sabie bl'smyth west yard
	May:	12	William: Poole servant to Mr Chevill Draper pit in the north Chappill
		23	A male Infant still borne of John Cotterill East y^rd
	June:	8	John Sonne of Richard Porter. pitt in ye East y^rd
	August	11	Elizabeth daught^r of William Ingall. pitt West y^rd
	Octob^r	14	Daniell sonne of John Athy pitt Midd^e Ile

* The Register from December 25, 1654, to January 28, 1655-6, is subscribed Capt William Easte, churchwarden.

THE REGISTERS OF ST. PETER'S, CORNHILL.

Yeare.	Month.	Day.	Names.
1655	Nouemb^r	3	John sonne of John Fowler pitt in ye South Ile
		20	Doct^r William ffairfax somtime p'son of this p'rish in ye Chansell by his wife
	Decemb^r	3	A femall Child still borne of Henry Stubfeilds Barb^r Chirurgion pitt In Library
		8	Judith daught^r of Capt: George Smith Grocer pitt in the Cross Ile
		15	Widd' Warren pitt in ye Easte yarde
		16	Jesp^r sonne of Richard Kinsman groc^r pitt in the Middle of ye West yarde
			Rachell wife of Henery Purser pitt west y^d
		23	John Kitchin seruant to Mr Woodward west y^d
		24	John sonne of Mr John Langley by his broth^r in the Chansell
	January	13	Elizabeth daught^r of Simon Reade pitt west yrd
		28	Joseph sonne of Tho: Jenings pitt East yard
	February	16*	Tho: Hill Marchantayl^r pitt west yard
			Francis sonne of Richard Blackborne drap^r pitt in ye Midle Ile by her pue
	March	2	Tho: sonn of Tho: Woodward pitt west yard
		21	Widd' Midleton pitt in west yard
1656		25	A femall Infant of Ralph Stokins west yard
	Aprill	18	James sonn of Robt Hyatt pitt south Ile
		16	Mathew sonn of Willm Lawson west yard
	May	2	Agnis daught^r of Mr Chitty pitt in Cross Ile
		20	James sonn of Anthony Sturt Hab^{r}dash^r pitt in ye North Ile by his Mother
		26	Mary daught^r of Francis Leonard Fishmong^r pitt in ye Library
		29	The wife of Mr Dauis pitt in west yard
	June	25	John: Sonne of Thomas: Tickner Pit in South Ile
	July	3	Mary: Webb pit in the East yard
		30	A female infant of Walter Yonge pit East yard
	August	9	Martha daughter of Ralph: Truncket pit Est yard
		27	Elizabeth Daughter of Henry Jorden pit west yard
	Septemb:	6	Andrew Bissell sonne of Mr Bissell pit west yard
		15	Sarah Daughter of John Wright pitt west yard
	Octob'	11	Heugh: son of Nicholas Dun: pit South Ile
		20	ffrancis Lyon Merchant at Mary Hill
	Novemb'	8	Hannah Daughter of Robt Hudson pit in the North: Chappill
		29	Christian wife of Edw: Bucher pit west yard
		11	Allis: Chamberlyn servant to M^{ris} Ber In the South Isle by her sonne
	January	26	Bethia daughter to Benjamen Claridge pitt west yard
		27	George Onely Vintner pit in ye library
	February	5	John: ffowler Vintner pit in ye Chancell
		19	Thomas Godfry of Essex, pit in ye west yard
		26	Judith daughter to Mr Abraham Sion Marchant North Chapell vaut
	March	4	Ralph son of Ralph Stoken pit in ye west yeard
1657		31	Elizabeth daughter of Jonathan Botham march^t pit in ye middle Ile

* The Register from February 16, 1655, to March 31, 1657, is subscribed Mr William Williams, churchwarden.

2 E

Yeare.	Month.	Day.	Names.
1657	May	2*	John Brickland porter at ye wayhouse west yard
		20	William sonn of Barnabie Dench Clothworker pit by the north doore
		25	Jenne Daughter of Ralph Stokin pit west yard
	June	29	Mary Weene servant to Mr Robbinson pit East yard
	July	27	Edward sonn of Edward ffrankton pit West yard
	August	8	Dorcas Daughter of Jarvis Smyth in middle Isle
		23	Susanna Daughter of Sammuell Purchis midle Isle
	Septemb^r	3	William Stuckey pit west yard
		3	M^{ris} Ann: Southwell Widdow pit in ye Chansell
		5	Thomas sonn of John ffrith pit in ye library
		5	Thomas sonn of James Oakes pit in ye North Isle
		22	Thomas Leake servant to Mr Leake pit East yard
	Octob:	5	Susan Cox servant to Mr James pit East yard
		17	Elizabeth Daughter of Mr Anthony Baley North Isle
	Nouember	7	Willyam Dorman Clarke of Andrew Hubbard in Lybrary
	Decemb^r	10	Sarah Spratberry pitt in ye west yard
		17	George sonn of John Rumney pit in ye south Chappell
		22	Ann: Daughter of Mr Lewis Biker in ye Chansell
		23	M^{ris} Katherin: Berkhed wid^o. pit in ye midd: Ile by husband
		24	Mary: Webb: servant to Mr Woodward pit East yard
	January	12	Susan: Mullit: Widdow pit west yard
		27	David sonn: of Benjamen: Clarridg pit west yard
	February	2	George: Pulcher servant to Mr Start pit East yard
		3	Thomas: Mothe Watchmaker pit East yard
		13	M^{ris} Oakes wife of James Oakes. pit North Ile
	March	15	W^m: sonn of W^m: Chamberlyn, Poulterer pit South Ile
		22	Mr Theophilus: Boulton by his children pit North Ile
1658		29	James Marsh pit in the west yard by his wife
	Aprill	2	Widdow Jones ye Blinde woman pit in the west yard
		21	Edward Chevill Brother to Mr John Chevill Draper pit North Ile
		26	Edward: Helme. Grocer in ye North Ile by his wife
	May	5	The wife of John: ffipps pit in ye Est yard
		26	Sarah the wife of Thomas: ffrith pewterer pit in ye library
		2	Sarah Blowe servant to Capt: Ostler pit in ye Est yard
		30	Richard Stokes servant to Tho: Seale pit in ye East yard
		31	John sonn of Thomas Griffin pit in ye East yard
	June	5	Thomas Spensely son to M^{ris} Biker pit in ye library
		29	Widdow Jarvis Aged ffourescore & Eyght pitt East yeard
	Julye	4	A still borne ffemale Child of m^r Clarkes pitt Southe Ile
		16	Mrs Hutchinson the wife of m^r Thomas Hutchinson Marchant taylor pitt in the north Ile
	August	3†	Samuell son of John Sturt Leatherseller Pitt in the north Ile by his Brother
		8	John Hill Brother to m^r Tho: Hill Marchant taylor pit in the north Chapell
	September	3th	Willyam ffipps servant to m^r Smith East yea^d
	October	8	Nickolis Dunn Cooke In the South Ile by his Child
			Widow Spiser pitt In the west yeard
		11	John Coocklow marchantayler pitt south Ile
		20	Male Infante of m^r Ordways in South Ile

* The Register from May 2, 1657, to July 16, 1658, is subscribed Mr Richard Kinsman, churchwarden.

† The Register from August 3, 1658, to June 28, 1659, is subscribed Mr William Crane, churchwarden.

THE REGISTERS OF ST. PETER'S, CORNHILL. 211

Yeare.	Month.	Day.	Names.
1658	October	22	m^r Rodgers Iukhorne maker In west yeard
		25	Thomas Jenings pitt In the West yeard
			A male Infant of m^r Lawsons in East yeard
	Nouember	2	Barbury daughter of Edward Archer west yeard
		3	Ann wyfe of willyam parker north Chapell
		16	A male Infant of m^r James Buck lieth in the ....
		17	dorithye daughter of m^r Leacocke In the South Chapell
	December	2	An ffemale Infante Sarah daughter of m^r frith In the Lybrary by her mother
		13	marye daughter of m^r Leacocke in South Chapell
		17	Sarah daughter of Thomas ffrith In the Lybrary
		27	Nathaniell Sonn of Thomas Woodard In west yeard
			Elizabeth daughter of Thomas Griffin In East yeard
	January	3	Nathaniell Sonn of Beniamin Clarridge west yeard
		13	Marye daughter of Tho. Woodward In west yeard
			Ann the wyfe of Edward pannell In the South Chapell
		25	Widdow Dauis pitt in the west yeard by her—*
	ffeberary	9	Elizabeth Billington widdow pitt west yeard
		10	Elizabeth Hudson widdow pitt South Chapell
		15	M^{ris} Desborough In the South Chapell by Husband
		19	John Rattliffe vintener In the west yearde
	March	2	Martha the wyfe of Clement Bacon Clarke. pitt In the East Churche yeard by her Children
		4	Gulburt Warrin Servant to m^r Willyams Esquyre pitt In the west yeard
		7	Elizabeth Stutfeild daughter to m^r Stutfeild pitt In the lybrary by his Children
		20th	John Sonn of Thomas and Ann Eles north Ile Grandffather
1659	Aprill	20th	the Sister of m^r Nuton pitt in the East yeard
	May	2	Steauen sonn of willyam dorman pitt in lybrary
			John sonn of m^r willyam Bookeye pitt in the Chansell Aged 5 years
		10	ffrances daughter of m^r Leanord, pitt in the Lybrarye
		23	willyam sonn of willyam Chamberlin pitt South Ile
			A ffemale stillborne Infant of Thomas Whitchkocke East yeard
	June	15	Samuell sonn of m^r Samuell Purchas In the midle Ile
		23	buried m^{rs} Mary Chittny At michaell Cor'hill
		28	buried m^{rs} marye Tyther In the Chauncell by her Chilldren
	Julye	14†	m^{rs} Smithe daughter to m^r Edward Helme In the northe Ile by Her father
		24	Margeret daughter to Richard barnestoue East yeard
		25	Susannah daughter to m^r Thomas powell and Susannah his wyfe Armorer In the South Chapell
		26	bridget the wyfe of m^r Tho. Seargaut in South Chapell
	August	5	Barnaby sonn of Barnaby denche In northe Ile by dore
		24	James sonn of Captayne willyam East in midle Ile
		30	Mary daughter of Anthony baylye pitt in the Southe Ile
	September	13	m^{rs} martha Blackmore the wyfe of m^r willyam Blackmore parson of peeters Churche pitt in Chauncell vper End
		16	male Chrisom Infante of w^m Hintons in South Chapell vper End
			male stilborne Infante of m^r presons in the Southe Ile

* Sic.

† The Register from July 14, 1659, to August 25, 1660, is subscribed Mr Willyam Hinton, churchwarden.

Yeare.	Month.	Day.	Names.
1659	September	20	mary Cobbam servant to the strong waterman New Church yeard
		30	Elizabeth Peeter a parish girle In the East yeard
	October	4	Allexsander King wthat* Criplegat pitt in Southe Ile
		7	Samuell sonn of m^r Quelch pitt In midle Ile
		12	Magdalin daughter of m^r Ordway pitt in Southe Ile
		30	Edward Eatenstall servant to m^r Best in west yeard
	Nouember	14	George Barker ffree of the Coopers pitt in west yeard
	December	8	Andrew Langlye brother to m^r John Langlye Esquyre pitt in the Cauncell* by his father
	January	11	A still borne male Infant of m^r Leacockes in South Chapell
		17	Willyam Hudson Sonn of m^r willyam Hudson Skinner pitt In the South Chapell by his ffather
		20	Hellin Coocke widdow pitt in the Lybrary
		23	George Ruse Searvant to m^r Bayes In the Church yeard
	ffeberary ffirst		John Alder sonn of m^r Alder pitt in the Northe Ile
		9	Mr Robert Gardiner pitt In the Chaunsell by his ffather
	Marche	21	John sonn of John wright of the teeth in the Churche yeard
1660	Aprill	24	Sarah daughter of Robert and Elizabeth Hyet Marchantayler pitt In the South Ile
	May the	6	m^r Whittneys sonn Robert in the Churchyard
		10th	willyam sonn of Richard Lucurs in midle Ile
		19th	Raph browne servant to m^r Woodward Cooke pitt In the west yeard he dyed of A ffeauer
		22th	Edward sonn of Edward ffrankett in west yard
		25	Lidyah daughter of Robert ffisher west yeard
	June	30	Hest the wyfe of m^r Thomas Helme in the north Ile
	Julye	30	Charles the sonn m^r Helme In the north Ile
		31	A male Chrisom Infant of m^r Grayes the west yeard
	August	10	Elizabeth daughter to Captine Robert Hudson South Chapell
		15	Thomas Griffen pitt In the west yeard
		17	Mr John Cason Esquire pitt in the Chaunsell
		25	Marye daughter of Mr Richard kinsman in the west yeard
	September	1†	Thomas Woodfort In the west yeard
		7	Charles sonn of Mr Varnham in west yard
	October	7	Widdow Athy In the Midle Ile by the Clarkes pew
		8	Margrett Ward servant to Mr Wilkox East
		23	Willyam Cole Servant to Mr Bookey in north Chapell
		25	John sonn of Mr Lewis Byker in Chaunscell
	Nouember	6	Hannah daughter of Mr Pryce In west yeard
		15	Sr Mathew Brande At west moulbe‡ by Hamton Court
		18	Mr Daniell Battin Marchantayler South Chapell
		30	John Athy searvant to Mr Athy in Northe Ile
	december	4	Gilbert Maddox baker In the South Ile
		22	Ann daughter of Willyam Rande In West yeard
1660	January	6	Blanch the daughter of Tho Hudson South Ile
		15	Mary Gentle daughter to Mr Jhon Gentle in midle Ile
		22	Samuel Atteway servant to Mr Abrathat in lybrary
	ffeberary	23	Willyam sonn of Henry Quelch draper midle Ile
	Marche	8	John sonn of Willyam Rande In west yeard
		12	Elizabeth daughter of John Smith in midle Ile

* Sic.
† The Register from September 1, 1660, to November 24, 1661, is subscribed Mr John Chevall, churchwarden.
‡ West Moulsey.

THE REGISTERS OF ST. PETER'S, CORNHILL. 213

Yeare.	Month.	Day.	Names.
1661	Aprill	26	Anna Infant daughter of John Brottway west ye'd
		8	Elizabeth daughter of w^m waythen In west yeard
		26	Elizabeth daughter of willyam wilson midle Ile
		17	Mary the wyfe m^r Robert waring In midle Ile
	May	10	Captaine Robert Hudson & m^{rs} mary his wyfe In the South Chapell by his ffather
		28	M^r dench the ffather of Barnaby dench north Ile by dore
	June	6	Mrs Elizabeth Welles the wyfe of m^r Thomas Welles Cordweyner In the Lybrary by the dore
		3	mary daughter of Christophor desborough South Chapell
		23	Katheriu daughter of m^r Haudson In the South Ile
		24	John Bradley servant to m^r Okes in the South Ille
		27	Mr Richard Garbrand in the South Chapell by vaught
	July	29	Richard ffitch Sarvant to m^r ffrankton in the west yeard
		10	Sarah Reason Servant to m^r Ordway in East yeard
		18	Thomas sonn of m^r Varnham In the west yeard
	August	9	Susanna Hollser pitt in the west yeard
		20	Willyam Hille pitt In the west yeard Aged 14
		22	m^{rs} Jane Hamon the wyfe of m^r Hamon In north Ile
		23	Robert sonn of m^r waring pitt In the midle Ile
		28	Robert Hyett marchantayler pitt In the South Ile
	September	14	Charles sonn of m^r Varnam In the west yeard
		18	m^r ffrancis walkott pitt in the midle Ile by wyfe
		28	Richard Harwood servant to m^r Bayley pitt South Ile
	October	10	Lankister Haward pitt In the Lybrary by church dore
		21	Richard Clarke Searvant to m^{rs} maddox In Lybrary
	Nouember	13	Nathan Sonn of w^m Iugall pitt in the west yeard
		22	Henry Jordin sonn of m^r Jordin In the west yeard
		24	Mary the daughter of Walter young
	Decem	4*	Mary ye daughter of Jarvis Smith pitt midle Ile
		5	Mrs Letteecia Bikar the wife of Mr Lewes Bikar Cittizen and Grocer of London Pitt in the Chancell
		13	Bridget ye daughter of Mr Harver pitt in ye West yeard
		31	Sarah daughter of Mr Wade pitt in ye library
	January	22	Robert Cowles pitt in the midle Ile
	ffeb.	5	m^{rs} Mary Norman the wife of m^r Thomas Norman Haberdaisher pitt in ye west yeard
		20	Mary Hinton daughter of m^r willyam Hinton In the Southe Chapell vaute
	March	10	william ye sone of Robert Clarke pitt in the west yeard
		13	Elizabeth Thuroughgood kinswoman of m^r Richard Thuroughgood pitt in ye Midle Ile
1662		27	Mary ye daughter of John Harbut pitt in west yeard
	Aprill	3	Robert Whittney Marchant Taylor pitt in the east yeard
		5	Ann Best the wife of Hugh Best vintner pitt in the Library by ye Church dore
		13	Charles Best ye sonne of Hugh Best ventner pitt in the Library by his mother
		20	Thomas ye sonne of Thomas Hichooke west yard
		22	A male abortiue of Mr Samuell Hinton Iron Monger pitt in ye south Chapell by ye vault
		24	Elizabeth ye daughter of Nicholas Bendy Cittizen and Salter of London pitt in ye Midle Ile

* The Register from December 4, 1661, to July 17, 1662, is subscribed Mr Jeames Blatt, churchwarden.

Yeare.	Month.	Day.	Names.
1662	Aprill	26	A still borne male Infant of Edward Gardner pitt in the west yeard
	May	6	Mr Edmund Tooly Innholder pitt in ye Library
		14	Alce the wife of Walter younge pitt east yerd
		15	Ellin the wife of Mihill Middlewhite of Bromely in ye Countey of Kent Tanner pitt in east yeard
		26	John Mills a Lodger at ye spread Eagle a Suffolk man: had his wound in the head by Wrastlinge the parish had a warant from the Cittie Coroner Deacently to inter his body: his pitt is in the west yeard
	June	8	Sara ye daughter of W^m & Sarah Hopkins Barbar Churgion pitt in west yeard
		8	Sarah ye daughter of John wright pitt in the west yeard
	July	17	w^m ye sonne of w^m Wise pitt in ye Midle Ile
		30*	Thomas Powell Armorer pitt in ye south Chapell
	August	4	Thomas ye sonne of Anthony Bayly Clothworker pitt in ye south Ile
		17	Abraham Jacksone haberdasher pit in ye South Chappell
		22	Elizabeth ye daughter of M^r william Sherington Marchant pitt in ye south chaple valt
		26	Joseph Cooke the sonne of John Cooke Scrivener pitt in the north Ile
	Sept.	5	Thomas ye sonne of John sturt Pitt in ye north Ile
		26	Samuell ye sonne of Jeams Blatt pitt in ye south Ile
		28	Henery Paucefoot Marchant taylor pitt in the west yeard
	October	6	Elizabeth ye daughter of Ralph Stocken
	Novem	16	Judah ye daughter of John Scot Clothworker pitt in ye west yeard
		25	Edward Porter a younge Man from the Bull head pitt in ye west yeard
	Decem:	24	Richard Johnsone Butcher pitt in ye south Ile
		28	Joseph ye sonne of Tho: Woodward Cooke pitt in ye west yeard
	January	6	Judah ye wiffe of John Scot Clothworker pitt in ye west yeard
		26	Ann Hope Widdow pitt in the west yeard of the†
	ffeberay	the 1	John Hope Servant to m^r Scott In the yea'd . . . .
		12	Sussanna Hutt daughter of m^r Hutte pitt in west yeard
1662	March	12th	Willyam sonn of Symond Coules Cooke in midle Ile
		25	Samuell Printe Gentleman kinsman to Cowles in midle Ile
1663	Aprill	2	Joseph the Sonn of Henry Quelch pitt in midle Ile
	May	25	Anthony Groue servant to widow Rodgers pitt in ye west yeard
	June	11	Robert midleton servant m^r James, pitt west yeard
		24	Charles sonn of Mr Saunders pitt in north Ile
	Septemb:	20th	John Clark sonn of Henry Clark Barber Surgeon buried in the South Ile by his mother
		23th	Buried in the West church yard a male chrisome Infant of m^r Waithams
	Octob^r	7	Sarah: Daughter of Mr Robert Hudson and Elizabeth his wife in the South Chappill by her ffather and mother
		7	John Cotterum son of Mr Cotteram in the middle Isle by his grandfathers pew

* The Register from July 30, 1662, to May 7, 1664, is subscribed Mr Nicholas Bendie, churchwarden.

† Sic.

Yeare.	Month.	Day.	Names.
1663	Octob{r}	7	The Widdow Hall In the west yard
		21	Edward Pansford brother to M{ris} Woodward pit west yard
		23	Walter sonn of John Smyth Clothworker Pit in the middle Ile
	No:ber	4{th}	William Rucell Sonn of m{r} Rucell Groser Pit in the west yard
		6{th}	James ffuller Servant to m{r} King Pitt in the middle Ile by the Churchwardens pue
		19	Buried a male Infant of m{r} John Prices in the new church yard
	January	3	Anne daughter of M{r} Parkers in the North Chappell by her Mother
		21	Grace Haggitt daughter of William Haggitt pit West yard
	ffebr:	16	Robert Hasler pit in the west yard
	March	8	Alice Clarke the wife of John Clarke Stationer pit in the west yard
		20	Charles Bookey the sonne of William Bookey Merchantaylor in the North Chappell
		24	The widow Perkinson in the west yard
1664	March	28	Sarah daughter of Thomas Woodward Cooke pit in the west yard
		29	James sonne of James Oakes pit in the North Ile
			Richard sonne of m{r} Cliffe Marchant in the South Chappell
	Aprill	26	Richard sonne of Richard Kinsman Grocer pitt in the west yard
		30	Thomas sonne of Robert Rowland Armorer pitt in the South Ile
	May	3	Henry Glue servant to m{r} Tillard Vintner pitt in the west yard
		7	Henry Linney Clothworker pitt in the west yard
		18*	Richard Stringer servant to m{r} Dench pitt att the lower end of the North Ile
		25	Edward sonn of John Alder Draper pitt in the North Ile
		28	Elizabeth daughter of Thomas Wheeler pitt in the west yard
	June	7	Mary Shipham daughter of Edward Shipham pitt in the Cloisters
		10	William Hopkins Barberchirurgeon pitt at the vper end of the South Ile
	July	8	Richard sonne of Thomas Hickocke pitt in the west yard
		29	Honor Prescott pit in the Chancell
	August	4	Hanah daughter of Thomas Lacocke Marchantaylor pit in the South Chappell
		28	John sonne of Tobias Garbraud flishmonger pitt in the South Chappell
		29	Anne daughter of James Turland pitt in the middle Ile
		31	James Evens Cutler pitt in the South Ile
	Septemb:	14	George sonn of John Ordway Vintner pitt in the South Ile
		15	Lewis Biker Grocer pitt in the Chancell
		15	Edward sonn of m{r} Saywell pitt in the west yard
		22	Mary Stringer pitt at the lower end of the middle Ile
	October	2	Vrsula daughter of m{r} Saywell pitt in the west yard
		6	Anne Allgood pitt in the South Chappell
		16	Susan daughter of Thomas Blackeburne pitt in the South Ile

* The Register from May 18, 1664, to March 18, 1664-5, is subscribed M{r} Ralph Trunckett, churchwarden.

Yeare.	Month.	Day.	Names.
1664	October	17	Mr Saxfeild Almes man of the Grocers pitt in the South Ile
		28	Anne daughter of William Holden pitt in the west yard
	Novemb:	26	Jackeson Smith a poore child left vpon Mr Wickses stall the 25° November pitt in the west yard
	December	13	Margarett daughter of Thomas Nicholas Ironmonger pitt in the middle Ile
	January	10	Richard sonne of William Ingall Cooper pitt in the West yard
		12	Thomas Leake Wyer drawer pitt in the East yard
	ffebruary	2	Peter sonne of m^r Cliffe Marchant pitt in the South Chapple
		3	A still borne male infant of William Dutton Tallowchandler in the Cloisters
		5	Daniell Maxfeild Haberdasher pitt in the North Chappell vnder the seacond stone
		8	A still borne male infant of John Rumney in the South Chappell
		9	John Buckley Haberdasher pitt in the west yard
		14	John Symonds Cooke pitt in the South Chappell
		17	A still borne female infant of Henry Smith Clothworker pitt in the East yard
		21	Thomas Hutchinson Merchantaylor pitt in the North Ile
		23	James sonne of James Bucke pitt in the North Ile att the lower end
		28	Anthony sonne of John Sturt Leatherseller pitt in the North Ile
	March	3	Mary daughter of John Vttinge Marchant pitt in the west Church yard
		8	Robert sonne of John Vttinge Marchant pitt in the west Church yard
		13	John Alden a poore man who died sudenly in the streete pitt in the East Church yard
		19	John sonne of John Price Skinner pitt in the middle Ile
1665	Aprill	2	James Marsh a parrish Child pitt in the East Church yard
		3	Joseph sonne of Thomas Eeles Haberdasher pitt in the East Church yard
		12	Mary daughter of Richard Cliffe Marchant pitt in the South Chappell
		16	Jone James the wife of Joseph James pitt in the East Church yard
		23	William sonne of William Waytham Haberdasher pitt in the west yard
	May	2	Judith daughter of Thomas Barber Scrivenor pitt in the East yard
	June	6	Charles sonne of John Symonds Cooke pitt in the South Chappell
	July	12	Temperance the daughter of Walter Younge Sexton in the new Church yard. plague
		17	Martha daughter of Walter Younge Sexton in the new Church yard. plague
		18	Margery Purchase wife of Samuell Purchase Vpholder pitt in the Middle Ile att the lower end
		21	Elizabeth daughter of Walter Younge Sexton in the new Church yard. plague
		22	John sonne of John Rumney Armorer pitt in the East yard. plague

THE REGISTERS OF ST. PETER'S, CORNHILL.

Years.	Month.	Day.	Names.
1665	July	22	Robert Parker servant to John Bayes Clockemaker in the new Church yard. plague
		24	Mary Merrill servant to William Merrill Inholder, in the new Church yard. plague
		29	William Taylor servant to m^r Chitty March^t pitt in the East yard. plague
	August	1	Richard Wattes servant also to the said m^r Chitty, in the East yard. plague
			Mary daughter of Walter Younge Sexton in the new Church yard. plague
		5	Sarah Barber servant to m^r Hall Cheesmonger in the new Church yard. plague
		7	Sarah daughter of m^{rs} Castle in the new Church yard. plague
		11	Edward Shipham Turner pitt in the Cloisters neare the great Church yard doore
		12	Anne daughter of John Rumney Armorer pitt in the East Church yard. plague
		13	Martha daughter of Edward Beeston in the new Church yard. plague
		14	Barbarah daughter of Alice Barker widdow pitt in the West yard. plague
		14	Jane the wife of John Rumney Armorer pitt in the East yard. plague
		17	Robert Hall Marchantaylor pitt in the West Church yard. plague
		18	George sonne of John Rumney Armorer pitt in the East yard. plague
		18	Thomas Catherall a lodger in the Green yard, pitt in the new Church yard. plague
		19	John Browne Haberdasher pitt in the East yard. plague
		19	Adrian Duckett Mercer pitt in the west Church yard
		19	Richard Bolton servant to Henry Chittie Marchant in the East yard. plague
		20	Sarah daughter of Edward Saywell pitt in the west yard. plague
		23	Agnes the wife of John Moone Marchant pitt in the vault in the South Chapple
		24	Ellen Hall widow pitt in the west Church yard
		28	Benjamin sonne of Thomas Lacocke Marchantaylor pitt in the South Chapple
		29	Thomas sonne of Thomas Lacocke Marchantaylor pitt in the South Chapple. plague
		31	Henry Lacocke kinsman to the said Thomas Lacocke pitt in the west yard. plague
		31	John Rumney Armorer pitt in the East yard. plague
	Septemb:	2	Joseph sonne of the worp^l Doctor Thomas Hodges Rector of this p'ish pitt in the Chancell
		5	James Thurland Weaver pitt in the middle Ile
		6	Elizabeth Reynalds servant to to Thomas Lacocke pitt in the west yard. plague
		7	Isaac Willmatt servant to John Bayes Clockemaker pitt in the west yard. plague
		7	Edward Saywell Cheesemounger pitt in the west yard. plague
		8	Margarett daughter of William Ingoll Cooper pitt in the west yard

2 F

Yeare.	Month.	Day.	Names.
1665	Septemb:	9	William sonne of William Ingoll Cooper pitt in the west yard
		9	Elizabeth daughter of Thomas Hickocke Cooke pitt in the west yard
		10	Samuell sonne of Samuell King pitt in the South Chappell
		10	Lidia Dearmore daughter of Mr Dearmore pitt in the west yard
		13	Constance Maddox widow pitt in the South Ile. plague
		13	Judith Matchell servant to m^r Osler pitt in the west yard
		14	A still borne female infant of Thomas Woodward Cooke in the west yard
		18	Elizabeth Watson widow pitt in the west yard. plague
		18	John Welles pitt in the west yard
		18	William Holond servant to John Silke pewterer pitt in the west yard. pl:
		19	. . . . * Welles widow pitt in the west yard
		21	Elizabeth daughter of Thomas Lacocke Marchantaylo^r in the South Chaple. pl:
		21	Sarah How servant to m^{rs} Maddox pitt in the west yard. plague
		22	Samuell sonne of Thomas Lacocke pitt in the South Chappell. plague
		22	Edward sonne of Thomas Hickocke Cooke pitt in the west yard. plague
		22	Benjamin sonne of m^r Lawson pitt in the west yard. plague
		23	Thomas Brearcliffe kinsman to Timothy Rosse pitt in the Cloisters. plague
		23	Elizabeth the wife of John Dearmore pitt in the west yard. plague
		24	Susan walker pitt in the west yard. pl:
		25	John Bayse Clockemaker pitt in the west yard. plague
		25	Margarett wife of Edward Hickocke in the west yard. plague
			John Stewart servant to Timothy Rosse in the west yard. pl:
			Katherine the wife and Katherine the daughter of Euclid Speidell
		25	Susan wife of Thomas Ticknell pitt in the South Ile. pl:
		28	A boy found dead in the Greene yard pitt in the west yard. pl:
			Susan daughter of Susan Howard widow pitt in the Cloisters
		29	Tameris daughter of Jacob Hadley pitt in the west yard. plague
		30	Mary daughter of Samuell King pitt in the South Chapple
	October	2	Joshua sonne of Jacob Hadley pitt in the west yard. pl:
		2	Thomas Brasier a distracted man found dead in the greene yard pitt in the west yard. pl:
		3	Susan Howard widow pitt in the Cloisters
		4	Elizabeth daughter of John Wade pitt in the Cloisters
		4	Elizabeth ffisher widow pitt in the west yard. plague
		6	Abell sonne of Ralph Trunkett Cooke pitt in the Cloisters. pl:
		6	Richard Nettleton Butcher pitt in the South Ile. pl:
		6	Moses Paswater servant to Thomas Ticknell pitt in the west yard. pl:

* Sic.

THE REGISTERS OF ST. PETER'S, CORNHILL.   219

Yeare.	Month.	Day.	Names.
1665	October	8	Thomas Martinscraft servant to Thomas Blackburne Marchantaylor pitt in the East yard
		9	Marcy the wife of William Lawson. pitt in the west yard
		9	Katherine Stawes servant to John Ordway Vintner pitt in the East yard. pl:
		10	John sonne of Samuell Purchase Vpholder pitt at the lower end of the Middle Ile
		12	Hellen Barton pitt in the East yard. pl:
		13	John Paston servant to John Clarke Stationer pitt in the East yard. pl:
		13	Margarett daughter of William Lawson pitt in the west yard. pl:
		13	Jacob Hadley Haberdasher pitt in the west yard. pl:
		13	William Hadley brother to the said Jacob pitt in the west yard. pl:
		13	Mary Hadley his Sister in the west yard. pl:
			John sonne of Thomas Lane in the South Chapple. pl:
		14	Thomas Lacocke Marchantaylor in the South Chapple. pl:
		15	Jacob sonne of Jacob Hadley in the west yard. pl:
		16	Richard sonne of Alexander Venner Marchantaylor pitt in the South Ile
		17	Samuell sonne of William Dormer pitt in the Cloysters
		24	Marsy Lawson the wife of William Lawson pitt in the west yard. pl:
		25	Joane winter widow a pentioner pitt in the East yard
		25	Peter pope servant to Mr Cole Stationer pitt in the west yard. pl:
		27	William Lawson and Richard his sonne pitt in the west yard. pl:
		28	Mary daughter of John Welles pitt in the west yard. pl:
		28	David Blare stranger in the East yard
			Jane daughter of John Welles pitt in the west yard. pl:
	Novemb:	1	William Blakemore ffishmonger pitt in the Cloisters
		1	John sonne of William Dormer pitt in the Cloisters
		2	Edward sonne of Henry Higgins Haberdasher pitt in the Cloisters
		2	Anne Coleman servant to John Atwood pitt in the East yard. pl:
		7	Thomas Blackeborne Marchantaylor pitt in the South Ile. pl:
		9	Mary wife of mr Searle in the west yard. pl:
		9	Ellen wife of Angell de Molder pitt in the East yard. pl:
		13	Thomas sonne of Thomas Searle Butcher. pitt in the Cloisters. pl:
		22	Joseph sonne of William Lawson pitt in the west yard. pl:
			Mary wife of Richard ffuller Draper pitt at the lower end of the middle Ile. pl:
		25	Elizabeth wife of James Blott Draper pitt in the South Ile
	Decemb:	1	Amy Marshall sister in Law to William Merrill pitt by the vestry house
		6	Nathaniell Higgins Haberdasher pitt in the Cloisters
		11	Peter Cole Stac'oner whoe hanged himselfe beinge distracted. pitt in the East yard
		11	William sonne of Jacob Clarke pitt in the middle Ile
		12	John Chapman pitt in the East yard. pl:
		18	Richard sonne of Nicasius Russell pitt in the South Ile

Yeare.	Month.	Day.	Names.
1665	Decemb:	23	Mary wife of John Ireland pitt in the Cloisters. pl:
		31	Edward Smith servant to the said John Ireland pitt in the west yard. pl:
	January	4	John Ireland Clothworker pit in the Cloisters. pl:
	ffebr.	17	William Williams Cordwynder late Dep^{ty} of Bishopsgate ward pitt in the Chancell
1666	Aprill	6	Susan Powell widow pitt in the South Chappell
	May	20	John and Elizabeth Alder Twins children of John Alder Draper pitt in the North Ile
		31	Anne daughter of william Langam pitt in the Middle Ile
	June	30	Elizabeth Robbins widdow pitt in the South Chappell. pl:
	July	4	Twoe still borne Male infants of Richard Armstrong pitt in the East yard
		25	Ralph Allin Vintner pitt in the west yard
	August	23	ffrances Williams the Relict of Mr Deputy Williams in ye Chancell nere her husband
		31	Richard Rowland an Infant Sonn of Robert Rowland in the South Ile
	Septem	21	Richard Mason an Infant Sonn of John Mason ffruiterer in the West Churchyard
	October	28	Jone Wallis Spinster Sister to Mrs Tronckett in Leadenhall street in the middle Ile
	Novem.	20	A Male stil borne Child of Samuel Poole in the West yard
	Decem.	14	A man found dead in Mr Chamberlins Celler in Grace-church street. in the West Churchyard
	Februa'	13	Leonard Pilkington servant to Barnaby Dunch in Leaden-hall street Cheesmonger. in the West Churchyard
		19	Elizabeth Daughter of James Buck in the North Ile

BURYED IN ALL THIS YEARE—16.

1538.

Sundry weddings in the times of King Henry, of King Edward, and Queen Mary.

WEDDINGS.

Yeare.	Month.	Day.	Names.
1538	Janua	19	Wedding of Richard Holland: And Anne Boro. Janua 19
1539	Maye	11	Wedding of William Beed: And Alice Johnson. May 11
		11	Wedding of Richard Miles: And Elizabeth Wallis. 11
	June	1	Wedding of John Bell: And Katherine Taylor. June 1
		8	Wedding of Robert Yans: And Katherine Hudsonne. ye 8
		15	Wedding of William Duns: And Katherine Tailer. ye 15
		22	Wedding of John Horton: And Rose Burname. ye 22th
		22	Wedding of Richard Juet: And Katherine Averell y^o 22
	Julie	20	Wedding of Christopher Drope: And Ellen Jackson. July 10
	August	3	Wedding of John Hunt: And Margaret Edam. Aug. 3
		17	Wedding of Symon Ponder: And Dorety Children. 17
	Septem	1	Wedding of John Richardes: And Margaret Watten
		7	Wedding of William Hyde: And Annes Walker ye 7
	October	23	Wedding of John Horton: And Annes Prestwitch
	Nouem	8	Wedding of Elisaunder Bricket: And Katherine Rice
		16	Wedding of John Leame: And Alice Greenwood
	Janua	18	Wedding of Oliuer Herman: And Alice Little. Jan 18
1540	Aprill	18	Wedding of George Finch: And Elizabeth Seygar
	June	6	Wedding of Maynerd Frere: And Margaret Jousonne
	Julie	4	Wedding of John Bennet: And Margery Dyrtney
	August	18	Wedding of George Okeley: And Christian Turner
	Octobe	31	Wedding of Nicholas Elysander: And Fraunces Gates
	Nouem	7	Wedding of Robert Yerson: And Isabell Tyffenne
	Janua	23	Wedding of John Seyger: And Elizabeth Jousonne
1541	Maye	15	Wedding of John Long: And Elizabeth Robinsonne
	Julie	18	Wedding of Thomas Borrow: And Annes Marshall
1542	August	14	Wedding of Thomas Eswell: And Annes Laxtonne
	Septem	18	Wedding of Edward Cutchborn: And Ellyn Wattson
1543	June	4	Wedding of Thomas Milles: And Grace Edgertonne
		11	Wedding of John Brewer: And Elizabeth Bittinson
		18	Wedding of Syr Christopher Morrys: And Mrs Eliza: Clifford
	Julie	9	Wedding of William Bucher: And Margaret Dyckenson
	August	20	Wedding of William Midleton: And Jane Tomsonne
	Octobe	19	Wedding of Richard Kyrke: And Jane Attrill. Octo: 19
	Janua	14	Wedding of John Tanner and Jane Spead
1544	Aprill	8	Wedding of John Spacy: And Emme Mathew. April 8
		10	Wedding of William Walker: And Joane Warde

THE REGISTERS OF ST. PETERS, CORNHILL.

Years.	Month.	Day.	Names.
1544	Julie	23	Wedding of John Elders : And Julian Nicholsonne the 23
	Septem	11	Wedding of William Gaith : And Elizabeth * . . .
	Octobe	20	Wedding of Thomas Kelby : And Joane Watring
1545	Maye	6	Wedding of Edward Thomson : And Julian Elders
	Septem	21	Wedding of William Ball : And Maude Tod
1546	Maye	3	Wedding of Abell Kitchiu : And Margaret Grey
		17	Wedding of Arcules Burton : And Elizabeth Pennill
		17	Wedding of John Jackson : And Annes Stamper
	August	29	Wedding of William Evanes : And * . . .
	Octobe	10	Wedding of Thomas Dauis : And Joane Hooker
1547	August	10	Wedding of William Blower : And Allis Halesbery
	Septem	29	Wedding of Thomas Horsley : And Elizabeth Olin
	October	1	Wedding of John Kellyn : And Anne Thorpe. October 1
		9	Wedding of Peeter Kingnam : And Annes Feeld the 9
		9	Wedding of Robert Stoney : And Elizabeth Ellingame
	Nouem	26	Wedding of John Euered : And Katherine Candyne
	Janua	16	Wedding of William Reado : And Elizabeth Lightman
1548	Aprill	8	Wedding of Thomas Bagly : And Joane Parson
		16	Wedding of William Trotter : And Joane Westgate
	Maye	15	Wedding of Thomas Brygges And Elizabeth Towley
	Julie	8	Wedding of Thomas Hutherstoll : And Barbara Hill
		12	Wedding of a Baker to Waites mayd : both vnnamed
1549	Maye	12	Wedding of Andrew Scarlet : And Katherine Yong
	June	24	Wedding of John Lockly : And Ellen Oliuer
	Julie	14	Wedding of Jeames * . . . . And Katherine * . . . .
	Octobe	6	Wedding of William Mese : And Julian Gourley
		28	Wedding of John Lambe : And Annes Jesper
	Nouem	24	Wedding of Vincent Heyward : And Annes Weller
	Janua	13	Wedding of Richard Tomsonne : And Katherin Blower
	Februa	16	Wedding of Edward Gunne : And Annes Childe
1550	Aprill	29	Wedding of Richard Kersy : And Elizabeth Brady
	Maye	6	Wedding of Roger Ponder : And Margery Lynniall
	June	1	Wedding of Anthony Fletcher : And Anne Cleffe
		8	Wedding of Robert Stokes : And Emme Egam
	Julie	27	Wedding of Christopher Collyer : And Alice Horsey
	Nouem	19	Wedding of Thomas Gough : And Ellen Trotte
	Decem	9	Wedding of William Spencer : And Margaret Melledy
	Janua	30	Wedding of Robert Packe : And Jeane Hyntonne
	Februa	1	Wedding of Richard Southwood : And Anne Masely
1551	Aprill	26	Wedding of Richard Jonsonne : And Elizabeth Houghton
	Maye	23	Wedding of Edward Mascoll : And Alice Cappes
	June	17	Wedding of John Askew : And Bridget Feeld
		28	Wedding of John Watkines : And Annes Bentry
	Julie	14	Wedding of Nicholas Skern gentleman : And Alice Stoke-maid
		20	Wedding of John Stoupe : And Annes Personne
	August	2	Wedding of John Makebray curat : And Ellen * . . . .
		16	Wedding of John Waller : And Joane Moyed
	October	13	Wedding of Thomas Wood : And Elizabeth Rayndales
	Februa	3	Wedding of Thomas Palfryman : And Annes Keyling
		3	Wedding of Rowland Whallyn : And Margaret Mushrymp
		4	Wedding of Edward Barker : And Margaret Steuenson
1552	Aprill	26	Wedding of Syr Harry Hubblethorn : And Elizabeth Fuller
	Maye	15	Wedding of Fraunces Nottingam : And Mary Halliwell

* Sic.

Yeare.	Month.	Day.	Names.
1552	Maye	18	Wedding of Thomas Ofley : And Katherine Lewis
	Julie	17	Wedding of Roger Holle : And Fraunces Horton
	Octobe	9	Wedding of Edward Walker : And Joane Hunt. October
		16	Wedding of John Blower : And Elizabeth Mathew
	March	2	Wedding of Thomas Spert : And Alice Croeford
1553	Octobe	30	Wedding of William Lawes : And Katherine Towe
	Nouem	13	Wedding of William Hoog : And Cisly Yonge
	Janua	20	Wedding of Richard Brown : And Margaret Woodward
1554	Aprill	3	Wedding of Anthony Fletcher : And Annes Keble
		22	Wedding of John Mannering : And * ... vnwritten
		24	Wedding of Robert Jourdane And Joane Gybbyns widow
	Maye	27	Wedding of Robert Ive : And Jane Harris
	August	12	Wedding of Richard Morris : And Annes Snepe
	Septem	4	Wedding of Robert Janes : And Pepercorne * ...
	Janua	14	Wedding of John Early : And Katherine Lawse
		14	Wedding of Richard Chamber : And Emme Gorley
1555	Aprill	23	Wedding of William Ryshmond : And Mary Smith
	Maye	12	Wedding of Thomas Wallis : And Joane Malyn
	June	9	Wedding of Roger Saunder : And Alice Smith
		30	Wedding of Anthony Adamson : And Margery Neuell
	Julie	21	Wedding of Blase Sawlter : And Collis Smith
	Septem	1	Wedding of Edward Welch : And Margery Wright
	Octobe	8	Wedding of John Mason : And Margery Tymes
		15	Wedding of Robert Feerichard : And Katherin Fresingfeld
		22	Wedding of Richard Steuen : And Ellen Jarman
	Janua	29	Wedding of John Hudsonne : And Elizabeth Grigges
	Februar	4	Wedding of Thomas Hayles : And Anne Porter
1556	Maye	4	Wedding of John Malyn : And Margaret Greane
		5	Wedding of Thomas Phillip : And Joane Barbor
	August	3	Wedding of Peeter Axson : And Luce Brisley
		11	Wedding of John Haule : And Alice Tipper
	Septem	30	Wedding of Steuen Millet : And Elizabeth Morgane
	Nouem	14	Wedding of John Still : And Margaret Kyrke
	Decem	15	Wedding of Edward Kibby : And Ellen Goffe
1557	June	13	Wedding of Richard Rosse : And Annes Hodge
		26	Wedding of John Burchall : And Katherin Doegood
		27	Wedding of Hillary Wapolle : And Joane Garret
	Julie	11	Wedding of William Wright : And Ellen Dauis
	Octobe	31	Wedding of Lawraunce Axson : And Margaret Tipper
	Nouem	21	Wedding of Christopher Rosse : And Elizabeth Goonne
		23	Wedding of William Parker : And Margaret Peell
	Februa	3	Wedding of Thomas Goorley : And Mary Portway
1558	Aprill	15	Wedding of Rowland Oker : & Sibell Averell
		25	Wedding of William Freeman : And Rose Dawes
	Maye	2	Wedding of Hugh Price : And Elizabeth Neuell
		8	Wedding of John Stourtonne : And Alice Daniell
	Julie	3	Wedding of William Butler : And Elizabeth Jonson
		31	Wedding of Edward Hodgesonne : And Margery Whittingam
	Nouem	7	Wedding of John Richardson : And Joan Weller

* Sic.

1558.

𝔚𝔢𝔡𝔡𝔦𝔫𝔤𝔢𝔰 beeginning at the raigne of our most noble Queene & vertuous Elizabeth.

Yeare.	Month.	Day.	Names.
1558	Nouem	20*	Wedding of Dauy Amoe, & Jone More the 20th of Nouember 58
		26	Wedding of Lawraunce Goffe, and Annes Lecroft the 26th
	Januar	18	Wedding of Ralph More, and Elizabeth Adlington: January 18
		19	Wedding of John Haull Trumpetor, and Ellen Foote Widowe
		22	Wedding of John Lamberd, and Ellen Hide Widowe the 22th
1559	Aprill	23	Wedding of John Pearson: and Isabell Bingly, the 23 of Aprill
	May	22	Wedding of John Web: and Alice Haull widow: May the 22th
	August	12	Wedding of Thomas Lawraunce: And Annes Morton the 12th
	Septem	3	Wedding of Harry Elsmar: And Jone Jones. September ye 3
		10	Wedding of Thomas Parkins: And Maudelyn Williames
		17	Wedding of Raynold Dowson: And Katherine Hallywell
	Nouem	5	Wedding of William Bowlyn gentleman: And Lady Annes Hilton
		5	Wedding of one not written downe to one † . . . Walkers widow
		12	Wedding of Thomas Ouerinde, and Jone Yonge: Nouember ye 12
	Decem	10	Wedding of William Hewat: And Mary Rosse. December the 10
	Janua	19	Wedding of Jeames Normanton: And Anne Thackhome the
		23	Wedding of William Chapman: And Jone Mittin, the 23th of
		29	Wedding of John Jonson: And Anne Walker. January the 29th
	Februa	1	Wedding of George Midleton: And Elizabeth Wood. February 1
		23	Wedding of Richard Lambe gentleman: And Elizabeth Lynsey
		25	Wedding of John Dyxon: And Katherine Preestman. Febru: 25
			SUMME—12
1560	May	21	Wedding of Thomas Leame: And Mary Boulton. Maye the 21
		29	Wedding of Thomas Perfew: And Christian Turnar: the 29

* The Register from November 20, 1558, to April 17, 1600, is subscribed Will'm Ashebnold, Robert Warden, Mark Scaliet.
† Sic.

THE REGISTERS OF ST. PETER'S, CORNHILL. 225

Yeare.	Month.	Day.	Names.
1560	June	9	Wedding of Edmond Lymcocke: And Alice Gates: June the 9th
		13	Weding of one Hoult: And a woman vnnamed; incuria scriptoris
	Julie	14	Wedding of Edward Ager; gentleman: And Mabell Wroth. the 14
	Septem	2	Wedding of John Jones: And Alice Richardson. September the 2
		4	Wedding of Foulke Health: And Katherine Sturman, the 4th
		5	Wedding of John Presye: And Annes Gonne. September the 5
	October	1	Wedding of Thomas Malyn Brownbaker: And Annes Goodale widoe
		2	Wedding of Harry Tipper: And Jone Faith. October the second
		13	Wedding of Gyles Farneworth: And Annes Vrselys, the 13th
	Nouem	24	Wedding of Thomas Sherson: And Ellen Vintener. Nouembr 24
	Decem	3	Wedding of John Daulton: And Jone Crofte. December the 3
	Janua	4	Wedding of John Bewter: And Elizabeth Goodale. January 4
		19	Wedding of Edmond waules: And Jone Westwood. the 19th Jan
	Februa	1	Weding of William Yong: And Anne Wheatly. February the first

SUMME—16

1561	May	20	Wedding of John Philpot preacher: And Jone Woolleynes. May 20
	June	9	Wedding of William Keltridge: And Jone Stanly. June the 9
		30	Wedding of Edmond Clarke: And Joane Garner. June the 30
	Septem	21	Wedding of William Ratting: And Elizabeth Allyn. Septemb. 21
	Janua	10	Wedding of Robert Hunter: And Annes Itchin. January the 10
		24	Wedding of William Maunsfeld: And Ellen Browne. the 24th
		26	Wedding of William Leynthall: And Isabell Richman the 26th
		26	Wedding of Nicholas Warren: And Gyllian Waite the 26th

SUMME—8.

1562	Aprill	10	Wedding of Walter Vpton: And Elizabeth Chapman the 10th April
	June	6	Wedding of Thomas Spencer: And Jone Hatly. June the 6th
	Nouem	26	Wedding of John Abowen: And Jane Inggould. Nouember the 26
	Janua	25	Wedding of Richard Moth: And Betteris Backe. January 25th

SUMME—4.

| 1563 | Aprill | 21 | Wedding of Jeames Chapman: And Margery Throwly. April 21 |

2 G

Yeare.	Month.	Day.	Names.
1563	Aprill	25	Wedding of Ralph:* And Margery Packer. Aprill the 25th
	May	2	Wedding of Thomas Bland: And Rose Bellynger, May 2
		25	Wedding of Thomas Beane: And Jone Typper. May the 25th
	June	20	Wedding of Edmond Burchall: And Grace Stanes, June 20
		24	Wedding of John Bourn: And Anne Craddocke. June ye 24
		24	Wedding of George Cuttler: And Christian Egles June ye 24
	August	29	Wedding of Richard Tucking: And Elizabeth Marshall. August 29
	Janua	9	Wedding of John Mascall: And Ellen Green: January ye 9th

SUMME—9.

1564		15	Wedding of Edward Hayes: And Wynnefrid Hodge Aprill 9th
	Aprill	9	Wedding of John Tompson: And Katherine Dowson. Aprill 9
		9	Wedding of Robert Fishman: And Katherine Richardson. the 15
		16	Wedding of Mathew Willson: And Jane Bell. Aprill the 16
		30	Wedding of William Ayre: And Ellen Stallocke the 30th
	Maye	29	Wedding of William Reeue: And Katherine Barbor. May 29
	June	7	Wedding of William Patynson: And Jone Lewtely: June 7
		21	Wedding of John Dorden: And Annes Estweeke: June the 21
		26	Wedding of Robert Chaderton: And Margaret Luntly. ye 26
	October	16	Wedding of Libeus Barnard: And Fraunces Jackson Widow
	Nouem	4	Wedding of Robert Richardson: And Margaret Haruey. the 4
		11	Wedding of Richard Jorden: And Alise Isharwood. Nouember 11
		19	Wedding of Robert Hinton: And Mabell Hause. the 19th
		19	Wedding of William Grymes: And Eddy Cobby: the 19th
	Februar	11	Wedding of Rice Jones: And Elizabeth Preest. Feb: 11

SUMME—15.

1565	May	5	Wedding of William Bennet: And Jone Richardson. May 5
		6	Wedding of Harry Howe: And Jone Vinclent. May the 6th
		17	Wedding of Michaell Weston: and Elizabeth Halle. May 17th
	Julie	5	Wedding of John Bryan: And Anne Phillippes, Julye the 5th
	Septem	10	Wedding of Fraunces Talemacke: And Anne Lambe Septem. 10'
	October	14	Wedding of John Knight: And Jone Grane: October the 14
		22	Wedding of Robert Tailor: And Rose Stonehouse. October 22

* Sic.

THE REGISTERS OF ST. PETER'S, CORNHILL. 227

Yeare.	Month.	Day.	Names.
1565	Nouem	24	Wedding of Barnard Jeronimus: And Alice Ashton. Nouem 24
	Februa	23	Wedding of Roger Walker: And Alice Dunne Widdowe. Februa 23

SUMME—9.

1566	June	24	Wedding of John Knipe: And Isabell Wylkenson. June the 24
	Nouem	11	Wedding of Thomas Catmore: And Margaret Dunmoe. Nouem. 11
		30	Wedding of John Daye: And Betteris Welche. November. 30
	Janua	19	Wedding of Thomas Allen: And Aune Thawthes. January 19
		26	Wedding of Edward Dauis: And Margaret Okely. Janua. 26

SUMME—5.

1567	Maye	11	Wedding of Walter Haukyns: And Elizabeth Bowland. May 11
	June	1	Wedding of Thomas Bowland: And Alice Synkefeeld: June 1
		8	Wedding of Robert Steale: And Alice Hope, June the 8th
		22	Wedding of Fraunces Futerell: And Ellen Lister: June 22th
	Septem	12	Wedding of William Bleach: And Margarett Willson wyddowe
	Decem	22	Wedding of Fraunces White: And Katherine Skynner, Decem 22
	Janua	18	Wedding of John Allen: And Mary Cottrell: January the 18th
	Februa	1	Wedding of John Boomer: And Jone Westgate: February 1
		10	Wedding of Thomas Tailor; And Jane Euerton: February 10
		22	Wedding of Harry Cowdall: And Susan Bayles, the 22th
		29	Wedding of William Bromly: And Margery Cannon
1568	Aprill	25	Wedding of William Hickmore: And Elizabeth Fuller. Aprill 25
	Maye	9	Wedding of Thomas Wheeler: And Sara Hodge. May the 9th
	June	27	Wedding of John Stanly: And Jone Hynde. June 27th
	August	22	Wedding of John Fraunces: And Clare Ansell. August 22th
	Octobe	25	Wedding of Jeames Hill: And Jone Haukyns. October 25th
	Decem	28	Wedding of William Fell: And Margaret Haull. Decem. 23
	Februa	14	Wedding of Jeames Hoult: And Rose Crofte. February 14

SUMME—7.

1569	Julie	18	Wedding of Symon Williames: And Elizabeth Mathew
	Octobe	15	Wedding of Christopher Halle: And Alice Goslyng. Octo. 15
		23	Wedding of Roger Knight: And Elizabeth Green. Octob. 23

Yeare.	Month.	Day.	Names.
1569	Nouem	12	Wedding of Nicholas Morgraue: And Annes Clarke. Nouem 12
	Janua	17	Wedding of John Dregot: And Elizabeth Satchfield. Janu. 17
		23	Wedding of Godfry Willson: And Elizabeth Mease. Janua. 23
		28	Wedding of Richard Estricke: and Jone Daldron. January 28

SUMME—7.

1570	March	29	Wedding of Thomas Langly: And Jone Bowser. March 29
	Aprill	3	Wedding of Robert Haull: And Alice King. Aprill the 3
		9	Wedding of William Tompson: And Jone Owin. Aprill the 9th
	Maye	20	Wedding of John Pearson: And Margaret Coole. May the 20
	June	17	Wedding of Edward Baker: And Alice Chapman. June 17
		18	Wedding of Thomas Colley: And Elizabeth Jonson. June 18
	Julie	2	Wedding of Nicholas Sparnne: And Jone Harrison. Julie 2
	Septem	10	Wedding of Thomas Euington: And Jone Speed. Septemb. 10
	Janua	21	Wedding of Richard Dylling: And Elizabeth Bennet. Jan. 21
		29	Wedding of Willlam Hodson: And Alice Harris. Janua. 29

SUMME—10.

1571	Aprill	28	Wedding of John Housman; And Elizabeth Chapman
	Maye	1	Wedding of Thomas Watton; And Ellen Byrd. May the 1
		7	Wedding of Thomas Phillippes: And Grace Westraw, the 7th
		13	Wedding of John Hewgle: And Mary Malison: May the 13
		14	Wedding of John Dockerell: And Rachell White: May the 14
	Julye	8	Wedding of George Gunby: And Elizabeth Thwaites
		8	Wedding of Rowland Gybson: And Jane Jones. July the 8th
		15	Wedding of Robert Barton: And Elizabeth Laye: July the 15
	August	27	Wedding of William Yong: And Amy Webbe: August the 27
	Septem	2	Wedding of Hugh Thomas: And Margaret Paynter
		3	Wedding of Thomas Borrowe: And Marian Pelsant
	October	7	Wedding of Anthony Neue: And Annes Webster: the 17th October
	Nouem	4	Wedding of Thomas Bynnell: And Jone Plummer: Nouem: 4
	Decem	16	Wedding of George Monday: And Annes Averell daug: of John Averell
	Janua	20	Wedding of Thomas Jordane: And Mary Ball. January 20th
	Februa	4	Wedding of John Rayment: And Jone Corse: Februa 4th

SUMME—16.

THE REGISTERS OF ST. PETER'S, CORNHILL. 229

Yeare.	Month.	Day.	Names.
1572	Aprill	20	Wedding of Dauy Croft: And Jane Richmond. April 20th
	June	22	Wedding of Richard Foord: And Elizabeth Armeson. June 22
		30	Wedding of Bryan Luntlowe: And Jane Turner. June 30
		30	Wedding of William Thomas: And Elizabeth Luntlowe
		30	Wedding of William Blacke: And Anne Luntlow. June the 30
	Julye	3	Wedding of Thomas Lambe: And Annes Durbridge. July the 3
	Nouem	25	Wedding of William Aushum: And Anne Wroth. Nouemb. 25
	Janua	17	Wedding of Robert Jarratt: And Sara Wheeler. Janua. 17
		27	Wedding of Thomas Symkins: And Martha Smith. Jan: 27

SUMME—9.

1573	Aprill	12	Wedding of William Gurnett: And Catherine Course. Aprill
		26	Wedding of Richard Armestrong; And Ellen Tedder. Aprill 26
	Maye	24	Wedding of Thomas Abington: And Annes Robinson. May 24
		31	Wedding of John Malyn: And Margery Atkinson. May 31
	Julye	19	Wedding of Humphrey Hurlestone: And Anne Macham
	August	30	Wedding of John Locke: And Elizabeth Watton: August 30
	Septem	6	Wedding of William Reeue: And Margaret Satchfield. Sept. 6
	Octobe	25	Wedding of Lawraunce Ward: And Margaret Townly. Octo. 25
	Nouem	15	Wedding of Thrustone Bufford: And Annes Dyckson. Nou. 15
	Decem	18	Wedding of Thomas Bushell: And Anne Winspere: Decem: 18
	Janua	15	Wedding of Thomas Luntlowe: And Mary Brooke. Janua. 15
	Februa	6	Wedding of John Tailor: And Margaret Richardson: Febru: 6
		14	Wedding of William Foden; And Annes Lambe. February 14
		20	Wedding of Thomas Weanewright: And Cisly Russell the 20
		21	Wedding of Edward Edwardes: And Mary Bradwynne

SUMME—15.

1574	Maye	23	Wedding of Nicholas Burdicke: And Elizabeth Coorse.
	Julye	22	Wedding of Thomas Adlyn: And Elizabeth Jenninges: July
	Septem	20	Wedding of Richard Cooke: And Ellen Mascall Widowe
		28	Wedding of Thomas Whitchead: And Elizabeth Dowsonne
	Octobe	17	Wedding of Mr Richard Kingsmeale: And Mrs Elizabeth Stonehouse. by licence
	Nouem	4	Wedding of Christopher Miller: And Annes Smith Widow
		28	Wedding of John Cadye: And Elizabeth Porder Widowe
	Janua	22	Wedding of Roger Doodly: And Elizabeth Hill. January 22

Yeare.	Month.	Day.	Names.
1574	Februa	6	Wedding of Morris Dauy: And Joane Willis: February 6th
		8	Wedding of John Malyn Armorer: And Ellen Steeuens Feb. 8
		14	Wedding of William Mager: And Anne Brizly. February 14

SUMME—11.

1575	Maye	15	Wedding of John Heppy: And Elizabeth Daldron, May: 15
		28	Wedding of John Beckinsall: And Bridget Wethwat. May 28
	June	27	Wedding of Robert Domkin: And Elizabeth Walker: June 27
	Julye	10	Wedding of John Lambe: And Elizabeth Thurske. July 10
	Janua	16	Wedding of Mr Hugh Gold: And Anne Cockes: Janua 16
	Februa	19	Wedding of Thomas Gee Haberdasher: And Mary Hassall
	March	4	Wedding of Robert Lecroft: And Margery Howse. March 4
		5	Wedding of Thomas Edmondes: And Elizabeth Byllem

SUMME—8.

1576	Aprill	26	Wedding of Robert Warden: And Annes Jans Widow. Aprill
	May	5	Wedding of Jeames Jordaine: And Alice Stokes Widowe
		7	Wedding of John Hasellwood: And Barbara Warren
		14	Wedding of William Blackwell: And Jone Gold. May 14
		15	Wedding of William Brickhead: And Affera Lawrence
		16	Wedding of Fraunces Lynsell: And Mary Filall. May 16
	August	19	Wedding of Dauy Powell: And Mary Dowson. August 19
	Septem	23	Wedding of Perciuall Burton: And Jone Hobson. Septe. 23
		24	Wedding of William Richemond: And Elizabeth Hill
	Octobe	21	Wedding of Harry Whitmore: And Rose Ford. October 21
	Nouem	5	Wedding of William Hattrell: And Annes Berry. Noue. 5
	Janua	27	Wedding of Thomas Nutbrowne: And Jone Wright. Janu. 27

SUMME—12.

1577	Aprill	11	Wedding of John Rayment the yonger: And Annes Newman
		14	Wedding of William Wilde Draper: And Annes Cartwright
		28	Wedding of Barnaby Watson: And Jone Clarke: Aprill 28
	Maye	12	Wedding of William Drew Merchant Tailor: And Blanch Write
	Julye	8	Wedding of Jeames Bennet Clothworker: And Sibell Lewes
		13	Wedding of Robert Hall, Mercer: And Margery Lecroft widow
	Septem	4	Wedding of Lawrance Shingleton: And Margery Jackson
	Nouem	14	Wedding of George Gunby Scriuenor. And Elizabeth Rauens
	Decem	8	Wedding of John Beckinsall: And Elizabeth Richardsonne
		15	Wedding of Hugh Brinckhurst: And Anne Holland. Decem. 15

THE REGISTERS OF ST. PETER'S, CORNHILL. 231

Yeare.	Month.	Day.	Names.
1577	Janua	23	Wedding of William Stiche: And Bennet Bennet Widow
		26	Wedding of John Gregory Baker: And Susan Lister. Janu: 26
	Februa	2	Wedding of William Strange: And Jane Price: February 2
		2	Wedding of Melchisedecke Bennet: And Alice King: Febru: 2
		3	Wedding of William Burton Stacioner: And Anne Lyard. 3
		9	Wedding of Jeames Isacke: And Jone Powell. February 9th

SUMME—16.

1578	Aprill	1	Wedding of Thomas Dowll: And Anne Cooper Widowe
	Maye	19	Wedding of John Mewiter Duchman: And Alice Spence
		25	Wedding of Libeus Swanne: And Katherine King. May 25
	August	17	Wedding of George Hubbersted Taylor: And Katherine Chapman
	Septem	14	Wedding of John Stonehouse Letherseller, And Marye Satchfeld daughter of Gilbert Satchfeld White Baker
	October	26	Sonday: Wedding of John Howell Habberdasher: And sonne of John Howell: to Margaret Hamore, daughter of Roger Hamore
	Nouem Fœlix atq: faustum coniugium δόξα Θέο	2	Sonday: Wedding of William Averell Merchant Tailor, of this parish: And Gyllian Goodale daugh: of Robert Goodale Brown baker of this p'ish
		23	Sonday: Wedding of William Harding sonne of Robert Harding: And Elizabeth Hill the daughter of John Hill. Nouember the 23th
	Februar	8	Sonday Wedding of Barthollomew Norton sonue of John Norton Joyner: And Alice Atkinson daughter of Richard Atkinson. Februa. 8
		15	Sonday: Wedding of John Dixon Armorer, sonne of Thomas Dixon: And Margaret Steeuens daughter of Richard Steeuens Armorer
		15	Sonday: Wedding of Richard Sanborn Barbor soune of Dauy Sanborn: And Isabell Walker; daughter of Edward Walker Carpenter
		22	Sonday: Wedding of John Sutton Carpenter sonne of John Sutton cuntryman: And Margaret Fynar daughter of Roger Fynar

SUMME—12.

1579	Aprill	6	Thursday: Wedding of Mr Fraunces Lamberd Grocer: a widower: And Mrs Anne Bricket of this Parish allso widowe Aprill 6
	Maye	4	Monday: Wedding of Peeter Shanke bacheler: sonne of John Shanke And Grace Euannes a mayden, the daughter of Richard Euannes
		6	Wedensday. Wedding of Richard Sturman bacheler, sonne of John Sturman Poulter: And Elizabeth Daniell daughter of William Daniell
		10	Sonday: Wedding of Robert Barnard Poulter, a widower: And Katherine Jans, a maiden, daughter of Robert Janes of London Poulter

Yeare.	Month.	Day.	Names.
1579	Maye	17	Sonday: Wedding of Thomas Jurden widower and white baker: And Sara Paucke daughter of Robert Paincke of London Shoemaker
	Julie	13	Monday Wedding of John Strawghon bacheler, sonne of Nicholas Straughon: And Annes Bridgeman daughter of Thomas Bridge
	Septem	24	Thursdaye Wedding of Mr John Palphreman of the Queenes chappell And Mrs Mary Pearpount of London Widow. Septem 24
	Nouem	23	Monday: Wedding of Thomas Kynnaston Widower & Merchant tailor And Alice Slade Widow, the late wife of Harry Slade
	Decem	13	Sonday Wedding of Robert Hubbersted Merchant Tailor sonne of Thomas Hubbersted: And Alice Chapman daughter of Wm Chapman poulter
		14	Monday: Wedding of Godfrey Lambright widower a stranger born: And Susan Crompe wch went for a maid, daughter of Thomas Crompe fletcher
	Februa	23	Satterday: Wedding of Thomas Rone bacheler; sonne of Robert Rone yeoman: And Jone Pigot a maiden daughter of John Pigot yeoman

SUMME—11.

1580	Maye	1	Sonday: Wedding of Robert Barnes Barber sonne of Thomas Barnes Ripper: And Elizabeth Peele a maid daugh: of Thomas Peele Woollwinder
		11	Wedensday: Wedding of Richard Popeiay bacheler sonne of John Popeiay Yeoman: And Annes Carter a maiden daug: of John Carter Yeoman
	June	26	Sonday: Wedding of Arthure Tonney, sonne of Edward Tonney of Norfolke: And Anne Yong daughter of Robert Yong of Bristow
	August	28	Sonday: Wedding of Richard Cherriot Merchant Tailor sonne of John Cherriot of Hamshire: And Katherine Lynneall, daug: of phillip Lynneall
	Nouem	10	Thursday: Wedding of Siluester Vittle of Gyllingam sonne of Richard Vittle yeoman: And Fraunces Barker, daugh: of Edward Barker
	Decem	12	Monday: Wedding of Robert Burnell Baker: And Isabell Meares daughter of Miles Meares. Marryed by Licence from Mr Gardners

SUMME—6.

1581	Julie	2	Sonday Wedding of Randoll Squire Dyer: sonne of John Squier of Darbyshire: And Mary Elkin daughter of John Elkyn of North Hamptonsher
	Octob.	9	Monday. Wedding of John Tallis an old man of 70 Yeares: And Jone Hunt daughter of Robert Hunt being a maiden of 23 Yeares
	Febru	5	Monday: Wedding of Robert Cooper of London Armorer sonne of Wm Cooper: And Elizabeth Newman the daughter of John Newman

SUMME—3.

1582	Maye	6	Sonday: Wedding of Robert Knowles Letherseller sonne of Ciprian Knowles: And Jone Hamman daughter of William Hammon

THE REGISTERS OF ST. PETER'S, CORNHILL. 233

Yeare.	Month.	Day.	Names.
1582	Maye	13	Sonday: Wedding of Geffrey Gylberd waterbear,* sonne of Harry Gylberd: And Ellen Dyckens daughter of Wm Dyckens
	August	13	Monday: Wedding of Mr Thomas Townson widower of London Carpenter: And Margaret Chatterton widow, by a Licence
	Decem.	7	Monday: Wedding of Harry Thompson bacheler of London Grocer And Margery Cotten late wife of George Cotten Grocer

SUMME—4.

1583	Aprill	3	Wedensday: Wedding of Richard Bottombe of London Clothworker sonne of Nicholas Bottombe: And Maudelyn Crooke dau: of Robert Crooke
		25	Thursday: Wedding of William Smith sonne of John Smith Husbandman: And Bridget Newman daughter of Thomas Newman
	Maye	12	Sonday: Wedding of Christopher Jackson sonne of Christopher Jackson: And Ellen Carpenter the daughter of John Carpenter
		13	Monday: Wedding of John Domelaw sonne of Richard Domelaw purveyor of the Queenes wynes, & Christian Chatterton dau: of Robert
	June	2	Sonday: Wedding of George Hollman sonne of Richard Holman, grocer And Jane Yong daughter of Mr Gregory Yong Grocer, a maiden
		9	Sonday: Wedding of John Randoll sexton of this Church, sonne of Leonard Randoll: And Jane Kennan daughter of William Kennan
		24	Monday: Wedding of Frances Donwell bacheler of London Armorer, And Annes Conningam the daughter of John Conningam
	Julye	15	Monday Wedding of Michaell Genyens of London Grocer, sonne of Thomas Genyens Girdler: And Elizabeth Goffe dau: of Lawrance
	August	5	Monday. Wedding of John Cooke cuntryman sonne of William Cooke And Elizabeth Jonson daughter of Rouland Jonson. August 5th
		11	Sonday Wedding of Richard Stokes of London Vpholster sonne of Robert Stokes: And Elizabeth Jones widow late wif of John Jones
		19	Monday: Wedding of Mr William Hammersly fishmonger a widower And Anne Lamberd widow, late wif of Fraunces Lamberd Grocer. p' Li.
	Septem	1	Sonday. Wedding of Thomas Sympson Grocer a bacheler, sonne of Thomas Sympson: And Elizabeth Downes daugh: of John Downes p' Li.
	Octobe	20	Sonday. Wedding of Richard Copland Merchant Tailor sonne of Wm Copland: And Ellen Rosier the daughter of Roger Rosier: by licence
	Nouem	3	Sonday: Wedding of John Barnerd Merchant Tailor, sonne of Thomas Barnerd: And Betteris King daughter of John King
		4	Monday: Wedding of Rafe Seare of London Tallow Chan-

* Sic.

Yeare.	Month.	Day.	Names.
			dler, sonne of Ralph Seare: And Sibbell Johnson, daughter of Harry Jonson
1583	Nouem	4	Monday. Wedding of John Faccam sonne of Nicholas Faccam: And Margaret Friar a maiden, the daughter of Anthony Friar
		11	Monday: Wedding of Thomas Allen Carpenter: sonne of Thomas Allen: And Alice Bennet late wif of Melchisedech Bennet
	Februa'	18	Tuesday: Wedding of Thomas Jones widower of London Goldsmith And Christian Lawraunce mayden daugh' of Richard Lawrance

Summe—18.

1584	June	1	Monday: Wedding of John Grean Cooke sonne of John Grean: And Alice Porter, daughter of William Porter Merchanttailor
	Septe'	27	Monday. Wedding of Edward Merefeeld Inhoulder in Southwarke And Annes Foden widow, late wif of Wm Foden Inhoulder
	Decem	8	Tuesday Wedding of Mr Thomas Lewner of Greyes Inne: And Mrs Mary Wroth, mayden: daughter of Mr Wm Wroth Mercer
	Februa	14	Sonday. Wedding of william Wigges bacheler, of London Turner And Katherine Clarke the daughter of Thomas Clarke
1585	May	16	Sonday. Wedding of Thomas Foord, bacheler sonne of Thomas Foord Yeoman: And Margaret Miner maiden: daugh: of Richard Miner
	Julie	9	Friday: Wedding of Mr Lawrance Goffe of London Draper: And Mrs Margaret Millian, late wif of Mr John Millian bricke maker p'. Li.
	Septem	1	Weddensday: Wedding of John Budley Skynner: sonne of John Budlye: And Elizabeth Goffe, daughter of Mr Lawrence Goffe
		19	Sonday: Wedding of William Lecroft bacheler of London Armorer sonne of Thomas Lecroft: And Mathie Garnet, daugh: of Wm Garnet
	Octobe	3	Sonday. Wedding of Richard Wetheryd of London Baker, sonne of Christopher Wetheryd: And Margaret Hilles dau. of Thomas Hilles
	Decem	9	Thursday: Wedding of William Cacy Broker, a widower, And Katherine Green mayden daugh: of John Green of Suffolk. p' licence
	Janua	6	Thursday: Wedding of Ralphe Riche, sonne of Thomas Riche: And Jane Allen a maiden daughter of William Allen. p' Licence
		17	Monday: Wedding of William Price Widower of London shoemaker: And Mary Gough the daughter of Mr John Gough minister
	Februa	6	Sonday. Wedding of Richard Burton bacheler. of London shoemaker sonne of John Burton: And Elizabeth Dickenson dau: of Benedict Dick:
		7	Monday. Wedding of Mr George Greame widower, and Browne baker: And Thomazen Railton Widow, late wif of Rowland Railton

Summe—10.

THE REGISTERS OF ST. PETER'S, CORNHILL.   235

Yeare.	Month.	Day.	Names.
1586	Aprill	7	Thursday: Wedding of Mr Robert Smith widower, of London Merchant Tailor: And Katherine Webbe a Widdow. by Licence
	Maye	1	Sonday: Wedding of John Edgent of west Tilbery, Widower: And Emme Lambe maiden daughter of John Lambe Habberdasher
		19	Thursday. Wedding of Mr Gamaliell Woodford of Loudon Grocer And Mrs Joyce Fowke daug: of Mr Roger Fowke Esquire, by Licence
		29	Satterday: Wedding of George Pounter of Essex yeoman. Widower And Alice Manning late wif of Thomas Manning yeoman
	June	5	Sonday: Wedding of Thomas Lewes bacheler of London Armorer sonne of William Lewis: And Charitie Burchenshaw dau: of Randoll B:
		12	Sonday: Wedding of Mr William Moorton sonne of Mr Wm Moorton Esquire: And Mrs Jane Kyrton maiden daugh. of Mr Thomas Kirton Esq
		13	Monday: Wedding of m^r Humphrey Smith Esquire a widdower: And Mrs Hursula Luson a maiden, daughter of Mr Walter Luson Esquire, p' Lic.
	Julye	3	Sonday: Weding of Benedict Nix bacheler, and Blacke smith: And Elizabeth Cathron a mayden; the daughter of Leonard Cathron
		7	Thursday: Wedding of Mr Thomas Colfe widower of London Grocer And Anne Grey Widdow late wif of John Grey Marchant venture^r
	Octobe	3	Monday: Wedding of Mr Richard Hewson widower of London Skynner And Mrs Heath Widow, late wif of Mr Foulke Heath Skynner
		16	Sonday: Wedding of Nicholas Tailor bacheler & Tallow Chaundler sonne of Thomas Tailor: And Joice Stodderd late wif of Phillip Stodderd
		30	Sonday: Wedding of Andrew Treuis plummer sonne of William Treuis yeoman: And Dennys Satchfeld daugh: of Gilbert Satchfeld baker
	Janua	22	Sonday: Wedding of Ralph Bird bacheler of London Baker sonne of Harry Byrd yeoman: And Elizabeth Agborow daug: of Edward Agboroe
		29	Sonday: Wedding of Jeames Shene bacheler Waterman sonne of Wm Shene: And Elizabeth Brigges maiden daughter of Harry Brigges
		30	Monday: Wedding of John Maddocke Widdower of London, Saulter (and) Anne Dowell widdowe late Wif of Thomas Dowell Seriant
	Februa	20	Monday: Wedding of Richard Waight of London poulter, sonne of Harry Waight: And Elizabeth Pegrom daughter of John Pegrom
		26	Sonday: Wedding of Hugh Parry of London Skynner, sonne of Harry Parry yeoman: And Elizabeth Roodes widowe, daugh: of Wm Tibbold
		26	Sonday: Wedding of Jeames Thorogood of London, poulter sonne of Jeames Thorogood: And Effam Adlington daugh: of John Adlington

SUMME—18.

Yeare.	Month.	Day.	Names.
1587	Maye	23	Tuesday: Wedding of M{r} Edward Caunt of London Fishmonger: And Katherine Ellis a maiden the daughter of Thomas Ellis Yeoman
	June	15	Thursday: Wedding of Peeter Hodgsonne of London Vphoulster, sonne of William Hodgsonne: And Anne Cooper daug: of John Cooper Yeoman
		18	Sonday: Wedding of John Pedder of London Merchant Tailor, sonne of Thomas Pedder: And Jane Bowefeeld daugh: of Richard Bowfeld
		19	Monday: Wedding of Lawrence Euannes of London Cutler, sonne of Richard Euannes: And Lettis Warren late wif of John Warren Armorer
	Julye	4	Tuesday: Wedding of M{r} John Thorogood sonne of M{r} William Thorogood And M{rs} Jane Wroth daughter of M{r} William Wroth of London, Merce{r}
	Septem	3	Sonday: Wedding of Robert Thrower of London Vintner, sonne of John Thrower: And Susan Ruggell daughter of Phillip Ruggell yeoman
		11	Monday: Wedding of William Reynoldes of London Barbor Surgion sonne of John Reynoldes: And Anne Chamberlane Widow of John Cham: p' Lic.
		25	Monday: Wedding of Oliuer Jones of London Dyer sonne of Roger Jones gentleman: And Elizabeth Atkinsonne a Maiden: the 25{th}
		25	Monday: Wedding of Thomas Maull of London Merchant Tailor, sonne of Richard Maull: And Anne Atkinsonne a maiden allso
	Octobe	1	Sonday: Wedding of Thomas Blayne of London Merchant Tailor, sonne of John Blayne: And Alice Killingworth daugh: of Richard Killingworth
	Nouem	26	Sonday: Wedding of George Marrowll of London Carpenter sonne of Arthure Marroull: And Alice Walker daugh: of Edward Walker Carpente{r}
	Janua	14	Sonday Wedding of Robert Lockson gardiner, sonne of Richard Lockson of London Brewer: And Alice Stullingflet daug: of Robert Stullingflet
	Februa	18	Sonday Wedding of Roger Whetstone bacheler, sonne of John Whetstone Yeoman: And Elizabeth Johnson mayden daugh: of Thomas Jonsonne

SUMME—13.

1588	Aprill	2	Tuesday: Wedding of William Shores widower of London Bowyer And Alice Stanly a Widdow: they weare married by Licence
		14	Sonday: Wedding of Richard Tite Bacheler; sonne of Mathy Tite And Grace Whartonne maiden daugh: of Robert Wharton Yeoman
		21	Sonday: Wedding of Frances Smith of London Skynner, sonne of George Smith: And Jane Taylor daughter of Thomas Tailo{r}
		23	Tuesday: Wedding of Roger Filewood bacheler; sonne of Roger Filewood Yeoman: And Dorothy Abdell the daughter of John Abdell yeoman
	Maye	1	Wednesday: Wedding of Richard Clarke of London Shoomaker sonne of Robert Clarke: And Katheryne Benton daughter of Thomas Benton

| Yeare. | Month. | Day. | Names. |

1588 Julye 15 Monday Wedding of Thomas Williamson sonne of Robert Williamson Yeoman: And Bridget Swanne daughter of Libbeus Swan yeoman

Augus 31 Satterday: Wedding of Thomas Ager widower of London Clothworker: And Agnes Stanton widowe of St Alphedg parish, by licence

Octobe 7 Monday: Wedding of John Pickering sonne of Richard Pickering, And Elizabeth Welch daughter of William Welch, Yeoman

10 Thursday: Wedding of John Nowell of London Marchant Tailor sonne of Jeames Nowell: And Margaret Tompson widow of Paule Thom.

13 Sonday: Wedding of Richard Crue of London Vpholder sonne of John Crue: And Katherine Yong daughte^r of Anthony Yong vpholste^r

Nouem 3 Sonday: Wedding of Jeames Orred Laborer, sonne of George Orred yeoman of the cuntry: And Alice Mason daughter of William Mason

10 Sonday: Wedding of Christopher Hubberthorn sonne of Lancelott Hubberthorn: And Dorothy Withnall daughter of John Withnall

18 Monday: Wedding of Hillary Turner of London Draper sonne of Peeter Turner Grocer: And Jone Lamberd dau: of Frances Lamberd

Februa 2 Sonday: Wedding of William Corden of London Tallow Chandler sonne of Vryon Corden: And Jone Malyn daugh: of John Malyn Armore^r

SUMME—14.

1589 May 19 Monday: Wedding of Mr John Jackman of London Clothworker: sonne of Arthure Jackman Clotbier: And Mary Cockes dau: of Mr Edward Cockes

Julye 6 Sonday: Wedding of Jeames Titly Carpenter: sonne of Robert Titly of Lancashire. And Margaret Brooke daugh: of Harry Brooke yeoman

Septem 8 Monday: Wedding of William Hudson of London Skynner, sonne of Robert Hudsonne: And Jane Garnet daugh: of Richard Garnet

Nouem 30 Sonday: Wedding of Christopher Felkyn of London Draper sonne of Hugh Felken yeoman: And Fraunces Lidley dau: of Edmond Lidlye

Februa 23 Monday: Wedding of Beniamin Farre, sonne of Walter Farre of great Bursted in Essex: And Elizabeth Jonson daugh: of Robert Jonsonne

SUMME—5.

1590 Aprill 26 Sonday: Wedding of Anthony Williamson of London Merchant Taylor: And Elizabeth Sturman late wif of Richard Sturman, Fishmon:

Julie 5 Sonday Wedding of Fraunces Atton of London Barbor, sonne of Edward Atton: And Susan Couchman daug: of Lawrence Couch.

15 Wedensday: Wedding of Walter Cooke Merchant Tailor sonne of John Cooke: And Margaret Paine daugh: of John Payne. yeoman

Yeare.	Month.	Day.	Names.
1590	Julie	20	Monday: Wedding of John Browne of London Draper sonne of Anthony Browne Carpenter, And Elizabeth Cauket dau: of John Cauket
	Octobe	19	Monday: Wedding of John Groome sonne of John Groome of the cuntry Yeoman: and Jone Barber daughter of Leonard Barber yoman
		19	Monday: Wedding of Robert Eueling sonne of George Eueling: And Susan Yong daughter of Mr Gregory Yong of Loudon Grocer
	Janua	10	Sonday: Wedding of John Pyewell of London Saulter sonne of Thomas Pyewell: and Jone Harris daugh: of George Harris
		24	Wedding of John Lawe of London Merchant Tailor sonne of Richard Lawe: And Elizabeth Willson daugh: of John Willsonne

SUMME—8.

1591	Aprill	17	Satterday: Wedding of Hugh Powell sonne of Thomas Powell And — Hutchenson the daughter of Christopher Hutchenson
		18	Sonday: Wedding of John Hayese widower & bedell of Bride well And Betteris Farrer a mayden daughter of Ambrose Farror Yeoman
		22	Thursday: Wedding of William Woodford of London Shoomaker. And Anne Hazeler the daughter of Ralphe Hazeler Yeoman
		28	Wedeusday: Wedding of Mr Randoll Damport Esquire Justice of peace And Mrs Katherine Gardner late Wif of Mr Thomas Gardner
	Maye	9	Sonday: Wedding of Richard Christian Cittizen and Shoemaker of London: And Jone Smith the danghter of John Smith yeoma'
		16	Sonday: Wedding of John Gothridge Widower of Loudon Gardner and Amye Maddox a mayden daughter of John Maddox yeoman
	Janua	6	Thursday: Wedding of Mr Jerome Horsey Esquire sonne of Mr William Horsey: And Elizabeth Hamden dau: of Mr Griphin Hamden
		16	Sonday: Wedding of Fraunces Brown bacheler sonne of Thomas Brown and Mary Burket the daughter of Harry Burket yeoman

SUMME—8.

1592	March	28	Tuesday Wedding of Henry Richardson of St Edmondes in Lumbard street: And Katherine Caunt of this parish, widow of Mr Edward Ca'nt
	Maye	7	Sonday: Wedding of William Haslet of Clements Danes Taylor, And Margaret Boote of this Parish. Mr Gregory younges Mayd Grocer
	June	18	Sonday: Wedding of Mr George Hussey gentleman sonne of Mr John Hussey of Sussex: And Mrs Jane Dearing daug: of Mr John Dearing gentle:
	August	27	Sonday: Wedding of William Jones of St Michaelles vpon Cornhill And Anne Claye wyddow of Clarkenwell, by licence Curie Cantuar:
	Octobe	12	Tuesday Wedding of Richard Foxe of Allhallowes in

Yeare.	Month.	Day.	Names.
			Thames street Grocer And Anne Villiares of this Parish daughter to Mr Hammerslye
1592	Nouem	10	Sondaye: Wedding of Anthony Moxon of St Gyles at Creeplegate And Annes Allenson of this Parish Mr Hassalde his maide
	Decem	3	Sonday: Wedding of Thomas Lawson of St Katherines: And Margery Allen of this Parish, Mr Thomas Walthall his maid
	Janua	3	Wedensday: Wedding of Ralphe Bridges of St Clements Danes Tailor: And Susan Linsey of this Parish daugh: to Mrs Linsey widow
	Februa	18	Sonday: Wedding of John Lewis of Greenwich: And Mabell Stewart, a mayden seruant with Mr Mascoll at the Bull in this parish
1593	Maye	27	Sunday Wedding of John Morris one Fishstreet hill: And Katherine Yong a maiden daughter of Mr Gregory Yong Grocer, by Licence
	Octobe	28	Sonday: Wedding of John Griphin of St Olaues in Southwarke And Martha Porter of this parish daughter of Widow Porter
		30	Tuesday: Wedding of Henry Needam of this Parish Barber Chirurgian: And Anne Kyrke widow in the Minorites, by Licence of Can:
	Janua	1	Sonday Wedding of William Chapman of St Mathies in Friday street Salter: And Elizabeth Sallisbury of this parish widow, by Licence
	Februa	10	Sonday: Wedding of John Steuanes seruant to Richard waight poulter of this Parish: And Jone Huckle his seruant allso; by Licence from Mr Red

SUMME—5.

1594	May	13	Monday. Wedding of Symon Yeomanes of the Parish of St Buttolphes at Belingsgat: And Mary Barkly of this Parish Mr Atkinsones maid, p' Lic.
		13	Monday: Wedding of Thomas Bury of Andrewes Vndershaft Tailor: And Elizabeth Careles widow of this Parish from out the Waygh house by banes
	Septem	9	Monday: Wedding of Robert Oldam seruingman of this Parish: And Aime Bolton of this Parish widdow late Wif of Mr Bolton smith
		17	Tuesday: Wedding of William Hartridge of this parish Draper: And Margaret Cooke of St Margets in new fish street widow, by Licence Ca.
	Octobe	6	Sonday: Wedding of Richard Vinar of St Lawrannce in the Jury: And Anne Hassald daugh: of Richard Hassald deceased of Kithermister by Licence Ca:
		13	Sonday: Wedding of Nicholas Keford of this Parish seruant to Mr Rayment And Grace Stewart of this Parish, seruant with Thomas Kynnaston. Ba.
	Februa	17	Monday: Wedding of John Ward of Allhallowes Staynings Merchant tailor And Hester Reene of this Parish Widowe: Married by bannes thrise asked

SUMME—7.

1595	Maye	18	Sonday: Wedding of Thomas Parlor of St Faithes vnder Paules Tailor And ffraunces Clifford of this Parish a maiden. Married by bannes

Yeare.	Month.	Day.	Names.
1595	Octobe	9	Thursday: Wedding of Mr Thomas Bellingeam of the County of Sussex And Mrs Margaret Gardner of the same County, Widdow. by Licence
	Nouem	16	Sunday: Wedding of Barnard Baker of Allhalowes in Hoony Lane, of London Haberdasher: And Elizabeth Faukes of this Parish maiden. by Licence Lo:
	Janua	6	Tuesday: Wedding of Symon Fryar of this Parish, of London Skynner: And Margaret Yong of this Parish a maiden seruant wth Mr Thomas Cockaines. by ba.

Summe—4.

1596	Maye	31	Monday: Wedding of Walter Roades of St Michaelles vpon Cornhill Carpenter: And Tabitha Heling of this Parish a maiden: by bannes
	Julye	4	Sonday: Wedding of Arthure Bray of Allhallowes Staynings Cooper, And Katherine Price of this Parish a maiden seruant wth Mr Atkinson. by ban.
		12	Monday: Wedding of John Packer of Dionice Backe Churche. Taylor: And Elizabeth Haull of this Parish seruant with Mr Dorington, by ban.
		18	Sonday: Wedding of Edward Sharpe of Brainford: And Christian Luddington of this Parish a maiden seruant with Mr Loxon. by bannes
	Nouem	14	Sonday: Wedding of Roger Ferris of Stepny Parish Sailer: And Katherine Hammond widowe. By Licence vacante sede Episcopali*
	Decem	13	Sonday: Wedding of Thomas Bourn of Basingstowe, And Agnes Powell daughter of Dauy Powell Merchant Tailor, by licence, sede vacante
	Februa	6	Sonday: Wedding of Christopher Frisingfeeld of St Michaelles vpon Cornhill. And Jone Sale of this Parish: by Licence Can.
		6	Sonday: Wedding of William Bromley of this Parish Poulter sonne of Wm Broomly. And Mathew Barnet maiden of this p'ish

Summe—8.

1597	Maye	8	Sonday: Wedding of Richard Vnderwood of St Edmundes in Lumbard street Haberdasher: And Jane Elsworth of this parish: by banes
	Octobe	3	Monday: Wedding of John Walker of St Bennets by Paules wharfe And Marget Hatford of this Parish Mr Sallomons mayd. B.
	Janua	29	Sonday: Wedding of Edward Smith of St Dunstanes the west And Annes Montegue maiden of this Parish, by bannes

Summe—3.

| 1598 | June | 25 | Sonday: Wedding of Thomas Ward of St Clements Danes: And Ellen Rose of this Parish Mt Hugh Goldes maid: by bannes |
| | Octobe | 24 | Tuesday: Wedding of Thomas Robinson of St Michaelles vpon Cornhill Brasier. And Alice Cokain of this Parish: by bannes |

---

* Richard Fletcher, D.D., Bishop of London, died June 15, 1596. His successor, Richard Bancroft, D.D., was not elected till April 21, 1597.

THE REGISTERS OF ST. PETER'S, CORNHILL.

Yeare.	Month.	Day.	Names.
1598	Octobre	31	Tuesday: Wedding of William Hooker of St Peeters in Cheap Goldsmith: And Elizabeth Cumber widow of this Parish: by ba'nes
	Decem	3	Sonday: Wedding of Thomas Cole of St Mary White Chappell, and Alice Warman of this Parish a maiden: by Bannes
	Februa	18	Sonday: Wedding of Thomas Bull of this Parish Poulter, And Susan Mayes maiden of this Parish allso, by Bannes

SUMME—5.

1599	Aprill	22	Monday: Wedding of Samuell Wiborn of Rochester in Kent: And Mary Read of this Parish Mr Doctor Ashboldes maid by Bannes
		22	Monday: Wedding of George White of St Giles without Creeplegate, yeoman: And Mary Vane of this Parish: by licence of Canturbury
	Julie	22	Sunday: Wedding of Jeames Barnard of White Chappell silke Weuer: And Mary Colly of this parishe a maiden, by bannes
	August	21	Tuesday Wedding of John Mercer of this Parish a Habberdasher and Isan Cockes of this Parish allso a maiden: by Bannes asked
	Septem	2	Sunday, Wedding of Hugh Morris of St Johnes vpon Walbrooke, bedell of the skynners, and Joane Carre of this Parish, by bannes
		30	Sunday Wedding of Thomas Embres of St Gregories Parish Cooke; and Jane Watson of this Parish. Mr Askewes maid: by licence Cantua.
	October	21	Sunday: Wedding of George Standly of St Faithes Parish Merchant Tailor; And Joane Segar of this parish maiden; by bannes
	February	2	Wedding of Edward Tewed, and Jane Wood, by certificat of bannes thrise asked both in Waltamstow and in Chinkford
		3	Sunday, Wedding of Edward Blane of Bennets at Paules Wharfe Tailor: And Marget Richardson of this Parish. ba'nes
	March	24	Monday: Wedding of Peeter Haule of Allhallowes in Lumberd street: And Margaret Thompson of this Parish by Licence
1600	Aprill	17	Thursday: Wedding of Edward Childe of Cole Church: And Barbara Carill widow of this Parish by Licence Cantua.
	Maie	18*	Sunday Wedding of William Stanly Tailor of St Bartholomews by the 'xchange: And Jane Rose of this Parish by bannes
	June	16	Monday Wedding of Edward Leatherborow of Couentry: And Cibell Pywell of this Parish; by bannes thrise asked
	Julie	13	Sunday. Wedding of William Huddleston of St Bottolph at Bishoppes gate: And Margery Edmonson of this p'ish. bannes

---

* The Register from May 18. 1600, to November 26, 1602, is subscribed Will'm Asheboold, Mark Scaliet, John Caunt, churchwardens.

Yeare.	Month.	Day.	Names.
1600	Julie	13	Sunday: Wedding of William Poole of Great Allhallowes And Margaret Haukenson of this Parish by bannes
		22	Tuesday Wedding of Christopher Bond of St Martens Outwitch: And Anne Roberts of this Parish by bannes
	August	3	Sunday: Wedding of Edward Bromly; of St Katherines And Maudlyn Booky of this Parish by bannes thrise
		18	Sunday: Wedding of Richard Loe of St Sepulchers wthout Newgate: And Katherine Elsworth of this parish. bannes
	October	15	Weddensday: Wedding of Thomas Sleepe of St Sepulche^{r}s And Jone Lee shee said widdow of the same parish by licence Lond.
	Februa	1	Sunday. Wedding of William Jones of this Parish poulter and Katherine Androwes of this Parish allso. by Bannes
		2	Monday Wedding of Jeames Pickborn of this parish poulter And Alice Bromely of this Parish allso by bannes asked
		16	Monday Wedding of Robert Shittleworth of the parish of St Sepulchers, and Barbara Childe of this parish by bannes
1601	Maye	5	Tuesday Wedding of Jeames Buttler of St Mary Sommersett, And Jane Randoll widdow of this parish by bannes asked
	Septem Ba.	27	Sunday: Wedding of Robert Ovenden sailer of this parish; and Katheren Steueus a maiden daughter of Mrs Malin by bans
	October Li.	15	Sunday Wedding of Dauid Kendricke of St Margetts Pattens Chaundler, And Elizabeth Overton of this parish. L. D. L.
	Nouem Ba:	1	Sunday Wedding of Fraunces Wilkinson of St Michaells by Wood street, and Margaret Stables of this Parish m^r Meares maid
	Febru: Li.	11	Thursday Wedding of Nathaniell Chambers of Windsor in ye Countie of Barkshire And Elizabeth Heelin of this parish. Lic. Can.
	Ba.	14	Sunday Wedding of Henry Lunne of St Giles without Creplegate, and Jane White of this parish a maiden. by Bannes
1602	June	15	Tuesday John Brattle of St Olaues in Southwarke, Grocer, And Sarra Wilde of this Parish Mrs Turkes daughter. L. B. C.
		17	Thursday Richard Babington of Brunningam in Warwickeshire Habberdasher. And Sara Tench of this parish. by Li. D. L.
	August	22	Sunday Edmund Potter of Mary White Chappell: And Anne Stroker of this parish Mrs Satchfeld her nurse, by bannes
	Septem	5	Sunday Richard Talbut of St Buttolphes wthout Bishopesgate: And Elizabeth Lane of this parish. by banns
		12	Sunday Edward Chambers of this parishe Carpenter: And Susan Willmor of this parish allso Mr Recordes maid. by bannes

Yeare.	Month.	Day.	Names.
1602	Nouem	26	Friday. Thomas Dauis of St Peeters ad vincula in her Maties Tower of London: And Martha Griffith of this parish. bans
	Decem	12*	Sunday: Robert Bolton of this Parish merchant Tailor: And Allice Brown of this Parish allso Mr Cason his maid. by banes
	Janua	18	Tuesday: James Jordane of this Parish porter of the Waigh house And Margery Green of this Parish allso widow, by Licence. facul.
		23	Sunday Roger Bradshaw of Benets ffinks Carpenter And Jone Morris of this Parish widow. By bannes thrise asked
1603	Aprill	14	Thursday: Alexander Fowle of Maidstone in Kent gentleman, And Dorothie Wastnes of the said Town gentlewoman. Licence Cant.
	June	15	Wedensday: William Barley of this parish booke seller: And Mary Harper of this parish allso, by bannes thrise asked
		26	Sunday: George Hales of St Andrewes in Holborn Tailor And Elizabeth Graues of this parish Mrs Waightes kinswoman. bans
	Julie	17	Sunday Jhon Martir of Mary White Chappell: And Katherin Bromely of this parish Mr Pywalles maid, by bannes asked
	Nouem	30	Wedensday: Jhon Deushire of Allhallowes Lumberdstreet, And Jone Trowell of this parish Mr Sacheuerelles seruant, by Licence Cant'
	Decem	4	Sunday: Richard Fowler of Barking parish, And Saraa Blase of this parish Mrs Turkes maid, by bannes three tymes asked
		5	Monday: Robert Chambers of allhallowes Stayninges Bricklayer, And Jone Bradshaw of this parish Widow, by bannes
		18	Sunday: Jhon Woodhaull of Bennets Finke Chirurgian, And Saraa Stauclic of this parish widow, by Licence of Cantur:
	Janua	9	Thursday: Richard Dowson Butcher, of St Olaues Southward † And Alice Kidwell Mrs Turkes maid seruant, by Bannes asked
	Februa	12	Sunday Richard Money of St Bennet Paules Wharf: And Dorothie Medowes of this Parish Mr Seamans seruant, by bannes
		20	Shroue Monday. Thomas Powle of St Gregories by Paules' groce^r And Susan Bridges of this parish Widow Mrs Linsaies daughter. banus
	March	1	Thursday. Thomas Stone of St Sauiours in Southwarke gent. And Alice Pickborn of this parish widow Mrs Bromlyes dau. Licen. D. L.
1604	Aprill	10	Tuesdaie in Easter Weeke John Lee Embroder of St Benets by paules wharf: And Isabell Arland of this Parish Mr Marris maid. ban'es
	May	13	Sunday Thomas Holmes of this Parish Barbor: And

---

* The Register from December 12, 1602, to November 22, 1604, is subscribed Will'm Asheboold, parson, Henry Holdsworth, Thomas Salomon.
† Sic.

Years.	Month.	Day.	Names.
			Thomasyn Jones of this Parish also, Mr Jones his daughter a Barber. banes
1604	May	21	Monday. Mr John Hay of Hestermounsex in Sussex Esquire And Mrs Anne Colstone of Laiton in Essex widow, by Licence, faculties
	June	17	Sunday: Rice Dauis of St Olaues Southwarke felt maker: And Anne King of this Parish Mr Deputie Walthalles maid. by banes
		24	Sunday: Cutbert Crackplace of this Parish: And Anne Whitcraft of this parish allso, Mrs Maxfeldes syster, by Bannes
	Julie	15	Sunday: John Yates of Stevenes in Colman street Coachman & Margaret Haule of this parish Mrs Chamberlaines sister: by bannes
	Septem	9	Sunday: Thomas Price of St Giles without Creple gate bucher And Christian Wiat of this Parish allso Mrs Walkers tapster banes
	October	1	Monday: John Bland of Buttolphes Bishopsgate Carpenter And Kathern Parker of this Parish Mrs Parkers syster, by bannes
		11	Thursday: William Hardcastle of this Parish Tailor. And Margaret Leget Widow out of Pallmers house Bodymaker; by banes
	Nouem	22	Thursday Mr George Caluert of St Martines in the feeld gentleman. And Mrs Anne Mynne of Bexler in Hertford shire, by Licence Cant.
	Decem	12*	Wedding of Owen ffisher of this Parish Cobler; And Margery Nicholson widow of this Parish allso. vppon Weddensday: by Banes
	Janua	4	Monday: John Barker of Saint Michaelles Cornhill Haberdasher And Elizabeth Paue sister to Mrs Stocke of this Parish. banes
	Febru:	12	Shroue tuesday: Richard Holmes of Steuens in Colman street: And Mary Marrow of this Parish daughter of George Marow Carpenter. ba.
1605	Aprill	21	Sunday. Valentine Luddington of this Parish Armorer: And Anne Richardson of this Parish: Mr Kinges maide, by Banes
	June	2	John Smalmaune of St John Walbrooke & Elizabeth Tenche sister to M^ris Parker of this p'ish were married by Bannes
	August	11	Thomas Key of St Martins Outwich & Sarah Garnet sister to Peter Whitman of this p'ish, were married by Bannes
	October	28	John ffoster of Sepulchers p'ish & Dorithie Kennistone of this p'ish were married by License from Caunterburic dated Octob^r 4 1605
	Nou'eb^r	21	William Tompsonne of St Katherins Creechurch & Jone Powell of this p'ish were married by Bannes
	Decemb^r	5	ffrancis Scotte gent. in ye countie of Yorke & Sarah Kettle of this p'ish were married by Licence from Caunto^r dat. dece'b^r 5. 1605
	Febru:	2	Steeuen Sutton of Sepulchers p'ish and Allice Peirce of this p'ish were married by Bannes

* The Register from December 12, 1604, to October 16, 1606, is subscribed Will'm Asheboold, parson, the marke of T I Thomas Jones.

THE REGISTERS OF ST. PETER'S, CORNHILL. 245

Yeare.	Month.	Day.	Names.
1606	May	11	John Luddingtonne of Ethelborow p'ish : and Elzabeth Andrews of this p'ish were married by bannes
		18	Robert Smith of St Dunstouns in ye east: and Jone Waters of this p'ish were married by bannes
	June	2	John Graunger Yeoman de le Scullerie Regis' Matie and Judeth Seely of St Marie Actes ; were maried by license fro' Can^t: da^t 24
		3	William Carpenter of this p'ish, & An Tiror of St Giles w^{t}hout Creplegate, were married by License from Cant^r da^t ye 26 of this mo'*
		12	Rowland Reynoldes of this p'ish: & Elzabeth Newman of St Michells Cornhill, were married by L: from Can^t: da^t ye 3 of June 1606
		26	William Johnsonne of St Albones in Woodstreet & Elzabeth Powell of this p'ish were married by Bannes
		26	Andrew Blake of Strowde in Kent, & An Kempston of St Nicholas in Roffen in Kent, Were married by Lic : from Caunte^r dat the 24 of June 1606
	July	27	Thomas Layland and Vrsley Hall both of this p'ishe Were maried by Bannes
		27	Jeames Davis of St Buttols Algate and Thomasine Vincent of this p'ishe were maried by Bannes
	October	3	Edward Whitacres and Jalian* Scotte of St Peter Paules Wharfe were maried by License from Caunte'
		16	Thomas Wither of St Michaell Cornhill and Jone Boyse of St Alhollowes the Great by License from Caunte^r
	Nouember	2†	Thomas Lyford of Wingfeild in Barksheere and Ann Burcher of the same place by License from Caunte'
	December	14	John Carter of Sherborne in the countie of Oxford Yeomane and Alice Hayes of Reddinge in the countie of Barksheere Widd' late wife to Ralph Hayes, whilst hee liued of the same sheere Clothier were maried by Lic : from Ca'
	Februarie	12	Nathaniell Burte of Sepulchers p'ishe Sadler and An Solloman daughter of Thomas Sollomon of this p'ishe were maried by License from the Bish: of London
		13	Beniaminne Buckhurst of stratford Bow in Com' Midd: Barge man and Alice Gladdinge Widd': late wif' to Rowland Gladdinge were maried by License Caun'
[1607]	Julie	2	Peter Eastbrooke of Hornchurch in Essex and Elzabeth Blatch of Walthan in the same count^e were maried by L : fr : Can'
	August	9	William Caunte of St Giles in the fields and Katherin Webb of this p'ishe were maried by Bannes
	Nouember	1	Robert Moorcock of St Steuens p'ishe and Margret Collier of this p'ishe were maried by Bannes
	Januarie	3	William Hopkins of Margret New fish streete and Alice Heskey of this p'ishe were maried by License from Ca'
		17	Edward Bywater of Criplegate brasier and Alice Maxfeild of this p'ishe were maried by License from Caunte'
1608	Aprill	24	Jeames Rodwell of the p'ishe of St Michaell Bassashawe

* Sic.
† The Register from November 2, 1606, to November 1, 1608, is subscribed Will'm Asheboold, parson, Chrystopher Vertew, ffrances Colynge.

Yeare.	Month.	Day.	Names.
			and Katherine Dennes of this p'ishe were maried by Banes
1608	May	29	William Clason of St Giles att Criplegate and Elzabeth Sutton of this p'ishe were maried by Bannes
	July	10	William Woodward of the p'ishe of St Martines in the Vintric and Elzabeth Cumber of this p'ishe were ma': by Ba:
	October	3	Bigley Carlton of this p'ishe and Rebecca Edge of St Gabriell ffanchurch,* were maried by License from London
		9	John Whiniard and Ann Pippine both of this p'ishe were maried by Bannes
		23	Giles Seager of St Hellens p'ishe Shoomaker and Ann Brian of this p'ishe were maried by Bannes
	Nouember	1	Jasper Ouldham of St Peters the Poore and Elzabeth Chapman of this p'ishe were maried by License from Ca'
		6†	Ephram Palmur and Ann Counstable both of this p'ishe were maried by Bannes
	December	4	Roger Powell of St Katherin Creechurch and Joane Peerson of this p'ishe were maried by Bannes
	Januarie	9	John Reynolds of this p'ishe and Susanne Iken of Mildreds in the poultrie were maried by License from Caunte'
1609	May	14	Robert Whitlocke of this p'ishe and Elizabeth Leuton of this p'ishe were Maried by Bainnes
		21	Richard Hubberstee, of this p'ishe and Marie Kinge of this p'ishe were Maried by Bainnes
	August	31	Robert Parker of the Countie of Sandw^{ch} in conterb'* haberdashor, and Abigall Bassocke in the Countie of Sandw^{ch} and came from the spread eagle in gratious st'
	Nouember	20	Zephaine Saires of St Edmunds in Lumberstreete, haberd^r and Nazareth Vaghan Widd': of this p'ishe L: Caun'
		30	Mathew Hollingburie Armorer and Katherine Holdsworth both of this p'ishe from hir fathers, License from Mr K. office
	December	3	Jeames Miller, of St Katherine Creechurch and Bridgett Mathew of this p'ishe were maried by Bainnes
		14	Owin Bett of the p'ishe of St Michaell in Woodstreete scriuener, and Allice Wheeler the daughter of John Wheeler, in the p'ishe of St Dunstons in the East Goldsmith, were maried by Licence from Caunterburie
	Januarie	23	William Pease, of this p'ishe and Marie Sollomon of this p'ishe from hir fathers by bainnes
	Februarie	4	John Lewis of St Brides p'ishe, and Allice Angie, of this p'ishe were maried by bainues
		21	Steephen Turrett of Chelmeford in Essex Brewer and Elizabeth Eue, daughter of Weston Eue, of Leaden Rooden, in Essex, were maried by License from Caunt'
1610	Aprill	9	Christopher Shartine, of St Olaues in Southwarke and Doritie Wolford of this p'ishe were maried by ba'
		29	Henry Dawes, of this p'ishe and Agnis Barritt of St Marie White Chapple were maried by bainnes

* Sic.
† The Register from November 6, 1608, to January 13, 1610, is subscribed Will'm Asheboold, parson, John Parker, Stephen Robberts.

THE REGISTERS OF ST. PETER'S, CORNHILL.

Yeare.	Month.	Day.	Names.
1610	May	15	William ffelo, of the p'ishe of St Leonard Eastcheepe and Marie Rose, of this p'ishe were Maried by bainnes
	July	8	Sunday Edmund Hassell of St Dennis Backchurch and Elizabeth Dickson of this parish by baines
	Janua^{r}y	13	Sunday Married Richard Robinson of St Laurence Pountney and Lewis Weauer of this p'ish by baynes
	ffebrua'y	3*	Sondaie Henric Planncon Dutchman of this parish and Margrett Weaver of this parish by Lycence Cant'
1611	Aprill	7	Sondaie William Blowfeild and Elizabeth Holland both of this p'ish. banes
		14	Sondaie Thomas Tayler of Bocking in Essex, & Judith Tann' of this p'ish by banes
		20	Sondaie Henrie Mascall of Hatfeild in Hartfordsheere & Katherine Steeuens of This parish by bannes
		22	Tewsday John Sutton & Elizabeth Peas both of this p'ish by bannes
	June	6	Thursday John ffell of Alhollous Barking & Margerie Badcock of y^s p'ish lycenc'
	October	8	Tewsday John Steevenson of St Dunstons west Blacksmith, & Allice Bett of St Michells in woodstreete, ye daughter of Edward Bett in ye cont' of Caunt' by lycence by Do^r Edwards
	December	4	Wend: John Maggott of St Sauiours in southwarke and Deonis Tunbridge both† of this parish by bannes
		11	Wend: Thomas Hinde of this parish & Jeane Middleton of y^s p'ish ly: Caut'
	ffebruary	5	Tews: John Bark^r of St Michells Cornehill & Hannah Snape of y^s p'ish by banes
1612	May	3	Sonday Nicholas Weston of St Olaues and Margerie Coop' of this p'ish s^{r}vante to Mr Langhlie in Cornhill lynnen drap' by baynes
	June	1	Mond: William Well of St Olaues Southwarke and Rose Cope of this parish by bannes
	August	23	Sonday Christopher Coop' of this p'ish, and Grace Olliuer of the p'ish of Bray in the Countie of Barkesheire by bannes
	October	18	Sonday Will'm Sheppard & Sarah Smith both of this p'ish lycen' Cant'
	January	26	Tewsd: Thomas Weygod Cooke and Alce Collyns by bannes both of this p'ish
		31	Sonday Edward Sherman & Margery Hunter both of this p'^{sh} by bannes
1613	Aprill	18	Sonday Roberte Payne & Alce Bryan both of this p'^{sh} by bannes
	June	20‡	Sonday Richard Phillips of the p'ish of Allhallowes Stayninges and Margret Poole of this parish by banes
	Julye	1	Thursd: Dauid Blake of the tower liberties ffarrier and Margery Hardwine of this parish by banes
	August	29	Sonday Thomas Porter of Mountneysinge in the county of Essex yeoman and Sara Stellyman of Heybridge in the said com' by lycens from my lo: B: of Caunterb^{r}y

* The Register from February 3, 1610, to Aprill 18, 1613, is subscribed Will'm Asheboold, parson, John Cason, churchwarden.

† Sic.

‡ The Register from June 20, 1613, to March 8, 1613-14, is subscribed Will'm Asheboold, parson, Robert Bell, John Pywall.

Yeare.	Month.	Day.	Names.
1613	September	2	Thurs: Peter Hassard of St Benites Sherchogg and Anna Edge of St Gabrill ffanchurch London by lycenc' lo: L: office
	October	17	Sonday William Taylor and Margaret Gibson servan^t to Valentine Luddington both of this parish by baynes
	November	25	Thursd: ffranncis Lownes of St Michells Querren and Martha Salter of St Michells Woodst: by lycence fro' Mr Kempe
	January	16	Sonday ffranncis ffynimore Joyner of St Albones Woodstreete and Dorytie Barber of this p'ish by baynes
		20	Thurs: Rowland Leake of Thistleworth in the Com' of Midd' gen' and Ann Wescott of St Martin Ludgate by licenc' Ni: Kemp
	ffebruar	24	Thursday Thomas Waight of this p'ish scriuon^r and Susann Stellowman of Woodh^{a}m Mortym^r in ye con' of Essex by licen' Ni: Kemp
	March	8	Tusday Thomas Cakebread of the p'ish of St Nicho: Olaues shomaker and Isbell Barnes of this p'ish by banes
1614	May	2*	Monday Edward Lyster of St Marie Aldermanburie and Ann Walthall of this p'ish wido' by lycence from N: K:
		8	Sonday Thomas Seymore and Joane Wright both of this parish by banes
		29	Sonday Tobias Waideson of St Olaues in Southwarke and Alce Graye of this p'ish by Banes
		22†	Sonday John Laborne of St Margrett Pattens in Roode lane and Anne Lynnacers of this p'ish by banes
	June	23	Thursday John West of St Dunstones in the east and Bridget Ashboold daught^r of Mr Docto^r Ashboold by lycence N. K.
	July	14	Thursday Edward Masters of St Michells Cornhill and Alce Warman of that p'ish by lycence from Nicho. Kemp.
	September	15	Thursday Daniell Barker of St Mary Bow p'ish and Mary Leacrofte, widd' of this p'ish by lycence from Mr Kempes office
		22	Thursday George Cleave of this p'ish and Alce Stanstall of St Savors in Southwarke by lycence fro' Mr Kempes
	October	23	Sonday Humphery Streete of S^t X'pofers by the Exchange & Rebecca Burge of this p'ish by lycence from Mr Kempes office
	December	19	Monday Jesper Goodwine of Darkinge in the Com' of Surry gent. and Jane Carleton of Chersey in the saide com' by lycence M^r K.
	January	1	Sonday Alexander Symondes of London Cooke and Susan Baker both of this parrishe by lycence from Mr Kempes
		22	Sonday Edward Wager of St Margetts p'ish westmin' and Margret Congrie of this p'ishe widd' by bane
	February	12	Sonday Jaruice Huchinson of this p'ishe porter and Elizabeth Dawes of Hackney parrish by banes
1615	Aprill	10	Monday John Scotton of the p'ish of St Martines Vinterie and Ann Millit of Bridewell precincte by lycence fro' m^r Weston office

* The Register from May 2, 1614, to September 7, 1615, is subscribed Will'm Asheboold, parson.

† Sic.

THE REGISTERS OF ST. PETER'S, CORNHILL.

Yeare.	Month.	Day.	Names.
1615	Aprill	23	Sonday Thomas Carter of the p'ishe of St Buttols Bishopsgate and Grace Caudwell of this parrishe by banes
	May	2	Tuesday Peeter Markeham of the p'ish of St Buttols Algate & Susan Johnson of this p'ish by licence from Mr Kempes
	June	10	Satterday Barker Browne of the p'ish of Mary Alderma'berrie and Tomazine Parrie of that p'ish by lycence from Nich. Weston
		15	Thursday Thurstano Symondes of Camberwell in Com' Surrie and Martha Savage of St Michels Queenehith by lycenc' Cant'
		26	Monday X'pofer Dynes of ye p'ish of St Olaves Juery and Elizabeth Westwood of This p'ish by lycence from Nicholas Westons off.
	July	9	Sonday Roberte Allen of the p'ish of St Androwes vndershaft and Alce Hinde of this p'ish by banes being 3 asked
	August	14	Monday Samuell Dalton of the p'ish of Stepney and Mary Rich of that p'ish also by lycence from Nicholas Weston
	Septemb^r	7	Thursday Anthony Scrarbricke of the p'ish of Dunstones west and Jeane Glascocke of Hatfeild in Com' Essex by lycen' Ro: Kempe
		14*	Thursday Samuell Man of the p'ish of St Leonardes ffoster lane and Sarah Sachfeild of this p'ish by lycence. N: W:
		21	Thursday Roberto Standish and Hanna ffrier by banes
	January	14	Sonday Tho. Kyndall and Elizabeth Treauers by banes
	March	18	Monday Thomas Rochedale sayler of this p'ish and Jone Heyman widdow of the p'ish of Stepny by lycence from Nicho: Kemp
1616	Aprill	16	Thursday Ephraim Hopkinson & Alice Harris by banes
		23	Tuesday† Thomas Mullett and Elizabeth Sherrington by banes
	May	5	Sonday Will'm Beard and Gyles Roache by banes
	Julie	9	Tuesday Hughe Brumlie & Mary Wildes by lycence from N: K:
		24	Wensday Thomas Love & Alice Bankes by lycence fro' N: Kemp
	December	26	Thursday Lawrence Hayes & Isabell Jackson by lycence fro' N: K:
		29	Sonday John Webb & Abbigale Newsam by banes
	January	26	Sonday Roger Whittacars & Jeane Maddox by bane
	ffebruary	2	Sonday Richard Hubberstead & Katherin Kinge by banes
	March	6	Thursday Andrew Carter and Ellen Wright by banes
1617	Aprill	22	Tuesday Thomas Bassell & Rose Bullardine by banes
	May	11	Sonday Anthony Williames & Elizabeth Gybbes by banes
	June	10	Thomas Pitt and Ann Colinge by lycence fro' N: K:
	Julie	28	Monday John Moth and Mary Bridges by banes
	Septem^r	29	Monday Will'm Bygraue and Joane Smith by banes
	October	5	Sonday Tho. Rixbie and Katherin Wilkins by banes
	ffebruary	2	Monday Richard Hewes and Joane Hancocke by banes

* The Register from September 14, 1615, to November 18, 1619, is subscribed Will'm Asheboold, parson, John Langley, churchwarden.
† Sic.

Yeare.	Month.	Day.	Names.
1617	ffebruary	12	Thursday Thomas Church & ffrancis Merryweath' by lycen' N: K.
1618	Aprill	7	Tusday Richard Denman and Ann Harrison by banes
		13	Monday Rob'te Carpenter & Elizabeth Collins by lycence fro' N: W.
		20	Sonday Richard Baxster & Elizabeth Bridges by lycence fro' N: W.
	May	26	Twesday William Hodgeson & Elizabeth Busby by lycence from N: K.
	July	27	Monday Jeromy Draper And Dorrithie ffoster by lycence fro' N: K.
	January	14	Thorsday M' W'm Drurie gent & M'rs Judeth Payne by banes
		18	Thursday Will'm Catlyn & Alice Pully by lycence from N: W.
	Februa'y	9	Tuesday Will'm Blackborow & Hester Jeffrey by lycence from N: K.
1619	March	30	Tuesday Will'm Hawkins & Ma'y J:anson by lycence from N: W.
	May	31	Monday Dauie Evans and Annis Ancocke by banes
	July	22	Thursday Gyles Rolles and Temperance Blinco by lycence fro' N: W.
		22	Thursday Walter Scott and Elizabeth Thimble by lycen' fro' N: W.
	August	12	Thursday John Gregorie and Rose Coop' by lycence from N: K.
	Septem'	30	Thursday Joseph Reeue and Jeane Lyttelton by lycen' fro' N: W.
	October	26	Tuesday ffrauncis Senior and Ann Dyer by lycen' fro' N: K.
		28	Thursday Nicholas Relfe and Mary Hudson by lycen' fro' N: K.
	Nouem'	1	Monday William Dauis and Elizabeth Man by banes
		15	Monday William Remnant & Alice Walter by lycen' fro' N: W.
		18	Thursday George Colpete & Elizabeth Harte by lycen' fro' N: K.
		24*	Wensday Daniell Ball & Proteza Culverwell by banes
		31	Tuesday John Morehowse & Constance Richardson by banes
	Janua'y	13	Thursday Samuell Swone & Ellenor Wattes by lycence
	ffebrua'	13	Sonday Henery Parkehurst & Mary Besouth by banes
	March	6	Monday Richard Bettesworth & Mary Lucas by lycence
1620	Aprill	24	Monday Richard Ashman & Joan Belinger by banes
	May	2	Tuesday Richard Chypp & Ellin Church by Banes
	June	8	Tuesday John Pywall & ffrancis Abbott by lycence
	Julie	20	Thursday Anthony Remnante & Catherin Drewe by lycence
	August	11	Fryday John Bunsey and Margret Kelly by lycence
	October	4	Wedensday John Tharpe & Ann Thornton by lycence
		17	Tuesday X'pofer Kyllimbecke & ffrauncis Parker by banes
		26	Thursday Richard Goodlade & Elizabeth Peeke by banes
	Nouemb'	12	Sonday Robert Gardner & Jeane Ashboold by lycence
	ffebruary	4	Sunday Anthony Poole & Lucretia Hill. by Banes
1621	Aprill	15	Sonday Jefferie Johnson & Joane Ramphem by Banes

* The Register from November 24, 1619, to April 4, 1622, is subscribed Ro: Dumvill, curat.

THE REGISTERS OF ST. PETER'S, CORNHILL. 251

Yeare.	Month.	Day.	Names.
1621	Aprill	29	Sonday Willm Poole & Alice Hayle by Banes
	May	13	Sonday Henery Branes & Joane Rees by Banes
	June	4	Monday John Whiffyn & Emme Haselwood by lycence
	August	7	Tuesday Roberte Ansecker & Mary Lawson by Banes
		19	Sonday Edward Peppen & Elizabeth Sheppard by lycence
		29	Wedensday Robert Browne & Jone Whitelocke by lycence
	October	21	Sonday Richard Dickinson & Judeth Robinson by Banes
	Decemb^r	26	Wedensday Robert Oneby & Elizabeth Harvie by lycence
		27	Thursday Thomas Eve & Sarah Harford by lycence
1622	Aprill	4	Thursday Peeter Weightman & Jeane Batcheler by lycenc'
	May	16*	Thursday Joseph Coop' & Margaret Williames by lycence
	June	10	Monday John Jackson & Margaret Steevens by banes
	Julie	25	Thursday Thomas Hill & Jone Poynte^r by banes
	Decemb	8	Sonday William Haswell & Katherin Sherman by banes
		26	Thursday Phillip Meade & Dorritie Reynoldes by lycence
		29	Sonday James Goodale & Ellyn Mynor by banes
	January	19	Sonday James March and Ellyn Portter by banes
	February	2	Sonday Richard ffrench & Mabell Musgrave by lycence N: W:
1623	Aprill	15	Tuesday George Butterfeild & Jone Grimmer by banes
	May	29	Thursday Humphrey Poole & Sara Aylett by lycence N: K:
	June	3	Tuesday Edward Elrington esq^r & Anne Sotherton gent. N: K:
		23	Monday William Moulton minister & Elizabeth Brocket by autho'
	Julie	13	Sonday John Cooke and Alice Symons by banes
		30	Wedensday Edward Deave & Elizabeth Browne by lycence N: W:
	Septem^r	14	Sonday Mathewe Kinge & Elizabeth Sharpe by banes
	October	28	Tuesday Robert Maddyson gent. & Deborah Drap' by lycence N: K:
	December	7	Sonday John Morlie and Elizabeth Powell by banes
	January	6	Tuesday William Norly and Mary Chambers by banes
		25	Sonday Thomas Carter & Mary Hudson by lycence N: K:
	February	5	Thursday Willm Bennett & Beatrice Bannister by lycence N: W:
		9	Monday John Mvmford & Elizabeth Okely by lycence N: K:
		28	Satterday Samuell Wilkinson gent. & Anne George by lycen'
1624	Aprill	14†	Wedensday Roger Dale gent of the County of Rutland and Elizabeth Wood by licence from N. Kempe
		29	Thursday William Thew of St Brides p'ish and Margarett Ellis of this p'ish by banes
	May	2	Wedensday John Mayhew of St Buttolphes Aldersgate & Judith Elliot of this p'ish by licence N. K.
	June	16	Wedensday George Buckley of ye p'ish of St Mary Bowe london: and ffrauncis Hayward widow by licence N: K.
		24	Thursday Willm Gilberte gent. of Grayes Inne and Elizabeth Gilbert of St Grigories by Powles lycence N: K.

* The Register from May 16, 1622, to February 28, 1623, is subscribed francis White.
† The Register from April 14, 1624, to November 1, 1631, is subscribed Phillip Mead, churchwarden.

Yeare.	Month.	Day.	Names.
1624	July	13	Tuesday Walter Williams of St Brides p'ish and Johan flinche of this p'ish by banes
		28	Weddensday Henry Kente and Richell Cooke both of the p'ish of St Andrewe Holborne by licence N. K.
	August	17	Tuesday Thomas Carpenter of St Andrewes vndershafte and Anne Triggs of this p'ish by banes
		29	Sonday George Kirkeman of Newington butts in ye County of Surr' & Susanna Anderson by banes
	Septemb	1	Weddensday John Canne of ye p'ish of Wolchurch and Elizabeth Rowe of this p'ish by banes
	October	10	Sonday William Browne of the p'ish of St Leonardes Shoreditch & Anne Tiggins of this p'ish, Banes
		31	Sonday William Wodhowse of the p'ish of Stepney and Mary Ship of this p'ish by banes
	November	4	Thursday Willm Rotheram and Suzanna Carpender both of Nebworth in com' Hert' by ly'ence N. Weston
	Decemb'	7	Tuesday Willm Lake gent. and M^{ris} Elizabeth Twedy gentlewoman by Licence from Robt Christian
		9	Thursday John Slauter of ye p'ish of St Sepulcher Sadler and Mary Slauter of this p'ish wid' by lycence Edm' Scott
	January	26	Weddenday Henry Harris and Anne Richesonne both of this p'ish by banes
	ffebruary	26	Satterday George Lee yeoman and Suzanna Samford mayden both of ye p'ish of Chigwell in the County of Essex by Lycence from Nich: Weston
1626	March	29	Tuesday John Derrivall Mercer and Elizabeth Norris mayden both of the County of Essex lycence N: W.
			Tuesday Thomas Barnejam of the p'ish of Butolph Algate and Katherine Warrin of this parish by lice'se from the faculties
		31	Thursday Thomas Brittin and Elizabeth moore by banes
	Aprill	30	William Michell of Botolph Bishops gate & Ann Wilkenson of this p'ish by banes
	August	21	Married Nicholas Hooker and Sara Tedder by license from the faculties
	December	28	Thomas ffowler and Mary Symonds of St Martins in the feilds by license from ye facul:
1627	January	1°	Married Samuell ffasset Preacher of St Georges in Southwarke and Elizabeth Shaw of this p'ish by license fro' ye faculties
		8	Robert Hudson and Elizabeth Reynolds both of this Parish by license from the faculties
		15	Daniell Hill of S^t Du'stones in the East and Elizabeth Reynolds widdow of this parish by license from the faculties
		23	Married Richard Bigley of St Katherine Creechurch and Mary Snode of this p'ish by ban':
1628	May	7	John Griggs of the parish of Ann Blackfriers and Ann Eeles of this p'ish married by banes
	July	24	Silvester Price and Elizabeth Ellcott married by lycense from the faculties
	August	20	Peter Garfoote and Rebecca Carter married by banes
	Septemb	28	Richard Walcot and Ellen Martine by banes
	October	06	Thomas Blackwell and Joane Staffold by license from the flaculties

THE REGISTERS OF ST. PETER'S, CORNHILL.

Yeare.	Month.	Day.	Names.
1628	January	08	George Browne and Blanch ffelton by license from the ffaculties
1629	Aprill	07	John Clarke and Mary Wannell married by banes
		12	John Warner and Elioner Burt married by banes
	May	19	Married Henry Staphith and Katherine Woodstocke by lycence from Mr Hunts Register
		26	Married Henry ffarefax and Margerett Willamote by lycense from the faculties
	January	11	Married Anthonie Leete and Elizabeth Gilmate by license from the faculties
		15	Thomas Woollard and Collatt Hargrave by Banes
		24	Humiliation Hinde and Elizabeth Phillips by Banes
	February	07	John Warren and Elizabeth White by License from ye faculties
1630	March	30	William Cash and Elizabeth Ellum by License from ye faculties
	Aprill	17	The Right Hono^{ble} George Earle of Desmond & m^{ris} Bridget Stanhope Marryed by Lycense from The Facultyes
		27	Married Thomas Haughton and Sara Bee South by banes
	June	10	Nicholas Heighmore and Anne Wroth by licence from the faculties
	December	12	Married William Williams and ffaith Butler widdow by license from the ffaculties
		30	Married Anthonie Sautleger of the countie of Kent Esqr and Dame Barbara Thornhurst of Westham in Essex, widdow by lycense from the faculties
	January	27	Married William Shipp and Elenor Howell by Banes
			Married John Painter and Dorothy Laycock by lycense from the ffaculties dated the 17° of November 1630
	March	10	Married Richard Hewes and Dorothy Wongan by license from the faculties
1631	Aprill	12	Married William Dennin of ye p'ish of Stepney Sawy^r: And Ann Warren of this parrish widdow by license from the ffaculties
	May	19	Married Thomas Kinge of Stepney, Vintne^r and Margarie Greene of this p'rish by license from ye ffaculties
			Married Thomas Harrison of ye p'ish of Bennett ffink Taylo^r & Elizabeth ffetherstone by license from ye ffaculties
		26	Married John Cotton of Rickmondsworth Tanne^r. and Venus Levat of ye same place by license from ye ffaculties
		30	Married Jo^n: Carnock Marrine^r & Margerie Munday both of Whitechappell p'ish by license from ye faculties
	Septemb^r	29	Married Thomas Spilsbery and Sarah South both of this parrish by Banes
	October	2	Married ffrancis Beadesley Grocer and Elizabeth Beadle widdow both of St Martins p'ish in the Vintry by Lycense from the ffaculties
		9	Married Humphrey Clark of St Ethelboroughes p'rishe & Margaret Harman of this p'rish by Baynes
		24	Married The r^t wor^{ll} William ffayrfax Esquire sonne of the r^t hono^{ble}: Thomas Lord viscount ffayrfax of Emelay. and the r^t wort^{ll}: the Lady Abigall Waterhouse widdowe of the p'rish of St Dunstans in the west by license from the faculties

Yeare.	Month.	Day.	Names.
1631	Novembr	1º	Married John Winterborne Haberdasher of the p'ish of Saint Hellens and Elizabeth Dawney of this p'ish widdow by license from the faculties
	february	9*	Married William ffowkes of the p'rishe of Bromley and Judith Bateman of this parrish by Banes
			Married George Waldren and Margrett Duncock of Eastham by license from the ffaculties
1632	Aprill	2º	Married Jon Sparks and Elizabeth Anbery both of St Martins in the feildes. by license from ye faculties
			Married Henry Tanner of St Buttolphs Algate and Elizabeth Miles of this p'ish, by license from the faculties
		5	Married Henrie Tailor of Bennett Pauls wharfe and Mary Mathews of this p'rish by license from the faculties
		19	Married Jon Serch of St Mary Woolchurch and Joyce Newey of this parrish. by Baynes
	Maie	6	Maried Josias Plumpton of Eastham in Essex and Elizabeth † of this parish by banes
		10	Maried Zacharie Specke and Jone Nightingale both of this parish, by banes
	Julie	5	Maried John Marsh of Botolphs Algate and Judith Bingam of this parish, by license from ye ffaculties
	June	11	Maried Thomas Cole minister in Kent and Anne Androwe widowe by licence from the ffaculties
		16	Maried William More of St Dionis Backchurche & Anne ffarrer of this parish by banes
	Decemb	21	Maried Allen Baker and Abigail Webb both of this parish by banes
		4	Maried Edward Mann of Alhollowes Lumberstreete and Rebecca Sachfeild of this parish by licence from the ffaculties
		26	Maried George Brogham of Thistleworth & Mary Waters of St Leonards ffoster lane by licence from the faculties
	Janua	22	Maried Timothie Younge and Elizabeth Lusher both of this parish by licence from the ffaculties
	February	20	Maried Thomas Biddle of Totnam Highcrosse and Elizabeth Whitlocke of this parish by licence from ye faculties
	March	5	Maried Richard Wintner of ye parish of St Gregories and Bridgett Rider of this parish by licence from ye ffaculties
		11	Maried Thomas Jones minister in Kent and Elizabeth Goodwin of the same countie by licence from ye ffaculties
1633	Maie	2	Maried John Duckott of St Marie Whitechappell & Anne Staines of this parish by banes
		24	Maried Jorden of Martinns Ludgate and Jane Abdy of this parish by banes
	Julie	25‡	Maried Mr Thomas Hodges minister & Mris Elizabeth Turner of St Martins in ye ffeilds, licence, Hunt
	August	6	Maried John Squire of Mildreds Bredstreete and Dorothie Sparkes of this parish by baines

* The Register from February 9, 1631, to May 24, 1633, is subscribed George Henlie, churchwarden.
† Sic.
‡ The Register from July 25, 1633, to March 1, 1635, is subscribed Jon. Meade, churchwarden.

THE REGISTER OF ST. PETER'S, CORNHILL. 255

Yeare.	Month.	Day.	Names.
1633	Novemb	1	Maried Thomas Hutchinson & Elizabeth Hitchcock p' licence from ye ffaculties
		24	Maried Thomas Kingston & Marie Starkey p' licence from ye ffaculties
	February	12	Maried Henrie Aires and Elizabeth Grove p' licence from ye ffaculties
1634	April	7	Maried Nathaniell Williams of St Mary Whitechaple & Marie Tiggins of this parish p' licence ffaculties
	Septemb	16	Maried John Mills and Margarett Watsonn of Eastham p' licence of ye faculties
		20	Maried George Abell and Margerie Coolie of this parish p' banes
	October	7	Maried Edward Browne of Ingerstone & Hester Barden of this parish p' banes
		30	Maried Nathan Hardinge of ye County of Bucks & Susann Deane of ye County of Hertf. p' licence facult'
	Januar	19	Maried Jarrett Birkhead of St Margaritts in Westm' and Abigaile Whitacre p' licence from ye faculties
	ffebruary	2	Maried Richard Jones of Katherine Colmans & Anne Rawbon by banes
1635	Marche	31	Maried W^m ffisher of St Marie Somerset & Rachell Sachfeild p' licence from ye faculties
	Aprill	7	Maried William Edmonds & ffrances Dane of ye County of Kent p' licence from ye faculties
			Maried Thomas Harris of St Botolph Bishopsgate and Joane Perriman p' banes
		14	Maried Roland Mather of St Albans Woodstreet and Elizabeth Gibson p' licence London
		26	Married John Shipton of Rumford & Prisilla Robinson p' Banes
		31†	Married John Greene & Edeth his wife of this p'rish p' banes
	July	6	Maried Richard Cox & Luce Woodward p' licence ex facult'
	Septemb^r	1°	Maried Jo^n Emerson Curate of Horsham & Margery Poulson p' licence from ye faculties
	february	19	Maried Jo^n Martin & Joane Allit p' licence ex facult'
		25	Married francis Bird & Suzan Browne p' license ex facult'
		28	Married Rob't Barnham & Elizabeth Henley p' licence ex facult'
		29	Maried Tho. Agar & Mary Rigbey p' licence de facult'
	March	1	Maried Wm Rawson & Margaret Graues p' licence de faculties
1636	May	22*	Married John Glynn & Dorathy Atkins p' banes
	January	20	Married John Wetherell and Sara White p' lycense
		29	Married Ambrose Langley & Eliz. Winch p' lycense
	february	30†	Married francis Parker & Ann Marson p' lycense
1637	June	16	Maried Symon Aston & Elizabeth Collet p' banes
	July	2	Maried Richard Laye & Dorathy Watson p' Banes
		8	Married James Hughes & Ann Smith p' lycense
		9	Married Edward Cotton & Jone Careless p' lycense
		24	Married Reynold Costion & Jone Bowdle p' baynes

* The Register from May 22, 1636, to October 15, 1639, is subscribed Henry Watson, churchwarden.
† Sic.

Yeare.	Month.	Day.	Names.
1637	Septem^r	21	Married Thomas Bedum & Kath: Watson of this p'ish p' lycense
		29	Married Timothie Munns & Anne Smith p' Baynes
	Octob'	26	Married Rob't Pomfrett & Ann Ashton p' Baynes
	Nouem^r	14	Married Wm Leapine & Mary Sneaton p' lycense
	Decem^r	7	Married Henryco Strudwick & Ann George p' Lycense
1638	March	27	Married John Browne & Alice Dell p' lycense
			Thomas Conn and Judith Merick p' lycense
	Aprill	3	Married William Dolton & Elizabeth Wattes p' lycense
	May	10	Humfry Sturt & Sarah Spilsbery p' license
		13	Married Peter White & Mary Young p' lycense
	June	29	Married Edmund Wood & Elizabeth Austen p' banes
	July	17	Married Christopher Chattrice & Mary Bingham p' license
		21	Married Gilbert Taylor & deionis Hilman p' Lycense
		25	Married Wm Mounstey & Susanna March p' lycense
	August	2	Married Wm Hicks & Margery Dauis p' license
	Septemb	25	Married Walter Symonds & Mary Golefer p' license
	Nouemb	5	Married Will' Hitchcok & Elizabeth Price p' lycense
		13	Married Elias Clark & Sarah Taudy p' banes
1639	March	25	Married Symon Silk & Alice Warner p' lycense
	Aprill	4	Married Thomas Kesar & Mary Woodward p' license
		25	Married Wm Shipley & Mary Bosworth p' banes
		22	Married Patrick Grady & Susan Smith p' license
	May	14	Married Christopher Clapham & Margaret Moyle p' license
		23	Married John Foster & Ann Mawkett p' license
	June	11	Married Thomas Birkhead & Katharin Wayt p' license
	July	10	Married George Painter & Alice Worrall p' lycense
	August	4	Married Rich. finch & Joane Stirt p' banes
		7	Married Edmond Elsonn & Joane Debbed. p' license lond'
	Octob^r	6	Married Joⁿ Witherall & Mary Keene p' license lond'
			Married Phillip Witherall & Jane Baylie p' license Lond'
		15	Married Hugh Tress & Judith Bingham widd' p' license Arch'
	Nouemb^r	6*	Peter Edmin & Eliz. Norris p' banes
		26	Thomas Ellis & Bridget Bingham p' license Lond'
			Will' Williams & Jane Middleton p' license Archbpp
	January	29	Wm Smith & frances Horne p' banes
	February	10	Joⁿ Booker & frances Ward p' license Archbpp
		13	Mr Rich. Engham & Eliz. freshwater p' license Archbpp
		20	Married Joⁿ Simpson & Eliz. Swift p' license Lond'
1640	June	22	Henry Taylo^r & Dorathie Debbit p' license Lond'
		28	Wm Scott & Anne Allen p' Banes
	July	28	Thomas North & frances Sikes p' Banes
	August	23	frances Andrewes & Katharen Hudds p' Banes
	Septem	3	Roger Singer and Elizabeth Sexton p' Lycense
		15	John Langley & Elizabeth Middleton p' lycense
		29	Mathew Bunnyon & frances Rawlyns p' banes
	Octobe^r	14	Edmond layfield & Ann King p' lycense
		22	Will'm Diston & Ellen Sharp p' lycense
		25	Robert foster & frances Seaborne p' lycense
	Nouemb'	10	Phillipp Wilson & Deborah Tirrell p' lycense
	Decemb'	24	Robert Hayes & Parnell Aldersey p' lycense

* The Register from November 6, 1639, to March 17, 1644, is subscribed Walter Golifer, churchwarden.

THE REGISTERS OF ST. PETER'S, CORNHILL. 257

Yeare.	Month.	Day.	Names.
1640	Decemb^r	29	Mr Wilborne & Martha lenthall p' lycense
		19	Rich Wokeham & Margaret Boswell p' lycense
	february	11	Paull Wright & Ann Ellington p' lycense
			Wm Warren & Elnor Wolfe p' Banes
		14	Roger Ingland & Alice Brookes p' lycense
	March	2	Tho: Cole and Susan Tidder p' lycense
1641	June	6	Isaack Woodward & Dorathy Sea p' Banes
	Septemb^r	9	Nicholas Steuens & Elizabeth Starkey p' lycense
		16	William Patrick & Susan Swetman p' banes
		23	Edward Payne & Elizabeth Heyward p' lycense
	Octob^r	12	John Marlow and Martha Robinson p' lycense
	Decemb^r	27	Baptist Crosse & Mary Clarke p' lycense
	January	26	George Allen & Ann Stacy p' Lycense
1642	Aprill	18	Thomas Salmon & Alce Ozbourne p' lycence
	June	26	William Holmes & Margeret Layton p' banes
	Octob	6	Robert Em'ims & Mary Conclade p' lycense
	Novemb	17	Thomas Price & Katherine ffearfax p' banes
	February	2	William Grover & Alice Greenbanke p' license
1643	October	18	Steven Dowell & Martha Norton p' banes
		21	Lenard Grigg & Mary Lewis p' banes
	November	7	Robert Hyron & Elisabeth Grinnoway p' banes
		30	Thomas Borke & Martha Kinge p' banes
	December	26	Tymothy Skerind & Margeret Bawe p' banes
1644	March	17	Mathias Harding & Elisabeth ffuller
	April	25*	Nicholas Atkins & Ann Clarke
	May	5	Thomas Jeffry & Mary Shoreditch
		14	Stephen Burrows & Jeane Midsley
		22	Morris Evans & Mary Creswell widd'
	June	1	Theophilus Luddington & ffrancis Oder
		10	John Read and Ann †
	August	15	William Mabbot and Dority Gleane
	October	24	John Nicholes and Ann Keele of this parish
	November	18	William Chamberlayne & Elisabeth Pitts
		24	John Coxes and Alse Beadle of this parish
		25	Robert Cooke and Katherine Dennis
	January	20	Thomas Pargiter and Tomsin Dickens
	February	6	Augustine Pollard and ffrancis Parke
1645	Aprill	7	John Butt and Eedy Turfett of this parish
	May	15	Thomas ffountayne and Alce Vnderwood
	July	10	m^r Perrigrin Pellam and Dame Katherine Vanlower
		24	Edward Starkey and Constance Herrin
	Novemb'	24	Thomas Rogers & Sarah Seller
1646	March	26	Mathew Norris of Ware And Ann Edmonds
	May	19	Mr John Cooke Counsellour and m^{rs} ffrancis Barr of †
	June	4	Thomas Skipper & Ann Cornwell
		8	Wm Elliot & Joane Judd, at Clem^t Danes
		8	Josua Bateman and Grace Cannon of Dagnam
	Decemb	26	Richard Wright of Maudline Milk street and Ann Hayden of this parish
	January	6	Josua Kirbey minister of Roade parish in Southampton And Mary Ballom of Wilsdon
		12	John Gerey and Elisabeth Sabin of Andrew Hubbert ‡

* The Register from April 25, 1644, to February 11, 1646, is subscribed Thomas Handson, churchwarden.
† Sic.   ‡ (?) St. Andrew's, Holborn. See also entry January 26, 1657.

2 L

Years.	Month.	Day.	Names.
1646	February	11	Barnard* of Mary Maudelines and Mary Risley of this parish
		16†	Edmund Cooke and Mary Watson of Georges Buttoll Lane
			Thomas Robinson and Elizabeth Ostedell of Amo't‡ p'sh
1647	Aprill	29	Robert Julian and Mary B'ewitt of Waltam Abby
	July	1	John Harding Marriner and Rachell Damore in the County of Kent
	Septem^r	28	Gilbert Maddox and Mary Starkey Widdow
	Octobe^r	4	Thomas Moore and Mary Reynoldes of Monesend§ in Essex
		11	John Moore and Lorie Collins of Rumford
	Decemb^r	27	Thomas Griffine Pewterer & Mary Woodward both of this parish
	ffebrua^r	17	Beniamine Warner and Katherine Wright
1648	Aprill	3^d	Nicholas Robinson and Sara Stephens of East Ham
		17	Samuell Grant and Sara Hower of Martins in the ffeeldes
	May	16	Phillip Harwood of Bristall Marriner and Mary Averill of Alhallowes staynng
	October	23	William Barnard and Sara Michell Bedford
	Novem^r	16	John Hungerford and Margarett Duckett of Nutfeeld in Surrey
	Decemb^r	28	William Hayward and Avis Wandling of Waltham in the County of Essex
1649	July	18	Beniamine Hinton of London and Elizabeth Ogle of Northampton
	August	26	Thomas ffrith and Sara Wells of this parrish
	Septem^r	25	John Cumbard & Mary Greene of Nvistocke§ Essex
	Octobe'	14	Thomas Pimlett & Ellinor Richardson of Ethelbo'
	Novem	7	Edward Key & Joane ffetherstone of Erith
	ffebru^r	12	John Bowrey & Judith Lester of Wapping
1650	Octob^r	22	Thomas Phillips and millisent smith of wolwich in kent
	Janua^r	5	Robert fairechild and Mary Treate daughter of Richard Treat by Giles Cripplegate
1651	March	31	John Wildborough of Hatfeild Bradocke in Essex and Hester Hudson
	May	23	Richard Ward & Anne Boroughs of Wapping
	June	2	William myles & sarah Church of Sepulchers
		4	James scail & Joane flipp of mucking§ in Essex
	Decem^r	22‖	William Titimouse and Anne Pertus of Ingerston in ye County of Essex
	Janua^r	1	Hugh Joanes and susan Land of mildreds in the Poultry
	ffeb^r	13	George branch and Elizabeth North
	March	9	George brodgate and Mary Pearle
		18	Thomas strato and Paskey Prideaux
1652		25	Robert Swan and Amy williamson hadly place
	July	7	John Graues & Marie Greene of Addin Jernon§
		10	William Hare & Elizabeth Smith of Dunstons in the east
		18	William Martin & Marie Wade of Woodbridg in the Counte of Suffolke

* Sic.
† The Register from February 16, 1646, to June 4, 1651, is subscribed Mr Lewis Biker, churchwarden.
‡ (?) Ainho for Aynho.
§ (?) Mountnessing—Navestock—Mucking—(?) for Theydon Garnon. See entry April 5, 1660.
‖ The Register from December 22, 1651, to March 30, 1654, is subscribed Mr William Hamon, churchwarden.

THE REGISTERS OF ST. PETER'S, CORNHILL. 259

Yeare.	Month.	Day.	Names.
1652	Augus	18	Joseph sumner and Joyce stallowbrace of Waltham in the County of Essex
	Octob	8	John nichols and mary murlwell of Billerykey in the County of Essex
	ffebrewy	24	William Crane and Mary Cock of Barkin in the Countie of Essex
1653	March	31	Thomas Blackborne and Susan Holmes
	July	25	John Gray and Sarah Tiller. Dedford in the Countie of Kent
	July	31	Henry Ballard & Joanna Owen: Giles: Cripple:
	August	3	Richard Addames & Eliz: Aust Countie Esex
		28	John Derron ye elder of Mary Bow and Ann Hynton of this p'ish
	Septemb	27	Joshua Clift: and Mary Mayld
		27	Joshua Bateman and Margaret Bowne of Barkin in ye Countie of Esex
	Decemb	27	William Wither of Clements Inn, Lawyer; and Abigall Roach: little minuories
	Octob	31	William Allin Ship Carpenter of Maudlin Barmundesbie.† And Dorothy Jones Spinster, by Thomas Andrews Alderman and one of the Justises of the peace in London
	Januu:	10	Henry Stutfeild Dyer of little Alhollowes and Elizabeth Blackmore of Stephens Walbrooke by Thomas Adkins A'derman and one of the Justises of the peace in London
1654	March	30	Moris Gethin of Alhollowes Bredstreete and Mary Kendricke widdow of the p'ish of Hackney
	Aprill	18*	Richard Porter and Mary Thompson: by Thomas Andrewes Alderman and one of the iustises of the peace in London
	May	1	William Johnson and Mary Blicke by Thomas ffoote Alderman, and one of the iustises of the peace in London
	June	13	Thomas Pilkinton of Katherin Colemans: Merchant and Hannah Broomewich of Peeters on Cornehill, by John Wolliston Alderman and one of the iustises of the peace in London
	July	27	Thomas Burton marriner of Stepney and Easter Taylor spinster of the tower liberties by Justis Swallow in Rosemary Lane
	August	10	Jeffrie Heath: of Steevens Colemanstreete and Elizabeth Dixon of Hartford by Recorder Steele
	Novembr	23	John White of Clemt Danes Shooemaker and Katherine Sharpe Spinster
		30	George Wheeler a Wheelewright and Joane Hall both of Hartlie Wintley in ye Countie of Southampton
1655	July	3	Richard Yapp of Laurance Jury Habberdasher and Christian Manskill Spinster of Stratford Bowe by Alderman Andrus one of the Justices of peace of the Citty of London
		4	Thomas Thorntone weauer and Elizabeth doniClifte Spinster both of Gylses Criplegate London by Justice Bloomer
		19	Henry quelch Oyleman and Jane Collins Spinster by Tho.

* The Register from April 18, 1654, to November 2, 1655, is subscribed Captayne Willyam East, churchwarden.
† St. Mary Magdalen, Bermoudsey. See entry February 2, 1659.

Yeare.	Month.	Day.	Names.
			Andrewes Alderman and one of the Justices of peace in London
1655	July	24	Willyam Gillye Lining draper & Sarah Pott by Christopher Packe Alderman & one of the Justices of peace in London
		27	John Heathe marchant and Rebeckah Golifer widow by Tho. Adkins Alderman & one of the Justices of peace in London
	August	13	John Godsell marriner & Margeret Grant widd' In the parish of Wapping by Sr Tho. Vyner Alderman one of the Justices of peace london
	September	24	Thomas Budd miller & Mathew larkin Spinster both of this parish by Tho. Adkins Alderman & one of the Justices of peace of the City of London
	October	1	m^r Jerimy dyke minester of parrindon In the County of Harford* & Marye Andros widd' In the parish of Peeters one Cornhill by Th° Andros Alderman one of the Justices of peace
	October	24	Lanslatt Chapman Coale marchant & Margeritt Allinn both of little Alhallowes by Tho. Andrewes Alderman & one of the Justices of peace in the City of London
		25	Mr Samuell ffearCloth minester of houghton Conquest In Bedfordshire & m^{rs} ffrances ffolter of Ketton In Suffolke by Justyce Bacon
	November	2	daniell W^{m}alet† mercer of Allowes† Lumbert streete & Marye midleborne spinster of Clements with out Temple bar by Justice Ceeling In the County of Middlesex
		24‡	John Smith wine Coper of Algate Parish & Sarah Porter Spinster of this parish. by Tho. Andrewes Allderman one of the Justice peace In the City of London
	January	21	daniell Evington widdoer & Sarah Cooper Spinster both of the parish of Hackney by John lyle Justyce of peace In ffeilde lane
		29th	Enocke Peate, Steauens Coleman streete Chandler & Barbery Salter spinster Gregery parish by Tho. Andrewes of the Justice of peace london
	ffebary	27	Nathaniel yearely Joyner & margery Abell Spinster both of Steues§ Colman streete by Th° Andrewes Allderman and one of the Justices of peace of the Cittye of London
		26	Allaxsander Beale sarvingman & Sisly pace Spinster of peeters one Cornhill by Th° Andrewes Alldreman & one of th^e Justices of peace in the City london
	Marche	13	Willyam porter mearser of Oxfford & Ann Robinson spinster of dounstons In the East by Thomas Adkins Alderman and one of ye Justices of peace in the City of London
1656	Nouember	11	Robart warner Souldier & Katherin Steverson Spinster of Steauen Colemanstreete by Alderman Adkins one of the Justices of peace of London
1657	June	16	Thomas Lancaster marriner & dennis Saule widdow of Poplar maried In this Parish of peeters

* There is no place of this name in Hertfordshire. Query whether it should not be Parndon in Essex.   † Sic.

‡ The Register from November 24, 1655, to July 29, 1657, is subscribed M^r. Richard Kinshman, churchwarden.   § St. Stephen's.

THE REGISTERS OF ST. PETER'S, CORNHILL.

Yeare.	Month.	Day.	Names.
1657	Julye	2	John Skidmore of Algate Carpenter And marye Nickoles of peeters parish one Cornhill Spinster
	September	2	Beniamin Smith yeaman & widdower of the parish of Butthalles Allgate [And] Hannah Hamendin widdow of the same
	October	11	Edward Christean wine Cooper And Elizabeth Huggins both of this parish
	October	11	Same daye Willyam Andrewes osler And Prudence Sammon Spinster both in this parish
	Nouember	5	willyam watson Husbandman And Annafrind bill Spinster both of waltham Abby In Essex
		10	Beiamen Spooner Butcher of dedford & Ance doged Spinster of this parish
		10	daniell Minnames linn' draper & Elizabeth Smithe Spinster by Justice Andrewes Ald'
	January	26	Edmond wade Marriner of Stepney parish & Sarah dorman of Andrew Huberd both single parsons
1658	May the	11	John Rigby in the parish of Oliues In Southwarke and Susanna Tayler of Clemt^s East Chip
		31	Peeter dobsen and Sarah Stevins of butthale Algate
	June the	3	Edward Golding & Elizabeth lawin of Waltham Abye
	Julye	29	Nicolas Robinson widdower of Stansted Hartfordshere And Mary . . . nisson widdow of Essindon same Co'nty
	August	31*	willyam Evans of Oliues harte Streete Coocke And ann warner Spinster of peeters Cornhill
	September	9	Edmond . . ynde of dower widdower And Elizabeth woodCocke Spinster of Hackny parish
	October	11	Arthur Baldwin of Gyles Criplegate And Jane Reade of woolchurch both Single parsons
	december	20	John Barritt of Lymhowse Shipwrihte & Mary Perkins widdow
	ffebeuary	17	Edward fillipes And Barbery payne both of Edmonton In the County of Essex
1659	Aprill	14	Edward Scrivenor Coocke & Elizabeth Smithe Spinster
		26	Mr Allixsander Hodge Minister of Thomas Exiter In devanshire & m^{rs} Hanah blackmore Peeters In Cornhill
	May	26	ffrancis walkott widdower & Ellin Butler Spinster
	June	2	John Games And Katherin Sheremane of Barking in Essex
		28	Henry Long of Margeret Moyses And Margerett Ricketts of the parish of peeters one Cornhill
	August	23	John Ashlye widdower & Susan Banke Spinster of Stepny
	Septemb^r	6	Clement Bacon Clarke of peeters parish of Cornhill widdower And Margett Aris widdow of the same parish
		8	Thomas Crawly widdower of Bednall greene In the parish of Stepnye yeaman & Amye powell widdow of Algate parish
			John Hamon batcheler And mariner & marye lofte widdow both of Stepny parish by m^r blackmore
	Ot'ber	6	Joseph Cooper and dorithy Atlee of mychaell Queene Hyne† wharfinger single parson of that parish
		24	Symon White & Sarah Willitt of peeters Cornhill

* The Register from August 31, 1658, to September 17, 1660, is subscribed M^r. Willyam Hinton, churchwarden. † Sic.

Yeare.	Month.	Day.	Names.
1659	Nouember	15	Timothy Alsop of plimoth marchant & Martha Sedghicke of marye Summarsit Spinster
	December	29	Robert Grifton of Rumford Butcher in the County of Essex and Jone ffuller [of] Larrance ould Jurye Spinster
	ffeberary	2	Richard Bryant marchant of Toolyes parish And Elizabeth Stokson widdow of Barmousby parish
			Same day John Weatheraut And Rose Clarke of gregories
		16	John Childes of Toolyes parish & Jone Morly of this parish
1660	Aprill	5	Richard Gunner of Teydon* Grernone & Joane Lea of much-hallanbury* both In the County of Essex spinster
	May the ffirst		Willyam Blackmore parson of peeters parish one Cornhill and Mrs Marye Chewny both att Mary Islingtone Church By Mr Tayler
	Maye the	17	Peeter Barricke and dorithy delton of popeler In this County of Midlesex both single persons
		24	George Coleman of Rotherridge & Abygall dobins of Rotheriffe single persons
			John daye of Epping Carpenter and Margett dodson of ffydon gardener spinster both of Essex
	September	17	John Mantill bachellr of diuonis Backcherch And Edith Roberds spinster of Stt martins Iu the ffeilds
		27†	John Slater Coocke & Dorithy Badger Spinster both of gruwidge by mr Tayler
1661	May	2	Thomas More of Lambeth whitstur and widowr and Martha Bent of this parish Spinster by Lycense from the ffacultyes
	June	13	John Clare Clothworker of the parish of Alhallowes Bred-streete and Jeane‡ of mary Somersett Spinster by Lycense from the ffacultyes
	August	20	Ezekiell Hopkins of Hackney Clarke and Mary Triplett of Hacknye Single woman
		22	Robert Meadowes of Barking in Essex widoer [&] Eliza-beth Tayler of wapping widdow by Lycense from the facul:
1662	Aprell	8	Edmund ffarrington of Martin outwich Marchand and Sarah Githin of Mary Islington Spinster by licence from ye ffaculty
		29	Thomas Cooper of ye parish of St Michall Queene hith Salter and Emm Clifte of ye parish of St Giles Criple-gate spinster by Banes
	May	8	Ralph Smart of Chesome in the County of Hartford fell-monger & Mary Hutchinson of the same parish by Licence from the ffackultyes
	July	24	John Cottram Grocer and Sarah Bikar spinster by Licence from the ffackultyes
	August	7	walter younge Cordwainer and Bridget Stone spinster by three severall Lords dayes publiched in this parish Church
1662	August	12	John Heather of parish of St Michy le Querne celibig & Jeane Earle of St Leonards forster lane Puellæ by licence from ye ffackultyes

* Theydon Garnon—Great Hallingbury.
† The Register from September 27, 1660, to February 19, 1662, is subscribed Mr James Blatt, churchwarden. ‡ Sic.

Yeare.	Month.	Day.	Names.
1662	September	18	Thomas Carr of ye parish of St Alholowes hony lane girdler and Elizabeth Stephens of S^t sepul'cers Spinster by licence from ye fackulties maried by m^r Goldman minister of Okindon in Essex
	October	2	Robert Hate of Shorne in Countey of Kent, husbandman & Jone Massey of ye same widdow by licence from ye faculties
	ffeberary	11	wilyam Willyams Eillzbeth Booker of Sp^eeny in the parish In the parish* of S^{tt} peeters one Cornhill by Lycense ffaculty
		19	John Mator ffranseman of Warrick lane And Mary Tappin of this parish by Deane Hodgis parson by Lycense ffrom the ffacultyes
	March	3†	Toby Comer of Gabryell ffenchurch And Sarah Parker of S^{tt} Lawrance By Lycense from the ffacultyes
1663	Aprill	21	Edward Gray and Elizabeth Bolton of Stepney by Licence from the ffacculties
	Septem :	19th	Jonathan Atherton of Ratcliffe mariner and Sarah ffirebread of Ratcliffe Spinster married by license from the Faculty office Mr Wills the lecturer
		30th	John Hunsden of Harford and Susan Pettitt of the same married by license from the Faculty office by m^r Ramsden curate
	October	14th	Edward Randall of the parish of Hellington in the Countie of Midilsex Malster and Eliz. Bisley of the same parrish Spinster by license from the faculty offis by Mr Ramsden, Curate
		11th	John Bartlet of Newgate market and Grace Pitts of this p'ish Married by Mr Mandrill p' licence
		19th	Thomas Winfeild of the p'ish of Camerwell in Surry and Margaret Tanner of the p'ish of Abchurch in London : beinge published Three Lords dayes according to the Canuon by Deane Hodges married
	October	28th	William Trunckit Sonne of Ralph Trunckit ffree of Drapers & Elizabeth Daughter of m^r Rigworth Statinor in Cornhill by Leicance from the ffaculties Maried by the Deane
	Nouember	12th	Thomas Wood of St Oliues Southwork Porter and Susana Daniell Widow of St Margreat new ffish Streete by Leicence from the ffaculties by m^r Wills Lecterer of this parish
1663	Nouember	15th	Richard Buterfeild Mealeman of Stepney p'ish and Susana Abram of Engerston by Leicence Spinster Maryed by the deane
1663	Decemb'	17	William Wild Esquire and Martha Hayse by Liccense from the ffaculty office by Deane Hodges
	January	21	Thomas Coston of St Michaell Querne and Elizabeth Chester of this parrish by banes
1664	Aprill	14	Thomas Haslam of the parrish of St Michaells Cornhill Leatherseller and Mary Bowers of the parrish of St Andrewes Holborne by banes
	May	17	Richard Kenricke of Islington and Rebecca Gethin of the same place by License

* Sic.
† The Register from March 3, 1662, to November 15, 1663, is subscribed Nicolas Bendye, churchwarden.

Yeare.	Month.	Day.	Names.
1664	Decemb	8	Edward wise of St Pauls Covent Garden gent. and Elizabeth Castle of this parrish by License
1665	May	4	William Hester Marchantaylo^r and Martha Medhops Spinster both of this p'ish by banes
		22	Phillipp Coleby of whitehall gent. and Mary Mores widow by License
			Henry Standish married to Sarah Ward by License the 2^d Nov: 1665
1666	Aprill	15	William Parker Clothworker and Mary Chamberlaine Spinster both of this parrish by License
	May	31	William Burgesse of St Martins Orgars widdower and Anne George of St Mary Bothawe by License; by Thomas Hollinsworth
	July	5	William Aylworth als Alyworthy of St Katherines Tower, batcheller and Mary Steward of St Michaell Queenhith Spinster by banes by Richard Hollingworth

INDEX OF NAMES.

A.

Abbot, William, 87.
Abbott, Frances, 250; James, 177.
Abdell, Dorothy, 236; John, 236.
Abdy, Jane, 254.
Abell, George, 255; Margery, 260.
Abington, Thomas, 229.
Abotes, William, 197.
Abowen, Daniel, 13, 125; Joane, 124; John, 10, 13, 15, 119, 121, 122, 125, 127, 225; Joseph, 121; Joshua, 119; Mary, 125; Samuel, 10, 125; Tobith, 15, 125.
Abram, Susan, 263.
Abrathapp, James, 203; Susan, 203.
Abrathaps, James, 202.
Abrathat, James, 93; Mary, 93; Mr., 212.
Abrathatt, James, 91, 204; Mary, 204; Mr., 204; Susan, 91.
Acklaude, Elizabeth, 198.
Acton, Mary, 205; William, 39.
Actonne, Francis, 39.
Adames, Anne, 127; John, 107; Katherine, 156; Mr., 110; Nicholas, 4; Richard, 127; Theophilus, 5; William, 115.
Adams, Richard, 127.
Adamson, Anthony, 223.
Addames, Richard, 259; Thomas, 122.
Addis, Anthony, 109.
Ade, Mr., 152.
Adey, Mary, 207; Thomas, 207.
Adkins, Thomas, 259, 260.
Adlin, Jane, 14; John, 14.
Adling, John, 121.
Adlington, Effham, 11, 235; Elizabeth, 17, 224; Hanibal, 11; Harry, 14; John, 10, 11, 12, 13, 14, 15, 16, 17, 123, 124, 129, 135, 235; Katherine, 10; Margaret, 15; Nicholas, 15, 129; Robert, 16; Susan, 10, 115; Thomas, 12.
Adlingtone, Cananell, 9.
Adlingtonne, 161.
Adlyn, Margaret, 113; Mr., 15; Thomas, 15, 229.
Adye, Thomas, 96.
Affenne, Thomas, 115.
Affley, Elizabeth, 9; Susan, 9.
Afort, John, 106.
Agar, Thomas, 255.
Agboroe, Edward, 235.
Agborow, Elizabeth, 235.
Ager, Edward, 225; Richard, 13; Thomas, 120, 237.
Agers, Sir Anthony, 164.
Agnies, John, 202.
Aires, Henry, 255.
Aish, Edward, 98; Elizabeth, 98.
Alcocke, Ralph, 158.
Alden, John, 216.
Alder, Edward, 100, 215; Elizabeth, 103, 220; John, 97, 100, 101, 103, 212, 215, 220; Mary, 97, 103; Mr., 212; Susan, 101.
Aldersey, Parnell, 256.
Aldred al's Tapster, William, 4.
Alisander, Mr., 127.
Alise, Thomas, 146.
Alkin, Mary, 77; Thomas, 77.
Allaby, Edward, 188; Elizabeth, 188.
Allam, Francis, 127; Margaret, 127.
Allen, Alice, 135; Anne, 256; George, 257; Jane, 234; John, 227; Margaret, 112; Margery, 239; Richard, 114, 163; Robert, 249; Thomas, 27, 227, 234; William, 234.
Allenson, Anne, 239.
Allgood, Anne, 215.
Allin, Katherine, 27, 133; Ralph, 220; Robert, 29; Thomas, 29, 133; William, 259.
Allinn, Margaret, 260.
Allins, Thomas, 135.
Allison, Francis, 190.
Allit, Joane, 255.
Allstone, Jeane, 112; John, 7.
Allyblaster, Thomas, 181.
Allyn, Elizabeth, 225.
Alsop, George, 75, 181; Timothy, 261.
Alsopp, George, 76, 186; Jane, 76; John, 76.
Ambrose, Anne, 171.
Amee, Davy, 224.
Ames, Thomas, 116.
Amie, John, 91; Mary, 91; Sarah, 91.
Amis, John, 90.
Am'y, John, 89; Sarah, 89.
Amys, Nicholas, 186.
Anbery, Elizabeth, 254.
Ancocke, Anne, 250.
Anderson, Luce, 161; Susan, 252.
Andrew, Anne, 67; Elizabeth, 64, 170; Richard, 63, 64, 66, 67, 170; Thomas, 63; William, 66.
Andrewe, Anne, 254.
Andrewes, Francis, 256; Thomas, 259, 260, 261; William, 261.
Andrews, Thomas, 259.
Androes, Elizabeth, 25; Margaret, 131; Mathew, 136; Richard, 136; Robert, 25, 128, 131.
Andros, Mary, 260; Thomas, 260.
Androw, Godfry, 129; Katherine, 129.
Androwe, Elizabeth, 245.
Androwes, Elizabeth, 61; Joane, 158; Katherine, 242; Richard, 61; Robert, 23, 153, 163; Susan, 23, 128; William, 162.
Androws, Marie, 56; William, 56.
Andrus, Alderman, 259.
Ange, George, 149.
Anger, William, 12.
Angie, Alice, 246.
Ansecker, Robert, 251.
Ansell, Clare, 227.
Anthonie, Lawrence, 189; Rebecca, 189.
Anthony, 75.
Anwicke, John, 7; Susan, 9.
Apot, James, 112.

2 M

INDEX OF NAMES.

Appelby, Samuel, 136; William, 136.
Apprice, Richard, 119.
Ap Robertes, William, 161.
Ap Thomas, Griphin, 125.
Archer, Barbary, 205, 211; Edward. 203, 205, 206, 207. 211; Elizabeth, 207; Richard, 91, 203.
Ardinge, Richard, 166.
Aris, Margaret, 261.
Arland. Isabel. 243.
Armeson, Elizabeth, 229.
Armestrong, Anne, 207; Richard, 229.
Arnit. James, 196.
Armstone, Alice, 97; Richard, 97.
Armstrong, Richard, 220.
Armstronge, Anne, 103; Richard, 103.
Arnwaie, Richard, 60.
Arnwaye, Grace. 164; Marie, 59; Richard. 59, 164.
Ash. Edward, 97; Jacob. 97.
Ashbold. Bridget, 32; Cicely, 45; Elizabeth, 43; Henry. 38, 54; Mr., 16, 241; William, 32, 34, 38, 43, 45.
Ashboold. Bridget, 248; Cicely, 180; Dr., 156, 175, 178, 248; Elizabeth, 161; Henry, 156; Jane, 51; Joane, 250; Mr., 182; Mrs., 169; William. 50, 51, 54, 144, 161, 179, 180.
Ashby, Jone, 196.
Ashe, Hugh, 116.
Asheboold. William. 8. 49, 51, 53. 56. 57, 59, 62. 63, 113, 150, 152, 155, 157, 160. 161, 162, 163, 165, 166, 169, 170, 172, 224. 241, 243, 244, 245, 246. 247. 248, 249.
Ashlies. Thomas, 65.
Ashly, John, 140.
Ashlye, John, 261.
Ashman. Richard. 250.
Ashpoole, Mrs., 193.
Ashton, Alice, 227; Anne, 256.
Aske, Peter Van, 137.
Askeu, William, 153.
Askew. Alice. 150; Christopher, 159; Edmund. 150; Frances, 162; John. 222; Mary, 41, 57, 162, 167; Mr., 145, 152; Mris., 162; Richard, 58; Thomas, 109; Tobias, 57, 58; William. 41, 162.
Askewes. Mr., 241; Mrs., 159.
Assley, Richard, 8.
Astine, Thomas, 79.
Astmore. John, 18.
Aston, Simon, 255.
Atherton, Jonathan, 263.
Atbey, John, 93; Phineas, 93.
Athie, Daniel, 95; Jane, 97; John, 95, 97.
Athy, Daniel, 208; Isaac, 97; Jacob, 97; John, 97. 208. 212; Mr., 212; Widow, 212.

Atkenson, John, 2.
Atkinnes, Christopher, 1.
Atkinnson, Margaret, 5.
Atkins. Dorothy, 255, John, 126; Nicholas, 257; Thomas, 126.
Atkinson, Alice. 231; Edward, 2, 4, 5. 22, 26, 29, 31, 126, 127, 136; Elizabeth, 29, 117; Ellen, 18; James, 31; John, 4; Julian, 109; Margaret, 5, 110; Margery, 124, 229; Mary, 136; Mr., 138, 239, 240; Nicholas, 26; Peter, 18. 124; Phebe, 4; Richard, 108, 231; Rowland, 108; Salomon, 5; Sarah, 147; Sibell, 26; Thomas, 4; Vincent, 22; William, 106.
Atkinsonne, Anne, 236; Elizabeth, 236; Nicholas, 6.
Atkynnes, Mr., 107.
Atkynson. John, 106; Thomas, 109.
Atlee, Dorothy, 261.
Atteway. Samuel, 212.
Atton, Edward, 237; Francis, 237.
Attrill, Jane. 221.
Atwood. John, 219.
Auddy. Mary, 94; Thomas, 94.
Aude, John, 185; Mris., 186; Susan, 74; Thomas, 74, 186; Widow, 186; William, 74. 185.
Audly, Martha, 14; William. 14.
Auling, Mary, 13.
Aunsell, John. 112.
Aunswell, Joanne, 116.
Aushum, William. 229.
Auskame. John. 112.
Austen. Anne. 113; Elizabeth, 198, 256; Thomas. 192, 198; Tobiah. 192; William. 192.
Austine, Elizabeth, 70, 73; John, 70, 180; Richard, 73; Thomas, 68, 70. 73, 180, 203; William. 68.
Aust, Elizabeth. 259.
Austonne. Martha, 8.
Avenon, Margery. 127.
Averell, Anne, 20, 228; Bartholomew, 35; Elizabeth. 2, 23, 45. 117, 130, 148; Gillian, 145; Henry, 8, 115; Jane, 6; Joane, 4; John, 2, 3, 4, 6, 7, 8. 24, 106. 111, 115, 120. 126, 228; Katherine. 221; Margaret, 3, 126, 154; Margery, 43; Martha, 37; Mathew, 25, 31, 139; Mr., 62; Parnell, 29; Rebecca, 41; Richard, 40. 143; Sibell, 223; Susan, 21; Thomas, 89; William, 7, 20, 21, 23, 24, 25, 28, 29. 31, 34, 35. 37, 39, 40, 41, 43, 45, 52, 130. 131, 139, 143, 145, 148, 154, 161, 231.
Averill, Mary, 258.
Avery. Alice, 112; Edward, 112; Richard. 107; Roger, 112.

Averye, Edward, 7.
Avison, alias Parten, Margery, 151.
Awbery, Arthur, 199.
Awnsell, Sarah, 8.
Awssle, Thomas, 7.
Axam. Richard, 114.
Axon, Elizabeth, 18, 119; Lawrence, 15, 16, 18, 124, 125; Margery, 15; Marrian, 122; Susan, 16, 124.
Axonne. Elizabeth. 11; Gregory, 13; Margaret, 9; Rachel, 10; Richard, 8; Sarah, 12.
Axson, Lawrence, 223; Peter, 223.
Axsonne, Lawrence, 124; Luce, 14. 124; Rachel, 125; Thomas, 125.
Axton, Lawrence, 115; Mr., 119; Sarah. 119.
Axtonne, Lawrence, 9; Thomas, 13.
Aylett, Sarah, 251.
Aylworth, alias Alyworthy, William, 264.
Aymis. John, 93; William, 93.
Ayre, William, 226.

B.

Baall. Harry. 110.
Babington. Elizabeth, 102; Margaret, 102; Richard, 102, 242.
Backe, Betteris, 225.
Bacon, Anne, 113, 182; Clement, 77, 182, 190, 200, 211, 261; Justice, 260; Martha, 211; Nicholas, 200; William, 77. 190.
Badcock, Margery, 247.
Badcocke, Vincent, 117.
Badger, Dorothy, 262.
Bagley. Edmund, 5, 116; Thomas, 6.
Bagly, Thomas, 222.
Baines, Frances, 18; Richard, 18.
Baker, Abigail, 206; Adam, 142; Alexander. 185; Allen, 193, 206, 208, 254; Anne, 8; Barnard, 240; Edward, 228; Eleanor, 98; Elizabeth, 193; Henry, 11; Jane, 7; Robert, 98; Susan, 9, 248.
Bakon, Anna. 68; Clement. 61, 63, 66, 68, 71, 74, 170, 174, 181; Jeremy, 174; John, 63; Martha. 71. 74; Mr., 173, 176; Nicholas, 66; Thomas, 63, 71, 181.
Bakonn, Clement. 64; Jeremy, 64.
Baldwin, Arthur. 261.
Bale, Catherine, 131.
Baley, Anthony, 210; Elizabeth, 210.
Ball, Daniel, 250; Elizabeth, 23; Humphry, 21, 23; John, 108; Margaret, 107; Mary,

INDEX OF NAMES.

228; Mandlyn, 139; Rebecca, 21; Richard, 4, 109; William, 131, 139, 222.
Ballard, Henry, 259.
Ballom, Mary. 257.
Bancroft. Richard, 240.
Banes, Grace, 147; Mary, 13; Mrs., 146; Richard, 22; Thomas, 154.
Banister. Elizabeth, 78; Stephen, 78.
Banke, Susan. 261.
Bankes, Alice. 249.
Bankes, *alias* Kerner, John, 106.
Bannester, Rebecca, 147.
Bannister, Beatrice, 251.
Barbar, Maudelin, 15; Paul, 15; Simon, 117.
Barber, Dorothy. 248; George, 181: Jone, 238; Judith, 216; Leonard, 238; Margaret, 101, 102, 103; Sarah, 217; Thomas. 101, 102, 103, 216.
Barbor, Elizabeth, 133; Joane, 223; Katherine, 226; William, 125, 133.
Barden, Hester, 255.
Barkar, Lea, 155; William, 155.
Barker, Alice, 217; Barbara, 217; Daniel, 248; Deborah. 93; Edward, 222, 232; Frances, 232; George, 91. 93, 121, 203, 212; John, 244, 247; Mary, 91, 193, 203; Mr., 204; Timothy, 3; William, 107.
Barkly, Mary, 239.
Barley, Jone, 162; Katherine, 54; Marie, 56, 165; Mr., 167; William, 54, 55, 56, 162, 165, 243.
Barlow. Margaret, 6.
Barnard. Amy. 196; Daniel. 13; Frances, 134; Henry, 180; Hugh. 55, 162; James, 241; Judith, 12; Libias, 12, 134. 226; Margaret, 180; Mr., 196; Richard, 35, 56, 162; Robert, 231; Susan. 120; William, 258.
Barnejam, Thomas. 252.
Barnerd, John. 233; Thomas, 233.
Barnes, Alice. 73; Elizabeth, 67, 70, 73; Isabel, 248; Robert, 232; Thomas, 67, 70, 73, 179, 232.
Barnestone, Margaret, 211; Richard. 211.
Barnett, Henry, 63; Margery, 177; Mathew, 240.
Barnfeld, William, 145.
Barnham. Robert, 255.
Barnsdale, Edward, 111.
Barr, Frances, 257.
Barret, John, 146.
Barricke, Peter, 262.
Barritt, Agnes, 246; John, 261.
Barron, Richard, 161.
Barrow, Susan, 15; Thomas, 15.
Barrowe, Anne, 55; Richard, 55.

Bartlet, John, 263.
Bartleye, George, 127.
Barton, Hellen, 219; Joane, 196; Robert, 228.
Basse, Thomas, 175.
Bassell, Thomas, 249.
Bassocke, Abigail, 246.
Batchelor, Elizabeth, 174; Jane, 251.
Bateman, George. 115; Joshua. 257, 259; Judith, 254; Thomas, 184.
Bates, Barbary, 193.
Batten. Daniel, 74; Humphry, 74; Katherine, 74.
Battes, John, 111.
Battin, Daniel, 212.
Bawcomb, Edward. 187.
Bawcombe, Edward. 73, 74, 75; John, 75; Sarah, 73. 74. 75; Thomas. 74.
Bawe. Margaret, 257.
Baxster, Richard, 250.
Baxter, Elizabeth, 11.
Bayes, John, 217; Mr., 212.
Bayle, William, 131.
Bayler, Anthony, 98; Elizabeth. 98.
Bayles, Susan. 227.
Bayley, Mr., 213.
Baylic, Jane, 256.
Bayly. Alice, 130; Anne, 103; Anthony, 99, 100, 103, 214; Joice, 103; Mathew, 99; Thomas, 100, 214.
Baylye, Anthony, 99, 211; Mary, 99, 211; Philip, 108.
Baynes, Elizabeth, 14; John. 14; Richard, 12, 22, 136; Ursula, 22.
Bayse, John, 218.
Beadesley, Francis, 253.
Beadle, Alse, 257; Elizabeth. 253.
Beale, Alexander. 260.
Beane, Mr., 116, 118; Thomas. 226.
Beard, William, 249.   [230.
Beckinsall. Bridget, 125; John, Beckinsalles, John. 124.
Bedford, Clare, 174; Lucy (Countess of), 55; Sarah Michel, 258.
Bedhouse. Elizabeth, 175.
Bedum, Thomas, 88, 198, 256.
Beed, William, 221.
Beeston, Edward, 217; Martha, 217.
Belinger, Joane, 250.
Bell, Elizabeth, 109; Ellen. 108; Emme, 2; Father. 109; Jane, 226; John, 109, 221; Mary. 2; Mr., 85, 163, 192; Richard, 3, 109; Robert, 62, 169, 247; Thomas, 4, 109; William, 183.
Bellaune, Alice, 11.
Bellingeam, Thomas, 240.
Bellinger, William, 118.
Bellynger, Rose, 226.

Ben. William, 157.
Bendie, Colinge, 97; Hannah, 95, 208; Nicholas, 95, 97, 208, 214.
Bendy, Edward. 102; Elizabeth, 94, 102, 213; Francis, 92, 207; Nicholas, 92, 94. 99, 101, 102, 207, 213; Samuel, 99; William. 99.
Bendye. Nicholas, 98. 263.
Benet, James. 125.
Bennet, 231; Alice, 20, 234; Elizabeth. 228; James, 230; Joane. 23; John, 60, 221; Katherine. 25; Melchisedeck. 20, 21, 23, 24, 25, 129, 130, 231, 234; Michel, 60; Peter, 12; Robert, 21; William, 226.
Bennett, William, 251.
Bent, Martha, 262.
Bently, John, 105, 133.
Benton, Katherine, 236; Thomas, 236.
Bentry. Anne, 222.
Ber, Mris., 209.
Berkhed, Katherine, 210.
Berrie, Mrs., 176; Thomas, 175.
Berriman, Sarah, 179.
Berry, Anne, 230.
Berryman, John, 126; William, 126.
Bertonne. Anne, 107.
Besouth. Mary. 250.
Best, Anne, 213; Charles, 213; Hugh, 90, 91, 199, 204, 213; Jane, 204; John, 6; Mr., 204, 212; William, 199.
Beston, Mary, 15; Susan, 15.
Bett, Alice, 247; Edward, 247; Owen, 246.
Bettesford, Sir Peter, 195.
Bettesworth. Sir Peter, 195; Richard. 250.
Beuan, vp, Davy, 127.
Bewchampe, 173; Mr., 159.
Bewter, John, 225.
Bibbey, Alice, 87; Dorothy, 89; Mary, 88, 199; William, 87, 88, 89, 90, 198, 199, 201.
Bibby, Alse, 201; William, 201.
Biddle, Thomas, 254.
Bigley, Richard, 252.
Bikar, Letitia, 213; Lewis, 213; Sarah. 262.
Biker, Anne, 87, 210; Hannah, 92; John, 87, 89, 198, 200, 212; Lettice. 90, 204; Lewis, 92 195, 198, 200, 204, 210, 212, 215, 258; Mr., 91, 197; Mrs., 195, 210; Richard, 205; Samuel, 91; Sarah, 90.
Bilborough, Robert, 14, 15; William, 14.
Bill. Anna Frind, 261.
Billam, Dorothy, 14; Richard, 14.
Billin, George, 184.
Billing, Francis, 182; George, 182, 184; Jane, 185;

INDEX OF NAMES.

John, 125; Katherine, 125; Sarah, 184; Widow, 185.
Billinge, Alice, 71; Francis, 71; George, 68, 71; Jane, 68.
Billingsley, Henry, 10, 11.
Billingslie, Henry, 115.
Billingsly, Henry, 51; Sir Henry, 54; Richard, 51.
Billington, Elizabeth, 211.
Billowes, Martinque, 29; Peter Van, 29.
Billowis, Martingue. 184; Daniell, 135; Peter, 134, 135.
Bingam, Judith, 254.
Bingham, Anne, 79, 196; Bridget, 256; Edmond, 66; George, 68, 178; John, 77; Josias, 80, 196; Judith, 72, 74, 256; Mary, 256; Mr., 183, 196; Paul, 74, 198; Rebecca, 72, 196; Sarah, 179; Thomas, 66, 67, 68, 72, 74, 77, 79, 80, 82, 172, 174, 175, 178, 179, 181, 187, 192, 196, 198; William, 82.
Bingly, Isabel, 224.
Binkes, Susan, 155.
Binlye, Mr., 114.
Birchwood, Thomas, 159.
Bird, Francis, 255; Harry, 135; Margery, 140; Ralph, 135, 235.
Birdsol, Mr., 205.
Birkehead, Bridget, 207; Thomas, 83, 207.
Birkett, Bridget, 85; George, 85; John, 198; Thomas, 85, 198.
Birkhead, Bridget, 197; Elizabeth, 191; Jarrett, 255; John, 86; Mr., 197; Thomas, 84, 86, 191, 192, 197, 206, 256.
Bishop, Sir William, 193.
Bisley, Elizabeth, 263.
Bissill, Andrew, 209; James, 95; Katherine, 95; Mr., 209.
Biston, Anne. 100; Edward, 100, 101; Henry, 101.
Bittinson, Elizabeth, 221.
Blackborn, Richard, 100; Susan, 99; Thomas, 99.
Blackborne, Charles, 99; Francis, 95, 209; John, 98; Richard, 92, 93, 95, 99, 204, 209; Simon, 92, 204; Thomas, 98, 101, 259; Timothy, 101.
Blackborow, William, 250.
Blackburne, Elizabeth, 97; Francis, 103; Paul, 98; Richard, 97, 98, 102, 103, 104; Susan, 100; Thomas, 100, 219.
Blacke, William, 229.
Blackeborne, Thomas, 219.
Blackeburne, Susan, 215; Thomas, 215.
Blackemore, James, 107.
Blackgrave, Elizabeth, 102; Isabella, 102; William, 102.
Blacklie, Mary, 84; Ralph, 84.

Blackmore, Chewning, 101; Elizabeth, 259; Hannah, 261; Martha, 93, 202, 205, 207, 211; Mary, 101; Mr., 261; Sarah, 92, 203; William, 92, 93, 101, 202, 203, 205, 207, 211, 262.
Blackwell, Thomas, 252; William, 230.
Bladwell, Robert, 158.
Blage, Anne, 124; Elizabeth, 128; Richard, 108; William, 124, 128.
Blagraue, Isabel, 100; William, 100.
Blagroue, John, 207.
Blagrow, Isabel, 96; Mary, 96; William, 96.
Blake, Andrew, 245; David, 247.
Blakemore, William, 219.
Blakmore, Martha, 94; William, 94.
Blalocke, John, 141; William, 141.
Bland, Elizabeth, 113; John, 244; Peter, 40; Robert, 40; Thomas, 226.
Blane, Edward, 241.
Blare, David, 219.
Blase, Sarah, 243.
Blatch, Elizabeth, 245.
Blatt, James, 213, 214, 262; Samuel, 214.
Blayne, John, 236; Thomas, 236.
Bleach, William, 227.
Bleache, Edward, 14, 121; Margaret, 119; William, 14, 121.
Blewitt, Mary, 258.
Blicke, Mary, 259.
Blinco, Temperance, 250.
Blofeild, Elizabeth, 58, 165; Judith, 59; Richard, 58, 59, 165.
Bloomer, Justice, 259.
Blott, Elizabeth, 89, 92, 93, 200, 204, 219; James, 89, 90, 91, 92, 93, 94, 96, 99, 100, 199, 200, 201, 219; John, 89, 90, 91, 199; Mary, 92; Mr., 202, 204; Samuel, 94; William, 90, 96, 201.
Blowe, Sarah, 210.
Blower, Anne, 17; Christopher, 16; John, 223; Katherine, 222; Robert, 16, 17; William, 222.
Blowfeild, Marie, 61; Mrs., 69; Richard, 61, 170; William, 247.
Blunt, Alice, 121; Robert, 121.
Bofeild, Marie, 196.
Boghhan, George, 126; Robert, 126.
Bolton, Anne, 239; Elizabeth, 263; George, 82; Mr., 239; Richard, 217; Robert, 243; Theophilus, 82, 198; Thomas, 198.
Bomer, John, 155.
Bond, Christopher, 242; John, 135; Richard, 135.

Bonde, Richard, 128.
Bondes, Martin, 170.
Bonnell, Richard, 7.
Boofeild, James, 176.
Booker, Anne, 89; Elizabeth, 263; John, 89, 256.
Bookey, Charles, 215; Elizabeth, 97; John, 95; Mr., 212; William, 95, 97, 215.
Bookeye, John, 211; William, 211.
Booky, Maudlyn, 242.
Boomer, John, 161, 188, 227; Jone, 161, 188.
Boote, Margaret, 238.
Booth, Agnes, 198; Elizabeth, 202; John, 198; Thomas, 202.
Boothe, Thomas, 90, 201.
Bording, Julian, 16; Nicholas, 16.
Borke, Thomas, 257.
Boro, Anne, 221.
Boroughs, Anne, 258.
Borow, Deborah, 4; Elizabeth, 14; Emme, 2; Joane, 3; Mary, 3, 108; Thomas, 14, 123.
Borrow, Anne, 118; Jane, 15; John, 116; Margaret, 108; Thomas, 5, 15, 116, 221.
Borrowe, John, 7; Master, 108; Thomas, 228.
Bostocke, Giles, 170; Margaret, 115.
Boston, Thomas, 145.
Bosworth, Mary, 256; Thomas, 185.
Botham, Elizabeth, 97, 209; Jonathan, 97, 209; Mary, 97; Mr., 208.
Bothe, Thomas, 201.
Botlie, Anthony, 63; Katherine, 63.
Botly, Anthony, 170, 182; Katherine, 170, 182.
Bottombe, Nicholas, 233; Richard, 233.
Boulstone, Mary, 114.
Boulten, Mary, 77; Theophilus, 77.
Boulton, George, 194, 195; James, 79; Mary, 224; Mrs., 190; Robert, 56; Theophilus, 79, 84, 85, 190, 193, 195, 210; Thomas, 84; William, 56.
Bourn, John, 226; Mary, 51; Peter, 53, 158; Thomas, 51, 53, 158, 240.
Bourne, Margaret, 56; Robert, 199; Thomas, 56.
Bowdle, Jone, 252.
Bowen, Anne, 49; Edward, 49, 152; John, 12, 14; Joshua, 14; Mary, 14.
Bower, Lady Anne, 112; John, 108.
Bowers, Mary, 263.
Bowfeld, Jane, 236; Richard, 236.
Bowing, Sarah, 11.
Bowker, John, 198; Margaret, 198.

INDEX OF NAMES.

Bowland, William, 227 ; Thomas, 227.
Bowlyn. William, 224.
Bowmer. Elizabeth, 9.
Bowne, Margaret. 259.
Bowrey, John, 258.
Bowser, Jone, 228.
Bowyar, Harry, 118.
Bowyer, Em. 24 ; Harry, 24 ; Sir William, 107, 140, 152.
Boyce, Sir Edward, 67 ; Katherine, 67.
Boyse, Jone, 245.
Braddington, Elizabeth, 154.
Braddocke. Anne, 70 ; Elizabeth, 70, 185 ; Thomas, 70, 178, 185.
Bradford, Martin. 169.
Bradley, John, 213.
Bradock, Thomas, 186.
Bradocke. Anne, 185 ; Samuel, 184 ; Thomas, 184, 185.
Bradshaw, Jone, 243 ; Roger, 155, 243.
Bradwynne, Mary, 229.
Brady, Elizabeth, 222.
Bramich. Isaac, 81, 191 ; Mary, 192 ; William, 81, 191, 192.
Bramwich, Hannah, 86 ; Mr., 191, 196 ; William, 86.
Branch, George, 258.
Brand, Sir Mathew, 193, 212 ; William, 193.
Braues, Henry, 251.
Brasier, Thomas, 218.
Brathwyth, John, 100; William, 100.
Brattle, John. 242.
Brawdy. Bridget, 145.
Bray, Anne, 41, 144, 203; Arthur, 240 ; Jane, 45 ; John, 34; Richard, 42 ; Thomas, 36, 39; William, 34, 36, 39, 41, 42, 45, 144.
Brearcliffe, Thomas, 218.
Breton. Mr., 159.
Brett, Francis, 169.
Brewer, John, 221.
Brewin, John, 150 ; Mary, 45 ; Mr., 167 ; Roger, 45, 47, 149, 150, 166; Robert, 47, 149,150; Thomas, 166.
Brewine, Mary, 167; Roger, 167.
Brian, Alice, 27 ; Anne, 246 ; John, 22, 27 ; Robert, 22.
Brickendale, William, 5.
Bricket. Alice, 135 ; Anne, 231 ; Elisaunder, 221; George, 135; Hamlet, 9, 14, 17, 123, 124 ; Joyce, 5, 123 ; Mary, 9, 124 ; Nicholas, 6 ; Thomas, 14; William, 17.
Brickhead, William, 230.
Brickhed, John, 119.
Bricking, John. 115.
Brickland. John, 206, 210 ; Susan, 206.
Bridgeman, Anne, 232 ; Thomas, 232.
Bridges, Elizabeth, 250 ; John, 173 ; Judith, 66 ; Mary, 249 ; Nicholas, 66, 173, 174; Ralph, 239 ; Susan. 243.
Brigges, Elizabeth, 235; Harry, 235.
Bright, Anthony, 23 ; Garthred, 5 ; Richard, 127 ; Mable, 4 ; Sallomon, 19, 23.
Brighte, Mr., 108.
Bruckhurst, Hugh, 230.
Briscow, Anne, 89 ; John, 89.
Brisely, Richard, 107 ; Thomas, 107.
Brisket, Ledewicke, 22 ; Philip, 22.
Brisley, Luce, 223.
Brislye, John. 1, 112 ; Katherine, 119.
Brittain, Elizabeth, 46 ; Robert, 51 ; Susan, 48 ; Walter, 46, 48. 51.
Brittane, Elizabeth, 164; Hable, 56, 161 ; Susan, 163; Walter, 56, 161, 162, 163, 164.
Brittin, Thomas, 252.
Brizely, John, 123.
Brizly. Anne, 230.
Brocke, Anne. 204 ; John, 92 ; Philip. 91, 92, 203 ; Rebecca, 91, 203.
Brockell, Valentine. 110.
Brocket. Elizabeth, 231.
Brodgate. George, 258.
Brogham, George, 254.
Bromefeeld, Richard, 8.
Bromely, Alice. 19, 242 ; Audrian, 23 ; Elizabeth, 24 ; Foulke. 16, 27 ; Katherine, 243 ; William, 16, 19, 23, 24, 27.
Bromley, William, 240.
Bromlie, Henry, 157; Widow, 51.
Bromly. Adrian, 132; Alice, 47 ; Edward, 242 ; Mrs., 243 ; Richard, 48, 168 ; William, 47, 48. 132, 149, 227.
Bromlyes, Mr., 141.
Brommidge, Mrs., 195 ; William, 194.
Brond, Stephen, 110.
Bronscom, Alexander, 75 ; Paul, 75.
Brooke, Harry, 237 ; Julius. 47; Margaret. 237 ; Mary, 229 ; William. 47.
Brookes, Alice. 257.
Broome, Christopher, 84 ; Elizabeth. 84.
Broomewich, Hannah, 259.
Brottway, Anna, 213; John, 213.
Brounescome, Alexander, 68 ; Effym, 68 ; Francis, 68.
Brownfeeld, William, 9.
Brown, Alice, 243 ; Anne. 12 ; Ellen, 154; Francis, 238 ; Richard, 223 ; Thomas. 14, 143, 148, 154, 238 ; Wilfrid, 11.
Browne. Anne, 86 ; Anthony, 238 ; Barker, 249 ; Dorothy, 85, 195 ; Edward, 13, 255 ; Elizabeth, 105, 251 ; Ellen, 225 ; George, 258 ; John, 80, 114, 190, 195, 197, 217, 238, 256; Mary, 50 ; Nicholas, 196 ; Ralph, 212 ; Rebecca, 77; Richard, 77; Robert, 251; Susan, 255 ; William, 50, 80, 85, 86, 190, 195, 252.
Brudges. Anthony, 124 ; Mathew, 124.
Brug or Brugge, Anthony, 17 ; Mathew, 17.
Brumlie, Hugh, 249 ; Margery, 177.
Brumstone. Alexander, 77, 186 ; Elizabeth, 77 ; Paul, 186.
Brunskyll, Michel, 169.
Bryan. Alce, 247 ; Anne, 25 ; Blanche. 174 ; Grace, 133 ; John, 25, 131, 133, 226 ; Robert. 131.
Bryant, John, 128 ; Richard, 262.
Brygges, Thomas, 222.
Bucher, Christian, 209 ; Edward, 209 ; Margaret, 118 ; William, 221.
Buck, Elizabeth, 220 ; James, 211, 220.
Bucke, James. 204, 216 ; Tabitha, 204.
Buckhurst, Benjamin, 245 ; Lord, 162.
Buckingham, George, 78.
Buckley, George. 251 ; John, 216.
Buckocke, Daniel, 67. 70, 177 ; Deborah, 70; Francis, 70, 177 ; Margaret, 67.
Buckstone. Myles. 184.
Budd, John. 91, 92, 202 ; Susan, 91, 202 ; Thomas, 92, 260.
Budlye, John, 234.
Bufford. Thrustone, 229.
Bufill, Elizabeth, 174.
Bull, Thomas, 241.
Bullardin. Anthony, 171.
Bullardine, Rose, 249.
Bulson. William, 111.
Bunny, Henry. 168.
Bunnyon, Mathew. 256.
Bunsey, John, 250.
Burch, Anne. 131 ; John, 131.
Burchall, Edmond, 226 ; John, 223.
Burche, Elizabeth, 122.
Burchenshaw, Charitie, 12, 235; Jone. 135 ; Randoll, 12, 144, 235 ; Rowland. 155.
Burcher, Anne, 245.
Burchewood, Elizabeth, 45 ; Thomas, 45.
Burchly, Edward, 140 ; James, 140.
Burchwood, Anne, 47; Sarah, 51; Thomas, 46, 47, 49, 51, 54, 150.
Burd, Anne, 98 ; Richard, 98.
Burden, Nicholas, 186, 187 ; Samuel, 186.

INDEX OF NAMES.

Burdicke, Nicholas, 229.
Burdsall, John, 202.
Burge, Rebecca, 248.
Burgesse, William, 264.
Burgis, Charles, 91, 204; William, 91.
Burke, Mr., 101.
Burkehead, Ellen, 179; George, 67, 68, 176; Henry, 179; Jane, 68; John, 68; Sarah, 67; Thomas, 181.
Burket, Harry, 238; Mary, 238.
Burkett, George, 60, 62, 65, 170; John, 65, 172; Sarah, 62, 170.
Burkin, John, 117.
Burnall, Nicholas, 9.
Burnam, Anne, 15, 122; Clement, 9, 12, 15, 131, 133; Edward, 14, 121; John, 10; Richard, 9, 105; Robert, 12, 133; Sibell, 131.
Burname, Rose, 221.
Burnell, Anne, 113; Robert, 232.
Burr, Bridget, 68; Nicholas, 68, 184.
Burrows, Stephen, 257.
Burt, Christopher, 194; Eleanor, 253; Elizabeth, 82, 191. 199, 200; Francis, 79, 82, 84, 86, 191, 195, 200, 204; John, 79; Mrs., 196.
Burte, Anne, 74; Elizabeth, 71, 74; Francis, 71, 74, 190; Mr., 186; Nathaniel, 245.
Burton, Andrew. 69; Apoline. 59; Arcules, 222; Elizabeth. 189; George, 199; Hercules, 3; John, 69, 86, 109, 189, 196, 199, 234; Mary, 71; Mr., 185; Percival, 230; Richard, 3, 234; Thomas, 259; William, 59, 71, 165, 231.
Bury, Thomas, 239.
Busay, Erasing, 107.
Busbey, John, 201.
Busby, Elizabeth. 30, 32, 134, 250; John, 30, 32, 134, 135, 136; Simon, 136.
Bushell, Thomas, 229.
But, Catherine, 136; John, 136.
Buterfeild, Richard, 263.
Butler, Alexander, 88, 89. 198, 203; Deborah, 204; Elizabeth, 89, 115; Ellen, 70, 182, 261; Faith, 253; Frances, 66, 88, 182; James. 64, 66, 70, 76, 169, 177, 182, 190, 197; Jockaminshaw, 169; Mathew, 10; Mr., 163, 205; Susan, 9, 114; Thomas, 120; William, 76, 223.
Butt, John, 257.
Butterfield, George, 251.
Buttler, Edward, 93; Elizabeth, 93; Faith, 201; Jane, 152; James, 152. 242.
Buttres, John, 190; Mary, 190.
Buttris, Anne, 75; Elizabeth, 77; Francis, 75; John, 75, 77.

Buttrisse, Elizabeth, 82; John, 81, 82.
Buzbie, *alias* Coghin, Elizabeth, 95
Byche, Robert, 115.
Bygrane, William. 249.
Byker, Lewis, 88, 92, 200; Mary, 88, 200.
Byllam, Clement, 119; Elizabeth, 13; Mr., 119.
Byllem, Elizabeth. 230.
Byngham, Judith. 70; Sarah, 70; Thomas, 70.
Bynnell, Thomas, 228.
Byrchewood, Anne, 150; Thomas, 150.
Byrd, Ellen, 228; Harry, 235; Richard, 134; Simon, 105; William, 134.
Bywater, Edward, 245.

C.

Cabbage, Weston, 157.
Cacy, William, 234.
Cade, Elizabeth, 172.
Cadye, John, 229.
Cage, Anthony, 30. 134; Christian, 142; Cornelius, 103; Ellen. 30. 134, 142; John, 142; Margaret, 103; Martha, 30. 134.
Cakebread, Thomas, 248.
Caluar, Grace, 11, 118; Sarah, 119.
Caluert, George, 244.
Campe, William. 152.
Candley. Anne, 10.
Candyne, Katherine, 222.
Canne, John, 252.
Cannon, Grace, 257; Margery, 227.
Capell, Dorothy. 208.
Cappes, Alice. 222.
Careles, Elizabeth, 239; John, 142.
Careless, Jone. 255.
Carendine, Henry, 194.
Carles. Mr., 142.
Carlill, Barbara, 241; Richard, 149.
Carleton or Carlton. Anna, 75; Bigley, 59, 62, 64, 66, 69, 80, 179, 186, 246; Hannah, 66; Jane, 248; John, 69; Mary, 64; Mr., 75; Rebecca, 62, 69; Samuel, 59.
Carnock, John, 253.
Carpender, Susan, 252.
Carpenter, Ellen, 233; John, 109, 233; Robert, 250; Thomas, 252; William, 245.
Carr, Thomas, 262.
Carre, Joanne, 241; William, 114.
Carsey, Elizabeth, 4; Katherine, 4.
Cartar, John, 108; Sarah, 109.
Carter, Andrew, 249; Anne, 232; Edward, 189; Elizabeth, 81; George, 138; John, 78, 122; Mary, 4, 83; Rebecca. 252; Robert, 79; Sarah, 3, 206; Thomas, 78, 79, 81, 83, 189, 192, 249, 251; William, 138.
Cartewright. Edward. 68, 69, 72, 173; Elizabeth, 72; Sarah, 68; Susan, 69, 72.
Cartwright, Anne, 52, 230; Edward, 183, 188; Elizabeth, 183; Susan, 188.
Caruaden, Robert, 106.
Caruet, Margaret, 119.
Carye, Harry, 125; Nem, 125.
Caryon, Elizabeth, 109.
Casebolt, Thomas. 107.
Cash, William, 253.
Cason, Barbara, 168; Dorcas, 76; Edward, 76; Isaac, 58, 165; John, 53, 58, 59, 76, 159, 165, 166, 168, 181, 212, 247; Marie, 53, 159; Mr., 72, 74, 177, 243.
Casonne, Joane, 165; John, 57; Nicholas, 163.
Cassell, Simon, 110.
Castle, Edward, 4; Elizabeth, 263; Katherine, 4; Mrs., 217; Sarah, 217.
Casun, John, 205.
Catche, Garret, 121.
Cater, Adam. 3, 109; Christian, 35; Elizabeth, 29; Ellen, 31; John, 3, 28. 29, 31, 33, 35, 39, 139; Mary, 39; Peter, 28, 33; Samson, 4.
Catherall, Thomas, 217.
Cathron, Elizabeth, 235; Leonard, 235.
Catlyn, William, 250.
Catmore, Thomas. 227.
Catterell, Elizabeth, 94; John, 94.
Caudell, John, 150.
Caudwell, Grace, 249.
Cauket, Elizabeth, 238; John, 238.
Caunt, Edward, 11, 32, 35, 130, 134, 138, 175, 236, 238; Elizabeth, 48; Ellen, 43, 145, 152; John, 11, 39. 42, 43, 45. 48, 50, 139, 140, 144. 145, 150, 151, 152, 162, 241; Katherine, 32, 238; Margaret, 42, 134, 144; Mary, 39, 139; Zachary, 118.
Caunte, John, 164; William, 245.
Cayne, Lettonish, 110.
Cecling, Justice, 260.
Chaderton, Robert, 18, 226; Thomas, 18.
Chadocke, William, 161.
Chadwicke, Charles, 124; Elizabeth, 124.
Challener, Francis, 36; Maudelin, 36.
Challenor, Nicholas, 195.
Chamber, Benjamin, 91; James,

INDEX OF NAMES. 271

77 ; Richard, 223 ; William, 77, 91.
Chamberlain, Colly, 123 ; John, 123.
Chamberlaine, Anne, 89 ; Elizabeth, 91 ; Margery, 79 ; Mary,264 ; Mrs., 244 ; Robert, 79, 205 ; William, 89, 91.
Chamberlane, Anne, 236 ; John, 236 ; William, 94.
Chamberlayne,Anne,202; Mary, 90 ; William, 90, 202, 257.
Chamberlen, Elizabeth, 102 ; William, 102.
Chamberlin, Grace, 100 ; John, 139 ; Mr., 100, 220 ; Rebecca, 101 ; Robert, 95 ; William, 95, 97, 211.
Chamberline, Edward, 90, 203, 204 ; Elizabeth, 91, 93, 99 ; Jane, 92 ; John, 99 ; Mary, 205 ; Mr., 166, 204 ; William, 90, 91, 92, 93, 99, 203.
Chamberlyn, Alice, 209 ; John, 183 ; Robert, 172, 183 ; Thomas, 98 ; William, 98, 207, 210.
Chambers, Charles, 84, 193 ; Edward, 242 ; Henry,76, 78, 80, 84, 85, 86, 189, 192, 193, 194, 195 ; James, 76, 80, 189, 190 ; Katherine, 149 ; Mary, 78, 190, 251 ; Nathaniel, 242 ; Robert, 243 ; Samuel, 85 ; 194 ; Sarah, 86 ; William, 189.
Chandeler, Grace, 199.
Chaplin, Mary, 197.
Chapman, Alice, 228, 232 ; Anne, 60 ; Daniel, 69 ; Edward, 9, 166 ; Eleanor, 72, 74 ; Elizabeth, 225, 228, 246 ; Ellen, 75 ; George, 116 ; Henry, 60, 61, 72, 74, 75, 77, 187, 188, 189 ; James. 74, 188, 225 ; Joane, 116 : John, 1, 117, 219 ; Katherine, 231 ; Lanslatt, 260 ; Mr., 169 ; Mrs., 200 ; Peter, 44 ; Prudence, 42 ; Ralph, 75 ; Robert, 1 ; Samuel, 77 ; Thomas, 72 ; Timothy, 118 ; William, 42, 44, 49, 60, 61, 113, 224, 232, 239.
Chapmanne,George.10 ; Robert, 2 ; Timothy, 9 ; William, 165.
Chare, John, 167.
Charkes, John, 67.
Charles, Ann, 171.
Charlton. William, 162.
Chart, Sarah, 154.
Charter, Mrs., 166 ; Richard, 59. 165, 166 ; Susan. 165 ; Thomas, 59, 166.
Chatterisse, Christopher, 88 ; Joseph, 88.
Chatterton. Christopher, 233 ; Margaret, 233 ; Robert, 129, 233.
Chattertonne, Anne, 11, 119 ; Sarah, 12.

Chattrice, Christopher, 256.
Chatwine, John, 58 ; Thomas, 58, 165.
Chaunce, Adam, 134 ; Joane, 134.
Chenery, Joane, 69 ; John, 69 ; William, 69.
Cherriot, John, 232 ; Richard, 232.
Chester, Elizabeth, 263.
Cheswick. Anne. 82 ; James, 84, 194 ; John, 81, 82, 83, 84, 194 ; Judith, 81.
Chesworth, Barberie, 86 ; John, 86.
Chetta', Sarah, 79 ; Thomas, 79.
Cheuall, John, 101 ; Robert, 101.
Cheuell, John, 94 ; Richard, 94.
Cheval, Elizabeth, 93 ; John, 93 ; Susan, 93.
Chevall, John, 91, 99, 100, 212 ; Susan, 91, 100.
Chevell, Daniel, 99 ; John, 97, 99 ; William, 97.
Chevill, Edward. 210 ; John, 95, 98, 210 ; Joseph, 98 ; Lawrence, 95 ; Mr., 208.
Chewney, Mary, 201 ; Nicholas, 201.
Chewny, Mary, 262.
Chidley, Anne, 111.
Childe, Anne, 222 ; Barbara, 242 ; Edward, 150.
Childes, John, 262.
Children, Dorothy, 221.
Chills, Conrad, 68 ; Elizabeth, 68 ; James, 68.
Chiswick, Anne, 192 ; John, 192.
Chittey, Abraham. 207, 208 ; Henry, 207, 208.
Chittie, Abraham, 95 ; Agnes, 95 ; Henry, 95, 217.
Chitty, Agnes, 97. 209 ; Henry, 97 ; Mr., 209. 217.
Chittny, Mary, 211.
Christeau, Edward. 261.
Christian, Richard, 238; Robert, 252.
Christmas, Robert, 117.
Church, Anne, 67, 177 ; Appelyna, 173 ; Ellen, 250 ; Frances, 71, 179 ; Mary, 65 ; Mris., 185 ; Sarah, 258 ; Thomas, 67, 71, 173, 177, 179, 183, 250 ; William, 65.
Churche, Frances, 69 ; Thomas, 69.
Churches, Thomas, 178.
Chypp, Richard, 250.
Clapham, Christopher, 256.
Clare, John, 262.
Claridge, Benjamin. 88, 89, 209 ; Bethia, 209 ; Elizabeth, 88 ; Hannah, 88 ; Jonathan, 89 ; Mr., 204, 208.
Clark, Benjamin, 200; Dorothy, 199 ; Elias, 256 ; Henry, 214 ; Humphry, 253 ; John, 199, 214 ; Mr., 100, 199 ; Rebecca, 200 ; Sarah, 196.

Clarke, Adrian, 208 ; Alice, 6, 215 ; Ambrose, 5, 116 ; Anne, 103, 228, 257 ; Anthony, 7, 116 ; Barbara, 76, 199 ; Bridget, 103 ; Dorothy, 84 ; Edmond, 225 ; Edward, 89, 110; Elizabeth. 5, 69, 81, 85, 89, 116,199; Frances, 102; Henry, 90, 91, 202, 208 ; Jacob, 102, 219 ; Jane. 11 ; Joane. 6, 90, 202, 230 ; John, 8. 69, 76, 78, 81, 84, 85, 91, 103, 113, 116, 130, 174, 207. 215, 219, 253 ; Katherine. 10, 234 ; Lawrence, 9 ; Lucressa, 168 ; Margaret, 152 ; Mary, 8. 257 ; Maudelin, 13 ; Mr., 204. 210 ; Misteris, 119, 169 ; Prudence, 5, 115 ; Richard. 5. 6. 12. 213, 236 ; Robert. 78, 103, 163, 213,236; Rose, 262 ; Sir Rowland, 126 ; Silvester, 13, 119 ; Thomas, 6. 7, 116, 118, 152, 234 ; William, 13, 111, 213, 219.
Clarridg, Benjamin, 199. 201, 210 : David, 210 ; Jonathan, 199 ; Sarah. 201.
Clarridge, Benjamin. 208, 211 ; Bethia, 208 ; Mr.. 205 ; Nathaniel. 211 ; Rebecca, 208.
Clason, William, 246.
Clawyer, Amy, 123.
Clay. Abraham, 201.
Claye, Anne, 238.
Cleanlie, Simon, 167.
Clearton, Grace. 111.
Cleaton, Anne, 198 ; Richard, 198.
Cleave, George. 248.
Cleent. Rachel. 11.
Cleffe, Anne, 124, 222; William, 124.
Clerke, Elizabeth. 4.
Clerkson, George, 59.
Cliffe, Mary, 216; Mr., 215, 216 ; Peter, 216 ; Richard. 215, 216.
Clifford, Anne, 151; Eliza, 221 ; Frances. 239.
Clift, Joshua, 259.
Clifte. Emm, 262.
Clifton, Elizabeth. 134 ; William, 134.
Clint. William, 13.
Cloinge, Anne, 162 ; Francis, 162.
Cloise, Daniel, 140 ; John, 140.
Clyfton, Elizabeth, 170.
Clynt, John, 122.
Contes, Joane, 114.
Cobbam. Mary, 212.
Cobby, Eddy, 226.
Cocher. Mary, 107.
Cock. Mary, 259. [48.
Cockaine, Martha, 48 ; Thomas.
Cockeram, John. 103 ; Leticia, 103; Samuel, 103: Sarah, 103.
Cockes. Agatha, 126 ; Anne, 20, 126, 230 ; Edward, 10, 12. 13, 114, 120, 124,126, 237; Harry,

INDEX OF NAMES.

20, 126; Izan, 241; John, 108; Joseph, 174; Mary, 13, 237; Thomas, 12, 108.
Cockings, William, 196.
Coghin, *alias* Buzbie, Elizabeth, 95.
Cokain, Alice, 240; Dorothy, 42; Joseph, 44; Robert, 147; Thomas, 42, 44, 147.
Cokaines, Samuel, 46; Sarah, 40; Thomas, 40, 46, 240.
Cokely, 186.
Cole, Mr., 176. 219; Nathaniel, 197; Peter, 219; Susan, 201; Thomas, 201, 241, 254, 257; William, 197, 212.
Coleby, Philip, 264.
Coleman, Anne, 219; Elizabeth, 72; George, 262; Thomas, 175, 201.
Coles, Simon, 101.
Colfe, Thomas, 205.
Coling, Anne, 43; Barbara, 46; Elizabeth, 54; Francis, 33, 36, 38, 41, 43, 46, 54, 75, 153, 182, 188, 191, 199; Gabriel, 38; Mary, 36; Peter, 33; Richard, 75; William. 191.
Colinge, Anne, 249; Elizabeth, 77, 162; Francis, 77, 160, 162; Mr., 168; Peter, 160.
Colle, Anne, 120.
Collect, Richard, 145.
Collet, Elizabeth, 225.
Colley, Thomas, 228.
Collier, Margaret, 245.
Collins, Elizabeth, 250; Jane, 259; Lorie, 258.
Collman, Anne, 189.
Colly, Mary, 241.
Collyer, Christopher, 222.
Collyns, Alce, 247; Ellen, 180.
Colpete, George, 250.
Colstone, Anne, 244.
Colyng, Francis, 48; Jane, 48.
Colynge, Francis, 53, 56, 155, 161, 162, 245.
Comer, Toby, 263.
Commyn, James, 128; Robert, 128.
Comptonne, William, 109.
Conclade, Mary, 257.
Congrey, Margaret, 50; Richard, 50.
Congrie, Margaret, 248; Richard, 169. [256.
Conn, John, 87; Thomas, 87, Conningam, Anne, 233; John, 233.
Connoway, John, 189.
Connyers, Elizabeth, 109; John, 109; Marmaduke, 109.
Conway, Elizabeth, 76; John, 76, 184, 187; Katherine, 184; Sarah, 76; William, 76.
Coocke, Hellen, 212.
Coocklow, John, 210.
Cooke, Alice, 38, 156; Bartholomew, 17; Edmund, 258; Ellen, 127; Hamlet, 120;

John, 37, 40, 125, 214, 233, 237, 251, 257; Joseph, 206, 214; Margaret, 151. 239; Mary, 206; Richard, 17, 127, 229; Richell, 252; Robert, 125, 257; Thomas, 125; Walter, 37, 38, 40, 151, 152, 156, 237; William, 125, 233.
Coole, Margaret, 228.
Coolefox. Anne, 110.
Coolie, Margery, 255.
Cooling, Elizabeth, 203; Francis, 84. 203, 205; Margaret, 202; Mr., 200.
Cooper, —, 138; Anne, 231. 236; Christopher, 247; Edmond, 157; Elizabeth, 95. 208; Henry, 90, 91, 92, 95, 208; Joane, 22; John, 236; Joseph, 251, 261; Margaret, 247; Marten, 33; Mr., 157; Mris., 169; Oliver, 135; Richard, 33; Robert, 26, 232; Rose, 26. 250; Sarah, 91, 208, 260; Simon, 152; Susan, 92. 208; Thomas, 22, 90, 137, 201, 262; William, 232.
Coorfe, John, 11, Robert, 11.
Coorse, Elizabeth, 229; John, 123; Katherine, 110; William, 123.
Coot, Mary, 11.
Coote, John. 10.
Cootes, Edward, 10; Hester, 118; Joane. 5; John, 118; Mathew, 119; William, 11, 118.
Cope. Rose, 247.
Copland, Richard, 233; William, 233.
Coppocke, John, 205.
Corbit, Francis, 176.
Corden, Vryon, 237; William, 237.
Corker, William, 173.
Cornelis. Anne, 17; Elizabeth, 22; Frances, 20, 129; Hicrome, 17, 25; Jerome, 20, 22, 129, 131; John, 25, 131.
Cornwell, Anne, 257.
Corse, Joane, 228; Samuel, 10.
Corser, Ellen, 125; John, 19, 125; Margaret, 122.
Corzer, Elizabeth, 26; Joane, 128; John, 22, 26, 128; Katherine, 22.
Cosby, Lawrence, 120; Widow, 126.
Cosse, —, 5.
Costion, Reynold, 255.
Coston, Frances, 197; Thomas, 263.
Cotes, John, 117. [233.
Cotten, George, 233; Margery, Cotteram, John, 214; Mr., 214.
Cotterell, Anne, 88; James. 92; John, 88, 89, 90, 91, 92, 201; Mary, 201.
Cotterill, John, 203, 208; Simon, 203.

Cottering, Anne, 112.
Cottes, Ester, 9; John, 7; Katherine, 6.
Cotton, Edward, 255; George, 20, 126, 127, 128, 129; John, 253; Robert, 20, 126.
Cottram, John, 101, 262; Sarah, 101.
Cottrell, Anne, 199; John, 199; Mary, 227.
Cotts, John, 121.
Couchman, Lawrence, 237; Susan, 237.
Coucny, Robert, 134.
Coules, Simon, 100, 214; William, 100, 214.
Coult, Alice, 5.
Counstable, Anne, 246.
Couper, Oliver, 124.
Course, Catherine, 229.
Courson, John, 13; Richard, 13.
Coursonne. Jane. 115.
Cowdall. Harry, 227.
Cowes, Joseph, 54, 161; William, 54, 161.
Cowles, Robert, 213.
Cowlie, Richard, 155.
Cowper, Henry, 89. 199; John, 199; Mary, 89, 199; Richard, 202.
Cowsley, Hannah, 56; William, 56.
Cox, Richard, 255; Susan, 210.
Coxe, Anne, 7; Edward. 7, 9; William, 9.
Coxes, John, 257.
Coxon, —, 130, 131; Mathew, 124; William, 124.
Crackplace, Cuthbert. 244.
Craddocke, Anne, 226.
Cradle, Harry, 121.
Craft, Hugh, 117; William, 117.
Craftes, Sarah, 207.
Crafton, Mary, 3; William, 110.
Cramphorne, Elizabeth, 75; Ralph, 75; Robert. 75.
Cranaway, Ellen, 126; Thomas, 126.
Crane, William, 210, 259.
Crant, John, 27, 132; Thomas, 27.
Crawley, Thomas, 261.
Creeke, Doctor, 55.
Creswell, Mary, 257.
Crocford, Alice, 223.
Croft, Baptist, 91, 203; Davy, 229; Gabriel, 91, 203; John, 91, 203.
Crofte, Elizabeth, 42; Joane, 225; Percival, 42; Rose, 227.
Crofton, John, 1; William, 2.
Crompe, Susan, 232; Thomas, 232.
Crooke, Maudelyn, 233; Robert, 233.
Croone, Jacob, 86; John, 200; Mr., 203; Richard, 198; William, 86, 87.

INDEX OF NAMES. 273

Crosse, Baptist, 257.
Crostand, Harry, 106.
Crouch, Anne, 170; Joane, 208.
Croughton, Gabriel, 109; John, 109.
Crow, Christian, 133; John, 133; William, 135.
Crowder, Dorothy, 205; Jane, 81; Phillis, 81.
Crue, John, 237; Richard, 237.
Cullimer, Mr., 122; Thomas, 121.
Cullymer, Harry, 13.
Culnerwell, Ekezial, 66; Richard, 66.
Culverwell, Proteza, 250.
Cumbard, John, 258.
Cumbars, Elizabeth, 45; Thomas, 45, 46, 147, 148.
Cumber, Elizabeth, 241, 246.
Cumbers, Elizabeth, 148; Thomas, 148.
Curling, Richard, 113.
Currant, Cicely, 126.
Curson, Elizabeth, 18; Richard, 14, 18, 122.
Cursonne, Augustus, 115; John, 9, 112, 114, 115.
Curteys, Thomas, 115.
Custings, Elizabeth, 83; Henry, 81, 83; Marie, 81.
Cut, Barbara, 113; Edward, 4, 124; Elizabeth, 14; Harry, 9, 10, 12, 13, 14, 16, 17, 19, 20, 124; Joane, 16, 113; Judith, 19; Mary, 124; Mathew, 12; Phebe, 13; Richard, 20; Sarah, 13; Thomas, 10; William, 9, 112.
Cutchborn, Edward, 221.
Cutt, Barbara, 8; George, 113; Harry, 124; Joane, 124; John, 117, 125; Phebe, 124.
Cutterell, John, 147.
Cuttes, Harry, 14, 15; Joane, 8; John, 14; Martha, 15; Mary, 65.
Cuttler, George, 226.

D.

Daie, Martha, 85; Ralph, 85.
Daldron, Alice, 111; Elizabeth, 230; Henry, 39, 140; Joane, 228; John, 39, 120, 140; Thomas, 126.
Daldronne, Marian, 116.
Dale, Roger, 251; Thomas, 118; William, 133, 145.
Dalton, Ellen, 7; John, 4; Samuel, 249.
Daltonne, Elizabeth, 6.
Damore, Rachel, 258.
Damport, Randoll, 238.
Dams, Mr., 173.
Dancaster, Mr., 142.
Dane, Frances, 255.
Daniell, Alice, 223; Elizabeth, 203, 231; Jeremy, 203; Mary, 203; Susan, 263; Thomas,

50; Walter, 50, 151; William, 231.
Darlton, Lady Elizabeth, 55.
Dauid, George, 117.
Dauie, Elizabeth, 178; Jane, 178.
Dauis, Edward, 227; Elizabeth, 53; George, 52; Hellen, 138, 223; Humphry, 138; James, 245; John, 134, 175; Katherine, 29; Margery, 256; Mr., 209; Rice, 244; Richard, 67, 175; Susan, 67; Thomas, 52, 222, 243; Widow, 211; William, 250.
Dauldorn, John, 115.
Dauisonne, Joane, 6.
Dauldron, Elizabeth, 115; Ellen, 121; Mr., 128.
Daulton, John, 8, 113, 225; Margaret, 106; Mr., 118; Richard, 11; Thomas, 11.
Dauy, Alice, 124; Bevan up, 127; Edmond, 124; Morris, 230.
Davis, Robert, 208.
Dawes, Elizabeth, 248; Henry, 246; Rose, 223.
Dawney, Edmond, 191; Elizabeth, 254.
Dawson, Edward, 65, 66, 69, 71, 177; Katherine, 66; James, 194; Lawrence, 65; Margaret, 69, 71; Mr., 73; Thomas, 177; Thomazine, 71.
Daye, John, 227, 262.
Dayne, Mary, 5.
Dayrell, Walter, 168.
Deane, Sir John, 54; Susan, 255.
Dearing, Jane, 238; John, 238.
Dearmore, Elizabeth, 218; John, 218; Lidia, 218; Mr., 218.
Denve, Edward, 251.
Decheborn, John, 108.
Dehouay, John, 12; Sidrach, 12.
Deiane, Joseph, 5.
Dekisar, Katherine, 146; Peter, 146.
Delas or Delasse, Eve, 136; Nicholas, 136.
Delton, Dorithy, 262.
Demaie, Jane, 169.
Dench, Barnaby, 97, 99, 210, 211, 213; Mr., 215; William, 97, 210.
Denham, Richard, 198.
Denman, John, 67, 174; Joseph, 183; Richard, 67, 174, 250.
Dennes, Katherine, 246.
Dennin, William, 253.
Dennis, Katherine, 257.
Deushire, John, 243.
Derham, Francis, 199.
Derrivall, John, 252.
Derron, John, 259.
Desborough, Christopher, 88, 213; Judeth, 89; Mary, 88, 213; Mrs., 211; Nicholas, 90·

Desborrow, Christopher, 201; Mr., 200.
Desbrough, Mr., 197.
Desmond, George (Earl of), 253.
Dethick, Gilbert, 22; Harry, 27; Robert, 29; William, 22, 24, 25, 27, 29, 129.
Deuill, James the, 121.
Deyne, Grizel, 4.
Dicheborn, William, 3.
Dickens, Tomsin, 257.
Dickenson, Benedict, 234; Elizabeth, 234; John, 51; Widow, 51.
Dickinson, Richard, 251.
Dickson, Elizabeth, 247; Margaret, 164.
Digby, Sarah, 82.
Dilling, Elizabeth, 18; Richard, 18, 125; William, 125.
Diston, William, 256.
Dix, Joseph, 93; Mary, 93.
Dixon, Adam, 147; Elizabeth, 259; John, 128, 147, 231; Robert, 112; Thomas, 147, 207, 231.
Dobes, Anne, 117.
Dobins, Abigail, 262.
Dobsen, Peter, 261.
Dockerell, John, 228.
Docket, John, 125; Nicholas, 125.
Dod, Briant, 59; Mathew, 186; William, 59.
Dodman, John, 119.
Dodsall, Marrian, 91; Mary, 91; Richard, 91.
Dodson, John, 206; Margaret, 262; Mr., 204.
Doegood, Katherine, 223.
Doged, Anoe, 261.
Dolfin, William, 111.
Dolton, Hannah, 60; Sarah, 61, 168; William, 60, 61, 168, 256.
Domelaw, John, 233; Richard, 233.
Domkin, Robert, 230.
Doniclifte, Elizabeth, 259.
Donwell, Francis, 233.
Doodly, Roger, 229.
Doodman, John, 116.
Dordeu, John, 226.
Dorington, Barbara, 148; Francis, 50, 154; Izan, 43; John, 43, 46, 50, 148, 154; Mr., 240; Thomas, 46.
Dorman, Sarah, 261; Stephen, 207, 211; William, 207, 210, 211.
Dormer, John, 219; Samuel, 219; William, 219.
Dorrington, Barbara, 45; John, 45.
Dorton, Elizabeth, 58; William, 58.
Doublebeare, Haunce, 108.
Doue, Agnes, 195.
Dover, John, 184.
Dow, John, 205.

2 N

Dowell, Anne, 235; Stephen, 257; Thomas, 235.
Dowle, Thomas, 132.
Dowll. Thomas, 231.
Dowlphin, William, 127.
Downes, Elizabeth, 49, 113, 233; Frances, 106; John, 233; Katherine, 106; Reynold, 108; Thomas, 49, 150.
Dowson, Elizabeth, 146; George, 10; John, 10, 11, 121, 128; Katherine, 226; Mary, 230; Philip, 7, 114; Raynold, 224; Richard, 243; Susan, 11, 128.
Dowsonne, Anne, 9, 118; Elizabeth, 229; Mary, 7.
Doyley, Francis, 200.
Drables, Anne, 41; George, 142; Henry, 37, 142; Robert, 37, 41, 138, 142.
Draper, Deborah, 251; Eve, 161; Jeremy, 250.
Drawater, Anne, 182.
Dregot. John, 228.
Drew, William, 230.
Drewe, Catherine, 250.
Drope, Christopher, 221; Harry, 109; Joan, 3; John, 2, 106; Mr., 116; Thomas, 3.
Druric, William, 250.
Dublebeer, Egbert, 3.
Duckett, Adrian, 217; John, 254; Margaret, 257.
Dudmanne, Giles, 9.
Duin, William, 78.
Dumber, Augustine. 114.
Dumvile, Ro., 69, 474, 177, 250.
Dun, Anne, 95; Hugh, 209; Nicholas, 95, 209; William, 78.
Dunch, Barnaby, 220.
Duncock, Margaret, 254.
Dundas, Duncan, 174.
Dunmoe, Margaret, 227.
Dunu, Hugh, 96; Nicholas, 96, 210.
Dunne, Alice, 227.
Duns, William, 221.
Durdant, Elizabeth, 15; Ellen, 17; Margaret, 124; Robert, 16; Thomas, 15, 16, 17, 124; William, 15.
Dured, Dorothy, 110.
Dutton, William, 216.
Dweight, Robert, 175; William, 175.
Dwight, Mary, 86; Peter, 84; William, 83, 84, 86, 183, 185, 193, 196.
Dwoight, Peter, 193; William, 193.
Dwoit, Elizabeth, 86, William, 86.
Dychebourn, John, 109.
Dyckens, Ellen, 233; William, 233.
Dyckenson, Margaret, 221.
Dyckson, Anne, 229.
Dye, Elizabeth, 194.
Dycath, Anne, 200.

Dyer, Anne, 250.
Dyke, Jeremy, 260.
Dylling, Richard, 228.
Dylton, Francis, 16; Richard, 16.
Dynes, Christopher, 249.
Dynn, Francis, 182; Margaret, 74; Martha, 74, 197; William, 74, 182, 191.
Dynne, Francis, 123; Margaret, 188; William, 188.
Dyrtney, Margery, 221.
Dytchborn, Edward, 113.
Dyxon, Joane, 110; John, 224.
Dyxonne, John, 7.

E.

Eachell, Edward, 166.
Eamnes, Ester, 94; Richard, 94.
Early, John, 223.
East, Benjamin, 94; Elizabeth, 90, 208; James, 89, 211; John, 199; Mary, 93, 96, 206; Thomas, 93; William, 89. 90, 91, 93, 94, 96, 199, 201, 206, 208.
Eastbrooke. Peter. 245.
Easte, Captain William, 96, 208, 211, 259.
Eastfeeld, Anthony, 117; Elizabeth, 5. 117.
Easton, Hester, 185; Mr., 185.
Eastwecke, John, 118.
Eatenstall, Edward, 212.
Eaton, Robert, 206; Thomas, 183.
Eatonne, Anne, 108.
Edam, Margaret, 221.
Edge, Anne, 248; Luce, 190; Rebecca, 246.
Edgeat, John, 235.
Edgertonne, Grace, 221.
Edhowse, Thomas, 175.
Edmond, Ralph, 188.
Edmondes, Evan, 42; Jane, 183; John, 42; Ralph, 182, 183; Samson, 182; Thomas, 230.
Edmonds, Anne, 257; William, 255.
Edmonson, Margery, 241.
Edward, Peter, 177.
Edwardes, Dinah, 75; Edward, 15, 229; Elias, 15; Elizabeth, 115; John ap, 124; Robert, 72, 75; Susan, 72, 75; William, 168.
Edwards, Doctor, 247; George, 77; Mr., 190; Robert, 77, 83, 183, 190, 192, 194; Susan, 83, 192; Thomas, 183.
Edwin, Edward, 108; Emme, 107; Joane, 107.
Edwinne, Luce, 2; Ralph, 4.
Edwyn, Leonard, 108; William, 108.
Eeles, Anne, 102, 103, 252; John, 102; Joseph, 102, 103, 216; Thomas, 102, 103, 216.
Eells, Anne, 97; Thomas, 97.

Egam, Emme, 202.
Egles, Christian. 226.
Eglesfeeld, Judith, 11.
Eglestou, Clement, 193.
Eglestone, Giles, 192.
Eldertonne, William, 4; Mr., 111.
Elders, John, 222; Julian, 222.
Eldrington, Christopher, 2.
Eles, Anne, 211; Humphry, 99; John, 211; Thomas, 99, 211.
Eliot, Margery, 106.
Elkin, John, 232; Mary, 232; William, 116.
Ellcott, Elizabeth, 252.
Ellerington, Edward, 125.
Elles, Thomas, 98.
Ellingame, Elizabeth, 222.
Ellington, Anne, 257.
Elliot, Judith, 251; William, 257.
Ellis, Katherine, 236; Margaret, 251; Thomas, 236, 256.
Ellison, James, 205.
Ellum, Elizabeth, 253.
Elme, John, 207.
Elmer, Edmond, 114.
Elmhurst, Ellen, 152; William, 52, 152, 153.
Elrington, Edward, 251.
Elringtonne, Susan, 5.
Elsmar, Harry, 224.
Elsonn, Edmond, 256.
Elsworth, Jane, 240; Katherine, 242.
Eluerington, Edward, 113.
Elysander, Nicholas, 221.
Embres, Thomas, 241.
Emerson, John, 255.
Em'ins, Robert, 257.
Emmes, James, 93; Richard, 93; Mr., 207.
Emms, Richard, 207; Susan, 207.
Engeham, Thomas, 173.
Engham, Richard, 256.
English, Simon, 105.
Esfeld, Giles, 136.
Estricke, Richard. 228.
Estweeke, Anne, 226.
Eswell, Thomas, 221.
Euannes, Emme, 120; Grace, 231; Lawrence, 147, 236; Richard, 231, 236.
Eue, Elizabeth, 246; Weston, 246.
Eueling, George, 39, 238; Robert, 37, 39, 238; Susan, 37.
Euered, John, 222.
Euerid, Widow, 119.
Euerite, William, 112.
Euerton, Elizabeth, 11; Jane, 227; John, 11.
Euertonne, John, 119.
Euington, Thomas, 228.
Evans, Anne, 101, 181; Davy, 250; Elizabeth, 65, 73, 199; James, 67, 73, 176; John, 65, 67, 73, 170, 176, 181, 199; Mr., 59, 164; Morris, 257.
Eve, Thomas, 251.
Evens, James, 215; John, 202.

Everall, Edward, 99 ; Thomas, 99.
Evered, Dorothy, 4.
Evins, Amy, 98 ; Joseph, 98 ; Katherine, 98.
Eyanes, William, 222.
Eyre, Harry, 112.

F.

Fables, Thomas, 126.
Faccam, John, 234 ; Nicholas, 234.
Fairechilde, Robert, 258.
Fairfax, Dorothy, 207 ; George, 81 ; Mary, 78, 83 ; William, 78, 81, 83, 84, 207, 209.
Faith, Joane, 225 ; Richard, 126 ; Thomas, 126.
Fannt, Bryde, 6.
Farefax, Henry, 253 ; William, 195.
Farewell, James, 196.
Farmer, Elizabeth, 159.
Farneworth, Giles, 225.
Farninean, Anthonet, 162.
Farre, Benjamin, 237 ; Walter, 237.
Farrer, Ambrose, 238 ; Anne, 254 ; Betteris, 238.
Farringdon, Edward, 47 ; Thomas, 47.
Farrington, Edmund, 262.
Fasset, Samuel, 252.
Faukes, Elizabeth, 240.
Fayrfax, William, 253 ; Thomas (Viscount), 253.
Feake, Elizabeth, 84 ; Henry, 82, 84 ; John, 82 ; Mr., 191.
Fear Cloth, Samuel, 260.
Fearen, Anne, 171 ; Godfry, 66, 173 ; John, 66, 171, 172.
Fearfax, Katherine, 257.
Fearue, Anne, 96 ; William, 96.
Fecie, Elizabeth, 12.
Federston, John, 105.
Feeld, Anne, 222 ; Bridget, 222 ; Mary, 3, 107 ; Mr., 141 ; Thomas, 141.
Feerichard, Robert, 223.
Feilding, Katherine, 165.
Felken, Christopher, 237 ; Hugh, 237.
Fell, Brian, 71, 72, 74, 75, 76, 78, 181, 188 ; Edward, 138 ; Elizabeth, 71, 72, 74, 75, 76, 188 ; John, 247 ; Margaret, 76, 78 ; Marie, 74 ; Richard, 138 ; Samuel, 71, 181 ; William, 227.
Fellowes, Peter, 83 ; Theophilus, 83.
Felo, William, 247.
Felton, Blanch, 253 ; Bose, 106 ; Stephen, 2.
Fen, Henry, 78 ; Thomas, 78.
Fenn, Anne, 87, 197, 202 ; Hannah, 84, 193 ; Jane, 89, 199 ; Mary, 76 ; Susan, 81 ; Thomas, 76, 79, 81, 84, 87, 189, 193, 197, 199, 202, 207.
Fenricke, John, 187.
Fenton, Alice, 50 ; Roger, 50.
Ferland, Anne, 101 ; James, 101.
Ferris, Roger, 240.
Ferychard, Anne, 8 ; Susan, 9.
Fetherstone, Elizabeth, 253 ; Joane, 253 ; Sir Richard, 105.
Fewterell, John, 13.
Fewterer, Elizabeth, 14 ; Francis, 14.
Fewtrell, John, 120.
Fidens, John, 18 ; Mary, 18.
Figes, Elizabeth, 202 ; Mr., 206 ; Thomas, 90, 202.
Filall, Mary, 230.
Filewood. Roger, 236.
Fillipes, Edward. 261.
Finar, Richard, 13.
Finard, Roger, 137.
Finch, George, 221 ; John, 21 ; Richard, 256.
Finche, Elizabeth, 21 ; Joane, 19 ; John, 19, 252.
Finer, Anne, 120 ; Richard, 120.
Fipp, Joane, 258.
Fipps, John, 208, 210 ; Ursley, 208 ; William, 210.
Firebread, Sarah, 263.
Fisher, Elizabeth. 77, 218 ; Goodman, 161 ; Hannah, 86, 197 ; John, 81, 89, 164, 193 ; Joseph, 190 ; Lidia. 87, 212 ; Marie, 81 ; Owen, 164, 244 ; Robert, 77, 83, 86, 87, 190, 197, 200, 206, 211 ; Roger, 193 ; Samuel, 90 ; Sarah, 83, 200 ; Widow. 164 ; William. 89, 90, 129, 255.
Fishman, Katherine, 141 ; Robert, 122, 226.
Fitch, Richard, 213.
Flammocke, Henry, 8, 114 ; Misteris, 120 ; Thomas, 6 ; William, 6.
Flaxmoore, Joane, 205.
Fletcher, Anne, 7 ; Anthony, 111, 222, 223 ; Elizabeth, 7 ; Emme, 111 ; John, 111 ; Richard (Bishop of London), 240 ; Thomas, 5.
Flewet, Richard, 8.
Flower, Elizabeth, 14, 120 ; Margaret, 13 ; Richard, 13, 14.
Flye. Thomas, 111.
Foaldington, Edward, 79 ; John, 79.
Foden, Anne, 234 ; John, 126 ; William, 126, 132, 229, 234.
Foldington, Edward, 188 ; Mary, 188.
Folter, Frances, 260.
Foord, Richard, 229 ; Thomas, 234.
Foote, Ellen, 224 ; Thomas, 259.
Ford, Rose, 230.
Fordom, Margaret, 8
Forest, Mary, 153 ; Robert, 111 ; William, 153.
Forringdon, Edward, 51, 149, 150 ; Mary, 150 ; William, 51.
Forster, Sarah, 100 ; William, 100.
Foster, Dorothy, 250 ; George, 60 ; John, 60, 244, 256 ; Marie, 191 ; Robert, 256 ; William, 108.
Fouldington, Anne, 182 ; Edward, 182.
Fouler, Sir Jasper, 190 ; John, 95 ; Mr., 110.
Foulke, Katherine, 146.
Fountayne, Thomas, 257.
Fowke, Joyce, 235 ; Roger, 235.
Fowkes, William, 254.
Fowle, Alexander, 243.
Fowler, Anne, 103 ; Edward, 118 ; Elizabeth, 93 ; Jesper, 169 ; John, 93, 96, 97, 207, 209 ; Joshua. 96 ; Mary, 97 ; Richard, 243 ; Sarah, 93 ; Thomas, 252.
Fox, Richard, 238 ; Robert, 142 ; Thomas, 157.
Francklin, Edie, 76 ; Patience, 75 ; William, 75.
Franckton, Edward, 97.
Francton, Anna, 101 ; Edward, 101.
Frankett, Edward, 212.
Franklin, Edward, 100, 103 ; Mary, 100 ; Richard, 108 ; Susan, 100.
Franklyn, Richard, 126.
Frankton, Edward, 98, 99, 102, 103, 210 ; Elizabeth, 103 ; Habberda, 98 ; Mr., 213 ; Susan, 98, 99.
Fraunces, John, 227.
Freeman, Elizabeth, 78 ; Isabell, 82, 85, 191 ; John, 83 ; Ralph, 80 ; Simon, 78, 80. 82, 83, 85. 191 ; William, 253.
Fremond, John, 122 ; Susan, 122.
French, Richard, 251.
Frere, Maynerd, 221 ; Robert, 106.
Fresingfeeld, John, 1 ; Luce, 1.
Fresingfeld, Katherine, 223.
Freshwater, Elizabeth, 256.
Frezingfeld, Maudelyn, 125.
Friar, Anthony, 234 ; Blanche, 139 ; John, 47 ; Margaret, 234 ; Mark, 139 ; Mary, 48 ; Mr., 143 ; Robert, 45 ; Simon, 45, 47, 48 ; William, 105.
Frier, Hannah, 249.
Frisingfeeld, Christopher, 240 ; William, 3.
Frith, Alice, 86 ; Elizabeth, 96, 203, 208 ; John, 210 ; Mary, 197 ; Nathaniel, 87 ; Ralph, 86, 87, 197 ; Sarah, 96, 98, 210, 211 ; Thomas, 96, 97, 98, 208, 210, 211, 258.

Frizingfeld, Anne, 136.
Fry, Elizabeth, 179.
Fryar, George, 122; Mark, 136; Mary, 152; Simon, 152, 240; Thomas, 109.
Fryerson, Margaret, 72, 180; Priscilla, 72, 180.
Fryre, Alice, 107.
Fuller, Elizabeth, 222, 227, 257; James, 215; Joane, 262; John, 99; Mary, 219; Mr., 122; Richard, 219; William, 99.
Fundling, Elizabeth, 106.
Fussell, Richard, 163.
Futerell, Francis, 227.
Futrell, Elizabeth, 122; Frances, 122.
Fynar, Margaret, 231; Roger, 231.
Fynimore, Francis, 248.
Fyrth, Ralph, 82.

G.

Gaith, Peter, 106; William, 222.
Galhampton, John, 90; Katherine, 90, 203; Mrs., 203.
Gall, Robert, 133; Thomas, 133.
Gallantley, James, 91.
Gallatle, Anne, 205; Henry, 205; Hester, 93; James, 93, 205.
Gallatley, Henry, 92; James, 92.
Galouwy, Thomas, 51.
Games, John, 261.
Ganne, Mrs., 110.
Garbrand, John, 102, 215; Margaret, 102; Mary, 104; Richard, 213; Tobias, 102, 215.
Gardiner, Robert, 212.
Gardner, Christopher, 15, 28; Edward, 214; Elizabeth, 112; Francis, 26; Jacob, 191; Jane, 178; Jeremy, 16, 198, 205; John, 182; Katherine, 238; Margaret, 240; Mr., 121, 139, 232; Richard, 26, 28; Robert, 18, 127, 178, 182, 250; Thomas, 14, 15, 16, 18, 127, 137, 143, 238.
Garfoote, Peter, 252.
Garford, Elizabeth, 93, 96; John, 94, 206; Mary, 93, 205; Walter, 93, 94, 96, 205, 206, 208.
Garner, Joane, 225.
Garnet, Jane, 237; Mathie, 234; Richard, 237; Sarah, 244; William, 234.
Garret, Elizabeth, 60; Joane, 223; Thomas, 60.
Garritt, Anne, 57; John, 58; Robert, 59; Thomas, 57, 58, 59.
Gates, Alice, 225; Elizabeth, 3, 4; Frances, 221; John, 4; Mary, 6.
Gatward, Anne, 84; Elizabeth, 68, 69, 71, 73, 76, 189, 199; Henry, 73, 181; John, 71; Thomas, 63, 69, 71, 73, 76, 84, 181, 189; William, 69.
Gathward, Thomas, 178, 180; William, 178.
Gatwood, Edward, 78; Marie, 193; Mr., 169; Thomas, 67, 78, 171, 174, 193.
Gaynesford, Mary, 76; Nicholas, 76; Thomas, 76.
Gee, Thomas, 230.
Genninges, John, 107; Lawrence, 27; Mibell, 27.
Genyens, Michael, 233; Thomas, 233.
Gentle, John, 212; Mary, 212.
George, Anne, 251, 256, 264.
Gerard, William, 107.
Gercy, John, 257.
Gest, Ellice, 168.
Gethin, Moris, 259; Rebecca, 263.
Gewen, Anne, 62; Christopher, 62, 64, 67; Elizabeth, 64; William, 67.
Geyst, Ellice, 61.
Gibbon, Robert, 111.
Gibbs, Ignatius, 205.
Gibson, Alice, 225; Elizabeth, 255; Margaret, 248.
Gibbynues, Joane, 3.
Giger, Anne, 107.
Gilbert, Anne, 200; Elizabeth, 251; William, 251.
Gillam, Thomas, 196.
Gillye, William, 260.
Gilman, Thomas, 196.
Gilmate, Elizabeth, 253.
Gilpin, Henry, 88, 198.
Githin, Sarah, 262.
Gittens, Davy, 125.
Gladdinge, Alice, 245; Rowland, 245.
Glascocke, Jane, 249.
Gleane, Dorothy, 257.
Gleene, John, 199.
Glouer, John, 120.
Glye, Henry, 215.
Glynn, John, 197, 205, 255; Martha, 205; Thomas, 197.
Goddard, Edward, 47, 50, 53, 152, 154, 158; Frances, 50, 152; Margaret, 47, 158; Marie, 53, 173; Richard, 173.
Godfrey, Elizabeth, 93; Thomas, 93.
Godfry, Mary, 97; Thomas, 97, 209.
Gofe, Lawrence, 18.
Goffe, Allen, 65; Anne, 7, 114; Edward, 11, 126; Elizabeth, 5, 12, 233, 234; Ellen, 223; Jane, 13; John, 65; Katherine, 6, 14; Lawrence, 6, 7, 11, 13, 14, 15, 16, 126, 140, 198, 199, 206, 224, 233, 234; Margaret, 15, 140; Mr., 126, 135, 139; Samuel, 14; Sarah, 199; Sibell, 121; Thomas, 111.
Gold, Agatha, 19, 128; Anne, 40; Christopher, 38; Edward, 132; Elizabeth, 41; Hugh, 19, 20, 21, 23, 30, 31, 32, 35, 37, 38, 40, 41, 47, 128, 132, 135, 141, 152, 230, 240; James, 47, 152, 200; Joane, 230; John, 20, 35, 132; Margaret, 132; Mary, 32; Mr., 146; Phebe, 21, 132; Richard, 20, 132; Robert, 37, 141; Thomas, 30, 135.
Golding, Edward, 261.
Goldinge, Anne, 165; Henry, 165.
Goldman, Mr., 263.
Goldstone, Alleyn, 111.
Goldwell, Thomas, 181.
Golefer, Anne, 192; Elizabeth, 86, 197; Henry, 87, 198; John, 88; Mary, 256; Rebecca, 88; Thomas, 89; Walter, 86, 87, 88, 89, 90, 192, 196, 197, 198.
Golifer, Joseph, 90; Rebecca, 260; Walter, 89, 90, 256.
Gollifer, James, 78; Walter, 78.
Golliver, Walter, 199.
Goner, William, 187.
Gonne, Alice, 225; Edward, 113, 117; Harry, 108; Susan, 112; Thomas, 6, 113.
Gooche, Ellen, 36; Robert, 36.
Goodale, Anne, 6, 8, 225; Denis, 3; Elizabeth, 225; Gyllian, 7, 231; James, 251; Joane, 6; Margaret, 7; Mary, 115; Robert, 7, 8, 114, 129, 231; Susan, 8, 129; Thomas, 109.
Goodlade, Richard, 250.
Goodwin, Edward, 154, 155, 156; Elizabeth, 254; Lettice, 44; Mr., 155; Richard, 44; Susan, 155, 189.
Goodwine, James, 57, 163; Jesper, 248; Margaret, 175; Peter, 166; Richard, 56, 57, 162, 163, 166, 170, 175, 181; Walter, 57, 163.
Goodwinne, Blaze, 5; Dionice, 7.
Goodwyn, George, 196; Peter, 48; Richard, 48.
Goodwynne, Elizabeth, 6.
Goollifer, Anne, 80; Walter, 80.
Gooune, Elizabeth, 223.
Goorley, Thomas, 223.
Gore, John, 92, 199, 204.
Gorley, Emme, 223; John, 112.
Gorom, Mary, 201; Mr., 201.
Gorum, John, 89; Mary, 89.
Goslyng, Alice, 227.
Gothridge, John, 238.
Gothwod, Thomas, 170.
Gouch, Ellen, 138; Robert, 138.
Gough, George, 11; John, 13, 116, 234; Martha, 10; Mathew, 115; Mr., 12, 115, 116; Ruth, 12; Samuel, 10, 118; Thomas, 10, 11, 13, 222.
Gould, Margaret, 23.
Gouldstones, —, 110.

INDEX OF NAMES. 277

Goulsonne, Anne, 122.
Gourley. Elizabeth, 114; Julian, 222; Katherine, 2.
Gowers, Jonathan, 194.
Gozhe, Thomas, 6.
Grace, George, 81; Hannah, 92; Hunt, 92; James, 46; Katherine, 29; Peter, 29; Richard, 46, 148.
Grady, Patrick, 256.
Graffam, Jesper, 135; John, 135.
Grane, Joane, 226.
Granger, Joane, 126; John, 186; Lady, 54; Simon, 126.
Grant, Margaret, 260; Samuel, 258.
Grassham, Robert, 119.
Gratrix, Isabel, 74; Joane, 74; William, 74.
Graue, Anne, 75, 76; Joseph, 75, 76, 187; Mary, 75; Paul, 76.
Grauener, Isabel, 166; Thomas, 166.
Graues, Amy, 72; Anne, 72, 73; Eleanor, 172; Elizabeth, 79, 243; Ellen, 62, 171; John, 258; Joseph, 61, 62, 63, 65, 70, 72, 73, 79, 161, 171, 172, 195; Margaret, 63, 170, 255; Sarah, 73; Susan, 61; William, 195.
Graunger, Joane, 20; John, 245; Katherine, 18; Simon, 18, 20.
Graunt, John, 193.
Graves, Francis, 77; Hannah, 85; John, 81; Joseph, 77, 81, 83, 85; Mr., 197; William, 83.
Gray, Edward, 263; Ellen, 192; John, 94, 95, 97, 98, 160, 259; Mr., 160; Rebecca. 94; Samuel, 9; Sarah, 95; Thomas, 97; William, 9, 160.
Graye, Alce, 248; John, 171; Mr., 212.
Greame, George, 234.
Grean, John, John, 27, 234.
Greane, Margaret, 223; Robert, 107.
Green, Anne, 129; Edward, 30; Elizabeth, 34, 227; Ellen, 226; Hugh, 125; John, 30, 34, 128, 150. 234; Katherine, 234; Margery, 243; Richard, 125; William, 116, 129, 152.
Greenbank, Alice, 257.
Greene, Edith, 255; John, 255; Margery, 253; Mary, 258.
Greenhalf, Francis, 58; Jane, 58.
Greenhall, Elizabeth, 56; Francis, 56.
Greenick, Sarah, 198.
Greenwood, Alice, 221.
Gregory, John, 231, 250.
Grey, Alexander, 91; Anne, 235; John, 133, 235; Joseph, 91; Margaret, 222.

Griffen, Marie, 94; Thomas, 94, 212.
Griffin, Elizabeth, 96, 211; John, 97, 210; Judith, 99; Mr., 190; Robert, 202; Thomas, 95, 96, 97, 99, 210, 211.
Griffine, Jonas, 93; Thomas, 92, 93, 204, 258.
Griffith, John, 154; Martha, 248; Parnell, 154.
Grifton, Robert, 262.
Grigg, Leonard, 257.
Grigge, Thomas, 206.
Grigges, Elizabeth, 223.
Griggs, John, 252.
Grigman, George, 104; Susan, 104.
Grimes, Christopher, 66; Mary, 66.
Grimmer, Joane, 251.
Grinnoway, Elizabeth, 257.
Griphin, Abraham. 43, 146; John, 41, 43, 47, 146, 147, 239; Morris, 142; Parnell, 41.
Grobbe, Robert, 109.
Groobbe, Mary, 112.
Groome, John, 238; Oliver, 148.
Groue, Anthony, 214; Edward, 107; Jane, 207; Joane, 107; Lettice, 2, 106; Robert, 1.
Grove, Elizabeth. 255; Robert, 79, 191; Elizabeth, 255.
Grover, William, 257.
Gryffen, Owen up Davy ap, 124.
Grymes, Christopher, 65; Joyce, 65; William, 226.
Gryphin, John, 142.
Guillefer, Mr., 194; Walter, 84.
Gulleuer, Anne, 83; William, 83.
Gullifer, Walter, 208.
Gunby, Anne, 111; Elizabeth, 22, 124, 127, 132; Ellen, 36; George, 15, 16, 20, 21, 22, 23, 25, 26, 28, 36, 40, 124, 127, 132, 142, 155, 156, 228, 230; Hugh, 40; James, 20; John, 15, 155; Margery, 16; Mary, 26, 142; Mr., 142; Percival, 28, 155; Richard, 21; Robert, 23; Susan, 40.
Gunne, Anne, 4; Charles, 110; Edward, 7, 222; John, 6, 8; Margaret, 7, 110; Sarah, 5; Susan, 5.
Gunner, Richard, 262.
Gunston, Frances, 133; Robert, 133, 138.
Gunstone, Alice, 138; Frances, 24; George, 27; Robert, 24, 26, 27; William, 26.
Gurley, William, 3.
Gurnett, William, 229.
Gutter, James, 200.
Gybbens, John, 109.
Gybbes, Elizabeth, 249.
Gybbiunes, Ellen, 2.
Gybbius, Daniel, 66; Katherine, 66.

Gybbon, Mr., 110.
Gybbyunes, Joane, 3.
Gybbyus. Joane, 223.
Gybson, Rowland, 228.
Gylberd, Geoffrey, 233; Harry, 233.
Gylder, John, 131.
Gyles, Anne, 4, 7, 110.
Gylman, William, 182.
Gylstone, Wynfred, 107.
Gyrling, John, 128; Robert, 128.
Gyttin, Hugh, 141.

H,

Hacket, John, 196; Mrs., 196.
Haddon, John, 125.
Hadley, Anne, 167; Jacob, 101, 218, 219; Jameris, 218; Joshua, 101, 218; Mary, 219; William, 219.
Hadly, Robert, 112.
Hafford, Katherine, 139.
Haggar, Anne, 72; Susan, 72; Thomas, 72.
Hagger, Anne. 73, 75; Henry, 76; Thomas, 73, 75, 76.
Haggitt, George, 215; William, 215.
Haiborn, Jane, 114.
Hailes, Anne, 15; James; 15; Nicholas, 21; Stephen, 21, 120, 124.
Haines, Constance, 2.
Haire, Jane, 120.
Haise, Grace, 118; Samuel, 118.
Hales, Elizabeth, 42, 146; George, 243; Stephen, 20; Thomas, 42, 146.
Halesbery, Alice, 222.
Hall, Andrew, 121; Anna, 80, 200; Charles, 101; Elizabeth, 70, 72, 86, 95; Ellen, 217; Emme, 88, 200; Francis, 70, 71, 180; George, 7; Grace, 92, 93, 96, 206; Hannah, 96; Jane, 72; Joane, 259; John, 92, 93, 95, 96. 97, 98, 99, 101; Martha. 93; Mary, 97; Mr., 167, 194, 217; Peter, 170; Peter Leden, 29; Robert, 88, 217, 230; Samuel, 87, 200; Susan, 77; Thomas, 7; Widow, 215; William, 77, 80, 82, 85, 86, 87, 88, 99, 193, 194. 200, 206.
Halle, Christopher, 227; Elizabeth, 226; Grace. 94; Roger, 106; William, 94.
Halliwell, Katherine, 2; Mary, 222; William, 2.
Hallward, Joane, 4.
Hallwood, Edward, 33; Elizabeth, 33.
Hallywell, Katherine, 224.
Halton, Elizabeth, 92; Robert, 92.

INDEX OF NAMES.

Hamlet, Judith, 6; Sarah, 181.
Hamlyn, Anne, 16; John, 16.
Hamden, Elizabeth, 238; Griphin, 238.
Hamendin, Hannah, 261.
Hammersly, Anne, 137; William, 137, 140.
Hammersley, William, 233.
Hammerslye, Mr., 239.
Hammon, Joane, 232; William, 207, 232.
Hammond, Anna, 86, 188; Katherine, 240; Stephen, 188; William, 86, 94.
Hamon, Jane, 213; John, 261; Judeth, 89; Mr., 94, 213; Sarah, 92; William, 89, 92, 94, 258.
Hamond, Benet, 91; Mr., 99; Samuel, 88, 199; William, 87, 88, 91, 199.
Hamor, George, 79; Susan, 79.
Hamore, Margaret, 231; Roger, 231.
Hampsonne, Alice, 6.
Hampton, Joane, 189; Ralph, 189.
Hanbury, Christopher, 200.
Hancocke, Joane, 249; John, 118, 138; Walter, 132.
Handson, Anne, 94; Katherine, 213; Mr., 213; Samuel, 90; Thomas, 90, 94, 201, 257; Ursula, 94.
Handsonn, Alice, 85; Thomas, 85.
Handsonne, Jane, 89; Thomas, 89.
Hannam, Richard, 12.
Hannis, Elbright, 179, 181, 184; Elizabeth, 170; Joane, 179; Margaret, 166; Mr., 173, 183; Richard, 166, 170; Robert, 177; Sarah, 177; Thomas, 173; Widow, 188.
Hannys, Christian, 198.
Hanscombe, Elizabeth, 7.
Hanson, Alice, 199; Anne, 92, 93, 94, 206; Benjamin, 90, 201; Edward, 94; Elizabeth, 88; Jane, 199, 203; John, 93; Mr., 93, 200, 203; Thomas, 88, 89, 90, 92, 93, 94, 95, 195, 199, 201, 203, 206.
Hansoun, Thomas, 83.
Happy, Ellen, 109.
Harbert, Elizabeth, 101; John, 101.
Harbut, John, 213; Mary, 213.
Hardcastle, Margaret, 57; Mr., 57; Richard, 57; William, 244.
Hardestoe, George, 85; Mr., 85, 194.
Harding, Elizabeth, 69, 72, 76, 201; Giles, 82, 84, 86, 87, 195; Hannah, 69; Hester, 66, 176; James, 72; John, 70, 79, 197, 258; Joshua, 90; Judith, 87; Margaret, 82;

Mathew, 66, 69, 70, 72, 76, 79, 82, 86, 90, 176, 201, 202, 257; Robert, 231; Sarah, 76, 86; William, 84, 231.
Hardinge, George, 199; Hannah, 172; Mathew, 172, 192; Nathan, 255.
Hardwin, Giles, 51; James, 46, 48, 51, 53, 148, 150, 154; Mr., 58; Susan, 46, 148; Thomas, 48, 150.
Hardwine, Anna, 64; James, 163; 165; Margery, 247; Mathew, 64.
Hare, Elizabeth, 141; John, 31, 141; Sarah, 31; Susan, 142; William, 258.
Harford, Sarah, 251.
Hargrave, Collatt, 253.
Harman, Dorothy, 197; John, 197.
Harley, Hester, 57; James, 57.
Harlow, Anne, 69; Elizabeth, 69, 175; James, 68, 69, 175; Joane, 110.
Harlowe, George, 58; James, 58.
Harman, Anne, 70; Elizabeth, 70, 71, 75; John, 70, 71, 75, 187, 193, 198; Margaret, 253; Mary, 75; William, 71.
Harmar, Elizabeth, 205; William, 205.
Harmer, Elizabeth, 92; William, 92.
Harper, Mary, 243.
Harries, Christian, 165.
Harriman, Edmond, 87; John, 87, 201; Sarah, 201.
Harris, Alice, 40, 228, 249; Ambrose, 119; Anne, 103, 182; Christian, 49, 190; David, 140; Elizabeth, 8, 117; George, 121, 238; Henry, 76, 184, 252; Hester, 12, 71, 72, 73; James, 73, 76, 181; Jane, 223; Joane, 238; John, 40, 43, 46, 49, 103, 150, 178; Lidia, 79; Margaret, 86; Margery, 46, 150; Mary, 83, 195; Nathaniel, 81.
Harris, Richard, 69, 71, 72, 73, 79, 81, 83, 86, 117, 181, 183, 195; Thomas, 255; William, 10.
Harrison, Anne, 250; Joane, 228; Mr., 110; Thomas, 253.
Harrisone, Winifred, 13.
Harman, Dorothy, 87; John, 87.
Harrood, Bridget, 95; Dudley, 95, John, 95.
Harl, Dorothy, 106.
Harte, Cicely, 163; Elizabeth, 250.
Hartridge, Anne, 33; Elizabeth, 32; George, 130, 143; John, 26, 130; Mary, 35; Thomas,

40; William, 26, 29, 32, 33, 35, 37, 40, 129, 132, 133, 144, 239.
Haruey, Frances, 51; Joane, 49; Margaret, 226; Simon, 49, 51.
Haruy, Alice, 120; James, 128.
Harver, Bridget, 213; Mr., 213.
Harvie, Andrew, 74; Anne, 74; Elizabeth, 251; Katherine, 74.
Harwood, Ellen, 129; Katherine, 107; Patrick, 129; Philip, 258; Richard, 213.
Haselbury, Goodman, 108.
Hasellwood, John, 130.
Haselwood, Emme, 251.
Haslam, Thomas, 263.
Hasler, Robert, 215.
Haslet, William, 238.
Hassald, Anne, 239; Eleanor, 32; Elizabeth, 16; Harry, 25; John, 16, 24; Joshua, 24; Luce, 26; Martha, 16, 30; Mr., 41, 42, 148, 151, 155, 239; Percival, 16, 18, 19, 20, 24, 25, 26, 28, 30, 32, 34, 151, 152; Richard, 239; Thomas, 16; Zachary, 19.
Hassall, Anne, 15, 123; Harry, 142; John, 15, 123, 131; Joshua, 142; Luce, 137; Mary, 230; Mr., 147; Percival, 15, 131, 137, 142; Thomas, 15.
Hassard, Peter, 203, 248.
Hassell, Edmund, 247.
Haswell, William, 251.
Hate, Robert, 263.
Hatford, Margaret, 240.
Hatherstoll, Thomas, 222.
Hatherstoole, Barbara, 4.
Hatly, Joane, 225.
Hatrill, Thomas, 87.
Hatte, John, 111.
Hatton, Abraham, 73; George, 69, 180; John, 66, 173; Joseph, 67, 179; Rebecca, 69, 73; Richard, 64; Roger, 64, 66, 67, 69, 71, 73, 173, 179, 180, 183, 187; Thomas, 183.
Hattrell, William, 230.
Haughton, Henry, 88; Thomas, 88, 253.
Haukenson, Margaret, 242.
Haukes, Elizabeth, 38; Henry, 35; John, 21, 24, 27, 31, 35, 38, 127; Thomas, 21, 24, 127; William, 31.
Haukyns, Joane, 227; Walter, 227.
Haule, John, 223; Margaret, 244; Mr., 204; Peter, 158, 241.
Haull, Alice, 224; Elizabeth, 240; Isabel, 8; John, 224; Margaret, 227; Robert, 228.
Hause, Mabel, 226.
Haward, Lankister, 213.
Hawes, Elizabeth, 156.

INDEX OF NAMES. 279

Hawkeridge, Nathaniel, 88; William, 88.
Hawkes, Thomas, 193.
Hawkins, William, 250.
Hawward, John, 110.
Haxsbee, Robert, 168.
Hay, Jane de, 154; John, 244.
Hayden, Anne, 257.
Hayes, Alice, 245; Anne, 15; Edward, 133, 226; Isabel, 14; John, 14; Lady, 54; Lawrence, 249; Luke, 12; Mary, 12; Ralph, 245; Richard, 11; Robert, 256; Samuel, 10; Winifred, 133.
Hayese, John, 238.
Hayle, Alice, 251.
Hayles, Richard, 16; Stephen, 16; Thomas, 223.
Hayleward, Joane, 110.
Haynes, Harman, 185.
Hayse, Joane, 14; Martha, 263; Richard, 13, 118; Stephen, 14; Thomas, 110.
Hayward, Frances, 251; Hugh, 135; Joane, 5; Katherine, 107; Luce, 114; Rooke, 135.
Hazards, Mr., 194; Mrs., 195.
Hazeler, Anne, 238; Ralph, 238.
Hazelfoote, Thomas, 35; William, 35, 258.
Healinge, Zachary, 180.
Health, Foulke, 225.
Heard, John, 135; Timothy, 135.
Hearon, Robert, 164.
Hease, Goodman, 120.
Heath, Anne, 2; Francis, 133; Fulke, 131, 153, 235; Jeffery, 259; Mary, 2; Mr., 16, 131; Mrs., 235.
Heathe, John, 260.
Heather, Jane, 69; John, 69, 262.
Heelay, Mary, 9; Zachary, 9.
Heclin, Elizabeth, 242; Peter, 152.
Heeling, John, 49; Peter, 49.
Heely, Henry, 10.
Heelys, Thomas, 111.
Heiborn, George, 114.
Heighmore, Nicholas, 253.
Heiwood, Richard, 115.
Heling, Tabitha, 240.
Hellmes, Edward, 61; Margaret, 61.
Helm, Edward, 202; Margery, 202.
Helme, Anne, 69, 177; Charles, 212; Edward, 67, 69, 70, 71, 175, 177, 210, 211; Gawen, 191; Hest, 212; John, 67, 175; Katherine, 191; Margery, 69, 70, 71; Mr., 212; Stephen, 201; Thomas, 212; William, 70.
Helmes, Abraham, 59, 167; Edward, 59, 60, 63, 65, 66, 167; Katherine, 63; Mr., 167, 168; Thomas, 65.

Helye, Richard, 8.
Helyn, Anne, 107.
Hemmings, Mr., 195.
Henley, George, 82, 87, 198; John, 82; Mary, 198; Samuel, 87.
Henlie, Dorothy, 83; George, 83, 254.
Henly, Daniel, 90; Elizabeth, 255; George, 90, 200.
Henlye, George, 88; Joseph, 88.
Hennag, Alice, 197; Thomas, 197.
Henricke, Audrian, 177.
Hensonne, Harry, 121.
Heppy, John, 230.
Hepworth, Adam, 2; George, 116; John, 2; Robert, 2; Thomas, 105; William, 1, 105, 106.
Herbert, Elizabeth, 103; John, 103.
Herby, Edward, 54; Katherine, 54.
Hercocke, Anne, 116.
Herd, Susan, 6.
Herman, Oliver, 221.
Hern, Anthony, 13.
Herrin, Constance, 257.
Heskey, Alice, 245.
Hester, William, 264.
Heton, Thomas, 45, 148; William, 45, 148.
Hewat, William, 224.
Hewes, Richard, 249, 253.
Hewet, Ellen, 142.
Hewgen, John, 16.
Hewgle, John, 228.
Hewson, Richard, 235.
Heyes, John, 117; Lawrence, 116.
Heyley, Elizabeth, 185.
Heyman, Joane, 249.
Heyton, Roger, 110.
Heyward, Elizabeth, 257; Hugh, 135; Vincent, 222.
Heywood, Anne, 115; John, 116; Luce, 8; Richard, 10; Vincent, 117; Widow, 118.
Hichooke, Thomas, 213.
Hickes, Dorcas, 205; John, 205.
Hickback, Edward, 98; Thomas, 98.
Hickman, Anne, 55; Ellen, 57, 171; Joseph, 55, 57, 158, 167, 171; Sarah, 158.
Hickmore, William, 227.
Hickmot, Edward, 28; Francis, 28.
Hickocke, Edward, 218; Elizabeth, 103, 218; Margaret, 101, 103, 218; Richard, 101, 215; Thomas, 101, 103, 215, 218.
Hickockes, Thomas, 96.
Hicks, William, 256.
Hide, Ellen, 224.
Hieron, John, 197.

Hiet, Elizabeth, 99; Robert, 99; Sarah, 99.
Higgenbotham, Elizabeth, 86; Thomas, 86.
Higgines, Alice, 166.
Higgins, Edward, 219; Elizabeth, 87; Henry, 219; John, 88; Martin, 85, 86, 87, 88, 195; Mary, 206; Mr., 87; Nathaniel, 219; Robert, 85.
Hill, Alice, 13, 129, 203; Anne, 6, 121; Barbara, 222; Daniel, 252; Edward, 10; Elizabeth, 199, 229, 230, 231; Ellen, 197; Flora, 87; George, 115; Grace, 129; James, 130, 227; John, 10, 14, 44, 61, 115, 121, 124, 129, 130, 210, 231; Lucretia, 250; Mary, 124; Mr., 65, 170, 172; Nicholas, 60, 61, 63, 65, 171, 172; Richard, 88, 94; Robert, 65, 172; Susan, 14; Thomas, 87, 88, 196, 209, 210, 251; Ursula, 7; William, 60, 198.
Hillarsdin, Amy, 93; Penelope, 93; William, 93.
Hille, William, 213.
Hillersden, Amy, 95; Frances, 95; Mr., 208; William, 95, 208.
Hilles, Grace, 12; John, 7, 9, 147; Margaret, 234; Thomas, 1, 234.
Hilliard, Anne, 92; Thomas, 92.
Hilman, Deionis, 256.
Hilton, Lady Anne, 224; Robert, 184.
Hind, Thomas, 195.
Hinde, Alce, 249; George, 183; Humiliation, 253; Isaac, 173; John, 118; Mr., 186; Richard, 187; Thomas, 61, 62, 170, 171, 178, 187, 247; William, 61, 170.
Hine, William, 135.
Hinton, Anne, 115; Benjamin, 91, 258; Elizabeth, 93; John, 90; Mary, 100, 213; Robert, 226; Samuel, 213; William, 90, 91, 93, 100, 211, 213, 261.
Hippe, Elizabeth, 18; John, 18.
Hippey, John, 20, 21, 128; Rebecca, 21; William, 20, 128.
Hiron, John, 87, 202; Mr., 196.
Hisfeld, Anne, 139; Giles, 139.
Hisfelde, —, 142.
Hitchcock, Elizabeth, 255.
Hitchcocke, Thomas, 192.
Hitchcok, William, 256.
Hix, Dorcas, 92; John, 92.
Hixe, Richard, 120.
Hobson, Joane, 230.
Hodge, Agnes, 2; Alice, 118; Alexander, 261; Anne, 223; Edward, 113; Harry, 7, 112; Isabel, 111; James, 5, 32, 136, 137; Joane, 110; John, 2; Joseph, 217; Mr., 112,

INDEX OF NAMES.

113, 115, 116, 173; Nicholas, 2; Richard, 2, 3, 4, 5, 7; Rowland, 4, 113; Sarah, 3, 227; Susan, 113; Thomas, 217; Timothy, 4; William, 115; Winifred, 226.
Hodges, Dean, 102, 263; Thomas, 254.
Hodgeson, Elizabeth, 69, 70, 71, 72, 74; Francis, 69, 176; John, 34, 72; Margaret, 68; Peter, 34, 138; Robert, 71, 72; William, 35, 68, 69, 70, 74, 176, 250.
Hodgesonne, Anne, 36; Edward, 223; Elizabeth, 32; Francis, 30; Peter, 32, 36; William, 30.
Hodgson, Margaret, 135; William, 135.
Hodgsonne, Peter, 236; William, 236.
Hodson, William, 228.
Holden, Anne, 103. 216; Nicholas, 154; Richard, 103; William, 216.
Holdsworth, Frances, 55; Henry, 20, 25, 27, 30, 33, 35, 39, 149, 152, 153, 158, 243; John, 30, 144; Jonas, 33, 158; Katherine, 246; Margaret, 35; Mary, 20; Mr., 159; Richard, 158; Susan, 24; Thomas, 39, 55, 56, 149, 161, 162, 164; William, 149.
Hole, John, 6.
Holland, Anne, 102, 128, 230; Benjamin, 37; Elizabeth, 247; John, 102, 128; Lucy, 201; Richard, 221; Thomas, 178, 201; William, 2, 3.
Holle, Roger, 223.
Holliday, Mr., 81.
Hollifeeld, John, 113.
Hollingburie, Mathew, 246.
Hollingworth, Richard, 264.
Hollinsworth, Thomas, 264.
Hollis, Katherine, 1.
Holliwell, Elizabeth, 136; Joane, 3; Thomas, 1; William, 1.
Hollser, Susan, 213.
Hollys, Katherine, 2.
Hollywell, John, 127, 136.
Holman, George, 233; Richard, 233.
Holmes, Dorothy, 184; James, 68, 184; Jane, 72, 184; John, 168, 182, 202; Margaret, 89; Mary, 68, 72; Mr., 169, 188, 189, 198; Richard, 68, 72, 184, 244; Susan, 259; Thomas, 243; Ursula, 185; Widow, 185; William, 89, 184, 202, 257.
Holond, William, 218.
Holsworth, Alice, 18; Diana, 23; Elizabeth, 17, 153; Henry, 17, 18, 21, 23, 24, 144, 149; Margaret, 21.

Holton, Elizabeth, 202; John, 205; Mr., 206.
Homes, Mr., 194; Robert, 202, 205, 206.
Hoog, William, 223.
Hooke, Marie, 81; Roger, 81, 191.
Hooker, Joane, 222; Nicholas, 252; William, 241.
Hope, Alice, 227; Ann, 214; John, 214.
Hopkins, Elizabeth, 192; Ezekiel, 262; Richard, 101; Samuel, 102; Sarah, 100, 101, 102, 214; William, 99, 100, 101, 102, 168, 192, 214, 215, 245.
Hopkinson, Ephraim, 249.
Hopkynnes, John, 121.
Hord, Mr., 193.
Horne, Frances, 256; Susan, 195; William, 181, 186.
Hornebuckle, Anne, 84; William, 84.
Horsey, Alice, 222; Elizabeth, 2; Emme, 106; Jerome, 238; William, 238.
Horsley, Katherine, 107; Robert, 109; Thomas, 222.
Horson, Emma, 1; Robert, 1.
Horton, Frances, 223; John, 106, 109, 221.
Horwood, Christopher, 2.
Hosseziar, Cicely, 6.
Houghton, Dorothy, 91; Elizabeth, 222; John, 91; Mary, 123; Robert, 91.
Houldsworth, Anne, 31; Henry, 28, 31; Katherine, 27; Susan, 28.
Houlsworth, Richard, 25; William, 25.
Hoult, —, 225; Anne, 106; James, 227.
Housman, John, 228.
Houster, Richard, 107.
How, Percival, 197; Sarah, 218.
Howard, Susan, 218.
Howe, Harry, 226.
Howell, Eleanor, 253; John, 231.
Hower, Sarah, 258.
Howse, Margery, 230.
Hubbard, Andrew, 210.
Hubberd, John, 38, 135; Richard, 38, 135.
Hubberstead, George, 171; Richard, 249.
Hubbersted, Alice, 22; Edward, 24; Elizabeth, 23; George, 20, 22, 24, 26, 141, 231; John, 26; Katherine, 197; Richard, 141; Robert, 20, 23, 232; Thomas, 232; Widow, 184.
Hubberstee, Richard, 246.
Hubbersteed, —, 68; George, 141.
Hubbersteid, Alice, 65; George, 65.

Hubberthorn, Christopher, 237; Lancelot, 237.
Hubblethorn, Anne, 111; Sir Henry, 111, 222; Lady, 110.
Huberd, Andrew, 261.
Hucheson, Mr., 207.
Huchins, Anne, 66; Luke, 66; Thomas, 66.
Huchinson, Jarvice, 64, 171, 248; Stephen, 64, 171.
Huckle, Joane, 239.
Huckslie, Toby, 3.
Huddleston, William, 241.
Hudds, Katherine, 256.
Huddson, George, 50; Thomas, 50.
Hudnoll, John, 89, 199; Martin, 89.
Hudson, Alice, 131; Anne, 79; Benjamin, 86; Blanche, 212; Daniel, 81; Elizabeth, 86, 94, 153, 206, 211, 214; George, 37, 50, 58, 59, 74, 143, 145, 182; Hannah, 209; Hester, 258; Jane, 39; John, 78, 93; Katherine, 182; Margaret, 191; Mary, 91, 96, 145, 208, 213, 250, 251; Mr., 89, 91; Robert, 91, 93, 94, 95, 96, 208, 209, 214, 252; Captain Robert, 212, 213; Sarah, 95, 214; Susan, 37, 143; Thomas, 50, 59, 212; William, 39, 78, 79, 81, 86, 90, 131, 146, 153, 191, 201, 206, 212.
Hudsonn, Robert, 195; William, 85.
Hudsonne, Anne, 53; George, 41, 53, 160; Joane, 3; John, 223; Katherine, 37, 221; Mary, 41, 43, 58; Robert, 40, 237; Thomas, 160; William, 37, 43, 237.
Huet, Elizabeth, 140; Mr., 140.
Huggins, Anne, 59; Elizabeth, 59, 168, 261.
Hughes, James, 255.
Hughson, Katherine, 153.
Hulce, Thomas, 75, 78, 184.
Humpden, Elizabeth, 88; Henry, 88.
Humphrey, Richard, 112.
Humstone, Francis, 161.
Hungerford, John, 258.
Hunsden, John, 263.
Hunt, Elizabeth, 206; Joane, 223, 232; John, 20, 126; Mr., 253; Robert, 20, 126.
Hunte, John, 118.
Hunter, Anne, 40, 136, 146, 155; Edward, 27, 29, 30, 31, 33, 36, 39, 40, 51, 56, 58, 132, 139, 146, 153, 155, 157, 161, 167; Elizabeth, 10, 36, 39, 56, 115, 139, 153; Fulke, 11; Grace, 58; John, 20; Margery, 247; Mary, 58; Mr., 142; Richard, 30; Robert, 20, 27, 117, 157, 225; Susan, 29; Thomas, 136; William, 33.

INDEX OF NAMES. 281

Hupton, George, 1 ; Thomas, 1.
Hurlestone, Humphry, 229.
Hurst, Rowland, 122.
Hurt, Henry, 86, 201 ; John, 86 ; Mr., 189, 196 ; Samuel, 192.
Husbands, Elizabeth, 205; Mr., 204, 205 ; Mrs., 207 ; Rebecca, 93 ; Richard, 93, 207.
Hussey, George, 238 ; John, 238.
Hutchenson, Christopher, 238 ; Cuthbert, 157.
Hutchinson, Jarvis, 190 ; Mary, 262 ; Mr., 207 ; Mrs., 210 ; Thomas, 210, 216, 255.
Hutsonne, William, 4.
Hutt or Hutte, Mr., 214 ; Susan, 214.
Hutton, Harry, 118 ; John, 107.
Huxley, Hercules, 2.
Hyatt, James, 94, 96, 206, 209 ; Robert, 94, 96, 206, 209.
Hyckmote, Elizabeth, 124.
Hyde, John, 111 ; William, 221.
Hyet, Elizabeth, 95, 97, 212 ; Mary, 95 ; Robert, 95, 97, 212, 213 ; Sarah, 212.
Hylles, Anne, 8.
Hynde, Jane, 200 ; Joane, 227.
Hyne, Margery, 31, 135 ; William, 31.
Hynton, Anne, 259 ; George, 106 ; Griffet, 109 ; Philip, 97 ; Richard, 98 ; Samuel, 94, 97 ; William, 94, 98, 99, 109.
Hyntonne, Griphet, 107 ; Jane, 222.
Hyron, Elizabeth, 200 ; John, 200 ; Robert, 257.

I.

Idle, Anne, 109 ; Edward, 4 ; Ellen, 2 ; Emma, 1, 105 ; George, 1 ; Margery, 106 ; Robert, 109.
Iken, Susan, 246.
Ibrain, Anne, 117.
Ilbraine, Elizabeth, 11; Katherine, 117.
Ingall, Elizabeth, 208; Nathan, 100, 213 ; Richard, 216; William, 99, 100, 208, 213, 216.
Ingerham, Thomas, 174.
Inggould, Jane, 225.
Ingham, Mary, 173 ; Thomas, 173.
Ingland, Roger, 257.
Inglott, Elizabeth, 94 ; William, 94.
Ingoll, Margaret, 97, 217 ; Richard, 101 ; William, 97, 101, 217, 218.
Ingram, Anne, 87 ; Marie, 87 ; Robert, 87.
Inman, Anne, 10 ; James, 136 ; Joane, 136 ; John, 10, 12, 116,
119, 131 ; Katherine, 144 ; Margaret, 116.
Innocent, Edward, 105.
Ireland, Elizabeth, 101 ; John, 101, 103, 220 ; Mary, 103, 220 ; Thomas, 131.
Irish, John, 109.
Isaackson, Margaret, 89 ; Randolph, 89.
Isacke, James, 231.
Isby, Arthur, 190.
Isharwood, Alice, 226 ; James, 118 ; Margaret, 115.
Isherwood, James, 11 ; Thomas, 10.
Itchin, Anne, 225.
Ive, Robert, 223.
Izard, Thomas, 198.

J.

Jackman, Arthur, 237 ; John, 237.
Jackson, Christopher, 233; Ellen, 221 ; Frances, 226 ; Isabel, 249 ; Joane, 113 ; John, 222, 251 ; Margery, 230 ; Samuel, 158 ; Susan, 116 ; Thomas, 118 ; William, 112.
Jacksone, Abraham, 214.
Jacksoune, Anne, 120 ; Lewce, 8 ; Margery, 2.
Jacob, Anne, 116 ; Mr., 116 ; Rose, 140.
Jacobson, Abraham, 147 ; Mr., 155 ; Peter, 147, 154 ; Sarah, 147.
Jacobsonne, Peter, 45, 165 ; Sarah, 45, 165.
Jakes, Anne, 87 ; Thomas, 87.
Jales, —, 108.
James, Andrew, 87 ; Anna, 89 ; Elizabeth, 80. 91, 193 ; Ellen, 1 ; Joane, 216 ; John, 1, 80, 83, 86, 87, 88, 89, 91, 93, 193, 194, 205 ; Joseph, 216 ; Mr., 210, 214 ; Peter, 88 ; Sarah, 93, 205 ; Thomas, 86.
Jance, Edmund, 3 ; Emme, 2 ; Joane, 120 ; John, 107, 120 ; Katherine, 8, 111 ; Mr., 120 ; Robert, 2, 123.
Janc, Joseph de, 111.
Janes, John, 7, 156 ; Robert, 223.
Janusonne, William, 162.
Jans, Anne, 230 ; Gabella, 1 ; Harry, 2 ; John, 3, 10 ; Philip, 5 ; Robert, 1, 231.
Janson, John, 166 ; Katherine, 59 ; Mary, 250 ; Mr., 172, 174 ; William, 59, 166.
Jansonne, John, 57 ; William, 57.
Jarman, Ellen, 223.
Jarmice, Paul, 176.
Jarratt, Robert, 229.
Jaruis, Margery, 3.
Jarvis, Widow, 210.

Jaunce, William, 7.
Jeames, John, 29, 78, 90 ; Mathew, 90 ; Samuel, 90.
Jefferisse, Philip, 94 ; Thomas, 94.
Jefferson, Harry, 121.
Jeffry, Thomas, 257.
Jelley, Thomas, 183.
Jeninges, Joseph, 95 ; Robert, 169, 173 ; Sarah, 181 ; Thomas, 94, 95.
Jenings, John, 208 ; Joseph, 209 ; Thomas, 208, 209, 211.
Jennettes, James, 63, 65, 68, 171 ; Martha, 65, 174 ; Peter, 68 ; Robert, 63, 171.
Jenninges, Elizabeth, 229.
Jennings, Charles, 98 ; Marie, 57 ; Robert, 55, 57 ; Samuel, 96 ; Sarah, 55 ; Thomas, 96, 98.
Jenntts, James, 61.
Jennynges, James, 121.
Jenoure, Henry, 58 ; John, 58.
Jentyll, Mathew, 7.
Jeronimus, Barnard, 227.
Jesper, Anne, 222.
Joanes, Davy, 124 ; Hugh, 258 ; John, 24 ; Mary, 29 ; Thomas, 24, 29, 122.
Joelen, John, 16 ; William, 16.
Johnson, Alice, 221 ; Elizabeth, 87 ; Ellen, 115 ; Jeffery, 250; John, 78 ; Margery, 114 ; Mary, 64 ; Mrs., 182, 190 ; Richard, 87 ; Rowland, 118 ; Susan, 249 ; Thomas, 80 ; William, 64, 259.
Johnsone, Richard, 214.
Johnsonne, William, 245.
Jones, Alice, 161, 188 ; Doggon, 125 ; Dorothy, 259 ; Edward, 35 ; Elizabeth, 233 ; Evan, 125 ; Gillian, 30 ; Gregory, 22, 131 ; Isaac, 84, 86 ; James, 179 ; Jane, 228 ; Joane, 234 ; John, 225, 233 ; Katherine, 132 ; Margaret, 86 ; Mary, 63, 172 ; Mathew, 166 ; Maudelin, 68, 72 ; Mr., 59, 60, 164, 165, 167, 244 ; Morgan, 147 ; Nicholas, 28 ; Oliver, 236 ; Peter, 178 ; Rice, 226 ; Richard, 172, 255 ; Robert, 35, 164 ; Roger, 236 ; Rowland, 161 ; Thomas, 20, 22, 25, 26, 28, 30, 34, 35, 128, 131, 132, 134, 137, 155, 167, 188, 192, 197, 234 ; Thomazine, 244 ; Ursula, 34, 137 ; Widow, 210 ; William, 35, 63, 67, 68, 72. 173, 174, 175, 178, 179, 181, 192, 238, 242.
Jonson, Anthony, 5, 111 ; Daniel, 155 ; Elizabeth, 223, 228, 233 ; Harry, 234 ; John, 105, 120, 224 ; Katherine, 6 ; Richard, 112 ; Rowland, 238 ; Sibell, 224.

2 o

INDEX OF NAMES.

Jonsonne, Elizabeth, 221, 236, 237; Ellen, 7; John, 105; Margaret. 221; Richard, 222; Robert, 107, 237; Thomas, 236.
Jordain, Edward, 11; Grace, 14; John, 12; Mary. 13; Robert, 12, 13, 14; Sarah, 13.
Jordaine, Henry.101; James.230;
Jordan, Abraham, 24; Alice, 153; Dorothy, 122; Elizabeth, 94, 206; Henry, 12, 94, 103, 206; James, 24, 125, 153; Mary, 133, 206; Robert, 12, 133, 135; Sarah, 103.
Jordane, Anne. 14; James, 18, 126, 128. 243; Joane, 115; Meg. 45; Mrs., 37; Robert, 14, 223; Susan, 18, 125; Thomas, 228; Widow, 152.
Jorden, Alice, 96, 97, 100, 102; Anne, 12; Elizabeth, 96, 97, 209; Fulke, 11; Henry, 94, 96, 97, 98, 100. 102, 209; Mary, 94, 102; Richard, 226; Robert, 11; —— 254.
Jordin, Henry, 213; Mr., 213.
Jud, John, 14; Ursula. 14.
Judd, Joane, 257.
Judde, Anne, 108; George, 109; John, 113.
Judge, Joane, 14; Mary, 8; William. 14.
Judson. Bridget, 123; John, 122, 123.
Judsoune, Richard, 221.
Juet, Richard, 221.
Juggle, Elizabeth. 138; John, 138.
Julian, Robert, 258.
Jurdaine, Alice. 162.
Jurdan, James, 164; Margery, 164.
Jurden, Thomas, 232.

K.

Kamyman, Margaret, 106.
Katch, Constance, 198; John, 89; Mr., 89.
Keble, Anne, 223.
Keech, Judith, 198.
Keele, Anne, 257.
Keely, Martha, 116; Sarah, 117.
Keene, Mary, 256.
Keford, Nicholas, 239.
Kelby, Thomas, 222.
Keling. John, 110; Sarah, 5.
Kellet, John, 17; Rebecca, 17.
Kelley, James, 15; John, 15.
Kelly, Anne, 123; Elizabeth, 149; John, 123, 124; Margaret. 250; Peter, 8; Robert, 48, 123, 149; Sarah, 48; Susan, 124.
Kellyn, John, 222.
Kelsall, Hugh, 1.

Kelsam, Winifred, 2.
Kelsye. Anne, 2; John, 2.
Keltridge, William, 222.
Kember, Christopher, 102; Constance, 102.
Kemble, Anne, 104; Richard, 104; Thomas, 104.
Kempe, George, 90; Nicholas, 248, 249, 251; Roger, 249; Rose, 90.
Kempston, Anne, 245.
Kempton, Anne, 158.
Kendall, Jacob, 1; James. 106; Jane, 1; Robert, 117; Thomas, 185.
Kendricke, David, 242; Mary, 259.
Kenneston, Mrs., 60.
Kenniston, Alice, 177; Dorothy, 244; Susan, 169.
Kenricke, John, 189; Richard, 263.
Kente, Henry, 252.
Kenuan, Jane, 233; William, 233.
Kerbee, Anne, 161.
Kersey, Richard, 222.
Kesar, Thomas, 256.
Kettle. Mr., 55; Sarah, 244.
Key, Edward, 258; Samuel, 189; Thomas, 244.
Keyes, Peter, 56.
Keyling, Anne, 222.
Kibby, Edward, 223.
Kidwell, Alice, 243.
Killingworth, Alice, 236; Richard, 236.
Kinesman, John, 98; Richard, 98; Sarah, 98.
King, Alexander, 212; Alice, 228, 231; Anne, 244. 256; Betteris, 233; Elizabeth. 53; Elphin, 11; John, 55. 233; Judith, 20, 22. 127; Katherine, 231; Margaret, 197; Mary, 218; Mr., 215; Richard, 20, 22, 127; Samuel, 218; Thomas, 10.
Kinge, Anne, 56, 163; James. 98; John, 56, 57, 163, 167, 172, 178; Katherine, 249; Marie, 246; Martha, 257; Mr., 165, 244; Samuel, 98; Thomas, 57, 253.
Kingnam, Peter, 222.
Kingsman, Mr., 197, 200; Richard, 87, 88, 89, 199; Sarah, 88; William, 89.
Kingsmeale, Richard. 229.
Kingston, Thomas, 255.
Kinnistone. Susan, 164.
Kinnston, Mrs., 56.
Kinshman, Richard, 260.
Kinsman, Jane, 94. 206; Jesper, 96, 209; Martha. 90; Mary, 90, 112; Richard, 90, 91, 94, 96, 206, 209, 210, 212, 215.
Kinson. William, 156.
Kirby, Joshua, 257.

Kirke, John, 1; Margaret, 1; Thomas. 2.
Kirkman, George, 252.
Kirton, Jane, 235; Thomas, 235.
Kitche. John, 200.
Kitchen, Abel, 222; John, 209.
Kittle, Edward, 163.
Knight, Edward, 112; Hannah, 10; Jane, 13; Joane, 6, 15, 120; John, 6, 15, 226; Mary, 6, 15, 122; Robert, 12; Roger, 227; Sarah, 101; William. 101, 154.
Knipe, John, 227.
Knowelles, Lord William, 55.
Knowleman, Wilmore, 172.
Knowles, Ciprian, 132; Robert, 132.
Kyllimbecke. Christopher, 250.
Kynaston. Thomas, 22.
Kyndall, Robert, 173.
Kynnaston, Anne, 28; Dorothy, 31; Elizabeth, 127; Ellen, 129; Francis, 29; John, 127; Katherine, 32; Margaret, 38; Owen, 23; Thomas, 23, 26, 28, 29. 31, 32, 38, 137, 151, 232, 239; William, 26, 129.
Kyndall, Thomas, 249.
Kynsman, John. 119.
Kyrke, Anne, 239; Mabel, 5; Margaret, 105, 223; Richard, 221; Thomas, 7.

L.

Laborne. John, 248.
Lacock, Dorothy, 102; Thomas, 102.
Lacocke, Benjamin, 217; Elizabeth, 218; Hannah, 215; Henry, 217; Samuel, 218; Thomas, 215, 217, 219.
Ladbrooke. Anne, 120.
Laister, William, 106.
Lake, Abigail, 91; John, 91; Thomas, 91; William, 252.
Lalache. Joane, 107.
Lambart, Francis, 181.
Lambe, Adam, 11, 120, 122; Alice, 13, 120; Anne, 226, 229; Barnard, 134, 137; Christopher, 10, 116; Emme, 5, 111, 235; Jane, 9, 107; John, 4, 6, 8, 105, 115, 118, 178, 222, 230, 235; Mary, 11; Maudelyn, 137; Paul, 8; Richard, 10, 11, 224; Susan, 8; Thomas, 6, 181, 229; William, 10, 12, 115.
Lamberd, Anne, 233; Francis, 231, 233, 237; Joane, 126, 237; Johu, 224; Mr., 126.
Lambright, Godfry, 232.
Lamebt, Benjamin, 60; John, 60.
Lamerson. Richard, 114.
Lamyman, Maye, 106.

INDEX OF NAMES. 283

Lancaster, Elizabeth, 60 ; Thomas, 260.
Land, Susan, 258.
Lane, Elizabeth, 242 ; John, 219 ; Thomas, 219.
Langdone. Thurstone, 107.
Langam, Anne, 220 ; William, 220.
Langeley, James, 95; John, 95.
Langhlie, Mr., 247.
Langley, Ambrose, 255 ; Anne, 59, 191. 195 ; John, 59, 66, 70, 77, 88, 89, 90, 173, 191, 198, 200. 201, 209, 249, 256 ; Martha, 70, 90, 198, 201 ; Mr., 197; Philip, 77; Richard, 88.
Langlie, Andrew, 74 ; Elizabeth. 63 ; John, 63, 65, 68, 74; Judith, 65 ; Richard, 68.
Laugly, Jane, 205 ; John, 61, 205 ; Thomas, 228.
Langlye, Andrew, 212; John, 212.
Launglee, Androwe, 163.
Lapley, John, 179.
Larkin, Mathew, 260.
Lasselles. Margaret, 108.
Latheman, William. 111.
Launglee, Grisogo, 57 ; John, 57 ; Mr.. 58.
Laurence, Thomas. 161.
Lauson, Richard, 97 ; William. 97.
Lawdry, Elizabeth. 109.
Lawe, John, 238 ; Richard, 238.
Lawes, Katherine, 2 ; William, 223.
Lawin, Elizabeth. 261.
Lawrance, Christian, 234 ; James, 143 ; Joane, 143 ; Richard, 234.
Lawraunce, Thomas, 224.
Lawrence, Affera, 230 ; Dorothy, 178 ; Judith, 117 ; Richard, 110 ; William, 174.
Lawse, Elizabeth, 2 ; Harry. 114 ; Joane, 110 ; John, 3, 57 ; Katherine, 223 ; Ralph. 4, 114 ; William, 111, 118.
Lawson, Benjamin, 99, 218 ; Joseph, 93, 219; Marcy, 219 ; Margaret, 100, 219 ; Margery, 92 ; Martha, 96 ; Mary, 91, 251 ; Mathew, 96, 209 ; Mr., 211, 218 ; Richard, 219 ; Thomas, 239; William, 91, 92, 93, 96, 99, 100, 209, 219.
Laxtonne, Anne. 221.
Laycock. Dorothy, 253.
Laye, Elizabeth, 228 ; Richard, 255.
Layfield, Edmond, 256.
Layland, Thomas, 245.
Laysee, William, 118.
Layton, Margaret, 257.
Lea, Francis, 58 ; Joane, 262.
Leacocke, Benjamin, 91, 204 ; Elizabeth, 92; Hannah, 100 ; Mary, 211 ; Mr., 98, 100, 211, 212 ; Thomas, 91, 92, 96, 100, 204.

Leacrofte, Mary, 248.
Leadall, Richard. 165.
Leake, Arthur, 41, 42 ; John, 42, 166 ; Mr., 210 ; Rowland. 248; Thomas. 210, 216.
Leame, Anne, 114 ; Christopher, 9 ; John, 221 ; Robert, 10 ; Thomas. 115, 224.
Leanord. Frances, 211 ; Francis, 99 ; Mr., 99. 211.
Leapine, William, 256.
Leatherborow, Edward, 241.
Leave, John. 196.
Lecock, Benjamin. 93; Dorothy, 97 ; Mr., 96, 206 ; Thomas, 93, 97.
Lecocke, Mary, 98 ; Samuel, 95 ; Thomas, 95, 98.
Lecraft, Samson, 151.
Lecrafte, Mr., 141.
Lecroft, Anne, 158, 224 ; Ellen, 46, 160 ; Katherine. 54 ; Margaret, 116 ; Margery, 30, 230 ; Mary. 34, 37 ; Mathew, 143 ; Mr.. 38, 150, 151. 156 ; Richard. 40. 48, 156 : Robert, 18, 36, 124, 230 ; Samson, 46, 48, 50, 52, 54, 151, 156, 158. 160; Sarah, 50, 151 ; Thomas. 234; William, 30, 31, 34, 36, 37, 40, 52, 143. 148, 234.
Lee, Anne, 64, 87, 147 ; Frances, 60 ; Francis. 60, 64 ; George. 252 ; Joane, 242 ; John, 87. 243 ; Mr., 170 ; Peter, 87 ; Thomas, 87, 88 ; William, 88.
Leechland, Jane, 180 ; William. 178, 180.
Leese, Ralph, 164.
Leete, Anthony, 253.
Leget, Margaret, 224.
Leigh. Ruth, 54 ; Thomas. 54, 55, 160.
Lemott, John, 166, 167 ; Mary, 167.
Leneman, Margaret, 112.
Lenford, Katherine, 94 ; William, 94.
Lenthall, Martha, 257.
Lenton. Elizabeth. 246.
Leonard, Frances, 95 ; Francis, 95, 97, 209 ; Mary, 95, 97, 209.
Lester, George, 11 ; Jane, 155 ; Judith, 258.
Levat, Venus, 253.
Lewes, Alice, 30 ; Harry, 5 ; John, 157 ; Sibell, 230; Thomas, 30.
Lewis, Joane, 5 ; John, 239, 246; Katherine, 223 ; Mary, 33, 257 ; Randoll, 37 ; Thomas, 33, 37, 110, 235 ; William, 235.
Lewkner, William, 132.
Lewner, Thomas, 234.
Lewtely, Jone, 226.
Leycraft or Leycrafte, Richard, 57 ; Sampson, 57 ; Thomas, 59, 165.

Leycroft, Elizabeth, 60, 167 ; Thomas, 60, 166, 167.
Leycrofte, Richard, 112 ; Sampson, 168.
Leynthall, William, 225.
Liddington, Elizabeth, 53, 156 ; Thomas, 53, 155, 156.
Lidley, Edmond, 237 ; Frances, 237.
Lightbrain, Anne, 10.
Lightman, Elizabeth, 222.
Lile, Martha, 186.
Lilliard, Thomas, 112.
Lillie, Thomas, 39.
Lindsey, Katherine, 105.
Linney, Henry, 215.
Linsaies, Mrs., 243.
Linsay, John, 108.
Linsey, Edward, 78 ; Elizabeth, 78 ; Grisell, 11 ; John, 14 ; Katherine, 138 ; Mrs., 157, 239; Susan, 14, 239; Thomas, 105, 138.
Liuthweight, Alice, 175.
Lipson. Celitie, 131 ; Peter, 131.
Lister, Dina, 28 ; Dorothy, 139; Elizabeth, 17; Ellen, 227 ; John, 7, 9, 17, 19, 21, 23, 25, 28, 116, 117, 130, 137, 139 ; Judith, 33 ; Lucres. 25 ; Margaret, 23 ; Peter, 19, 130 ; Richard, 111 ; Susan, 231 ; William, 21, 33, 130.
Little, Alice, 221.
Living. William, 196.
Lock. Barbara, 201.
Locke, Blanche, 16 ; John, 16, 229 ; Mr., 151 ; Mrs., 151.
Lockey, Blanche, 123 ; John, 123.
Lockly, John, 222.
Lockson, Alice, 125 ; John, 123 ; Margery, 18, 123, 125 ; Richard, 18, 125, 236 ; Robert, 125, 236 ; Thomas, 125.
Locksonne, Thomas, 123.
Lodge, Harry, 12 ; Sir Thomas, 12.
Loe, Richard, 242.
Lofte. Mary, 261.
Loudon, John, 148.
Long, George, 88 ; Henry, 261 ; John, 221 ; Sarah, 88.
Longe, George, 88.
Longshaft, John, 117.
Lotis, Joane. 110.
Loton, Henry, 198.
Louell, John, 105.
Love, Thomas, 249.
Lownes. Francis. 248.
Loxon, Isabel, 164 ; Mr., 51, 150, 154, 240; Richard, 123, 125, 160.
Lucas, Mary, 250.
Lucurs, Richard, 212 ; William, 212.
Lucust, Richard, 164.
Lucy, Alice, 139 ; Richard, 36 ; Thomas, 36, 139.
Luddington, Anne, 62 ; Chris-

INDEX OF NAMES.

tian, 240; Susan, 57, 167; Theophilus, 257; Thomas, 165; Valentine, 57, 62, 165, 167. 244, 248.
Luddingtonne, Elizabeth, 56, 162; John, 245; Valentine, 56, 58, 162.
Lukener, Ellen, 160; Roger, 160.
Lukner, Edward, 132.
Lunne, Henry, 242.
Luntley, Thomas, 121.
Luntly, Elizabeth, 126; Margaret, 226; Thomas, 121, 124.
Luntloes, Mr., 15.
Luntlow, Anne, 229.
Luntlowe, Bryan, 229; Elizabeth, 229; Thomas, 229.
Lusher, Anne, 69, 76, 183; Elizabeth, 62, 254; Isabella. 92; Mary, 78, 193; Mr., 78; Mrs., 200; Moody, 63, 206; Richard, 71, 189; Sarah, 80; Sibell, 64, 69, 71, 81; Thomas, 62, 63, 64, 66. 69, 71, 76, 78, 80, 81, 92, 167, 179, 183, 189, 193, 197, 200, 202.
Luson, Ursula, 235; Walter, 235.
Luther, Sir Anthony. 206; Thomazine, 206.
Lyard, Anne, 231.
Lyford, Thomas, 245.
Lyle, John, 260.
Lylly, Roger, 106.
Lymcocke. Edmond, 225.
Lyne. John, 129; William, 129.
Lyngar, James, 143.
Lynnacers, Anne, 248.
Lynne, Hugh, 116.
Lynneall, Katherine, 232; Philip, 232.
Lynniall, Margery, 222.
Lynsay, Grizell, 119; Joane, 115; Mr., 116.
Lynsell, Francis. 230.
Lynsey, Elizabeth, 224; Erasmus, 2; George, 17; Grace, 1; Joane, 7; John, 1, 2, 120, 137; Margery, 7.
Lynthwaight, Mr., 169.
Lynthweight, Alice, 175; James, 175.
Lynzey, —, 130; Elizabeth, 172; George, 123.
Lyon, Francis, 209.
Lyster, Edward, 248.
Lyttelton, Jane, 250.

M.

Mabbet, William, 91.
Mabbot, William, 257.
Mabbott, Anne, 208; William, 208.
Mabbutt, William, 204.
Mabletonne. Mary, 110.
Macham, Anne, 299.
Mackaris, Anne, 196.
Mackerell, John, 107.
Macree, John, 191.

Macrell, John, 3.
Maddesonne, Anne, 8.
Maddestone, Anne, 112.
Maddison, Elizabeth, 74; Jane, 76; Lionel, 74; Ralph, 74, 76.
Maddocke, Anne, 136; John, 136, 235.
Maddokes, Gilbert, 94; Hannah, 94.
Maddox, Amy, 238; Constance, 218; Gilbert, 202. 204, 212, 258; Hannah, 202; Jane, 249; John, 238; Mary, 204; Mrs., 213, 218; Richard, 172.
Maddyson, Robert, 251.
Mader, Gilbert, 114.
Madewell, Anne, 3.
Madison, Deborah, 75; Elizabeth, 75; Mr., 187; Robert, 75.
Madox, Gilbert, 95; William. 95.
Mager, Alice, 19, 125; Elizabeth. 128; Grace, 131; John, 131; Mr., 130; William, 19, 125, 128, 230.
Maggott, John, 247.
Maier, William, 135.
Maiors, Mr., 124.
Makebray, John, 222.
Malen, Anne. 147; Ellen, 153; John, 10, 12, 130, 131, 153; Thomas, 10, 39. 147, 160.
Malin. Griselic. 10; Joane, 13; John. 13, 14. 15, 122, 138; Margaret, 14; Mrs., 242.
Malison. Anne, 132; Mary. 228; Robert, 129, 132.
Mallison, Frances, 117.
Mallisonne, Frances, 9.
Malyn, Joane, 223, 237; John, 11, 119, 121, 168, 223, 229, 230, 237; Margaret, 122; Mrs., 142; Thomas, 11, 225.
Man, Elizabeth, 250; Samuel, 249.
Mande, Walter, 47; William, 47.
Mandrill, Mr., 263.
Mane, Margery, 146; Mother, 147.
Manes, Mother, 41.
Mann, Edward, 254.
Mannering, John, 223; Margaret, 111.
Manning, Alice, 235; Thomas, 235.
Mansfeld, Thomas, 132.
Manskill, Christian, 259.
Mantill, John, 262.
Mapletonne, Ellen, 6; Sarah, 5.
March, Ellen, 73; James, 73, 251; Susan, 256.
Marc, John, 186.
Margerets, Anne, 89; Robert, 89.
Margrane, Nicholas, 124; Sarah, 18, 124.

Markcham, Peter, 249.
Marlow, John, 257.
Marow, George, 47, 50, 137, 145, 244; Katherine, 145; Mary, 244.
Marrall, George, 32; Mary, 32.
Marris, Mr., 243.
Marroull, Arthur, 236; George, 236.
Marrow, Edward, 47, 155; Ellen. 46, 155; George, 42, 46. 155, 156, 157; Margaret, 137; William, 50, 155.
Marrys, John, 50, 151.
Marsh, Anne, 54; Eleanor, 199; Isabel, 202; James, 190, 199, 202, 206, 210, 216; John, 254; Leonard, 203; Margaret, 206; Robert, 203; Thomas, 54.
Marshall, Amy, 219; Anne, 221; Elizabeth, 226; Mathew, 126; Thomas, 110.
Marson, Anne, 255.
Marten, Amery, 132; Anne 109; Thomas, 105.
Martin, Edward, 67; John. 67, 255; Robert, 33; William, 258.
Martine, Ellen, 144, 252.
Martinscraft, Thomas, 219.
Martir, John, 243.
Maruell, Radegund, 166.
Marwood, Elizabeth, 94; Francis, 94, 208; Mr., 208; William, 208.
Mascall, Ellen, 229; Henry, 247; John, 226; Mary, 115; Sarah, 5.
Mascoll, Frances, 222; Elizabeth, 8, 116, 118, 138; Joane. 110; John, 11, 14, 118, 121; Mary, 9; Mr., 13, 14, 139, 239; Robert, 138, 140; William. 12, 13, 119.
Mase, Mr.. 140; Thomas, 114.
Masely, Anne, 222.
Mason, Alice, 237; Anne, 102, 103; Henry, 190; John, 78, 102, 103, 220, 223; Mr., 89; Richard, 103. 220; Robert, 78; Thomas, 187; William, 237.
Masonne, George, 124.
Masse, Thomas, 8.
Massey, Isabel, 9; Joane, 263.
Masson, Alice, 133; John. 133.
Masters, Anne, 70, 178; Edward, 248; John, 70; Thomas, 70.
Matchell, Judith, 218.
Mather, Rowland, 255.
Mathew, Anne, 5, 111; Bridget, 246; Elizabeth, 4, 223, 227; Ellen, 8, 117; Emme, 221; Jane, 4; John, 109; Margaret, 109; Richard. 6, 111, 112, 117.
Mathewes, Barbara, 57; Thomas, 56, 57.

INDEX OF NAMES. 285

Mathews, Mary, 254.
Mator, John, 263.
Matram, Elizabeth, 115; Stephen, 116.
Maull, Richard, 236; Thomas, 236.
Maunsfeeld, Ellen, 115.
Maunsfeld. William, 225.
Mawkett, Anne, 256.
Maxfeeld, John, 46.
Maxfeild, Alice, 243; Anne, 57, 191; Bartholomew, 180; Daniel, 216; Elizabeth, 55; John, 55, 57, 163, 180, 191.
Maxfeld, Bartholomew, 47; Daniel, 54; John, 47, 49, 54, 148, 149, 150, 157, 160; Mrs., 244.
May, John, 15; Richard, 99; Robert, 15.
Maye, John, 122; Mayes, Susan, 241.
Mayhew, John, 251.
Mayid, Mary, 259.
Mayne, Thomas, 122.
Mead, John, 85, 194; Margaret, 83, 193; Philip, 82, 83, 181, 192, 193, 251.
Meade, Dorothy, 73, 77. 79, 190; Jane, 73; Philip, 73, 77, 79, 82, 179, 190, 251, 254.
Meadowes, Robert, 262.
Meares. Anne, 86; George, 86; Henry, 83, 193; Isabel, 232; Katherine, 83, 194; Mary, 77; Miles, 232; Mr., 242; M^{rs}. 191; Robert, 85, 198; Walter, 49, 82, 194; William, 49, 77, 82, 83, 85, 86, 189, 193, 194. 198.
Mense, Elizabeth, 228; William, 119, 122.
Medelyn, John, 112.
Medhops, Martha, 257.
Medowes, Dorothy, 243.
Meers, Alexander, 202; Anne, 202.
Megges. William, 113.
Meires, Alexander, 71; Margaret, 187; Sarah, 68, 71, 74; Walter. 174, 178; Widow, 187; William, 68, 71, 74, 178.
Meirs. Mathew, 174; Mrs., 174.
Melledy, Margaret, 222.
Melway, Nicholas, 164.
Mempris, Deborah, 70; Elizabeth, 70, 72; Jacob. 67, 72 197; Thomas, 67, 70, 72, 179, 187.
Memprisse, Robert, 186; Thomas, 186.
Mercer, Anne, 66, 178; Elizabeth, 49; Jane, 68; John, 49, 60, 63, 177, 241; Mary, 72; Stephen, 59, 60, 62, 63, 66, 68, 72, 177, 178; Thomas, 59.
Meredith, Davy, 129; Richard, 129.

Merefeeld, Edward. 234.
Merial, Nicholas. 143.
Merick. Judith, 256.
Mericke. Joane, 119; William, 5.
Merrick, Thomas, 206.
Merricke. George, 119; William, 119.
Merrill, Anne, 102; Mary, 102, 217; William. 102, 217, 219.
Merryweather, Frances, 250.
Mese, Mr., 12; William, 12, 222.
Mewes, Margaret, 117.
Mewiter, James. 231.
Mewter, John. 20; Sibell, 20.
Michaell, Mother, 119; Robert, 113.
Michell, William, 252.
Michem, Robert, 158.
Middleton. Elizabeth. 82, 256; Jane, 247, 256; John, 71, 82, 83, 188, 205; Margaret, 71; Robert, 83; Thomas. 71.
Middletoun, John, 193.
Middletonne, Edward, 58; Robert, 58.
Middlewhite, Ellen, 214; Mihill, 214.
Midleborne, Mary, 260.
Midleton. Anne, 72; Elizabeth, 106; George, 224; Jane, 70, 77, 189, 203; John, 72, 77. 80; Mr., 70, 166; Mrs., 183; Oliver, 118; Richard, 70, 203, 206; Robert, 214; Thomas, 189; Widow, 209; William. 221.
Midletonne, Katherine, 114.
Midsley. Jane. 257.
Miers, Mrs., 196.
Mihell, Simon, 125; Susan, 125.
Miles, Elizabeth, 254; Katherine, 15, 105; Richard, 221; Robert, 15.
Miller, Anne, 22; Christopher, 229; James, 246; Mr., 206; Richard, 22.
Milles, Elizabeth, 14; George, 13; James, 120; Robert, 14; Rosamund, 120; Thomas, 221; Tobith, 136; William, 136.
Millet, Stephen, 223.
Millian, John, 234; Margaret, 234.
Millit, Anne, 248.
Mills, Esdras, 93; John, 214, 255.
Milner. John, 161; Robert, 161.
Mils, Esdras, 206.
Miner, Margaret, 234; Richard, 234.
Miunames. Daniel, 261.
Minors, Ellis, 157.
Mittin, Joane, 224.
Molder, Angell de, 219; Ellen, 219.
Mole, Frances, 71, 73, 74, 76,

189; George, 76, 78, 189; Henry, 71; Howard, 73; Hugh, 40, 157; John, 71, 73, 74, 76; Mary, 43, 156; Richard, 40, 43, 156, 157.
Molsonne. Frances, 5.
Monday, George, 228.
Mondye, Jeronomy, 111.
Money. Richard, 243.
Montegue, Anne. 240.
Moorcock, Robert, 245.
Moore, Agnes, 217; Dorothy, 170; Elizabeth, 252; Hannah, 64; John, 183, 217, 258; Joseph, 67, 174; Mary, 61; Mr., 110; Prudence. 60; Thomas, 60, 61, 63, 64, 67, 170, 174, 258; William, 63.
Mooreheu, Widow, 189.
Moorehowse, Anne, 78; John, 78, 80; Mr., 194; Samuel, 80.
Moorton, William, 235.
More, Alice, 129; Anne, 15, 190; Dorothy, 59; James, 14, 15, 125; Jone. 224; Marie, 155; Mathy, 125; Ralph, 224; Thomas, 15, 59, 125, 262; Walter, 110; William, 129, 254.
Morehouse, John, 83, 191; Sarah, 83.
Morehowse, Elizabeth, 86; John, 86, 250.
Moreton, Edward, 68; George, 68.
Mores, Mary, 264.
Morgane, Elizabeth, 223.
Morgraue, John, 14; Nicholas, 18, 180, 228; Sarah, 130; William. 14.
Moris. Apeline, 40; John, 40; Mr., 134.
Morlie, John. 251.
Morly, Joane, 262.
Morow, George, 34; Margaret, 34.
Morrell, Thomas. 121.
Morrice, John, 168.
Morries, Elizabeth, 166; Hugh, 166.
Morris, Sir Christopher, 108; Constant. 123; Dorothy, 76; Elizabeth, 11; Hugh, 241; Jane, 25, 198; Joane, 243; John, 34, 35, 148, 239; Lady, 110; Lady Margery, 106; Mr., 52; Mrs., 190; Richard, 123, 223; Thomas, 49; William, 76.
Morrow, George, 36, 39; Jane, 36; Katherine, 39.
Morrys, Sir Christopher, 221.
Morton, John, 167.
Mortimor, Anne, 56; John, 56.
Morton, Anne, 176, 224; Christopher, 75; Elizabeth, 75, 183; George, 62, 63, 64, 75, 176, 177, 180, 183; John. 64, 177; Mary, 63; Susan, 62.

INDEX OF NAMES.

Mortonn, Christopher, 75; Elizabeth, 72, 75; George, 66, 72, 75.
Moseley, Anne, 192; Edward, 87; Thomas, 87; William, 192.
Mosse, Anne, 106; Hugh, 130; Richard, 130.
Mote, Anne, 204; Elizabeth.197.
Moth, John, 249; Richard, 225.
Mothall. Susan, 78; William, 78.
Mothe, Thomas, 210.
Mould, Mr., 186; Richard, 205.
Moule, Joane, 202; Richard, 202.
Moulton, William, 251.
Moustey, William, 256.
Mountford, Elizabeth, 188; John, 188, 201.
Moxon, Anthony, 239.
Moyce, Mathew. 179.
Moyle, Margaret, 256.
Mucey, Erasmus, 86, 87; John, 87.
Mullat, Thomas, 198.
Mullet, Anne, 71; Elizabeth, 66, 69, 71, 184; Hugh, 72; Thomas, 65. 66, 69, 71, 72, 181, 184; William, 65.
Mullett. Katherine, 68; Thomas, 68, 249.
Mullit, Susan, 210.
Mumford, Francis, 181.
Munday, Margerie, 253; Richard, 43, 145; William, 1, 43, 106, 145.
Munde, John, 1; Margaret, 1.
Munke, George, 137; Joseph, 36; Richard, 36; Thomas, 137.
Muuus, Timothy, 256.
Muus. Mr., 87.
Murlwell, Mary, 259.
Musgrave, Mabel, 251.
Mushrempe, William, 110.
Mushrymp, Margaret, 222.
Mvn, Thomas, 204.
Myles, Katherine, 2; William, 258.
Mylles, Rose, 108.
Mymford, John, 251.
Myn, Nicholas, 151.
Mynn, Denis, 86; John, 82, 86; William, 82.
Mynne, Anne, 244.
Mynor, Ellen, 251.
Myntton, William, 172.

N.

Naddle, Jane, 44; John, 42, 145; Rowland, 42, 44, 145.
Natt, Thomas, 201.
Neale, Alice, 121.
Needam, Anne, 44; Dorothy, 111; Elizabeth, 117; Henry, 42, 44, 239.
Nettleton, Richard, 218.
Neuby. Elizabeth. 146.
Neue, Anthony, 228.

Neuell, Elizabeth, 223; John, 6; Margery, 223.
Newball, John, 178.
Newell, Edward, 158, 159, 160; Mary, 159.
Newey, Joyce, 254.
Newman, Anne, 134, 207, 230; Bridget, 233; Elizabeth, 232. 245; John, 232; Peter. 207; Priscilla, 207; Roger, 117; Thomas, 134, 233.
Newsam, Abigail, 249.
Newton, Peter, 88, 90, 198; Phebe, 90; Priscilla, 88.
Nicholas, Elizabeth, 101, 102; Margaret, 101, 216; Thomas, 101, 102, 216; William, 102.
Nicholer, John, 257.
Nicholles, Edmond, 16; Jane. 6.
Nichollson, Joane, 120; John, 105; Michael, 8, 42.
Nichollsonne, Joane, 10.
Nichols, John, 259.
Nicholson, Aholinb, 47, 159; Alice, 131; Bezaleell, 34; Edmond, 122; Edward, 134; Frances, 112; James, 122. 131. 140; Joane. 138; Margery, 244; Michael, 34, 42, 47, 149, 157, 159; Rebecca, 149; Robert, 134; Sarah, 159; Thomas, 111.
Nicholsonne, Julian, 222.
Nickoles, Mary, 260.
Nickolles, Beasce, 164.
Nicolls, William, 183.
Nightingale, Joane, 254.
Nihill, John, 118.
Nisson, Mary, 261.
Nix. Benedict, 235.
Noble, Edward, 19; Robert, 132; Thomas, 19, 132.
Norden, John, 37; Martha, 37.
Norly, William, 251.
Norman, Anne, 106; Hannah, 205; John, 61, Mary, 61, 89. 92, 195, 213; Mathew, 91; Mr., 172, 206; Robert, 61, 64, 173, 195; Samuel, 64; Sarah, 92; Thomas, 89, 91, 92, 205, 213.
Normanton, James, 224.
Normavell, William, 162.
Norris, Alexander, 15; Elizabeth, 252, 256; Isabel, 107; John. 15; Mathew, 257; Nathaniel, 77, 190; Samuel, 77, 190.
North, Elizabeth, 258; Thomas, 256.
Nortly, Robert, 174.
Norton, Bartholomew, 231; Bridget, 200; Ellis, 53; Henry, 53; John, 149, 231; Martha, 172, 257; William, 197.
Nottingam, Francis, 222.
Nowell, James, 237; John, 237.
Nulm, Robert, 92.
Nurse, Elizabeth, 204.
Nutbrowne, Thomas, 230.

Nuton, Mr., 211.
Nutt, Thomas, 207; William, 206.
Nuttall, Mr., 206.

O.

Oakes, James, 97, 210, 215; Mris., 210; Thomas, 97, 210.
Oder, Frances, 257.
Odium, *alias* Cartwright, Anne. 52; John, 52.
Offley, Elizabeth, 11; Mabel, 7; Margaret, 117; Robert, 6; Thomas, 6, 11.
Offly, Elizabeth. 117.
Ofley, Thomas, 223.
Ogar, Thomas, 171; William, 171.
Ogle, Elizabeth, 258.
Okeley, Anne, 57; George, 221; Joane. 163; Thomas, 57, 168.
Okely, Elizabeth, 251; Joane, 54; Margaret, 227; Thomas, 54, 181.
Okeye, Effam, 55; Mr., 63; Thomas, 55.
Oker, Rowland, 223.
Okes, Anna. 95; Elizabeth, 96; James, 95, 96, 98; Mr., 213.
Oldam, Elizabeth, 44; Robert, 44. 145, 239.
Olin, Elizabeth, 222.
Oliner, Elizabeth, 149; Ellen, 222; Isaac, 149.
Olliuer, Elizabeth, 114; Grace, 247.
Oneby, Robert, 251.
Onely. George, 209.
Oner, Henry, 206.
Only, Elizabeth, 97; George, 97.
Orde, Edward, 172.
Ordway, Alice, 102; Benjamin, 99; George, 102, 215; Henry, 103; John, 102, 215, 219; Magdelin, 212; Mr., 210, 212, 213.
Ordwaye, John, 100; Marcye, 100.
Orred, James, 237; John, 237.
Orton, Elizabeth. 133; John, 28; Libeus, 29; Raudoll, 28, 29, 133.
Osborne, Anne, 87, 90; Gabriel, 88; Grace, 89; John, 198; Mary, 88; Mr., 58; Thomas, 87, 88, 89, 90, 198, 207.
Osler, Mr., 218.
Ostedell, Elizabeth, 258.
Ostler, Captain, 210; Mr., 204.
Oton, Alice. 120.
Ouerinde, Thomas. 224.
Ouerton, Ellen, 10; John, 10; Lawrence, 35, 145; Nicholas, 135; Sibell, 35, 145; William, 135.
Oulden, Dorothy, 190.

INDEX OF NAMES. 287

Ouldham, Jasper, 246.
Ovenden, Robert, 242.
Overton, Elizabeth, 242.
Owen, Joanna, 259; Katherine, 141; Thomas, 107,
Owin, Jone, 228.
Ownly, George, 208; James, 208.
Oxeley, Susan, 5.
Oxgall, Margaret, 8.
Oxley, Anne, 4; Ralph, 121.
Ozbourne, Alice, 257.

P.

Pace, Cicely, 260.
Packe, Christopher, 260; Robert, 222.
Packer, John, 240; Margery, 226; Mary, 104; William, 104.
Packington, Peter, 3.
Packyuton, Anne, 107.
Padmoore, Anne, 77; John, 77.
Padmore, Francis, 79; James, 81, 198; John, 79, 81, 84, 198; Mary, 84, 199.
Page, Elizabeth, 51, 153; Thomas, 51, 153, 155; William, 116.
Paginton, Joane, 118; Richard, 1, 121.
Pain, Alice, 151.
Paine, Richard, 165.
Painter, George, 256; Jane, 129; John, 253; Nicholas, 129.
Paintill, Anne, 4.
Pakington, Emme, 2.
Palfreman, Richard, 6.
Palfryman, Thomas, 222.
Pallfryman, Mary, 117.
Pallmer, Daniel, 10, 118; Ellen, 55; Joane, 115; John, 55; Leonard, 41; Mary, 120; Rose, 116; Sebastian, 41; William, 10.
Palmer, Elizabeth, 43; Ellen, 160; Henry, 55; Joane, 112; John, 135; Richard, 135; Sebastian, 43; William, 55.
Palmur, Ephram, 246; Henry, 161; William, 161.
Palphreman, Anne, 126; John, 232; Mr., 134; Thomas, 126, 137.
Pancefoot, Henry, 214.
Panck, Ben, 87; Sarah, 87.
Pancke, Robert, 232; Sarah, 232.
Pane, Elizabeth, 244; Susan, 54; William, 54.
Pannell, Anne, 211; Edward, 211.
Pansford, Edward, 215.
Parchement, Richard, 26.
Parchment, Alice, 135; Anne, 30, 143; Elizabeth, 42; Katherine, 131; Margaret, 143; Mary, 143; Maudelin, 39; Peter, 26, 30, 83, 39, 42, 131, 139, 143; Susan, 33, 139; William, 139, 148.
Pargeter, Thomas, 557.
Parkar, John, 160; Mr., 153., Susan, 160.
Parker, Francis, 257.
Parkchurst, Henry, 250.
Parkens, Francis, 145; Margaret, 145.
Parker, Anne, 98, 128, 211; Edward, 46, 52; Elizabeth, 96; Frances, 48, 250; Francis, 255; Jane, 58; John, 43, 46, 48, 50, 52, 55, 56, 57, 58, 121, 128, 162, 163, 246; Katherine, 244; Maister, 108; Margaret, 58, 109; Margery, 112; Mary, 96; Mr., 215; Mrs., 244; Richard, 8; Robert, 217, 246; Samuel, 97; Sarah, 263; Susan, 43; William, 55, 94, 96, 97, 98, 112, 211, 223, 264.
Parkins, Thomas, 244.
Parkinson, Henry, 187.
Parlor, Thomas, 239.
Parradine, Mr., 64.
Parrey, Jane, 91; John, 90; Robert, 91.
Parreys, William, 202.
Parrie, Thomazine, 249.
Parrott, Dorothy, 169.
Parry, Harry, 235; Hugh, 235.
Parson, Joane, 222.
Parsonne, Ellen, 107.
Parton, Anne, 16; Edmund, 171; Edward, 161; Elizabeth, 146, 161; Francis, 15, 16, 146; Goodwife, 151, 178; John, 15, 122; Margery, 15.
Partridge, Anthony, 66; Denis, 34; John, 111; Mary, 66; Stephen, 34.
Pasmore, Margaret, 202; Mr., 202.
Paston, John, 219.
Paswater, Moses, 218.
Pateman, Henry, 93; Mary, 94; Randolph, 93, 94.
Pateshall, William, 138.
Patrick, William, 257.
Pattison, John, 107.
Patty, Anne, 87; Margaret, 87.
Patynson, William, 226.
Paucfreman, Mary, 5.
Pauet, Edward, 139; John, 139.
Paullmer, Rose, 8; William, 119.
Paulmer, Elizabeth, 9; Rebecca, 11; William, 12.
Payne, Alice, 108; Anne, 168; Barbary, 261; Deborah, 130; Edward, 257; Iddyr, 206; John, 237; Judith, 250; Margaret, 237; Mrs., 169; Robert, 247; William, 130.
Paynter, Margaret, 228; Robert, 106.
Payste, Anne, 61; Audrian, 61.
Pearce, Francis, 165; Mr., 204.
Pearle, Mary, 258.
Pearpount, Mary, 232.
Pearse, Andrew, 90; Edward, 90; Mary, 111.
Pearson, Anne, 112; John, 224, 228.
Pearsye, Isabel, 112.
Peas, Elizabeth, 247; Mary, 81, 191; Martha, 88; Mr., 196; William, 81, 88, 191.
Pease, John, 70, 76, 92, 183; Luke, 62; Margaret, 68, 177; Mary, 70, 73, 76, 78, 85, 176, 192, 194; Mr., 200; Rebecca, 86; Samuel, 90; Thomas, 73, 200; William, 62, 68, 70, 73, 76, 78, 85, 86, 90, 176, 177, 183, 192, 194, 200, 205, 246.
Peate, Enock, 260.
Peck, Elizabeth, 100; John, 97, 98, 100; Katherine, 98; Mary, 97, 98.
Pecke, Katherine, 100.
Pedder, Ellen, 41, 145; John, 41, 46, 49, 138, 139, 145, 146, 147, 157, 158, 166, 175, 236; Katherine, 138; Simon, 49, 157; Thomas, 236.
Peeke, Elizabeth, 250.
Peele, Elizabeth, 232; Thomas, 232.
Peell, Margaret, 223.
Peerson, Joane, 246.
Peeter, Barbery, 97; Dionis, 59; Edward, 65; Eleanor, 84; Elizabeth, 212; Evans, 100; Gerson, 50; Henry, 86; Jane, 167, 195; John, 63, 65, 92, 94, 173; Judith, 96, 98; Margaret, 97; Mary, 89, 92; Nicholas, 100; Robert, 100; Roger, 38; Simon, 88; Susan, 92; Walter, 98; William, 99.
Pegrom, Elizabeth, 235; John, 235.
Peirce, Alexander, 91; Alice, 244; Andrew, 91, 92; Rebecca, 92.
Pellam, Peregrine, 257.
Pelsant, Marian, 228.
Pembrooke, Katherine, 204.
Penifather, Harry, 108.
Penn, James, 88; Samuel, 87; Thomas, 87, 88, 89.
Pennelton, Joane, 129; William, 129.
Pennicke, Frances, 189.
Pennill, Elizabeth, 222; John, 206.
Pennington, Robert, 201.
Penny, John, 136; Thomas, 136.

INDEX OF NAMES.

Peppen, Edward, 251.
Pepper, Alice. 118; Christopher, 117; Mr., 116; William, 116.
Percifall, Jone, 132.
Peregrine, Hugh, 58.
Perfew, Thomas, 224.
Perkins, Elizabeth, 197; Mary, 261.
Perkinson, Deborah, 86; Henry, 80, 82, 84, 86, 88, 193, 198, 203; Jane, 82; John, 88; Widow, 215.
Perriman, Joane, 255.
Perry, Elizabeth, 138; John, 138; Judith, 204; Thomas, 90; William, 90, 204.
Perryn, Anne, 124.
Persey, Francis, 44; John, 44; Thomas, 44.
Person, Roger, 106.
Personne, Anne, 222; Ellen, 115; Thomas, 113.
Persy, Francis, 47, 49, 145, 146, 148, 149, 160; James, 49, 160; John, 146; Thomas, 148; Ursly, 145; Walter, 47, 148.
Pertus, Anne, 258.
Peter, Anna, 63; Edward, 199; Elizabeth, 90; Hannah, 88, 206; Henry, 86; Jean, 60; John, 89; Juventa, 58; Judith, 100; Lidia, 94; Mary, 89, 94; Sarah, 93; Stephen, 102; Susan, 93.
Petronilla, —, 1.
Pettie, Effam, 74; Mary, 74; Ralph, 74.
Pettite, Ralph, 184.
Pettitt, Susan, 263.
Phillip, Fulke, 19, 131; Grace, 127; Thomas, 18, 19, 127, 131, 165, 223.
Phillipes, Elizabeth, 176.
Phillippes, Anne, 4, 226; Elizabeth, 122; Joane, 121; John, 15; Mathew, 15; Rachel, 16; Thomas, 15, 16, 228.
Phillips, Elizabeth, 253; Grace, 14; Humphry, 79; Richard, 247; Thomas, 14, 79, 258; William, 93, 205.
Philpot, John, 223.
Pickborn, Alice, 53, 243; James, 51, 53, 155, 242.
Pickborne, Alice, 161; James, 161.
Pickering, Francis, 205; John, 237; Richard, 237.
Piggot, Emmory, 175; John, 174, 182.
Piggott, Elizabeth, 175; John, 175, 192; Richard, 163; Robert, 163; Thomas, 163, 205.
Piggottes, John, 176, 177.
Pigine, Anthony, 167.
Pigot, Edward, 48, 156; Elizabeth, 27, 42, 154; Joane, 232; John, 30, 232; Mr., 155, 160;
Thomas, 26, 27, 30, 42, 48, 140, 154, 156.
Pigott, John, 183; Mris., 183.
Pike, Jone, 142.
Pilkington, Leonard, 220; Thomas, 259.
Pimlett, Thomas, 258.
Pingle, Ciprian, 28; Jane, 25; Lionel, 27; Richard, 24, 25, 27, 28, 133; William, 24.
Pippine, Anne, 246.
Pistoll, Sarah, 97; Thomas, 97, 208; William, 208.
Pitt, Thomas, 249.
Pitts, Elizabeth, 257; Grace, 263.
Planckney, Edward, 162.
Planncon, Henry, 247.
Plasterer, Elizabeth, 115.
Plombaire, Jerome, 5.
Plomer, Elizabeth, 76; Martha, 78; Mr., 189; Thomas, 76, 78.
Plommer, Alice, 6; Grisell, 5.
Plummer, Jone, 228; John, 125; Katherine, 157; Mrs., 158; Thomas, 157.
Plumpton, Brian, 86; Josiah, 86, 254.
Pollard, Augustus, 257.
Pomfrett, Robert, 256.
Ponder, Roger, 110, 222; Simon, 221; Theophilus, 5.
Poole, Anthony, 250; Humphry, 251; John, 198; Margaret, 247; Mr., 203; Mrs., 203; Ralph, 86; Richard, 86; Samuel, 220; William, 208, 242, 251.
Poole, alias Vander la poole, Daniel, 153; Sophia, 153.
Pope, Abraham, 24; Agnes, 142; Balthasar, 142; Daniel, 21, 147; David, 19; Jeremy, 142; Jerome, 31; Mary, 27, 142; Peter, 219; Salamon, 26; Susan, 23, 143; Waldron, 19, 21, 23, 24, 26, 27, 31, 142, 143, 147.
Popeiay, John, 232; Richard, 232.
Porder, Elizabeth, 229; Mr., 143; Parson, 175; Richard, 122.
Portas, Harry, 130; William, 130.
Porter, Alice, 6, 234; Ambrose, 17; Anne, 56, 98, 223; Catherine, 121; Edward, 17, 124; Elizabeth, 9, 99, 116; Frances, 125; George, 123; Gregory, 16, 124; Joane, 5, 16, 111, 116, 123; John, 14, 96, 123, 208; Katherine, 13, Lewis, 56; Margaret, 151; Margery, 125; Martha, 15, 239; Mary, 96, 97; Oliver, 108; Richard, 7, 17, 96, 97, 98, 99, 100, 116, 124, 208, 259; Sarah, 260; Thomas, 8, 112, 116, 247; Widow,
239; William, 15, 17, 20, 123, 124, 127, 135, 234, 260.
Portington, Thomas, 106.
Portler, John, 197.
Portor, Edmond, 101; Nicholas, 103; Mary, 100, 103; Richard, 98, 100, 103; Robert, 101.
Poriter, Ellen, 251.
Portway, Mary, 223.
Pott, Misteris, 119; Sarah, 260.
Potter, Anne, 174; Edmund, 242; Richard, 174; Simon, 174.
Poulson, Margery, 255.
Poulter, Anne, 162, Elizabeth, 151.
Pountell, Timothy, 4.
Pounter, George, 235.
Powell, Agnes, 240; Amy, 261; Anne, 20; David, 19, 20, 23, 25, 28, 30, 33, 37, 41, 45, 133, 142, 143, 147, 151, 157, 230; Edward, 53; Elizabeth, 30, 97, 245, 251; Hannah, 98; Humphry, 53, 158; Hugh, 238; Joane, 28, 231, 244; Katherine, 37, 157; Mary, 95; Maudlyn, 23, 133; Mr., 141, 142, 143, 147, 181; Mrs., 51, 53, 75; Richard, 19, 41, 143, 157; Roger, 246; Susan, 33, 97, 98, 211, 220; Thomas, 25, 45, 95, 97, 98, 142, 211, 214, 238.
Powle, Thomas, 243.
Pownter, Stephen, 119.
Poyntell, John, 109.
Poynter, Jone, 251.
Pratt, William, 182.
Preagle, Thomas, 180.
Preast, Mary, 27.
Preene, Robert, 61; Thomas, 61.
Preest, Elizabeth, 3, 226; Ellen, 6; Emme, 2; Isabel, 4; John, 6; Katherine, 4; Richard, 5; Robert, 27; Thomas, 7, 105, 130.
Preestman, Katherine, 224.
Preist, Joane, 121; Margaret, 5.
Prentize, Arnold, 61, 62, 169; Jone, 61, 169; Sarah, 62.
Prescott, Honor, 215.
Presons, Mr., 211.
Pressey, Robert, 11; Susan, 9; Thomas, 11.
Pressie, Susan, 115.
Presson, John, 135; Katherine, 135.
Pressy, Henry, 10.
Preste, Francis, 105; Thomas, 105.
Prestly, John, 25; Peter, 25.
Preston, Richard, 127; William, 127.
Presye, John, 225.
Price, Davy, 191; Elizabeth, 100, 101, 103, 256; Hugh,

INDEX OF NAMES.

228; Ignatius, 3; Jane, 231; John, 31, 100, 102, 216; Joseph, 102; Katherine, 240; Mary, 102, 167; Mr., 215; Philip, 141; Sarah, 103; Silvester, 252; Thomas, 244, 257; William, 31, 147, 234.
Prideaux, Paskey, 258.
Prime, Robert, 57, 163; Sarah, 60; Thomas, 57, 59, 60, 163, 164; William, 59.
Printe, Samuel, 214.
Prisley, Jone, 167.
Pristie, Widow, 59.
Probe, William, 154.
Procter, Samuel, 201; Susan, 183; Thomazine, 208.
Pryce, Hannah, 212.
Pulcher, George, 210.
Pullner, John, 3.
Pully, Alice, 250.
Purchas, Samuel, 211.
Purchase, John, 219; Margery, 216; Samuel, 216, 219.
Purchass, Samuel, 97; Susan, 97.
Purches, John, 99; Samuel, 99.
Purchis, Elizabeth, 98; Samuel, 95, 98, 210; Susan, 210; Thomas, 95.
Purleuant, Harvey, 34; Thomas, 34.
Purlevant, Anne, 164; Marie, 164; Thomas, 164.
Purlivent, Thomas, 180.
Purret. —, 132.
Purser, Henry, 209; Rachel, 209.
Pye, Prosper, 187; William, 111.
Pywall, John, 62, 169, 247, 250.
Pywalles, Mr., 243.
Pywell, Frances, 162; John, 41, 166, 238; Jone, 166; Sarah, 41; Sibel, 241; Thomas, 199, 238; William, 162.

Q.

Quelch, Andrew, 98; Henry, 98, 99, 100, 212, 214, 259; Joseph, 100, 214; Mr., 212; Samuel, 212; William, 99, 212.
Quiby, John, 111.

R.

Railton, Clement, 122; Rowland, 122, 133, 234; Thomazine, 234.
Raiment, John, 29; Katherine, 29.
Rainscroft, Elizabeth, 157.
Ramphem, Joane, 250.
Ramsden, Mr., 263.
Rand, Katherine, 28; William, 28.
Randall, Edward, 263.
Rande, Anne, 212; John, 212; William, 212.
Randole, Katherine, 34.

Randoll, Anne, 21, 130; James, 29, 135; Jane, 32, 242; John, 21, 22, 28, 29, 32, 34, 38, 130, 135, 139, 142, 143, 144, 152, 157, 233; Katherine, 34, 139; Leonard, 233; Susan, 28, 144; Thomas, 32.
Rankin, Joane, 189; Thomas, 183.
Ranking, Thomas, 63.
Rastells, Mrs., 192.
Ratcliffe, John, 93.
Rates, Robert, 165.
Ratliff or Ratliffe, James, 94, 208; John, 94, 208.
Ratsdale, Dorithy, 35, 141; Francis, 39; John, 41; Margaret, 43, 47, 146; Martha, 32, 141; Peter, 141; Susan, 137; William, 32, 35, 37, 39, 41, 43, 45, 47, 134, 137, 141, 146, 153, 158.
Rattliffe, John, 211.
Ratting, William, 118, 225.
Rauens, Elizabeth, 230.
Rawbon, Anne, 255.
Rawlyns, Frances, 256.
Rawson, William, 225.
Rayman, John, 136; Margery, 125.
Rayment, Alice, 35; John, 24, 27, 31, 35, 128, 129, 133, 138, 140, 142, 228, 230; Jone, 128; Margery, 24, 129; Mr., 145, 147, 239; Thomas, 27.
Rayndales, Elizabeth, 222.
Rayne, Edward, 86; Margaret, 86.
Read, Deborah, 95; Elizabeth, 95; James, 3; Jane, 193; John, 257; Mary, 241; Simon, 95.
Reade, Elizabeth, 96, 209; Jane, 261; Simon, 96, 209; William, 222.
Reader, Katherine, 186.
Reason, John, 107; Sarah, 213.
Reckener, Lawrence, 3.
Recknar, William, 6.
Recknoll, Margaret, 114; Stephen, 113.
Record, Anne, 29, 144; Barbara, 145; Blanch, 37; Elizabeth, 38; Erasmus, 40; John, 29, 37, 38, 40, 48, 50, 52, 144, 145, 157; Mr., 156, 242; Nicholas, 52, 157; Robert, 50, 157.
Reddish, Frances, 30; Francis, 30.
Redman, Christopher, 152.
Reed, Randulph, 105.
Reene, Hester, 239.
Rees, Joane, 251.
Reene, Joseph, 250; William, 226, 229.
Rekener, Larence, 108.
Relfe, Nicholas, 250.
Remnant, William, 250.
Remnante, Anthony, 250.
Renolds, Mr., 89; Samuel, 90; Thomas, 90.

Reuses, Edward, 132; John, 132
Reynalds, Elizabeth, 217.
Reynoldes, Dorothy, 52, 251; Joane, 107, 160; John, 85, 86, 187, 236; Martha, 66; Mary, 258; Parnell, 48; Rowland, 48, 52, 55, 57, 60, 61, 66, 160, 161, 170, 187, 245; Sarah, 61, 170; Thomas, 57, 85, 86; William, 60, 236.
Reynolds, Elizabeth, 59, 89, 199, 252; John, 246; Martha, 188; Ralph, 88, 198; Rowland, 59, 188, 189; Susan, 194; Thomas, 59, 87, 88, 89, 194, 198, 199.
Rhodes, Arthur, 82; Susan, 82.
Rice, Katherine, 221.
Richardson, Alice, 225; Anne, 29, 164, 244; Constance, 250; Eleanor, 258; George, 124; Henry, 238; Isabel, 2; John, 109, 117, 223; Jone, 226; Katherine, 226; Lewes, 117; Margaret, 229, 241; Mr., 56, 156, 169; Mrs., 188; Peter, 157; Richard, 13, 119, 121; Robert, 226; Thomas, 121; William, 3.
Richardsonne, Thomas, 116.
Richardsonne, Elizabeth, 11, 119, 230; George, 119; Lewes, 10; Peirce, 161, 164; Richard, 13; Thomas, 4, 9.
Rich, Mary, 249.
Riche, Ralph, 234; Stephen, 111; Thomas, 284.
Richeman, John, 120; Jonas, 114; Leonard, 112, 120; William, 118.
Richemanne, John, 6.
Richemond, Dorothy, 12; Margaret, 8; William, 10.
Richemonde, Isabel, 7; William, 230.
Richesonne, Anne, 252.
Richman, Harry, 7, 120; Isabel, 225; Richard, 98.
Richmaune, Susan, 11.
Richmond, Elizabeth, 134; Hierome, 10; Jane, 229; John, 113, 181; Margaret, 115; William, 134.
Richmonde, Elizabeth, 6.
Ricketts, Margaret, 261.
Rickworth, Elizabeth, 187.
Rider, Adam, 36; Bridget, 254; Elizabeth, 36.
Ridgely, Edward, 150, 159; Rachel, 159.
Ridgley, Edward, 55, 56, 58, 59, 153, 163, 165, 166; Margaret, 58, 165, 166; Mrs., 166; Walter, 56, 58, 163.
Ridgsley, Edward, 57; John, 57.
Rigbey, Mary, 255.
Rigby, John, 261.
Rigge, William, 117.
Rigsby, Hamlet, 159.

2 P

INDEX OF NAMES.

Rigworth, Elizabeth, 263; Mr., 263.
Rikecord, John, 148; Malliard, 148.
Rikeworth, John, 151.
Risley, Mary, 258.
Rixby, Thomas. 249.
Roache, Abigail, 259; Giles, 249.
Roades, Arthur, 86; Marie. 86; Walter, 240.
Roads, Mr., 194.
Robartes, Stephen, 169.
Robberts, Stephen, 246.
Robbins, Elizabeth, 220; Mephibosheth, 207.
Robbinson, Mr., 210.
Robens, Edward, 201; Mephibosheth, 201; William, 201.
Roberds, Edith, 262.
Robertes, Alice. 142; Cadwallader, 130; Jone, 147, 157; Josias, 141; Stephen, 142, 145, 147, 157.
Roberts, Anne, 242; Elizabeth, 104; Edward, 197; Henry, 49; Joane, 41; John, 104; Mary, 104; Samuel, 49; Stephen, 41, 57, 163, 165.
Robins, Edward, 89; Mephibosheth, 88, 89; William, 88.
Robinson, Abigail, 69, 183, 195; Anne, 136, 229, 260; Arthur, 54, 58, 60, 61, 168; Blanche, 133; Dorothy, 91; Elizabeth, 58, 168; Henry, 60, 87, 89, 90, 91, 92, 195, 198, 202; Jane, 31; Jeremy, 79; John, 87, 89; Judith. 251; Margaret, 61, 91; Marie. 60, 76, 180; Martha, 64, 257; Miles, 60, 62, 64, 66. 69, 73, 76, 79, 180, 183, 186, 187; Nicholas, 258, 261; Priscilla, 255; Rebecca, 195; Richard, 21, 22, 31, 133, 144, 247; Sarah. 62; Thomas, 22, 60, 240, 258; William, 21, 54, 133.
Robinsonne, Arthur. 56, 57, 59, 104; Elizabeth. 221; Luke, 59; William, 56.
Robottam, John. 116.
Robuck, Roger, 194.
Rochedale, Margaret, 158, 172; Thomas, 249; William, 158, 172, 173.
Rochdale, Margaret, 65; Thomas, 65.
Roddes, Joyce, 111.
Roddocke. Elizabeth, 108.
Rodemaker, Abraham. 130; Anne, 130; Isaac, 130; John, 130.
Rodes, Arthur. 195; Marie, 195; Robert, 1; William, 158.
Rodgers, Mr., 211; Widow, 214.
Rodwell. James, 245.
Rogers, Elizabeth, 185; John, 28, 173; Lucy, 14; Peter, 173, 180, 185; Thomas, 257.
Roise, George, 198.

Rolf, Mr., 200.
Rolfe, John, 88; Sarah, 88.
Rolles, Giles, 250.
Rolph, Hannah, 89; John, 89.
Rombat, Godfry, 15.
Romney, Anne, 92; John, 92.
Rone, Robert, 232; Thomas, 232.
Roodes. Elizabeth, 108, 235; Emme, 2; Robert, 3.
Rookesech, John, 112.
Rose, Alice, 180; Ellen, 240; Jane, 241; Marie, 247; Wyniffreth, 180.
Rosier, Ellen, 233; Roger, 233.
Rosse, Christopher, 223; Mary, 224; Mr., 97; Richard, 223; Thomas, 8, 120; Timothy, 218.
Rotheram, William. 252.
Rott, Judith. 207; Thomas, 207.
Rowe, Elizabeth, 252.
Rowell, Ellen, 141.
Rower. George, 109.
Rowland, Deborah, 101; Elizabeth. 102. 103; John, 175; Richard, 220; Robert, 101, 103, 215. 220; Thomas, 102, 215.
Rowles, Edward. 162.
Rowley, James, 151.
Rowse, Anne, 108.
Royce, John, 85, 194; Margaret, 85, 194.
Roys, Anne, 196; John, 87, 196; Katherine, 196; Margaret, 196.
Royse, John, 86; Katherine, 86; Thomas, 198.
Rucell, Mr., 215; William, 215.
Rudcarke. Agnese, 108.
Rugby, William, 98.
Ruggell, Philip, 236; Susan, 236.
Rumle. George, 94; John, 94.
Rumley, George, 207; John, 207.
Rumleye, John, 93.
Rumey, John, 99; Thomas. 99.
Rumney. Anne, 217; George, 98. 100, 210, 217; Jane. 96, 217; John, 96. 98, 100, 210, 216, 217.
Ruse, George, 212.
Russell, Anne. 103, 206; Cisly, 229; Francis. 94; John, 94, 206; Mary, 205; Marssy, 206; Nicasius, 103, 219; Richard, 103. 206, 219; Sarah, 94; Thomas. 9; William, 201, 205.
Rutter. Jonne. 123; John, 77; Mary, 77; Mr., 192.
Ryshmond, William. 223.

S.

Sabey, John, 202; Magdelen, 89; William, 89, 90, 202.
Sabie, Maudlin, 208; William, 208.

Sabin, Elizabeth, 257.
Saby, Daniel, 92; James, 89; William, 88, 89, 92, 199, 204.
Sacheucrell, Francis, 138; John, 138; Mr., 243.
Sachfeild, Edward, 57; Mris., 186; Rachel, 255; Rebecca, 254; Richard. 56, 57, 172, 185; Sarah, 249; Widow, 185.
Sachfilde, Richard, 63, 170.
Sacker, Marie, 162; Richard, 162.
Sadler, Jacamine, 132.
Saijon, Abraham, 102; Judith, 102; Mary, 102.
Saires, Zephaine, 246.
Sakary, Julian, 107.
Sale, Jone, 240.
Sallisbury, Elizabeth, 239.
Sallomon, Anne. 38; Henry, 44; Jelyan. 174; John, 144; Mary, 40; Mr., 240; Nicholas, 146; Richard, 36, 146; Thomas, 33. 36. 40, 44, 144, 146, 168, 174, 178.
Salmon, Thomas, 257.
Salomon, Thomas, 152, 243.
Salsbury, Daniel, 141; Elizabeth, 16; Robert, 16, 141; Susan, 141.
Salter, Barbery, 260; Jeffry, 167; John, 167; Martha, 248.
Samford, Susan, 252.
Sammon, Prudence, 261.
Sanders, Robert. 165.
Sanford, Jane. 69, 177; Phillis, 69; Robert, 67, 69, 176, 177.
Sanforde, Margaret, 70; Phillis, 70; Robert, 70.
Santleger, Anthony, 253.
Sapp, Elizabeth. 76; John, 76; Mary. 76.
Sappes, Elias, 71; John, 71; Mary. 71.
Satchfeeld, Andrew, 44; Dionice, 12; Gilbert, 6, 10, 12, 13; Henry, 38; John, 35, 38, 41, 46; Katherine, 13; Mary, 6, 46; Richard, 10, 41; Thomas, 42.
Satchfeild, Elizabeth, 59, 199, 200; Hester, 60; Mr., 196; Richard, 59, 60.
Satchfeilde, Mrs., 81.
Satchfeld, Anne, 134; Cisly, 146; Dennys, 235; Elizabeth, 32, 228; Gilbert, 9, 12, 125, 134, 231, 235; Henry, 140; John. 32, 35. 42, 44, 135, 140, 146, 148. 150; Margaret, 229; Martha, 48, 160; Mary, 148, 231; Mr., 142; Mrs., 242; Rebecca, 50; Richard, 48, 50, 51, 54, 150, 160; Thomas, 12; William, 9, 54, 134.
Satraw, Dorothy. 111.
Sauage, William, 136.

INDEX OF NAMES. 291

Sauidge, Susan, 167.
Sauill, Sarah, 151.
Saule, Denis, 260.
Saull, Connoway, 207.
Saunder, Roger, 223.
Saunders, Charles, 214 ; John, 2, 107 ; Mr.. 214; Ralph, 108; Randoll, 3 ; Robert, 2, 105 ; Thomas. 3.
Savage, Martha, 249.
Sawell, Eleanor, 92.; John, 92.
Sawfor, Joane, 117.
Sawllmond, Alexander, 122.
Sawlter, Blase, 223.
Saxfeeld, Elizabeth, 5.
Saxfeild, Mr., 216.
Saxfeld, Gilbert. 7 ; John, 7.
Say, John, 1 ; William, 1.
Saye, John, 105 ; William, 105.
Sayer, Nicholas, 151.
Sayon, Abraham, 98; Judith, 98.
Saywel, Eleanor, 206 ; John, 206.
Saywell, Edward, 215; Frances, 97; John. 95, 97, 99 ; Mr., 215 ; Sarah, 95, 217 ; Ursula, 215 ; William. 99.
Scaliet, Mark, 8, 49, 113, 150, 153. 224, 241.
Scaliot, Mark, 19. 23, 25, 130, 146 ; Paul, 19, 25, 130 ; Susan, 23, 146.
Scarlet, Andrew, 222.
Scath, John, 141.
Scherly, Thomas, 110.
Sekot, George. 14 ; William, 13.
Sekott. Thomas, 12.
Scot, Anne, 14, 134 ; John, 15, 214 ; Judah, 214 ; William, 14, 15.
Scott, Edmond, 252 ; John, 101; Judith, 101 ; Mr. 214 ; Walter, 250 ; William, 256.
Scotte, Francis, 163, 244 ; Julian, 245.
Scotton. John, 248.
Scrarbricke, Anthony, 249.
Scremshy, John, 141 ; Mr., 141.
Scruier, John, 105.
Scrivenor, Edward, 261.
Sea, Dorothy, 257 ; Richard. 88 ; Susan, 88.
Seaborne, Frances, 256.
Seager, Giles, 246.
Seale. Thomas, 210.
Seall, James, 258.
Seaman, James, 153 ; Mary, 196 ; Mr., 243 ; Robert, 159 ; Thomas, 153, 159.
Seare, Ralph, 233.
Seares, Nicholas, 80 ; Susan, 80.
Seargant, Bridget, 211 ; Thomas, 211.
Searle, Mary, 219 ; Mr., 219 ; Thomas, 219.
Sedall, William, 146.
Sedghicke, Martha, 261.
Sedgwick, Elizabeth, 94 ; Nathaniel, 94.

Seely, Judith, 245 ; Richard, 109.
Segar, Joane, 241 ; Margaret, 2 ; William, 108, 110.
Seger, John, 137 ; Rowland, 106 ; Sarah, 137.
Segers, Jone, 132.
Seirle, Isabel. 56 ; John, 56.
Selby, John, 196.
Seller, Sarah, 200, 257 ; William. 4.
Selman, Robert, 94, 121.
Selwin, Anne. 93 ; Robert, 23.
Semer. —, 108.
Sener, Christopher, 197.
Senior, Francis. 250.
Serch, John, 254.
Seres, Nicholas, 194, 195, 201 ; Susan, 201 ; William. 194.
Sergant, Bridget, 73 ; Thomas, 73.
Sergeant, Thomas. 197, 202.
Seriant, Thomas, 205.
Sericant, Susan, 79 ; Thomas, 79.
Sesmer, Edmund, 162.
Seuerne, William, 182.
Seward, Awdry, 124.
Sexton, Elizabeth, 256.
Seygar, Elizabeth, 221.
Seyger, John, 221.
Seymore, Thomas, 248.
Seyr, Ralph. 28 ; William, 28.
Shanke, John, 231 ; Peter, 231.
Sharp, Ellen, 256.
Sharpe, Edward, 73, 240; Elizabeth, 71, 73, 251 ; Katherine, 259 ; John, 71, 73.
Shartine, Christopher, 246.
Shaw, Anne, 200 ; Elizabeth, 79, 252 ; Jasper, 196 ; Ralph, 41 ; Robert, 79, 196, 200 ; Roger, 41.
Shawe, Anne, 82 ; Elizabeth, 192 ; Mr., 194 ; Robert, 82, 192.
Shearemanne, Joane, 11.
Sheding, Ralph, 116.
Sheffeild, Francis, 164.
Shene, James, 235 ; William, 235.
Shenton, Joane, 95 ; Samuel, 95, 96.
Shepheard, Elizabeth,49; Sarah, 97 ; Susan. 97 ; Thomas, 49 ; William, 97.
Shepie, Elizabeth, 151; Robert, 151.
Sheppard, Elizabeth, 251; Jane, 61 ; William, 61, 247.
Sheppy, Helena, 41 ; Katherine, 39; Margaret, 36; Mary, 31; Robert, 31, 32, 36, 39, 41 ; William, 32.
Shepy, Barbara, 140 ; Jane, 42 ; Joane, 48 ; Katherine, 141 ; Margaret, 46, 148 ; Robert, 42, 46, 48, 140, 141, 148; William, 140.
Sheremane, Katherine, 261.

Sheres, Alexander, 121.
Sherington, Elizabeth, 214 ; William, 214.
Sherman, Edward, 181, 247 ; Katherine, 251.
Sherrington, Elizabeth,100, 101, 103, 249 ; Mary, 101 ; William, 99, 100, 101, 103.
Sherson, Thomas, 225.
Shersonne, Mary, 10.
Sheyfeld, Edward, 110.
Shingleton, Lawrence, 140, 230; Margery, 145.
Ship, Mary, 252.
Shipp, Adam, 165 ; John, 165 William, 176, 192, 253.
Shippe, Alice, 182 ; John, 105 ; William, 182.
Shipdon, Edmond, 190.
Shipham, Edward, 215, 217 ; Mary, 215.
Shipton, John, 255.
Shittleworth, Robert, 242.
Shoreditch, Mary, 257.
Shores, William, 236.
Shorte, Margaret, 184; William, 184, 188.
Shute, Anna, 100, 103 ; Francis, 100 ; Samuel, 100, 103.
Sibblis, Judith, 200.
Sibley, Mathew, 199 ; Mr., 199.
Sibthorpe, Christopher, 205.
Sidgwicke, Elizabeth, 207 ; Nathaniel, 207.
Sikes, Anne, 201 ; Frances, 256; Marie, 194 ; Robert, 85 ; William, 85, 194, 201.
Silk, Anne, 86, 87, 196, 201 ; John, 81, 87, 196, 197, 201 ; Samuel, 196 ; Simon, 256.
Silke, Christian, 90 ; John, 79, 84, 86, 88, 89, 90, 91, 200, 202, 203, 218 ; Marie, 86, 200 ; Susan, 89 ; Vincent, 84.
Simonds, John, 96 ; Mary, 96 ; Mr., 86.
Simons, Christopher, 94 ; John, 93, 94 ; Mary, 93.
Simpson, John, 256.
Singer, Robert, 256.
Sion, Abraham, 209 ; Judith, 209.
Skeell, Anne, 43, 146 ; Ralph, 42 ; Sarah. 41, 146 ; William, 41, 42, 43, 141, 146, 147.
Skerind, Timothy, 257.
Skern, Nicholas, 222.
Skidmore, Anne, 80 ; Edward, 80 ; John, 260.
Skipper, Thomas, 257.
Skolding, Edward, 133 ; John, 133.
Skynner, John, 45 ; Katherine, 227 ; Margaret, 45.
Slade, Alice, 232 ; Harry, 232.
Slake, John, 134.
Slanter, Anne, 68 ; John, 68 ; Mary, 68.
Slater, Jeffery, 60; John, 60, 61, 262 ; Richard, 61.

INDEX OF NAMES.

Slauter, Anne, 179; Caudewell, 63; Flowrance, 172; John, 63, 65, 171, 172, 175, 178, 179, 181, 252; Margaret, 170; Mary, 65, 252.
Sleepe, Thomas, 242.
Slinge, William, 107.
Smalmanne, John, 244.
Smart, Ralph, 262.
Smith, Agatha, 15; Alexander, 71, 204; Alice, 223; Anne, 29, 94, 101, 136, 229, 255, 256; Benjamin, 261; Collis, 223; Dorcas, 96, 100; Edward, 16, 123, 220, 240; Elizabeth, 80, 99, 101, 212, 258; Ellen, 125; Elybath, 99; Frances, 30, 141; Francis, 236; George, 84, 175, 236; Captain George, 209; Hager, 59; Henry, 100, 101, 216; Humphry, 32, 137, 235; Jackeson, 216; Jarvice, 96, 100, 213; John, 14, 15, 16, 18, 28, 80, 92, 94, 97, 99, 100, 101, 102, 123, 124, 125, 126, 139, 196, 203, 204, 205, 206, 212, 233, 238, 260; Jone, 238, 249; Joyce, 71, 73, 205; Judith, 14; Katherine, 32, 39; Martha, 229; Mary, 100, 201, 213, 223; Milicent, 258; Miles, 194; Mr., 210; Peter, 12, 110; Randall, 184; Rebecca, 85, 87, 195; Richard, 18; Robert, 6, 38, 39, 235, 245; Samuel, 155; Sarah, 84, 247; Simon, 79; Susan, 256; Thomas, 71, 73. 75, 77, 79, 80, 84, 85, 87, 100, 102, 190, 191, 195, 198, 199, 204; Ursula, 38; Walter, 32, 77, 190; Widow, 41; William, 28, 29, 30, 32, 38, 75, 100, 136, 141, 199, 233, 256.
Smithe, Anne, 99; Elizabeth, 261; John, 99, 125; Mrs., 211; Peter, 82; Richard, 99; Sarah, 81; Thomas, 81, 82.
Smithes, Ellen, 13; John, 204; Mr., 127.
Smiththicke, Ellen, 70; Margaret, 70; Mr., 174; Thomas, 65, 70.
Smyth, Dorcas, 210; Elizabeth, 208; George, 208; Jarvis, 210; John, 208, 215; Mary, 207; Sarah, 208; Thomas, 207, 208; Walter, 215.
Snape, Edward, 167; Elizabeth, 167; Hannah, 247; John, 163.
Sneaten, Mary, 256.
Snepe, Anne, 223.
Sneton, Thomas, 122.
Snode, Mary, 252.
Snowe, Harry, 120.
Socke, Mrs., 168.
Sodaine, Katherine, 113.
Sollomon, Anne, 245; John, 26; Marie, 246; Thomas, 26, 29, 245.

Sommer, William, 107.
Sommers, Joane, 107; Peter, 170; Stephen, 107.
Sotherton, Anne, 251.
Sound, James, 116.
Sourall, Joane, 106.
South, Sarah Bee, 253; Sarah, 253.
Southwell, Anne, 65, 69, 70, 71, 73, 74, 210; Elizabeth, 77, 80, 189; John, 74, 75, 187; Joseph, 83; Margaret, 67; Mary, 73; Mrs., 175; Ralph, 65, 67, 69, 70, 71, 73, 74, 75, 77, 79, 80, 83, 170, 173, 187, 188, 189; Richard, 79; Susan, 71; Thomas, 70; William, 75, 188.
Southwood, Richard, 222.
Spacy, John, 221.
Spalding, Anne, 45; Edward, 44; Wilfrod, 38, 44, 45.
Spann, John, 177.
Sparkes, Dorothy, 254.
Sparks, John, 254.
Sparune, Nicholas, 228.
Sparrat, Anne, 108.
Sparrey, Josiah, 86.
Sparrow, Alice, 205; Jane, 85; Josiah, 85.
Speck, Joane, 199; Zachary, 199, 254.
Speed, Elizabeth, 108; Ellen, 106; Hannah, 200; Harry, 106; Jone, 228; Thomas, 200.
Speidell, Euclid, 118; Katherine, 118.
Spence, Alice, 231; Anne, 186; Francis, 126; Margery, 126.
Spencer, Anne, 84, 86; John, 84, 86; Thomas, 225; William, 222.
Spensely, Thomas, 210.
Spenser, John, 85; Marie, 85.
Spert, Robert, 105; Thomas, 223.
Spilsberie, Thomas, 182.
Spilsbery, Sarah, 256; Thomas, 197, 253.
Spilsburie, Thomas, 85, 194.
Spiser, Widow, 210.
Spooner, Benjamin, 261.
Sporling, Nicholas, 126.
Sporlynge, Lawrence, 81; Nicholas, 81.
Spradbury, Edward, 190; Thomas, 190.
Spratberry, Sarah, 210.
Sprentar or Sprenter, John, 155.
Squier or Squire, John, 232, 254; Randoll, 232.
Stabbye, John, 109.
Stables, Margaret, 242.
Staffold, Joane, 252.
Staines, Anne, 120, 254; William, 120.
Stallocke, Ellen, 226.
Stallord, Hannah, 90.
Stallowbrace, Joyce, 258.
Stamford, Mary, 107.

Stamper, Anne, 222; George, 108.
Stancer, Gregory, 143.
Staudish. Henry, 264; Robert, 171, 249.
Standly, George, 241; John, 14; Rowland, 14.
Stanes, Grace, 226.
Stanhop, Sir Edward, 51.
Stanhope, Bridget, 253.
Stanley, James, 21; John, 21, 126; Margery, 126.
Stanly, Barnaby, 128; Friz, 129; James, 127; John, 15, 17, 19, 23, 29, 124, 127, 128, 129, 227; Jone, 225; Margery, 19; Susan, 23, 127; Thomas, 15, 17, 124; Ursula, 23; William, 241.
Stanniper, John, 2.
Stansall, Peter, 155.
Stanstall, Alce, 248.
Stanton, Agnes, 237; Elizabeth, 128; John, 128; William, 197.
Staper, Etheldra, 1; Joane, 2, 3; Richard, 2; Rowland, 1.
Staphith, Henry, 253.
Staple, Edward, 117; Mr., 102.
Starkey, Edward, 257; Elizabeth, 257; Marie, 255, 258.
Starling, Frances, 150; James, 150.
Start, Anthony, 94, 207; James, 94, 207; Mr., 210.
Stauclie, Abigail, 158; James, 53, 158; Sarah, 53, 158, 243.
Stawes, Katherine, 219.
Stayner, Harry, 15; William, 15.
Steale, Robert, 227.
Steele, Recorder, 259.
Steeuen, Richard, 7.
Steeuens, Ellen, 230; Katherine, 247; Margaret, 231; Richard, 231.
Steevens, Margaret, 251.
Steevenson, John, 247.
Stellowman, Susan, 248.
Stellyman, Sarah, 247.
Stephen, Mr., 172, 173.
Stephens, Alexander, 194; Elizabeth, 263; Sarah, 257.
Stepney, Abraham, 156.
Stert, Anthony, 95, 96, 208; Elizabeth, 208; James, 96; John, 95, 208.
Stetfeild, Henry, 208; John, 208.
Steuanes, John, 239.
Steuannes, Edward, 10; John, 9, 10; Margaret, 9.
Steuen, Richard, 223.
Steueues, Edward, 10; Richard, 13.
Steuenues, Francis, 13; John, 11; Richard, 13; William, 11.
Steuens, Anne, 115; Edward

INDEX OF NAMES.

160; Francis, 138; James, 14, 121; Joane, 126; John, 37, 115, 126, 138; Katherine, 14, 242; Mr., 12, 153; Nicholas, 257; Philip, 12, 129; Richard, 12, 14, 121, 122. 129, 138; William, 37, 122, 138.
Steuenson, Margaret. 202.
Stevens, Anne, 8.
Steverson, Katherine, 260.
Stevins, Sarah, 264.
Steward, John, 39; Joyce, 34; Mary. 172, 264; Moses, 36; Robert, 61, 171.
Stewart, Grace. 239; John, 218; Mabel, 239; Mary, 154; Moses, 154; Robert, 154; William, 154.
Stiche, William, 231.
Still, John, 223.
Stirt, Humphry, 200; Joane, 256; Sarah, 200.
Stoakes, Bryde, 7.
Stocke, Mr., 51, 147, 163, 167; Mrs., 224.
Stockemeed, Alice, 3; Mary, 5.
Stocken, Elizabeth, 214; Ralph, 214.
Stocking, Ralph, 94; Richard, 94.
Stockinge, Barbara, 102; Ralph, 102.
Stockmede, Thomas, 4.
Stodder, Mary, 66; Richard, 66.
Stodderd, Joice, 235; Philip, 132, 134, 235; Walter, 134.
Stoke, Alexander. 108.
Stokely, Anne, 139.
Stokemaid, Alice, 222.
Stoken, Jane, 98; Ralph, 98, 209.
Stokes, Alice, 230; Benjamin, 14; Bryde, 115; Jane, 15; John, 109; Judith, 5, 115; Mr., 109; Richard, 6, 210, 233; Robert, 110, 123, 222; William, 15, 233.
Stokin, Benjamin, 206; Elizabeth, 99; Jane, 210; Ralph, 99, 206, 209, 210.
Stokson, Elizabeth, 262.
Stollard, Sarah, 203; Thomas, 203.
Stonar, Elizabeth, 147.
Stone, Alice, 58, 162; Bridget, 262; Charles, 60; Helen, 56, 161; John. 57; Thomas, 56, 57, 58, 60, 161, 243; William 161.
Stonehouse, Anne, 9, 114; Elizabeth, 229; George, 9, 114, 122; James, 12; John, 231; Nicholas, 10; Rose, 226; Walter, 11.
Stoney, Robert, 222.
Stookes, Benjamin, 121; Emme, 121.
Stott, John, 109.

Stoupe, John, 222.
Stourtonne, John, 223.
Stowell, Jone, 207.
Strachie, William, 146.
Strafford, James, 161; Sarah, 161.
Straunge, William, 231.
Stranguidge, Joane, 204.
Strato, Thomas, 258.
Straughon, John, 232; Nicholas, 232.
Straunge, John, 12.
Strayne, William, 169.
Street, William, 3.
Streete, Humphry, 248.
Stretch, Elizabeth, 83; Richard, 83, 194.
Stringer, Mary, 215; Richard, 215.
Stroker, Anne, 242.
Strudwick, Henry, 256.
Stuard, Edward, 124; Elizabeth, 124; Mary, 42; Robert, 36, 39, 42, 43; William, 43.
Stuart, John, 144; Robert, 144.
Stubbs, William, 198.
Stubfeild, Henry, 209.
Stuckey. William, 210.
Stullingflet, Alice, 236; Robert, 236.
Sturdy, Dyna, 174; James, 174.
Sturgion, Margery, 114.
Sturman, Anne. 34; Elizabeth, 237; Grace, 28; James, 25; John, 113, 125. 231; Katherine, 225; Margaret. 29; Mary, 31, 111; Nicholas, 5, 125; Richard, 4, 22, 24, 25, 28, 29, 31. 34, 132, 136, 231, 237; Thomas, 3, 24; William, 22, 117, 132.
Sturmanne, John, 7; Mary, 6.
Sturt, Anthony, 209, 216; Frances, 102; Humphry, 256; James, 209; John, 92, 93, 97, 98, 102, 210, 214, 216; Joseph, 102; Samuel, 97, 98, 210; Thomas, 214.
Stutfeild, Elizabeth, 211; Henry, 250; Mr., 211.
Styrman, John, 175.
Sucklyne, Richard, 110.
Sumner, Joseph, 258.
Sutle, Thomas, 162.
Sutton, Alice. 66; Elizabeth, 24, 62, 70, 73, 132, 139, 246; Isaac, 61, 62, 63, 64; John, 22, 24, 27, 34, 62, 64, 66, 70, 73. 132. 134, 139, 154, 173, 185, 194, 231, 247; Margaret, 180; Mary, 63, 64; Nicholas, 61; Sarah, 73; Stephen, 244; Susan, 27, 154; William, 34, 154.
Swallow, Justice, 259.
Swan, Bridget, 237; John, 130; Katherine, 155; Libeus, 130, 155, 161, 237; Robert, 258.

Swanne, Libeus, 231; Mr., 141.
Swetman, Susan, 257.
Swift, Elizabeth, 256; Jane. 52, 159; Richard, 50, 52, 153, 159.
Swifte, Jane, 159; Richard, 158, 159.
Swinehoe, James, 194.
Swingefeeld, Thomas, 111.
Swingfeeld, Anne, 117; Edward, 8. 11; Harry, 110.
Swinkfeeld, Edward, 118; Giles, 119; John, 10.
Swone, Samuel. 250.
Swyngfeeld. Anne, 117.
Swyukfeeld, Mary, 6.
Symcock, Sarah, 192.
Symkins, Thomas, 229.
Symmes, Margaret, 113.
Symmon, Alice, 51; Thomas. 51.
Symmones, James, 49; Mr., 151; Thomas, 49.
Symon, Mr., 141.
Symon, or Seaman, Edward, 54; Thomas, 54.
Symondes, Alexander, 64, 70, 73, 172, 248; Elizabeth, 113; John, 70, 97; Mary, 73; Susan, 70, 73; Thomas, 63; Thurstan. 249; William, 63.
Symonds, Charles, 100, 216; Edward, 98; John, 98, 99, 100, 216; Mary, 252; Susan, 99; Walter, 256; William, 98.
Symones, Alexander, 65, 178; John, 178; Nicholas, 138; Samuel, 65.
Symons, Alexander, 67, 69, 176, 178; Alice, 251; Elizabeth, 100; John, 100; Mary, 183; Nicholas, 40, 144; Susan, 67, 69, 176, 183, 186; Thomas, 40; Widow, 185; William, 69.
Sympson, or Sympsonne, Anne, 119; Thomas, 233.
Symson, Richard, 155.
Synagree, Austine, 182.
Syngerly, John, 115.
Synkefeeld, Alice, 227.
Synnocke, James, 54.

T.

Tailer, Abel, 39; Daniel, 50; Joane, 121; John, 39, 50; Katherine, 221; Thomas, 121; William, 110.
Tailor, Abacucke, 36; Abel, 39, 158; Christian, 43; David, 44; Griffet, 107; Henry, 254; John, 36, 39, 43, 44, 46, 153, 157, 158, 229; Mary, 46, 153; Mrs., 158; Nicholas, 137, 235; Robert, 226; Thomas, 135, 157, 227, 235; William, 112.

294 INDEX OF NAMES.

Talbut, Richard, 242.
Talemacke, Francis, 226.
Tallis, John, 232.
Talmach, Frances, 119.
Tandy, Sarah, 256.
Tanner, Henry, 203, 254 ; John, 221 ; Judith, 247 ; Margaret, 263.
Tappin, James, 91 ; John, 89 ; Mary, 90. 263 ; Thomas, 90, 201 ; Thomas Walter, 201 ; William, 89, 90, 91.
Tapping. Elizabeth, 93, 94 ; John. 91, 202 ; Martha. 93 ; Sarah, 92 ; William, 89, 91, 92, 93, 94, 202.
Tapster, *alias* Aldred, William, 4.
Tarleton, Mr., 206.
Tarlton, George, 207.
Tatam, Boniface, 162.
Tauernor, Jane, 111.
Taven, James, 185.
Tayler, Elizabeth, 262 ; Mr., 262 ; Susan, 261 ; Thomas, 247.
Taylor, Abraham, 120 ; Easter, 259 ; Ellen, 142 ; Henry, 256 ; Hugh, 64 ; Jane. 70, 178 ; John, 63, 64, 65, 67, 69, 70, 81, 106, 171, 177, 183, 201 ; Jone. 69, 70, 183 ; Joyce, 136 ; Katherine. 221 ; Mary, 67, 177 ; Nicholas, 136 ; Peter, 81 ; Richard, 63, 69, 171, 181 ; Susan, 13 ; Thomas, 178 ; William, 217, 248.
Tedder, Ellen, 229 ; Sarah, 252.
Tench. Sarah. 242.
Tenche, Elizabeth, 244.
Tepkyn, John, 108.
Tewed, Edward, 241.
Thackhome, Anne, 224.
Tharpe, John, 250 ; Lawrence, 8.
Thawthes, Anne, 227.
Thew, William, 251.
Thickpenny, Leonard, 137.
Thikneys, Mary, 200.
Thimble, Elizabeth. 250.
Thomas, Elizabeth, 129 ; Hugh, 228 ; Joane, 110 ; Mr., 129 ; William, 229.
Thomlinson, Alice, 15 ; Mathew, 15.
Thompson, Elizabeth, 117 ; Henry, 176, 233 ; John, 109 ; Margaret, 208, 241 ; Mary, 259.
Thompsonne, Thomazine, 194.
Thomson, Anne, 12 ; Edward. 222 ; Henry, 149 ; Lancelot, 152 ; Mary, 4 ; Maudelyn, 117 ; Richard, 4, 12, 13 ; Thomas, 13.
Thomsonne, Maudlyn, 5 ; Stephen, 116 ; William. 6.
Thornell, Mary, 23 ; Thomas, 23.

Thornhurst, Lady Barbara, 253.
Thornton, Anne, 105, 250 ; Jane. 106 ; Joane, 111 ; Robert, 33, 108.
Thorntone, Thomas. 259.
Thorogood, Alice, 44, 158 ; Anne, 35. 42, 148 ; Bartholomew, 51 ; Cicely. 49, 158 ; Daniel, 32, 38 ; Effam, 41 ; Elizabeth, 93 ; James. 31, 33, 35. 38, 41, 42, 44, 49, 50, 51, 148, 158. 235 ; John, 31, 32, 33, 236 ; Joseph. 93 ; Mary, 94 ; Richard, 93, 94 ; William, 236.
Thoroughgood, Richard, 93 ; William, 93.
Thorowgood, Benjamin, 91 ; Edward, 167 ; Elizabeth, 85 ; James, 148 ; Jane, 201 ; Mr., 139 ; Richard, 88, 89, 91. 92, 95 ; Simon, 80, 85, 88, 195 ; Susan, 80 ; William, 95.
Thorp, Thomas, 127.
Thorpe, Anne, 222 ; John, 196 ; Thomas, 9, 105, 121.
Thorton, Anne, 33.
Thrawer, Henry, 38 ; Robert, 38.
Thrower. Edward, 32 ; Elizabeth. 109 ; John, 236 ; Robert, 32, 34, 137, 140, 236 ; Susan, 137.
Throwly, Margery. 225.
Thurland, James, 217.
Thurman, Edward, 207.
Thuroughgood, Elizabeth, 213 ; Richard, 213.
Thurske, Elizabeth, 230.
Thwait, Judith, 124 ; Stephen, 124.
Thwaite, Alice, 115 ; Mary, 115.
Thwaites, Elizabeth, 228 ; John, 120 ; Margery, 112.
Thayres, Anthony, 178 ; Bridget, 178.
Tibbald, Mr., 22 ; Philip, 14 ; William, 14.
Tibbold, Anne, 123 ; Jesper, 16 ; Jone, 135 ; Robert, 125 ; William, 15, 16, 125, 126, 135, 235.
Tickener, Robert, 206 ; Thomas. 206.
Ticknell, Susan, 218 ; Thomas, 218.
Tickner, Appolonia, 92 ; George, 96 ; John, 95, 209 ; Lawrence, 208 ; Robert, 93 ; Thomas, 92, 93, 95, 96, 209.
Ticknor, Lawrence, 81 ; Michael, 81.
Ticstopher, Anne, 79 ; Henry, 80 ; William, 79.
Ticstover, William, 78.
Tidder, Susan, 257.
Tiggin, Thomas, 189.
Tiggins, Anne, 252 ; Margaret, 75 ; Marie, 255 ; Tabitha, 183 ; Thomas, 75, 183.

Tillard, Anne, 101. 103 ; Christopher, 101, 103 ; Mr., 215 ; Thomas, 101.
Tiller, Sarah, 259.
Tillman, Edward, 153 ; Ellen, 154 ; Nicholas, 51, 153, 154 ; William, 51.
Tillowe, Anne, 120.
Tilman, Edward, 49 ; Nicholas, 49.
Tippe, Ellen, 114 ; Harry, 114.
Tipper, Alice, 223 ; Elizabeth, 105 ; Harry, 115, 225 ; Jone, 2 ; Margaret, 223 ; Thomas, 3, 108.
Tiror, Anne, 245.
Tirrell, Deborah, 256.
Tite, Mathy, 236 ; Richard, 236.
Tither, Edward, 206.
Titimouse, William, 258.
Titly. James, 237 ; Robert, 237.
Tixtofer, John, 75 ; Thomas, 75.
Tixtover, Elizabeth, 76 ; Thomas, 76, 82 ; William, 82.
Tocock, Jane, 192 ; Thomas, 192.
Tococke. Jane, 82 ; Thomas, 82.
Tod, Jone, 145 ; Maud, 222.
Tomelay, Christian, 199.
Tompson. Anne, 121 ; Christopher, 125 ; Henry, 72, 133 ; John, 226 ; Margaret, 111, 237 ; Mary, 78 ; Mr., 177 ; Robert, 78, 80, 190 ; Thomas, 72, 186 ; Thomazine. 72, 74 ; Valentine, 125 ; William, 74, 186, 228.
Tompsonne, William. 244.
Tomson, Charles, 106 ; Elizabeth, 201 ; Joane. 118 ; John, 114 ; Mary, 118 ; Richard, 118, 125 ; Thomas, 125 ; William, 177.
Tomsonne, Elizabeth, 8 ; Jane, 221 ; Richard, 222.
Tonney, Arthur, 232 ; Edward, 232.
Tooley, Edmond, 81, 191, 202, 203, 204 ; Elizabeth, 191 ; Jane, 204 ; Mrs., 191 ; Robert, 203 ; Rose, 81, 202.
Toolie, James, 193.
Tooly, Edmond, 214.
Toomes, Alexander, 32 ; John, 32, 35, 137.
Towe, Katherine, 223.
Towers, Katherine, 91 ; Leonard, 91, 92, 203 ; Peter, 91, 92, 203 ; William, 159.
Towerson, Christian, 39 ; William, 39, 141.
Towley, Elizabeth, 222.
Townly, Margaret. 229.
Townsend, Ellen, 117.
Townson, Thomas, 223.
Trase, Jane, 128 ; William, 128.
Trasler, John, 96 ; Mathew, 96 ; Sarah. 96.
Tratter, Julie, 6.
Travesse, Basshaw, 163.

INDEX OF NAMES. 295

Treate, Mary, 258; Richard, 258.
Treaton, James, 113.
Treuuers, Elizabeth, 249.
Trodway, John, 99; Thomas, 99.
Tresor, Elizabeth, 120.
Tress. Hugh, 256.
Tresse, Hugh, 198.
Trevis, Andrew, 149, 235; Margaret, 149; William, 235.
Triggs, Anne, 252.
Triplett, Mary, 262.
Trisse, Anne, 112.
Tronckett, Mrs., 220.
Trotte, Ellen, 222.
Trotter, Elizabeth, 7; John, 4; William, 222.
Trougton, Frances, 109.
Trowell, Jone, 248.
Truket, Abraham, 94; Ralph, 94.
Trulace, Deborah, 171.
Trumkett, Ralph, 92; Rebecca, 92.
Trumkitt, Abel, 92; Ralph, 92.
Truncket, Martha, 209; Ralph, 98, 209; Susan, 98.
Trunckett, Anne, 95; Martha, 97; Ralph, 95, 97, 102, 215; Rebecca, 95.
Trunckit, Ralph, 263; William, 263.
Trunckitt, Mary, 204; Ralph, 204.
Trunket, Mary, 91; Ralph, 90, 91; Sarah, 90.
Trunkett, Abel, 218; Mary, 93; Ralph, 93, 205, 218.
Tuchborn, Ellen, 106.
Tucker, Arthur, 167; Mr., 164; Mris., 184; Thomas, 175, 176.
Tucking, Richard, 226.
Tulie, Edmond, 77; Robert, 77.
Tunbridge, Deonis, 247.
Tupper, Margaret, 1.
Turberfeld, Morgan, 111.
Turfett, Edward, 257.
Turfrey, George, 88; Richard, 88, 199.
Turke, Anne, 134; Harry, 134; Mrs., 242, 243; Samuel, 49.
Turland, Anne, 215; James, 215.
Turnar, Christian, 224.
Turner, Alice, 136; Amy, 57; Christian, 221; Christopher, 13; Elizabeth, 11, 38, 94, 119, 254; Hillary, 33, 36, 38, 40, 42, 44, 47, 49. 51, 53. 57, 237; Humphry, 47; Jane, 153, 229; Jeffery, 153; John, 12, 14, 15, 51, 93, 94, 120, 121; Joice, 123; Mary, 14, 42, 94; Mr., 56; Palmer, 55; Peter, 162, 237; Richard, 136; Sibel, 93, 94; Susan, 36; Thomas, 49, 53; William, 15, 33, 44. 55.
Turnere, Anne, 57; Hillary, 57.
Turnpeny, Thomas, 110.
Turret, Stephen, 246.
Twedy, Elizabeth, 252.
Twist, Roger, 157.

Twistleden, Alice, 106.
Tyffenne, Isabel, 221.
Tyggius, Anne, 174; Elizabeth, 68; Tabitha, 68; Thomas, 68, 174, 177.
Tylluer, Ellen, 48; Richard, 48.
Tymes, Margery. 223.
Typper, Jone. 226.
Tyther, Edward, 65, 67, 68, 174, 181; Francis, 67, 174; Honor, 65; Mary, 211; Susan, 68.
Tythers, Edward, 177.

U.

Ubanke, Thomas, 105.
Udall *alias* Woodall, John, 56, 161; Katherine, 161; Margaret, 56.
Udoueall, John, 174.
Unckles, Osman, 197.
Underwood, Alce, 257; Richard, 240.
Upley, Margaret, 2.
Upperhend, Anne, 116.
Upton, Elizabeth, 148; Mary, 122; Walter, 123, 225.
Urselys, Anne, 225.
Utting, Amy, 102; John, 102.
Uttinge, John, 216; Mary, 216; Robert, 216.
Uxlaye, Giles, 7.
Uxley, Katherine, 3.
Uxly, Elizabeth, 113.

V.

Vaghan, Lewes, 107; Nazareth, 246.
Vale, Michael, 146.
Valler, Robert, 119.
Vales, John, 108.
Vandebrooke, Mr., 187; Susan, 187.
Vandeleare, Jesper, 125.
Vandenhamble, John, 121.
Vandeweruen, Charles, 110.
Vandort, Cornelis, 21; Katherine, 21.
Vane, Mary, 241.
Vanhoeke, Bartholomew, 16; Daniel, 17; Paul. 16.
Vanlower, Lady Katherine, 257.
Vansalt, Isaac, 43, 159; John, 43, 159.
Vanvphowen, Gilbert, 43; Peter, 43.
Varnam. Ralph, 50.
Varne. John, 137; Margaret, 137.
Varnham, Benjamin, 100; Charles, 212, 213; Joseph, 100; Mr., 212, 213; Ralph, 50; Thomas, 213; William, 100.
Vauhon, Michael, 208.
Venner, Alexander, 101, 102, 219; Elizabeth, 101, 102; Richard, 102; William, 219.

Verney, James, 117.
Verteu, Christopher, 53.
Vertew, Christopher, 160, 161, 245; Mr., 155.
Vertu, Christopher, 35, 37, 43, 156, 160; Elizabeth, 35; James, 37; John, 43; Margaret, 160; Peter, 156.
Vertue, Bridget, 75; Christopher, 75, 166, 188, 189; Grace, 188; John, 75, 189; Mr., 146, 164; Mrs., 168.
Vigor, Stephen, 91; Walter, 91.
Villiares, Anne, 239.
Vinar, Richard, 239.
Vincent, Thomazine, 245.
Vinclent, Jone, 226.
Vintener, Ellen, 225.
Vittle, Richard, 232; Silvester, 232.
Vleskchawer, Gyllam de, 134.
Voulmer, James, 173.
Vowell, Epham. 195; John, 163. 180; Mr., 174, 191; Thomas, 163.
Vowelles, Mr., 68.
Vyner, Harry, 130; Thomas, 130; Sir Thomas, 260.

W.

Wade, Edmond, 261; John, 118; Marie, 258; Mr., 213; Sarah, 213.
Wager, Edward, 248.
Waideson, Tobias, 248.
Wnight, Alice, 45; Anthony, 47; Elizabeth, 43; Fulke, 36, 140; Gyllian, 225; Harry, 32, 41, 149, 235; Margery, 40, 153; Mr., 151, 155; Mrs., 243; Richard, 32, 34, 36, 38, 40, 41, 43, 45, 47, 140, 147, 149, 153, 235, 239; Simon, 38; Thomas, 34, 114, 248.
Waitham, Mr., 214.
Wakefeeld, Mr., 13; Mrs., 13.
Wakefeild, Arthur, 58, 165; Mathew, 165.
Walcot, Francis, 197; John, 197.
Walcote, Francis, 207; Thomas, 207.
Walcott, Elizabeth, 76; Francis, 76, 183, 185. 198; Jane, 198; John, 76; Mary, 183; Sarah, 183.
Waldron, George, 254.
Wales, Daniel, 260.
Walker, Alice, 9, 236; Anne, 221, 224; Audrian, 108; Edward, 8, 9, 10, 11, 12, 17, 120, 127, 130, 170, 223, 231, 236; Elizabeth, 4, 10, 118, 206, 230; Ellen, 12, 171; Francis, 91, 206; Isabel, 7, 231; Jane, 106; Joanne, 176; John, 15, 17, 20, 130, 240;

INDEX OF NAMES.

Walkott, Francis, 213, 261.
Walkur, Francis, 204; Mary, 204.
Wall, Thomas, 140.
Wallay, Nicholas, 11.
Wallen, John, 179.
Waller, John, 222.
Walley, Thomas, 12.
Wallis, Elizabeth, 221; John, 107; Jone, 220; Thomas, 223.
Wallmesly, Alice, 142.
Wallonne, Susan, 9.
Wallthall, Elizabeth, 27; John, 38; Katherine, 37; Thomas, 38, 40, 44, 142, 157; William. 25, 27, 31, 33, 36, 164.
Walltholl, John. 208.
Wally, Thomas, 119.
Walnesly, Ellis, 136.
Walstall, Thomas, 77.
Walthall, Anne, 40, 248; Cisly, 152; Deputy, 244; Dinah, 138; Katherine. 139; Lucas, 36; Luke. 61, 62. 169; Margaret, 80; Marion, 137; Mary, 61, 126; Roger, 55, 137, 163; Thomas, 25, 33. 37, 56, 131, 139, 163, 168, 204; William, 30, 62, 126, 131, 138, 152.
Walter, Alice, 250.
Walton, John, 158; Richard, 129; Robert, 129.
Wandling, Aris, 258.
Wanton, Alice, 106; Thomas, 1.
Wapolle, Hillary, 223.
Ward, Andrew, 195; Frances, 256; Isabel. 196; Joanne, 221; John, 239; Lawrence, 229; Margaret, 89, 199, 212; Mary, 87, 200; Peter, 56; Richard, 258; Samuel, 87, 198; Thomas, 56, 89, 199, 201, 240; William. 198.
Warde, Andrew, 106; Anne, 107; Joanne, 193.
Warden, —, 134; Anne, 144; Margaret, 171; Mr., 148, 156; Robert, 8, 144, 165, 224, 230.
Wardman, Mark, 137; William, 137.
Warenn, Rebecca, 95; Robert, 95.
Waring, John, 99; Mary, 97, 213; Mr., 213; Rebecca, 97; Robert, 97, 99, 100, 213.
Warman, Alce, 248; Alice, 241; Bennet, 51, 163; Elizabeth, 55; George, 58; Harry, 47, 150; Joanne, 48, 160; Mr., 157; Stephen, 53; Susan, 50; William, 47, 48, 50, 51, 53, 55, 58, 150, 160, 163.

Warner, Alice, 256; Anne, 177, 261; Benjamin, 258; Christopher, 193; Elizabeth, 82, 192; Ellen, 69; John, 80, 82, 86, 88, 89, 192, 193, 195, 197, 200, 253; Katherine, 69; Margaret, 128; Mary, 89, 200; Richard, 177; Robert, 128, 260; Sarah. 86, 195; Splenden. 69, 177; William, 88.
Warren, Ade, 1; Ananias, 157; Anne, 253; Barbara, 230; Christopher, 84. 149; Elizabeth, 131, 176, 179; George. 157; Gyllian, 118; Isaac, 83, 86, 194; Jane, 77; Jesper, 14; John, 14, 15, 17, 21, 25. 84. 123, 131, 138, 179, 190, 236. 253; Lettice, 236; Luke, 64; Nicholas, 118, 225; Peter. 77, 80, 83, 86; 194; Rebecca, 80; Richard, 21. 64. 182; Susan, 17; Widow, 209; William, 1, 15, 149, 158, 175, 176, 257.
Warrin. Gulbart, 211; Katherine, 252; Rebecca, 94; Richard, 207; Robert, 94, 207.
Warrington. Edward, 106.
Wastall. Deborah, 79; Thomas, 79.
Wastell, Esther, 81; Mr., 85, 192; Thomas, 81.
Wastnes, Dorothy, 248.
Waters, Jone, 245; Mary, 254.
Waterhouse, Lady Abigail, 253.
Waterhowse, Alice, 192.
Watkines, John, 222.
Watkiunes. Anne, 7; Jane, 4; Katherine, 6; Rachel, 4.
Watkyn, Katherine, 120.
Watkynnes, John, 114.
Watlam. Margery, 136; Philip, 136.
Watring, Joanne, 222.
Watson, Adam 19; Anne, 180; Barnaby, 19, 21, 24, 26, 29, 33, 132, 137, 156, 204, 230; Christopher, 184; Dorothy, 255; Elizabeth, 29, 87, 130, 156, 197, 218; Henry, 75, 87, 180. 181, 189, 255; Joane, 86, 191, 198; John, 24, 26, 130, 186; Katherine, 256; Mary, 87, 258; Mr., 196, 199; Rebecca, 89, 186; Samuel, 88; William, 21, 86, 87, 88, 89, 132, 197, 198, 200, 261.
Watsonn. Margaret, 255.
Wattam, Martha, 10; Mathew, 117; Philip, 127; Susan, 116; Thomas. 117.
Watten, Margaret, 221.
Wattes, Eleanor, 250; Elizabeth, 256; Richard, 217.
Watton, Elizabeth, 229; Thomas, 228.

Wattonne, Susan, 9.
Wattson, Ellen, 221.
Waules, Edmond, 225.
Wavthan, Deborah, 103; William, 103.
Waygood, Thomas, 181.
Waylye, Richard, 115.
Wayt, Katherine, 256.
Waytham, William, 216.
Waythen, Elizabeth, 213; William, 213.
Weanewright, Cisly, 122; Thomas, 229.
Weathernut, John, 262.
Weaver, Lewis, 247; Margaret. 247.
Web. —, 157; Elis. 42. 44, 146; Elizabeth, 44, 146, 155; John, 42, 224; Mrs., 155; Richard, 155; Widow. 188.
Webb. Abigail. 66, 69, 71. 74, 254; Ellis, 148; Goody. 179; John, 66, 68. 69, 71, 74. 177, 185, 188, 204, 240; Katherine, 245; Martha, 69, 74, 177. 185; Mary. 68. 204. 209, 210; Michael, 64. 173. 177, 178; Mr., 170; Nehemia, 71; Richard, 56, 165; Thomazine, 178; William, 56, 165.
Webbe, Amy, 228; Elizabeth, 55; Ellis, 45, 48; Joane, 110; John, 185, 186; Katherine, 235; Mary, 186; Nehemiah. 185; Richard, 55; Robert, 48; William, 45.
Webster, Anne, 228.
Weebrooke, Francis, 154; Jozen, 154; Katherine, 154.
Weight, Mrs., 169; Richard. 165.
Weightman, Alce, 169; Cyslic, 175; Elizabeth, 56, 62, 168; Jane, 57; Peter, 56, 57, 59. 60, 62, 162, 164, 166, 168. 169, 175, 178, 179, 251; Prudence, 59, 164. 166.
Weket, Thomas, 1; William, 1.
Welch, Dorothy, 101; Edward, 223; Elizabeth, 101, 237; Ellen, 116; Robert, 101; William. 237.
Welche, Betteris, 227.
Well, William, 247.
Wellen, Margaret, 172; Marie, 164; Nathaniel, 54, 152, 160, 164, 172; Phebe, 153; Thomas, 54, 160.
Weller, Anne, 222; Barbara, 108; Joanne, 161, 223; Lucy, 112; Maude, 108; Thomas, 112.
Welles, Elizabeth, 213; Jane, 219; John, 218, 219; Mary, 219; Thomas, 213.
Welles, or Wells, Alice, 105; Isabel. 140; John, 140.
Wellham, Elizabeth, 208.
Wellinge, William, 162.

INDEX OF NAMES. 297

Wells, John, 87 ; Sarah, 258 ; Susan, 87 ; Thomas, 95, 207.
Welsh, Edmund, 55.
Wendrit, Alice, 122 ; John, 122.
Wenewright, John, 22; Thomas, 22.
Wenlock, Elizabeth, 74, 181 ; John, 181 ; Joshua, 74.
Weulocke, Elizabeth, 71, 73, 178 ; John, 71, 178 ; Joshua, 73, 179.
Wenman, Elizabeth, 55 ; Sir Ferdinand, 55.
Wenwright, Anne, 19 ; Thomas, 19.
Wessell, John, 31.
West, Alice, 134 ; Andrew, 92 ; Harry. 125 ; John, 125, 175, 248 ; Margaret, 3 ; Thomas, 134 ; William, 92.
Westbrucke, Anne, 204.
Westcoott, Elizabeth, 58 ; Thomas, 58.
Westcott, Anne, 248 ; John, 64 ; Margaret, 60 ; Mary, 189, 201 ; Mrs., 190 ; Thomas, 60, 64, 185, 189.
Weste, John, 186.
Westerbe, Robert, 106.
Westgate, Anne, 112 ; Joane, 222, 227 ; John, 112, 146 ; Margaret, 151.
Westkott, John, 174 ; Mary, 62 ; Thomas, 62, 174.
Westlic, Frances, 156.
Westly, Joane, 149 ; John, 46, 148 ; Robert, 46, 148, 149.
Weston, Anne. 55, 162 ; Michael, 226 ; Mr., 248 ; Nicholas, 167, 247, 249, 252 ; Robert, 55, 57, 162, 165, 167 ; Tobias, 57, 165 ; Valentine, 147 ; William, 164.
Westone, Nicholas, 59 ; Richard, 59 ; Robert, 59.
Westonn. Richard, 167 ; Robert, 167.
Westra, Joane, 110.
Westraw, Elizabeth, 11 ; Ellen, 9 ; Grace, 228 ; Joane, 4, 5, 111 ; Judith, 10 ; Mary, 188 ; Robert, 111 ; Thomas, 12, 121, 188 ; Timothy, 111, 188.
Westrawe, Richard, 13.
Westwood, Elizabeth, 249 ; Jone, 225 ; Richard, 128.
Wetherall, Edward, 90 ; James, 91 ; John, 90, 91 ; Philip, 90.
Wetherell, John, 255.
Wethers, Elias, 138 ; Harry, 138.
Wetheryd, Christopher, 234 ; Richard, 234.
Wethwat, Bridget, 230.
Wetwood, Ralph, 59 ; Robert, 59.
Weuer, Haunce, 116.
Weygod, Thomas, 247.

Whaley, Deborah, 186 ; Mrs., 186 ; Thomas, 186.
Whalie, Anne, 72 ; Deborah, 72 ; Thomas, 72, 179.
Whaly, Deborah, 69, 70 ; Thomas, 69, 70.
Whallyn, Rowland, 222.
Wharton, Robert, 185 ; Thomas, 63.
Whartonne, Grace, 236 ; Robert, 236.
Whatman, Richard, 7.
Whaylsley, Thomas, 202.
Wheatly, Anne, 225.
Wheeler, Alice, 246 ; Elizabeth, 215 ; George, 259 ; Joane, 13, 119 ; John, 196, 246 ; Sarah, 229 ; Thomas. 215, 227.
Whetstone, John, 236 ; Roger, 236.
Whichcote, Thomas, 97.
Whiffyn, John, 251.
Whighte, Thomas, 108.
Whighted, Ralph. 109.
Whiniard, John, 246.
Whitacre, Abigail, 255.
Whitacres, Edward, 245.
Whitbourn, Christian, 90 ; Robert, 90.
Whitburne. Robert, 202.
Whitchkocke. Thomas, 211.
Whitcraft, Anne, 244.
White, Doctor. 180 ; Elizabeth, 37, 253 ; Francis, 67, 70, 177, 227, 251 ; George, 241 ; Harry. 131 ; Jane, 242 ; John, 197, 259 ; Peter, 256 ; Rachel, 228 ; Richard, 122, 196 ; Sarah, 197, 255 ; Simon, 261 ; Susan, 174 ; Thomas, 37, 195, 197 ; Walter, 195.
Whitehead, Elizabeth, 142 ; Thomas. 229.
Whitehorse, Robert, 205.
Whitelocke. Emmanuel, 66 ; Jone, 251 ; Mary, 64 ; Robert, 64, 65, 66 ; William, 65.
Whiteshead, Elizabeth, 199 ; John, 185, 197.
Whitlock, Margaret, 60 ; Robert, 60.
Whitlocke, Elizabeth, 58, 174, 254 ; Grace, 193 ; Margaret, 168 ; Margery, 62, 185 ; Mary, 172 ; Robert, 58, 62, 168, 172, 173, 174. 184, 185, 246 ; William, 173.
Whitman, John, 163 ; Peter, 163, 244.
Whitmann, John, 57 ; Peter, 57.
Whitmore, Harry, 230.
Whitney, John, 87 ; Margaret, 93 ; Richard, 91 ; Robert, 87, 88, 89, 90, 91, 93, 95, 199, 202, 203 ; Thomas, 88, 90, 199, 202.
Whittacars, Roger, 249.
Whittaker, Robert, 207.

Whittingam, Margery, 223 ; Timothy, 9 ; William, 9.
Whittingham, Elizabeth, 74 ; Jane, 181 ; Mary, 74, William, 74, 181.
Whittington, Mr., 203.
Whittney, Mr., 212 ; Robert, 212, 213.
Whorde, Joane, 206.
Whorewood. Thomas, 155.
Whorton, Elizabeth, 64 ; Martha, 65 ; Mary, 67, 174 ; Thomas, 64, 65, 67, 174.
Wiat, Christian, 244.
Wibo, John, 172.
Wiborn, Samuel, 241.
Wickam, William, 143.
Wickersham. Elizabeth, 104 ; Susan. 104 ; Thomas, 104.
Wicket, Jane. 2.
Wickham, John, 126.
Wicks, Mr., 216.
Wifen, John, 19 ; Sarah, 19.
Wiges, Anne, 137 ; Katherine, 135 ; William, 135, 137.
Wigganhance, Elizabeth, 159.
Wigges, or Wigs, Anne, 30 ; William, 30, 234.
Wikkes, Grace, 99; William, 99.
Wilborne, Mr., 257.
Wild, William, 263.
Wildborough, John, 258.
Wilde, Sarah, 242 ; William, 230.
Wildes, Mary, 249.
Wilkenson, Anne, 252.
Wilkins, Anne, 198 ; Francis, 198 ; Katherine, 249.
Wilkinson, Francis, 242 ; Gillian, 118 ; Harry, 157 ; John, 126 ; Samuel, 251.
Wilkinsonne, Anne, 13.
Wilkox, Mr., 212.
Willamot. Christopher, 177 ; Simon, 177.
Willamote, Margaret, 253.
Willes, Thomas, 87.
Willett, Elizbeth, 156.
Willey, Anne, 110.
Williames, Anne, 54, 160 ; Anthony, 249 ; Edward, 179 ; Elizabeth, 6 ; Harry, 133 ; James, 136 ; John, 47, 161 ; Katherine, 133 ; Maudelyn, 224 ; Roger, 47, 54, 160, 161, 173 ; Simon, 227.
Williams, Anthony, 67, 174, 176 ; Christian, 208 ; Deputy, 220 ; Elizabeth, 67 ; Frances, 220 ; Margaret, 251 ; Maudeline, 163 ; Mr., 208 ; Nathaniel, 255 ; Richard, 163 ; Robert, 67, 176; Roger, 179 ; Walter, 252 ; William, 96, 220, 253, 256.
Williamson, Amy, 258 ; Anthony. 237 ; Edmund, 92, 94, 95, 207 ; Elizabeth. 95, 208 ; Hellen, 167 ; James. 167 ; Jane, 92 ; Joane, 115 ; Ka-

2 Q

INDEX OF NAMES.

therine, 92, 94, 207; Robert, 237; Thomas, 237; William, 208.
Willimot, Anne, 182; Christopher, 65; Simon, 65.
Willimott, John, 64; Simon, 62, 64, 178, 180.
Willis, Anne, 151; Jane, 44; Joane, 230; Richard, 42, 44, 151, 156.
Willitt, Sarah, 261.
Willmatt, Isaac, 217.
Willmott, James, 67; Simon, 67.
Willow, Elizabeth, 115.
Wills, Mr., 194, 263; Thomas, 202.
Willson or Willsonne, Alice, 142; Christopher, 125; Daniel, 22; Elizabeth, 238; Ellen, 8, 44, 155; Godfry, 228; Isabel, 112; John, 106, 125, 238; Margaret, 227; Margery, 22; Mathew, 226.
Willy or Willye, Alice, 17; Anne, 19; Cicely, 40; Elizabeth, 24; John, 27; Mary, 30; Richard, 17, 19, 21, 24, 27, 30, 36, 40, 128, 136; Samuel, 36.
Willyams, Mr., 211; William, 263.
Willyes, Daniel, 46; Nathaniel, 46.
Willymotts, Simon, 183.
Wilson, Alice, 139; Daniel, 127; Elizabeth, 213; James, 139; John, 176; Margery, 127; Philip, 256; Thomas, 155; William, 213.
Winch, Elizabeth, 189, 255; Nathaniel, 78; William, 78.
Winckefeeld, Ellen, 8.
Wincrappe, John, 2.
Winfeild, Thomas, 263.
Winne, Joane, 203.
Winspere, Anne, 229.
Winter, Joane, 219.
Winterborne, John, 254.
Wintner, Richard, 254.
Wintrop, Ade, 1; Alice, 1.
Wintrope, Bridget, 3; Susan, 5.
Wise, Clara, 101; Frances, 101; William, 101, 214.
Wisewald, Thomas, 141.
Wiston, Joane, 121; Margaret, 117.
Witham, Daniel, 197.
Wither, Thomas, 245; William, 259.
Witherall, James, 205; John, 88, 94, 197, 205, 256; Marie, 94; Philip, 256; Sarah, 197.
Withnall, Dorothy, 237; John, 237.
Witter, Christopher, 47; George, 45, 47; Mr., 147; Susan, 45.
Woddcroffe, Mr., 176.
Wodford, Gamaliel, 131; Joane, 131; Mr., 136.

Wodforde, Deputy, 146.
Wodhowse, William, 252.
Wodward, Joseph, 101; Sarah, 101; Thomas, 101.
Wokeham, Richard, 257.
Woldrig, Mr., 176.
Woleston, Captain, 200.
Wolfe, Eleanor, 257.
Wolford, Dorothy, 246.
Wolgate, Sarah, 176.
Wolleston, Richard, 204.
Wolliston, Bro., 207; John, 259.
Wolridge, William, 176.
Wongan, Dorothy, 253.
Wood, Anne, 7; Edmund, 256; Edward, 10, 119; Elizabeth, 13, 224, 251; George, 11, 191; Jane, 241; John, 111; Richard, 191; Robert, 12; Susan, 9; Thomas, 25, 222, 263; William, 25.
Woodall, John, 55; Katherine, 55.
Woodard, Humphry, 80; Jone, 139; Nathaniel, 211; Sarah, 80; Thomas, 211.
Woodart, Bartholomew, 77; Humphry, 77.
Woodcocke, Daniel, 14; Elizabeth, 197, 261; John, 18; Katherine, 12; Margery, 18; Richard, 14; William, 14, 119.
Woodford, Anne, 20; Foulke, 33; Gamaliel, 19, 20, 23, 33, 168; Mrs., 168; Thomas, 19; William, 23, 238.
Woodfort, Thomas, 212.
Woodgate, Elizabeth, 206.
Woodhaull, John, 243.
Woodine, Goodman, 56.
Woodleaf, John, 144; Mr., 144.
Woodnorth, Rebecca, 93; Richard, 93, 94.
Woodnoth, Mr., 98; Richard, 208.
Woodstocke, Katherine, 253.
Woodward, Anne, 99; Dorothy, 184; Elizabeth, 74, 184; Humphry, 74, 76, 82, 84, 184, 188, 196, 197; Isaac, 257; John, 84, 197; Joseph, 214; Lucy, 255; Margaret, 223; Mary, 82, 97, 99, 196, 209, 210, 211, 256, 258; Mr., 209, 210; Mris., 215; Nathaniel, 98; Sarah, 197, 215; Thomas, 97, 98, 99, 209, 211, 214, 215, 218; William, 76, 188, 246.
Wooldridge, Mr., 156.
Woollard, Thomas, 253.
Woolleynes, Jone, 225.
Worrall, Alice, 256; Elizabeth, 126; John, 126.
Worthington, Jone, 130; John, 130.
Wotton, Thomas, 175.
Wrath, George, 9; Jane, 9; Peter, 9; Thomas, 10; Sir Thomas, 9.

Wratting, Elizabeth, 144.
Wreuche, Joane, 121; John, 121.
Wright, Alice, 51; Anne, 44; Bartholomew, 6, 111; Edmond, 1; Edward, 126; Elizabeth, 92, 99, 126, 158; Ellen, 249; Harry, 4; Joane, 4, 230, 248; John, 2, 44, 51, 52, 92, 93, 96, 98, 156, 158, 162, 205, 209, 212, 214; Katherine, 258; Margery, 114, 223; Mary, 93; Mr., 208; Paul, 257; Richard, 130, 257; Robert, 1, 110, 116; Sarah, 96, 209, 214; Thomas, 3; Walter, 52, 162; William, 99, 223.
Wrighte, Elizabeth, 3, 7.
Write, Blanch, 230; Elizabeth, 3; Joan, 2.
Wroth, Anne, 26, 229, 253; Dionise, 128; Dorothy, 120; Elizabeth, 120; Jerome, 34; John, 176, 197; Mabel, 13, 225; Mary, 234; Mr., 134, 170, 178, 194; Richard, 34; Robert, 26; William, 7, 128, 234, 236.
Wyborne, Elizabeth, 193.
Wylkenson, Isabel, 227.
Wyner, Edward, 185.
Wyng, Elizabeth, 114.
Wyntrop, Adam, 3.
Wyntrope, Catherine, 4.

Y.

Yans, Robert, 221.
Yapp, Richard, 259.
Yates, James, 208; John, 244.
Yearely, Nathaniel, 260.
Yeates, Umphery, 174; William, 169.
Yeomanes, Susan, 239.
Yeomans, John, 187.
Yerson, Robert, 221.
..., ynde, Edmond, 261.
Yong, Alce, 99; Alice, 13; Anne, 10, 119, 123, 138, 232; Anthony, 11, 12, 13, 14, 15, 16, 123, 237; Bartholomew, 9; Edward, 16; Elizabeth, 7, 12, 113; Gregory, 9, 10, 12, 13, 14, 15, 21, 115, 116, 126, 231, 233, 238, 239; Jane, 233; John, 10, 12, 14, 121; Joseph, 91; Katherine, 11, 15, 129, 222, 237, 239; Margaret, 115, 240; Martha, 99; Mary, 12, 126; Mr., 16; Philip, 112; Rachel, 8; Robert, 13, 129, 232; Stephen, 14, 126; Susan, 14, 116, 171, 238; Thomas, 11, 21, 91, 119, 148; Walter, 99; William, 12, 15, 121, 223, 228.
Yonge, Alice, 174; Anthony, 9; Cisly, 223; John, 98;

Jone, 224; Mrs., 154, 174; Philip. 6; Walter, 98, 209; Widow, 156.
Yopus, Jerard, 148.
Young, Alce, 100; Bridget, 100; Christopher, 87; Elizabeth, 86, 87; Mary, 100, 213, 256; Mr., 195; Temperance, 101; Thomas, 88; Timothy, 86, 87, 88, 198; Walter, 100, 101, 213.
Younge, Alce, 214; Bridget, 102; Elizabeth, 56, 112; George, 56, 58, 163; Gregory, 165; John, 79, 190; Martha, 216; Mary, 102, 190, 217; Robert, 58; Temperance, 216; Timothy, 85, 254; Walter, 102, 214, 216, 217, 262; Widow, 170.

ERRATA ET CORRIGENDA.

Page 86, line 17, *insert* " and."

Page 135, line 1, *for* " sonue," *read* " sonne."

Page 231, in margin, *for* " Θéo," *read* " Θéψ."

Page 257, note ‡, *for* " (?) St. Andrew's, Holborn." *read* " St. Andrew Hubbard, Eastcheap."

Page 281, column 3 last 2 lines, *read* " Rowland, 233; Sibell, 234."

Page 284, column 3 line 34, *read* " Marnell, Radegund, 106."

Page 287, column 1 last line, *read* " Parchment, Alice, 138;"

Page 287, column 2 line 7, *read* " Pargeter, Thomas, 257."

Page 288, column 3, *add* " Prestwitch, Anne, 221."

Page 288, column 3 last line, *read* " 100, 102, 103, 256."

www.ingramcontent.com/pod-product-compliance
Lightning Source LLC
Chambersburg PA
CBHW030809230426
43667CB00008B/1135